O9-BTN-697

Quiet Revolution in the South

Quiet Revolution in the South

THE IMPACT OF THE VOTING RIGHTS ACT, 1965–1990

CHANDLER DAVIDSON AND
BERNARD GROFMAN, EDITORS

PRINCETON UNIVERSITY PRESS
PRINCETON, NEW JERSEY

Published by Princeton University Press, 41 William Street,
Princeton, New Jersey 08540
In the United Kingdom: Princeton University Press, Chichester, West Sussex

---

Library of Congress Cataloging-in-Publication Data

Quiet revolution in the South : the impact of the Voting Rights Act, 1965–1990 / Chandler Davidson and Bernard Grofman, editors.
p. cm.
Includes bibliographical references and index.
ISBN: 0-691-03247-5 — ISBN 0-691-02108-2 (pbk.)
1. Afro-Americans—Suffrage—Southern States. 2. Voter registration—Southern States. 3. Afro-American politicians—Southern States. 4. Elections—Southern States. 5. Southern States—Politics and government—1951– I. Davidson, Chandler. II. Grofman, Bernard.
JK1929.A2Q54 1994
324.6′2′08996073075—dc20 93-38961

This book has been composed in Times

Princeton University Press books are printed on acid-free paper and meet the guidelines for permanence and durability of the Committee on Production Guidelines for Book Longevity of the Council on Library Resources

Printed in the United States of America

1 2 3 4 5 6 7 8 9 10

1 2 3 4 5 6 7 8 9 10
(Pbk.)

IN MEMORY OF

JUSTICE THURGOOD MARSHALL

"AND WE MUST TAKE THE CURRENT WHEN IT SERVES, OR LOSE OUR VENTURES"

CONTENTS

FIGURES

ACKNOWLEDGMENTS

WE ARE GRATEFUL to a host of people and institutions who have contributed to this book. The research project leading to it was made possible by National Science Foundation Grants #SES 88–9090392 and SES #88–13931 to Chandler Davidson and Bernard Grofman. While we had substantial funding from the National Science Foundation's Law and Social Sciences Program, once it was divided among eight state projects and a number of more specialized investigations whose results will be reported elsewhere, the amount allocated to any single project was small. It was only through the willingness of very busy scholars and attorneys to work essentially without compensation for their own time that this book was possible, and we thank them sincerely.

We would like to express our gratitude to the Sociology Department of Rice University for a seed grant to this enterprise from the department's Walter and Helen Hall Fund. Also at Rice we thank Elizabeth Lock, Cathy Monholland, and Michelle Packer for their excellent editorial assistance, and Twyla Davis, director of the Social Sciences Computer Laboratory, who was most helpful in translating the files of our contributors into a common program. Nancy Dahlberg, then Sociology Department secretary, was extremely helpful in the early stages of the project. Rita Loucks, the Sociology Department coordinator, has provided outstanding support in ways too numerous to mention. Sandy Perez went far beyond the call of duty, often late at night, in word processing parts of the manuscript, including the many tables. Patsy Garcia, too, provided valuable word processing assistance. Carolyn Liebler and Shay Gregory offered excellent clerical help. At the University of California, Irvine, School of Social Sciences, we thank Dorothy Gormick for invaluable bibliographic and proofreading assistance, and Ziggy Bates, Tu Duong, and Cheryl Larrson of the Word Processing Center for help with manuscript typing and conversion of data files. Cindy Crumrine deserves praise for her conscientious reading of the manuscript—and for her attention to the multitude of details contained in the many tables in this book. Michèle Pavarino provided excellent proofreading and indexing help.

Aid in the form of advice and criticism at various stages of the research process has come from many colleagues, including Joaquin Avila, Alwyn Barr, Numan V. Bartley, Patricia Bass, Bruce Cain, William Chafe, Armand Derfner, Robert Erickson, Luis Fraga, James Gibson, Keith Hamm, Gerald Hebert, Gordon Henderson, Tom Holm, Sherrilyn Ifill, Samuel Issacharoff, Franklin Jones, Pamela Karlan, Clifton McCleskey, Neil R. McMillen, Richard Murray, Richard Niemi, Barbara Phillips, Lawrence Powell, Robert Pratt, Jewel Prestage, John Sproat, Carol Swain, Susan Welch, Leslie Winner, and Raymond Wolfinger. We owe a special debt of gratitude to David Brady for having suggested this project to us one day in 1987. Finally, we are grateful to Malcolm DeBevoise, our editor at Princeton University Press, for his encouragement and continued interest in the enterprise.

This volume is part of a larger project that resulted in three conferences in 1990: one at Rice University, funded by the National Science Foundation and resulting in this volume; one at the University of California, Irvine, entitled "Modeling Race and Electoral Politics," cosponsored by the UCI Interdisciplinary Focused Research Program in Public Choice; and one at the Brookings Institution—funded by the Rockefeller Foundation and sponsored by the Brookings Program in Governmental Studies—whose proceedings are published as Bernard Grofman and Chandler Davidson, eds., *Controversies in Minority Voting: The Voting Rights Act in Perspective* (Washington, D.C.: Brookings Institution, 1992). We wish to thank these institutions and in particular the people involved in the three conferences for their support.

Quiet Revolution in the South

EDITORS' INTRODUCTION

CHANDLER DAVIDSON AND BERNARD GROFMAN

PRESIDENT LYNDON B. JOHNSON signed the Voting Rights Act on 6 August 1965. Enacted to enforce the Fifteenth Amendment, the statute consists of both permanent features that apply to the United States as a whole and temporary features—special provisions—that largely apply to specific jurisdictions.[1] The initial duration of its nonpermanent parts was five years. However, Congress extended them in 1970, 1975, and 1982, in each case with some important amendments to the act. Initial passage and each subsequent extension occurred with substantial bipartisan support.

Extensions were necessary because many white officials continued to resist the full incorporation of blacks and certain language minorities into the polity. As direct disfranchising strategies were frustrated by the act, officials relied on more subtle mechanisms of vote restriction aimed primarily at preventing minority voters from electing the candidates of their choice. Widely employed throughout the South, these mechanisms included the submergence of minority voting strength in at-large or multimember districts and the gerrymandering of district lines. The story told in the chapters of this book is largely the story of the "quiet revolution" in voting rights that has occurred since 1965.[2]

Because the most frequent and the most severe discrimination against minorities in the United States has occurred against blacks in the South, the special provisions of the act have been targeted particularly toward that region. From 1965 to the present, seven of the eleven states of the former Confederacy, including all five Deep South states, have been continuously covered entirely or in large part by the act's special provisions: Alabama, Georgia, Louisiana, Mississippi, South Carolina, Virginia, and forty of the hundred counties of North Carolina. Since 1975 Texas, an eighth former Confederate state with the largest black population of any southern state and the second largest Mexican-American population in the nation, has also been covered by the act's special provisions.[3]

Most of these states at one time or another employed a statewide literacy test, exclusive white primary elections, a poll tax, and a majority runoff requirement. These states were also more likely than others to employ at-large municipal election systems.[4] The use of such systems was much more widespread in these states than in the rest of the nation when the Voting Rights Act was passed, which Wolfinger and Field at the time attributed to the fact that in the South, "most municipal institutions seem to be corollaries of the region's traditional preoccupation with excluding Negroes from political power."[5]

We have chosen to focus on the eight southern states covered by the act's special provisions because the Voting Rights Act has had its greatest impact in the South and because, almost without exception, it is in these states that the key conceptual underpinnings of vote dilution have come to be defined through litigation challenging election practices.

The Basic Research Goals

In anticipation of the twenty-fifth anniversary of the act in 1990, with funding from the National Science Foundation's Law and Social Science Program, we commissioned comprehensive studies of several facets of southern black political participation. These studies included research on gains in black registration, systematic state-by-state investigations of the relationship between the act and the electoral success of racial minorities for municipal office in each of the eight states,[6] and a study of black representation in southern legislatures and congressional delegations.[7] Each state chapter was to be written by students of that state's electoral history, including at least one lawyer and one political scientist, sociologist, or historian. Many of the authors, as it turned out, had had direct experience with voting rights litigation as attorneys or as expert witnesses.[8]

The central aims of the project reflected the two major purposes of the act. We wanted to determine what effect it had in *enfranchising blacks* in the South. We also wanted to know its impact on black representation by *preventing the dilution of minority votes*. Regarding dilution, we were particularly interested in whether the act enabled blacks (and Mexican Americans in Texas) to win local office.

More specifically, the task we set for the authors of the state chapters had five components. First, we asked them to cover the main voting rights developments in their state from Reconstruction to modern times in a relatively brief compass but to give special attention to the post–World War II period. Without this prelude, the significance of the events from the 1960s on would be difficult to appreciate.

The second component stems from the fact that the Voting Rights Act is complex and open to different readings; there has consequently been a considerable development over the past two decades of case law devoted to its interpretation. Voting rights litigation in the states discussed in this book has been voluminous. We asked the authors of the eight chapters to review the major constitutional and statutory cases in their state related to the act and also to discuss section 5 enforcement issues in the state.

Third, we wished to address a long-standing controversy over the precise effects of at-large election systems on local minority representation. Unfortunately, no research design that could definitively resolve the issue had been used by any of the numerous scholars in the debate. To attack the problem, we required the authors to generate a comprehensive longitudinal data base for cities in their state that would enable them to distinguish—in large part, at least—the consequences of multimember-district elections from the impact of other factors.

The fourth task concerned the direct effect of the Voting Rights Act on the election of minority candidates to local office. If, as we anticipated, our data revealed that the abolition of at-large election structures increased minority candidates' chances of winning, we wanted to find out whether the act caused the adoption of district systems. To investigate the role of law—including the activities of voting rights organizations and attorneys—in promoting change, we required our authors to make an inventory of all litigation challenging at-large city council elections in the state over the previous twenty-five years. Our data include information on both the organizations and the individual attorneys involved in instigating such litigation.[9]

The fifth component allowed us to address a debate over how easy it is for minority candidates to win office in majority-white districts at the local level. The conventional view has been that minority success in these districts is difficult, especially when the white voters make up a substantial majority.[10] But recent claims to the contrary have raised a controversy on this point.[11] The authors of the state chapters have compiled evidence on the relationship between minority population in districts in a multidistrict system and the likelihood of minority electoral success, with an eye to determining what minority population proportion is sufficient to provide minority voters with a realistic opportunity to elect their candidates of choice at the local level.[12] The result is the most comprehensive data base extant with which to explore this question.

Previous Research on the Voting Rights Act

A survey of research on the Voting Rights Act reveals that while a number of useful studies of one aspect or another have been reported, no attempt has been made to understand the broad contours of its effects. And even the limited efforts to gauge its impact have often suffered from shortcomings in conceptualization, method, or both. We are struck, for example, by the dearth of hard evidence on the extent to which the remarkable gains in black officeholding in the South, and in Mexican-American officeholding in Texas and other southwestern states, could be attributed directly to the Voting Rights Act.[13] Most of the best scholarship has addressed legal or constitutional issues and has appeared in law-related journals, or it has been written from a nonquantitative or a journalistic vantage point.[14]

With some important recent exceptions,[15] most empirical work on the act's effects on minority representation has been either anecdotal or of a relatively low level of methodological sophistication. While there is a very important body of research that has examined minority officeholding under different election methods, those articles do not systematically investigate when and how changes in election type came about.[16] Also, remarkably, even the most basic facts about the implementation of the act, such as the number and results of post-1982 section 2 cases brought under it, have never been compiled, perhaps because many of these cases did not result in published opinions or were settled out of court before trial.[17]

It is true that many informative statistics have been made available in the various reports on the act's enforcement, published by the U.S. Commission on Civil Rights, and in the reports of groups such as the Southern Regional Council and the

Lawyers' Committee for Civil Rights Under Law. But much data that are publicly available, such as those contained in a list of Justice Department preclearance objections, have never been systematically examined to see what the consequences of Justice Department intervention have been.[18] Moreover, there has been too little thought given, even when statistics are published, to the overarching question of how the act's several mechanisms have directly or indirectly influenced minority registration and voting, on the one hand, and minority officeholding, on the other.

Our book is an attempt to remedy this situation. It gathers data systematically on southern voter registration and officeholding, keeping firmly in mind the questions of whether the Voting Rights Act has been responsible for the remarkable upsurge in black participation and electoral success, and, if so, how. We believe that the findings of our project constitute the best answer so far to the question of the Voting Rights Act's effect on minority representation in the South at the local level.[19]

The act's effect on black enfranchisement is treated by Alt in chapter 12. Alt's work is an advance over that of scholars who considered black registration separately from that of whites. He recognizes that the two are bound together in a dynamic system in which whites' behavior depends on blacks' potential to form a majority of the electorate in a jurisdiction. Following in the footsteps of Key, Alt explores the hypothesis that white efforts to reduce black electoral participation have traditionally depended upon the size of the black population. He provides a careful longitudinal investigation of the changing black-white registration ratio, which is the single most accessible measure of potential black voter mobilization in comparison with that of whites, and provides a comparison of that ratio with what would be expected if whites and blacks registered at equal rates relative to their pool of eligible voters. Alt's multivariate modeling allows him to assess the relative short- and long-run effects of several factors on changes in black and white registration, including the use of literacy tests, poll taxes, and the sending of federal registrars to various southern counties as authorized by the Voting Rights Act.

A different analytical framework allows us to examine systematically, using a quasi-experimental design, the impact of election type on changes in local minority officeholding. This framework is applied in the eight individual state chapters. In addition, chapter 11 presents data on the relation between black population concentration and black officeholding in the legislatures and congressional delegations of all eleven states of the former Confederacy, including the three states not covered by section 5 of the act.

The Controversy over Barriers to Minority Representation

A major purpose of the chapters on representation is to resolve an issue that since the 1970s has been sharply debated in academic journals and courtrooms. The refusal of the controversy to subside is undoubtedly tied to its continuing practical importance. The question goes to the heart of the meaning of racial and ethnic representation in a democratic polity and how that representation is best achieved under the constraints imposed by considerations of fairness, constitutional norms, and statutory mandates. Chapter 1, which provides a brief introduction to voting rights case law, illuminates the importance of this question, and chapter 10 discusses the question in detail. But a brief description of it now is useful as well.

Most American local and state election schemes are basically of three kinds: at-large, single-member district, and *mixed* systems—the latter combining features of the first two. In an at-large system, all the contested seats on a governmental body, such as a city council, county commission, or school board, are filled by voters in the jurisdiction at large. If there are eight seats to be filled, all voters have eight votes and theoretically have a chance to influence who gets elected to all eight seats. In a single-member-district system, by contrast, the city is divided into geographical districts, and voters in each district, like voters in congressional elections, are limited to a vote for a single candidate running to represent their district. In a mixed system, some of the seats are voted on at large, and some by district.

In the nation and in the South, single-member districts or wards were widely used in the late nineteenth century. The Progressive movement (1896–1920) introduced the at-large election as a substitute for voting by ward, ostensibly to foster "good government," a notoriously vague idea.[20] In the North the imposition of such election procedures made it much less likely that European ethnics—many of them impoverished immigrants recently arrived from Ireland and from southern and eastern Europe—would be elected from the heavily ethnic wards. In the South, at-large elections were often seen as a way to make it harder for blacks, and sometimes poor whites as well, to win office. From the Progressive Era to the 1970s, the proportion of at-large elections in the nation's local election systems increased. They became especially common in the South.[21]

Students of local government structure have long known that at-large elections, whatever their benefits might be, disadvantage ethnic minorities, especially when there is strong resistance by the majority to minority officeholding.[22] In particular, scholars of southern politics have pointed to dramatic instances where district election structures in majority-white jurisdictions were changed to at-large ones in anticipation of minority officeholding.[23] In the 1970s social scientists conducted research that corroborated this commonsense idea. About the same time, expert witnesses for minority plaintiffs challenging at-large elections were citing this research in arguing that at-large elections, when whites were in the majority and voted overwhelmingly against minority candidates, prevented the election of those candidates even when they had strong and cohesive support in their own communities. District elections, by contrast, often enabled minority candidates to win.

An article written in 1981 reviewed fourteen studies of the effects of at-large elections on minority representation between 1969 and 1981 and found that eleven supported the conventional view that at-large and other multimember-district elections, ceteris paribus, reduced the representation of black officeholders.[24] An unpublished study that same year found that eighteen of twenty-three published and unpublished studies also supported the conventional view.[25] The occasional study that did not find at-large elections to disadvantage minority candidates could usually be accounted for by small sample size or flawed methods, such as inclusion in the data base of cities with very small minority populations.[26] A text on political participation summed up the scholarly consensus in 1991 by observing that while some authors had denied the impact of at-large elections on minority officeholding, "there is persuasive evidence that the electoral structure has a significant, perhaps even dominant, impact on the extent of [minority officeholding]."[27]

Until 1981, the only approach to the question had been to examine samples of at-large, mixed, and single-member-district cities at a single point to see whether there were fewer minority officials on council, proportionally, in cities using one election type instead of another. The results were typically presented in a contingency table or a regression equation. This cross-sectional method, however, has serious shortcomings even when used correctly, which it sometimes was not.

One problem is that several other factors besides the election system can affect minority officeholding. Some factors can be measured without difficulty and with their effects controlled in a cross-sectional design. Among these are the size of the city's minority population and the socioeconomic differences between blacks and whites. Another factor, whose effects are more difficult to control, is minority residential segregation; it has typically not been measured in cross-sectional studies because segregation data are difficult to obtain for sizable samples of cities.[28] Other variables are also difficult to gauge. One is the existence of racially gerrymandered district boundaries in ward-based or mixed-system cities, which can lead to an underestimation of the differences in minority representation between at-large and district cities.

To resolve these and other problems of the cross-sectional research design, Davidson and Korbel conducted a longitudinal study of jurisdictions before and after a change from an at-large to a district or mixed system to determine what kind of election rules provided the most equitable minority representation. The advantage of this approach—especially when effects are measured immediately before and after the change in election rules—is that very little change takes place in the cities aside from the change in election structure. Thus the effects of other factors that could influence minority officeholding are held constant.

Davidson and Korbel examined the forty-one cases of political jurisdictions, including cities, they could identify as having changed from at-large plans in Texas during the 1970s. The proportion of minority officeholders in the forty-one units increased from 10 to 29 percent after the change occurred: from 6 to 17 percent for blacks and from 5 to 12 percent for Mexican Americans.[29] As a result, both minority groups were represented in rough proportion to their percentage in the population in the forty-one units as a whole; before the change, they had been underrepresented, roughly speaking, by a factor of three. The findings in this longitudinal research, combined with those of corroborating studies using the cross-sectional method, seemed to vindicate the conventional view, at least so far as blacks were concerned.[30] (Some authors, however, while admitting that at-large elections disadvantaged Mexican Americans, questioned whether single-member-district remedies generally benefited them.)[31]

The controversy was revived in 1987 by Thernstrom, who claimed that whites had become increasingly accepting of minority candidates. And as it is the tendency of whites to bloc vote against minority candidates that gives at-large elections their force in diminishing minority officeholders, the implication of Thernstrom's claim was that at-large elections were not terribly different in their effects on minority officeholding from district elections. Consequently, most minority voters no longer needed the protections of the Voting Rights Act.[32] Although Thernstrom presented only the sketchiest of anecdotal evidence for her hypothesis, the spectacular success in 1989 of a few minority officeholders in predominantly white jurisdictions shortly after her book appeared gave some credence to her view. The mayoral victories of David Dinkins, John Daniels, and Norman Rice in New York City, New Haven, and Seattle, respectively, and Douglas Wilder's election as governor of Virginia were especially noteworthy.

More systematically gathered evidence also appeared to underscore Thernstrom's point. Welch, in the most comprehensive cross-sectional study that uses data from the 1980s rather than the 1970s, looked at the effect of election type on minority representation in 1988 in predominantly white cities of 50,000 or larger with at least 5 percent black or 5 percent Hispanic population. She found that the gap in black officeholding between at-large and mixed or district cities had narrowed sharply, in comparison to findings from earlier research, including her own. To be sure, in the nation as a whole blacks were still somewhat less well represented in at-large than in single-member-district cities, and the gap was greater in the South than in the non-South. But black representation in at-large cities generally had risen significantly, she concluded.[33]

However, Welch noted that her study, like earlier ones addressing this issue, used the cross-sectional design after the time when many cities—particularly in the South—had abandoned the at-large election system, and she acknowledged that this fact presents a problem of interpretation.[34] The problem is that some of the previously at-large cities are now in the sample of district or mixed cities that are compared to the remaining at-large ones. If the cities that changed election forms were more resistant than average to black candidates when they were using at-large systems, then more recent findings of small differences between at-large and districted systems in cross-sectional data may be biased by what is called a *selection effect*.

There is at least prima facie evidence to suggest that such a bias is operative. The cities that have abandoned at-large elections through litigation or threat of it have typically been cities that are vulnerable to legal challenge for having systematically defeated black or Hispanic candidates. In consequence, the disappearance from the at-large category of many such cities could lead to mistaken conclusions about the impact of at-large elections on minority representation, if the analysis depends entirely on cross-sectional data. For this reason a longitudinal, or "before-and-after," design is clearly preferable, even though research on this issue has, almost without exception, continued to use cross-sectional data.

Previous longitudinal research has exibited shortcomings as well. Grofman has criticized Davidson and Korbel for failing to incorporate into their longitudinal design a control group consisting of a sample of cities that did not change their at-large structure during the period when other cities were changing theirs.[35] This precluded knowing whether minority representation had also increased in unchanged cities, which one would have expected if white voters' attitudes were changing in cities generally with the passage of time.[36]

In 1983 Heilig and Mundt presented longitudinal data based on a sample of 209 southern cities of at least 10,000 persons containing a black population of at least 15 percent.[37] They compared cities that retained their election structure in the 1970s (whether at-large, mixed, or district plans) with those which changed during the decade from at-large to either mixed or district plans. The cities that changed election structures had sharp increases in black officeholding, a finding that corroborated the findings by Davidson and Korbel. There was virtually no change in black representation in cities that maintained an at-large system during the same period, and relatively small gains in the cities that retained mixed or district plans.

While Heilig and Mundt's study represents an advance over Korbel and Davidson's, given its use of a control group of unchanged cities, it, too, has methodological problems. First, the cities' black equity scores (ratios) for the two time periods were not exactly comparable. Those for the earlier period were either means of the cities' scores over the entire decade of the 1970s or, alternatively, "for the years in the decade before the change to districts." Those for the latter were apparently based on a score at a single point in 1980 or 1981.[38] Second, like Davidson and Korbel, the authors failed to control for the effects of the city's black population percentage, a factor known to influence black officeholding. But perhaps the most serious problem with their design was pointed out by Engstrom and McDonald, who observed that the cities were not placed randomly in experimental and control groups. "This leaves open the possibility that another factor or factors may be responsible for both the change in the electoral system and the increase in the number of blacks elected to the councils," such as black political mobilization.[39]

To examine the impact of at-large elections by utilizing a design that would overcome some of the flaws in both the previous longitudinal and cross-sectional studies, we decided to conduct new research in each of the eight southern "section 5 states," focusing on city election system changes (and in three states, county changes as well) during the period when the Voting Rights Act may well have had its greatest effect on minority officeholding.[40] Our findings are based on data for two different times[41] in all cities above a certain population size[42] with a black population (or in Texas, black plus Hispanic population) of at least 10 percent.[43] Our analysis controls for the effects of minority population size by classifying cities as those with a minority population of 10–29.9 percent, 30–49.9 percent, and 50 or larger percent. The data base identifies the number of elected officials who were black (and in Texas and North Carolina, Hispanic and Native American, respectively) at each time and identifies the election system in use at each time.[44] Election type is classified as either at large, single-member district, or mixed.[45] In all of the state chapters the population thresholds of the analyzed cities are far below the 25,000 or 50,000 thresholds used in most of the earlier studies. Our response rate for cities above the requisite size and population minimum in each state is very near 100 percent.[46] Thus, our data base of over one thousand cities is considerably larger than that in virtually all earlier studies,[47] even though the cities are located in only eight states.[48]

In addition to measuring the impact of election systems on minority representation, we wanted to determine if the Voting Rights Act influenced changes in the cities' election structure. Therefore, for every lawsuit filed challenging at-large rules in a city (and, in three states, counties too), the data set includes the case citation, the name of the attorney bringing the lawsuit, the name of the sponsoring organization, if any, and information about the disposition of the case, including the final outcome.[49]

Moreover, for each instance where there was a change in election method over the period in question, information was collected about the factors that led to the shift. For most states, where the shift was not voluntary, the proximate legal cause is classified according to whether a section 5 preclearance denial by the Justice Department was involved, or alternatively, a Fourteenth Amendment or section 2 challenge. Many of the state chapters also distinguish cases where the threat of litigation influenced the decision, and a few also specify whether the change was brought about by referendum.

The Tables

There are several kinds of tables in this book, all of which appear at the end of the chapters' text. Chapters 1, 10, 11, and 12 contain tables whose formats are unique to each of the four chapters, and they are numbered sequentially, beginning with 1, as they are mentioned in the text. In contrast, the 8 state chapters (2 through 9) contain four types of tables: those whose format is virtually identical in all eight; those whose format is similar in all eight; those whose format is a variation of tables of the first two types; and those which are unique to a state chapter and are not a variation on any of the "standard" tables. Let us briefly describe and illustrate these four types in the eight state chapters.

First, there are five tables whose format is virtually identical from one state chapter to the next. They are numbered 1 through 5 in each chapter, and they contain data on city election structures and minority equity of representation.[50] They can be found in the table section of any of the eight state chapters, and the reader will find it easy to compare, say, Alabama's table 5 with Georgia's or South Carolina's table 5.

Second, there are tables whose format is similar in all eight chapters, but not quite so much so as in the first five tables, and so their data are only roughly comparable. These are numbered 6 through 10. Thus, tables 1–10 can be thought of as "standard" tables, although 1–5 are more similar to their analogues in other states than 6–10 are. A glance at table 6 for Texas and Georgia will illustrate this. The Texas table presents a more complicated data configuration than the Georgia table, although the tables both address similar questions about city election structures in their state. Again, table 10 in both the Texas and Alabama chapters gives the percentage of minority officeholders, but the Texas table focuses on the statewide officeholding population, while the Alabama table presents data only on legislative officeholding.

Third, there are tables that are variations of standard tables in the state chapters, and as such they are designated with an A. For example, three state projects collected data for county office and presented them in a format similar to that for cities in their states' tables 1–5. Tables 1A–5A in the three chapters present the county data. To take another example of a variation on a standard table, Alabama table 5A presents data on changed city election structures for a time period different from that in Alabama table 5, in order to illustrate the way in which the selection effect can bias data in cross-sectional studies. Or, to mention yet another example, the Louisiana project composed a set of variations to Lousiana tables 1–5 using voting-age population, rather than total population, for the percentage base, to see if their test results would be different. These variations, too, are designated as tables 1A–5A in the Louisiana chapter.

Fourth, there were a few tables in the state chapters that were not variations on standard tables. They were given numbers above 10. For example, Lousiana table 11 presents black registration rates for Louisiana parishes in 1964. No equivalent data were gathered by other state projects. While we believe the four kinds of tables in the state chapters will be easy for the reader to distinguish once the tabular data are examined, we nonetheless urge him or her to pay attention to the table titles, which give full and accurate descriptions of each table's contents—especially when analogous tables in two or more state chapters are being compared.

A word should be said about one table composed for each of the eight state chapters that is not included in this book. Designated as table Z, it is a listing of all lawsuits filed between 1965 and 1989 under the Fourteenth Amendment, the Fifteenth Amendment, or the Voting Rights Act by private plaintiffs or the Justice Department that challenged at-large elections in municipalities in these states, as well as the disposition of the case, the ensuing changes in election structures, if any, and the names of plaintiffs' attorneys and their organizational affiliations. Some of these tables (or variations on these tables) also contain information on challenges to county election systems as well. Because of the length of these tables, and the fact that table 8 in each state chapter makes use of much of the information in it for analytic purposes, we have chosen not to include table Z.

Nonetheless, it is archived along with the other data bases of this project, and can be obtained through the International Consortium for Political and Social Research at the University of Michigan.

The most important data on minority election success in the eight states provide the basis for tables 1–5 and their variations. Table 1 reports minority officeholding percentages in 1989 or 1990 for cities classified according to election type and minority population percentage. Table 2 reports minority officeholding percentages in terms of before-and-after comparisons (most commonly in 1974 and 1989) for cities that elected council at large at the beginning point of the study. The changes in minority representation in the cities that retained at-large systems over the entire period constitute a type of control for effects independent of change in election type. Table 3 refers only to cities with mixed election plans and reports the minority officeholding percentages in both the at-large and district components. Table 4 makes use of the data in table 1 to report two measures of minority representational equity in 1989 or 1990 for cities with each of the three election plans.[51] Both measures—one involving an arithmetic difference, the other a ratio—gauge proportionality of minority representation by comparing the percentage of minority officeholders on the governing body with the percentage of the total minority population in the jurisdiction. (A variation of table 4 in chapter 4—table 4.4A—substitutes minority voting-age population for minority total population in the state of Louisiana, thus providing a comparison between results using these two population measures.)

Table 5 makes use of the data in table 4 to report the ratio measure of minority representational equity for cities of the various types at both the beginning and the end of the period under study. It shows how equity has changed over time in cities that changed election plan and in those that did not.[52]

Among other things, these five tables allow us to develop a clear picture of the growth since the early 1970s in the number of black (and, in Texas, Hispanic) council members in cities with varying minority population proportions and election structures. The size of our data base allows us to establish with more confidence than would otherwise be possible the effect of the act on minority electoral success at the local level within individual southern states. Moreover, because our data permitted comparisons between changes in minority representation in the cities that retained at-large systems and those which did not, we can make some cautious inferences—as we do in chapter 10 for blacks—about how much of the growth in the number of minority officials is the result of change in election systems as distinct from change in other respects, including the willingness of whites to vote for minority candidates.

Tables 6 and 7 examine the racial characteristics of districts in relation to the race of the officeholder elected from those districts, in cities with single-member-district or mixed plans. They tell us how likely blacks are to be elected from districts with various percentages of whites and, in particular, how likely blacks are to be elected from majority-white districts. These two tables, then, are equivalent—for cities in the eight states—to various tables in chapter 11, which present similar information for legislative and congressional districts in all eleven southern states.

Table 8 contains a complete list, by city, of the reasons why cities changed to district or mixed plans during the period under analysis and enables us to estimate the extent to which the Voting Rights Act or Fourteenth Amendment litigation was directly responsible for abolition of at-large systems.[53] Thus, by examining table 8 in conjunction with table 5, we can model a three-step process in which voting rights litigation is either brought or threatened, which may lead to a change in election system, which in turn may lead to a change in minority electoral equity.

Table 9 focuses on disfranchisement. It contains a sobering list of each of the major disfranchising mechanisms used at some time between the end of the Civil War and the present era. Table 10 contains figures on black and white (and in Texas, Mexican-American and Anglo) registration at the time the Voting Rights Act was passed and in the late 1980s or early 1990s; it also contains figures on black and white officeholding in the 1960s and recent years. These data are presented as a percentage of total registrants and total officeholders (or, in some chapters, officeholders in each of the two statehouses), respectively, to provide a depiction of the changes in racial composition of these aggregates in the years since 1965.

Third- and Fourth-Generation Voting Research

As straightforward as our research goals were, they required a massive effort to gather and analyze several kinds of data and to situate them within a historical setting that gives them meaning. We nonetheless anticipate that some readers of this volume will charge us with not having addressed the question of whether the act has made a difference to ordinary southern blacks and Latinos. These readers will want to know: Has the federal guarantee of minority persons' right to vote and to elect candidates of their choice measurably changed their daily lives for the better?

We call *first-generation research questions* those having to do with minority enfranchisement, and *second-generation* those dealing with vote dilution and minority candidate electoral success. *Third-generation* issues concern the extent to which minority elected officials become an integral part of the political process: operating inside the system without being discriminated against, forming multiethnic coalitions, and working out resolutions to problems with fellow officials—in short, finding acceptance as active, influential players in the mainstream political game. *Fourth-generation* issues examine that game's output so far as minority citizens at the grass roots are concerned. Of concern here are the substantive policies that minority officeholders are able to get enacted and the impact these policies have on the life chances of their minority constituents. In these terms, it is clearly first- and second-generation questions that our project set out to answer definitively. By contrast, we asked the authors of the state chapters to ignore third- and fourth-generation problems. There were several reasons for this decision.

First and most obvious, the impact of the Voting Rights Act on minority registration and voting and the election of minority officials is a large and important topic in itself, requiring careful and time-consuming investigation. The act's impact has been the subject of much controversy. In particular, as we have already said, some scholars and political commentators claim that increased willingness of whites to vote for black candidates had by the 1980s largely obviated the need to make further changes in election methods. Only a comprehensive longitudinal data set on minority representation in southern jurisdictions, of the kind we have developed, permits this controversy to be adequately addressed.

Second, we are putting first things first. Before one can sensibly talk about policy consequences of the minority vote and minority officeholding, it is important to ascertain the pattern and causes of minority registration and electoral success. While it is widely assumed that the act has been responsible for increases in minority officeholding, there has been almost no systematic effort to test this assumption. The work reported in this book is the most extensive effort so far. We believe that it will, in itself, contribute to our understanding of law as an instrument of social change. In addition, we anticipate that it will facilitate an informed discussion of the act's implications for the theory of democratic representation. Until certain key factual issues are settled, however, we submit that such normative inquiry lacks guidance. In particular, we doubt the usefulness of an abstract debate over the merits of color-blind redistricting that ignores the issue of the prevalence of racially polarized voting and its effects in various types of election system.[54]

Third, relative to what is needed to study the policy consequences of black elected officials, our resources were prohibitively small. There have been a few serious efforts to answer third- and fourth-generation questions in selected southern jurisdictions, but this kind of research, even when focused on a small sample, requires a labor-intensive case-study approach carried out over a considerable period of time.[55] An attempt to provide a systematic answer to these questions based on an adequate, carefully selected sample of cities across the South would be a major undertaking—one, we believe, that would require at least the resources and time that went into our own project. In the absence of such an enterprise, comments on third-generation questions would necessarily be speculative. For this reason we encouraged our authors to forgo them.[56]

There is yet another reason why we decided not to pursue this line of inquiry here. Where the rights of long-excluded minority groups to vote and to elect candidates of their choice against concerted white opposition are concerned, we firmly believe that these two rights are not contingent on the groups' ability to demonstrate that their exercise results in measurable political incorporation or in policy benefits to the minority communities, even though common sense tells us that over time such results will come to pass. These voting rights can be justified—quite aside from their link to better police protection, job opportunities, and the like, in minority communities—solely on the basis of their power to confer full citizenship on the members of the group.[57]

Karst, the constitutional scholar, quotes Judge Learned Hand to make this point about the right to vote. "Of course I know how illusory would be the belief that my vote determined anything; but nevertheless when I go to the polls I have a satisfaction in the sense that we are all engaged in a common venture." Karst adds, "Voting is the preeminent symbol of participation in the society as a respected member, and equality in the voting process is a crucial affirmation of the equal worth of citizens."[58] What is true of voting is also true of electing candidates of choice. Where the ability to elect such candidates is systematically denied, a group long frozen out of the political process is denied the full measure of citizenship that has long remained beyond its grasp.

Tom McCain was one of the first blacks elected to office since Reconstruction in Edgefield County, South Carolina—home of racist firebrand Benjamin "Pitchfork Ben" Tillman and of long-time opponent of desegregation J. Strom Thurmond. Speaking in 1981, McCain said, "There's an inherent value in officeholding that goes far beyond picking up the garbage. A race of people who are excluded from public office will always be second class."[59]

We believe that the questions about whether black officeholding leads directly to political incorporation, whether it has immediate policy consequences, and if so in either case, under what circumstances, are important ones for social scientists to address.[60] However, to pursue them in this book, within the context of the history of black voting rights in the South, could easily muddy Karst's and McCain's distinction between, on the one hand, the justification of those rights on the basis of their conferring full citizenship and, on the other, justification on the basis of their enabling those who exercise them to achieve preferred policy goals. This confusion would be unfortunate.

All of these reasons, then, have militated against our attempting to answer third- and fourth-generation questions in this book.[61] Rather, the key issue we have tried to resolve is whether, during the first quarter century of its existence, the Voting Rights Act has made it possible for southern blacks (and in Texas, Mexican Americans) to vote without hindrance and to elect candidates of their choice.

The data sets that provide the basis for our authors' conclusions about the effects of the act on minority representation will be made publicly available through the computerized data archives of the Inter-university Consortium for Political and Social Research at the University of Michigan within six months of this book's publication. Thus, if there are disagreements with the conclusions reached by the authors, they can be debated with respect to a common comprehensive data base. Even more important, we see the comprehensive data base that has been generated by our authors as one of the project's lasting legacies, one that will be of use for some time to come, we hope, to students of voting rights and broader issues of race and politics in the South.[62]

Chapter Organization

Chapter 1 describes the legal context in which the recent battle for minority participation was fought. It attempts to show how the act evolved synergistically with the constitutional voting rights protections that were elucidated in a remarkable series of federal court decisions beginning in 1960 and continuing into the 1980s. Chapters 2 through 9 contain individual accounts of the impact of the act, particularly on local election systems, in the eight southern states covered entirely or in substantial part by the section 5 preclearance provision.

The data on voting rights litigation and minority officeholding in the eight state chapters are summarized and commented upon in chapter 10. Changes in city election structure are gauged. Then the effect of these changes on minority officeholding is measured. Further, the ability of blacks to win office from districts of varying black population proportions is examined. Taken together, this information allows inferences about the direct link between enforcement of the act and minority officeholding. Chapter 10 also contains a discussion of the issues that led us to adopt the longitudinal design that served as the unifying framework for the individual state chapters.

Chapter 11 examines the relationship between the black population proportion in state legislative and congressional districts in the eleven southern states and the ability of blacks to win election there. It provides an overview of minority legislative and congressional representation in the South (including states not covered under section 5) and links changes in minority representation to voting rights litigation and preclearance decisions. Chapter 12 answers the first-generation question of how the act affected the black-white registration rates in the eleven-state South. Chapter 13 summarizes and interprets the larger significance of the book's major findings.

PART ONE

The View from the States

CHAPTER ONE

The Recent Evolution of Voting Rights Law Affecting Racial and Language Minorities

CHANDLER DAVIDSON

THE VOTING RIGHTS of American ethnic minority groups are guaranteed primarily by two documents: the United States Constitution—especially the Fourteenth and Fifteenth amendments—and the Voting Rights Act of 1965. Some of the same principles are contained in both, but there are important differences between the two, including differences in coverage, legal standing of parties, methods of enforcement, and standards of proving discrimination.

This volume examines the effects of the Voting Rights Act. Yet the act, as it has evolved, is interwoven with constitutional voting rights law that grew out of a series of judicial decisions enunciating the rights of racial and language minorities as these groups were making an extraordinary push for inclusion in the American polity. An understanding of the act therefore requires an appreciation of the synergystic relation between the mandates of the act and those of the Constitution regarding the rights of minority voters. There has yet to appear a standard legal history of the modern development of minority voting rights, from the abolition of the white primary by the Supreme Court in 1944[1] to the Court's latest full-dress interpretation of the Voting Rights Act's prohibition of minority vote dilution in 1986.[2] In the absence of such a history, I will sketch the merest outline of one as a road map for reading the chapters that follow.

After the Civil War, southern states were required by the Military Reconstruction Acts of 1867 to adopt new constitutions granting universal male suffrage regardless of race as a precondition for readmission to the Union. The Fifteenth Amendment, ratified in 1870, seemed to guarantee blacks the franchise by prohibiting vote discrimination on the basis of "race, color, or previous condition of servitude."[3] Nonetheless, by the turn of the century white conservative officials had effectively nullified the black vote as a political force in the eleven states of the former Confederacy. The elimination of black suffrage was made possible by northern indifference to the plight of southern blacks after the Hayes-Tilden Compromise in 1877, southern intimidation of potential black voters, corruption and fraud at the ballot box, Supreme Court decisions striking down various provisions of the Enforcement Act of 1870 and the Force Act of 1871, and subsequent court decisions permitting southern states to rewrite their constitutions to exclude blacks by devices such as literacy and good character tests and the poll tax. The Fifteenth

Amendment, ignored by racist southern officials and racist courts, was a dead letter. As a weapon to protect black voting rights, another Civil War amendment, the Fourteenth, with its potentially powerful equal protection clause, suffered the same fate.

Southern blacks continued to fight for the franchise that had been promised them. The National Association for the Advancement of Colored People, founded in 1910, became the main organization through which the laws preventing black voting were attacked. The first significant breakthrough came in 1944, when the Supreme Court unanimously held that the Texas Democratic party's exclusive white primary elections violated the Fifteenth Amendment. It was not until passage of the Voting Rights Act, however, that the last major barriers to voting were breached.

Minority Vote Dilution

The original purpose of the act was primarily to destroy the remaining barriers to the full exercise of the black franchise. But the act would soon be used to confront a quite different problem: electoral devices that operated to restrict the impact of black votes. Their establishment was in many instances the result of white southern politicians' recognition after World War II that, since black enfranchisement was probably inevitable and the white primary no longer existed as a force to prohibit black voters from participating in the all-important nominating elections, new means would have to be found to limit black voters' effectiveness. The fear of black voting—and in Texas, of Mexican-American voting as well—led southern officials, years before the Voting Rights Act was passed, to enact laws to prevent minority candidates from gaining office when barriers to voting fell. Whites had used such laws in the nineteenth century both during and after Reconstruction to dilute or curtail the power blacks had obtained at the ballot box.[4]

The distinction between disfranchisement and dilution can be made as follows. Disfranchisement prohibits or discourages a group from voting—for example, through making it difficult to register, intimidating would-be voters from entering the polling booth, declaring ballots invalid for specious reasons, stuffing the ballot box, or inaccurately tallying votes. Dilution, on the other hand, can operate even when all voters have full access to the polling place and are assured that their votes will be fairly tallied.

Vote dilution is a process whereby election laws or practices, either singly or in concert, combine with systematic bloc voting among an identifiable group to diminish the voting strength of at least one other group. The idea is that one group, voting cohesively for its preferred candidates, is systematically outvoted by a larger group that is also cohesive. If both groups are cohesive or, in other words, vote as opposing blocs, then *racially polarized voting* exists. Dilution can occur as a result of polarization between Democrats and Republicans, between rural voters and urban ones, or between any other identifiable factions in the electorate.[5]

Ethnic or racial vote dilution takes place when a majority of voters, by bloc voting for its candidates in a series of elections, systematically prevents an ethnic minority from electing most or all of its preferred candidates—candidates who will probably be members of the minority group—in an election system to which there is a feasible alternative. Vote dilution not only can deprive minority voters of the important symbolic achievement of being represented by preferred members of their own group, it can deprive them of a committed advocate in councils of government. In doing this, it may also deprive them of the substantial benefits that government bestows—from streetlights to storm sewers, municipal employment to fire protection, fair law enforcement to efficient public transportation.

Several election rules or practices may have a dilutionary impact when used in a setting of racially polarized voting. One of the most familiar is the gerrymander, by which district lines are drawn either to diminish the proportion of minority voters in districts or, alternatively, to pack far more minority voters in a district than is necessary for their candidates to win, thus reducing the number of districts with a substantial minority population or voter preponderance. Another is the at-large election plan (a type of multimember district), which has instead of several single-member districts or "wards"—some of which might contain a majority of minority voters—only one district, all of whose members are chosen by an electorate in which the ethnic minority may also be an arithmetic minority. If voting is polarized, then the majority in an at-large system will be able to elect all its candidates, and the minority will not be able to elect any. Even if the degree of polarization is less than absolute, the ability of minority voters to elect their candidates can be severely diminished.

Yet a third election practice that sometimes dilutes minority votes is the majority-runoff requirement. A runoff is a two-stage election procedure whose second stage comes into effect only if no candidate wins a majority of the votes. In the first election, the white majority may split among several candidates, with the result that a candidate favored by the minority would obtain a plurality. Under a plurality-win arrangement (which is a very common one in U.S. cities), the minority candidate in this situation would win. Under a majority-win rule, however, a runoff is required if no majority is obtained in the first election. If in the runoff the white majority coalesces behind the white candidate who was runner-up in the first contest, the white bloc vote can often defeat the front-running minority candidate, even if the minority bloc is strongly behind that person. This arrangement has sometimes been adopted by white officials soon after minority voters enter the electorate in large numbers, or after a minority candidate has won or come close to winning under the plurality-win rule.[6]

A fourth dilution measure, of which there are two common types, is the anti-single-shot device. The first type operates in elections where all candidates run against each other and the top vote getters fill the available seats. The device restricts the ability of voters to single-shoot (sometimes called "bullet vote"), that is, to withhold votes for some candidates in order to help their favored one. Blacks, for example, have often decided as a group before an election that the white bloc vote will defeat their preferred candidate if blacks vote not only for their candidate but for as many others as they have votes to cast. So they decide on the candidate they will vote for while witholding votes for the other candidates, who are, in effect, her competitors. This strategy has often led to the election of a black in a polarized setting, although it requires black voters to forgo having a say in the election of other officials. The single-shot strategy is frustrated by the full-slate rule, requiring voters to cast all their available votes or to have their ballots invalidated. Another device is the numbered place system, whereby every candidate is required to declare for "place" 1, 2, 3, and so forth, on the ballot rather than run against all other candidates in a single contest. As voters can cast only one vote per place, this system prevents them from withholding votes from their favored candidate's competitors. It is sometimes resorted to when more straightforward prohibitions against single-shot voting are not feasible.[7] In a racially polarized setting, both anti-single-shot devices prevent a successful single-shot strategy to elect a minority candidate.

As Kousser has shown, southern white officials have long known the dilutionary effects of these arcane laws when used in a racially polarized setting.[8] While it is true that ordinary voters show little interest in the intricacies of voting laws, the politicos of even the smallest towns make it their business to understand how voting rules advantage some groups over others. This knowledge, after all, can powerfully influence who wins and who loses; and election results can affect how and to whom city contracts are let, on whose property the county airport will get built, how high the tax rate will be, who gets on the city payroll, in whose neighborhood the waste treatment plant will be located, or how aggressively environmental regulations will be enforced.[9] This practical political knowledge of election rules was used by southern whites against blacks from the end of the Civil War until disfranchisement, when the black vote was no longer a serious factor.[10]

But when it threatened to become one again, efforts were mounted throughout the former Confederacy to establish laws that would dilute minority voting strength. The chapters that follow provide detailed accounts of these efforts from the 1940s onward. The methods were the same ones that had been used during Reconstruction. Rosenberg provides a useful laundry list of the tactics—some disfranchising, some diluting—that whites have employed in recent decades when confronted by the prospects of black officeholding:

> When blacks attempted to run as candidates, discriminatory administration of neutral laws resulted in the following: abolition of the office; extension of the term of the white incumbent; substitution of appointment for election; increase in filing fees; raising of requirements for independent candidates; increase in property qualifications; withholding information on how to qualify; withholding or delaying required certification of nominating petitions. And finally, of course, there are the time-honored practices of gerrymandering, county consolidation, switching to at-large elections, and the like, which all can act to continue to deprive blacks of any political representation.[11]

The Alabama legislature in 1951, for example, enacted a full-slate law preventing single-shot voting, a law that applied to every election in the state.[12] The city of Tuskegee, with its large black population, was specifically mentioned by one white legislator who said the law was necessary because "there are some who fear that the colored voters might be able to elect one of their own race" to Tuskegee's city council.[13] But when the full-slate law proved insufficient to this end, the legislature went a step further by redrawing the city's boundaries to exclude virtually all of the city's black voters but none of its white ones. In *Gomillion v. Lightfoot* (1960) the Supreme Court held that the law violated the Fifteenth Amendment.[14] Justice Felix Frankfurter, who wrote the opinion, saw the boundary manipulation as vote denial rather than vote dilution,[15] but the decision called attention to the way in which drawing boundaries could affect the political strength of blacks; and Frankfurter cited one of the Court's earlier opinions, *Lane v. Wilson* (1939)[16] in holding that "the [Fifteenth] Amendment nullifies sophisticated as well as simple-minded modes of discrimination."[17] The quoted passage continues: "It hits onerous procedural requirements which effectively handicap exercise of the franchise by the colored race although the abstract right to vote may remain unrestricted as to race."

When the Voting Rights Act was passed, Alabama blacks began to vote in significant numbers. But the white registration rate also shot upward. Indeed, the net gain in white registration between 1964 and 1967 outstripped that of blacks, thanks to the efforts of Governor George Wallace and his followers. The fear of black officeholding in the state was no doubt partially responsible for this upsurge. Shortly after the Selma-to-Montgomery march the spring preceding passage of the act, a state senator pushed through a bill to require at-large commission elections in Barbour County, which till then had had districts. The reason he gave was to restrict the impact of "the block vote."[18] The first minority vote dilution suit, *Smith v. Paris*,[19] was filed in Alabama in 1966, challenging another switch in Barbour County elections—this one pertaining to the county's Democratic Executive Committee.

In 1947 the first southern black running against whites was elected to public office since the turn of the century. He won a seat on the Winston-Salem, North Carolina, Board of Aldermen under a ward system. Soon afterward a new district plan was adopted to restrict black officeholding to one ward out of eight.[20] After a black was elected in Wilson, a town in eastern North Carolina, in 1953 and 1955, the legislature changed the election plan from district to at large, resulting once more in an all-white council.[21]

These stratagems were harbingers of more widespread resistance to black officeholding in North Carolina, a state that has long prided itself on its relative moderation in racial matters. In 1966, shortly after the Voting Rights Act was passed, the general assembly in special session authorized almost half the state's counties' governing bodies to adopt at-large elections. Departing from past practice, the state would also require at-large elections in every school district in North Carolina.[22] In South Carolina between 1965 and 1973, eleven of nineteen counties that elected at least some members of their governing board from districts had switched to at-large systems.[23]

In Georgia, the legislature responded to a federal court order in 1962 requiring reapportionment by presenting a plan that maintained single-member districts in most areas of the state but that created multimember districts in counties with more than one state senator, which included Fulton County, with its heavily black areas. During debate on the bill, a senator had warned his colleagues of the danger that a black might be elected in Fulton County under a single-member-district scheme. The plan was narrowly averted only hours from election day by a court order holding that the scheme violated the state constitution's prohibition of multimember elections in senate races; thus Georgia's first black senator since Reconstruction was subsequently elected.[24]

When the Supreme Court struck down the Georgia county-unit system, a malapportionment mechanism that diluted the votes of blacks, among others, the legislature passed majority-vote and numbered-place requirements in all state and federal elections. The bill, introduced in 1963, thus changed the plurality requirement in as many as 100 of the state's 159 counties. The law's sponsor spoke openly of its purpose "to thwart election control by Negroes and other minorities." In 1968, shortly after passage of the Voting Rights Act, the legislature extended the majority-vote requirement to many municipalities.[25] In Louisiana several police juries—the county governing bodies in the state—switched from district to at-large elections in the late 1960s and early 1970s.[26]

Soon after *Brown v. Board of Education* the Texas legislature began passing laws with increasing frequency that enabled school districts and cities to adopt the place voting system. One purpose, according to a student of place voting, was to prevent the election of minority officeholders by preventing single-shot voting.[27] In 1966, as a result of court-mandated reapportionment, the legislature gerrymandered district lines to dilute minority votes. It also imposed a minority-runoff requirement for school board elections in Houston, site of the state's largest school district, after two blacks and a white liberal had won election under the plurality rule. In the same period conservative Democrats set in motion an effort to shift elections for state office to off years. When the effort succeeded in the early 1970s, voter turnout, which had gradually been rising since the abolition of the state's white primary in 1944, decreased in state elections by about one-third.[28] In Mississippi in 1962, as black voter registration drives were beginning, the legislature passed a law requiring a large number of municipalities to elect aldermen on an at-large basis.[29] In Virginia, the legislature blatantly diluted the black vote in its 1964 reapportionment plan by creating a two-member senate district in Richmond and by joining the city of Richmond, 42 percent black, with Henrico County to form an eight-person multimember house of delegates district that was only 29 percent black.[30]

In short, there was widespread hostility among southern whites to black officeholding before passage of the Voting Rights Act—a hostility that found ready expression in legislation designed to curtail minority political strength even as the civil rights movement was expanding it. Once the act was passed, efforts to undercut blacks' newly gained voting strength continued, not only by creating at-large or multimember districts in many kinds of jurisdictions but by gerrymandering existing single-member districts to restrict the possibility of black (and Mexican-American) officeholding.[31] These efforts continued into the 1980s, and if they have begun to diminish, it is at least partly because the evolution of voting rights law has made them more difficult and more costly to white officials in southern jurisdictions.[32]

Vote Dilution and the Constitution

The Supreme Court's involvement in the question of vote dilution followed on the heels of *Gomillion*, the case that originated in Tuskegee, Alabama, where blacks were gerrymandered out of the city's municipal boundaries. The Court held in a case originating in Tennessee, *Baker v. Carr* (1962),[33] that legislative apportionment was justiciable. In *Reynolds v. Sims* (1964),[34] decided the year before the Voting Rights Act was passed, it held that because Alabama legislative districts contained unequal numbers of voters, the state's apportionment diluted the votes of inhabitants of the heavily populated districts and thus violated the equal protection clause of the Fourteenth Amendment. The Court required the legislature to reapportion itself on the basis of population equality.

In *Reynolds*, Alabama plaintiffs had sued to rectify the dilution of white suburban votes by a rural-dominated legislature at a time when few blacks could vote in that state.[35] Race was not explicitly at issue. Nor was it in *Fortson v. Dorsey*,[36] a Georgia dilution case that the Supreme Court decided in 1965. Rejecting a claim by Georgia voters that a combination of single-member and multimember legislative districts diluted the votes of residents of the multimember districts, the Court nonetheless said that while multimember districts were not inherently unconstitutional, they might be if they operated "designedly or otherwise . . . to minimize or cancel out the voting strength of racial or political elements of the voting population."[37] The Court was silent as to how that might happen.

Black plaintiffs then filed class actions trying to convince the courts that multimember districts, including at-large election systems, did in fact violate their constitutional rights.[38] These cases typically invoked the Fifteenth Amendment and the equal protection clause of the Fourteenth Amendment (claiming that plaintiffs' right to equal political participation was denied), and they sought as a remedy the creation of single-member-district plans. But not until 1973 did the Court hold that unconstitutional minority vote dilution had been proven. In *White v. Regester*,[39] an action filed in Texas by Mexican-American and black voters who challenged multimember legislative districts in Bexar County and Dallas County, respectively, after the 1970s round of redistricting, the Court unanimously found for the plaintiffs. However, its reasoning as to why the districts were unconstitutional was vague. The Court cited a number of factors: the long history of state-sanctioned discrimination against blacks in Texas and the history of discrimination against Mexican Americans as well; the small number of blacks and Mexican Americans elected to office in Dallas and Bexar Counties, respectively; and the existence of a powerful white-dominated slating group in Dallas that ignored blacks' interests and engaged in racial campaign tactics to defeat candidates of blacks' choice. The Court also cited cultural and language barriers that had depressed Mexican-American registration and Bexar County legislators' lack of responsiveness to Mexican-American interests. It pointed to the existence of the majority-vote and numbered-place rules as enhancing the opportunity for racial discrimination in the counties' multimember settings. There was no indication, however, that the Court considered any of the items on this laundry list to be determinative. It simply approved the trial court's conclusion based on its examination of the "totality of the circumstances." Taken together, the high court said, they revealed that blacks and Mexican Americans "had less opportunity than did other residents in the district to participate in the political processes and to elect legislators of their choice."[40]

The vagueness of the opinion bothered voting rights lawyers, especially inasmuch as the justices did not even try to explain why the record in *White* differed from an earlier case with similar facts, in which the Court had found for the defendants.[41] A subsequent circuit court opinion, *Zimmer v. McKeithen*,[42] systematized the facts to be considered in a dilution case and, drawing on *White*, listed eight criteria as relevant. Four of these it called "primary" and four others "enhancing." But, like *White*, it did not specify determinative factors: "The fact of dilution is established," the Court said, "upon proof of the existence of an aggregate of these factors."[43]

The heavy burden of proof plaintiffs in these cases were required to shoulder is indicated by the list of "*Zimmer* criteria."

> Where a minority can demonstrate a lack of access to the process of slating candidates, the unresponsiveness of legislators to their particularized interests, a tenuous state policy underlying their preference for multimember or at-large districting, or that the existence of past discrimination in general precludes the effective participation in the election system, a strong case is made. Such proof is enhanced by a showing of the existence of large districts, majority vote requirements, anti-single shot voting provisions, and the lack of provision for at-large candidates running from particular geographical subdistricts.[44]

In spite of this burden, minority plaintiffs in the years following *White* filed a number of constitutional challenges to at-large election schemes throughout the eight states covered by section 5—at least forty from 1973 through 1980. City councils, county commissioners' courts, and school boards—often in large cities—were the main targets of these suits, which were litigated primarily by attorneys with the Legal Services Corporation, the American Civil Liberties Union, the Lawyers Committee for Civil Rights Under Law, the NAACP Legal Defense Fund, the Mexican American Legal Defense and Educational Fund, the Southwest Voter Registration Education Project, and various private attorneys who began to specialize in voting rights cases. In some instances the U.S. Department of Justice also filed suit or was involved as intervenor or amicus curiae.[45]

The task of the plaintiffs was formidable. Because *White* and *Zimmer* presented a list of relevant factors without specifying any as determinative, plaintiffs' lawyers tried to cover all the bases. They hired experts to investigate the racial history of the jurisdiction's major institutions, the history of its electoral system, and the socioeconomic situation of minorities compared to that of the majority in recent decades. The experts conducted detailed demographic studies of the ethnic groups to establish whether single-member districts would in fact remedy the vote dilution that existed under the challenged at-large system. Experts closely examined many kinds of statistics on local government hiring of minorities over time, government responsiveness to minority concerns, and government appointments to boards and commissions. They scrutinized newspapers and other documents for signs of racial appeals to white voters in elections involving minority candidates. They developed and applied methodological and statistical techniques for measuring such things as racial polarization and residential segregation—techniques that were sometimes refined after courtroom cross-examination by defense lawyers and criticism by opposing experts. Lawyers submitted interrogatories to officials requesting numerous records. They deposed potential witnesses. "Visuals" presenting many kinds of social science data were constructed. By the time these cases went to trial, the evidence, marshaled and systematized by lawyers and expert witnesses for both sides, often resembled huge, historically framed ethnographies of the jurisdiction's race relations and politics, sometimes spanning many decades.

The burdensome nature of these cases at the trial court level alone should be obvious from this description. The data-gathering process sometimes had to be extended when cases were appealed and then remanded to the trial courts for further fact-finding. In the intervening period, statistics might become dated as the factual situation evolved or new statistical sources became available. In the case that was ultimately styled *City of Mobile v. Bolden*,[46] black plaintiffs' lawyers filed suit in 1975 challenging the city's at-large election system; the case worked its way to the Supreme Court, which announced its decision in 1980 and remanded the case to the district court for further factual findings. The case was reheard in 1981 after extensive new evidence by four expert witnesses for the plaintiffs and the Justice Department and was finally decided in 1982. The first elections under the new district plan were held in 1985, ten years after the case was originally filed. Plaintiffs' lawyers logged 5,525 hours and spent $96,000 in out-of-pocket fees, which were exclusive of expenses incurred by Justice Department lawyers after the department intervened and the costs of expert witnesses and paralegals.[47] While *Bolden* was not typical, many other Fourteenth Amendment cases also involved massive data collection efforts and bounced back and forth between district and appeals courts for years.

The Origins of the Voting Rights Act of 1965

In 1940 approximately 3 percent of the black voting-age population in the South was registered to vote, which was about the same proportion it had been forty years earlier.[48] After World War II that figure began to rise, and by 1964 it stood at 43.3 percent. However, in many areas, particularly where the racial caste system was strongest, white resistance to black voting was adamant. Blacks who attempted to register risked economic reprisals, violent repression, and sometimes death. In spite of courageous efforts by civil rights groups and local black leaders to increase registration and in spite of the Civil Rights Acts of 1957, 1960, and 1964, with their relatively weak voting provisions, little progress was made enforcing the Fifteenth Amendment in the areas of greatest resistance—five southern states with large black populations: Alabama, Georgia, Mississippi, North Carolina, and South Carolina. In 1964 average black registration in the five was 22.5 percent; in Mississippi it was 6.7.[49]

Lyndon Johnson's decision in late 1964 to press forward with a voting rights statute reflected a combination of factors: the inability of previous civil rights laws to crack white resistance to black voting,[50] a changing climate of public opinion outside the Deep South, the heroism exhibited by many civil rights activists, Johnson's concern with his place in history as well as his genuine desire to guarantee black voting rights, and calculations of Democratic advantage at a point when white southern support for the Democratic national ticket was eroding. Barry Goldwater's 1964 sweep of the Deep South, a bastion of Democratic strength since Reconstruction, had underscored the erosion.

About the same time Johnson reached his decision, the Southern Christian Leadership Conference, a civil rights group led by the Reverend Martin Luther King, Jr., chose Selma, Alabama, to be the battleground for a do-or-die push for black voting rights. Another civil rights group, the Student Nonviolent Coordinating Committee, and the Department of Justice had been working unsuccessfully for some time to register black voters in Selma and surrounding Dallas County. The drive, launched on 2 January 1965, provoked violence against the demonstrators and eventually led to the deaths of one black and two white protesters. The national outrage over the brutality of Alabama lawmen and of white terrorists galvanized Congress to enact Johnson's bill by a very large margin, even in the face of bitter resistance from most southern white congressmen.[51]

Provisions of the 1965 Voting Rights Act, as Amended

Until the 1980s the key components of the original act were the temporary provisions contained in sections 4 through 9, which were renewed and amended in 1970, 1975, and 1982, the last time for a period of twenty-five years.[52] They will come up again for congressional consideration in 2007. As with its original passage in 1965, extensions and amendments of the act in all three years reflected a strong bipartisan consensus, although there were initial attempts by presidents Nixon and Reagan in 1970 and 1982, respectively, to sabotage extension of various important provisions of the act.[53]

In 1965 the most imposing barrier to the black franchise was the literacy test in the seven southern states of Alabama, Georgia, Louisiana, Mississippi, North

Carolina, South Carolina, and Virginia. Even when fairly employed, this test often kept a disproportionate number of blacks from registering, since the South's unequal school system had provided blacks with an inferior education. But it was not always fairly administered, and then the effects were even more discriminatory than they otherwise would have been. Section 4 of the act contained a triggering formula that originally abolished literacy tests for a five-year period in any state or subdivision that used a test or similar device as a voting requirement on 1 November 1964 and had a voter registration rate on that date (or a voter turnout in the 1964 presidential election) of less than 50 percent of the voting-age residents. Between 1965 and 1975 six southern states and much of a seventh were the primary areas covered by this formula: Alabama, Georgia, Louisiana, Mississippi, South Carolina, Virginia, and forty counties in North Carolina.

A major expansion of section 4 coverage occurred in 1975, when an additional language-minority trigger formula was added. A jurisdiction would be covered according to this formula if more than 5 percent of the voting-age citizens belonged to a single language minority group (defined as Asian Americans, American Indians, Alaskan natives, and persons of Spanish heritage), if, furthermore, fewer than 50 percent of voting-age citizens had voted in the 1972 presidential election, and if that election had been conducted only in English. Jurisdictions thus covered were required to provide election materials, including ballots, in the appropriate language in addition to English.[54] This new formula brought under the umbrella of section 4 the state of Texas—also a part of the old Confederacy, with its large black and Mexican-American populations—as well as the entire states of Alaska and Arizona and a number of counties in other states.

Section 5, which pertains only to the jurisdictions covered as a result of section 4's triggering formula, froze in place all voting statutes, pending federal approval of proposed changes. Jurisdictions were required to submit to the Attorney General (who normally had sixty days to object) or to the U.S. District Court for the District of Columbia all proposed changes having to do with voting that were in force before coverage. In the areas originally covered, the freeze date was 1 November 1964. In others, it was a later date, depending on when coverage first occurred. The proposed changes would be "precleared" for approval, each jurisdiction separately, after federal scrutiny of the particular facts if and only if the changes did not have the purpose or effect of denying or abridging the right to vote on account of race, color, or (after 1975) language-minority status. Section 5 preclearance requirements have, at one time or another, covered all or part of twenty-two states, although the focus has consistently been on the South. Today, section 5 covers nine states entirely and counties in seven additional ones.[55]

Sections 6 and 7 gave the Attorney General authority to appoint federal officials as voting examiners, or "registrars," who could be sent into jurisdictions covered by section 4 to ensure that legally qualified persons were free to register in federal, state, and local elections. Section 8 provided for the Attorney General to assign, when needed, federal observers to oversee the actual voting process in covered jurisdictions. Section 9 spelled out the procedures for challenging lists of eligible voters drawn up by federal registrars.

Other sections of the original act instructed the Attorney General to challenge the constitutionality of the poll tax as a voting requirement in the four states that still retained it for state elections (it had just been outlawed at the federal level by the Twenty-fourth Amendment, ratified in 1964); prohibited, under threat of penalty, interfering with the voting rights of qualified voters or engaging in voting fraud; and spelled out in detail the meaning of *vote* or *voting* for purposes of the act.[56] In *South Carolina v. Katzenbach* (1966)[57] the Supreme Court found constitutional all those sections of the act challenged by the state of South Carolina, including most of section 4 and all of section 5.

Vote Dilution Issues under Section 5 of the Act

Initially the key provisions of the Voting Rights Act were those dealing with voter registration. For almost four years after passage, the Justice Department did not apply the section 5 preclearance mechanism to proposed changes in voting laws that threatened to dilute minority votes. The situation changed dramatically as a result of *Allen v. State Board of Elections*,[58] a 1969 Supreme Court decision based on suits filed in Virginia and Mississippi. The facts in Mississippi were particularly egregious. The 1966 legislature, without public debate, passed a package of election laws that would diminish black voting strength. Among them was a bill requiring at-large election of all county boards of supervisors and boards of education. A senator explained that the change from wards to countywide elections would protect "a white board and preserve our way of doing business."[59] Lawyers for black voters argued that these bills should have been cleared with the Justice Department under section 5; Mississippi disagreed. After reviewing the Voting Rights Act's legislative history, the Supreme Court held that preclearance was required, reasoning that the act "gives a broad interpretation to the right to vote, recognizing that voting includes 'all action necessary to make a vote effective.'"[60]

Preclearance decisions are not subject to judicial review. Thus section 5, as interpreted by *Allen* in 1969, gave the Justice Department unprecedented authority to monitor election procedure in covered areas for evidence not only of disfranchisement but of vote dilution and to force compliance. Whereas the department had not objected to a single instance of vote dilution before 1969, it began to object that year and continued to do so thereafter with increasing frequency,[61] signaling to the multitude of covered jurisdictions that attempts to make dilutionary changes in their election laws would encounter difficulties.

Allen was a tremendously important decision for two reasons. By interpreting section 5 as requiring preclearance of election changes that could affect black representation as well as black voting, it gave the Justice Department's review powers a much broader scope than they otherwise would have had. But equally as important, in this decision the Court expanded the notion of vote dilution beyond that developed in the reapportionment cases—where an *individual's* vote was diluted by virtue of unequally populated districts—to include the dilution of a group's vote by any number of devices, including submersion in an at-large election system. The expanded idea of dilution in *Allen* was implicit in *White v. Regester* in 1973, although the Court was still struggling to articulate it.[62] Indeed, the idea would not be spelled out precisely by the Court until *Thornburg v. Gingles*,[63] decided more than a decade later. But minority vote dilution as a group-based phenomenon was clearly the target of the Fourteenth Amendment voting rights cases growing out of *White* and *Zimmer*; and so in an important sense the Voting Rights Act from 1969 on has influenced the development of the constitutional case law on this subject. As the Fourteenth Amendment was the primary weapon by which minority plaintiffs could attack at-large elections and other multimember districting schemes that diminished their voting strength until section 2 was amended in 1982, the synergistic relation between the U.S. Constitution and the act is obvious.

The reach of section 5 in protecting against dilution was limited in four respects, however. First, its coverage was restricted to a minority of the states and to a small number of jurisdictions within several of these. In 1981, for example, all or parts of twenty-two states were covered by the preclearance provisions, but only nine (seven in the South) were entirely covered, and in the remaining thirteen states, ten had fewer than six covered counties. Second, dilutionary laws on the books at the time jurisdictions were first covered by section 5 could not be challenged unless officials proposed changes. In many instances, dilutionary laws already in place simply remained unchanged. Third, when officials decided to pass a dilutionary law, they sometimes failed to submit it to the Justice Department or the Washington, D.C., court for preclearance, despite the section 5 requirement to do so. Once enacted, the changes might escape detection indefinitely. This was especially a problem in the early years of the act. Fourth, under the standard enunciated by the Supreme Court in *Beer v. United States* (1974),[64] only those proposed electoral changes in covered jurisdictions that were "retrogressive" or, in other words, would actually diminish minority voting strength from what it had been, were prohibited under section 5. Thus if the election law to be supplanted by the proposed change already diluted minority voting strength and the proposed change would not dilute it more, the change was permissible.[65]

In short, while section 5 was enforced by the Justice Department with growing effectiveness from the early 1970s on, especially with respect to state legislative redistricting, and while it undoubtedly prevented numerous dilutionary devices from being implemented, it was an instrument with serious limitations. These limitations led plaintiffs and their lawyers to continue to press suits in the federal courts, claiming that election structures violated the constitutional right of the minority group to an equal opportunity to elect candidates of its choice.

Bolden and the Amendment of Section 2

City of Mobile v. Bolden was a major turning point in the evolution of voting rights law, both constitutional and statutory. The Supreme Court in 1980 handed down the decision, sending shock waves through the voting rights community. A plurality of the badly divided Court held that the Fifteenth Amendment prohibited only formal barriers to registration and voting—not vote dilution. And it held that a Fourteenth Amendment violation required a showing of racially invidious purpose in creating or maintaining a dilutionary system such as at-large elections. The decision indicated, in the words of two voting rights lawyers, that "the justices confronted the lingering problem of adjudicating at-large vote dilution cases caused by the lack of clearly enunciated standards, but no five justices could agree on a solution."[66]

The intent requirement seemed to be the straw that would break the camel's back in voting rights cases, where the load borne by the plaintiffs' camel was already heavy. It was not simply one more burden equal in importance to the eight other *Zimmer* factors. Often the at-large system, like that in Mobile, had been established at the turn of the century as part of a Progressive Era reform package described by its advocates as a "good government" measure but often intended to get socialists, blacks, and white ethnic or working-class representatives off city council.[67] The likelihood was remote that plaintiffs in these cities could uncover "smoking guns" indicating reformers' racial intent more than half a century after the fact. In some cities there were not even extant public records or newspaper accounts that described the events leading to the adoption of such reforms. While this was not true for Mobile, the complexity of that city's racial politics in the early twentieth century was such that, when forced to present evidence of racially discriminatory purpose after the case was remanded to the district court, plaintiffs' lawyers and the Justice Department, intervenor in the case, felt compelled to hire three historians to comb the record—which stretched back to the early nineteenth century—for months. The results of this research led to the discovery of evidence of discriminatory intent in the *Bolden* case and an ultimate victory for the plaintiffs. But the hundreds of hours of historical research that might go into the discovery of incriminating racial motives would very likely have been prohibitive in most cases.

Faced with the new *Bolden* requirements, the voting rights bar mobilized the national civil rights lobby to press for a statutory response to the Court's decision. As fate would have it, the Voting Rights Act was coming up for renewal in 1982, and civil rights strategists decided to try to convince Congress to amend section 2—a permanent feature of the act covering the entire nation—to restore the *White-Zimmer* factors as the criteria for proving minority vote dilution. While this tactic appeared in 1981 to be a long shot, given the recent election of Ronald Reagan as president and his appointment of a quite conservative attorney general and assistant attorney general for civil rights—William French Smith and William Bradford Reynolds, respectively—it ultimately succeeded. In 1982 the Voting Rights Act was extended and the amendments to section 2 that the voting rights bar sought were made, thanks partly to clarifying compromise language introduced by Republican senator Robert Dole of Kansas. The amendment passed both houses of Congress by veto-proof majorities, despite strong initial opposition of the White

House and the continued spirited opposition of such Republican stalwarts as senators John East of North Carolina and Orrin Hatch of Utah. President Reagan signed the amended bill into law.[68]

As amended, section 2 explicitly prohibited any voting procedure that so much as resulted in members of the protected classes having "less opportunity than other members of the electorate to participate in the political process and to elect representatives of their choice." The law went on to say that "the extent to which members of a protected class have been elected to office in the State or political subdivision is one circumstance which may be considered: *Provided*, That nothing in this section establishes a right to have members of a protected class elected in numbers equal to their proportion in the population."[69] Shortly thereafter, ironically, the Supreme Court in *Rogers v. Lodge*[70] softened its intent standard to the extent that plaintiffs' burden of proof was essentially what it had been in *White* and *Zimmer*. By the end of 1982, therefore, amended section 2 enabled either the Justice Department or private plaintiffs to sue jurisdictions anywhere in the nation without having to prove intent.

Vote Dilution and Section 2 of the Voting Rights Act

Yet another irony in the train of events set in motion by the plurality ruling in *Bolden* became manifest when the Court gave its interpretation of amended section 2 in *Thornburg v. Gingles* (1986). In a decision written by Justice William Brennan, the Court adopted criteria for claims of at-large dilutionary effects similar to those proposed in a law review article by James Blacksher and Larry Menefee, plaintiffs' lawyers in *Bolden* whose criticism of *White* focused on its lack of judicial manageability.[71] Thenceforth, the Court held, claims of dilutionary effects under section 2 must meet a three-pronged test. First, the minority group must be "sufficiently large and geographically compact" to constitute a majority in at least one single-member district. Second, the group must be "politically cohesive," or in other words, tend to vote as a bloc. Third, the majority must also vote "sufficiently as a bloc to enable it . . . usually to defeat the minority's preferred candidate."[72] This test, which was significantly different from the *White* standards, streamlined the evidentiary requirements for minority plaintiffs.

With the exception of one feature—the Court's introduction of a population size and geographic compactness standard for minority groups that was not explicitly contained in the statute—the new test for dilution was immediately welcomed by most voting rights lawyers as a major advance.[73] Many dilution cases were filed in the 1980s, some of which were settled out of court in a manner favorable to plaintiffs, as the chapters to come make clear. Many at-large jurisdictions in the South (and to a lesser extent in the Southwest), having seen the handwriting on the wall, decided to adopt at least some single-member districts before someone filed a section 2 case in their locale, just to be on the safe side. As a city attorney in Texas whose municipality had shifted to single-member districts put it, "Because of recent changes in the law, [our city] felt a voluntary move to single-member districts to be more efficient from an economic and political standpoint."[74]

Conclusion

The Voting Rights Act of 1965, one of the most important civil rights statutes in American history, is part of a struggle for the minority franchise reaching back across centuries. Since its enactment, it has evolved beyond its original primary purpose of securing the black franchise (see table 1.1). Congress and the federal courts have gradually developed a theory of voting rights—one that extends to certain language minorities as well as to blacks—that includes protection against vote dilution. Constitutional protection is found in the language of the Fourteenth Amendment, so long as minority plaintiffs can show under the preponderance of the evidence an intent to diminish their voting strength through racial gerrymanders, at-large election systems, and the like. Vote dilution is also subject to protection under the Voting Rights Act, both in sections 2 and 5. Under both sections intent to discriminate need not be proved.[75] The achievement of these protections is a long and complicated story, not easily captured in statistics, although the authors of the essays in this volume present a good many of them. In fact, as the chapters that follow demonstrate, there is not one single story but at least eight: one for each southern state covered by section 5. To speak even more accurately, there are thousands of stories, each detailing the amazing efforts by determined men and women in communities throughout the former Confederacy to make good on this nation's promise of an inclusive democracy. While the research reported here only hints at these rich and varied local histories, it makes clear, through its integrated design and, chapter by chapter, its reiteration of common themes, how important the Voting Rights Act of 1965 has been its first twenty-five years.

TABLE 1.1
Major Legal Developments Involving Vote Dilution, 1960–1990

Year	*Development*	*Significance*
1960	*Gomillion v. Lightfoot*	Disfranchisement through racial gerrymandering is unconstitutional.
1962	*Baker v. Carr*	Legislative reapportionment is held justiciable.
1964	*Reynolds v. Sims*	Alabama legislature must reapportion itself under "one-person, one-vote" principle.
1965	Voting Rights Act is passed	Jurisdictions covered by section 5 must preclear voting changes.
1965	*Fortson v. Dorsey*	Multimember districts might possibly be unconstitutional in some cases.
1966	*South Carolina v. Katzenbach*	Voting Rights Act is constitutional.
1969	*Allen v. State Board of Elections*	Laws potentially causing minority vote dilution are subject to section 5 preclearance.
1970	Voting Rights Act is extended, amended	Section 5 remains in force.
1973	*White v. Regester*	Invoking "the totality of the circumstances," Court invalidates a legislative plan that diluted minority voting strength.
1973	*Zimmer v. McKeithen*	*White* standards are codified into eight factors.
1975	Voting Rights Act is extended, amended	Section 5 is expanded to cover language minorities and hence some other states (including Texas).
1976	*Beer v. United States*	Retrogression standard applies to section 5.
1980	*City of Mobile v. Bolden*	Evidence of discriminatory intent is required in Fourteenth Amendment and section 2 dilution cases.
1982	Voting Rights Act is extended, section 2 amended	Congress adopts a "results" standard for section 2 cases.
1982	*Rogers v. Lodge*	*Bolden* standards are softened in Fourteenth Amendment dilution cases.
1986	*Thornburg v. Gingles*	Three-prong dilution test in section 2 cases is established; polarized voting is the linchpin.

CHAPTER TWO

Alabama

PEYTON McCRARY, JEROME A. GRAY, EDWARD STILL, AND HUEY L. PERRY

WHEN COLONEL AL LINGO'S state troopers charged onto the Edmund Pettus Bridge in Selma, Alabama, on Sunday, 7 March 1965, their violent assault on unarmed civil rights demonstrators unwittingly dealt the cause of white supremacy a mortal blow. Television cameras recorded the entire scene as troopers attacked with nightsticks and tear gas, to the cheers of white onlookers, and Sheriff Jim Clark's mounted posse chased the panic-stricken demonstrators back across the bridge.[1] That footage on the evening news, followed by a mass march from Selma to Montgomery and the deaths of two civil rights workers at the hands of Klansmen and their sympathizers, prompted Congress to demand federal intervention in the black struggle for voting rights. President Lyndon B. Johnson personally addressed the Congress, urging passage of the administration's voting rights bill and stirring a nationwide television audience with an eloquent defense of political equality for southern blacks.[2]

Alabama was at the heart of the resistance to minority voting rights. Only 19 percent of the black voting-age population was registered in 1964, the lowest proportion in the South except for Mississippi. By contrast, 69 percent of the white voting-age population was registered. Discriminatory application of a literacy test—a requirement that two registered voters "vouch" for each new applicant—and a cumulative poll tax were the most effective tactics used to inhibit black political participation.[3]

The recently enacted Civil Rights Act of 1964 prohibited use in federal elections of different qualifications for blacks and whites, or disqualification of applicants for minor errors, and made a sixth-grade education prima facie proof of literacy.[4] The Alabama Supreme Court, charged by state law with responsibility for the literacy test, then developed a new set of short-answer quizzes; these were struck down, in turn, by the federal courts.[5]

The Voting Rights Act, passed by Congress a few months after the Selma-to-Montgomery march, was a watershed in the history of Alabama politics. By suspending literacy tests and the voucher system, this powerful new statute moved the state far along the road to universal suffrage.[6] The threat that federal examiners might intervene in the registration process throughout the state, as they did in a few counties that had registered virtually no blacks, helped persuade white officials to give up their discriminatory manipulation of registration laws.[7] The federal courts also struck down state court injunctions that would have prevented registrars in several black-belt counties from complying with the act.[8] Elimination of the state poll tax by federal court action also made it easier to add new voters to the rolls.[9] By October 1967, 248,432 blacks (52 percent of the black population) had registered in Alabama, more than doubling the black registration rate in only three years.[10] The fact that most blacks could now vote, in turn, brought a dramatic reduction in the use of traditional white supremacist rhetoric in most areas of the South. Because of the extraordinary strength of the George Wallace movement, however, Alabama was among the slowest to put away old habits. As late as the 1970 gubernatorial runoff against the moderate incumbent, Albert Brewer, Wallace's charge that his opponent was the candidate of "the bloc vote (Negroes and their white friends)" helped him come from behind and eke out a narrow victory over the governor.[11]

The effort of Wallace and his supporters to mobilize white voters after 1965 had, in fact, facilitated a great expansion in white registration in Alabama, now that the literacy test and the poll tax were gone. In absolute numbers the new white voters actually outstripped new black voters: 276,622 whites registered between 1964 and 1967, bringing the proportion registered to 90 percent.[12] In all except a few localities, blacks remained a political minority; outside of black-majority jurisdictions, no blacks were elected to public office.[13]

When the Voting Rights Act was adopted, most Alabama jurisdictions already used citywide or countywide elections designed, together with a "numbered-place" requirement, to dilute black voting strength. The state could thus prevent black officeholding without having to change its election laws (and thus be subject to the preclearance provision of section 5). Politicians in Alabama, as in the rest of the South, had long understood that at-large elections enable a white majority—if it chooses to vote as a cohesive bloc—to prevent minority representation altogether.[14] Black officeholding in Alabama was achieved, by and large, only as a result of successful voting rights litigation challenging the use of at-large elections.

The First Vote-Dilution Lawsuit

Barbour County, which George Wallace called home, was among those still electing county commissioners by single-member district in 1965. Shortly after the Selma-to-Montgomery march, Senator James S. Clark of Barbour County pushed through the legislature a bill that required at-large elections for the county commission.[15] The local paper quoted him as saying that one of the reasons for switching to countywide elections was "to lesson [*sic*] the impact of any block vote."[16] Clark, a Wallace floor leader in the legislature, used the term *block vote* as a code word for the black vote, as was customary in the 1960s.[17]

Barbour County's change from district to at-large elections for the county commission escaped federal detection until 1978.[18] When party officials attempted the same change in 1966 for the Barbour County Democratic Executive Committee, however, it sparked the very first minority vote-dilution lawsuit, *Smith v. Paris*.[19] Veteran civil rights lawyer Fred Gray, who had been a close associate of Martin Luther King, Jr., from the Montgomery bus boycott of 1955 to the Selma demonstrations in 1965, filed the case as a cooperating attorney of the NAACP Legal Defense and Education Fund. On behalf of the county's black citizens, Gray alleged that the elimination of ward elections by the executive committee was intentional discrimination designed to dilute the black vote, and thus violated the Fourteenth and Fifteenth amendments.[20]

For many years voters in each of sixteen districts had chosen their own representatives in the party primary, with only five members elected on an at-large basis. Between the passage of the Voting Rights Act and 21 February 1966, however, the number of blacks on the registration rolls increased from 723 to 3,100, approximately one-third of the total county electorate. In four districts blacks were now a majority of the registered voters.[21] After six blacks filed as candidates for the county executive committee, the incumbents adopted a resolution requiring all members to run countywide, rather than just within their districts.[22]

The plaintiffs were fortunate that their lawsuit was before Judge Frank Johnson, the legendary federal district judge in Montgomery who had heard most of the important civil rights cases in Alabama for more than a decade. The "clear effect of the resolution" adopted by the county executive committee, declared Johnson, was that "predominantly Negro beats now have their representatives determined for them by the predominantly white majority of voters in the county as a whole."[23] In that first election the black candidates received a majority of the votes cast in their districts but lost countywide. The defendants conceded that at-large elections had a discriminatory impact, disputing only the claim that the executive committee acted with a racial motive.[24]

As to motive, Judge Johnson's experience with racial attitudes in Barbour County went back to 1959, when he had ordered George Wallace, then a circuit judge in Barbour County, to allow the staff of the U.S. Commission on Civil Rights to examine voter registration records. Preston Clayton, Wallace's personal attorney in the earlier dispute, was now attorney for the County Democratic Executive Committee.[25] The court, however, saw the elimination of ward elections as just another in a history of efforts by Alabama whites to keep blacks from power. "If this court ignores the long history of racial discrimination in Alabama," declared Johnson, "it will prove that justice is both blind and deaf."[26] Johnson outlawed future use of the at-large scheme because "its passage was racially motivated" and thus violated the Fifteenth Amendment.[27] The Fifth Circuit Court of Appeals upheld Johnson's finding of unconstitutionality, and ordered new elections to be held on a single-member-district basis in 1968.[28]

Amazingly, the Barbour County Democratic Executive Committee defied both courts. At a meeting on 17 February 1968, the committee voted to elect new members in the May primary on an at-large basis, without requiring candidates to reside in a particular district.[29] "The majority of people in Barbour County," Senator Clark explained, wanted "to keep the Democratic Committee on an at-large basis and 'free from federal intervention.'"[30]

This time the United States government sued the Barbour County Democratic Executive Committee, charging that the resolution "was adopted with the purpose and effect of diminishing the effectiveness of the Negroes' vote."[31] This appears to be the first vote-dilution case filed by the Department of Justice, and the first in which it challenged the adoption of at-large elections as a violation of section 5 of the Voting Rights Act.[32] Seeing this case as "a sequel to *Smith v. Paris*," the court found the 1968 resolution "purposeful discrimination against Negroes in violation of the Fourteenth and Fifteenth Amendments."[33] When a new election was held on a single-member-district basis, four blacks were elected to the Barbour County Democratic Executive Committee.[34]

The history of racial discrimination mattered a great deal in Judge Johnson's court. His willingness to make judicial findings of invidious intent seems to have been based, in part, on his personal knowledge of that history. This tendency to focus on the question of motivation was more pronounced among federal judges in Alabama than elsewhere, for reasons that appear rooted in the individual biographies of the judges themselves. Vote-dilution lawsuits in the state for the next two decades, in any event, often turned on historical evidence of discriminatory intent. This historical evidence is worth a closer look.

The History of Discrimination in Alabama Politics

The Reconstruction Period

In 1867, two years after the end of the Civil War, the United States government sought to "reconstruct" the southern states by requiring the election of new constitutional conventions. Blacks were able to register freely, but many whites who had supported the Confederacy were disqualified under the terms of the Fourteenth Amendment. The convention elected under the new suffrage requirements was overwhelmingly Republican; it left voter registration open to blacks and continued, for a time, the restrictions on former Confederates.[35]

The state government elected under the new constitution, like the convention that had preceded it, was dominated by white Republicans, a majority of whom were residents of Alabama before the Civil War. These "scalawags," as native white Republicans were called by hostile white Democrats, represented predominantly white counties, especially in the northern half of the state. Northern whites who had moved to Alabama after the war ("carpetbaggers," in the Democratic lexicon), tended to represent black-majority constituencies, especially in the plantation counties of the south.[36] Except in counties or city wards where their race was in the majority, however, black officeholders were rare.[37]

The Democrats often used violence and intimidation as political weapons. During a special legislative election in 1869, for example, Mobile Democrats wheeled a piece of field artillery from a firehouse and trained it on a crowd of perhaps a thousand blacks waiting to cast their ballots. The crowd scattered without waiting to vote; the Democrat won the election.[38] The Ku Klux Klan was active in rural areas of the state between 1868 and 1872, beating and killing Republican leaders, burning their houses, lynching several blacks, and sending armed bands of as many as 160 white horsemen to break up Republican political rallies and intimidate voters.[39]

In the 1874 elections the Democrats again used violence and intimidation to secure permanent control of Alabama state government. In Mobile white horsemen shot down black voters on their way to the polls, killing one, wounding four, and intimidating countless others. Another major election riot in black-majority Barbour County left three dead and over forty wounded.[40] Systematic use of political violence, intimidation, and economic coercion played a pivotal role in the Democrats' "redemption" of Alabama from Republican rule.[41]

Minimizing the Effectiveness of Black Voting

The likelihood of federal intervention prevented the Democrats from simply disfranchising blacks and made it necessary to find alternative methods of assuring white supremacy.[42] The first legislature controlled by the Democrats enacted a statute designed, among other things, to punish election fraud. Under the new law, changing the preferences marked on a voter's ballot, bribing a voter, deterring a voter from casting his ballot, or failing to open the polling place at all—practices in which white election officials or party representatives routinely indulged—were illegal, but were only misdemeanors. The statute made it a felony, however, to vote more than once for any office during an election.[43] Democrats charged that blacks—but not whites—were often guilty of voting "early and often." "It is an established fact that a white man cannot easily vote more than once at one election," said one legislator during debate over the bill, because whites "do not all look alike."[44]

The prohibition on multiple voting was clearly intended as a device to limit primarily black election fraud, and perhaps to intimidate honest black voters as well. "Governor Houston has approved the new election law for the State," reported the *Montgomery Advertiser*: "Good-bye to negro repeating and packing of negroes around the Courthouse on election day."[45]

Democrats in Montgomery and Selma persuaded the legislature to remove predominantly black sections from each city's boundaries, so that whites would have a safe majority.[46] Mobile Democrats pushed successfully for the adoption of at-large elections for the county school board, replacing a "limited vote" procedure enacted in 1871 to allow minority representation. The new system of countywide elections eliminated black, as well as white Republican, membership on the school board.[47]

With the exception of a few predominantly white counties, most county commissions were already elected at large in Alabama.[48] Thus only in the black belt was white domination of local governing bodies in jeopardy. In 1876 the Democratic legislature eliminated elections altogether for county commissions in eight black-majority counties, authorizing the governor to appoint county commissioners. In several counties the legislative delegation was still Republican, and these bills were passed over their opposition.[49] The legislature also set unusually high security bonds for elected officials in certain black-belt counties, and Democrats tried to assure through community pressure that no whites would help Republicans raise the money for these bonds. The governor could then appoint a Democrat to the vacant office. The legislature also abolished the criminal court in black-majority Dallas County, solely because the judge was a black Republican, and created a new court to perform the same functions.[50]

Thereafter county commissioners and election officials in these counties were Democrats committed to the principle of white supremacy. Often they refused to open the polling places at all, or kept them open for only a few hours, in overwhelmingly black precincts. They used wholesale election fraud to win congressional, legislative, and gubernatorial races, regularly casting black votes intended for Republican or Populist candidates on behalf of their own conservative Democratic ticket, and justifying these tactics as a necessary evil to prevent a return to the "horrors" of Reconstruction.[51]

Widespread outcry against the conservatives' use of black votes in 1892 to defeat the Populist gubernatorial candidate, who was, after all, a white man, led the Alabama legislature to adopt an alternative approach: a restrictive voter registration and election law. Drafted by A. D. Sayre, a powerful committee chairman from black-majority Montgomery County, the bill authorized the governor to appoint all registration boards, provided that voters could register only in the month of May, and required the voter to produce his registration certificate in order to vote. Ostensibly a "reform" bill because it provided an official secret ballot for the first time instead of relying on the traditional "party ballot," it actually created a de facto literacy test. The complex form of the ballot, in which candidates were arranged alphabetically without party labels, was designed to confuse those who could not read well; illiterate or semiliterate voters could be assisted only by an election official and could remain in the voting booth only five minutes.[52] The complexities of casting the new official ballot were widely recognized as providing a "legal and honest way of preventing Negro control in the black counties."[53]

The Sayre Law cut black voter participation dramatically, to be sure: Kousser estimates that turnout among blacks dropped from 64 percent in 1892 to 42 percent in 1894. White participation also declined from 80 to 67 percent in the same period, however, and the decline was greatest among whites who had supported the Populist party in 1892. Thus the secret ballot "reform" broke the back of Alabama Populism and prepared the way for the wholesale disfranchisement of blacks and poor whites in 1901.[54]

Disfranchisement

By the late 1890s southern white conservatives no longer feared federal intervention to enforce the voting rights extended to blacks by the Reconstruction amendments. Northern whites were often disenchanted with the principle of Negro suffrage, and the theme of sectional reconciliation was dominant in the literature of the period. The Spanish-American War and U.S. intervention in the Philippines led a growing number of Americans to speak of the "white man's burden" to rule colored peoples throughout the world. The Supreme Court, reflecting (or perhaps even leading) this drift to the right, accepted the idea that state-sanctioned racial segregation was not unconstitutional.[55]

When the conservative wing of the Alabama Democratic party took firm control of state politics in 1900, it called an election for delegates to a constitutional convention to eliminate the black vote. Against the opposition of the few surviving Populist and Republican delegates, the convention enacted a cumulative poll tax, a literacy test, a long residency requirement, and required gainful employment for the past year.[56] Another provision disfranchised persons convicted of a variety of specific crimes, usually misdemeanors perceived by delegates as more often committed by blacks than whites.[57] These disfranchising devices were effective. In 1900 there were over 180,000 blacks eligible to vote in Alabama; by 1 January 1903, there were fewer than 3,000. Many whites, especially poorer whites, also lost their right to vote: over 230,000 whites qualified in 1900, but only 191,000 were registered at the beginning of 1903. As a result of disfranchisement, voter turnout in the presidential election of 1904 was only 24 percent of adult males. This figure represented an estimated 19 percent reduction among whites, when compared with the 1900 election, but an extraordinary 96 percent reduction in black voter turnout.[58]

"But if the Negroes did learn to read, or acquire sufficient property, and remember to pay the poll tax and to keep the record on file," notes Woodward, "they could even then be tripped by the final hurdle devised for them—the white primary."[59] As in other states, Alabama laws regulating primary elections allowed party officials to determine the rules for voting, thus providing the legal fiction that it was the party, not the state legislature, that limited participation to whites.

The possibility that litigation might persuade the federal courts to strike down the disfranchising devices enacted in 1901 was still a concern, even after the Supreme Court refused to take action in *Giles v. Harris*.[60] With the white primary as an insurance policy against such legal threats, however, white supremacy seemed to be safe at last. Then black-majority counties that had relied on gubernatorial appointment of county commissioners to maintain white supremacy felt safe in returning to popular elections, and many other counties switched to district elections.[61] The state legislature also adopted a new municipal code requiring larger cities to use ward elections for city council seats.[62]

The return to a ward system caused a brief controversy in Mobile, where close to two hundred blacks remained on the voter registration rolls, many in the overwhelmingly black seventh ward.[63] In 1908 opponents of Mayor Pat Lyons accused his "machine" of using the black vote to elect its aldermanic candidate in what was supposed to be a white primary. The mayor's supporters did, in fact, seem unusually tolerant, for their day, of black voting rights. In the next session the business-oriented Mobile legislative delegation, avoiding open reference to the race issue and employing the "good government" arguments common to advocates of at-large elections elsewhere, began the drive that culminated in the adoption of a commission form of government in 1911. Adopted at least in part to prevent Lyons from capitalizing on his strength in the overwhelmingly black seventh ward, the commission system eliminated the election of council members by single-member districts and thus added a new layer of insurance against black electoral influence.[64]

The Restoration of Black Voting Rights

For decades the multilayered system of discriminatory election laws enacted between 1893 and 1911 denied Alabama's black citizens any voice in the election of state or local officials. In 1944, however, the Supreme Court struck down the white primary in *Smith v. Allwright*.[65] Thereafter, the federal courts offered an arena where blacks might sometimes find vindication of their political rights.

Immediately blacks in Mobile, Birmingham, and the college town of Tuskegee began to register in larger numbers and tried unsuccessfully to vote in the Democratic primary. The governor and legislature pushed through a state constitutional amendment, drafted by Representative E. C. Boswell, that gave local registrars greater discretion to disqualify prospective voters. Black citizens in Birmingham, represented by local black attorney Arthur Shores with the assistance of the NAACP Legal Defense Fund, and in Mobile, represented by Chicago attorney George Leighton of the American Civil Liberties Union, successfully challenged the "Boswell Amendment" in federal court.[66]

Subsequently, however, the legislature adopted and voters ratified a new constitutional amendment prescribing a uniform registration application to be drawn up by the Alabama Supreme Court. Designed to accomplish the same goal of minimizing black voter registration by requiring applicants to fill out a complex, legalistic form and read portions of the Constitution, the new amendment was adopted in a deliberately quiet campaign and was not challenged in court for a decade.[67]

In addition to its continuing effort to prevent blacks from registering and voting, the Alabama legislature developed new tactics to minimize the effectiveness of black voting strength. The most flamboyant approach was conceived by state senator Sam Engelhardt of Macon County to deal with the rapidly growing black electorate of Tuskegee, the county seat and home of famed Tuskegee Institute.[68] Engelhardt persuaded the legislature to redraw Tuskegee's municipal boundaries in such a way that virtually all blacks found themselves residents of the rural portions of Macon County.[69]

Because the discriminatory purpose of his "Tuskegee gerrymander" was so obvious, it was immediately challenged in court in *Gomillion v. Lightfoot*.[70] On behalf of the local black political organization, the Tuskegee Civic Association, Montgomery attorney Fred Gray, with the assistance of the NAACP Legal Defense

Fund, challenged the act in federal court. The plaintiffs lost in the trial court because Judge Johnson felt obliged to follow the strong precedents against entering what Justice Felix Frankfurter had called the "political thicket" of redistricting.[71] On appeal, however, the plaintiffs won a unanimous victory before the Supreme Court. Although "cloaked in the garb of the realignment of political subdivisions," the gerrymander had the "inevitable effect" of depriving black citizens of the right to vote in municipal elections, according to Justice Frankfurter's opinion, which found that Engelhardt's legislation was "solely concerned with" the achievement of this racially discriminatory goal.[72]

The Perfection of Vote-Dilution Measures

Far less obvious in its racial purpose, and perhaps for that reason not challenged in court, was an "anti-single-shot" law Engelhardt persuaded the legislature to apply to all Alabama municipalities in 1951. Under the municipal election code, some cities used a *simple* at-large system that made it possible for a politically cohesive minority group to elect one representative if several council seats were to be filled in the same election. In order to accomplish this goal, the minority group must concentrate its votes on one of the candidates, and not cast the full number permitted. This practice, which increases the mathematical weight of the vote for the preferred candidate, is called single-shot, or "bullet," voting.[73] Engelhardt's law made single-shot voting impossible by disqualifying any ballot not including a full slate of preferences. As one black-belt legislator explained, the bill was necessary because "there are some who fear that the colored voters might be able to elect one of their own race to the [Tuskegee] city council by 'single shot' voting."[74] This is the first modern example of an Alabama statute designed explicitly to dilute minority voting strength.

Engelhardt's full-slate law remained in effect until 1961, when the Alabama legislature replaced it with another statewide law accomplishing the same purpose by requiring the use of numbered places for all elections.[75] Single-shot voting is impossible if each candidate is required to qualify for a separate *place* or *post* (i.e., place no. 1, place no. 2, and so forth). Because every seat on the governing body is filled through a head-to-head contest in which only one vote can be cast, there is no way to increase the mathematical weight of one's ballot by denying votes to other candidates.[76]

Democratic party leader Frank Mizell of Montgomery explained both the dangers of single-shot voting and the advantages of the place requirement to the State Democratic Executive Committee. "If you have a group of people who want to vote as a bloc, whether they be negroes or otherwise," he said, "it would be easy under the single shot voting for all of them to come in, to put a scallowag [*sic*] or put a negro in there." Mizell reminded his colleagues of "increasing Federal pressure" from the Department of Justice, which sought to "register negroes en masse, regardless of their criminal records." In light of changing circumstances, concluded Mizell, "it has occurred to a great many people, including the legislature of Alabama, that there should be numbered places."[77]

By the time the Voting Rights Act was adopted, Alabama had perfected a system of local and state laws that, for most jurisdictions, required at-large elections, numbered places, and a majority vote, making it virtually impossible for blacks to elect candidates of their choice without substantial white crossover voting. In a handful of counties or municipalities with substantial black majorities, unrestricted voter registration would inevitably give black voters effective majorities at the ballot box. Otherwise, only a change to district elections could provide black voters with an opportunity to elect representatives of their choice. With a few rare exceptions, such changes occurred over the next quarter century only as a result of successful voting rights litigation or objections by the Department of Justice.

Implementation of the Voting Rights Act

Section 5 Review by the Department of Justice

In the first few years after passage of the act, the Department of Justice concentrated on attacking barriers to registration, to participation in elections, and to filing of candidacies.[78] Not until 1969 did the Supreme Court make clear that section 5 required *all* proposed voting changes, including measures that could dilute minority voting strength, to be precleared by the Department of Justice before implementation.[79] Thereafter the Voting Section of the department, guided by evolving federal case law, scrutinized the adoption of potentially dilutive electoral procedures.[80]

The Attorney General first objected to a dilutive device in Alabama on 9 July 1971. The Jefferson County legislative delegation had imposed a numbered-place requirement on the election of Birmingham city council members shortly after the council appointed black attorney Arthur Shores to a vacant seat. Until then, Birmingham's at-large system was among the few in the state exempted from the 1961 numbered-place requirement; thus it would have been possible for Shores to win election in 1971 without substantial white crossover voting. Sponsored by Representative Bob Gafford, long an ardent segregationist and Wallace supporter, the bill's purpose was, according to the *Birmingham News*, "to minimize chances of election of Negroes to the council by forcing them to run head-to-head with white candidates for specific places."[81]

Most municipalities already used at-large elections and numbered places before 1965 and thus had no need to enact new laws that would require preclearance. Three small cities did adopt district elections in order to secure approval of annexation plans to which the department had objected.[82] Phenix City found itself confronting a Justice Department objection when the local legislative delegation tried to shorten the terms of unpopular city commissioners by imposing staggered terms. Knowing that it was under section 5 scrutiny, the city switched to a mayor-council form of government; it included two at-large seats but, at the request of the black community, three single-member districts.[83] One black council member was elected from the 62 percent black district.[84]

Approximately one-third of Alabama's county commissions were elected by single-member districts in 1965; sixteen sought to adopt at-large elections during the next two decades.[85] The Department of Justice objected to eleven of these changes and precleared the remainder because the black population was either too small or too geographically dispersed to constitute a black-majority district. Justice also objected to the adoption of at-large elections for three county school boards.[86]

Section 5 review was sometimes the cause of changes to district elections in Alabama. In most jurisdictions, however, the principal means of securing equitable election plans was through litigation. A number of federal court decisions in the early 1970s signaled that black plaintiffs in such cases would receive a fair hearing.

The Influence of Sims v. Amos *and* White v. Regester

In 1972 a three-judge panel decided in *Sims v. Amos* to outlaw further use of multimember districts in the apportionment of seats in the Alabama legislature, at least in part as a remedy for racial vote dilution.[87] Newspaper coverage of public reaction to the decision displayed widespread agreement among attorneys, legislators, local officials, and political observers that elimination of multimember districts would substantially increase black representation.[88] Implementation of the court's districting plan in 1974 increased the number of black legislators from two to fifteen.[89]

Three weeks after the court struck down multimember districts as racially discriminatory in *Sims v. Amos*, the Selma city council discovered that it had to change its method of elections. Because the city's population had passed the 20,000 mark by 1970, the state's municipal election code required Selma to choose between going to ward elections or cutting the number of council seats from ten to five. The black community petitioned for acceptance of single-member districts, and city council members agreed. Mayor Joe Smitherman seems to have played a role in persuading the council to choose ward elections, despite their recognition that such a change would "lead to the election of the council's first black members."[90]

Two communities apparently switched on their own initiative to district elections; the change even seems to have been motivated, in part, by a desire to provide minority representation. In 1972 the college town of Auburn adopted a mixed plan, with two members elected by each of four wards, plus a council president elected citywide.[91] More surprising was the switch to single-member districts in the state's capital city. Under the leadership of Mayor James Robinson, Montgomery adopted the mayor-council form of government with nine single-member districts. According to a recent study, "Montgomery adopted districts as the price to be paid for black assent to, and Justice Department approval of, a referendum to change from a commission to a strong-mayor system."[92] The county's two white state senators successfully fought to eliminate all at-large seats on the grounds that "having at-large councilmen would discriminate against blacks since the city has a greater percentage of whites," warning opponents that the federal courts might strike down the new law if at-large seats were included.[93]

Two weeks earlier, on 18 June 1973, the Supreme Court had for the first time found the use of at-large elections, together with numbered-place and majority-vote requirements, unconstitutional on the grounds of racial vote dilution in a Texas redistricting case, *White v. Regester*.[94] In the same year the Fifth Circuit set forth specific guidelines by which trial courts should decide such vote-dilution lawsuits in a Louisiana case, *Zimmer v. McKeithen*.[95] Alabama politicians now had fair warning that the at-large numbered-place system was open to legal challenge.

The Creation of an Alabama Voting Rights Bar

Thereafter, a new generation of voting rights lawyers challenged the use of at-large elections in community after community; when successful, as they usually were, these lawsuits transformed the racial politics of Alabama beyond recognition. Most of the work was done by young Alabama whites, educated at the University of Alabama Law School but affiliated with public-interest legal organizations, such as the NAACP Legal Defense and Educational Fund and the American Civil Liberties Union.[96] The Voting Section of the Department of Justice brought numerous cases; most of its attorneys handling Alabama cases were young whites from outside the South.[97] The so-called voting rights bar proved to be far more successful than its opponents were, at least in part because plaintiffs' attorneys and lawyers from the Justice Department were specialists who knew more about case law in this complex field than did those who represented state and local defendants.

The ability of private attorneys to bring successful voting rights litigation, which as a rule involved heavy expenses and a lengthy appeals process, was dependent on their ability to recover reasonable fees and expenses. In *Sims v. Amos*, the court had awarded the plaintiffs' attorneys fees under the established theory that lawyers representing class-action members in public-interest litigation acted as "private attorneys general" in seeking enforcement of federal law.[98] This prospect was thrown into doubt in 1975 by a Supreme Court decision in an unrelated case.[99] Congress revised the Voting Rights Act in 1975 to clarify its intention that private attorneys successfully representing the claims of minority voters receive expenses and reasonable fees for their time.[100]

White attorneys took great pains to consult closely with local black plaintiffs, most of whom were members of the Alabama Democratic Conference (ADC), the leading statewide black political organization. In 1972 loyalist party chairman Robert Vance, who had persuaded the State Democratic Executive Committee to remove the white supremacy symbol of a rooster from its campaign literature only six years earlier, persuaded fellow whites on the committee to bring blacks into the Alabama Democratic Party; ADC president Joe Reed of Montgomery became the party's vice-chairman for minority affairs.[101] By the 1980s Jerome Gray, ADC field director, worked closely with plaintiffs' attorneys in virtually all Alabama voting rights litigation, and ADC members provided most of the financial support.[102]

Initially the going was uncertain. In the fall of 1973, black plaintiffs in Pickens County challenged the use of at-large elections for the county commission, school board, and Democratic executive committee. The court required the school board and party committee plans, which were adopted after 1965, to be submitted for preclearance; the Department of Justice objected to the use of at-large and numbered-place requirements for both.[103] The county had long elected its commissioners by districts in the Democratic primary, however, using at-large elections only in the general election. The court required reapportionment of the district lines to comply with one-person, one-vote standards for the all-important primary, but let the at-large system stand for the general election. This decision was upheld on appeal.[104]

Fairfield, a small city in Jefferson County, was 48 percent black. Its city council was elected at large, with two seats to be filled by residents of each of six wards, and a council president to be elected without regard to residence. In 1968 blacks elected six council members; in 1972, however, whites won all thirteen seats. A suit was subsequently filed by blacks. Although Judge Sam Pointer did not conclude that the at-large system was intentionally discriminatory, he found that voting was racially polarized to a substantial degree, and ruled for the plaintiffs. The appeals court declared that finding at-large elections discriminatory in effect due to polarized voting was not sufficient to outlaw their use.[105] Judge Pointer then decided in favor of the city, and was upheld on appeal.[106]

Judge Frank Johnson in 1974 found in favor of the plaintiffs in a challenge to at-large council elections in Dothan, but stayed proceedings for a year because a black had been elected citywide.[107] On the basis of similar evidence, on the other hand, he outlawed the use of at-large elections for the Montgomery County commission.[108] Judging from these early cases, the standards of proof in dilution cases were still in flux.[109]

Challenging At-Large Elections in Mobile

The Alabama case that played the most important role in shaping national voting rights law was *Bolden v. City of Mobile*.[110] In 1975 black plaintiffs led by octagenarian Wiley L. Bolden, a voting rights activist since the days of the white primary, filed their challenge to the at-large election of three city commissioners, a system that had resulted in the total exclusion of blacks from office. Shortly thereafter a white state senator introduced a mayor-council bill that would require election to seven district seats and two at-large posts. The senator later testified that district elections provided the only way black voters could secure representation in

Mobile city government; he included the at-large seats in the hope of winning the support of "certain established members of the community."[111] Nevertheless, the conservative daily newspaper opposed any use of ward elections, explaining that the plan would have the effect of "assuring representation from the black community."[112] The bill did not pass.

Judge Virgil Pittman cited the defeat of this plan as evidence that the at-large system was being maintained with a racially discriminatory purpose. He also found that the city government was unresponsive to the black community in the delivery of municipal services, that city police continued to be guilty of brutality against blacks in law enforcement, that city agencies were desegregated only by court order, that few blacks were appointed to boards or committees, and that socioeconomic disparities between blacks and whites continued to inhibit black political participation.[113]

The most compelling aspect of the plaintiffs' case, however, was expert testimony that racially polarized voting made it unlikely that black candidates could ever win office in citywide elections. In addition, observed the judge, "practically all active candidates for public office testified it is highly unlikely that anytime in the foreseeable future, under the at-large system, that a black can be elected against a white."[114]

Under the prevailing *Zimmer* standard, the court had little alternative but to find for the plaintiffs. The question of remedy was more troublesome; because commissioners under the existing plan performed specific administrative functions of a citywide nature, Judge Pittman found it necessary to order replacement of the commission system by a mayor-council form of government patterned after that established in Montgomery.[115]

Some lower federal courts were beginning to require proof of racial purpose, however, not just discriminatory impact, before striking down dilutive election structures. The appeals court ruled in 1978 that proof of discriminatory intent was required, but held that Judge Pittman's findings "compel the inference that the system has been maintained with the purpose of diluting the black vote."[116] In 1980, however, the U.S. Supreme Court overruled the lower courts in *City of Mobile v. Bolden* and surprised knowledgeable observers by setting forth an "intent standard" for judging vote-dilution lawsuits. In a plurality opinion by Justice Potter Stewart, the Court held that plaintiffs must prove at-large elections were adopted or maintained with a racially discriminatory *purpose*. Arguing that plaintiffs had not presented such "intent" evidence in the first trial, a majority of the justices agreed to remand the case to the lower courts.[117] When the case was tried a second time, expert testimony concerning the historical evidence discussed earlier in this chapter demonstrated to the court that racial concerns played a significant role in the adoption of at-large elections in 1911.[118]

The intent standard set forth by Justice Stewart in the Mobile case, however, had aroused a furor in national civil rights circles. In hearings before subcommittees in both House and Senate, voting rights lawyers, black political leaders, and an increasingly broad spectrum of white public officials urged Congress to revise the

Voting Rights Act in such a way as to eliminate the need for this sort of detailed historical inquiry. A revision of section 2, known as the *Bolden* Amendment, made clear that Congress intended that the courts outlaw election practices that were discriminatory in effect, without requiring proof of invidious racial purpose.[119]

Litigation by the Department of Justice

The Department of Justice sometimes had to go to court to defend its objections to voting changes covered by section 5.[120] In such cases the act places the burden of proof on the jurisdiction. One such case involved Hale County, Alabama, which had switched from district to at-large elections for its county commission pursuant to a 1965 statute adopted the day after it was assigned federal registrars under the act. The county, contrary to the law, did not submit the change for a decade. Although it was a black-majority county, half of its registered voters and a majority of those turning out to vote were white, due to the low participation rate of its poverty-stricken black citizens. Regression analysis by a Department of Justice expert demonstrated, furthermore, that voting was highly polarized along racial lines. The court found Hale County's at-large election system racially discriminatory in purpose and effect.[121] Other counties recognized that they could not sustain the burden of proof in a section 5 challenge and agreed to return to district elections.[122]

The department's two most difficult Alabama cases were Fourteenth Amendment challenges to the at-large election of commissioners in the black-belt counties of Marengo and Dallas. Both were filed in 1978 and tried before Judge W. Brevard Hand of Mobile, who had almost always found for defendants in civil rights cases. Judge Hand concluded in both cases that there was no evidence of discriminatory intent; although he found evidence that voting was racially polarized to a significant degree, he ruled that blacks were close enough to a majority of the electorate that they could win if they worked harder to turn out the vote.[123]

The appeals court, however, refused to attribute the exclusion of blacks to the failure of blacks to work hard enough. In both cases it viewed the lower level of registration and turnout among blacks as a lingering effect of past discrimination in education and employment, and thus a factor favoring the plaintiffs. More importantly, the overwhelming evidence of racially polarized voting in both cases, which made it clear that blacks could not expect to win countywide elections, led the appeals court to rule in favor of the plaintiffs. By 1988 effective remedies were put into place, and black citizens in Marengo and Dallas counties were able to elect representatives of their choice.[124]

The Winning Coalition

More victories were won by the private voting-rights bar, working in close coalition with the Alabama Democratic Conference. ADC members were the plaintiffs in *Burton v. Hobbie*, a legal challenge to the legislative redistricting plan enacted by the state after the 1980 census.[125] The Department of Justice objected to the initial plan on 6 May 1982, and to a new legislative plan on 2 August 1982, on the grounds that both reduced black voting strength by comparison with the previous system imposed by *Sims v. Amos*.[126] Chairman Joe Reed of the ADC was the principal drafter for the districting arrangements proposed by the plaintiffs, adopted by the legislature, precleared by the Department of Justice, and approved by the court for use in new elections in the fall of 1983.[127]

In *Harris v. Graddick*, black plaintiffs successfully challenged the underrepresentation of blacks among poll officials in the state.[128] ADC members gathered the lists of county poll officials and identified their race in exhibits used at trial, as well as testifying about conditions in their counties. Not only was the quantitative evidence of white domination of the administration of Alabama elections dramatic, but the case revealed ongoing evidence of racial animosity like that found two decades earlier.[129] After the plaintiffs won a preliminary injunction, the state agreed to appoint substantial numbers of black poll officials and to establish a program of training and certification for all those who worked at the polls; staff members of historically black Alabama State University were actively involved in the training program and in a voter outreach project targeting young black adults. The state also agreed to gather and maintain precinct-level voter registration data by race, and to provide the court with detailed records of its efforts to implement the numerous changes.[130]

In a case tried under the Constitution such as *Underwood v. Hunter*, initiated in the late 1970s but not decided by the Supreme Court until 1985, evidence of a racially discriminatory purpose is essential. A challenge to the section of the 1901 state constitution disfranchising individuals convicted of various enumerated "petty crimes," *Underwood* turned on historical evidence that the framers of this provision explicitly intended that it eliminate black voters in significant numbers. The state's defense was that in addition to disfranchising blacks, the provision was also intended to prevent many poor whites from voting. The trial court agreed with this reasoning but was reversed on appeal; in a unanimous Supreme Court opinion, Justice William Rehnquist ruled that the state could not discount the compelling evidence of racial intent in the record merely by showing that the convention was also motivated by distaste for the poor. In light of this evidence of discriminatory purpose, moreover, only a modest additional showing of disparate impact was necessary for the plaintiffs to prevail.[131]

The 1982 revision of section 2 of the Voting Rights Act makes it unnecessary for plaintiffs to prove discriminatory intent in order to win a dilution case. Nevertheless, black plaintiffs in Alabama managed to turn the intent standard into a weapon to advance minority voting rights on a wholesale basis. In *Dillard v. Crenshaw County*, black citizens challenged the at-large election of commissioners in nine counties in one consolidated lawsuit.[132] The linchpin of their case was evidence of discriminatory purpose in the adoption of the statewide anti-single-shot and numbered-place requirements in 1951 and 1961 discussed above. In addition, the plaintiffs' expert historian testified that a third of the state's counties shifted from district to at-large elections between 1947 and 1971, after blacks began to register and vote in large numbers. On the basis of this historical evidence, Judge Myron Thompson ruled that "the plaintiffs have shown a substantial likelihood of prevailing," and enjoined further use of at-large elections in those counties.[133]

All of the defendants adopted single-member district plans for their county commissions. Then the plaintiffs added all the municipalities and school boards where at-large elections still resulted in the dilution of black votes (in the end some 180 jurisdictions). Most agreed to settle on election plans acceptable to local ADC leaders. Many of the changes to district elections documented in the next section of this chapter emanate from *Dillard* and its progeny. In a few jurisdictions, settlement talks between ADC leaders and local officials led to the adoption of cumulative or limited voting plans rather than single-member districts. These remedies succeeded in providing a substantial degree of black representation throughout Alabama.[134]

Changes from At-Large to District Elections in Alabama

At the time the Voting Rights Act was adopted, as we have noted, the handful of black elected officials in the state were restricted entirely to communities in which blacks constituted a majority of the registered voters. Nor did the removal of legal barriers to registration and voting lead immediately to black representation in white-majority jurisdictions. In 1970 only two white-majority cities, Auburn and Birmingham, had elected a black at large.[135] By 1989, however, black officeholding in Alabama approached the level of proportional representation. To what factors must we attribute this extraordinary change?

The existing social science literature provides two alternative hypotheses. Some accounts argue that racial attitudes have changed so markedly in the South during the last two decades that whites are generally willing to vote for qualified minority candidates; thus the increase in black officeholding in Alabama cities between 1970 and 1989 might result from a decline in the degree of racially polarized voting.[136] Most empirical studies, however, indicate a strong correlation between the use of single-member districts and the election of racial and ethnic minority officials. This evidence suggests that the increase in black representation results largely from the abolition of at-large elections.[137] In order to test these conflicting hypotheses, we compare the method of electing municipal governing bodies with the degree of representation for blacks in Alabama city government over the last two decades.[138]

Our principal concern is to identify the racial effect of changing from citywide to district elections. We measure the degree of black representation by an equity ratio (the percentage of elected officials who are black divided by the proportion of the jurisdiction's population that is black).[139] Between 1970 and 1989, 37 of the 48 cities with 6,000 or more inhabitants having a population at least 10 percent black switched to single-member districts, and another 5 to mixed plans (see table 2.2).[140] As a result, the degree of black representation in white-majority cities using single-member districts increased from zero in 1970 to slightly better than proportional representation in 1989 (see table 2.5). For mixed plans, the small number of cases renders any conclusion suspect; the equity ratios are significantly lower than under single-member district plans, primarily because no blacks were elected to any at-large seats in those cities (see table 2.3).[141]

To control for the possibility that declining racial prejudice alone explains the dramatic increase in black representation, we sought to identify a control group of cities retaining at-large elections. The success of minority plaintiffs and the Department of Justice in eliminating at-large elections, however, complicates the analysis. By 1989 the use of at-large elections, once ubiquitous, had all but disappeared in Alabama.

Only 6 of the 48 cities in our sample retained at-large elections (see table 2.1). This is a small and arguably unrepresentative sample. Three of the 6 were black-majority cities where at-large elections should benefit rather than disadvantage blacks; predictably, blacks were more than proportionally represented in 1989 (see table 2.4). Only 3 of the 42 white-majority cities in our sample elected their councils at large. The fact that blacks had proportional representation in these 3 cities, as well as in the 36 using single-member districts (see table 2.4), should not be taken as proof that at-large elections are no longer racially discriminatory. Indeed, the fact that blacks were adequately represented in these cities helps explain why their at-large systems went unchallenged in the 1980s.[142]

Had our survey been conducted a mere two years earlier, in January 1987, our control group would have included 31 cities still using at-large elections. As the data presented in table 2.5A demonstrate, the 27 white-majority cities in this control group had only minimal black representation. In contrast, blacks in the 11 cities electing council members by single-member districts had proportional representation.[143]

Between 1970 and 1989, 42 of the 48 Alabama cities of 6,000 or larger switched from at-large to district or mixed plans. Litigation was the principal cause of these changes, accounting for 26 of the new district systems and 1 of the shifts to a mixed plan (see table 2.8). Four of the changes came in response to objections by the Department of Justice.[144] Thus, in 31 of the 42 changes, some degree of coercion was involved. Voluntary decisions by city leaders accounted for only 11 of the shifts to district elections.[145] In many of those instances, furthermore, jurisdictions were well aware of the possibility of lawsuits or objections by the Department of Justice.[146]

Our findings provide little support to the view that a significant increase in minority representation occurred in Alabama merely because white voting behavior had changed. (Indeed, in districted cities, we found only two instances out of

148 white-majority districts in which blacks were elected. See table 2.6.) Instead, we provide new evidence to reinforce the conclusion of most empirical studies that district elections played a major role in increasing black officeholding.

Conclusion

As long as at-large elections were in place, white majorities voting as a bloc were able to prevent black citizens enfranchised by the Voting Rights Act from winning local office. Most changes from at-large to district elections in Alabama resulted either from litigation or, to a lesser degree, objections by the Department of Justice. Although lawsuits won by the department played a key role in eliminating at-large elections in various black-belt counties, most of the changes were due to litigation by private attorneys. These changes substantially increased minority representation on local governing bodies, both rural and urban. Indeed, black representation in our sample has now reached the level of proportional representation in Alabama.

The act has played a critical role in this achievement. Its first great success, the enfranchisement of the black population, brought less immediate change in black representation to Alabama than to some other southern states, because state election laws already in place effectively diluted black voting strength. The evolution of case law in the voting area, however, ultimately provided civil rights lawyers with the weapons necessary to eliminate those barriers to minority representation. In most of the successful lawsuits in Alabama, historical evidence of discriminatory intent played a key role in the outcome. The story we have chronicled is controversial, we recognize, among those who believe that federal intervention with state and local control of elections in the South, either by administrative action or as a result of court decisions, is no longer warranted. In the best of worlds, effective minority representation would not depend on such intrusive legal action. Our findings make clear, however, that at least in Alabama, effective minority representation could have been achieved in no other way.

TABLE 2.1
Black Representation on Council in 1989 by Election Plan, Alabama Cities of 6,000 or More Population with 10 Percent or More Black Population in 1980

Type of Plan by % Black in City Population, 1980	N	*Mean % Black in City Population, 1980*	*Mean % Black on City Council, 1989*
SMD plan			
10–29.9	23	19	20
30–49.9	13	37	38
50–100	1	74	80
Mixed plan			
10–29.9	1	16	11
30–49.9	2	38	30
50–100	2	52	51
At-large plan			
10–29.9	3	20	20
30–49.9	0	—	—
50–100	3	68	74

TABLE 2.2
Changes in Black Representation on Council between 1970 and 1989, Alabama Cities of 6,000 or More Population with 10 Percent or More Black Population in 1980

Type of Change by % Black in City Population, 1980	N	*Mean % Black in City Population, 1980*	*Mean % Black on City Council*	
			Before Change (1970)	*After Change (1989)*
		Changed Systems		
From at-large to SMD plan				
10–29.9	23	19	0	20
30–49.9	13	37	0	38
50–100	1	74	0	80
From at-large to mixed plan				
10–29.9	1	16	11	11
30–49.9	2	38	0	30
50–100	2	52	0	51
		Unchanged Systems		
At-large plan				
10–29.9	3	20	0	20
30–49.9	0	—	—	—
50–100	3	68	46	74

TABLE 2.3
Black Representation in 1989 in Mixed Plans by District and At-Large Components, Alabama Cities of 6,000 or More Population with 10 Percent or More Black Population in 1980

% Black in City Population, 1980	N	*Mean % Black Councilpersons in District Components, 1989*	*Mean % Black Councilpersons in At-Large Components, 1989*
10–29.9	1	13	0
30–49.9	2	42	0
50–100	2	59	0

TABLE 2.4
Two Equity Measures Comparing Percentage Black on Council in 1989 with Percentage Black in City Population in 1980, Alabama Cities of 6,000 or More Population with 10 Percent or More Black Population in 1980

Type of Plan by % Black in City Population, 1980	N	*Difference Measure (% on Council − % in Population)*	*Ratio Measure (% on Council ÷ % in Population)*
		Changed Systems	
From at-large to SMD plan			
10–29.9	23	1	1.10
30–49.9	13	1	1.03
50–100	1	6	1.08
From at-large to mixed plan			
10–29.9	1	−5	0.69
30–49.9	2	−8	0.78
50–100	2	−1	0.98
		Unchanged Systems	
At-large plan			
10–29.9	3	0	1.00
30–49.9	0	—	—
50–100	3	18	1.09

TABLE 2.5
Changes in Black Representation on Council between 1970 and 1989, Alabama Cities of 6,000 or More Population with 10 Percent or More Black Population in 1980 (Ratio Equity Measure)

Type of Change by % Black in City Population, 1980	N	*Black Representational Equity on Council*	
		1970	*1989*
	Changed Systems		
From at-large to SMD plan			
10–29.9	23	0.00	1.10
30–49.9	13	0.00	1.03
50–100	1	0.00	1.08
From at-large to mixed plan			
10–29.9	1	0.11	0.69
30–49.9	2	0.00	0.78
50–100	2	0.00	0.98
	Unchanged Systems		
At-large plan			
10–29.9	3	0.00	1.00
30–49.9	0	—	—
50–100	3	0.46	1.09

TABLE 2.5A
Changes in Black Representation on Council between 1970 and 1986, Alabama Cities of 6,000 or More Population with 10 Percent or More Black Population in 1980 (Ratio Equity Measure)

Type of Change by % Black in City Population, 1980	N	*Black Representational Equity on Council*	
		1970	*1986*
	Changed Systems		
From at-large to SMD plan			
10–29.9	4	0.00	1.00
30–49.9	7	0.00	1.00
50–100	0	—	—
From at-large to mixed plan			
10–29.9	2	0.35	1.06
30–49.9	2	0.00	0.79
50–100	2	0.00	0.87
	Unchanged Systems		
At-large plan			
10–29.9	21	0.00	0.32
30–49.9	6	0.00	0.26
50–100	4	0.49	1.09

TABLE 2.6
Black Representation in Council Single-Member Districts in 1989, Alabama Cities of 6,000 or More Population with 10 Percent or More Black Population in 1980

% Black Population of District	N[a]	*Mean % Black Population in Districts, 1980*	*Mean % Black Councilpersons in Districts, 1989*
0–29.9	139	8	0
30–49.9	9	41	22
50–59.9	0	—	—
60–64.9	2	61	100
65–69.9	17	67	100
70–100	38	82	100

[a]Racial composition of single-member districts was not available for the following cities (each of which had five districts): Athens, Brewton, Lanett, Prichard, and Russellville.

TABLE 2.7
Black Council Representation in Single-Member Districts in 1989 by Racial Composition of District, Alabama Cities of 6,000 or More Population with 10 Percent or More Black Population in 1980

Racial Composition of District	N	*Mean % Black Population in Districts, 1980*	*Mean % Black Councilpersons in Districts, 1989*
Black majority[a]	57	74	100
White majority	148	10	1

[a]There were no districts in the 50–59.9 percent black range.

TABLE 2.8
Cause of Change from At-Large to Mixed or District Plan between 1970 and 1989, Alabama Cities of 6,000 or More Population with 10 Percent or More Black Population in 1980

City	*Did Lawsuit Accompany Change?*	*Reason for Change*
	Changed to Single-Member Districts	
Alabaster	No	Objection of Department of Justice to annexations in 1977; objection withdrawn in 1983 upon submission of a single-member-district plan.
Alex City	No	Objection by Department of Justice to annexations in 1986; withdrawn upon submission of a single-member-district plan in 1987.
Andalusia	No	Voluntary change to single-member districts in 1988, at the request of the black community.
Athens	Yes	*Dillard v. Crenshaw County;* consent decree implemented in 1988.
Atmore	Yes	*Dillard v. Crenshaw County;* consent decree implemented in 1988.
Attalla	No	Ordinance, 1988; supported by local black leaders; in 1984 Attalla had switched from at-large elections to a mixed plan, also voluntarily.
Bay Minette	No	Objection by Department of Justice to annexations in 1986; withdrawn upon submission of single-member-district plan in 1987.

(*continued*)

TABLE 2.8 (*Continued*)

City	*Did Lawsuit Accompany Change?*	*Reason for Change*
Brewton	Yes	*Dillard v. Crenshaw County;* consent decree implemented in 1988.
Decatur	Yes	*Dillard v. Crenshaw County;* consent decree implemented in 1988.
Demopolis	Yes	*United States v. City of Demopolis;* consent decree implemented in 1986.
Enterprise	Yes	*McClain v. City of Enterprise;* consent decree implemented in 1986.
Eufaula	Yes	*Dillard v. Crenshaw County;* consent decree implemented in 1988.
Florence	Yes	*Dillard v. Crenshaw County;* consent decree implemented in 1988.
Gadsden	Yes	*Adams v. City of Gadsden;* consent decree implemented in 1986.
Greenville	No	Legislation upon request of local chapter of Alabama Democratic Conference.
Guntersville	Yes	*Dillard v. Crenshaw County;* consent decree implemented in 1988.
Huntsville	Yes	*Grayson v. Madison County;* consent decree implemented in 1988.
Jackson	Yes	*Elliott v. City of Jackson;* consent decree implemented in 1985 (3 districts; 2 members per district).
Jasper	No	Legislation adopted following unsuccessful challenge to at-large elections (*Chapman v. Nicholson*).
Lanett	Yes	*Reese v. Yeargan;* consent decree implemented in 1988.
Leeds	Yes	Objection by Department of Justice to annexations in 1985; subsequently sued in *Dillard v. Crenshaw;* consent decree implemented in 1988.
Mobile	Yes	*Bolden v. City of Mobile;* plaintiffs won at trial; court-ordered legislation implemented in 1985.
Montgomery	No	Legislation adopted in 1973 as a result of voluntary action initiated by Mayor James Robinson and the

TABLE 2.8 (*Continued*)

City	*Did Lawsuit Accompany Change?*	*Reason for Change*
		county's legislative delegation; change approved in referendum and implemented in 1975.
Northport	No	Voluntary change at request of black community; implemented in 1988.
Opelika	Yes	*Lee County Branch of NAACP v. City of Opelika;* consent decree implemented in 1986.
Opp	Yes	*Dillard v. Crenshaw County;* consent decree implemented in 1988.
Pell City	Yes	*Dillard v. Crenshaw County;* consent decree implemented in 1988.
Prichard	No	Legislation adopted voluntarily at the behest of black-majority city government.
Prattville	Yes	*Dillard v. Crenshaw County;* consent decree implemented in 1988.
Russellville	Yes	*Dillard v. Crenshaw County;* consent decree implemented in 1988.
Sheffield	Yes	*Dillard v. Crenshaw County;* consent decree implemented in 1988.
Sylacauga	No	Voluntary change adopted at the request of black community.
Talladega	Yes	*Taylor v. City of Talladega;* consent decree implemented in 1988.
Tarrant City	Yes	*Dillard v. Crenshaw County;* consent decree implemented in 1988.
Troy	Yes	*Henderson v. City of Troy;* consent decree implemented in 1986.
Tuscaloosa	Yes	*Mallisham v. City of Tuscaloosa;* consent decree implemented in 1985.
Tuscumbia	Yes	*Dillard v. Crenshaw County;* consent decree implemented in 1988.
		Changed to Mixed Plan
Anniston	No	Legislation prompted by threat of litigation by Department of Justice.

(*continued*)

TABLE 2.8 (*Continued*)

City	*Did Lawsuit Accompany Change?*	*Reason for Change*
Auburn	No	Legislation; voluntary change in 1972; liberal sentiment in a university town.
Bessemer	Yes	*Tolbert v. City of Bessemer;* consent decree implemented in 1986.
Phenix City	No	Objection by Department of Justice to adoption of staggered terms, combined with local dissatisfaction with existing city commissioners; under pressure from black leaders, and aware of federal scrutiny, legislative delegation adopted a mixed plan, which was precleared in 1977.
Selma	No	1970 census showed Selma's population was over 20,000; state municipal code required Selma to use districts or cut the size of its council; aware of federal court rulings concerning at-large elections, and pressed by black leaders, council agreed to a mixed plan with 5 double-member districts and an at-large council president; in 1980s council was reduced to 1 member per ward and ward lines were redrawn pursuant to court order in a one-person, one-vote lawsuit brought by whites; in 1988 legislation adopted with consent of city government created 8 single-member districts, with the council president continuing to be elected at large.
SUMMARY	Yes 27 (64%) No 15 (36%)	

TABLE 2.9
Major Disfranchising Devices in Alabama

Device	Date Established	Date Abolished
Restricting voter assistance	1893	1988[a]
Literacy test, voucher system	1901	1965[b]
Poll tax	1901	1966[c]
Long residency requirement	1901	1972[d]
Petty crimes provision	1901	1985[e]
White primary	1902	1944[f]
Registrar discretion in judging applicant's interpretation of state or federal constitutions	1946	1949[g]
Court-prepared educational test	1951	1964[h]

[a] *Harris v. Siegelman,* 695 F. Supp. 517 (M.D. Ala. 1988).

[b] Voting Rights Act.

[c] *United States v. Alabama,* 252 F. Supp. 95 (M.D. Ala. 1966).

[d] Unconstitutional in light of *Dunn v. Blumstein,* 405 U.S. 330 (1972).

[e] Ruled unconstitutional in *Underwood v. Hunter,* 730 F.2d 614 (11th Cir. 1984), *aff'd,* 471 U.S. 222 (1985).

[f] Unconstitutional in light of *Smith v. Allwright,* 321 U.S. 649 (1944).

[g] *Davis v. Schnell,* 81 F. Supp. 872 (S.D. Ala. 1949), *aff'd,* 336 U.S. 933 (1949).

[h] *United States v. Hines,* 9 Race Rel. L. Rep. 1332 (N.D. Ala. 1964) [Sumter County]; *United States v. Cartwright,* 230 F. Supp. 873 (M.D. Ala. 1964) [Elmore County]; and *United States v. Parker,* 236 F. Supp. 511 (M.D. 1964) [Montgomery County].

TABLE 2.10
Black and White Registered Voters and Officeholders in Alabama, Selected Years[a]

	Black		White	
	N	%	N	%
Registered Voters				
1964[b]	92,737	9	935,695	91
1966[c]	246,396	17	1,192,072	83
1992[d]	373,205	22	1,335,837	78
Officeholders[e]				
State house				
1964	0	0	105	100
1966	0	0	105	100
1992	18	17	87	83
State senate				
1964	0	0	35	100
1966	0	0	35	100
1992	5	14	30	86

[a]Mean black Alabama population, 1960–90 = 26.8%.

[b]U.S. Commission on Civil Rights 1968.

[c]Southern Regional Council (Voter Education Project), "Voter Registration in the South, 1966."

[d]Data submitted by the state of Alabama in connection with its legislative and congressional redistricting plans, 1992.

[e]U.S. Commission on Civil Rights 1968; Joint Center for Political and Economic Studies 1990.

CHAPTER THREE

Georgia

LAUGHLIN McDONALD,
MICHAEL B. BINFORD,
AND KEN JOHNSON

THE IMPACT of the Voting Rights Act in altering the political environment in Georgia has been substantial. Dramatic changes have come in the registration of eligible black voters, and, with more equitable forms of voting, in the election of black candidates to office. The degree of change is all the more impressive given the background of intentional discrimination against black political participation in this state.

On the eve of passage of the act, fewer than a third of age-eligible blacks in Georgia were registered to vote.[1] The disparities were even greater in the state's twenty-three counties with black voting-age majorities, where an average of 89 percent of whites, but only 16 percent of blacks, were registered. Despite the fact that blacks were 34 percent of the voting-age population, there were only three black elected officials in the entire state, and they had been elected only in the preceding three years.[2] This exclusion from the normal political processes was not fortuitous; it was the result of two centuries of deliberate and systematic discrimination by the state against its minority population.

THE HISTORY OF DISCRIMINATION: THE EARLY YEARS

Blacks first got the right to vote in Georgia in 1867 as a result of federal military reconstruction.[3] The state held a constitutional convention the following year—roundly denounced by white Democrats as a "nigger–New England" convention—and formally guaranteed blacks citizenship, equal protection of the law, and the right to vote.[4] Because of the intense opposition of whites, the convention did not expressly guarantee the right of blacks to hold office.

At the ensuing elections, which were accompanied by an extremely high level of racial violence, twenty-five blacks were elected to the house and three to the senate. They were promptly expelled from office. Four mulattoes were also elected to the house and were originally targeted for expulsion, but they were granted the status of "honorary white men" and allowed to keep their seats.[5] Because of the expulsions, as well as continuing violence and white terrorism across the state,

Georgia was again placed under federal military reconstruction. The expelled blacks were returned to the general assembly, certain Democrats were disqualified under the Fourteenth Amendment, and control of the lower chamber returned to the Republicans.

The change in political fortune of blacks was short-lived. With the election of James Smith as governor in 1872, full control of the executive and legislative branches passed to white Democrats. This shift signaled that blacks were no longer a viable element in state politics and paved the way for the complete restoration of white supremacy. The state was assisted in its efforts by the U.S. Supreme Court, which weakened civil rights enforcement in a series of decisions, including *United States v. Cruikshank*[6] and *United States v. Reese*,[7] holding that the right to vote was a state-created, not a federal, right.

The "redeemed" legislature moved quickly to roll back Reconstruction and nullify the effects of black suffrage. It reimplemented proof of payment of the poll tax as a condition for voting;[8] abolished ward voting for the city of Atlanta, which had allowed the election of blacks to office; eliminated local elections altogether in majority-black McIntosh County; and abolished district elections for county school boards in favor of a system of appointments by white grand jury "elites."[9]

In 1873, the general assembly increased the residency requirements for voters in order to take advantage of the supposed itinerant habits of blacks and disfranchise them.[10] Local officials also closed their registration books except during planting time, when many blacks would find it difficult, if not impossible, to register.[11] Aside from these "legal" methods of limiting the black vote, the state resorted to such time-honored stratagems as intimidation, violence, vote buying, ballot-box stealing, and the use of "tissue ballots" that facilitated stuffing ballot boxes and altering the results of elections.[12]

The state adopted a new constitution in 1877. Robert Toombs, the acknowledged leader of the constitutional convention, consigned blacks to a status that was less than human when he boasted: "Give us a convention, and I will fix it so that the people shall rule and the Negro shall never be heard from."[13] The convention incorporated the new statutory residency requirements and added bribery and larceny to the list of disfranchising offenses that blacks were thought more likely to commit than whites.[14] But the main work of disfranchisement was the adoption of a cumulative poll tax, requiring proof of payment of past as well as current poll taxes as a condition for voting.[15] The tax could accumulate indefinitely and was described by one observer as "the most effective bar to Negro suffrage ever devised."[16]

The poll tax finally was abolished in Georgia in 1945.[17] Leaders of the general assembly assured their colleagues that repeal would increase white voter participation and would not affect the state's white primary.[18]

In an additional effort to consolidate power in the hands of ruling white Democrats, the legislature passed a law in 1890 giving party officials the duty of conducting primary elections.[19] This allowed parties to enact rules excluding blacks, which the Democratic party eventually did, thereby adopting into its formal rules what its general practice had been.[20] Since victory in the Democratic primary was tantamount to election, exclusion from the primary effectively eliminated blacks from meaningful participation in Georgia politics. Further exclusionary efforts included a law passed in 1894 that required registration by race on separate lists.[21] Given the climate of the times, this law merely facilitated fraud and discrimination against blacks.[22]

While the state moved relentlessly toward white hegemony, the Populist revolt of the early 1890s, led by Georgia firebrand Tom Watson, provided a countervailing tendency. The Populists, composed of agrarian masses and an emerging blue-collar proletariat, urged a united front of black and white farmers to oppose the oppressive forces of capitalist finance and industrialism. Its platform called for racial cooperation and justice, and repudiated race hatred and lynch laws. The Populist movement failed in Georgia by the middle of the decade—with Watson himself turning to virulent racism and anti-Semitism—in large measure because of the demagogic and destructive use of the race issue by other white state and local politicians at the time.[23]

As effective as the prior disfranchising measures were, the centerpiece of Georgia's efforts to deny the vote to blacks, the Disenfranchisement Act of 1908, came later.[24] Governor Hoke Smith's naming of the act in his message to the legislature left no doubt as to its goal.[25] This law provided for registration by any male who was sane, had no criminal record, had paid all taxes since 1877, had met the existing residency requirements, and had satisfied one of the following additional requirements: (1) had served honorably in wars of the United States or in the forces of the Confederate states; (2) had descended from persons who had such service records; (3) was of "good character" and could understand the duties of citizenship; (4) could read and write in English any paragraph of the state and federal constitutions or could understand and give a reasonable interpretation of any paragraph of such constitutions; or, (5) owned at least forty acres of land or property assessed for taxation at the value of at least five hundred dollars.[26]

Few blacks could meet any of these requirements as they were administered. They had not fought in wars in significant numbers, nor had their ancestors. The good character, literacy, and understanding tests, aside from the fact that they were designed to exclude uneducated blacks, were administered by white Democrats who made sure that blacks did in fact fail. Qualification through property ownership, given the disadvantaged economic position of blacks in the South, was for them a virtual impossibility. In *South Carolina v. Katzenbach* (1966)[27] the 1908 Georgia scheme was described as "specifically designed to prevent Negroes from voting." Five years after passage of the act, disfranchisement was intensified by a system of permanent registration requiring all voters to submit to examination by a board of registrars.[28] Since the boards were composed of whites who were hostile to black voting, many blacks were denied registration or were discouraged from even attempting it.[29]

A contemporary publication noted that Georgia had "closed the door of political hope in the faces of one million of its citizens."[30] A commentator writing more than twenty years later reported that following passage of the Disenfranchisement Act, there was "almost absolute exclusion of the Negro voice in state and federal elections."[31]

Abolition of the White Primary

The white primary was successfully challenged in Georgia in 1945 in *King v. Chapman*,[32] after the Supreme Court's decision in *Smith v. Allwright*[33] invalidated the white primary system in Texas. Eugene Talmadge, a candidate for governor the following year and a confirmed white supremacist, responded by orchestrating a series of challenges to blacks around the state for allegedly being improperly registered and thus ineligible to vote in the primaries.[34] These challenges were a stopgap measure and, despite their *in terrorem* effect, did not keep a significant number of blacks from the polls. The challenges collapsed under their own administrative weight, and most of the challenged blacks actually voted.[35]

The legislature made a final attempt to salvage the white primary in 1947. It enacted a white primary bill repealing all statutes linking the primary to the state in an attempt to remove the primary from state control and thus from federal judicial oversight. The bill was vetoed by Governor M. E. Thompson, who questioned the legality of the bill and said it was an invitation to fraud.[36]

After the White Primary: Black Mobilization and New Restrictions on Registration

The demise of the white primary set in motion two opposing forces in the state: mobilization in the black community and efforts by the white leadership to make the registration process more restrictive. In 1940, before the end of the white primary, estimates placed the black registration in Georgia at 20,000.[37] After its abolition in 1945, black voter-registration organizations sprang up across the state, including the All-Citizens Registration Committee of Atlanta (ACRC), which has claimed the distinction of being "the oldest continuous political education and registration organization of its kind in the South."[38] It was through the efforts of ACRC and other groups that 125,000 blacks, 18.8 percent of the eligible population, were registered by late 1947.[39] The political leadership of the state was not slow in responding to these political stirrings in the black community.

By the time Eugene Talmadge's son Herman became governor in 1948, the decision in *King v. Chapman* had made the outright exclusion of blacks from the primary no longer possible. Accordingly, the state turned its attention once again to making the registration process more difficult. In 1949, it passed a reregistration and purge law.[40] Voters who failed to vote in at least one election in a two-year period were automatically purged, unless they requested a renewal of their registration.

The most innovative feature of the new law was a requirement that all who sought reregistration on the basis of good character and understanding of the duties of citizenship—that is, those who could not qualify under the literacy provisions—were required to take a test and successfully answer ten of thirty questions. The law proved to be as burdensome to whites as to blacks, and as a result, the Talmadge administration secured passage of a bill allowing those registered under the preexisting statutes to remain on the voter rolls.[41]

The traditional leadership of the state felt a new urgency to shore up the state's registration laws and protect white supremacy when Congress enacted the Civil Rights Act of 1957, the first civil rights act since Reconstruction.[42] The act prohibited discrimination in voting and authorized the Attorney General to bring suit for injunctive relief. That same year, the Georgia General Assembly adopted a resolution calling for the repeal of the Fourteenth and Fifteenth amendments to the Constitution because they "were malignant acts of arbitrary power" and "are null and void and of no effect."[43]

In 1958, the state enacted a new registration act,[44] which incorporated the provisions of the old one but added an even more stringent test for the registration of those who could not read or write. They were required under the "good character and understanding" qualification to correctly answer twenty of thirty questions propounded by the registrar. The questions were difficult for even the best educated person to answer. They were an insurmountable barrier to illiterate blacks, particularly since the tests were administered by unsympathetic whites.[45]

Among the thirty questions were: What is a republican form of government? How does the Constitution of the United States provide that it may be amended? What does the Constitution of the United States provide regarding the suspension of the privilege of the writ of habeas corpus? How does the constitution of Georgia provide that a county site may be changed? How may a new state be admitted to the Union? One question, with no irony apparently intended, was: What does the Constitution of the United States provide regarding the right of citizens to vote? The thirty questions were rewritten and reduced to twenty in 1964, with fifteen correct answers considered a passing score.[46] Robert Flanagan, for many years the field director of the Georgia National Association for the Advancement of Colored People (NAACP), says that there was actually only one correct answer to each question, and that was "white folks ain't going to let black folks vote."[47]

The difficulty blacks had in registering under restrictive statutes that gave total discretion to hostile local officials, and the failure of existing civil rights laws to remedy the problem, were exemplified by Terrell County. Although it was 64 percent black, only 48 blacks—compared to 2,810 whites—were registered to vote in 1958.[48] The reasons for the disparities were simple. Registration was segregated; whites were given white application forms, and blacks were given green application forms. The white forms were processed, and the green forms were not. The literacy test was administered in a racially discriminatory manner, and blacks were held to a higher standard of literacy than were whites.

The Department of Justice brought one of its first suits under the Civil Rights

Act of 1957 against Terrell County in 1959, seeking an injunction against discriminatory local registration practices.[49] The case was bitterly contested, and although the department eventually won an injunction, only five blacks were added to the county voter rolls by 1960.

Despite the federal court order, opposition to black registration remained unabated in Terrell County, appropriately dubbed by civil rights activists "Terrible Terrell." In 1963, Sheriff Zeke Mathews locked up two Student Nonviolent Coordinating Committee (SNCC) workers engaged in voter registration on trumped-up charges of vagrancy. The federal court again stepped in and enjoined local officials from interfering with black registration efforts.[50]

Similar strong-arm tactics were used in nearby Sumter County, in which 44 percent of the population was black but only 8.2 percent of the black voting-age population was registered. Voting was segregated, and the Jaycees, an all-white organization, ran county elections. In 1963, four civil rights workers, John Perdew, Don Harris, and Ralph Allen of SNCC, and Zev Aeloney of the Congress of Racial Equality (CORE), were arrested because of their voter-registration and civil-rights activities and were charged with insurrection, at that time a capital offense in Georgia. A federal court eventually ruled the insurrection statute unconstitutional, ordered the four defendants admitted to bail, and enjoined their prosecutions.[51]

Clearly, if the problems of discrimination in voting were to be effectively redressed in places like Terrell and Sumter counties, some method other than the time-consuming, expensive, case-by-case litigation method of enforcing civil rights would have to be devised.

The County Unit System and the Statewide Majority-Vote Rule

Georgia's unique and complex county unit system was adopted in statutory form in 1917.[52] Described by Key as the "Rule of the Rustics," it applied to primary elections for United States senator and statewide offices.[53] This unique system institutionalized malapportionment and also served to minimize black political power.

Unit votes were assigned on the basis of the apportionment (in fact, malapportionment) of the Georgia House of Representatives. The candidate who received the highest number of popular votes in a county received all the county's unit votes. A majority of county unit votes nominated a senator and the governor, while a plurality of county unit votes nominated others. The system allowed for control by the rural counties and insured the containment of the voting power of blacks and other elements concentrated in the urban areas of the state, both of which were regarded with suspicion by the Democratic party.[54] The federal district court for the District of Columbia found that one of the purposes of the county unit system in Georgia was "to destroy black voting strength."[55]

The county unit system was a highly inequitable way of apportioning electoral power, and in 1963, in an opinion by Justice William O. Douglas, the Supreme Court, agreeing with the decision of the lower court, held that the county unit system violated the concept of "one person, one vote," which was the first use of the phrase.[56] The response of the state's white leaders to the overthrow of the county unit system was swift and predictable. Representative Denmark Groover, a former floor leader for segregationist governor Marvin Griffin, introduced a bill in the general assembly in 1963 requiring a majority vote for election to all county, state and federal offices.[57] The majority-vote law was enacted, with the support of the administration of Governor Carl Sanders, the following year.[58]

Prior to 1963, county officials—unlike statewide officeholders, who were selected under the county unit system—were nominated in primary elections conducted by the political parties. There was no statewide majority-vote requirement, and local party committees were free to determine whether a majority or a plurality vote would decide winners in their county's elections. The use of the plurality vote was widespread. Party officials estimated that as many as 100 of Georgia's 159 counties used a plurality vote, and that "it had been a 'toss up' between the two systems."[59]

Representative Groover was reported in several newspapers as saying the purpose of the majority-vote legislation was to "again provide protection which . . . was removed with the death of the county unit system" and to "thwart election control by Negroes and other minorities."[60] According to Groover, without a majority-vote requirement, "special interests and bloc groups" could control elections "by entering several candidates to split the field."[61] Speaking a week later, he warned that the federal government had been trying "to increase the registration of Negro voters" in Georgia and that his bill "would prevent the election by plurality vote of a candidate supported only by a local courthouse ring or by a bloc vote group."[62]

The general assembly also enacted a numbered-post provision to accompany the majority-vote rule requiring that candidates run for specific seats. The Supreme Court later ruled in a case from Burke County that the numbered-post law further enhanced minority vote dilution because it prevented a cohesive political group from concentrating on a single candidate.[63]

The majority-vote requirement was extended to municipalities in 1968,[64] but exempted from coverage were those whose charters expressly provided for plurality vote. More than fifty cities and towns that had plurality-vote provisions in their charters eventually adopted a majority-vote requirement, and often under overtly racial local circumstances—for example, after the near win, by a plurality vote, of a black to municipal office; after the resignation of a long-term white incumbent; after a black entered a contest with several white candidates who would likely split the white vote; or after an increase in black voter registration.[65]

The majority-vote requirement, currently under attack in *Brooks v. Harris*[66] and *United States v. Georgia*,[67] has survived two prior federal court challenges. The first was dismissed in 1971 as too speculative and not ripe for adjudication.[68] The second, an action to enforce section 5 brought by the Department of Justice, was also dismissed when it was discovered that the Attorney General had in fact precleared the majority-vote rule.[69] The evidence of purposeful discrimination discussed above, however, as well as evidence of the impact of the majority-vote requirement on the outcome of elections and its depressant effect on black candidacies, was not presented in either case. In the current litigation, the state has argued that Groover "did not have any power at all" in the general assembly, and that the majority-vote requirement was part of an election law reform bill pushed by the Sanders administration for nonracial reasons.[70]

The effect of abolition of the majority-vote requirement is to some extent speculative, for it is not possible to predict accurately, among other things, the extent to which whites would choose consensus candidates prior to the primary and impose the functional equivalent of a majority-vote requirement or would simply bolt the Democratic party in the event blacks were nominated in the primary and vote for white Republicans in the general election.[71] It seems likely, though, that abolition of the majority-vote requirement would result in an increase in the number of blacks nominated in the primaries, and thus elected in general elections, and would increase black political participation, including the number of black candidacies in majority-white jurisdictions.

Reapportionment: The Opening Round

A three-judge court in 1962 invalidated the apportionment of the Georgia General Assembly because it underrepresented the most populous counties.[72] The allocation system under the old arrangement insured that the smallest counties, containing less than one-fourth of the state's total population, comprised constitutional majorities in both houses. The court indicated that at least one house elected by the people had to be apportioned according to population. The general assembly went into a special session and reapportioned the senate into single-member districts on the basis of population, but it was very careful to devise procedures that would preclude blacks from being elected from the majority-black areas of Fulton County. Heeding the warning of house floor leader Frank Twitty that "district elections almost inevitably would lead to the election of a Negro in one of Fulton County's seven districts," the general assembly included a provision in the legislation requiring candidates in counties with more than one senatorial district to be elected at large on a countywide basis.[73]

The disfranchising provision was thrown into doubt, however, when legislative counsel advised the general assembly that at-large voting would violate the state constitution, which required senators to be elected from single-member districts. Twitty, vowing that he would "not . . . vote for anything that would automatically put a member of a minority race in the Senate," helped push through an amendment to the state constitution allowing at-large voting for senators in multidistrict counties.[74] The drawback of this tactic from its sponsor's point of view was that the constitutional amendment could not be presented to the voters for approval until the November general election—one month after the scheduled 16 October primary.

The stratagem to exclude blacks from the senate unraveled further when a would-be candidate challenged the at-large voting requirement for Fulton County in federal and state court. The federal court abstained, but Judge Durwood T. Pye of the Fulton County Superior Court issued an order less than seven hours before the polls were to open on election day holding that the at-large provision was in violation of the state constitution.[75] The elections were held on a district basis, and Leroy Johnson, a black attorney, defeated three white opponents for the majority-black District 38 seat. He went on to win the general election against a black Republican opponent and became the first black to serve in the general assembly since Reconstruction.[76] Horace Ward, another black attorney and presently a federal district court judge in Atlanta, won a second seat in the senate from a majority-black district in 1964.

The significance of the dispute over district as opposed to countywide voting in Fulton County, which Twitty and his colleagues thoroughly understood, is apparent from the district and countywide totals for Johnson's election. He got a majority of 70 percent of the votes in District 38, but only a plurality of 47 percent countywide.[77] Had countywide voting been in effect, Johnson would have been forced into a runoff, and given the prevailing pattern of racial bloc voting, he would doubtlessly have been defeated by his white opponent.

When the Supreme Court upheld the constitutionality of the Voting Rights Act of 1965, it described the voting practices of various southern states as "an invidious and pervasive evil which has been perpetuated . . . through unremitting and ingenious defiance of the Constitution."[78] Given its remarkable and relentless history of discrimination, that characterization was particularly accurate for Georgia.

The Voting Rights Act of 1965: A Watershed Event

The Voting Rights Act abolished Georgia's literacy test for voting, including its "good character and understanding" questions and a 1964 law requiring poll officials to be "judicious, intelligent and upright,"[79] and required the state under section 5 of the act to prove, before its new voting practices could be implemented, that they were not discriminatory.[80] This combination of abolition of barriers to registration and federal supervision of new voting procedures has had a profound impact on the state. Voter registration has increased dramatically, and black officeholding, while still disproportionately low, has steadily advanced.

The Increase in Black Voter Registration

The U.S. Commission on Civil Rights estimated that the number of blacks registered to vote in Georgia in 1964 was 270,000, or 27.4 percent of the eligible black citizens.[81] Figures from the Georgia secretary of state's office show that by 1980, 464,783 black registered voters were reported—69.7 percent of the black voting-age population. As of 1988, 644,500 registered blacks were on the voter lists. Data for black and white registration have shown consistently that since 1988 about 10 percentage points more eligible white voters register than black ones.

Some of the black increase can be traced to the early efforts of federal examiners appointed under the Voting Rights Act, who in 1967 registered 1,465 blacks in Terrell County, 475 in Lee County, and 1,448 in Screven County.[82] However, the main work of voter registration has been done by civil rights organizations such as the Voter Education Project (VEP), the Southern Christian Leadership Conference (SCLC), NAACP, SNCC, CORE, and literally hundreds of local black clubs and civic leagues from around the state.[83]

Although Georgia's literacy test was abolished by the act, and the state was prevented by section 5 from enacting new, equally discriminatory practices to take its place, the state's cumbersome registration process remains in place. Faithful to its white redeemer roots, Georgia's procedures are now needlessly complex. They place the burden of registration on the voter and vest enormous discretion in local officials. Registration, for example, may be conducted only at fixed sites designated by local registrars and must be advertised in advance.[84]

After passage of the Voting Rights Act, fraud and intimidation as methods of blunting black voter registration gradually faded away. They were replaced with what the director of VEP has described as "an adversarial relationship."[85] Local officials simply refused to designate additional registration sites in the black community or canceled previously authorized neighborhood registration drives.

Some of these restrictive practices have been challenged in state and federal court, but with mixed results. Blacks were successful in securing an injunction in 1980 under section 5 against the implementation of a new policy prohibiting neighborhood registration drives in DeKalb County, where only 24 percent of the black eligible voters were registered, as compared with 81 percent of eligible whites.[86] Blacks failed in their state court efforts to have additional registration sites designated in the black areas of Muscogee County, where 60 percent of whites, but only 48 percent of blacks, were registered. In a show of remarkable legal obfuscation and indifference to the depressed levels of minority registration, the state supreme court held that the plaintiff should have filed an action for mandamus, rather than declaratory judgment, and that the discretion of the local registrar in designating, or refusing to designate, registration sites was judicially unreviewable.[87]

In another case, *VEP v. Cleland*,[88] a federal court dismissed a statewide challenge to Georgia's registration system when the state agreed in the stipulation of dismissal that it would "encourage" registrars to appoint black deputy registrars and establish additional registration sites. While *VEP v. Cleland* did not succeed in restructuring the state's system of voter registration, VEP's director said it precipitated a change in the relationship between state officials and voter registration groups. "Since 1984 there has been more cooperation. I think Max Cleland [secretary of state] was hurt by the suit and realized the adversarial relationship was self-defeating. It's not ideal now, but at least we talk. It's definitely better."[89] As evidence of the thaw in relations, state and local officials entered into consent decrees in two subsequent cases facilitating access to voter registration by minority and poor citizens. In *Project VOTE! v. Ledbetter*,[90] the state consented to allowing registration at food-stamp distribution centers, and in *Spalding County VEP v. Cowart*,[91] the defendants agreed to establishing registration sites in the black community in Spalding County.

One improvement in the registration process would be a simplified system using mail-in registration and motor vehicle files. This change—inexpensive and easy to administer—would undoubtedly increase registration for all voters and reduce existing racial disparities.[92]

Changes in City and County Electoral Structures

To assess the impact of the Voting Rights Act in Georgia on local electoral systems (principally at-large elections), we surveyed in 1989–90 all cities in the state of 10,000 or more people that had 10 percent or more black population in 1980. Thirty-four cities met these criteria. We asked whether the cities had made changes in their method of elections in response to the act, and whether the changes were associated with increased minority officeholding.

Because of the historical significance of county government in Georgia, we also surveyed counties regarding the electoral changes they had made. A substantial number of counties in Georgia had changed their method of elections since 1965 from at-large to district voting. In order to include these jurisdictions in our study and make our analysis more comprehensive, we surveyed all counties in the state with 10 percent or more black population; 129 counties fit this standard, including a number of very small rural counties. By including city and county governments in our analysis, we feel confident that our conclusions are not limited to city environments but apply to both major types of local government affecting the lives of Georgians.

The survey was done by mail questionnaires, with a follow-up mailing and, when necessary, follow-up telephone calls. We were able to obtain the appropriate information for virtually all cities and counties. Local registrars and voting officials cooperated fully in the project.

We had originally wanted to learn, for each jurisdiction, the method of electing the governing body at three points—1964, 1980, and 1990. Preliminary discussions with election officials and civil rights workers, however, led us to select 1980 and 1990 as years for which accurate data on election methods and black officeholding could be obtained. Moreover, because many changes in Georgia election structure occurred between these two years, we believed we would have a good sample of jurisdictions for a before-and-after study of the results of those changes. We therefore tried to determine the election method—whether at large, district, or mixed—in the two years. If it had changed, we discovered when the change had occurred. We collected the racial and gender makeup of the council or commission in both pre- and post-change formats, although we do not report gender data here. We also sought information about whether the change was a result of litigation or threat of litigation, or was simply voluntary.

A Summary of Findings

We discovered a striking pattern of changes over time in electoral structures from at-large to district voting in the surveyed jurisdictions, for both cities and counties. The changes were particularly marked after 1982, the year in which section 2 of the Voting Rights Act was amended to make voting practices unlawful if they resulted in discrimination, whether intentional or not.[93] The switch from at-large to single-member-district or mixed plans invariably led to an increase in the number of black elected officials. In contrast, there was not a consistent increase in black officeholding in the jurisdictions that retained their at-large systems, nor was the black increase as great when it occurred. These changes correspond with the general findings in the social science literature regarding form of election and minority representation.[94]

Our findings are also consistent with the conclusions expressed by knowledgeable local observers of politics in some jurisdictions that have switched from at-large to district elections. According to one of the leaders in the drive for single-member districts in Baldwin County, "We've tried many, many times to get blacks elected [at large] and we've never been able to do it, even when most everybody turns out to vote. We finally made the decision that the only thing we could do was sue."[95] One of the two blacks elected to the Mitchell County Commission following a successful legal challenge to at-large voting in 1984 underscored the importance of district elections. "District voting, as we had alleged all the time, resulted in people being elected who really represent the community."[96]

The massive shift to district voting usually was caused by litigation or threat of it. Seventy-seven law suits were filed against the surveyed jurisdictions alone, challenging at-large elections under the Fourteenth and Fifteenth amendments, the preclearance provisions of section 5, and amended section 2. While the Justice Department played a key role in the enforcement of section 5, virtually all of the litigation challenging election structures was brought by civil rights organizations on behalf of the minority community.

Increased Minority Officeholding

The changes brought to Georgia's electoral systems by the Voting Rights Act have been broad and systematic, and are only now beginning to reveal themselves in increased electoral representation of blacks. That these changes have come from the passage and implementation of the act, and the parallel development of vote-dilution jurisprudence in constitutional litigation, is undeniable. Virtually every change was from a more dilutive to a more representative form of government. At-large elections were once the dominant form of election in both cities and counties in Georgia; now, single-member-district and mixed plans predominate.

Cities that changed to multimember plans also experienced increased black officeholding. These cities, and three additional cities with multimember plans in place before 1980, show how adopting minority-controlled districts increases black representation. With usually two to three members representing each district, these plans, by allowing voters of different districts to use the same polling place, permit small cities to have relatively large governing councils even when they have only a few voting precincts.

Of the 34 cities of 10,000 or more we surveyed, 29 reported previously having had an at-large system, but only 6 still maintained that method. We found evidence of legal action in 17 cities. (Twenty-three suits were also brought in cities with fewer than 10,000.) Table 3.8 shows that in many of the unsued cities making changes in their method of elections, litigation was threatened or was implicit in demands of the minority community for the abolition of at-large voting. In 1990, 9 of the surveyed cities reported pure single-member districts, and 12 had mixed plans. Over one-half of the changes occurred in the seven years following the amendment of section 2.

Of the 129 counties surveyed in our study, 115 had at-large systems prior to passage of the Voting Rights Act. Only 12 counties made changes to mixed or single-member-district plans between 1965 and 1980. By 1990, only 30 at-large systems remained. Over one-half of the changes have occurred since 1984. Fifty-seven of the counties—more than one-half of those making changes—faced direct legal challenges to their systems of electing commissioners. The other counties making changes often did so under the threat, direct or implied, of litigation.

Of the 30 counties retaining at-large voting, 9 used a sole commissioner form of government. The sole commissioner system, unused outside of Georgia, combines all county legislative and executive authority in a single official.[97] In majority-white counties where voting is racially polarized, the sole commissioner system, coupled with the state's majority-vote requirement, effectively denies blacks the equal opportunity to elect candidates of their choice to the legislative and executive branches of county government. Several of the single commissioner counties have sizable black populations; when an entire county is represented by one white male commissioner, the result there is substantial underrepresentation of minorities. Sole commissioner systems have come under increasing attack under section 2, and as a result, several jurisdictions have abandoned this form of government in favor of boards of commissioners elected from districts.[98]

Generally speaking, there is a moderate-to-strong correlation in both the cities and the counties between the proportion of the population that is black and the percentage of the governing body that is black. The Pearson product-moment correlations are .79 in the cities and .53 in the counties. Both of these correlations are substantially stronger than the relationship under the at-large form of election.

Our data from the thirty-four cities are presented in tables 3.1–3.7, and the county-level data are reported in the corresponding tables 3.1A–3.5A. Tables 3.1 and 3.1A show the expected connection between the proportion of the population that is black and the percentage of black officeholders. These two tables also show the continuing underrepresentation of blacks in majority-white jurisdictions under all plans. In only one instance, involving multimember district plans with low percentages of black residents, did the mean percentage of black officials meet or exceed the mean population figures. This anomaly was based on one case.

Tables 3.2 and 3.2A show the dramatic increase in representation in the last ten years in majority-white cities and counties that abandoned at-large plans, in contrast to those that did not. The 6 cities and 30 counties that retained at-large systems show only minimal increases in the level of black representation. Of the counties retaining at-large systems, only the 7 with majority-black populations showed a substantial increase, and this increase (7.8 percentage points) still leaves blacks woefully underrepresented. The remarkable lack of change in black representation in cities and counties that maintained at-large systems is quite significant. Without electoral changes and the potential empowerment of the black electorate that they provide, very little forward movement in the electoral fortunes of Georgia blacks would have occurred.

The source of black success in mixed plans is exhibited in tables 3.3 and 3.3A. In majority-white jurisdictions, the district arrangements reported there (and in table 3.6) were much more conducive to black electoral success than the at-large components. In short, most local black officials in these Georgia cities and counties were elected from single-member districts, either in pure district systems or in the district component of mixed plans. Tables 3.3, 3.3A, and 3.6 point to the conditions that encourage election of blacks in these districts: a sizable black population.

Tables 3.4 and 3.4A show two measures of black representational equity in 1990—the percentage of blacks on a government body compared to their percentage of the jurisdiction's population, expressed as a difference and as a ratio. Blacks were much more equitably represented on governing bodies in district systems than in at-large ones, by either measure.

Table 3.5 reports the degree of change in black representational equity between 1980 and 1990, using the ratio measure. Only cities that changed electoral systems after 1980 are included. The results are clear and consistent: changing from at-large to some variety of district plan markedly increased black representation on city councils. Unchanged cities had minuscule changes in black representation, however. Table 3.5A reports similar data from Georgia counties. Again, the evidence is clear. Changing the method of electing the county commission substantially increased black representation, particularly in majority-white counties. Counties that did not alter their election systems continued to show very low levels of black representation, even in majority-black counties. The results envisioned by those who see the Voting Rights Act as a weapon to attack vote dilution were occurring in Georgia in the 1980s.

The connection between a majority-black constituency and black electoral success in cities is obvious in tables 3.6 and 3.7. Multimember systems are included because there is evidence that these plans were introduced to provide at least some level of minority representation. Excluding multimember systems does not substantially affect the results of tables 3.6 or 3.7. While blacks occasionally won in majority-white districts, it was rare. Even in cities 50–59.9 percent black, only a little over one-half of the council members were black. As black majorities increased, so did black electoral success. Racially polarized voting may very well have accounted for the results in these tables.

To summarize, the empirical evidence reflects the strong impact of the Voting Rights Act on black electoral success in Georgia. Through the introduction of single-member-district and mixed plans, which the act facilitated, blacks have been able to sharply increase their representation. Even so, measures of equity show that in 1990 blacks were still underrepresented in all types of systems, and at all levels of black population.

Litigation and the Role of the Civil Rights Community

Georgia has had an extraordinary amount of voting rights litigation at the local level. Between 1974 and 1990 there were lawsuits challenging at-large systems in forty Georgia cities and fifty-seven counties, respectively. A few jurisdictions were sued more than once. Augusta, for example, was sued in separate actions by the U.S. Attorney General and private plaintiffs. In addition, cities and counties were often joined as defendants in the same suit. Bleckley County and Cochran, the county seat, for example, were both defendants in *Hall v. Holder*.

A review of the litigation makes at least two things clear. First, most changes in voting that occurred were forced upon the cities and counties by the preclearance process and by litigation (see table 3.8 for cities).[99] There is no basis for concluding that jurisdictions voluntarily abandoned past discriminatory practices. Second, most of the litigation was brought by the civil rights community itself. Of the 86 cases filed against a city or county, at least 68 were brought by the legal staffs of civil rights organizations: 54 by the American Civil Liberties Union; 5 by Georgia Legal Services; 4 by the Voter Education Project; 3 by the Southern Poverty Law Center; 2 by the Legal Defense Fund; 1 by the NAACP; and 1 by the Center for Constitutional Rights. In five cases, two or more of the organizations shared representation of the plaintiffs, and each organization is separately credited in the numbers listed immediately above. Three cases were brought by the Department of Justice.

Shift by Counties from District to At-Large Elections

The continuing effort by Georgia whites to exclude blacks from effective participation is particularly apparent in the shift by a number of counties from district to at-large voting soon after the passage of the Voting Rights Act. An intentional shift to a more dilutive form of elections in the face of the act cannot be interpreted as anything other than a continuing resistance to black political participation.

Although the vast majority of the state's counties elected their county government at large at the time of the act's passage, some did use single-member districts. Thirteen of those with significant black populations, which almost certainly would have had one or more majority-black districts as a result of increasing black registration, abolished district voting in favor of at-large elections after the passage of the act. The counties, with black populations ranging from 28 to 61 percent, were: Miller, Dooly, Calhoun, Clay, Early, Henry, Walton, Meriwether, Morgan, Newton, Twiggs, McDuffie, and Wilkes. Two additional counties, Bacon (13 percent black) and Crisp (40 percent black), switched from district to at-large voting in 1963 and 1964 respectively, but with implementation of the changes to take place after 1 November 1964, which later became the effective date for preclearance under section 5.

Since passage of the act, such changes in voting are presumed by law to be discriminatory.[100] Presumptions aside, in view of the 1962 senate reapportionment battle described earlier, there can be little doubt that local officials and their representatives in the general assembly were aware that at-large voting would make it more difficult for blacks to win elective office in these counties. Although the act required that at-large changes be submitted for preclearance, most of them were not.

All the above fifteen counties eventually returned to district elections, but only because they were forced to do so by lawsuits, threats of such, and/or Department of Justice denial of preclearance to their at-large systems.[101] After these counties returned to district elections 17 percent of the county commissioners elected were black.

One county with district elections before passage of the act that did not change to at-large voting was Seminole County. Its districts, which were grossly malapportioned, already discriminated against minority voters. The county's plan had been enacted in 1933,[102] and the most populous district, with the majority of the county's black voters, was over ten times larger than the smallest one. After local blacks filed a one-person, one-vote lawsuit, the court in 1980 ordered a new, properly apportioned plan into effect.[103] To no one's surprise, a black commissioner was elected after the new system was implemented.

Rogers v. Lodge *and the Acceleration of Change*

One of the most important modern voting cases in Georgia is *Rogers v. Lodge*,[104] a successful challenge to at-large elections in Burke County. *Pitts v. Busbee*,[105] a similar challenge to at-large elections in Fulton County, and *Paige v. Gray*,[106] the first successful challenge to at-large elections for a Georgia city (Albany), were earlier cases that set important precedents, but it was not until *Rogers* that much of the confusion over appropriate standards in vote-dilution cases was resolved and the change to district voting began to escalate throughout the state.

The first decision of the U.S. Supreme Court invalidating at-large elections on the grounds that they diluted minority voting strength was *White v. Regester*, a case from Texas.[107] In reaching its decision, the Court looked at a broad range of factors affecting minority participation, such as the history of discrimination, a depressed minority socioeconomic status, the small number of minorities elected to office, and so forth. The *White* analysis, which examined the effect of a challenged practice to determine its lawfulness, was applied in subsequent voting cases, including *Pitts v. Busbee* and *Paige v. Gray*.

In 1980, a sharply divided court in *City of Mobile v. Bolden*[108] held that minority plaintiffs must prove that a challenged voting practice was adopted or was being maintained with a racially discriminatory intent, and essentially repudiated *White*. *Bolden* was a highly controversial and much criticized decision.[109] In response to it, Congress amended section 2 in 1982 to provide that, whatever the standard of the Constitution, voting practices were in violation of the statute if their "result" was to discriminate on the basis of race or color.[110]

Two days after Congress amended section 2, the Supreme Court decided *Rogers v. Lodge* and essentially reversed its earlier decision in *City of Mobile*. While the Court continued to require proof of racial purpose, it said that such purpose could be inferred from circumstantial evidence: "discriminatory intent need not be proved by direct evidence. 'Necessarily, an invidious discriminatory purpose may often be inferred from the totality of the relevant facts.'"[111]

The decision in *Rogers* and the amendment of section 2 represented the renewal of a strong judicial and congressional commitment to equal voting rights. They also accelerated the pace of litigation and the adoption of district elections in Georgia.

The facts in *Rogers* were egregious, but Burke County was fundamentally no different from other counties in the state that had a significant black population and used at-large elections. All of them had a common history of discrimination; minorities were a depressed socioeconomic group; there were few, if any, elected black officials; voting was racially polarized; housing, churches, civic, and social organizations were largely segregated as a matter of practice. *Rogers* was a clear signal, as the subsequent litigation bore out, that every at-large system in the state was vulnerable to challenge under the Voting Rights Act.

Another factor contributing to change was that jurisdictions which lost in court were required to pay the costs and attorneys' fees of the prevailing plaintiffs. In *Rogers*, Burke County not only had to pay its own lawyers, but it had to pay the plaintiffs' attorneys $294,584.41.[112] Poor odds and the costs of losing were strong disincentives for jurisdictions to fight to keep their at-large systems. According to a survey of probate judges conducted by the *Atlanta Constitution*, "the threat of costly lawsuits is prompting more and more local officials to adopt district elections."[113]

The Supreme Court first construed amended section 2 in 1986 in *Thornburg v. Gingles*,[114] a case involving multimember legislative districts in North Carolina. The court simplified proof of vote dilution by focusing on whether voting was racially polarized and whether majority-black single-member districts could be created. As a result of the amendment of section 2 and the decisions in *Rogers* and *Gingles*, many jurisdictions in Georgia and throughout the South have bowed to the inevitable and have adopted less dilutive forms of elections. Linda Meggers, the director of the state's reapportionment office, described the change to district voting as "the most revolutionary change in Georgia since the Civil War. You're having a whole new distribution of power."[115]

Polarized Voting

Elections in Georgia in which voters have a choice between viable black and white candidates are, with occasional exceptions, polarized on the basis of race. This is true whether the definition of polarized voting is the one adopted by the Supreme Court of "black voters and white voters vot[ing] differently,"[116] or a more stringent definition, such as a majority of each race voting differently.

The fact that voting behavior may also be correlated with other factors, such as voters' socioeconomic characteristics or place of residence, or candidates' expenditures, is legally irrelevant to a section 2 racial bloc voting analysis. Not only are many of these factors themselves strongly related to race, but the Supreme Court held in *Gingles* that "all that matters under §2 and under a functional theory of vote dilution is voter behavior, not its explanation."[117] Thus, where black and white voters are actually voting differently, it is immaterial that nonracial factors may play a role in explaining voter behavior.

Reported decisions have explicitly or implicitly found polarized voting in a number of Georgia jurisdictions, including Bleckley County, where "the evidence conclusively established a pattern of racially polarized voting";[118] Burke County, where the evidence of bloc voting "was clear and overwhelming";[119] Carrollton, where voting was "racially polarized";[120] Colquitt County, where there was evidence of "racial bloc voting";[121] Albany, where the at-large system amounted to "the winner take all";[122] Fulton County, where "the government ha[d] never become equally open to participation by black and white members of the community";[123] Putnam County, where elections were characterized by "racially polarized white voting";[124] and Wilkes County, where "racial bloc voting exist[ed] in the county."[125]

A 1989 analysis by the ACLU confirmed the continuing existence of polarized voting in the state. The analysis was conducted as part of a challenge to the at-large, circuitwide election of superior court judges. The state, which contended that statutes affecting the election of judges were not subject to the Voting Rights Act, was ordered by a three-judge court to comply with section 5 and to submit for preclearance statutes enacted since 1 November 1964 affecting the election of forty-eight judgeships.[126]

The ACLU analyzed all known judicial, legislative, and at-large county office elections since 1980, in the counties affected by the litigation (principally those with substantial concentrations of black population) in which there was a "serious" black candidate, defined as a black who received at least half of the black vote in a primary or general election. Fifty-one elections from twenty counties were examined. Regression analysis showed that, on average, 86 percent of whites voted for the white opponent(s) of the black candidate.[127] Given such a pattern of voting, it is apparent why black candidates with strong black support have found it difficult to win majority-white districts. Conversely, it is equally clear why serious black candidates have enjoyed success primarily in those districts where members of their own race were in the majority.

The three most notable exceptions to the pattern of blacks losing in majority-white districts involved Andrew Young, elected to the then majority-white Fifth Congressional District in 1972; Robert Benham, elected to the court of appeals in 1984 and the state supreme court in 1990, becoming the first black ever to win statewide office in Georgia; and Clarence Cooper, elected as a member of the court of appeals in 1990.

In his 1972 contest, Young got 25.3 percent of the white vote. In 1981, however, after serving in Congress for three terms and as U.S. ambassador to the United Nations under President Carter, and after raising more money than in any of his previous campaigns, he got only 8.9 percent of the white vote in his successful runoff election against a white for mayor of majority-black Atlanta.[128] In 1990 Andrew Young ran for governor of Georgia, receiving 28.8 percent of the primary vote. In the required runoff election, he increased his share to 38.1 percent, far short of the majority he needed. Ecological regression analysis of the county returns showed strong evidence of racially polarized voting in both Young efforts that year. The slope of his regression lines mirrored that of Jesse Jackson's 1988 presidential primary bid in Georgia, indicating that in all these races, the black candidate received less than 26 percent of the white vote.[129]

Judicial elections are unique in that they are subject to considerable control by the bar and the political leadership of the state. Candidates are essentially preselected through appointment by the governor to vacant positions upon the recommendation of a judicial nominating committee dominated by the bar. The chosen candidate then runs in the ensuing election with all the advantages of incumbency. Judicial elections are low-key, low-interest contests in which the voters tend to defer to the choices that have previously been made.[130] Benham, following this pattern of preselection, was appointed by the governor to the court of appeals in 1984. He ran for the position in August of that year, and was elected with 58.5 percent of the vote. His election was unusual in that he faced three white opponents, whereas most court appointments have very little opposition.

Benham received special political treatment. According to state representative Tyrone Brooks, "the governor felt they could sell Benham in the white community, with the support of the bar and the Democratic leadership, because nobody knew he was black. The plan was to get out the vote in the black community in the traditional way, but to ignore race in the white community. Benham's picture could appear only on brochures distributed in the black community and there could be no endorsements of Benham by Maynard Jackson, Julian Bond, Jesse Jackson, or anybody in the civil rights community."[131] Ironically, but not surprisingly, the result of this consciously racial campaign was that Benham's election revealed very little racial polarization. Benham's election to the state supreme court in 1990 resulted from much the same strategy, and he was again successful.

In 1990, Clarence Cooper became the second black to win statewide judicial office by following Benham's strategy. He was appointed to the court of appeals and then ran for election to a full term. Ecological regression analysis showed strong similarities in racial voting patterns between the Benham and Cooper contests; white support for black candidates was decidedly greater than in either Andrew Young's 1990 or Jesse Jackson's 1988 statewide contest.

Legislative Reapportionment

The increased use of single-member districts in the general assembly, implemented as a result of litigation and section 5 review, has also resulted in a corresponding increase in the number of black legislators. Following decisions of the Supreme Court holding that the one-person, one-vote principle required a state to apportion both houses of its legislature on the basis of population, the district court in *Toombs v. Fortson*[132] ordered further reapportionment in Georgia. This litigation created a series of interim plans and special elections, and culminated in the adoption of single-member and multimember districts for the house.[133]

One of the first blacks elected was Julian Bond, former communications director of SNCC. After his election in 1965 but before he took office, he issued a SNCC-endorsed statement strongly critical of the Vietnam War and of continued racial discrimination in the United States. "We are in sympathy with and support the men in this country who are unwilling to respond to a military draft," the statement said, "which would compel them to contribute their lives to United States aggression in Viet Nam in the name of 'freedom' we find so false in this country."[134]

The statement was triggered by the death of Samuel Younge, Jr., a Tuskegee Institute student and navy veteran, who had been killed while trying to use the segregated bathroom of a local service station. According to Bond, "the irony of Younge losing the life he had offered his country over a segregated toilet" prompted the release of the antiwar statement by SNCC.[135]

Before the house convened, seventy-five members petitioned to have Bond excluded on the grounds that he could not validly take the oath of office to support the constitutions of the United States and Georgia. When he appeared for the swearing-in ceremony, Bond felt that "the hostility from white legislators was nearly absolute."[136]

In an action reminiscent of that of the general assembly of 1868, the house in 1966 passed, 184 to 12, a resolution that "Bond shall not be allowed to take the oath of office . . . and . . . shall not be seated as a member of the House of Representatives."[137] Undaunted, Bond ran in the special election to fill his vacant seat and was reelected by an overwhelming majority. He refused to recant his statement and was denied the oath of office a second time.

The U.S. Supreme Court held that he had been improperly excluded and his freedom of expression had been violated. The court found it unnecessary to reach the issue of whether Bond's exclusion had also been because of race. He was seated and served several terms in both the house and later the Georgia senate.

After the 1970 census, the state enacted a new legislative apportionment plan. Under the preclearance process, the Attorney General objected to the original plan because various discriminatory features—including multimember districts, numbered posts, a majority-vote requirement, and changes in the structure of potential black-majority single-member districts for the house—enhanced the possibility of discrimination against minority voters.[138] He also objected to the senate plan because of the potentially discriminatory way in which districts had been drawn in Fulton and Richmond counties.

Once again, the state was compelled by section 5 to construct a more racially fair reapportionment plan. The new plan corrected the objection to senate redistricting, increased the number of single-member house districts from 105 to 128, and reduced the number of multimember house districts from 49 to 32. The Attorney General approved the senate changes but rejected the house reapportionment plan again. He concluded that the house plan did not remove the objectionable combination of multimember districts, numbered posts, and the majority-vote requirement. The state resolved to take no further steps to rectify the matter. The Attorney General brought suit, and the state eventually lost. It was required to reapportion in conformity with section 5.[139] The general assembly adopted a new plan in 1974 and used fewer multimember districts. It provided for 180 house members elected from 154 districts. As a result of the 1974 changes, the number of blacks in the house increased from fourteen to twenty.

It is difficult to overstate the impact on minority officeholding of single-member-district elections for the general assembly. Of the six black state senators and twenty-two representatives, only one—Michael Thurmond, whose district included the university town of Athens—was elected from a majority-white (57 percent) district.[140] The remaining black members were elected from districts 56 percent to 99 percent black.

Congressional Reapportionment

Georgia's 1971 and 1981 congressional reapportionments were the products of intentional discrimination and are dramatic examples of the extraordinary lengths to which the legislature was prepared to go to exclude blacks from the congressional delegation. They also show how effective the preclearance provisions of section 5 have been in blocking certain forms of vote dilution and facilitating minority officeholding.

The congressional reapportionment enacted in 1931 was invalidated in *Wes-*

berry v. Sanders (1964)[141] because of severe malapportionment of the Fifth District, comprising Fulton, DeKalb, and Rockdale counties. This district was the largest in the state and contained 823,680 people, while the smallest district, the Ninth, had only 272,154 people—fewer than one-third as many as the Fifth. After *Wesberry*, the general assembly enacted a new plan with acceptable population deviations.[142] The apportionment process following the 1970 census was the first reapportionment subject to section 5 review.

The original 1971 plan discriminated in three distinct ways. First, it divided the concentration of black population in the metropolitan Atlanta area into the Fourth and Fifth districts to insure that the Fifth would be majority-white. Second, it excluded the residences of black persons from the Fifth District who were known to be potential candidates: Andrew Young, who had run in the previous Fifth District election in 1970; and Maynard Jackson, the vice-mayor of Atlanta. The homes of both men were located about one block from the new district line. The 1970 contest between Young and a white opponent, Fletcher Thompson, had been particularly divisive, and, according to a federal judge, was characterized by "racist campaign tactics."[143] Third, to maximize the chances of white control, the residences of whites who were recognized as potential candidates were included in the district bounds.[144] Although there is no candidate residency requirement in congressional elections, nonresidence would have been an obvious political obstacle.

The plan was submitted for preclearance, and the Attorney General objected to it. He said that he was unable to conclude "that these new boundaries will not have a discriminatory racial effect on voting by minimizing or diluting black voting strength in the Atlanta area."[145] Under the duress of section 5, the general assembly enacted a new plan in 1972, increasing the black percentage in the Fifth District from 38 to 44 percent and including the residences of Young and Jackson. The plan was precleared. Young, an adroit politician and campaigner, ran in the ensuing 1972 election and, with crossover support from progressive white in-town Atlanta neighborhoods, became the first black elected to Congress from Georgia since Reconstruction.[146]

When the state reapportioned its congressional districts after the 1980 census, it tried once again to minimize black voting strength in the metropolitan Atlanta area. The 1980 figures revealed that the state's ten congressional districts, while having become severely malapportioned since they were drawn in 1972, were still majority white, with the exception of the Fifth. This district contained a slight (50.33 percent) black population majority.

The new plan drawn in 1981 maintained white majorities in nine of the ten districts and increased the black population in the Fifth to 57.28 percent. Although majority-black in total and voting-age populations, the district actually contained a 54 percent white majority among registered voters. The state submitted the plan for preclearance and argued that the Fifth District's configuration could not be discriminatory because it increased the black percentage over the 1972 plan. The Attorney General did not agree, and denied section 5 approval.[147]

The state then filed a declaratory judgment action in the district court for the District of Columbia, arguing that under the retrogression standard of section 5, it was entitled to have its congressional reapportionment plan precleared. The Supreme Court had previously held in *Beer v. United States*[148] that the purpose of section 5 was to maintain the status quo in voting, and that a plan that was ameliorative instead of retrogressive could not violate the effect standard of the statute. The evidence at trial showed that the 1981 plan, while not technically retrogressive, was the product of intentional discrimination. The court denied preclearance, and the Supreme Court affirmed on appeal.[149]

Given the rich history of chronic vote discrimination against blacks, it is not surprising that the 1981 congressional redistricting process was influenced by race, despite the vigorous denials by white officials. What is surprising was the extent of that influence. Senator Julian Bond had introduced legislation that would have created a Fifth District that was 69 percent black. Several senators opposed the so-called Bond Amendment because it would, they said, cause "white flight," divide the congressional districts into "black and white," and "bring out resegregation in a fine county like Fulton and a fine city like Atlanta."[150] Nonetheless, the final plan adopted by the senate contained the Bond Amendment.

The leadership of the house rejected the Bond plan for the Fifth District. Joe Mack Wilson, chairman of the House Reapportionment Committee and the person who dominated the process in the lower chamber, frankly explained to his colleagues that "I don't want to draw nigger districts."[151] Wilson freely used the term "nigger," and he regularly characterized legislation of benefit to blacks as "nigger legislation." The District of Columbia court, in an extraordinary but factually based finding, concluded that "Representative Joe Mack Wilson is a racist."[152] The speaker of the house, Tom Murphy, while not as antagonistic in his language, was equally opposed to the Bond plan for the same reasons. "I was concerned," he said later, "that . . . we were gerrymandering a district to create a black district where a black would certainly be elected."[153] On the basis of these overt racial statements, as well as on the absence of a legitimate nonracial reason for adopting the plan, the conscious minimizing of black voting strength, and the history of discrimination in Georgia, the court concluded that the state's submission had a discriminatory purpose and violated section 5.

Forced yet again by the Voting Rights Act to construct a racially fair plan, the general assembly in a special session enacted an apportionment plan for the Fifth District with a black population exceeding 65 percent. The plan was approved by the court. In 1986, black civil rights activist John Lewis was elected in this district, defeating Julian Bond, a former SNCC colleague and the principal architect of the redistricting plan.

Conclusion

Against formidable odds, and checked at every turn, blacks in Georgia have made impressive advances in political participation. The number of black elected officials grew from 3 in 1964 to 495 in 1990.[154] During the same period, black registration increased from 270,000 to 608,000.

The Voting Rights Act was a decisive event in Georgia's political history and continues to be the major weapon in the civil rights armamentarium in the battle to bring about a more equitable role for blacks in the political system. Section 5 has successfully blocked the introduction of many new attempts at vote dilution. Section 2, since its amendment in 1982, has proved a potent force in challenging existing discriminatory practices.

The increase in black officeholding can in large measure be traced directly to the gradual demise of at-large elections and the implementation of single-member districts containing effective black voting majorities. These changes were neither self-executing nor voluntary, but were coerced through a combination of congressional legislation, favorable judicial decisions, the enforcement of the preclearance requirement, and litigation efforts of the civil rights and minority communities.

Significant racial disparities remain, however. Blacks are 25 percent of Georgia's voting-age population, but constitute only 7.6 percent of the elected officials in the state. Not only is black registration depressed, but black voter turnout is lower than white voter turnout. According to Bureau of the Census surveys taken after the 1988 presidential election, 53.2 percent of age-eligible whites in Georgia, but only 42.4 percent of age-eligible blacks, reported voting in the election.[155]

Bloc voting, evidence of a continuing racial schism, remains a political fact of life in the state, as does the use of election practices that enhance discrimination, such as at-large voting and the majority-vote and numbered-post requirements. The state's system of voter registration is needlessly rigid and cumbersome and is in need of overhaul. The fight for equal voting rights in Georgia, therefore, is far from over. Much remains to be done. But the Voting Rights Act, in conjunction with alert and active civil rights and minority communities, should continue to serve well the citizens of the state, both black and white.

TABLE 3.1
Black Representation on Council in 1990 by Election Plan, Georgia Cities of 10,000 or More Population with 10 Percent or More Black Population in 1980

Type of Plan by % Black in City Population, 1980	N	*Mean % Black in City Population, 1980*	*Mean % Black on City Council, 1990*
SMD plan			
10–29.9	3	23.5	15.0
30–49.9	6	44.1	33.3
50–100	0	—	—
Mixed plan			
10–29.9	0	—	—
30–49.9	9	40.9	32.2
50–100	3	57.8	45.8
MMD plan[a]			
10–29.9	1	27.4	30.0
30–49.9	6	43.0	31.9
50–100	0	—	—
At-large plan			
10–29.9	5	21.7	10.0
30–49.9	1	41.0	16.7
50–100	0	—	—

[a]These are multimember-district plans in which all councilpersons are elected from districts, but typically two or three members are elected per district.

TABLE 3.1A
Black Representation on Commission in 1990 by Election Plan, Georgia Counties with 10 Percent or More Black Population in 1980

Type of Plan by % Black in County Population, 1980	N	*Mean % Black in County Population, 1980*	*Mean % Black on Commission 1990*
SMD plan			
10–29.9	7	24.0	11.4
30–49.9	25	37.6	24.6
50–100	5	35.7	36.0
Mixed plan			
10–29.9	26	22.5	15.0
30–49.9	28	36.4	22.8
50–100	8	55.4	38.1
At-large plan			
10–29.9	18	17.2	2.2
30–49.9	5	40.8	10.0
50–100	7	61.4	27.6

TABLE 3.2
Changes in Black Representation on Council between 1980 and 1990, Georgia Cities of 10,000 or More Population with 10 Percent or More Black Population in 1980

Type of Change by % Black in City Population, 1980	N[a]	*Mean % Black in City Population, 1980*	*Mean % Black on City Council*	
			Before Change (1980)	*After Change (1990)*
		Changed Systems		
From at-large to SMD plan				
10–29.9	1	28.2	0.0	25.0
30–49.9	3	44.4	13.3	30.0
50–100	0	—	—	—
From at-large to mixed plan				
10–29.9	0	—	—	—
30–49.9	3	38.7	6.7	32.1
50–100	2	53.4	22.5	35.4
From at-large to MMD plan				
10–29.9	0	—	—	—
30–49.9	4	42.3	23.3	31.7
50–100	0	—	—	—
		Unchanged Systems		
At-large plan				
10–29.9	5	21.7	8.5	10.2
30–49.9	1	41.0	20.0	16.7
50–100	0	—	—	—

[a] The number of cities in table 3.2 is smaller than in table 3.1 because the change to an at-large plan in some cities occurred before 1980.

TABLE 3.2A
Changes in Black Representation on Commission between 1980 and 1990, Georgia Counties with 10 Percent or More Black Population in 1980

Type of Change by % Black in County Population, 1980	N[a]	*Mean % Black in County Population, 1980*	*Mean % Black on County Commission*	
			Before Change (1980)	*After Change (1990)*
		Changed Systems		
From at-large to SMD plan				
10–29.9	5	22.8	2.9	12.0
30–49.9	21	37.9	16.2	25.5
50–100	4	55.8	0.0	35.0
From at-large to mixed plan				
10–29.9	14	22.0	0.0	16.6
30–49.9	19	34.4	19.2	23.8
50–100	4	54.5	30.0	33.3
		Unchanged Systems		
At-large plan				
10–29.9	18	17.2	0.0	2.2
30–49.9	5	40.8	8.3	10.0
50–100	7	61.4	19.8	27.6

[a]The number of counties in this table is smaller than in table 3.1A because the change to an at-large plan in some counties occurred before 1980.

TABLE 3.3
Black Representation in 1990 in Mixed Plans by District and At-Large Components, Georgia Cities of 10,000 or More Population with 10 Percent or More Black Population in 1980

% Black in City Population, 1980	N	*Mean % Black Councilpersons in District Components, 1990*	*Mean % Black Councilpersons in At-Large Components, 1990*
10–29.9	0	—	—
30–49.9	9	41.5	12.0
50–100	3	44.6	38.9

TABLE 3.3A
Black Representation in 1990 in Mixed Plans by District and At-Large Components, Georgia Counties with 10 Percent or More Black Population in 1980

% Black in County Population, 1980	N[a]	*Mean % Black Commissioners in District Components*	*Mean % Black Commissioners in At-Large Components*
10–29.9	5	18.0	0.0
30–49.9	2	43.8	8.3
50–100	2	50.0	33.3

[a]Missing data reduced the number of mixed county plans for analysis.

TABLE 3.4
Two Equity Measures Comparing Percentage Black on Council in 1990 with Percentage Black in City Population in 1980, Georgia Cities of 10,000 or More Population with 10 Percent or More Black Population in 1980

Type of Plan by % Black in City Population, 1980	N	*Difference Measure (% on Council − % in Population)*	*Ratio Measure (% on Council ÷ % in Population)*
		Changed Systems	
From at-large to SMD plan			
10–29.9	3	−2.40	0.90
30–49.9	6	−9.91	0.74
50–100	0	—	—
From at-large to mixed plan			
10–29.9	0	—	—
30–49.9	14	−10.45	0.75
50–100	3	−11.87	0.78
		Unchanged Systems	
At-large plan			
10–29.9	5	−12.15	0.37
30–49.9	1	−24.30	0.40
50–100	0	—	—

TABLE 3.4A
Two Equity Measures Comparing Percentage Black on Commission in 1990 with Percentage Black in County Population in 1980, Georgia Counties with 10 Percent or More Black Population in 1980

Type of Plan by % Black in County Population, 1980	N	*Difference Measure (% on Commission − % in Population)*	*Ratio Measure (% on Commission ÷ % in Population)*
		Changed Systems	
From at-large to SMD plan			
10–29.9	7	−12.54	0.52
30–49.9	25	−11.43	0.66
50–100	5	−19.70	0.65
From At-large to mixed plan			
10–29.9	26	−13.34	0.68
30–49.9	28	−13.49	0.64
50–100	8	−18.67	0.69
		Unchanged Systems	
At-large plan			
10–29.9	18	−76.00	0.10
30–49.9	5	−30.40	0.25
50–100	7	−33.69	0.42

TABLE 3.5
Changes in Black Representation on Council between 1980 and 1990, Georgia Cities of 10,000 or More Population with 10 Percent or More Black Population in 1980 (Ratio Equity Measure)

Type of Change by % Black in City Population, 1980	N[a]	*Black Representational Equity on Council* 1980	1990
	Changed Systems		
From at-large to SMD plan			
10–29.9	1	0.00	0.89
30–49.9	3	0.30	0.68
50–100	0	—	—
From at-large to mixed plan			
10–29.9	0	—	—
30–49.9	3	0.17	0.83
50–100	2	0.42	0.66
From at-large to MMD plan			
10–29.9	0	—	—
30–49.9	4	0.55	0.75
50–100	0	—	—
	Unchanged Systems		
At-large plan			
10–29.9	5	0.39	0.47
30–49.9	1	0.49	0.40
50–100	0	—	—

[a] The number of cities in this table is smaller than in tables 3.1 and 3.4 because some changes in form occurred before 1980.

TABLE 3.5A
Changes in Black Representation on County Commission between 1980 and 1990, Georgia Counties with 10 Percent or More Black Population in 1980 (Ratio Equity Measure)

Type of Change by % Black in County Population, 1980	N[a]	*Minority Representational Equity on Commission*	
		1980	*1990*
	Changed Systems		
From at-large to SMD plan			
10–29.9	5	0.13	0.53
30–49.9	21	0.43	0.67
50–100	4	0.00	0.63
From at-large to mixed plan			
10–29.9	14	0.00	0.75
30–49.9	19	0.56	0.69
50–100	4	0.55	0.61
	Unchanged Systems		
At-large plan			
10–29.9	18	0.00	0.10
30–49.9	5	0.20	0.25
50–100	7	0.32	0.42

[a]These data exclude counties that changed plans prior to 1980 or that maintained single-member-district or mixed plans throughout this period. Thus the *N*s may be smaller than in tables 3.1A and 3.4A.

TABLE 3.6
Black Representation in Council Single- and Multimember Districts in 1990, Georgia Cities of 10,000 or More Population with 10 Percent or More Black Population in 1980

% Black Population of District	N[a]	*Mean % Black Population in Districts, 1980*	*Mean % Black Councilpersons in Districts, 1990*
0–29.9	65	13.2	0.0
30–49.9	8	38.7	25.0
50–59.9	13	54.6	53.8
60–64.9	8	62.3	75.0
65–69.9	4	65.7	100.0
70–100	35	85.3	94.3

[a]Of the 162 single- or multimember district cities in Georgia, we were able to obtain data on 133 districts. We received data from 26 of the 27 cities.

TABLE 3.7
Black Council Representation in Single- and Multimember Districts in 1990, by Racial Composition of District, Georgia Cities of 10,000 or More Population with 10 Percent or More Black Population in 1980

Racial Composition of District	N	*Mean % Black Population in Districts, 1980*	*Mean % Black Councilpersons in Districts, 1990*
Black majority	60	74.3	83.3
White majority	73	16.0	2.7

TABLE 3.8
Cause of Change from At-Large to Mixed, Single-Member-, or Multimember-District Plan between 1974 and 1990, Georgia Cities of 10,000 or More Population with 10 Percent or More Black Population in 1980

City	*Did Lawsuit Accompany Change?*	*Lawsuit/Reason for Change*
	Changed to Single-Member Districts	
Albany	Yes	*Paige v. Gray,* 1977
Milledgeville	Yes	*NAACP v. City of Milledgeville,* 1983
Newnan	Yes	*Rush v. Norman,* 1984
Waycross	Yes	*Ware County VEP v. Parks,* 1985
	Changed to Mixed Plan	
Americus	Yes	*Wilkerson v. Ferguson,* 1981
Atlanta	No	Legislative change
Augusta	Yes	*United States v. City of Augusta,* 1988
Bainbridge	No	Legislative change
Carrollton	Yes	*Carrollton Branch NAACP v. Stallings,* 1985
Columbus	No	City/county consolidation
Cordele	Yes	*Dent v. Culpepper,* 1988
Covington	Yes	*Newton County Voters League v. City of Covington,* 1977

(*continued*)

TABLE 3.8 (*Continued*)

City	*Did Lawsuit Accompany Change?*	*Lawsuit/Reason for Change*
Decatur	Yes	*Thrower v. City of Decatur, Georgia,* 1984
Douglas	Yes	*NAACP Branch of Coffee County v. Moore,* 1978
Dublin	Yes	*Sheffield v. Cochran,* 1975
Griffin	Yes	*Reid v. Martin,* 1986
Macon[a]	No	Legislative change after dismissal of lawsuit, *Walton v. Thompson,* 1975
Moultrie	Yes	*Cross v. Baxter,* 1984
Savannah	No	Legislative change
Statesboro	Yes	*Love v. Deal,* 1983
Thomasville	No	Threat of litigation
Valdosta	Yes	*United States v. Lowndes County,* 1984
Vidalia	No	Legislative change
SUMMARY	Yes 16 (70%) No 7 (30%)	

Sources: Legal research and interviews with civil rights attorneys.

[a] Macon was sued under section 2, but the lawsuit was unsuccessful. The subsequent change to a new system was legislative.

TABLE 3.9
Major Disfranchising Devices in Georgia

Device	*Date Established*	*Date Abolished*
Poll tax	1868; repealed in 1870; reenacted in 1871; made cumulative in 1877	1945[a]
Payment of taxes	1868	1931[b]
Durational residency requirements	1868; lengthened in 1873	1972[c]
Grand jury appointment of school boards	1872	Gradually by local referendums in individual counties, statewide in 1992[d]
White primary	By party rules, late nineteenth century	1945[e]
Disfranchising offenses	1877	Still in use[f]
Registration by race	1894	Still required
Literacy, good character and understanding tests	1908	1965[g]
Grandfather clause	1908	1915[h]
Property ownership alternative	1908	1945[i]
County unit system	By party rules, late nineteenth century; by statute, 1917	1963[j]
Thirty questions test	1949, revised 1958	1965[g]
Majority vote and numbered posts requirements	Late nineteenth century, local option; replaced by statute county- and statewide in 1964; operative for municipalities in 1968	Still in use

[a]Georgia Laws 1945, 129.
[b]Georgia Laws, 1931, 102.
[c]*Abbott v. Carter,* 356 F. Supp. 280 (N.D. Ga. 1972).
[d]Georgia Laws 1991, 2032 (approved by referendum on 3 November 1992).
[e]*King v. Chapman,* 62 F. Supp. 639 (M.D. Ga. 1945).
[f]Upheld in *Kronlund v. Honstein,* 327 F. Supp. 71 (N.D. Ga. 1971).
[g]Voting Rights Act of 1965, 42 U.S.C. §1973b.
[h]Georgia Laws 1908, 29 (providing expiration data).
[i]Georgia Laws 1945, 15.
[j]*Gray v. Sanders,* 372 U.S. 368 (1963).

TABLE 3.10
Black and White Registered Voters and Officeholders in Georgia, Selected Years[a]

	Black		*White*	
	N	%	N	%
Registered voters				
1964[b]	270,000	16.2	1,399,778	83.8
1966[c]	289,545	17.4	1,378,005	82.6
1990[d]	607,782	21.9	2,143,121	77.3
Officeholders[e]				
State house				
1964	0	0.0	100	100.0
1966	9	5.0	171	95.0
1990	27	15.0	153	85.0
State senate				
1964	2	3.6	54	96.4
1966	2	3.6	54	96.4
1990	8	14.3	48	85.7

[a]Mean black Georgia population, 1960–90 = 27.0%.
[b]Estimate reported by U.S. Commission on Civil Rights
[c]Southern Regional Council 1966.
[d]Secretary of state.
[e]All data on officeholding were provided by the clerks of the house and senate.

F O U R

Louisiana

RICHARD L. ENGSTROM,

STANLEY A. HALPIN, JR.,

JEAN A. HILL, AND

VICTORIA M. CARIDAS-BUTTERWORTH

> Historically, Louisiana's political environment has been hostile to the aspirations of blacks for equal political participation. Any alteration in this basic environment has been largely the result of "outside interference" in the form of federal intervention.
>
> —*Jewel L. Prestage and Carolyn Sue Williams*[1]

EFFORTS TO RESTRICT black participation in the governmental process have been a permanent feature of Louisiana's political environment. Prior to the Civil War the state's constitutions prohibited blacks, whether free or slave, from voting. Today, while allowed to vote, blacks must constantly challenge electoral schemes that dilute their new voting strength. Discriminatory election laws, in short, continue to be a serious problem in Louisiana. The fact that the nature of the discrimination has changed from disfranchisement to vote dilution, however, does reflect progress toward a more open electoral process.

This progress has been the consequence of one of the most significant manifestations of "outside interference" in Louisiana's political process—the federal Voting Rights Act. As a result primarily of that act, blacks now register to vote in Louisiana at a rate approaching, but still not equal to, that for whites. Among blacks of voting age, 66.9 percent were registered to vote at the beginning of 1990, compared to 72.6 percent of the whites, resulting in a registered electorate that was 26.2 percent black.[2] This new black voting strength has been the principal reason there were over five hundred black elected officials in Louisiana by 1990—about 11 percent of all elected officials.[3] There were twenty-four black members (22.9 percent) of the state's house of representatives and eight members (20.5 percent) of the senate in 1992. Blacks now serve on the governing boards of parishes (counties), municipalities, and education authorities throughout Louisiana. In the state's largest city, New Orleans, both the mayor and a majority of the city council are black. Although the registration and representation figures for Louisiana continue to be low when compared with the percentage of blacks in the state's population—30.8 percent in 1990—and although blacks still have to fight efforts to dilute their votes, the situation today is a major improvement over that in 1965, when the Voting Rights Act was adopted.

Vote Denial

On 8 March 1965, only a few months before President Lyndon Johnson signed the Voting Rights Act, the Supreme Court unanimously concluded that Louisiana was guilty of unconstitutionally depriving its black residents of their right to vote. In *Louisiana v. United States* the state was enjoined from continuing to require potential voters to pass its constitutional "interpretation" test.[4] This test required applicants for registration to "understand and give a reasonable interpretation" of a passage from either the three-volume state constitution or the federal Constitution.[5] It was the latest in a series of unlawful devices that the state had employed to disfranchise its black residents.

Their disfranchisement was initially straightforward. The state's first three constitutions—those of 1812, 1845, and 1852, as well as the secessionist constitution of 1861—simply restricted the franchise to white males who could satisfy other registration requirements.[6] The constitution of 1864, written by delegates from the federally occupied southern part of the state, did not lift this racial ban. Blacks were registered to vote, however, under the federal Military Reconstruction acts, and a report by the state board of registration in 1867 revealed that 65.2 percent of the state's registrants were black at that time. About 90 percent of the black males of voting age were reportedly registered in 1867, compared to less than half of the white males.[7]

The state prohibition on blacks voting was removed by the state constitution adopted in 1868, under which Louisiana was readmitted to the Union. This constitution was written by an elected convention in which half of the delegates were black. In 1870 the state legislature, also about half black at this time, required voters to register under the new requirements.[8]

Blacks were a significant political force in Louisiana during this period of black enfranchisement. They developed political organizations of their own, and participated actively in Republican party politics. Blacks were not only elected in large numbers to the state legislature, three were also elected to the statewide offices of lieutenant governor, superintendent of education, and state treasurer. One lieutenant governor, Pinckney Benton Stewart Pinchback, served briefly as governor. At the local level blacks served as mayors, sheriffs, assessors, tax collectors, coroners, and in a variety of other elective positions.[9]

Black enfranchisement and its consequence, an integrated elected elite, did not sit well with Louisiana's whites. New means were developed to minimize black participation. These methods could not be direct, as the old ones had been, because of the Fifteenth Amendment to the federal constitution, adopted in 1870. The new methods had to be "facially neutral," but they were effective nonetheless.

The Grandfather Clause

In 1896 blacks still constituted 44.8 percent of Louisiana's registered voters. Four years later they composed only 4.0 percent.[10] Their virtual elimination from the electorate was accomplished initially through the discriminatory application of a new registration law adopted in 1896 that required voters to register between 1 January 1897 and 1 January 1898. Black registration was reduced during this period by about 90 percent, leaving only 9.5 percent of the adult black males with the franchise.[11] This was followed by the adoption of new registration requirements in the constitution of 1898. According to its presiding officer, this constitution was written by a convention that had been called for one primary purpose—"the purification of the electorate."[12] As part of the scheme to accomplish this, it invented the now infamous "grandfather" clause.

The constitution of 1898 established an educational or property ownership requirement for voters. Applicants for registration were required to read and write, and to demonstrate this ability by completing without assistance a complicated application form (which demanded, for example, that the applicant express his age in years, months, and days), or alternatively, to own property with an assessed valuation of at least three hundred dollars and to have paid all taxes due on that property. Anyone registered to vote on or before 1 January 1867, however, as well as the son or grandson of any such person, was exempted from these new requirements, as were immigrants who had come to the United States after that date. Only 111 blacks qualified to vote under this exemption in 1898, compared to 37,877 whites.[13]

The intended effect of the new registration provisions was of course the disfranchisement of blacks. According to the convention's president, if the delegates had been free of federal constraints, they would have again provided explicitly for "the exclusion from the suffrage of every man with a trace of African blood in his veins."[14] The federal constraints, however, required only a slightly more complicated procedure. The convention's president undoubtedly spoke for the delegates when he commented on the new scheme:

> What care I whether it be more or less ridiculous? Doesn't it meet the case? Doesn't it let the white man vote, and doesn't it stop the negro from voting, and isn't that what we come here for?[15]

The purpose was achieved. By 1900, after a reregistration of voters based on the new requirements, blacks constituted about 4.0 percent of those registered, despite still comprising half of the state's population. Registration figures showed that while 29,189 whites had been exempted from the new requirements by the grandfather clause in 1900, not a single black person was any longer enfranchised as a result of that clause.[16]

The White Primary

Although Louisiana invented the grandfather clause, it was the Oklahoma version that was struck down in 1915 by the Supreme Court in *Guinn and Beal v. United States*.[17] The opinion, ironically, was written by the only person from Louisiana ever to sit on the Court, Chief Justice Edward D. White. Unable to rely any longer on that provision as a means to keep whites in and blacks out of the electorate, Louisiana in 1921 adopted new barriers to black participation. A new state constitution adopted that year contained two devices widely regarded as disfranchising mechanisms—the "interpretation" test and the white primary.[18] This layered approach was designed to minimize black participation. The interpretation requirement would be used to keep blacks from becoming registered, while any who did so would be precluded from voting in the only elections of any consequence in one-party Louisiana, the Democratic primaries.

The white primary so effectively prevented meaningful participation by blacks that the interpretation test was rarely needed prior to the 1950s. The state constitution did not explicitly preclude blacks from voting in primaries, but rather authorized political parties to require registered voters to possess "other and additional qualifications" as prerequisites to participating in the selection of party nominees.[19] The state's Democratic party decided that being white was an additional qualification. The white primary not surprisingly had a chilling effect on black interest in attempting to surmount the registration hurdle.[20] From 1921 to 1944, when the Supreme Court declared that whites-only primaries were unconstitutional, blacks never made up more than 1 percent of the state's registered voters.[21]

The "Interpretation" Test

Following the invalidation of the white primary, black registration increased in Louisiana. It did so, however, very unevenly, with substantial gains in some parishes and next to none in others. By 1964 just over 30 percent of voting-age blacks across the state were registered to vote, and they constituted 13.7 percent of all registered voters. Registration rates for the individual parishes that year, however, ranged from only 1.7 percent in Tensas to 93.8 percent in Evangeline. The distribution of parish-based registration rates for 1964, in deciles, is reported in table 4.11. Fewer than 20 percent of voting-age blacks were registered in twenty of Louisiana's sixty-four parishes, while over 70 percent were registered in eight.[22]

Much of the variation in registration rates can be accounted for by two variables, the location of the parishes and the potential black electorate within them.[23] This is highlighted by the two extremes, Tensas and Evangeline. Tensas, a northern parish, had a potentially large black electorate (60.7 percent of the voting-age population was black in 1960). In contrast, Evangeline, a French-Catholic parish in the southern part of the state, had a black voting-age population the same year of only 19.7 percent.

Black registration rates tended to vary *inversely* with the relative presence of blacks in the parish populations. This relationship was not unique to Louisiana,[24] but simply reflected the fact that in Louisiana, as in the South generally, "the greater the potential for meaningful black impact on politics in the immediate geographic area the more rigid were the barriers to such impacts."[25] The other relationship between the location of parishes and registration rates was a more uniquely Louisiana phenomenon. The southern part of the state, unlike the rest of the American South, is largely French Catholic. The white population in this area (known as Acadiana), while segregationist, was generally less hostile to blacks voting, a trait attributed to the influence of the Catholic clergy there. Blacks therefore faced fewer barriers to registration in most of the Acadiana parishes. As described by Wright, "Catholicism in southern Louisiana fashioned a different political perimeter for blacks living there. The record clearly indicates that black political participation was not enthusiastically sought or even welcomed. However, the evidence is just as clear that black participation was nonetheless tolerated."[26]

The demise of the white primary brought the interpretation test to the fore, and the different registration rates across the parishes undoubtedly reflected the different manner in which the "test" was applied by parish registrars.[27] Evidence demonstrating the racially selective application of the interpretation requirement was marshaled for twenty-one parishes in *United States v. Louisiana*, initiated by the federal government under the Civil Rights Act of 1960. Only one of the twenty-one parishes, Plaquemines, controlled by the archsegregationist Leander Perez,[28] was located in south Louisiana. In these selected parishes only 8.6 percent of voting-age blacks were registered at the end of 1962, compared to 66.1 percent of the whites.[29] The Supreme Court concluded that evidence of the application of the interpretation requirement in these parishes showed that it had been employed "not [as] a test but a trap."[30]

The test required applicants for registration to provide "a reasonable interpretation" of a section of either the federal or state constitution.[31] Enormous discretion was provided in its application. Parish registrars decided which applicants would be confronted with it, what constitutional passage they would have to interpret, and whether their interpretation was "reasonable." Needless to say, the discretion was abused; the test was a trap for black applicants. The evidence revealed a pattern of "regular, consistent, predictable, unequal application" so as to disfranchise black but not white residents in these parishes.[32]

In parishes in which substantial numbers of blacks had registered, the discriminatory application of the interpretation test was preceded by a purge of the black registrants.[33] This two-step approach to black disfranchisement was advocated in a pamphlet, *Key to Victory*, published by the Association of Citizens Councils of Louisiana and distributed to parish registrars by the state.[34] Louisiana law allowed any two registered voters to file affidavits challenging the registration of another person. This law was used by local white citizens councils to challenge the registration status of numerous blacks, along with a token number of whites. For example, in October 1956 the Citizens Council of Jackson Parish successfully challenged the registration of 953 of the 1,122 blacks registered to vote in that parish, along with 13 of the 5,450 whites. A federal district court found that "the challenges were based on alleged errors, omissions, and handwriting differences on the original application cards of the voters. These alleged deficiencies were not deficiencies under the standards applied by the registrar at the time these voters registered and the application cards of approximately 75 percent of the white voters who were not challenged contained similar deficiencies."[35]

Following the purges, registrars became more rigorous in their review of applicants' qualifications, or at least those of the black applicants. For example, in Jackson Parish during the period beginning just after the purge in October 1956 and ending in September 1962, the registrar rejected the applications of about 64 percent of the blacks but only 2 percent of the whites.[36]

The interpretation test, as noted above, was invalidated by the Supreme Court in 1965, just prior to the adoption of the Voting Rights Act. It was found to be discriminatory in purpose and effect and, therefore, a violation of both the Fourteenth and Fifteenth amendments. The Court concluded that it was a trap "sufficient to stop even the most brilliant [black] man on his way to the voting both."[37] Indeed, its purpose was so clear that many blacks were deterred from even attempting to register, knowing that the registrar would find any answers from a black applicant unsatisfactory.[38]

Despite the invalidation through litigation of several barriers to black disfranchisement, black participation in Louisiana's electoral process was still restricted as late as 1965. Litigation victories had been important, but they had not provided blacks with anything approaching equal access to the voting booth. It would take a more forceful form of "outside interference" for that to happen. The successful antidote to disfranchisement in Louisiana, as elsewhere, was the expanded federal protection authorized by the Voting Rights Act.

The Voting Rights Act

The act suspended the use of discriminatory tests and devices as a prerequisite for voting, authorized federal officials to register voters in selected areas (at the discretion of the Attorney General), and required "preclearance" for any changes in the election and registration laws in those states and local political subdivisions covered by section 5.[39] All of these provisions affected Louisiana. The impact was rapid and dramatic.

Louisiana was one of the seven states initially covered entirely or in large part by section 5. It was therefore precluded once again from simply substituting a new discriminatory trap for its invalidated literacy test. Black and white applicants for registration were to be treated equally beginning in 1965. To assist in the attainment of that goal, federal registrars were sent into nine of the parishes with the worst history of discrimination. By the fall of 1967 over 24,000 blacks had been added directly to the registration rolls in these parishes by the federal officials.[40] Their presence undoubtedly had a catalytic effect, as there were simultaneously "phenomenal increases" in black registration in parishes near those to which federal registrars had been sent.[41] By October 1967 overall black registration is reported to have increased by 84.2 percent. Blacks at that time constituted about 20 percent of the state's registered electorate, with just over half of voting-age blacks registered.[42]

Louisiana continued to be covered as the preclearance provision of the act was extended in 1970, 1975, and again in 1982. These extensions preserved the gains in black registration. Indeed, black registration continued to improve, with over 60 percent of voting-age blacks registered by the early 1970s, and close to 70 percent by the end of that decade.[43] As noted above, in 1990 about two-thirds were registered, comprising over a fourth of the state's registrants.

One consequence of the act therefore has been the virtual elimination of vote denial as an issue in Louisiana politics.[44] While racial disparities in registration rates remain, they are attributable largely to the socioeconomic disparities that continue to distinguish the black and white residents of the state, rather than to formal legal barriers or to the discriminatory behavior of local registrars. But while disfranchisement is now a thing of the past, the issue of "voting rights" is still very much alive in Louisiana. Efforts to combat discrimination in the electoral process have had to continue as blacks in Louisiana quickly learned that election systems could be arranged in ways that reduced their right to vote to a right to cast "meaningless ballots."[45]

Equal access to the voting booth is a necessary but not a sufficient condition for a fair electoral process. Louisiana unfortunately was not immune to efforts to minimize systematically, or dilute, the impact that black voters could have on election outcomes. This "second-generation" type of electoral discrimination had to be confronted as well.[46] Fortunately, the Voting Rights Act proved to be almost as powerful an antidote for this type as it had been for disfranchisement.

Vote Dilution

As the black vote in Louisiana grew, so did the number of black elected officials. There were over 100 in the state by 1972, over 200 by 1975, over 300 by 1978, and over 400 by 1984. The number in January 1990 stood at 527. Only two states, Alabama and Mississippi, had more.[47] This has been "the most striking payoff" from the registration gains reported above, as these officials were heavily dependent on black voters for their electoral support.[48] Indeed, almost all of them were elected from units (districts, cities, and so forth) in which blacks constituted a majority, as Louisiana's white voters have not been very receptive to black candidates.[49]

The payoff was not automatic, however. Resistance to integrating the elected elite continued. The state and various local governments adopted schemes that would impede the ability of blacks to use their new voting strength to elect black officials. Given the marked racial divisions in candidate preferences among Louisiana voters when they were presented with a choice between or among black and white candidates, the election of blacks has almost always depended on how electoral competition has been structured. Attempts to structure it to the disadvantage of blacks have been common.[50]

The major mechanisms for diluting the black vote have been elections held at large in majority-white political jurisdictions, the use of majority-white multimember geographic districts that submerge black voters, and the discriminatory delineation, or gerrymandering, of election district boundaries.[51] Both the preclearance requirements contained in section 5 and the general prohibition on dilutive electoral arrangements contained in section 2, as amended in 1982,[52] have served as important protections against these and other dilutive schemes in Louisiana. Had these protections not been available, there can be little doubt that the growth in the number of black elected officials in the state would have been severely attenuated.

Section 5

The preclearance requirement contained in section 5 precludes the state of Louisiana, as well as its local governments, from implementing any changes in laws relating to elections until those changes have been approved by either the Attorney General or the United States District Court in the District of Columbia. In this process, the state or local unit making the change has the responsibility of demonstrating that no discriminatory intent lies behind the alteration and that no discriminatory effect will result from it. The burden of proof, in short, rests with the governmental jurisdiction proposing the change.

The impact that this provision has had on Louisiana cannot be quantified for the simple reason that its major consequence has undoubtedly been its deterrent effect. There is no way to identify the number of times discriminatory changes would have been adopted had this requirement not been in effect, but the number must be large. Despite this deterrent effect, the Attorney General still found it necessary between 1965 and the middle of 1989 to issue sixty-six objection letters nullifying approximately two hundred of the changes that had been submitted for review. Eleven letters concerned changes proposed by the state government, and fifty-five, changes by local governments.[53] These objections have played a critical role in protecting the black vote from efforts to minimize its impact on Louisiana elections.

Among the most important objections under section 5 have been those preventing the state from implementing racially discriminatory districting plans for the state legislature. Objections were issued to the state's redistricting proposals following both the 1970 and 1980 censuses.

Both the house and senate plans adopted by the legislature in 1971 contained a mixture of single- and multimember districts that disadvantaged black voters. Multimember districts can be used to submerge black voters in large majority-white districts,[54] and the Attorney General identified a number of instances of these in Louisiana's proposed schemes. Concentrations of blacks sufficient to have formed majorities in single-member districts had simply been swallowed by larger majority-white multimember districts. The Attorney General noted that other black concentrations had been dissected by the proposed district boundaries, resulting in black voters being dispersed among majority-white districts. In one instance, a majority-black parish was joined with two majority-white parishes with which it was not even contiguous in order to form a majority-white state senate district. There were also instances of blacks being overconcentrated in a systematic fashion. For example, the only black person serving in the legislature at the time the plans were adopted, Dorothy Mae Taylor from New Orleans, was given a new nineteen-sided house district in which 33,364 of the 36,598 residents (91.3 percent) were black. Many of the black voters in this district could have helped to constitute a second black-majority district.[55]

The dilutive consequences of the legislature's schemes were so blatant that a federal district judge stated in 1971 that if the Attorney General had not objected to their implementation, he would have found them to be unconstitutional for, among other reason, "employing gerrymandering in its grossest form."[56] In response to Fourteenth Amendment–based "equal protection" challenges to these legislative acts, the judge ordered forthcoming legislative elections to be held under an alternative districting arrangement adopted by him.[57] This decision brought about a change in Louisiana's legislative election system that would be of profound importance to the state's blacks: the court-ordered arrangement relied exclusively on *single-member* districts.

Single-member districting unquestionably facilitated the election of blacks to the legislature.[58] By the end of the decade the voters in ten of these judicially imposed house districts and in two of the senate districts had elected black people as their representatives.[59] Since their imposition by the court, single-member districts have become a state constitutional requirement.[60]

The 1980 census necessitated another thorough revision of legislative districts. The state's plan for new senate districts, which contained five districts having a black population majority, was approved by the Attorney General's office, but the plan for the lower house once again failed to meet preclearance standards. The house plan was found to be unnecessarily retrogressive, even given the state's own districting criteria, as the number of black-majority districts was reduced from seventeen to fourteen. The state subsequently revised that plan, creating four more black-majority districts, and this second effort was granted preclearance.

The denial of preclearance to the legislature's redistricting products highlights the importance of section 5 in Louisiana. By 1990 there were fifteen state house districts and five senate districts in which blacks constituted a majority of the registered voters, and the voters in each of those districts (and only those districts) had chosen to be represented by a black legislator. It is extremely unlikely that there would have been twenty blacks serving in the legislature in 1990 had it not been for these section 5 objections and the federal court–ordered single-member districts.

The vast majority of the black elected officials in Louisiana serve in local legislative bodies. The fact that Louisiana ranked third in the nation in 1990 in the size of its black elected elite was due primarily to the 116 blacks elected to parish governing bodies, the 128 elected to local school boards, and the 173 elected to municipal councils.[61] As was the case with the state legislature, these numbers would also have been substantially lower had Louisiana not been subject to the preclearance requirement.

Probably the most important section 5 objections in Louisiana were the very first two, issued together on 27 June 1969. The state in 1968 had adopted statutes that authorized the election at large of the general governing boards (called police juries) and the school boards of parishes. These units had previously been required by state law to be elected through districts. The dilutive consequences of switching to at-large elections were obvious. Given the residential segregation of blacks, fairly drawn districting schemes would certainly have resulted in many majority-minority districts from which blacks would be elected. At-large elections, like the multimember state legislative districts, would have submerged this black voting strength within the overall white majority and often precluded the election of blacks.[62] These legislative acts were the first changes submitted for preclearance from Louisiana, and the Attorney General objected to both because of their dilutive nature. These objections, along with six others to subsequent attempts by specific police juries to switch to at-large elections in the early 1970s,[63] combined with the nearly forty objections the Attorney General had made to the redistricting schemes adopted by police juries and school boards following the 1970 and 1980 censuses, have been a critical factor in the successful conversion of black votes into black representation at the parish level.

Changes in Municipal Election Structures

Prohibiting these parish bodies from switching to at-large elections set an important precedent for cities as well. Indeed, municipal changes went in the opposite direction: from at-large elections to district or mixed plans (the latter containing both district and at-large seats). A survey in December 1989 of the state's eighty-seven municipalities having populations of 2,500 or more and in which blacks constituted at least 10 percent of the voting-age residents in 1980 revealed that one-half of the fifty-four cities that had at-large council plans in 1974 had adopted district or mixed plans by 1989 (table 4.12).[64] Whereas over 60 percent of the cities surveyed had an at-large plan in 1974, this arrangement was the least frequent of the three basic election types by 1989.

Many of these changes were stimulated by actual or expected legal challenges to the at-large system under either the Voting Rights Act or the Fourteenth Amendment. Local informants in nine of the twenty-seven cities switching from at-large systems stated that the change had been ordered by a court; in another four, change resulted from the voluntary settlement of a legal challenge; and in three others, it came from the threat of litigation (see table 4.8A). No information on the cause of change could be ascertained in the remaining eleven.

The shift to districts contributed to the increase in the number of black elected officials. Table 4.1A shows comparisons between the mean percentage of council seats held by blacks and the mean percentage of the voting-age population that was black in the surveyed municipalities, grouped by types of electoral systems and the percentage black. Two measures of how proportionately blacks were represented in 1989 are shown in tables 4.4 and 4.4A.[65]

Blacks were close to being, or were more than, proportionally represented in almost every category in 1989, according to table 4.4A. The only exceptions were the two categories (containing twenty-four cities in all) in which blacks were a minority of the voting-age population and elections were held at large. In 33.3 percent of these twenty-four at-large cities, blacks were completely absent from the council. This was true in only 3.3 percent of the cities using mixed systems and in none of the districted cities. The close correspondence between the black percentage of the voting-age population and number of black-held seats in the mixed systems was, in addition, due entirely to the districted portions of those systems. As disclosed in table 4.3A, blacks tended to be severely underrepresented in the at-large seats within these cities, but close to proportionately represented in the districted components, which contained some majority-black districts. These results demonstrate the critical importance of districts to black officeholding. While black representation in at-large systems overall was no longer as low as it had been, more equitable levels were achieved in municipalities that adopted districts. (See tables 4.2A and 4.5A for comparisons between 1974 and 1989.)[66] These results were not unique to Louisiana,[67] and were consistent with the well-established generalization that the less municipalities rely on at-large elections, the more proportionately blacks are likely to be represented within them.[68]

Although the Attorney General often objected to the districting plans proposed by police juries and school boards, only rarely did he object to the redistricting of municipal councils in Louisiana. As reported above, there was a close correspondence between black voting-age population percentages and black seat percentages in districted cities; in these municipalities, the percentage of majority-black districts was roughly proportional to the percentage of the voting-age population that was black. As with state legislative districts, there was a pronounced relationship between the racial composition of council districts and the race of the person elected to represent the district. Voters in majority-black districts almost invariably elected a black to represent them, while voters in majority-white districts elected whites (tables 4.6A and 4.7A).[69] As a consequence of the creation of the black-majority districts in these plans, the Attorney General rarely objected to them. Following the 1970 census he twice objected to efforts at revising the council districts in New Orleans, and he also objected to a redistricting in the city of Many. Only a single objection—to New Iberia's proposed districts—followed the next round of municipal redistricting based on the 1980 census.

New Orleans's second effort at redistricting in the 1970s became the subject of an important Supreme Court decision concerning section 5 preclearance criteria. The city council did not accept the Attorney General's decision and sought preclearance from the federal judiciary. The Supreme Court in *Beer v. United States* (1976),[70] its first review of a districting proposal under section 5, ruled in favor of the council. This decision affected far more than New Orleans, however, as the standard adopted in *Beer* seriously restricted the grounds upon which the Attorney General could deny preclearance generally.

At issue in *Beer* was the redrawing of the city's five single-member council districts and the continued use of at-large elections for two seats. This "five plus two" arrangement had been adopted in 1954 as part of a new city charter. The five districts had always been constructed by combining the seventeen wards of the city, which tended to follow a north-south pattern. By 1970 the city's blacks constituted 45 percent of the population and about 35 percent of the registered voters, and they tended to reside in an east-west pattern. The north-south districting configuration therefore dispersed the city's black vote across districts.

Despite the city's growing black electoral strength, no black had ever been elected to council, and the 1970s redistricting was controlled by whites. Not surprisingly, the council continued with a basically north-south districting scheme (although ward boundaries were now violated in order to comply with the one-person, one-vote rule). The result was two districts with black population majorities, but one was only 50.6 percent black. The other was 64.1 percent black and had a 52.6 percent black majority in voter registration. The black percentages among registered voters in the other four districts were 43.2, 36.8, 23.3, and 22.6.[71] After the Attorney General objected because of the dispersion of black electoral strength, the council sought permission from the federal district court in Washington, D.C., to use the plan.

A unanimous three-judge panel found, as had the Department of Justice, that the plan had a discriminatory effect, and refused to allow it to be implemented. The court concluded that the number of seats that blacks could expect to win under this plan, given the racially polarized voting patterns in the city, was considerably fewer than the number of seats that both the citywide black population and black registration percentages suggested as their "theoretical entitlement." The arrangement therefore was found to be an unjustified dilution of the black voting strength. The court also concluded, in response to an issued raised by the New Orleans blacks who had intervened in the case, that the two at-large seats, by themselves, diluted the city's black vote.[72]

The council appealed this decision to the Supreme Court, arguing that the at-large seats adopted in 1954 were not part of any voting change and therefore not covered by section 5, and that the district court had incorrectly adopted a rule that required districting plans to maximize black electoral opportunities. The Court agreed that the at-large seats were not part of the change and therefore should not be considered.[73] More important, however, was the Court's approach to the proposed division of the city into five districts.

In its review of the districting arrangement, a five-member majority adopted a new interpretation of section 5's purpose. The Court concluded that it was not a protection against dilutive changes per se, but only against *retrogressive* changes: it was the intent of Congress to ensure that "no voting procedure changes would be made that would lead to a retrogression in the position of racial minorities with respect to their effective exercise of the electoral franchise."[74] If a redistricting plan was not retrogressive—that is, not worse for blacks than the plan it was to replace—it should not be denied preclearance (unless the plan was clearly unconstitutional).[75] As for New Orleans's five proposed districts, the Court found that they were not retrogressive but ameliorative. The districting plan being replaced, at the time it was adopted in 1961, had contained only one district with a black population majority and none with a black voter registration majority. The city's new proposal included two districts with a population majority and one with a registration majority. It was therefore an "improvement" over the old arrangement and, the Court concluded, entitled to be precleared.

The *Beer* decision was, from the black perspective, an unfortunate step backward. The retrogression test established a *relative* vote dilution standard under section 5 rather than an absolute standard. In the words of one scholar, this approach to preclearance had the perverse consequence of "rewarding those jurisdictions with a history of the worst dilution of black electoral strength."[76] In addition, the Court's application of the retrogression criterion in *Beer* was itself problematic. The Court compared the racial composition of the districts in the city's proposed plan with those of the previous plan at the time that plan had been adopted (1961) rather than at the time it was revised (1973). The more appropriate comparison would have been with the districts as they stood at the time of revision. If the point of comparison is the time of initial adoption, then even plans that are in fact retrogressive could receive section 5 approval, given the usual ten-year period that elapses between redistricting efforts. In the New Orleans situation the comparison of the voter registration figures for the new districts with those for the old districts as of 1961, prior to the adoption of the Voting Rights Act, is particularly difficult to understand. Only about 17 percent of New Orleans's registered voters were black in 1961, compared to about 35 percent in 1973. It is hard to imagine how any set of districts proposed in 1973 would not be ameliorative if the comparison was to the 1961 figures.

The impact of *Beer*'s retrogression test was to restrict, at least for a while, the range of dilutive redistricting proposals that could be prevented from being implemented by the preclearance requirement.[77] This retrogression standard became less important, however, following the extension and amendment of the Voting Rights Act in 1982. Section 2 was revised to provide a "results" test for dilution, and the Attorney General held that changes creating arrangements that would violate the new results test would be denied preclearance under section 5. Nonretrogressive yet dilutive changes therefore could be objected to once again.[78]

The *Beer* decision highlighted two limitations of the preclearance requirement as a protection against dilution. First, section 5 applies only to *changes* in election procedures; it does not reach dilutive structures, such as at-large elections, that were in place prior to 1 November 1964. Second, until the 1982 amendment to section 2, changes could be dilutive and still precleared, provided they were not deemed to be retrogressive (or so blatant as to have been motivated by racial considerations). In Louisiana, however, blacks confronted with dilutive arrangements that were in place prior to 1965 or that have been granted preclearance by the Attorney General have had considerable success in overturning these schemes. The medium for these challenges has been the other provision of the Voting Rights Act mentioned above—the more general results test contained in section 2. Indeed, much of the effort at combating dilution in Louisiana since 1982 has relied on this provision.

Section 2

Section 2 was a relatively unimportant provision, at least in impact, before 1982. The Supreme Court had even held in *City of Mobile v. Bolden* (1980) that it was merely a restatement in statutory form of the Fifteenth Amendment prohibition on race-based disfranchisement and therefore was not a protection against dilution of the franchise.[79] The Court in *Bolden* also held that the Fourteenth Amendment, while a protection against dilution, prohibited only those schemes that had been adopted or retained for the purpose of diluting minority votes. Proof of the discriminatory effects of an electoral arrangement would not be sufficient for the plaintiffs to prevail on a Fourteenth Amendment claim; victory would require a demonstration of discriminatory motives as well.[80]

Bolden elevated seriously the burden of proof that black plaintiffs in Louisiana would have to meet in their constitutionally based challenges to dilutive schemes. Prior to *Bolden* the prevailing precedents, at least in cases involving claims of dilution by submergence in at-large or multimember districts, were *Whitcomb v. Chavis* (1971)[81] and *White v. Regester* (1973).[82] These cases had required not proof of discriminatory motives but demonstration by the plaintiffs that as a consequence of an electoral scheme, minority residents "had less opportunity than did other residents in the district to participate in the political process and to elect legislators of their choice."[83] Federal district courts in Louisiana had been instructed by an *en banc* decision of the Fifth Circuit Court of Appeals, *Zimmer v. McKeithen* (1973), to examine a variety of evidentiary considerations when determining whether this "opportunity" was in fact equal.[84]

The *Zimmer* decision blocked a shift from district to at-large elections for the East Carroll Parish police jury and school board that had been ordered by a federal district court in response to a complaint that the districts violated the one-person, one-vote standard. Blacks alleged that the initial malapportionment case had been a "sweetheart" white-on-white lawsuit, and challenged the constitutionality of the at-large remedy on dilution grounds. The Fifth Circuit agreed that the system would be dilutive in the East Carroll context. In reaching this conclusion, the court cited specifically the "protracted history" of discrimination against blacks in the parish, the persistent "debilitating effects" of previous disfranchisement schemes on black electoral participation, the "firmly entrenched state policy" in favor of district elections prior to the growth in the black electorate, and the fact that the at-large system in question required a majority vote for election to specific seats or places (thereby precluding "single-shot" voting). Under *Zimmer*, courts were instructed to examine "the confluence of factors" such as these to determine whether impermissible dilution was or would be present.[85]

There were a number of successful challenges to dilutive systems in Louisiana under the *Zimmer* standard. After the *Bolden* decision, however, constitutionally based litigation came to a virtual standstill. This halt to Fourteenth Amendment cases was not unique to Louisiana but a common phenomenon throughout the South, as many voting rights attorneys viewed litigation under *Bolden*'s intent requirement to be relatively useless.[86] Direct evidence of discriminatory motives would rarely be available, and judges were not expected to infer a racial intent readily from circumstantial evidence.[87]

Voting rights advocates proposed an amendment to section 2 as a way to minimize the impact of the *Bolden* ruling. The amendment was to provide a general statutory protection against dilutive schemes that would serve as an alternative to the now weakened constitutional protection. In a major lobbying victory, civil rights forces persuaded Congress in 1982 to prohibit electoral schemes that resulted in vote dilution, regardless of the purpose behind their use.[88] This revision gave new life to the fight against dilution, particularly in Louisiana.[89]

One of its first applications was in a successful challenge to the division of the state's eight congressional districts after the 1980 census. The New Orleans black community was split into two districts. Both of these districts, which extended into white suburban areas outside the city, had white population and voter registration majorities. New Orleans had a population of 557,482, which was only 0.06 percentage points over the ideal population size for a congressional district. Blacks constituted 55.3 percent of the city's residents in 1980. Therefore, a congressional district centered on the city could have been a racially competitive district in which black voters would have had an opportunity to elect a black to Congress.

The state chose instead to divide the city's black vote, placing about 43 percent of the black residents in the new First District and 57 percent in the new Second

District, each of which had a white incumbent. This division left blacks as only 29.5 percent of the population (and 21.4 percent of the registered voters) in the First, and 44.5 percent of the population (38.7 percent of the registered voters) in the Second. The division was accomplished geographically by a contorted boundary line that left the shape of the Second resembling a duck (fig. 4.1), prompting the scheme to be labeled derisively as a "gerryduck."[90]

The design of the districts was initially decided upon at an unofficial meeting attended by several legislators and other interested parties, but to which no blacks were invited. Although the group was conscious of the need to obtain section 5 preclearance and therefore avoided a configuration that was racially retrogressive, the dominant consideration was the impact the configuration of the districts would have on incumbents, all of whom were white. The "cracking" of the black vote could therefore charitably be viewed simply as a by-product of an incumbent protection plan. The plan was later formally adopted over the objections of all of the black state legislators. It was then granted preclearance by the Attorney General, despite an internal staff recommendation from Justice Department lawyers that an objection should be issued, because the state had failed to demonstrate the absence of a discriminatory purpose behind the division. (Blacks alleged, during the subsequent section 2 litigation, that this preclearance decision had been motivated by partisan politics. The plan was largely the result of the intervention of Louisiana's Republican governor, David Treen, in the interest of the Republican congressman from the New Orleans area, Robert Livingston. The decision to preclear the plan, despite the staff recommendation, was made by Republican political appointees in the Justice Department in response, blacks claimed, to Treen's lobbying for section 5 approval of the plan.)[91]

Only the 1982 congressional elections were held under this controversial districting arrangement, however. The following year a three-judge federal court in New Orleans ruled unanimously, in *Major v. Treen* (1983), that the plan was a violation of the new section 2.[92] Black plaintiffs characterized the arrangement as an "outrageous racial gerrymander," for which there were no legitimate nonracial explanations. They maintained that it was a conscious effort to accommodate the political ambitions of white incumbents at the expense of black voters. The state attempted to justify the arrangement by arguing that it reflected an effort to continue to locate two congressional districts in New Orleans and that its racial impact was therefore benign, not dilutive, in that New Orleans's blacks could influence the election of two members of Congress rather than one.[93] The court was not persuaded that the arrangement was benign, however, and held instead that the dissection of the city had been performed in a "racially selective manner" that would result in the dilution of the black vote. Neither the decision to continue to base two districts in New Orleans nor a desire to protect the electoral future of incumbents could justify this discriminatory result.[94] According to the court, "If [the] sundering of the black populace of New Orleans were allowed to stand, the effective independent impact of black voters would be unfairly and illegally minimized."[95]

Figure 4.1. New Orleans "Gerryduck" Congressional District

The crack in the black vote was repaired when the legislature, in a special session in late 1983, adopted a new congressional districting scheme for the New Orleans metropolitan area. This arrangement contained a district, the Second, that was located entirely within the city, and had both a black population and black voter registration majority (58.6 percent and 53.9 percent, respectively). This was not a "safe" black district, as many critics of the court's intervention complained, but it did provide potential black candidates with their first opportunity since Reconstruction to compete seriously for a congressional seat in Louisiana. A black state court judge, Israel Augustine, attempted to unseat the incumbent in the district, Democratic congresswoman Lindy Boggs, in the 1984 open primary. Although Augustine was the preferred choice of the black voters in that election, winning an estimated 64 percent of their votes, he won only a paltry 7 percent of the white vote and therefore lost to Boggs by a substantial margin.[96] Boggs, the most liberal member of Louisiana's congressional delegation, enjoyed considerable support from New Orleans blacks and did not face serious opposition again. In 1990, however, she announced her retirement from Congress, and the voters in the Second District chose a black, William Jefferson, to be her successor.

Section 2 has also been invoked in Louisiana to invalidate election systems that dilute through submergence. These efforts had been facilitated greatly by the Supreme Court's first decision involving the amended section, *Thornburg v. Gingles* (1986), in which multimember state legislative districts in North Carolina were found to have a dilutive effect.[97] They were facilitated further in Louisiana by the first post-*Gingles* decision of the Fifth Circuit Court of Appeals, which involved a Louisiana municipality. That decision, *Citizens for a Better Gretna v. City of Gretna*, handed down in 1987, contained important pronouncements concerning the plaintiff's burden of proof on the critical evidentiary issue of whether voting in the jurisdiction in question was "racially polarized."[98]

Blacks constituted about 30 percent of Gretna's population but no black had ever been elected to the city's at-large five-member council. Blacks had attempted to win seats on three occasions, but each attempt had failed because, as plaintiffs demonstrated, these candidates received only minimal support from the city's white voters. Additional evidence of black support for and white opposition to black candidates in Gretna was marshaled through an analysis of voting within Gretna in statewide elections involving black candidates. Plaintiffs claimed this pattern of voting precluded Gretna's blacks from electing candidates of their choice in the at-large context. The city attempted to rebut this evidence by arguing that some of the white candidates elected to the council had been supported by a majority of the black voters, and therefore blacks were electing candidates of their choice. The city argued that plaintiffs' focus on the fortunes of the black councilmanic candidates was misplaced and that the analysis of "exogenous" (i.e., noncouncilmanic) elections was irrelevant in a dispute involving a city's election system.

The Fifth Circuit, in upholding a district court judgment in favor of the plaintiffs, rejected the city's suggestion that as long as blacks supported some winning white candidates, their inability to elect a black was legally inconsequential. The court noted that the at-large elections in Gretna were five-seat contests in which each voter had five votes. Given that no more than one candidate in any councilmanic election had been black, it was "virtually unavoidable" that some white candidates would receive substantial black support. The fact that some of these white candidates were successful did not negate the existence of the veto white voters exercised over black candidates.[99] The plaintiffs' focus on the racial divisions in the vote for black candidates was found to be proper. The court concluded that elections involving "a viable minority candidate" provided the best context for determining whether the candidate preferences of whites and blacks diverged.[100] In addition, exogenous elections involving black candidates, because they provide information about "local voting patterns," were found to be relevant to the section 2 inquiry.[101]

The *Gretna* decision was an important precedent. Prior to the Supreme Court's decision in *Gingles*, defendants in vote-dilution cases typically argued that plaintiffs, in order to demonstrate that voting was "racially polarized," had to show that race was itself the cause of the voting divisions.[102] This argument was rejected in *Gingles* when the Supreme Court held that plaintiffs need show only the existence of the divisions, not the reasons for them.[103] Following *Gingles* the standard defense strategy was to argue, in effect, that as long as blacks were often on the winning side in white-on-white elections, they had no valid claim of dilution. The fact that blacks could not elect blacks was somehow cleansed of any discriminatory consequences by this ability to elect candidates of their "choice" in the white-on-white context. This argument was especially pernicious in light of the chilling effects that dilutive arrangements often have on black candidacies. Campaigns can be expensive in both time and money, and the probability of success is one factor that candidates, black or white, consider when deciding whether to run.

The Fifth Circuit's focus on black-on-white contests in *Gretna*, including those for other offices in which voters in the jurisdiction at issue participate, has virtually eliminated this argument as an efficacious defense in Louisiana.[104] Indeed, just such a defense was rejected the following year when a federal district court, based on evidence from numerous exogenous elections, found that voting in Louisiana's major suburban parish, Jefferson, was racially polarized. The finding was critical to the court's conclusion in *East Jefferson Coalition for Leadership and Development v. Parish of Jefferson* (1988) that the three-tiered election system (four single-member districts, two half at-large districts, and one parishwide district) employed to select the parish council had a dilutive result and therefore violated section 2.[105]

Section 2 and the Election of Judges

The section 2 case that may have the most profound impact in Louisiana, however, involves not the election of legislators but rather of judges. In *Clark v. Edwards* (1988), the systems through which judges are elected to serve on the state's basic trial courts—called judicial district courts—and on its intermediate courts of appeals, were challenged under section 2 by black plaintiffs.[106]

The systems at issue were at-large (jurisdictionwide) elections to specific places or divisions on the respective court, with winners determined by a majority-vote rule, with the top two vote recipients entering a runoff if no candidate received a majority in the first election. Blacks have been especially underrepresented in the state's judiciary. At the time of the trial in *Clark*, only 5 of the state's 178 district court judges and only 1 of the 48 court of appeals judges were black. Blacks had made numerous efforts to be elected to the bench, but their candidacies were consistently rebuffed by the state's white voters.[107] Relying heavily on the Supreme Court's *Gingles* decision, a federal district court in Louisiana found that black voters were being submerged in a number of the judicial jurisdictions, resulting in a dilution of their vote under section 2.[108]

The state attempted to remedy the dilution identified in *Clark* by proposing a constitutional amendment authorizing the election of judges through "subdistricts" within the geographical jurisdiction of each court. Only voters residing within a subdistrict would be able to vote for judges apportioned to that subdistrict, but candidates living elsewhere within the overall jurisdiction could run in any of the subdistricts. The state also adopted a districting scheme, contingent on approval of the amendment, through which forty trial judges and twelve appellate judges would have been elected by voters in majority-black districts. White incumbents who would be adversely affected by this new arrangement were provided with the option of assuming a new "senior" status, through which they could remain on the bench (retaining their salaries) without standing for reelection. When this arrangement was presented to the voters for their approval in October 1989, however, the proposed amendment was rejected in a racially divided response. An estimated 66.4 percent of blacks voting on the amendment voted in favor of it, but only 17.2 percent of the whites supported it.[109] Had the amendment passed, the number of black judges in Louisiana would have increased dramatically after the 1990 elections.

The subdistricting remedy was subsequently adopted by the federal court for ten trial court jurisdictions and one appellate court district. A total of nineteen trial court judges and one appellate court judge were to be elected from within black-majority subdistricts in these new arrangements.[110] While the *Clark* case was on appeal before the Fifth Circuit, the plaintiffs and the state settled the suit. Under the settlement, even more trial court judges and more appellate court judges would be elected from black-majority subdistricts than would have been in the federal court's remedial order.

The system for electing state supreme court judges was also challenged. There are seven members of this court, five of whom are elected from single-member districts, the other two from a two-member district (with staggered terms) made up of the City of New Orleans and three surrounding parishes, Jefferson, St. Bernard, and Plaquemine. No black was ever elected to the supreme court under this arrangement. The plaintiffs in this case, *Chisom v. Edwards*, later *Chisom v.*

Roemer,[111] asserted a standard claim of dilution by submergence, relying on the *Gingles* precedent. The four-parish two-member district was majority white in both population and voter registration. Given the racially polarized nature of voting within the four-parish area and the majority-vote requirement for election to the supreme court, blacks did not have a realistic opportunity of electing a black candidate of their choice within this district. If it were divided into two single-member districts, however, a district centered on New Orleans in which blacks would have a population and a registration majority could have been created. Plaintiffs argued that a New Orleans–based district would provide blacks with their first real opportunity to elect a candidate of their choice to the supreme court.[112]

The *Chisom* case was also settled in 1992, again while it was on appeal before the Fifth Circuit. Unlike the *Clark* case, the state had won the *Chisom* case in the federal district court. Although it was undisputed that no black candidate for any type of judgeship had been supported over a white candidate by white voters in any of the four parishes in the district, the federal judge concluded that there was an emerging crossover vote in the district, and therefore the black vote was not illegally submerged.[113] The case was settled, however, when the legislature created a new, temporary "supreme court" judgeship that would be filled in a 1992 election in which only New Orleans voters would participate.

The state constitution specifies that the state supreme court shall consist of seven justices, and therefore the new eighth member was to be elected, technically, to the state court of appeals and then assigned to serve on the supreme court. The eight-member court would then hear cases in rotating seven-member panels, with cases assigned to panels randomly. This is to be a temporary arrangement; the legislature is required to adopt, in 1998, a new districting plan containing a single-member district with a black voting-age majority that includes Orleans Parish in its entirety. This new districting arrangement will be in place starting with an election in 2000. If a vacancy should occur in one of the two seats in the existing First District prior to the year 2000, Orleans Parish voters only will vote in a special election to fill the seat.[114] This is the result of a compromise obviously intended to add a black justice to the court without abbreviating the term of one of the two white incumbents in the First District. A new black justice assumed the new seat on 1 January 1993, as only black candidates filed to run in the 1992 election for that position.

The *Chisom* case also served as the medium for an important Supreme Court decision in 1991 concerning section 2's application to judicial election systems. Following the trial court decisions in *Clark* and *Chisom*, the Fifth Circuit Court of Appeals held, in an *en banc* decision involving Texas judgeships, that section 2 did not provide a protection against dilution in the *judicial* election context. The majority in that case concluded that the language in subsection b concerning minority voters' opportunities "to elect *representatives* of their choice" was intended to exclude judges because judges, unlike other elected officials, were not "representatives."[115] The Supreme Court, in reviewing this issue in the *Chisom* context, held otherwise. Congress, the Court concluded, did not intend any exemption of judicial elections from this protection against vote dilution. The word *representatives* simply referred to "the winners of representative, popular elections," which included successful candidates in judicial elections.[116] Judicial election systems that dilute minority votes, therefore, are invalid under the Voting Rights Act.

Section 2 has become an important supplement to the preclearance requirement contained in section 5. Since its revision in 1982, section 2 has provided blacks in Louisiana with a means through which to challenge election systems not subject to the preclearance rule and, also, arrangements such as the 1981 congressional redistricting that are not retrogressive but are still viewed by blacks as discriminatory. The two sections together have proven overall to be very effective protections against dilution. The number of black elected officials in Louisiana today would be much smaller had it not been for these provisions.

Conclusion

Efforts to integrate the elected elite have been resisted by whites throughout Louisiana's history. This resistance was initially operationalized through schemes that disfranchised black voters. The first of these schemes explicitly established racial qualifications for voting; the later ones were "facially neutral" but discriminatory in application. This denial of the franchise on the basis of race was not successfully attacked in Louisiana until the adoption of the Voting Rights Act. Although there had been federal court decisions in favor of the plaintiffs in some voting rights cases prior to that act, it was the special provisions of the act that ultimately opened the franchise to Louisiana's black residents.

The consequent growth in the black vote did not end electoral discrimination in Louisiana, however. As the black vote expanded, a second-generation type of electoral discrimination became prevalent, the dilution of the black vote. Although the Fourteenth Amendment provides a constitutional protection against dilution, it requires plaintiffs to assume the difficult burden of proving racially discriminatory motives behind the use of these arrangements. In Louisiana as elsewhere blacks have had to rely heavily on the statutory protections of the Voting Rights Act to combat dilutive schemes. Both the preclearance provision of section 5 and the more general results tests contained in amended section 2 have provided critical protections against such schemes.

In 1990 Louisiana had the third largest number of black elected officials among the fifty states. This remarkable progress toward integrating the elected elite is the direct result of the Voting Rights Act. Both the enfranchisement of blacks and the subsequent protection against the virtual nullification of their votes were made possible by the act. This extraordinary form of "outside interference" in Louisiana was necessary to begin to open the electoral process to blacks. More remains to be done before blacks have a truly equal opportunity to participate politically, however, and any further progression toward that ultimate goal will undoubtedly be very dependent on the act's protections as well.

TABLE 4.1
Black Representation on Council in 1989 by Election Plan, Louisiana Cities of 2,500 or More Population with 10 Percent or More Black Population in 1980[a]

Type of Plan by % Black in City Population, 1980	N	*Mean % Black in City Population, 1980*	*Mean % Black on City Council, 1989*
SMD plan			
10–29.9	9	24.1	25.2
30–49.9	16	42.2	34.9
50–100	6	56.6	50.0
Mixed plan			
10–29.9	13	22.7	20.4
30–49.9	13	36.9	25.9
50–100	4	52.8	47.2
At-large plan			
10–29.9	16	17.5	10.0
30–49.9	7	39.7	20.0
50–100	6	63.8	53.3

[a]This table contains data on three cities not included in table 4.1A because this table employs a threshold of 10 percent black total population rather than voting-age population.

TABLE 4.1A
Black Representation on Council in 1989 by Election Plan, Louisiana Cities of 2,500 or More Population with 10 Percent or More Black Voting-Age Population (VAP) in 1980

Type of Plan by % Black in City VAP, 1980	N	*Mean % Black in City VAP, 1980*	*Mean % Black on City Council, 1989*
SMD plan			
10–29.9	12	21.9	28.6
30–49.9	14	38.6	34.5
50–100	4	55.0	55.0
Mixed plan			
10–29.9	19	22.3	21.0
30–49.9	11	39.4	35.6
50–100	0	—	—
At-large plan			
10–29.9	16	18.4	11.2
30–49.9	8	41.9	27.5
50–100	3	71.7	66.7

TABLE 4.2
Changes in Black Representation on Council between 1974 and 1989, Louisiana Cities of 2,500 or More Population with 10 Percent or More Black Population in 1980[a]

Type of Change by % Black in City Population, 1980	N	*Mean % Black in City Population, 1980*	*Mean % Black on City Council*	
			Before Change (1974)	*After Change (1989)*
		Changed Systems		
From at-large to SMD plan				
10–29.9	3	25.4	0.0	26.7
30–49.9	9	43.0	1.6	38.4
50–100	2	61.6	0.0	50.0
From at-large to mixed plan				
10–29.9	7	23.5	3.2	19.4
30–49.9	6	36.4	0.0	24.2
50–100	1	51.1	0.0	25.0
		Unchanged Systems		
At-large plan				
10–29.9	16	17.5	0.0	10.0
30–49.9	7	39.7	0.0	20.0
50–100	6	63.8	26.7	53.3

[a]This table contains data on three cities not included in table 4.2A because this table employs a threshold of 10 percent black population rather than voting-age population.

TABLE 4.2A
Changes in Black Representation on Council between 1974 and 1989, Louisiana Cities of 2,500 or More Population with 10 Percent or More Black Voting-Age Population (VAP) in 1980

Type of Change by % Black in City VAP, 1980	N	*Mean % Black in City VAP, 1980*	*Mean % Black on City Council* Before Change (1974)	*Mean % Black on City Council* After Change (1989)
		Changed Systems		
From at-large to SMD plan				
10–29.9	5	22.9	2.9	32.6
30–49.9	7	38.3	0.0	37.6
50–100	1	64.9	0.0	60.0
From at-large to mixed plan				
10–29.9	10	23.2	2.2	20.1
30–49.9	4	38.3	0.0	26.9
50–100	0	—	—	—
		Unchanged Systems		
At-large plan				
10–29.9	16	18.4	0.0	11.2
30–49.9	8	41.9	2.5	27.5
50–100	3	71.7	40.0	66.7

TABLE 4.3
Black Representation in 1989 in Mixed Plans by District and At-Large Components, Louisiana Cities of 2,500 or More Population with 10 Percent or More Black Population in 1980

% Black in City Population, 1980	N	*Mean % Black Councilpersons in District Components, 1989*	*Mean % Black Councilpersons in At-Large Components, 1989*
10–29.9	13	30.5	0.0
30–49.9	13	30.7	6.9
50–100	4	50.8	37.5

TABLE 4.3A
Black Representation in 1989 in Mixed Plans by District and At-Large Components, Louisiana Cities of 2,500 or More Population with 10 Percent or More Black Voting-Age Population (VAP) in 1980

% Black in City VAP, 1980	N	*Mean % Black Councilpersons in District Components, 1989*	*Mean % Black Councilpersons in At-Large Components, 1989*
10–29.9	19	29.2	2.1
30–49.9	11	40.3	18.2
50–100	0	—	—

TABLE 4.4
Two Equity Measures Comparing Percentage Black on Council in 1989, Louisiana Cities of 2,500 or More Population with 10 Percent or More Black Population in 1980[a]

Type of Plan by % Black in City Population, 1980	N	*Difference Measure (% on Council − % in City)*	*Ratio Measure (% on Council ÷ % in City)*
SMD plan			
10–29.9	9	1.1	1.04
30–49.9	16	−7.2	0.84
50–100	6	−6.6	0.88
Mixed plan			
10–29.9	13	−2.4	0.93
30–49.9	13	−11.0	0.70
50–100	4	−5.6	0.89
At-large plan			
10–29.9	16	−7.1	0.60
30–49.9	7	−19.7	0.52
50–100	6	−10.4	0.80

[a]This table contains data on three cities not included in table 4.4A because this table employs a threshold of 10 percent black total population rather than voting-age population.

TABLE 4.4A
Two Equity Measures Comparing Percentage Black on City Council in 1989, Louisiana Cities of 2,500 or More Population with 10 Percent or More Black Voting-Age Population (VAP) in 1980

Type of Plan by % Black in City VAP, 1980	N	*Difference Measure (% on Council − % in City VAP)*	*Ratio Measure (% on Council ÷ % in City VAP)*
SMD plan			
10–29.9	12	6.7	1.31
30–49.9	14	−4.1	0.89
50–100	4	0.0	1.00
Mixed plan			
10–29.9	19	−1.3	1.00
30–49.9	11	−3.8	0.90
50–100	0	—	—
At-large plan			
10–29.9	16	−7.1	0.62
30–49.9	8	−14.4	0.66
50–100	3	−5.0	0.93

TABLE 4.5
Changes in Black Representation on Council between 1974 and 1989, Louisiana Cities of 2,500 or More Population with 10 Percent or More Black Population in 1980[a] (Ratio Equity Measure)

Type of Change by % Black in City Population, 1980	N	*Black Representational Equity on Council*	
		1974	*1989*
	Changed Systems		
From at-large to SMD plan			
10–29.9	3	0.00	1.04
30–49.9	9	0.04	0.90
50–100	2	0.00	0.80
From at-large to mixed plan			
10–29.9	7	0.11	0.85
30–49.9	6	0.00	0.65
50–100	1	0.00	0.49
	Unchanged Systems		
At-large plan			
10–29.9	16	0.00	0.60
30–49.9	7	0.00	0.52
50–100	6	0.33	0.80

[a]This table contains data on three cities not included in table 4.5A because this table employs a threshold of 10 percent black total population rather than voting-age population.

TABLE 4.5A
Changes in Black Representation on Council between 1974 and 1989, Louisiana Cities of 2,500 or More Population with 10 Percent or More Black Voting-Age Population (VAP) in 1980 (Ratio Equity Measure)

Type of Change by % Black in City VAP, 1980	N	*Black Representational Equity on Council* 1974	1989
	Changed Systems		
From at-large to SMD plan			
10–29.9	5	0.12	1.40
30–49.9	7	0.00	0.99
50–100	1	0.00	0.92
From at-large to mixed plan			
10–29.9	10	0.08	0.90
30–49.9	4	0.00	0.70
50–100	0	—	—
	Unchanged Systems		
At-large plan			
10–29.9	16	0.00	0.62
30–49.9	8	0.06	0.66
50–100	3	0.56	0.93

TABLE 4.6A
Black Representation in Council Single-Member Districts in 1989, Louisiana Cities of 2,500 or More Population with 10 Percent or More Black Voting-Age Population (VAP) in 1980

% Black VAP of District	N	*Mean % Black Population in Districts, 1980*	*Mean % Black Councilpersons in Districts, 1989*
0–29.9	59	10.8	1.7
30–49.9	14	38.3	14.3
50–59.9	7	57.9	85.7
60–64.9	1	62.5	100.0
65–69.9	3	67.8	100.0
70–100	30	86.0	100.0

TABLE 4.7A
Black Council Representation in Single-Member Districts in 1989 by Racial Composition of District, Louisiana Cities of 2,500 or More Population with 10 Percent or More Black Voting-Age Population (VAP) in 1980

Racial Composition of District	N	*Mean % Black VAP in Districts, 1980*	*Mean % Black Councilpersons in Districts, 1989*
Black majority	41	79.3	97.6
White majority	73	16.1	4.1

'ABLE 4.8A
'ause of Change from At-Large to Mixed or District Plan between 1974 and 1989, Louisiana 'ities of 2,500 or More Population with 10 Percent or More Black Voting-Age Population in 1980

'ity[a]	Did lawsuit Accompany Change?	Year of Change	Results: District Seats (Number)	Results: At-Large Seats (Number)	Reason for Change[b]
		Changed to Single-Member Districts			
.mite	Yes	1984	5	0	Settlement
reaux Bridge	No	1976	5	0	Threat of lawsuit
lammond	Yes	1977	5	0	Court-ordered
iomer	Yes	1975	5	0	Settlement
.ake Charles	Yes	1974	4	0	Court-ordered
afayette	Yes	1975	5	0	Court-ordered
larksville	No	1978	5	0	—
linden	Yes	1978	5	0	Court-ordered
lonroe	Yes	1980	5	0	Court-ordered
hreveport	Yes	1978	7	0	Court-ordered
pringhill	Yes	1974	5	0	Settlement
allulah	Yes	1979	5	0	Court-ordered
'innfield	Yes	1982	5	0	Settlement
		Changed to Mixed Plan			
ogalusa	No	1978	5	2	—
ossier City	No	1977	5	2	—
roussard	No	1986	4	1	—
unkie	No	1984	4	1	Threat of lawsuit
ovington	No	1978	5	2	—
rowley	No	1974	8	1	Threat of lawsuit
onaldsonville	No	1975	3	1	—
retna	Yes	1987	4	1	Court-ordered
enner	No	1974	5	2	—
eesville	No	1978	4	2	—
atchitoches	No	1975	4	1	—
onchatoula	No	1980	4	1	—
aibodeaux	No	1975	3	2	—
lle Platte	Yes	1975	5	1	Court-ordered
SUMMARY	Yes 13 (48%)				
	No 14 (52%)				

[a] Voting age population by race was not provided in the 1980 census for Farmerville, a city which switched, der threat of a lawsuit, from at-large elections to a single-member-district system; therefore it is not included in s table.

[b] Some cities would not or could not supply reasons for the change.

TABLE 4.9
Major Disfranchising Devices in Louisiana

Device	*Date Established*	*Date Abolished*
Explicit racial exclusion	1812	1868[a]
Grandfather clause (educational and property requirements)	1898	1915[b]
White primaries	1921	1944[c]
Interpretation test	1921	1965[d]

[a]Congressional Reconstruction.
[b]*Guinn and Beal v. United States,* 238 U.S. 347 (1915).
[c]*Smith v. Allwright,* 321 U.S. 649 (1944).
[d]*Louisiana v. United States,* 380 U.S. 145 (1965).

TABLE 4.10
Nonwhite and White Registered Voters and Officeholders in Louisiana, Selected Years[a]

	Nonwhite		*White*	
	N	%	N	%
Registered voters				
1964	164,601	13.7	1,037,184	86.3
1967	303,148	20.2	1,200,517	79.8
1988	571,453	26.4	1,589,942	73.6
Officeholders				
1964	—	—	—	—
1969	64	1.0[b]	—	—
1988	524	11.1	4,196	88.9

Sources: Registration figures for 1964 and 1967 are based on United States Commission on Civil Rights 1968, 242–43. Registration figures for 1988 are based on the end-of-year report for that year by the Louisiana Department of Elections and Registration. Figures for the number of elected officials are taken from the Joint Center for Political Studies 1970 and 1989.

[a]Mean black Louisiana population, 1960–90 = 30.5%.
[b]Rough estimate.

TABLE 4.11
Black Voter Registration Rates for Louisiana Parishes, 1964

Registration as % of Black VAP[a]	*Parishes* N	%
0–10	13	20.3
10–20	7	10.9
20–30	8	12.5
30–40	8	12.5
40–50	5	7.8
50–60	7	10.9
60–70	8	12.5
70–80	4	6.2
80–90	3	4.7
90–100	1	1.6
TOTAL	64	99.9

Source: United States Commission on Civil Rights 1968, 240–43.

[a]Registration figures are for 3 October 1964.

TABLE 4.12
Municipal Election Systems, 1974 and 1989, Louisiana Cities of 2,500 or More Population with 10 Percent or More Black Voting-Age Population in 1980

Type of Election System	*1974* N	%	*1989* N	%
Districts	17	19.5	30	34.5
Mixed	16	18.4	30	34.5
At-large	54	62.1	27	31.0
TOTAL	87	100.0	87	100.0

CHAPTER FIVE

Mississippi

FRANK R. PARKER, DAVID C. COLBY, AND MINION K. C. MORRISON

"I OPPOSE the bringing of the negro back into politics, which . . . allowing the wards to select their Aldermen, will surely do," argued Mississippi state senator J. L. Hebron in 1906, during a debate on whether to change Greenville's electoral structure from at-large to district elections.[1] In 1962, the Mississippi legislature required all code charter cities with mayor–board of aldermen governments to switch from district to at-large aldermanic elections to prevent the election of black aldermen. "This is needed to maintain our southern way of life," a supporter of this legislation argued.[2] In Mississippi, exclusion of black representatives was at least one reason for the widespread adoption of at-large municipal voting. In this chapter we analyze the impact of the Voting Rights Act and litigation under it on changes from at-large to district city council elections, as well as on the election of black city council members in Mississippi. We do not discuss the impact of the act on other governmental structures, such as congressional, state legislative, and county redistricting, which has been discussed elsewhere.[3]

Intense social and political mobilization by blacks seeking the right to vote in the most "redeemed" of the former Confederate states significantly contributed to the passage of the Voting Rights Act.[4] The history of Mississippi race relations and black disfranchisement is therefore important for understanding the changes in black municipal political participation. The state came into the Union in 1817 and, unlike some other southern states, had essentially a one-crop cotton economy. Most slaves were occupied with hoeing and picking cotton "from sunup to sundown." This regimen was sustained by harsh regulations that amounted to a police-state apparatus. Notwithstanding factionalism among themselves, whites were in sufficient agreement on African-American inferiority to produce greater resistance to change in race relations than in any other state in the South.[5]

Despite the harshness of the slave system before the Civil War, the Reconstruction Act of 1867 enabled blacks to achieve some quick successes in political participation from 1867 to 1870. For example, they sent sixteen delegates to the hundred-member constitutional convention in 1868. From 1870 to 1875, they enjoyed their greatest participation in politics until the present period. Blacks teamed up with their white allies to control the legislature. In 1870, 30 of 107 representatives in the lower house and 5 of 30 senators were black.[6] In the 1870s, other blacks occupied national, state and local offices: there were 2 U.S. senators, a U.S. representative, a lieutenant governor, 5 secretaries of state, a superintendent of education, and 2 speakers of the state house of representatives. Blacks also controlled some county governments, notably in the Delta region. Nevertheless, in a state that was 54 percent black in 1870, black representation in government was never proportional to the black population.[7]

This period of participation ended in 1875, when blacks were disfranchised by fraud and intimidation, or co-opted into arrangements controlled by whites.[8] This de facto disfranchisement received the sanction of law in 1890 when a new constitution was written by an almost all-white convention. The convention adopted a cumulative poll tax of two dollars per year and a literacy requirement for voter registration (see table 5.9). The poll tax created an economic hardship for blacks and poor whites alike. The literacy provision—requiring an applicant to read, understand, or interpret any section of the state constitution (later changed to read, write, *and* interpret) to the satisfaction of the circuit clerk, a local white official—gave circuit clerks wide discretion to allow illiterate whites to vote and to prevent even literate blacks from doing so. Previously, blacks had made up a majority of the registered voters; by 1896 only 9 percent of adult blacks were registered to vote.[9]

These constitutional measures were reinforced by the adoption of party primaries to nominate candidates for office and the "white primary" rule that excluded blacks from these crucial elections. They were barred from participating in the Democratic primaries beginning in 1907.[10] In response both to the U.S. Supreme Court's decisions, in 1944 and 1954, respectively, that white primaries and racially segregated schools were unconstitutional and to growing black mobilization, Mississippi erected further barriers to black enfranchisement.[11] The legislature conditioned participation in party primaries upon adherence to "party principles," and the political parties adopted principles supporting racial segregation, in effect excluding anyone who did not support segregation. In addition, the legislature adopted statutes and constitutional amendments that strengthened the literacy test and added a "good moral character" test that required the names of persons applying for voter registration to be published in the local newspaper. Some blacks whose names were published were then evicted from their homes and fired from their jobs.

The systematic exclusion of blacks from electoral participation came under increasing attack in Mississippi as early as the 1940s. At that time, groups composed mainly of black professionals, such as clergy, schoolteachers, and doctors, along with the National Association for the Advancement of Colored People (NAACP), began to take independent action to secure voting rights and greater respect in general for blacks.[12] Their efforts culminated in the 1960s in a civil rights campaign for voter registration, school desegregation, and a wide range of other rights commonly denied blacks. The collective activation of their groups' resources resulted in broad mobilization for the acquisition of social and political goods.[13] In its organized form this activation occurred under the sponsorship of the NAACP, the Student Nonviolent Coordinating Committee, the Congress of Racial Equality, the Mississippi Freedom Democratic Party, the Council of Federated Organizations, and numerous local leaders. These forces worked with federal officials and civil rights lawyers to challenge Mississippi's racist laws and to seek new legislation to strengthen black rights. The Voting Rights Act is the crowning achievement of the civil rights agitation and litigation campaign.

Passage of the act in 1965 dramatically changed Mississippi politics. The most obvious change was the enfranchisement of blacks. But as Chief Justice Earl Warren stated in *Allen v. State Board of Elections*, a case interpreting the scope of the act, "the Voting Rights Act was aimed at the subtle, as well as the obvious, state regulations which have the effect of denying citizens their right to vote because of their race. . . . The right to vote can be affected by a dilution of voting power as well as by an absolute prohibition on casting a ballot."[14] The Voting Rights Act invalidated Mississippi's literacy test as well as other voter registration tests, and led to the abolition of the the poll tax in state elections; consequently, black registration increased sharply.[15] However, other obstacles to registration, such as the requirement of dual registration for state and municipal elections, and a prohibition against registrars enrolling voters outside their offices, remained in effect in Mississippi until the 1980s. Barriers that diluted black voting power were more resistant to change. After passage of the act, the goal of white segregationists was mainly to dilute black voting power, not only through legislation but through deceit, intimidation, and violence.[16]

The Impact of Litigation on At-Large Municipal Elections

Twenty-two of the twenty-six largest incorporated cities in Mississippi had at-large city council elections in 1965. Today most cities have changed to district-based election systems. This change is the product of a new, post-1965 voting rights movement that has relied primarily on litigation under the Fourteenth and Fifteenth amendments and the Voting Rights Act to mount court challenges to at-large election systems that dilute minority voting strength. To the extent that this new movement protests denials and abridgments of black citizens' right to vote, it reflects a historical continuity with the goals of the civil rights struggles of the 1960s. The success of the later movement resulted not only from black initiatives but from congressional legislation and Supreme Court decisions that made the litigation possible. The 1965 passage of the act, which broadly prohibited racial discrimination in voting, and the 1982 amendment to section 2, which eliminated the necessity of proving discriminatory intent in challenges to voting systems and adopted a more liberal "results" test, were key to the movement's success.

To study the impact of the act on municipal election structures and black officeholding, we have conducted research on litigation challenging at-large city council elections, including the collection of information on all lawsuits against Mississippi cities with at-large elections. Since many of these cases were unreported or were settled out of court, we surveyed legal organizations and attorneys filing voting rights cases in the state to obtain information on their lawsuits. For each case, we obtained the name of the city involved, the case name, the case particulars (date filed, date resolved), the attorneys for the plaintiffs, how the case was resolved, the legal basis for the case, and the type of election system challenged.

Between 1965 and 1989, seventy-one Mississippi cities of 1,000 or more with at least 10 percent black population switched from systems under which all the city council members were elected at large to either district elections or to mixed plans in which some council members were elected by district and others at large (see tables 5.8 and 5.11). Fifty-nine of the seventy-one cities went to district elections as a result of court injunctions in contested litigation, settlement of pending litigation, or threat of litigation; four (including three that were also targets of litigation) switched as a result of Justice Department section 5 objections to the adoption of at-large voting or to municipal annexations; and eleven switched voluntarily.

The Section 5 Preclearance Requirement

Section 5 requires covered states, including Mississippi, to submit all proposed new voting laws either to the U.S. Attorney General or to the U.S. District Court for the District of Columbia for preclearance before they can be implemented. The state has the burden of proving that the change is not racially discriminatory in purpose or effect. If the Attorney General objects or the court denies approval, the change cannot be implemented. In *Allen v. State Board of Elections*, the Supreme Court interpreted the section 5 preclearance requirement to cover not only changes affecting registration and voting, but also any changes that might dilute minority voting strength, including adoption of at-large elections.

The first municipal at-large election challenge in Mississippi was *Perkins v. Matthews*,[17] filed by the Jackson office of the Lawyers' Constitutional Defense Committee (LCDC), a national coalition of groups that opened offices in the South to assist the civil rights movement. In this case, black voters challenged Canton's switch in 1969 to at-large elections without section 5 preclearance. The city contended that although it had conducted the 1965 city elections under a district system, the 1969 change to at-large voting was not covered by section 5 because it was authorized by a state statute adopted in 1962, before section 5 went into effect. A three-judge district court agreed with the city's position and went on to rule that the change was not discriminatory, since black voters had an overwhelming majority in only one district. If one black alderman were elected, the district court reasoned, it "would, in practical effect, amount to nothing" because "the one Negro member of the board [of aldermen] would always be outvoted by the four white members."

On appeal, the Supreme Court reversed the district court's ruling.[18] The decision was significant for Voting Rights Act enforcement throughout the South because it reaffirmed the Court's ruling in *Allen* that all voting law changes adopted after 1965 must be precleared under section 5, and it expressly applied section 5 to changes in at-large municipal elections (as well as municipal annexations and polling place changes). The Court ruled that section 5 covers any change in actual voting practices since the effective date of the Voting Rights Act. Thus, because

Canton conducted district elections in 1965, the 1969 switch to at-large voting was a covered change. Further, the Court held that the question of whether Canton's changes were racially discriminatory was an issue specifically reserved by section 5 to the Attorney General or the district court for the District of Columbia to decide.

However important the Supreme Court's *Perkins* decision was to the issue of what changes are covered by section 5, it had little impact upon at-large voting structures in Mississippi. Most of the state's cities had adopted at-large voting before 1965, and their systems therefore were not subject to federal preclearance. As table 5.11 shows, only three cities were blocked by section 5 objections from adopting at-large elections after 1965, although undoubtedly the *Perkins* decision and these objections deterred some cities from switching to at-large voting. As a result, most at-large challenges in Mississippi have been based on the Fourteenth and Fifteenth amendments or, after 1982, on section 2.

Fourteenth Amendment Challenges

The first, and most important, Mississippi lawsuit challenging the constitutionality of at-large municipal elections was filed in 1973. *Stewart v. Waller*[19] is important not only because it was one of the first such lawsuits in the South, but also because it was the first multijurisdictional one, ultimately requiring thirty-one municipalities to abolish at-large voting. In 1962, as the state's first black voter registration drives of the decade were getting underway, the Mississippi legislature passed one of its first political "massive resistance" statutes, requiring all code charter municipalities (cities organized under the state's municipal code but not those municipalities incorporated under private charters from the legislature) with a mayor–board of aldermen form of government to elect all board members on an at-large basis. Previously, code charter municipalities over 10,000 in population were required to elect six aldermen by district and one at large, while those under 10,000 had the option of either electing five aldermen at large or four by district and one at large. To challenge the constitutionality of this statute, the Lawyers' Committee for Civil Rights Under Law—a national civil rights group with an office in Jackson—and the Washington law firm of Covington and Burling filed *Stewart* on behalf of eight black voters in four cities.

In 1975, a three-judge district court held that the statute violated the Fourteenth and Fifteenth amendments because it was adopted with "an intent to thwart the election of minority candidates to the office of alderman." The court's ruling was based on direct evidence of discriminatory motivation, the absence of an adequate nonracial explanation for the change, Mississippi's long history of official racial discrimination, and the foreseeable and actual impact of the law in defeating black candidates' efforts to win at-large municipal elections. The district court's 1975 injunction required thirty municipalities to revert to the district voting systems they had used prior to the enactment of the statute. In 1977 an additional city, West Point, which had been severed from the principal case, was also enjoined from holding at-large elections. The district court, however, rejected the plaintiffs' request to expand its injunction to cover all at-large municipal elections in Mississippi, holding that the constitutionality of at-large elections in municipalities that did not rely on the 1962 statute would have to be litigated on a case-by-case basis.

Stewart was atypical because there was direct evidence of discriminatory intent supplied by newspaper reports of the state senate floor debate on the statute. Most of the Mississippi lawsuits of the 1970s were litigated under what became known as the *White-Zimmer* standard, which did not require proof of discriminatory intent. In *White v. Regester*[20] the Supreme Court held that at-large voting violated the Fourteenth Amendment if minority voter plaintiffs could prove on the basis of a number of evidentiary factors that "the political processes leading to nomination and election were not equally open to participation by the group in question—that its members had less opportunity than did other residents in the district to participate in the political processes and to elect legislators of their choice." This decision was first implemented by the U.S. Court of Appeals for the Fifth Circuit in the Louisiana case of *Zimmer v. McKeithen*,[21] hence the *White-Zimmer* standard. Racially polarized voting, which was an element of the district court's decision in *White v. Regester* but which was not cited in the Supreme Court's decision, subsequently was added as an element of proof in the subsequent *White-Zimmer* line of cases.

Although this standard required a complex multifactor analysis, it nevertheless established a favorable legal standard for black plaintiffs to litigate at-large election challenges because it did not depend on proof of discriminatory intent. Between 1976 and 1980, twelve lawsuits were filed against eleven cities in Mississippi, challenging at-large city council elections for violating the Fourteenth Amendment. Seven of the twelve cases were settled with agreements to eliminate at-large elections and to institute district voting systems.

The Impact of *City of Mobile v. Bolden*

The first wave of legal attacks on at-large voting came to a screeching halt in 1980 with the Supreme Court's decision in *City of Mobile v. Bolden*.[22] Plaintiffs in Fourteenth Amendment challenges were now required to prove that the at-large system had been adopted or maintained for a discriminatory purpose, a difficult burden of proof. Even worse for voting rights plaintiffs, the court rejected as not probative of discriminatory intent the evidentiary factors (e.g., past history of discrimination, absence of minority officeholders, discriminatory election rules) on which the *White-Zimmer* line of cases was based.

The damaging impact of the *Mobile* decision on at-large election challenges throughout the South has been widely noted.[23] In Mississippi, district courts employing the *Mobile* intent standard for the first time rejected constitutional challenges to at-large voting in two of the four cities against which cases were pending—Jackson (*Kirksey v. City of Jackson*)[24] and Greenwood (*Jordan v. City of Greenwood*).[25] In a third case pending against the city of Hattiesburg, the Justice Department on its own motion dismissed its lawsuit challenging at-large city council elections after the *Mobile* decision, sending the district court a signal that the intent standard could not be met in that case and undermining the viability of a companion case filed by black voters.

The district courts ruled against black voter plaintiffs in the Jackson and Greenwood cases even though at-large voting had resulted in the total exclusion of black representation on the city councils of both cities and even though there was strong but circumstantial evidence that discriminatory intent had been a factor in the adoption and retention of at-large elections. In the Jackson case, both the district court and the court of appeals rejected as failing to prove discriminatory intent strong circumstantial evidence that at-large voting had been adopted and retained for racial reasons. Most damaging to the plaintiffs in this case, the courts refused to accept as relevant evidence an analysis of a 1977 referendum showing that 72 percent of the whites voted to retain at-large elections, while 98 percent of the blacks voted to change to district elections. The courts also excluded from consideration an opinion survey in which 61 percent of the white respondents who voted against the change gave at least one racial reason for their vote, and 44 percent gave two or more racial reasons, including unsolicited comments such as "I don't want a 'Nigra' representing me" and "blacks are human but whites are more efficient."[26] On appeal, the Fifth Circuit upheld the district court's decision to exclude this evidence for the reason that white voters' motives in retaining at-large elections were protected under the First Amendment from judicial inquiry. This ruling made it impossible to satisfy the *Mobile* requirement of proving discriminatory intent in cases in which at-large elections were adopted or retained by popular referendum because it excluded the voters' motivations from judicial consideration.

Section 2 Litigation

Responding to the outcry against the *Mobile* decision from civil rights groups and legal scholars, Congress amended section 2 in 1982 to prohibit voting practices that result in discrimination, regardless of the motivation behind them.[27] Congress's stated purpose was to restore the *White-Zimmer* legal standard, under which proof of discriminatory intent was not required. Then in *Thornburg v. Gingles*[28] the Supreme Court simplified the new section 2 standard even further by adopting a three-part legal test of discriminatory results based on proof that (1) a single-member district could be created in which minorities have a majority; (2) minority voters bloc vote for certain candidates; and (3) minority-preferred candidates usually are defeated by white bloc voting. The new section 2 standard, then, as interpreted by the Supreme Court in the *Gingles* decision, emphasizes proof of racially polarized voting that results in the systematic defeat of minority-backed candidates.

If the Justice Department's refusal to pursue its Hattiesburg case under the Fourteenth Amendment indicated that the case would be lost under the intent test, Congress's enactment of the section 2 amendment made the case winnable. In the first court ruling under the new section 2 standard in Mississippi—and one of the first in the South—the district court in *Boykins v. City of Hattiesburg*[29] ruled that Hattiesburg's at-large city council elections violated the section 2 standard. The court cited evidence of a history of official discrimination against black voters in Mississippi, statistical proof of racially polarized voting that resulted in the defeat of all black candidates, and election rules—including a majority-vote requirement, a prohibition on single-shot voting, a numbered-post system, and the absence of a district residency requirement—that disadvantaged black candidates. The district court also relied on data showing severe socioeconomic disparities between whites and blacks that hindered black political effectiveness, evidence of racial campaigning, and proof that white officials had been unresponsive to the needs of the black community.

All the Mississippi cases that had been lost under the *Mobile* intent standard were won or settled under the new section 2 results standard. The district court's earlier adverse decision against the black voter plaintiffs in the Greenwood case was vacated on appeal by the Fifth Circuit and remanded for reconsideration. The district court then reversed its prior ruling for the city and held that at-large voting violated section 2. The lawsuit against the Jackson City Council that was lost under the *Mobile* standard was refiled as a section 2 case, and in 1985—responding to newspaper advertisements that if the city's voters did not adopt a district voting system, the federal court would do it for them–Jackson's voters by referendum eliminated at-large voting and adopted ward elections.

The 1982 amendment has had great impact in eliminating at-large city council elections in Mississippi. Altogether, section 2 lawsuits were filed against forty-three cities. Four of these cities litigated, three unsuccessfully, and thirty-two settled the lawsuits. The remaining seven were still pending at the time of our survey. In addition, twenty-three other cities abandoned at-large voting voluntarily or under threat of litigation.[30] Indeed, it is likely that the successes in the section 2 cases may have persuaded cities that converted to district systems to change without the direct threat of litigation.

The Election of Black Council Members

Having reviewed the history of voting rights litigation in Mississippi, we now turn to a systematic analysis of black officeholding in the state's cities. In this analysis, we examine the relationship between council election systems and the election of black council members.

In the spring of 1989, to gather data for this study, we conducted a telephone survey of all Mississippi cities with 1980 populations of at least 1,000 (N = 148). Of the 145 cities that responded to the survey, our analysis considers only those with a black population of 10 percent or more (N = 133). The data include information on the type of electoral structure, the number of city council members, the racial composition of the city council, and the race of the mayor. For those cities with district elections, we have collected information about the date of change to this system and the racial composition of the council in 1980. We have supplemented our survey with information from sources such as the U.S. Bureau of the Census and the Joint Center for Political Studies' annually published *National Roster of Black Elected Officials*.

Table 5.1, showing black officeholding in 1989, confirms the findings of several previous studies: in cities with a black population of less than 50 percent, black council members were most likely to be elected in pure single-member-district systems and least likely to be elected in at-large ones; cities with mixed plans fell in between. In those Mississippi cities with *any* seats elected at large, blacks were less likely to be elected to council than in pure single-member-district cities.

Why do the mixed plans occupy the middle status? To answer this question, we compared the results of elections for single-member-district seats with at-large seats in the 43 cities with mixed plans (see table 5.3). We found that black officials in mixed systems were elected overwhelmingly from district seats. Indeed, in cities with a black population of less than 50 percent, no blacks were elected to the at-large seats under mixed plans, showing that at-large seats in mixed plans continued to dilute black voting strength, just as they did in pure at-large systems.

From the survey data and section 5 records obtained from the Justice Department, we were able to calculate the black percentage of the population in each single-member district in 40 cities (see table 5.6). In districts with a black population of less than 65 percent, blacks were dramatically underrepresented. In districts with a higher black percentage, blacks were elected in about the same proportion as their percentage of the city's population. Thus, even in single-member districts, blacks in Mississippi needed a supermajority to win elections.

A Longitudinal Measure of the Impact of Election Structures on Black Representation

In our cross-sectional analysis of cities discussed so far, we have shown a positive relationship between district elections and the presence of blacks on city councils—a fact noted in other such studies as well.[31] Although there have been only a few before-and-after studies of this relationship, they reached the same conclusion.[32] Nevertheless, one of these longitudinal studies lacked a control group of unchanged at-large cities. The other did not randomly assign cities to the experimental and control groups. On the other hand, as Davidson and Grofman argue in chapter 10 of this volume, cross-sectional studies also have serious methodological problems.[33] Our research remedies this by adopting the research design similar to that used in the other state chapters in this book: it compares the racial makeup of city councils before and after cities shifted from at-large to mixed or single-member-district plans in the period between 1974 and 1989; it then compares the racial makeup of councils in 1974 and 1989 in the control group of cities that retained their at-large system throughout the period.

By 1974, nine years had elapsed since passage of the Voting Rights Act, allowing time for the act's effect on black registration and mobilization to be felt. Nevertheless, Mississippi was still resistant to equal black participation in many ways.[34] In the 130 cities with at-large elections in 1974, there were very few black council members, and they were elected in cities that were virtually all black (see table 5.2).

In cities that later switched electoral structures, a dramatic change occurred in the black percentage on council (see table 5.2). In cities less than 50 percent black that switched to pure single-member districts or mixed plans, the proportion of black council members increased noticeably; in cities that did not switch, the increase was minimal. In cities less than 50 percent black, district voting led in every category to significant increases in numbers of black elected officials.

Since the black population ratio varies among city election types, a comparison of standardized measures of black "equity of representation" provides a clearer analysis of the impact of these changes than does the comparison in table 5.2. Table 5.4 presents two measures of representational equity in 1989—a ratio and a difference measure—for cities with different types of elections. Our findings can be summarized as follows: When the effects of the size of black population are controlled, blacks in majority-white cities were best represented in 1989 in pure district cities, less well represented in mixed ones, and least well represented in at-large ones.

Finally, we compare the three types of cities' equity ratios for 1974 and 1989 (see table 5.5). For all types of cities, these improve over time. Nevertheless, the improvement in black representation in majority-white cities changing to district or mixed plans was much greater than in cities that retained at-large elections.

Conclusion

Black electoral power was dramatically diluted in Mississippi cities following passage of the Voting Rights Act, largely due to the use of at-large elections. As our data show, the abolition of this system in many cities has brought about fairer representation for blacks. Majority-white cities that switched from at-large to single-member districts had the fairest representation, followed by cities with mixed electoral systems.

Most at-large systems in Mississippi cities have been eliminated through litigation under the Voting Rights Act and, prior to 1980, the Fourteenth Amendment. Moreover, section 5 was successfully used to block changes from ward to at-large elections.

Of the fifty-five lawsuits that were filed challenging at-large elections in Mississippi cities, only seven of them—*Stewart v. Waller* and the individual cases against Greenwood, Hattiesburg, Houston, Jackson (the first case filed in the state), West Point, and Woodville—actually went to trial on the merits of at-large challenges (exclusive of remedy hearings on a redistricting plan). The degree of resistance in these cases, however, should not be minimized. The state strenuously defended the 1962 statute at issue in *Stewart* even when it became patently obvious that the law was racially motivated. After that decision, resistance was strongest in the state's most populous cities, which had large black concentrations and the financial resources to pay their attorneys for years of resistance. The cities that most strongly resisted eliminating their at-large systems included Jackson, which bitterly contested the lawsuits against it through two separate trials and two appeals to the Fifth Circuit—litigation lasting from 1977 to 1985. Greenwood, Greenville, and Hattiesburg all fought to retain at-large elections from 1977 to 1984. After section 2 was amended and the demise of their at-large election systems seemed inevitable, all four cities in effect gave up. The Jackson City Council supported the 1985 referendum that created ward voting. The Greenwood council, although it did not settle, in the end did not contest the evidence that demonstrated a section 2 violation. Greenville agreed to a mixed four–two voting plan in 1984. Hattiesburg decided not to appeal the district court decision striking down at-large elections under section 2.

In resisting other applications of the Voting Rights Act, Mississippi created ingenious devices, engaged in persistent resistance, and, during the Reagan presidency, had the implicit support of a federal administration that was hostile to the act.[35] Mississippi racially gerrymandered its congressional and state legislative districts, and numerous counties gerrymandered their county election district lines after the 1970, 1980, and 1990 censuses. Between 1965 and 1980, fourteen of the state's eighty-two counties attempted to switch to at-large elections for county supervisor positions, twenty-two counties switched to at-large elections for school boards, and from 1966 to 1975 the legislature increased the number of multimember districts for the election of state senators and representatives.[36] Additionally, some cities annexed white residential areas to dilute black electoral strength.

Mississippi resisted in other ways. Under pressure from U.S. Senator Thad Cochran and Congressman Trent Lott, the Justice Department in 1981 violated its own procedures for preclearance when it withdrew an objection to a municipal annexation.[37] In a 1980 amicus curiae brief in *City of Rome v. United States*,[38] a Georgia case, Mississippi argued that section 5 was unconstitutional twelve years after the Supreme Court had sustained its constitutionality.

Approximately 125 years have passed since Mississippi blacks registered to select delegates to the constitutional convention during Reconstruction. Between that time and passage of the Voting Rights Act, Mississippi thwarted black voter registration with literacy tests, white primaries, and poll taxes as well as with violence and intimidation. After passage of the act, the state has used barriers to candidacy, relocation of polling places, denial of the ballot, racial gerrymandering, at-large elections, and annexations to deny or dilute black voting. Yet in spite of this massive and unceasing resistance, the act has advanced Mississippi toward the ideal expressed in the Fifteenth Amendment that "the right of citizens . . . to vote shall not be denied or abridged . . . on account of race, color, or previous condition of servitude."

TABLE 5.1
Black Representation on Council in 1989 by Election Plan, Mississippi Cities of 1,000 or More Population with 10 Percent or More Black Population in 1980

Type of Plan by % Black in City Population, 1980	N	*Mean % Black in City Population, 1980*	*Mean % Black on City Council, 1989*
SMD plan			
10–29.9	5	24	20
30–49.9	14	42	36
50–100	12	57	41
Mixed plan			
10–29.9	18	20	12
30–49.9	13	40	30
50–100	12	63	37
At-large plan			
10–29.9	20	22	9
30–49.9	15	35	9
50–100	24	71	49

TABLE 5.2
Changes in Black Representation on Council between 1974 and 1989, Mississippi Cities of 1,000 or More Population with 10 Percent or More Black Population in 1980

Type of Change by % Black in City Population, 1980	N[a]	*Mean % Black in City Population, 1980*	*Mean % Black on City Council*	
			Before Change (1974)	*After Change (1989)*
		Changed Systems		
From at-large to SMD plan				
10–29.9	5	24	0	20
30–49.9	14	42	0	36
50–100	11	58	0	43
From at-large to mixed plan				
10–29.9	16	20	0	11
30–49.9	13	40	0	30
50–100	12	63	5	37
		Unchanged Systems		
At-large plan				
10–29.9	20	22	0	9
30–49.9	15	35	0	9
50–100	24	71	23	49

[a]Two cities with mixed plans and one with a single-member-district plan listed in table 5.1 are excluded from this table because they had adopted their plans before 1974.

TABLE 5.3
Black Representation in 1989 in Mixed Plans by District and At-Large Components, Mississippi Cities of 1,000 or More Population with 10 Percent or More Black Population in 1980

% Black in City Population, 1980	N	*Mean % Black Councilpersons in District Components, 1989*	*Mean % Black Councilpersons in At-Large Components, 1989*
10–29.9	18	15	0
30–49.9	13	37	0
50–100	12	46	25

TABLE 5.4
Two Equity Measures Comparing Percentage Black on Council in 1989 with Percentage Black in City Population in 1980, Mississippi Cities of 1,000 or More Population with 10 Percent or More Black Population in 1980

Type of Plan by % Black in City Population, 1980	N[a]	*Difference Measure (% on Council − % in Population)*	*Ratio Measure (% on Council ÷ % in Population)*
		Changed Systems	
From at-large to SMD plan			
10–29.9	5	−4	0.84
30–49.9	14	−6	0.85
50–100	11	−15	0.74
From at-large to mixed plan			
10–29.9	16	−8	0.58
30–49.9	13	−11	0.74
50–100	12	−26	0.59
		Unchanged Systems	
At-large plan			
10–29.9	20	−13	0.41
30–49.9	15	−26	0.26
50–100	24	−21	0.70

[a]Two cities with mixed plans and one with a single-member-district plan listed in table 5.1 are excluded from this table because they had adopted their plans before 1974.

TABLE 5.5
Changes in Black Representation on Council between 1974 and 1989, Mississippi Cities of 1,000 or More Population with 10 Percent or More Black Population in 1980 (Ratio Equity Measure)

Type of Change by % Black in City Population, 1980	N[a]	*Black Representational Equity on Council* 1974	1989
	Changed Systems		
From at-large to SMD plan			
10–29.9	5	0.00	0.84
30–49.9	14	0.00	0.85
50–100	11	0.00	0.74
From at-large to mixed plan			
10–29.9	16	0.00	0.58
30–49.9	13	0.00	0.74
50–100	12	0.07	0.59
	Unchanged Systems		
At-large plan			
10–29.9	20	0.00	0.41
30–49.9	15	0.00	0.26
50–100	24	0.32	0.70

[a]Two cities with mixed plans and one with a single-member-district plan listed in table 5.1 are excluded from this table because they had adopted their plans before 1974.

TABLE 5.6
Black Representation in Council Single-Member Districts in 1989, Mississippi Cities of 1,000 or More Population with 10 Percent or More Black Population in 1980

% Black Population of District	N[a]	*Mean % Black Population in Districts, 1980*	*Mean % Black Councilpersons in Districts, 1989*
0–29.9	84	10	0
30–49.9	26	39	0
50–59.9	11	56	27
60–64.9	6	62	33
65–69.9	15	67	53
70–100	53	89	94

[a]Of the 347 single-member districts in Mississippi cities of 1,000 or more population with 10 percent or more black population, we were able to obtain usable data on 195.

TABLE 5.7
Black Council Representation in Single-Member Districts in 1989, by Racial Composition of District, Mississippi Cities of 1,000 or More Population with 10 Percent or More Black Population in 1980

Racial Composition of District	N	*Mean % Black Population in Districts, 1980*	*Mean % Black Councilpersons in Districts, 1989*
Black majority	85	79	74
White majority	110	17	0

TABLE 5.8
Cause of Change from At-Large to Mixed or District Plan between 1974 and 1989, Mississippi Cities of 1,000 or More Population with 10 Percent or More Black Population in 1980

City	*Did Lawsuit Accompany Change?*	*Reason for Change*
	Changed to Single-Member Districts	
Aberdeen	Yes	Consent decree
Belzoni	Yes	Settlement
Biloxi	No	Voluntary
Carthage	No	Voluntary
Charleston	Yes	Consent decree
Clarksdale	Yes	Consent decree
Columbia	Yes	Court order
Columbus	Yes	Consent decree
Gloster	Yes	Settlement
Greenwood	Yes	Court order
Grenada	Yes	Consent decree
Gulfport	No	Voluntary
Hattiesburg	Yes	Court order
Hazelhurst	Yes	Consent decree
Indianola	Yes	Settlement
Jackson	Yes	Settlement
Laurel	Yes	Consent decree
Leland	Yes	Settlement
Lumberton	No	Voluntary
Macon	Yes	Court order
Meridian	Yes	Settlement
Monticello	No	Voluntary
Newton	Yes	Settlement
Okolona	No	Threat of litigation
Picayune	Yes	Consent decree
Port Gibson	Yes	Settlement
Tutwiler	No	Voluntary
Vicksburg	No	Section 5 negotiation
West Point	Yes	Court order
Yazoo City	Yes	Consent decree
	Changed to Mixed Plan	
Bay St. Louis	No	Voluntary
Brandon	No	Voluntary
Brookhaven	Yes	Court order
Canton	Yes	Settlement
Centreville	Yes	Settlement

(*continued*)

TABLE 5.8 (*Continued*)

City	*Did Lawsuit Accompany Change?*	*Reason for Change*
Cleveland	Yes	Court order
Coffeeville	Yes	Consent decree
Collins	No	Voluntary
Crenshaw	Yes	Settlement
Crystal Springs	Yes	Settlement
Drew	Yes	Consent decree
Ellisville	Yes	Court order
Forest	Yes	Court order
Hollandale	Yes	Consent decree
Holly Springs	Yes	Court order
Houston	Yes	Court order
Itta Bena	Yes	Settlement
Kosciusko	Yes	Court order
Lexington	Yes	Court order
Louisville	No	Threat of litigation
Magee	Yes	Court order
Magnolia	Yes	Court order
Marks	Yes	Settlement
Mendenhall	No	Threat of litigation
Moss Point	Yes	Court order
New Albany	Yes	Court order
Oxford	Yes	Court order
Pass Christian	Yes	Court order
Pearl	Yes	Court order
Philadelphia	Yes	Court order
Pontotoc	Yes	Court order
Ridgeland	Yes	Court order
Ripley	No	Voluntary
Rolling Fork	Yes	Settlement
Sardis	Yes	Court order
Starkville	Yes	Court order
Tupelo	Yes	Court order
Tylertown	Yes	Court order
Water Valley	Yes	Court order
Wesson	Yes	Court order
Wiggins	No	Voluntary
SUMMARY	Yes 56 (79%) No 15 (21%)	

TABLE 5.9
Major Disfranchising Devices in Mississippi

Device	Date Established	Date Abolished
Literacy test: Must be able to read or understand or interpret any section of the state constitution (1890); amended to read *and* write any section *and* give a reasonable interpretation (1955)	1890	1965[a]
Poll tax	1890	1964 for federal elections;[b] 1966 for state elections[c]
Durational residence requirement: 2 years in state, 1 year in precinct (1890); amended to 1 year in state, 6 months in precinct (1972)	1890	1972[d]
Disfranchising crimes list	1890	Still in effect
Dual registration requirement (voters must register with both county registrar and municipal clerk)	1892	1984, 1987[e]
White primary	1907	ca. 1947[f]
Party principles loyalty oath	1947	1987[g]
Citizenship understanding test	1955	1965[h]
Prohibition on satellite registration	1955	1987[e]
Good moral character test	1960	1965[h]
Newspaper publication of names of applicants for registration; procedure for challenging moral character	1962	1965[h]

Sources: U.S. Commission on Civil Rights 1965; U.S. Commission on Civil Rights 1968; Parker 1990.

[a] Voting Rights Act of 1965, 42 U.S.C., Section 1973 et seq.

[b] Twenty-fourth Amendment to the U.S. Constitution.

[c] *United States v. Mississippi,* 11 Race Relations Law Reporter 837 (S.D. Miss. 1966) (three-judge court).

[d] *Graham v. Waller,* 343 F. Supp. 1 (S.D. Miss. 1972) (three-judge court) (limited to thirty days in state, county, and precinct).

[e] *Mississippi State Chapter, Operation PUSH v. Allain,* 674 F. Supp. 1245 (N.D. Miss. 1987), *aff'd,* 932 F.2d 400 (5th Cir. 1991).

[f] *Smith v. Allwright,* 321 U.S. 649 (1944).

[g] Mississippi legislature.

[h] Mississippi legislature, passed in July 1965 in hopes of evading coverage of the Voting Rights Act.

TABLE 5.10
Black and White Registered Voters and Officeholders in Mississippi, Selected Years[a]

	Black		White	
	N	%	N	%
Registered voters[b]				
1964	28,500	5.1	525,000	94.9
1968	181,233	23.6	589,066	76.4
1988	—[c]	32.5	—[c]	67.0
Officeholders				
1965	6	0.1	5,272	99.9
1968	29	0.5	5,249	99.5
1989	646	12.2	4,632	87.8

Sources: U.S. Commission on Civil Rights 1968; voter registration statistics of the Voter Education Project of the Southern Regional Council; Joint Center for Political Studies 1989.

[a] Mean black Mississippi population, 1960–90 = 37.4%.

[b] Voter registration statistics for 1964 and 1968 are estimates, and voter registration statistics for 1988 are based on census survey results and probably exaggerate the total number of registered voters, on which these percentage calculations are based, and the number of black registered voters.

[c] Black and white registration combined was 945,712 in 1988.

TABLE 5.11
Reasons for Changes from At-Large to Mixed and Single-Member-District Plans in Mississippi Cities of 1,000 or More Population with 10 Percent or More Black Population in 1980

Reason	N[a]
Injunction, contested litigation	29
Settlement of litigation	27
Threat of litigation	3
Voluntary, no litigation	11
Section 5 objection to switch to at-large voting	3
Section 5 objection to municipal annexation	1
TOTAL	74

[a] Three cities—Grenada, Kosciusko, and Lexington—that were required to revert to ward elections by litigation are listed twice. These cities later attempted to switch to at-large elections and were blocked by section 5 objections.

CHAPTER SIX

North Carolina

WILLIAM R. KEECH AND
MICHAEL P. SISTROM

> It has been the vogue to be progressive. Willingness to accept new ideas, sense of community responsibility toward the Negro, feeling of common purpose, and relative prosperity have given North Carolina a more sophisticated politics than exists in most southern states.
>
> —*V. O. Key, Jr.*[1]

KEY RECOGNIZED North Carolinians' self-conscious and self-perpetuated image of themselves as a "progressive plutocracy." For black Tar Heels, however, the long struggle for voting rights and racial equality has been a paradox. For example, North Carolinians have been taught to remember Governor Charles Brantley Aycock as the "education governor," bringing progressive reform in public education at the turn of the century.[2] Blacks might also recall that Aycock came to power as an advocate of black disfranchisement.

Similarly, in 1954 Greensboro, North Carolina, became the first city in the South to announce that it would comply with the Supreme Court's school desegregation edict. However, the Pearsall Plan, the state law passed in response to *Brown v. Board of Education*, provided that local school districts or individual schools within them could close down rather than desegregate. In 1971, after loss of federal funds and under court order, Greensboro finally integrated its public schools, making it one of the last in the region to do so.[3]

Among southern states, North Carolina has often been perceived as different, usually in a way that reflected favorably on it as more progressive or less blatantly racist than other southern states. The Voting Rights Act itself recognized that North Carolina was different by originally including fewer than half its hundred counties under coverage of the special provisions. Before the act was passed in 1965, an estimated 46.8 percent of the state's black voting-age population was registered, the most of any of the seven states originally covered.[4]

Clearly North Carolina's performance has been "better" in some respects, but there are limits to its racial progressivism. One observer contends that North Carolina, as "one of the few Southern states that has been moderate in race relations has been most effective in belittling the voting strength of a sizable black population."[5] Perhaps projecting the progressive image was a less blatant and therefore more effective way to maintain a system of white supremacy.

The groundbreaking 1984 lawsuit, *Gingles v. Edmisten*,[6] was a response to the facts that rates of black officeholding still lagged, state election law and local government were slow to reform, and racially polarized campaigns and voting still characterized North Carolina elections. Yet by now, a quarter century after the passage of the Voting Rights Act, the barriers of tradition have been substantially broken. The purpose of this chapter is to examine the effects of the act on black registration and officeholding in North Carolina. In general, we will show that there has been substantial progress, much of which resulted from the act. After a look at North Carolina politics, we will consider changes in voter activity and officeholding by race.

Demographic and Historical Context

North Carolina's black population is 22 percent of the total. Much of it is concentrated in the historical black belt in the eastern section of the state. There is also substantial black population in the cities of the Piedmont. These cities—Raleigh, Durham, Greensboro, Winston-Salem, and Charlotte—are the largest in what is still one of the least urban of American states.

North Carolina's Native American population, 1.1 percent of the total, is the largest east of the Mississippi, and is the second largest minority population in the state. It is concentrated in three counties—Robeson, Hoke, and Swain—in two of which it is a plurality. The Voting Rights Act in 1975 placed those counties under the new language-minority provisions.

Blacks played an important role on the political stage throughout the postbellum period. The state's Reconstruction constitution of 1868 established universal manhood suffrage, thus eliminating racial and property qualifications for voting. In the registration rolls created by the ruling Republicans in 1868, 36 percent of the new voters were former slaves.[7] The freedmen continued to register and cast ballots, with their turnout reaching 83 percent of registered blacks in the 1880 elections, surpassing the white rate.[8]

The restoration of county government under the new constitution and the existence of strong alternatives to the dominant Democratic party (Republicans and later the Republican/Populist Fusion movement) gave North Carolina blacks access to a variety of elected and appointed positions until the turn of the century. As a rule, "the darker the district"—whether city or county ward, legislative or congressional seat—the more frequent was its black representation. Four blacks represented the Second Congressional District, the "Black Second," between 1868 and 1901, serving a total of seven terms.[9] George White, the last of these, was the last black member of Congress until 1929, and the last from the South until 1973.[10]

These representatives were able to secure a measure of federal patronage for their black constituents, especially jobs as postmasters, recorders of deeds, tax collectors, and even collector of customs for the Port of Wilmington.[11]

Between 1876 and 1900, fifty-nine blacks sat in the state house and eighteen were elected to the state senate, all from districts drawn from sixteen majority-black counties. They were almost without influence in the white-dominated legislature, and were truly active only on "race issues" such as black education, election laws, and convict labor, but they did hold some important committee assignments.[12] Local black communities also captured county and municipal posts. Numerous blacks were elected as magistrates, and a handful became sheriffs and county commissioners. A scattering of black aldermen were also on the boards of several eastern and Piedmont cities, including Raleigh, Wilmington, Tarboro, and New Bern.[13] Still, white allies were unenthusiastic about black officeholding, and blacks never exercised political power commensurate with their numbers.

White Democrats, motivated by the specter of "Negro domination" and the desire for one-party hegemony, sought to eliminate this limited black political strength from the time Democrats regained control of state government in 1870 until the culmination of their efforts in the disfranchising constitutional amendments of 1900. They experimented with a number of intermediate steps both to deny the ballot to the blacks and poor whites who made up the Republican and Populist constituencies and to dilute black voting strength. In 1877 the general assembly replaced the popular vote with legislative control of county government. Other bills redrew ward lines in cities with heavy black populations, either to limit black influence to one district or to disperse it through several. This maneuvering, along with violent terror, gave the white Democratic minority control over the eastern black belt.[14]

One of the most effective early disfranchisement measures was the centralization of control over elections and the establishment of intricate procedures for voter registration. A new and highly partisan state board of elections supervised the appointment of local registrars and judges of elections. The key features of the statutes were the wide discretion granted to the local clerks, the specificity of the information required of the registrant, the limited time periods the books were open, and the provisions allowing challenges of a voter's qualifications to be made on the day of the election, thus making it more difficult for the challenged would-be voters to clear their record in time to vote.[15] Even where impartially administered, such laws significantly diminished turnout from their inception in the late nineteenth century to the 1960s.

The registration scheme, however, like the other election chicanery, was by no means foolproof. Since the techniques relied on discriminatory administration, a change in the control of state government might reverse the direction of discrimination in voter registration. Federal regulation of voter registration and elections, a feature of the narrowly defeated "Force Bill" of 1890, might eliminate the advantage entirely. In fact, Democrats lost control of the legislature in 1894 to a "Fusion" ticket of Populists and Republicans, which replaced the Democratic registration schemes with what Kousser has called "probably the fairest and most democratic election law in the post-Reconstruction South."[16]

With this law, the Fusion ticket prevailed again in the 1896 legislative elections, when Republican Daniel Russell won a four-year term as governor. But the Democrats regained the legislature in 1898 and reformulated the election law again. This time, however, Democratic leaders sought the permanent and constitutional elimination of blacks from the electorate. In the face of opposition from blacks and some white dissenters, the 1900 election returned a victory for Democratic gubernatorial candidate Charles Aycock and for a package of disfranchisement amendments that differed only in minor ways from those used in the rest of the South. The central provision was a requirement that "persons offering to vote shall be at the time a legally registered voter." In order to be registered, potential voters had to "be able to read and write any section of the constitution in the English language" and to have paid a poll tax.

Lawmakers faced a problem: one-fifth of the white population was illiterate and one-half of the adult black population was literate. A fair application of the test would have disfranchised over 50,000 whites and left almost 60,000 blacks on the rolls.[17] A grandfather clause excused voters from the literacy test if they had been entitled to vote in any state in 1867, or were a lineal descendent of such a person. (In order to be eligible for this possibility, voters had to be registered as such by 1908.)[18] North Carolina has never had a system of white primaries, and the poll tax was repealed as a requirement for voting in 1920. Thus the main institutional feature of black disfranchisement in North Carolina was the literacy test as a part of the registration requirement and the discretion granted to local registrars—precisely what was suspended by the Voting Rights Act of 1965.

The suffrage restriction mechanisms secured white supremacy and Democratic solidarity. The Fusion movement had collapsed, the Republican party turned lily-white, and black efforts to challenge the amendments in court failed. By 1910 almost no blacks voted, and white turnout had dropped substantially.[19] Apathy spread throughout the electorate as blacks all but disappeared from the public life of the state.

Black plaintiffs challenged the legality of the literacy requirement in court, but without success. In 1936, two black schoolteachers who had been prevented from voting sued their county registrar and the state for a judgment outlawing the literacy test. The state supreme court, limiting its inquiry to whether the test was correctly applied in the teachers' case, ruled that they were clearly literate and qualified to vote, a fact the defendants had admitted. The literacy test itself, however, was not struck down as a voting prerequisite. In a curious non sequitur, the court endorsed the test, saying that "this constitutional amendment providing for an educational test . . . brought light out of the darkness as to education for all people of the state. Religious, educational, and material uplift went forward by leaps and bounds."[20]

The courts continued to protect North Carolina's registration procedures through the 1950s. In 1959, the U.S. Supreme Court affirmed a decision by the state supreme court upholding the use of the literacy requirement.[21] In 1961, the state supreme court qualified its earlier rulings, striking down the practice of requiring registrants to write a chosen section of the North Carolina constitution from dictation, but it upheld the requirement that all applicants of uncertain ability be required to show a capacity to read and write a section of the state constitution.[22] The ruling seemed to have little effect in easing restrictions, as evidenced by 750 complaints filed by blacks in 1962 with the North Carolina Advisory Committee to the Civil Rights Commission, documenting discriminatory application of the literacy test.[23]

Meanwhile, the black electorate struggled to grow. In 1940 only 5 percent of the eligible black electorate was registered, but by 1956 the fraction had risen to one-fifth, by 1960 to one-third, and by 1965 to over 45 percent.[24] The proportions registered were lower in the heavily black counties in the east than in the whiter western counties. In 1960, in the twenty-three majority-black counties, fewer than 20 percent of eligible blacks were registered.[25]

In contrast, pockets of black voting and even black officeholding developed in some Piedmont cities. For example, in Winston-Salem a militant black labor union local began building a black electorate in the mid-1940s, and by 1947 a black was voted onto that city's board of aldermen, becoming the first black public official elected in North Carolina in this century. In Durham an upper-middle-class black community had begun a political organization in the 1930s. This group, which was associated with the city's black insurance and banking industry, increased the local black electorate until it became an important force in local elections, and by 1953 a black insurance executive had been elected to the city council. The tradition of black politics continued in these cities until, by 1960, 62 percent of Durham's eligible black population was registered, as was 54 percent of Winston-Salem's, 34 percent of Greensboro's, and 27 percent of Raleigh's.[26]

After blacks were elected to public office in several cities in the 1940s and 1950s, concerned whites borrowed from the earlier strategies of the 1870s and 1880s to dilute black voting strength by changing district lines or electoral systems. In Winston-Salem, the prospective election of a black led to a demand for citywide elections, but this was denied by the city council. After the election of a black to the board of aldermen in 1947, however, a new single-member-district plan was implemented. This arrangement split a previous two-member district and localized black influence in a single "safe" ward.[27] When a black won election in 1953 and 1955 in Wilson, a small city in eastern North Carolina, the legislature changed the city's electoral system from district to at large, and Wilson's city council became all-white again.[28]

The state legislature mounted a more concentrated effort to dilute black votes in the 1950s as the threat of the black vote loomed larger and the national legal campaign against disfranchisement gained momentum. While passing anti-integration legislation for the public schools, the general assembly also passed a law that would prohibit "bullet voting" in fourteen mostly eastern counties. The law invalidated votes cast for only one candidate in a multimember district, and was obviously aimed at black strategies of voting for a single black, thereby denying any of their votes to a competitor who might defeat him. (This act was declared unconstitutional by the federal courts in 1972.)[29] Lawmakers also turned aside a bill that would have made school board positions elective instead of appointive.

The Effect of the Voting Rights Act on Voter Registration

Section 2 of the Voting Rights Act prohibited all practices that denied or abridged the right to vote on grounds of race or color. Section 4 identified "covered jurisdictions" for special treatment if they used a literacy test and had had a black registration rate on 1 November 1964 or a black turnout rate in the 1964 presidential election of less than 50 percent. Six southern states were entirely covered on these grounds, and some forty of North Carolina's one hundred counties were covered by this presumption of discriminatory use of a test. Wake County, which includes Raleigh, the state capital, successfully sued for exemption, while Gaston County was denied exemption in an important case defining a limit on the possibilities of becoming exempt.[30] In the latter case, the Supreme Court held that the Gaston County black schools were so poor that no literacy test could avoid discriminating on the grounds of race.[31]

Literacy tests were automatically suspended in all covered counties. The act also provided that federal registrars or observers could under certain conditions be sent into covered jurisdictions by the Attorney General. Although the state's black leadership urged oversight from Washington, no North Carolina county was ever designated for federal examiners.[32]

Therefore, when we assess the direct consequences of the act on voter registration in North Carolina, we are assessing suspension of the literacy test in the covered counties. (The test continued to be used in some noncovered counties as late as 1970, the year that an amendment to the Voting Rights Act suspended literacy tests nationwide; the state board of elections did not instruct these counties to discontinue such use until December 1970.)[33] The political atmosphere may well have changed after passage of the act, and this may have affected behavior in both covered and uncovered jurisdictions. We do not have direct knowledge that literacy tests were suspended in the covered jurisdictions, although this is implied by the fact that no examiners were sent.

Thompson has carefully documented changes in voter registration in both covered and uncovered counties. He found that the percentage of eligible blacks registered to vote in the covered counties increased from 32.4 percent in 1964, before passage, to 54.0 percent in 1976—a change of over 20 percentage points. In the same period, white registration increased by only 3.1 points, to just over 80 percent. There was less than 1 percentage point net change in both white and black registration in forty matched counties that were not covered by the act.[34] There have been even more spectacular gains since 1965 in individual covered counties.

In thirty, black voter registration rates have doubled, while in seven, they have more than tripled; in three, blacks have become a majority of the registered electorate.[35]

Thompson's figures provide powerful support for the claim that coverage made a difference, even without external enforcement by federal examiners. They suggest also that section 4 standards (less than 50 percent black registration or total voter turnout) were reasonable ways to identify discriminatory use of the literacy test. A measure of what the act did *not* do for voter registration can be found in the continuing difference as of 1976 between black and white registration rates in both covered counties (54 and 81 percent, respectively) and uncovered ones (65 and 89 percent, respectively), and also in the difference between black registration rates in the covered and uncovered counties (54 and 65 percent, respectively).[36]

In the state as a whole, there has been a unique pattern of change since 1965. There has not been the dramatic statewide increase in black registration found in some states, such as Mississippi, where black registration was previously much lower than in North Carolina. Instead, there has been a convergence of black and white rates that reflects slow and steady growth of black registration and a slight decline in that of whites. The fraction of the electorate that was black grew from 18 to almost 27 percent in covered counties between 1966 and 1988, while the fraction grew from 12 to 15 in the uncovered counties in the same period. As of 1990 the statewide proportion of eligible blacks registered (63 percent) approached that for whites (69 percent), while 47 percent of the Native American population was registered.

The Effect of Section 5 on Election Laws

Section 5 demands that proposed electoral changes in covered jurisdictions be precleared—submitted for approval to the U.S. Attorney General or to the Federal District Court for the District of Columbia. Such changes include "any voting qualification or prerequisite to voting, or standard, practice, or procedure with respect to voting." According to Thernstrom, preclearance had originally a very limited aim, "guarding against renewed disfranchisement, the use of the back door once the front door was blocked,"[37] although, according to the Civil Rights Commission, "Congress intended to include a very broad range of subjects under section 5."[38]

There has been a variety of efforts in covered states to dilute the impact of the newly enfranchised black electorate by, for example, redrawing district lines or shifting from single-member districts to at-large elections. Some of the most flagrant of these efforts were in Mississippi.[39] In *Allen v. State Board of Elections* (1969),[40] the Supreme Court held that section 5 preclearance applied to such changes. Speaking for the Court, Chief Justice Warren said that the Voting Rights Act "was aimed at the subtle, as well as the obvious, state regulations which would have the effect of denying citizens their right to vote because of race."[41]

In response to the act's unprecedented challenge to prevailing practice, North Carolina quickly employed some of the strategies used by Deep South states to dilute the emerging black vote. The general assembly relinquished its central powers and authorized some localities to alter their election procedures. In a 1966 special session, the legislature authorized forty-nine boards of county commissioners that had had some form of election or residency requirements by districts to adopt an at-large election system. Twelve counties took immediate steps: six converted to at-large elections, and six changed the boundaries of their wards. The state also shifted from past practice and required at-large election of all school boards.

The North Carolina government's extensive revisions of election law took place under the purview of the Voting Rights Act and the preclearance requirements of section 5, but very few changes were submitted for review and none was objected to before 1971. Of the 88 changes in election law proposed between 1965 and 1971, only 12 were submitted, and all 12 were approved. In 1971 the Justice Department interceded in 6 cases to block the continued application of the literacy test, and it ruled on a few at-large election schemes, annexations, and the procedure for voting for multimember house and senate seats. According to Suitts's 1981 tabulation, there were 193 legislative acts passed by the general assembly between 1965 and 1979 affecting local electoral schemes in the forty covered counties. Of these, only about 20 percent were submitted for review under section 5.[42] Subsequently the number of such acts has risen, and, according to Justice Department data that do not entirely agree with Suitts's figures, a total of 4,416 changes were submitted from North Carolina between 1970 and 1987. According to the same data, 107 objections were interposed in the same period.[43] (Some apparent discrepancies between the tabulations may be due to the fact that Suitts's unit of analysis was individual laws, each of which may have included multiple changes in voting procedures.)

Although Suitts acknowledged some margin of error in his figures, he argued that "the overwhelming majority of legislative changes has not been submitted for review and does not comply with the law. . . . A benign explanation for these nonsubmissions has not been readily apparent."[44] He contended that North Carolina's failure to submit changes could not be attributed to ignorance of the act's requirements. The fact that some submissions have been made for each of the covered counties indicates that officials have made selective judgments about what needed to be submitted for review.

While North Carolina lawmakers were not eager to change the racial complexion of state politics, they may not have been as conspiratorial as Suitts implied. Given a Justice Department that did not vigorously act on its own interpretations, it was up to states and localities to initiate the process of preclearance. North Carolina had to wait along with the rest of the South for the language of the Voting Rights Act to be interpreted in the series of precedent-setting lawsuits of the late 1960s and 1970s—particularly *Allen*—over what kinds of legislative changes required preclearance. The increase in submissions in the 1980s suggests that *Gingles* helped to further clarify what issues were subject to preclearance. North

Carolina has the added confusion of having only forty of its one hundred counties covered by the federal mandate. Decisions regarding election law and the Voting Rights Act have thus rested with forty different elections boards and county attorneys, who have little or no supervision from the legislature or the state board of elections.

The Election of Blacks to Public Office

The remainder of this chapter assesses the consequences of the Voting Rights Act on the election of blacks to public office. This is, of course, only one of the consequences that might be investigated. There are many kinds of public policy results to be expected from the effective enfranchisement of the black population.[45] The election of blacks is by far the most easily measured—the main reason it is the focus of our attention. In effect, we are investigating in this section the effect of the Voting Rights Act on descriptive representation (based on race) rather than on substantive representation (based on interests and preferences). As Swain documents and explains, the relationship between descriptive and substantive representation of African Americans is far from simple. Fortunately, the election of blacks to public office is not the only way to assure that black interests are considered in public life.[46]

As the unique experience of the urban Piedmont showed and the subsequent history of the state in the wake of the Voting Rights Act continues to illustrate, white voters have not uniformly refused to vote for black candidates. Furthermore, a black electorate has often supported and at times provided the margin of victory for sympathetic white candidates.

As of 1990 there were 453 black elected officials in North Carolina serving in a variety of state, county, and municipal posts.[47] At each level of government the act's effect on black voting strength, districting arrangements, minority officeholding, and the relationship between minority candidates and white voters is different.

Statewide Executive and Congressional Office

Before the 1992 election, no blacks had been elected to statewide executive office or to Congress, though a few had run. Reginald Hawkins ran for the Democratic gubernatorial nomination in 1968 and 1972. He came in third both times, with 18.5 and 8 percent of the votes cast in the first primary, respectively. In 1976, Howard Lee, a black former mayor of majority-white Chapel Hill, narrowly led in the first primary for the Democratic nomination for lieutenant governor. But Jimmy Green (a white who had received 27.35 percent to Lee's 27.71) defeated Lee in the runoff by 56 to 44 percent. In 1977 Lee was appointed head of the state Department of Environment, Health and Natural Resources, a post he held for over four years. In February 1990 he was appointed to fill a vacancy in the state senate, and was elected to that post later in that year.

Lee's experience, along with that of some blacks running for congressional offices discussed below, contributed to a belief that runoffs reduced the chances for blacks to win nomination and election to public offices that they might otherwise win. In response to pressures from the black community, the state law was changed in 1989 to provide that a runoff be held only if the leading candidate in the first primary received less than 40 percent of the vote.

In 1990, Harvey Gantt, a black former mayor of majority-white Charlotte, sought the Democratic nomination for the United States Senate, and won the first primary with 37.51 percent, which was short of the new threshhold. Even though a second primary was called, forcing a two-person race between a white and a black, Gantt was able to win the nomination with almost 57 percent, showing that in a Democratic primary, a runoff provision does not necessarily disadvantage a black candidate in a majority-white electorate. In a race that commanded international attention, Gantt received 47 percent of the general election vote against three-term incumbent Jesse Helms, even though Gantt had led in some polls taken before the final week of the campaign. As the figures below indicate, Gantt's losing margin was similar to that of the three white candidates who had lost to Helms in earlier senate races, even though Helms introduced racial appeals in the campaign. (The main example was a television advertisement suggesting that white workers would lose jobs if the congressional civil rights bill supported by Gantt were to pass.)

1972	Helms	54%	Galifianakis	46%
1978	Helms	55%	Ingram	45%
1984	Helms	52%	Hunt	48%
1990	Helms	53%	Gantt	47%

Black candidates ran strong races to be the Democratic nominee for Congress in the Second District—38 percent black in 1980—but none won. In 1972, Howard Lee ran unsuccessfully against incumbent L. H. Fountain, who was first elected in 1952. In 1982, the year in which Fountain retired, H. M. "Mickey" Michaux ran first with 44 percent in the first primary to 33 percent for I. T. "Tim" Valentine. Valentine subsequently won the second primary with 54 percent and then won the general election; he has held the seat since that time. This election inspired much of the effort to create the threshold change for avoiding a second primary.[48] Valentine was challenged in the Democratic primary in 1984 by Kenneth Spaulding, a black, who lost with 48 percent.

Statewide Judicial Office

More than a dozen blacks have been elected to statewide judicial office. In the state judicial system, overhauled in the mid-1960s, there are three tiers that involve statewide election: the supreme court, the court of appeals, and the superior court.

Elections to all three are partisan. Vacancies are filled by gubernatorial appointments, which last until the next general election, at which time the seat is filled for the remainder of the original term.[49]

The supreme court has seven judges elected to eight-year terms. One of these judges, Henry Frye, is black. Justice Frye was appointed to fill a vacancy in 1983, elected in 1984, and reelected to a full term in 1988. The court of appeals has twelve judges elected for eight-year terms. Of these twelve seats, one has been occupied by black judges since 1978, and another since 1982. Blacks first came to these seats by appointment, but they have won five different statewide elections for the two seats. The only black to lose was a Republican appointee who lost to a black Democrat in the general election.

One seat on the court of appeals has been occupied continuously since 1982 by Judge Clifton E. Johnson, who was first appointed and then elected in that year, and reelected in 1990. The other seat has had four black occupants since 1978, when Judge Richard Erwin was appointed and subsequently elected. He resigned in 1980, and was replaced in 1981 by Judge Charles L. Becton, who was elected in 1984 and resigned in 1990. He was replaced by Judge Allison Duncan, a Republican, who was defeated for reelection by Judge James A. Wynn, Jr., another black, in that same year. Other than Judge Duncan, all were Democrats.

The trial level of the statewide judicial system is called the superior court. These judges are nominated in partisan primaries in electoral districts, but they are elected in statewide partisan elections for eight-year terms. The question whether to elect trial court judges from districts or statewide has been a serious and persistent one in North Carolina since Reconstruction. In 1868 the Republican-dominated constitutional convention first created a system of popularly elected superior court judges. The convention mandated that the elections be held in districts in order to ensure that Republican strength, which was concentrated in pockets across the state, would be protected. In 1875, after regaining control of the legislature, the Democrats amended the state constitution to shift to statewide election of superior court judges. This change was intended to increase Democratic power across the state, dilute the Republican strongholds, and prevent the election of black judges. Statewide election of superior court judges remained in place until it was amended by a 1987 lawsuit inspired by the Voting Rights Act.

The number of superior court judges is set by the general assembly. Before 1987, there were sixty-four "regular" judges, supplemented by from two to eight "special" judgeships. The special judgeships were created by the general assembly and the judges were appointed by the governor for four-year terms. Between 1900 and 1986, two blacks had served as "regular" superior court judges. One was Clifton Johnson, mentioned above, who was elected in 1978 and subsequently elevated to the court of appeals in 1982. The other was Terry Sherrill, who resigned in 1990 after he was convicted for cocaine possession. The special judgeships had been an important vehicle for the appointment of blacks in the 1960s and 1970s, but few became regular judges.[50]

The system of selecting superior court judges was changed in 1987 in response to several lawsuits filed under the Voting Rights Act. The first suit, *Haith v. Martin*,[51] decided in 1985, determined that the state had failed to submit for preclearance several acts regarding judicial election passed in the 1960s and 1970s. After subsequent submission, the Department of Justice rejected features involving numbered seats and staggered terms, both of which can sometimes operate to dilute black votes through frustrating the black strategy of single-shot voting.

The state changed the law in response to the numbered seat issue, but was challenging the decision on staggered terms when another suit was filed under amended section 2. *Alexander v. Martin*[52] challenged the use of staggered terms, large multijudge districts for primaries, and statewide general elections. The remedies under section 2 could be much broader than simply rejection of the proposed changes, as provided by the preclearance features of section 5, and the state responded to the suit by changing the law before a judgment was issued.

The new law was introduced by a black representative from Durham, and after it passed in 1987,[53] the relevant litigation was dropped. The legislation created nine new judgeships and eliminated the special judges. It subdivided six former single-county, multijudge districts into multiple districts providing for several safe black seats, and it eliminated staggered terms in these counties.[54] The law also split ten multicounty, multijudge districts into twenty single-judge districts, of which two had majorities of black or other minority groups.[55] Subsequently, eleven black judges and one Native American were elected to superior court. Two of the black judges were elected from seats that were not created especially to elect blacks.[56]

The experience with judgeships shows that it is possible for blacks to be elected statewide in North Carolina, a state with a black population of 22 percent. All of the elections have come after passage of the Voting Rights Act. Most of them have been a direct result of litigation under the 1982 amendments to the act, and have been based on nominations from districts designed to generate black nominees. Still, several elections, especially those to the supreme court and the court of appeals, demonstrate the possibility that blacks can win open statewide election under more normal circumstances. The general rule seems to have been for black judges to run for reelection as incumbents after initially gaining the office by appointment. Since judicial elections did not in the past involve much campaigning, they were not very visible. This fact as well surely helped blacks to win these statewide elections. However, this advantage for blacks may not last because partisan competition and open campaigning for judicial office have increased steadily in recent years.[57]

The General Assembly

Black representation in the state legislature increased substantially after 1968, when the first black in this century was elected to the house (see table 6.10). The number rose by 1990 to 5 blacks among 50 senators, and to 13 blacks among 120 house members. The largest jump was from 3 to 11 black members of the house after the 1982 election. There was also one Native American, representing Robeson County. The post-1982 changes followed the 1982 filing of *Gingles v. Edmisten*,[58] which was to become on the national level one of the most important cases implementing the Voting Rights Act, but change in North Carolina came before the decision was handed down.

The suit challenged the 1981 redistricting of general assembly seats and the provision of the North Carolina constitution that counties not be divided in creating election districts. The suit contended that the constitutional provision had been in use since 1967, without having been precleared as required by section 5. After the suit was filed, the state did submit the questioned practices, and both the constitutional provision and the 1981 districting plan were denied preclearance.

The general assembly responded to the objections by enacting a new redistricting plan that contained five majority-black house districts and one majority-black senate district. As indicated, the result was an increase of eight black house members, although no additional blacks were elected to the senate until 1984. The *Gingles* decision, which was handed down by the district court in 1984 (after the 1982 amendents to the Voting Rights Act became law), rejected the redistricting plan that had been adopted after the suit was brought. In a special session in 1984, the legislature adopted single-member districts in lieu of several former multimember districts, and postponed the primary elections until the new districts could be drawn. The increases that followed the *Gingles* decision were modest in the house (from eleven to thirteen by 1985), but more dramatic in the senate (from one to four by 1989).

The relationship between the act, the *Gingles* case, and increases in the number of blacks in the legislature is complicated. While the biggest changes came before the suit was resolved, it would be difficult and unreasonable to deny that they came in response to the filing of the suit. The mere existence of the act was not enough to bring very substantial changes in the election of blacks to the legislature. Private litigation under the act was necessary to get officials to request preclearance as required by section 5. Yet, the initiation of litigation was able to produce substantial changes even before a decision was issued. The court itself acknowledged the claim that the election of additional blacks in 1982 was a special case: "In some elections the pendancy of this very litigation worked a one-time advantage for black candidates in the form of unusual organized political support by white leaders concerned to forestall single-member districting."[59] Clearly the threat of litigation under the act is capable of generating changes even before a verdict. North Carolina legislators were doubtless mindful of the *Gingles* experience as they carried out the 1991 redistricting process.

Blacks have achieved an important presence in the general assembly in terms of policy impact and leadership positions.[60] Shortly after Harvey Gantt lost the 1990 election, which, had he won, would have made him the first black U.S. senator from the South since Reconstruction, Daniel T. Blue achieved a different historic first. A five-term (ten-year) member of the house, Blue was chosen speaker of that body. This choice of the Democratic house caucus made him the first black state house speaker in modern southern history.[61]

The more long-term effects of the Voting Rights Act on the general assembly remain to be seen. The results of the 1990 census have already begun another round of high-stakes redistricting for seats in Congress and in the state house and senate, perhaps the most significant redistricting since passage of the act. While largely beyond the scope of this essay, a more recently recognized and unanticipated effect of the shift to single-member legislative districts in southern states like North Carolina has been to narrow the reach of the black electorate by excluding blacks from larger multimember districts. This in turn has made some Democratic incumbents more vulnerable to Republican challengers. Some formerly heterogeneous multimember districts like Wake County (from which Representative Blue had been elected prior to the 1984 shift) have, in essence, been split into black Democratic, white Democratic, white Republican, and rural and urban districts.

County Commissions

We consider next the relationship between districting arrangements and the election of black and Native American officials in county governments. We begin with counties and follow with cities because counties are more comprehensive administrative units. Every citizen lives in one of these jurisdictions, while not every citizen is included in cities. While we concentrate on county commissions, blacks served in several other county-level offices as of 1990. In addition to the forty-four black county commissioners (roughly 5 percent of the total membership on county boards), there were sixty-four black members of county boards of education and four black sheriffs. Native American officeholding at the county level was limited to three members of Robeson County's seven-member commission and two members of the county board of education, all of whom were elected at large.

The series of tables comparing districting arrangements, minority population, and minority officeholding of counties are designated with an A, while those tables without an A refer to cities.[62] Table 6.1A shows that in 1989, nine out of ten counties had at-large systems for election of county commissioners. Among these counties, there was a positive relationship between the size of the black population in the county and the percentage of commissioners who were black, though at most a quarter of the commissioners were black, even in the eight majority-black counties. The fraction of officials who were minority was consistently less than the minority fraction of the population.

Only four counties had pure district systems. Curiously, none of them was one of the eight counties in which minorities were a majority of the population. The fact that blacks were so underrepresented in majority-black counties retaining at-large schemes would seem to indicate a situation ripe for change in districting arrangements. In the handful of counties with district elections, there was a much more nearly proportionate relationship between the black percentage in the electorate and on the county commission than in the at-large counties in the same population categories. The four counties with mixed systems fell in between.

Table 6.2A, containing longitudinal data, shows that there were small increases in black elected officials between 1973 and 1989 even in majority-white counties with unchanged electoral systems. This indicates that there were other changes besides electoral arrangements during the sixteen years covered by the table. We should keep in mind that the effects of these nonelectoral changes were also likely to to felt, to some degree, in the counties where the electoral arrangements were changed. Thus, not all changes in black officeholding in these locales can be attributed to the creation of districts. On the other hand, to the extent that the electoral changes were the result of preclearance objections or lawsuits, the counties in which these took place may have been especially resistant to black officeholding.

Still, there is clear evidence that electoral arrangements made a difference. In the three counties that changed from at-large to single-member status between 1973 and 1989, and in the four that changed from at-large to mixed systems, all of the black elected officials were elected after the change. Table 6.3A allows an assessment of the consequences of the electoral arrangements on minority officeholding in counties with mixed plans. In the four counties with both district and at-large components, most of the black commissioners were elected from the districts rather than from the entire county.

Two measures of representational equity are reported in tables 6.4A and 6.5A. One measures the *difference* between the minority percentage in the county population and on the commission, while the other measures the *ratio* of the same percentages. Blacks and Native Americans were consistently underrepresented on county commissions regardless of districting arrangements and time. Nevertheless, the equity measures confirm the observations of tables 6.1A and 6.2A that in majority-white counties single-member districts were the most proportionately representative system, followed by mixed systems. At-large plans were the least proportional. Comparing the equity ratios across time, as table 6.5A does, one can also see that while the ratios in the unchanged counties increased slightly, much more substantial increases occurred after the adoption of some form of district election.

Tables 6.6A and 6.7A allow a more detailed analysis of the influence of district elections in North Carolina counties. The tables compare percentages of minority populations with those of minority elected officials in each of the fifteen wards composing the four counties with single-member district plans. Within these few districts it appears that minorities needed a substantial majority (over 60 percent) before they could be assured of electing their own or of controlling county boards with people of their own ethnic group. (None of the three Native American counties employed district elections.)

City Councils

We now consider the relationship between districting arrangements and the election of black and Native American officials in North Carolina cities. The picture in many ways parallels that presented above for counties. There were 260 black city council members (around 10 percent of the total), 18 black mayors, and 19 black members of city school boards governing North Carolina cities, towns, and villages.

As table 6.1 shows, over 90 percent of city councils were elected at large, and in them the fraction of minority elected officials was minuscule, even in majority-black municipalities. As with counties, there was a very small number of cities with mixed or single-member district arrangements. These were the cities in which the percentage of minority council members approximated the minority percentage of the population.

Over time there have been dramatic increases in the fraction of black elected officials in most of the groups of cities with changed arrangements, regardless of the system adopted. As table 6.2 shows, in the great majority of cities there was no change in electoral arrangements, and in such cities there was much less of an increase in the proportions of minority officials than there was in the changed cities. Even in the 144 majority-black cities, the jump in black officeholding between 1973 and 1989 was many times higher in the changed as compared with the static at-large plans.

There was an important difference between city and county patterns that is not shown in the tables. For both counties and cities, some at-large jurisdictions had district residence or nomination requirements. Counties with these arrangements, like pure at-large systems, elected very few blacks. In the cities, however, this system did almost as well as single-member districts in producing minority officials. We speculate that this is because minority residential concentration was greater in cities than in counties. When a district is largely black, a candidate who must be a resident or nominated by residents is likely to be black. Under such circumstances, district residence or nomination with at-large election can approach the success possible in single-member districts in securing the election of blacks. We suspect that these conditions of black residential concentration in districts are more likely to exist in cities than in more sparsely populated counties.

In cities with mixed plans (table 6.3), districts produced substantially larger numbers of blacks than did the at-large system. This is not surprising, though it is an even more dramatic pattern than that found in the mixed systems in the counties. Of the fifteen black council members from the fourteen cities with mixed plans, only one was elected at large. Here too, we suspect that the districting arrangements paralleled segregated residential patterns in the cities more than in the counties. That is, we expect more black-dominated districts in cities than in counties, and therefore even more blacks are likely to be elected from districts under these circumstances. A comparison between counties and cities of the numbers of districts in each population category (tables 6.6A and 6.6) bears out this expectation.

In single-member districts in the counties, 27 percent of the districts had majorities composed of minority groups, while roughly 42 percent of such districts in the cities are dominated by minorities. Ironically, residential segregation of the races is important for allowing single-member districts to facilitate the election of blacks. In the absence of such segregation, single-member districts are far less effective in doing so. These points are illustrated by a Granville County case discussed below.

The equity scores for the changed cities (tables 6.4 and 6.5) were substantially higher than they were in the counties, but differences in scores among the three types of electoral systems were similar to those in the counties. In no case were minorities better represented than whites, but mean equity ratios in majority-white cities ranged between 0.82 and 0.98 for blacks and Native Americans combined in single-member district and mixed systems. In none of the at-large cities did the ratio rise above 0.14.

Tables 6.6 and 6.7 allow a more detailed analysis of the influence of district election in North Carolina cities. In contrast to the counties analyzed above, it was possible to elect blacks in city single-member districts where blacks were only a minority of the electorate. Not surprisingly, even larger proportions of council members were black in black-majority districts.

The fact that most North Carolina Native Americans lived in a cluster of towns retaining at-large plans makes it difficult to discuss multiethnic voting within district systems. We can, however, take a closer look at the towns in Robeson County, where the Native American population was concentrated. (All but the county seat of Lumberton operated without district elections.) The voter registration rates for blacks and Native Americans in these towns were both very high. Assuming that Native Americans, blacks, and whites have comparable opportunities to vote, Native Americans were more seriously underrepresented than blacks on the local boards.

The Role of Litigation

As indicated in tables 6.8 and 6.8A, most of the changes from at-large to single-member district or mixed systems in North Carolina counties and cities involved litigation or the threat thereof under section 2 as amended in 1982. Of the forty-nine (fifty-four) changes in county and city electoral systems that took place between 1973 and 1989 (1965 and 1991), twenty-nine (thirty-two) were induced by lawsuits and two (two) by threatened suits. Very few resulted from section 5 preclearance objections. Out of the thirty-four changes induced between 1965 and 1991 by real or threatened legal action, twenty-one occurred in covered jurisdictions, while five counties and eight cities not originally covered under section 5 were successfully sued under amended section 2.

There were very few suits on the county or city level before *Gingles*, and only five suits were filed while that case was pending in district court. Soon after *Gingles* was decided, however, the plaintiffs in a suit against Halifax County won a favorable decision.[63] In response to these decisions, at least thirty lawsuits were filed in the state pursuant to the Voting Rights Act, and at least five more controversies were resolved before filing by the threat of litigation. The use of at-large elections was challenged for at least twelve cities or towns, twenty counties, and seven boards of education. The majority of these suits were sponsored by the NAACP or the NAACP Legal Defense and Educational Fund. North Carolina's voting rights case law has been constructed largely by a group of committed black and white attorneys: Leslie Winner, Romallus Murphy, Ronald Penny, Angus Thompson, and a few others.

The results of the litigation have been basically favorable to the plaintiffs, resulting about half the time in a negotiated agreement regarding the use of some districts and some at-large seats before the case was even brought to trial. In only two lawsuits were plaintiffs offered no relief.[64] Of the county and city government controversies that have been resolved by the courts, thirteen resulted in pure district systems and nineteen in mixed ones. Four resulted in either limited voting or a combination of districts and limited voting, and two resulted in the elimination of the residency requirement that had been used in conjunction with at-large elections. In several jurisdictions, such as Guilford, Wilson, Halifax, and Paquotank counties, and in Elizabeth City, High Point, and Lexington, litigation was associated with the creation of majority-black districts from which blacks were elected.[65]

A limit on the possibility of using the Voting Rights Act to secure the representation of blacks has been defined in Granville County.[66] This county was 43 percent black, but a maximum of two of seven districts could be drawn with a black majority. The U.S. Court of Appeals for the Fourth Circuit overturned a district court decision that had mandated a limited voting system. Specifically, the district judge had provided for election of four and three seats at a time for staggered terms, but with each voter allowed only two votes per election. This was seen as a way to allow blacks to control more seats in a county where their substantial numbers were too dispersed to elect commissioners in proportion to their numerical strength. The argument was rejected by the higher court.[67]

Granville County had not contested the fact that the original at-large system was discriminatory, and the plaintiffs had agreed that the county's new plan for seven single-member districts was drawn as well as could be expected, but they still pushed for a limited voting scheme as an alternative. The appellate court rejected the district judge's decision to dismiss the county's plan as an overtly political ruling that substituted the judge's wisdom for the county's preference.

The influence of the Voting Rights Act has also been felt on the remaining twenty-five county commissions and city councils that appear to have shifted from at-large systems "voluntarily," that is, without the impetus of a lawsuit or threatened litigation. We suspect that the fear of possible litigation, especially in the post-*Gingles* environment, was enough to convince moderate white politicians who may have been wavering to undertake reform. Tables 6.8A and 6.8 reveal that all five of the counties and nine of the fifteen cities which shifted on their own (i.e., without a lawsuit filed) to single-member or mixed plans were subject to the direct scrutiny of the Justice Department under section 5. In retrospect, the fact that plaintiffs have tended to seek relief under section 2 does not diminish the perceived power of section 5 with its specific coverage. The minority population of the counties and cities that changed voluntarily is also, on average, about 9 percentage points higher than the minority population in the counties and cities undergoing legal action. While not a startling difference, the political incentives of a larger black population may have made the extra push of a lawsuit unnecessary.

A comparison of tables 6.8A and 6.8 also reveals that litigation inspired by the act appears to have been much more instrumental in altering county systems than municipal bodies. About three-fourths of the changes in county government were the result of lawsuits, while fewer than half of the new city systems had their genesis in court. While the voluntary counties were not geographically clustered, many of the cities that implemented changes on their own were large (over 25,000) and were located in the Piedmont region of the state (for example, Winston-Salem, Tarboro, Wilson, Raleigh, Cary, Charlotte, Greensboro, and Fayetteville). These facts bear out a general pattern in which the racial politics of the urban Piedmont has been relatively more progressive than in the rest of North Carolina.

The Granville case may be an important indicator for the future of litigation under the Voting Rights Act concerning methods of election in North Carolina. Specifically, the appellate ruling established the precedent for balancing plaintiffs' desires with the ability of local governments to comply within the bounds of reason and fairness. More generally, the case suggests that after the first wave of suits following *Gingles*, which aimed at some of the most obvious county and city targets, future legal battles will more likely occur in locales where there are not simple remedies for an underrepresentation of blacks in elective office. On the other hand, the evidence from tables 6.5 and 6.5A, in particular, on majority-black jurisdictions with at-large systems suggests that there are still many locales awaiting basic reform.

Conclusion

The Voting Rights Act of 1965 has had a substantial impact in North Carolina. It capped the sixty-five-year struggle of black Tar Heels to rebuild the political community destroyed by disfranchisement and opened up an entirely new realm of possibilities. Most immediately, the act facilitated substantial increases in black voter registration in the covered counties. On the other hand, the preclearance provisions were largely ignored by the state and the Justice Department until the 1970s. It took litigation to change this. The most notable cases targeted the judicial system and the state legislature, and the response was substantial.

The possibility of minority voters suing to demand preclearance obviously made a difference in the behavior of white officials. State resistance was not substantial in the case of the judicial system, and the state's resolution of the problem led to the withdrawal of the lawsuit. For the legislative changes, the state did not give up its resistance until *Gingles* was resolved. The 1982 amendments to section 2 have surely made a difference in North Carolina by calling attention to the possibility of the use of the act to block some changes and to secure others. The changes in the judicial election system show that substantial "voluntary" compliance may occur when litigation becomes a real option.

Recently, political and legal energies have been focused on North Carolina counties and cities, for it is in these jurisdictions that the act has opened up both the greatest opportunities and challenges for black electoral equality. Litigation inspired by the act has led to the adoption of districting arrangements that, in turn, have led to much more nearly proportional representation for blacks. For a variety of reasons, however, an overwhelming number of cities and counties have retained at-large elections, and blacks and Native Americans continue to be underrepresented on local boards, even when they are a majority of the population.

The North Carolina experience, however, raises questions about the common presumption that blacks cannot be elected in majority-white districts. On the statewide level, Harvey Gantt came as close to winning a U.S. Senate seat as had three previous white opponents of Senator Helms. Although nine of the judges elected statewide are products of a nominating system that is designed to assure the choice of a black, the fact remains that there are fourteen black judges elected statewide, and five of these are not products of such engineering. In 1991 five black members of the state house of representatives (including Representative Michaux) and the one Native American member were elected from majority-white multimember districts. The remaining eight black house members came from majority-black single-member districts. In the state senate Howard Lee and one other black senator served majority-white multimember districts. The other three black senators were elected from majority-black single-member districts.

There have also been important local examples of blacks being elected in majority-white districts. Howard Lee's election as mayor of Chapel Hill in 1969 (then about 13 percent black) was the first modern election of a black to such a position in a predominantly white community in the South. Harvey Gantt in 1983 was elected mayor of Charlotte, the state's largest city, which was then about 31 percent black. At this writing, the sheriff and the register of deeds of Wake County, the site of the state capital, are black, as is the district attorney for Orange and Chatham counties. However, as our discussion of local elections makes clear, blacks, whatever the election system, are still not elected to county boards and city councils to a degree that approaches their fraction of the population. This is particularly true in at-large jurisdictions.

North Carolina's progressive image has surely exaggerated the nature of the reality, as many of the observations in this essay make clear. It is true that the victories of Justice Frye, Speaker Blue, Representative Michaux, Senator Lee, Mayor Gantt, Sheriff Baker, and numerous other minority candidates prove that North Carolina whites are not consistently unwilling to support blacks for public office. But it cannot be ignored that in voting rights as in school desegregation, the state has also resisted movements toward racial equality and fairness. Many of the changes regarding voting rights issues would not have been made without the reality or the threat of litigation.

The Voting Rights Act has clearly reshaped North Carolina politics, both in increasing black participation and in securing procedural arrangements that facilitate the possibility of electing blacks to public office. North Carolina's experience a quarter century after passage of the act suggests both the importance of the federal mandate and the uniqueness of the state within the region. It is also clear that there are many perplexing issues regarding voting rights and political equality still to be faced.

TABLE 6.1
Minority Representation on Council in 1989 by Election Plan, North Carolina Cities with 10 Percent or More Combined Black and Indian Population in 1980

Type of Plan by % Minority in City Population, 1980	N	*Mean % Minority in City Population, 1980*			*Mean % Minority on City Council, 1989*		
		Black	*Indian*	*Black + Indian*	*Black*	*Indian*	*Black + Indian*
SMD plan							
10–29.9	0	—	—	**—**	—	—	**—**
30–49.9	9	39.8	0.2	**39.9**	39.3	0.0	**39.3**
50–100	4	47.2	8.8	**56.0**	44.0	2.8[a]	**46.8**
Mixed plan							
10–29.9	5	22.0	0.2	**22.2**	18.2	0.0	**18.2**
30–49.9	8	32.7	0.4	**33.1**	31.8	0.0	**31.8**
50–100	1	76.4	0.1	**76.3**	40.0	0.0	**40.0**
At-large plan[b]							
10–29.9	346	18.8	0.4	**19.2**	2.7	0.0	**2.7**
30–49.9	216[c]	38.2	1.0	**39.2**	5.3	0.0	**5.3**
50–100	140	56.5	9.0	**65.5**	8.5	0.7[d]	**9.2**

Note: In tables 6.1–6.7A, the "Black + Indian" percentages are not the summed row values of blacks and Indians. Rather, these percentages are derived from the raw data.

[a] Lumberton had one Native American on its nine-member board in addition to three blacks.

[b] The at-large cells include nineteen cities that were "other" systems, i.e., systems that had a residence requirement and/or nomination requirement.

[c] Durham had six members elected at large and six elected at large to wards. There were seven blacks on the board.

[d] Pembroke's board was 100 percent Native American. It was the only city other than Lumberton with Native Americans on the city governing body.

TABLE 6.1A
Minority Representation on Commissioners Court in 1989 by Election Plan, North Carolina Counties of 10 Percent or More Black and Indian Population in 1980

Type of Plan by % Minority in County Population, 1980	N	*Mean % Minority in County Population, 1980*			*Mean % Minority on County Commission, 1989*		
		Black	*Indian*	*Black + Indian*	*Black*	*Indian*	*Black + Indian*
SMD plan							
10–29.9	1	25.0	0.4	**25.4**	14.3	0.0	**14.3**
30–49.9	3	37.5	0.1	**37.6**	30.5	0.0	**30.5**
50–100	0	—	—	**—**	—	—	**—**
Mixed plan							
10–29.9	1	26.5	0.3	**26.8**	14.3	0.0	**14.3**
30–49.9	3	38.6	0.8	**39.4**	12.2	0.0	**12.2**
50–100	0	—	—	**—**	—	—	**—**
At-large plan[a]							
10–29.9	29	17.9	11.5	**29.4**	5.8	0.0	**5.8**
30–49.9	26	37.8	0.6	**38.4**	5.2	0.0	**5.2**
50–100	8	50.8	6.6	**57.4**	25.0	5.4[b]	**30.4**

[a] The at-large category includes thirty-four counties with "other" types of at-large systems, i.e., those combining at-large election with district residency and/or nomination requirements. Twelve of these had a 10–29.9 percent minority population, and about 6 percent of their board membership was minority. Sixteen had a 30–49.9 percent minority population, and just over 3 percent of their commissioners were minority. Six of these counties were majority black, and their boards were 20 percent minority.

[b] Robeson County had three Native Americans on its seven-member county commission, in addition to four whites. The population of the county was 35 percent Native American and 25 percent black. The commissioners were nominated by district but elected at large. Robeson was the only county with Native Americans on its governing body.

TABLE 6.2
Changes in Minority Representation on Council between 1973 and 1989, North Carolina Citie
with 10 Percent or More Combined Black and Indian Population in 1980[a]

Type of Change by % Minority in City Population, 1980	N[b]	Mean % Minority in City Population, 1980			Mean % Minority on City Council: Before Change (1973)			Mean % Minority on City Council: After Change (198		
		Black	Indian	Black + Indian	Black	Indian	Black + Indian	Black	Indian	Bla + In
Changed Systems										
From at-large to SMD plan										
10–29.9	0	—	—	**—**	—	—	**—**	—	—	—
30–49.9	6	40.7	0.2	**40.9**	5.2	0.0	**5.2**	36.0	0.0	**36**
50–100	3	54.9	0.0	**54.9**	5.6	0.0	**5.6**	47.6	0.0	**47**
From at-large to mixed plan										
10–29.9	5	22.0	0.3	**22.2**	8.3	0.0	**8.3**	18.2	0.0	**18.**
30–49.9	7	33.2	0.5	**33.7**	11.2	0.0	**11.2**	32.3	0.0	**32**
50–100	1	76.3	0.1	**76.4**	0.0	0.0	**0.0**	40.0	0.0	**40.**
Unchanged Systems										
At-large										
10–29.9	346	18.8	0.4	**19.2**	0.8	0.0	**0.8**	2.7	0.0	**2**
30–49.9	216	38.2	1.0	**39.2**	1.2	0.0	**1.2**	5.3	0.0	**5.**
50–100	140	56.5	9.0	**65.5**	1.9	0.0	**1.9**	8.5	0.7	**9.**

[a] The cells in this table submerge in the general at-large categories the cities in the "other" category of at-election and district residency and/or nomination requirements. Four cities shifted from simple at-large to "o at large, and two with majority-black populations went from having 0 to 60 percent minority membership on city boards. Four cities shifted from "other" to single-member districts. Two had a 30–49.9 percent min population and one was majority-black. In all three, the percentage of minority officials on city boards rose between 0 and 0.35 percent to almost 43 percent. Three cities shifted from "other" to mixed systems. In the cities 30–49.9 percent minority, the percentage of minority officials rose from 8.35 to 41.7 percent. Fifteen retained their "other" systems through 1989 and so remained "unchanged," but the percentage of minority offi rose. Twelve of these cities had a 10–29.9 percent minority population, and the percentage of minority offi increased from 5.4 to 13.1 percent. Two cities had a 30–49.9 percent minority population, and their percenta minority officials jumped from 8.4 to 37.5 percent. In the one majority-black city that retained its "other" sys the percentage of minority officials stayed at 20 percent.

[b] Five cities are excluded from this table because shifts from at-large systems occurred before 1973. The fiv composed of one mixed system and four single-member districts. The cities are Tarboro, Winston-Salem, Ral Plymouth, and Lumberton.

[c] This picture is somewhat distorted by lumping the "other" at-large and the simple at-large categories toge The two pure at-large cities in this cell went from 0 to 16.7 percent minority officials when they changed fro large to mixed. The one "other" at-large city lost minority representation (16.7 to 0 percent) when it shifted "other" at-large to mixed.

LE 6.2A

nges in Minority Representation on Commissioners Court between 1973 and 1989, North olina Cities with 10 Percent or More Combined Black and Indian Population in 1980[a]

of Change ; Minority ounty ılation, 1980	N[b]	Mean % Minority in County Population, 1980			Mean % Minority on County Commission: Before Change (1973)			Mean % Minority on County Commission: After Change (1989)		
		Black	*Indian*	*Black + Indian*	*Black*	*Indian*	*Black + Indian*	*Black*	*Indian*	*Black + Indian*
Changed Systems										
n at-large to SMD plan										
10–29.9	1	25.0	0.4	**25.4**	0.0	0.0	**0.0**	14.3	0.0	**14.3**
30–49.9	2	34.9	0.1	**34.8**	0.0	0.0	**0.0**	35.8	0.0	**35.8**
50–100	0	—	—	**—**	—	—	**—**	—	—	**—**
n at-large to mixed plan										
10–29.9	1	26.5	0.3	**26.8**	0.0	0.0	**0.0**	14.3	0.0	**14.3**
30–49.9	3	38.6	0.1	**38.7**	0.0	0.0	**0.0**	12.2	0.0	**12.2**
50–100	0	—	—	**—**	—	—	**—**	—	—	**—**
Unchanged Systems										
ırge plan										
10–29.9	29	18.5	1.6	**20.1**	1.8	0.0	**1.8**	3.4	0.0	**3.4**
30–49.9	25	38.8	0.9	**39.7**	3.2	0.0	**3.2**	4.7	0.0	**4.7**
50–100	8	50.8	6.6	**57.4**	5.0	0.0	**5.0**	25.0	5.4	**30.4**

The categories in this table submerge the 32 counties with "other" at-large systems (those with district lency and/or nomination requirements) into the overall at-large category. Four counties (all less than 30 ent minority) shifted from simple at-large to "other" at-large systems but still had no minority representation ıeir boards. Three counties (all 30–49.9 percent minority) shifted from "other" at-large to mixed systems. The entage of minority commissioners rose from 0 to 12.2 percent. Twenty-five counties retained their "other" at-; systems. The change in those 25 counties in minority officeholding over time very nearly paralleled that for ınchanged at-large counties without residence or nomination requirements.

Vashington and Cherokee counties were excluded because of the 1973 cutoff date. Washington adopted a SMD em before 1973. Cherokee had a SMD system until 1978 and then shifted to an at-large system.

TABLE 6.3
Minority Representation in 1989 in Mixed Plans by District and At-Large Components, North Carolina Cities with 10 Percent or More Black and Indian Population in 1980

		Mean % Minority Councilpersons in District Components, 1989			*Mean % Minority Councilpersons in At-Large Components, 1989*		
% Minority in City Population, 1980	N	*Black*	*Indian*	*Black + Indian*	*Black*	*Indian*	*Black + Indian*
10–29.9	5	31.0	0.0	**31.0**	0.0	0.0	**0.0**
30–49.9	8	35.9	0.0	**35.9**	3.1	0.0	**3.1**
50–100	1	50.0	0.0	**50.0**	0.0	0.0	**0.0**

TABLE 6.3A
Minority Representation in 1989 in Mixed Plans by District and At-Large Components, North Carolina Counties with 10 Percent or More Black and Indian Population in 1980

		Mean % Minority Commissioners in District Components, 1989			*Mean % Minority Commissioners in At-Large Components, 1989*		
% Minority in County Population, 1980	N	*Black*	*Indian*	*Black + Indian*	*Black*	*Indian*	*Black + Indian*
10–29.9	1	25.0	0.0	**25.0**	0.0	0.0	**0.0**
30–49.9	3	30.5	0.0	**30.5**	16.7	0.0	**16.7**
50–100	0	—	—	**—**	—	—	**—**

TABLE 6.4
Two Equity Measures Comparing Percentage Minority on Council in 1989 with Percentage Minority in City Population in 1980, North Carolina Cities with 10 Percent or More Combined Black and Indian Population in 1980[a]

Type of Plan by % Minority in City Population, 1980	N	*Difference Measure (% on Council − % in Population)* Black	Indian	Black + Indian	*Ratio Measure (% on Council ÷ % in Population)* Black	Indian	Black + Indian
		Changed Systems					
From at-large to SMD plan							
10–29.9	0	—	—	**—**	—	—	**—**
30–49.9	9	−0.5	−0.1	**−0.6**	0.98	0.00	**0.98**
50–100	4	−3.1	−6.0	**−9.2**	0.93	0.32	**0.84**
From at-large to mixed plan							
10–29.9	5	−3.7	−0.2	**−4.0**	0.83	0.00	**0.82**
30–49.9	8	−1.0	−0.4	**−1.5**	0.97	0.00	**0.96**
50–100	1	−36.3	−0.1	**−36.4**	0.52	0.00	**0.52**
		Unchanged Systems					
At-large plan							
10–29.9	346	−16.1	−0.4	**−16.6**	0.14	0.00	**0.14**
30–49.9	216	−32.9	−1.0	**−33.9**	0.14	0.00	**0.13**
50–100	140	−48.1	−8.2	**−56.3**	0.15	0.07	**0.14**

[a]This table includes five cities not included in tables 6.2 and 6.5, cities that changed prior to 1973.

TABLE 6.4A

Two Equity Measures Comparing Percentage Minority on County Commission in 1989 with Percentage Minority in County Population in 1980, North Carolina Counties with 10 Percent or More Combined Black and Indian Population in 1980[a]

Type of Plan by % Minority in County Population, 1980	N	*Difference Measure (% on Commission − % in Population)*			*Ratio Measure (% on Commission ÷ % in Population)*		
		Black	*Indian*	*Black + Indian*	*Black*	*Indian*	*Black + Indian*
				Changed Systems			
From at-large to SMD plan							
10–29.9	1	−10.7	−0.4	**−11.1**	0.57	0.00	**0.56**
30–49.9	3	−7.0	−0.1	**−7.1**	0.81	0.00	**0.81**
50–100	0	—	—	**—**	—	—	**—**
From at-large to mixed plan							
10–29.9	1	−12.2	−0.3	**−12.5**	0.54	0.00	**0.53**
30–49.9	3	−26.4	−0.8	**−27.2**	0.32	0.00	**0.31**
50–100	0	—	—	**—**	—	—	**—**
				Unchanged Systems			
At-large plan							
10–29.9	29	−12.1	−11.5	**−23.6**	0.32	0.00	**0.20**
30–49.9	26	−32.6	−0.6	**−33.2**	0.14	0.00	**0.13**
50–100	8	−25.8	−1.2	**−27.0**	0.49	0.83	**0.53**

[a]This table includes two counties not included in tables 6.2A and 6.5A, counties that changed prior to 1973.

Camden, a county with a mix of at-large and multimember districts, is treated as having a mixed plan in this table. Mitchell County shifted to at-large elections after 1989.

TABLE 6.5
Changes in Minority Representation on Council between 1973 and 1989, North Carolina Cities with 10 Percent or More Combined Black and Indian Population in 1980 (Ratio Equity Measure)

		Minority Representational Equity on Council					
		1973			*1989*		
Type of Change by % Minority in City Population, 1980	N	*Black*	*Indian*	*Black + Indian*	*Black*	*Indian*	*Black + Indian*
		Changed Systems					
From at-large to SMD plan							
10–29.9	0	—	—	**—**	—	—	**—**
30–49.9	6	0.12	0.00	**0.12**	0.89	0.00	**0.89**
50–100	3	0.10	0.00	**0.10**	0.87	0.00	**0.87**
From at-large to mixed plan							
10–29.9	5	0.38	0.00	**0.38**	0.83	0.00	**0.82**
30–49.9	7	0.34	0.00	**0.33**	0.97	0.00	**0.96**
50–100	1	0.00	0.00	**0.00**	0.52	0.00	**0.52**
		Unchanged Systems					
At-large plan							
10–29.9	346	0.04	0.00	**0.04**	0.14	0.00	**0.14**
30–49.9	216	0.03	0.00	**0.03**	0.14	0.00	**0.13**
50–100	140	0.03	0.00	**0.03**	0.15	0.07	**0.14**

TABLE 6.5A
Changes in Minority Representation on Commission between 1973 and 1989, North Carolina Counties with 10 Percent or More Combined Black and Indian Population in 1980 (Ratio Equity Measure)[a]

Type of Change by % Minority in County Population, 1980	N	*Minority Representational Equity on Commission*					
		1973			*1989*		
		Black	*Indian*	*Black + Indian*	*Black*	*Indian*	*Black + Indian*
		Changed Systems					
From at-large to SMD plan							
10–29.9	1	0.00	0.00	**0.00**	0.57	0.00	**0.56**
30–49.9	2	0.00	0.00	**0.00**	1.03	0.00	**1.03**
50–100	0	—	—	**—**	—	—	**—**
From at-large to mixed plan							
10–29.9	1	0.00	0.00	**0.00**	0.54	0.00	**0.53**
30–49.9	3	0.00	0.00	**0.00**	0.32	0.00	**0.31**
50–100	0	—	—	**—**	—	—	**—**
		Unchanged Systems					
At-large plan							
10–29.9	29	0.10	0.00	**0.09**	0.18	0.00	**0.17**
30–49.9	25	0.08	0.00	**0.08**	0.12	0.00	**0.12**
50–100	8	0.10	0.00	**0.09**	0.49	0.83	**0.53**

[a] Mitchell County changed from at-large elections before 1965.

TABLE 6.6
Minority Representation in Council Single-Member Districts in 1989, North Carolina Cities with 10 Percent or More Combined Black and Indian Population in 1980

% Ethnic Population of District	N[a]	*Mean % Minority Population in Districts, 1980*			*Mean % Minority Councilpersons in Districts, 1989*		
		Black	*Indian*	*Black + Indian*	*Black*	*Indian*	*Black + Indian*
Black							
0–29.9	30	15.2	1.6	**16.8**	3.2	0.0	**3.2**
30–49.9	15	37.3	3.8[b]	**41.1**	29.4	5.9	**35.3**
50–59.9	7	55.8	0.2	**56.0**	100.0	0.0	**100.0**
60–64.9	2	63.6	0.0	**63.6**	33.3	0.0	**33.3**
65–69.9	3	67.8	0.2	**68.0**	100.0	0.0	**100.0**
70–100	20	86.3	0.4	**86.7**	100.0	0.0	**100.0**
Indian							
0–29.9	76	45.1	0.1	**45.2**	51.1	0.0	**51.1**
30–49.9	1	34.4	46.6	**81.0**	0.0	100.0	**100.0**
50–100	0	—	—	**—**	—	—	**—**
Black + Indian							
0–29.9	29	15.0	1.3	**16.3**	0.0	0.0	**0.0**
30–49.9	14	35.6	1.5	**37.1**	31.3	0.0	**31.3**
50–59.9	8	55.1	0.3	**55.4**	100.0	0.0	**100.0**
60–64.9	2	63.6	0.0	**63.6**	33.3	0.0	**33.3**
65–69.9	3	67.8	0.2	**68.0**	100.0	0.0	**100.0**
70–100	21	83.8	2.6	**86.4**	96.6	3.4	**100.0**

[a]The number of seats does not match the number of districts because some districts elect multiple members. There are 77 districts and 90 seats.

[b]The Indian population percentage in this cell is inflated by one district in the town of Lexington that was 44.6 percent Indian. Excluding this district, the Indian population percentage for the 30–49.9 percent black population range was 1.2 percent.

TABLE 6.6A
Minority Representation in Commission Single-Member Districts in 1989, North Carolina Counties with 10 Percent or More Combined Black and Indian Population in 1980

% Ethnic Population of District	N	Mean % Minority Population in Districts, 1980			Mean % Minority Commissioners in Districts, 1989		
		Black	*Indian*	*Black + Indian*	*Black*	*Indian*	*Black + Indian*
Black							
0–29.9	7	12.0	0.2	**12.2**	0.0	0.0	**0.0**
30–49.9	4	36.6	0.3	**36.9**	0.0	0.0	**0.0**
50–100	4	63.4	0.1	**63.5**	100.0	0.0	**100.0**
Indian							
0–29.9	15	37.3	0.2	**37.5**	33.3	0.0	**33.3**
30–49.9	0	—	—	**—**	—	—	**—**
50–100	0	—	—	**—**	—	—	**—**
Black + Indian							
0–29.9	7	12.0	0.2	**12.2**	0.0	0.0	**0.0**
30–49.9	4	36.6	0.3	**36.9**	0.0	0.0	**0.0**
50–100	4	63.4	0.1	**63.5**	100.0	0.0	**100.0**

TABLE 6.7
Minority Council Representation in Single-Member Districts in 1989, by Ethnic Composition of District, North Carolina Cities with 10 Percent or More Combined Black and Indian Population in 1980

		Mean % Minority Population in Districts, 1980			*Mean % Minority Councilpersons in Districts, 1989*		
Ethnic Composition of District	N	*Black*	*Indian*	*Black + Indian*	*Black*	*Indian*	*Black + Indian*
Black Majority	32	76.5	0.3	**76.8**	95.2	0.0	**95.2**
Indian Majority	0[a]	—	—	—	—	—	—
White Majority	43	21.7	1.3	**23.0**	10.9	0.0	**10.9**
Black Plurality	1	49.8	0.9	**50.7**	100.0	0.0	**100.0**
Indian Plurality	1	34.5	46.6	**81.0**	0.0	100.0	**100.0**
White Plurality	0	—	—	—	—	—	—

[a]Native Americans were a plurality of the population in three North Carolina cities and a majority in thirteen, but all sixteen had at-large systems and so are excluded.

TABLE 6.7A
Minority Commission Representation in Single-Member Districts in 1989 by Ethnic Composition of District, North Carolina Counties with 10 Percent or More Combined Black and Indian Population in 1980

		Mean % Minority Population in Districts, 1980			*Mean % Minority Commissioners in Districts, 1989*		
Ethnic Composition of District[a]	N	*Black*	*Indian*	*Black + Indian*	*Black*	*Indian*	*Black + Indian*
Black majority	4	63.4	0.1	**63.5**	100.0	0.0	**100.0**
Indian majority	0	—	—	—	—	—	—
White majority	11	22.5	0.2	**22.7**	0.0	0.0	**0.0**

[a]There were no pluralities in counties.

TABLE 6.8
Cause of Change from At-Large to Mixed or District Plan between 1973 and 1989, North Carolina Cities with 10 Percent or More Combined Black and Indian Population in 1980

City	*Year of Change*	*Covered by Section 5?*[a]	*Did Lawsuit Accompany Change?*	*Reason for Change*
		Changed to Single-Member Districts		
Princeville	1977	Yes	No	Ordinance
New Bern	1985	Yes	No	Ordinance
Rocky Mount	1985	Yes	Yes	Settled
Wilson	1986	Yes	No	Ordinance
Elizabeth City	1986	Yes	Yes	Settled[b]
Dunn	1987	Yes	Yes	Consent decree
Freemont	1987	Yes	No	Ordinance, lawsuit threat
Goldsboro	1987	Yes	No	Ordinance
Clinton	1989	No	Yes	Consent decree
		Changed to Mixed Plan		
Raleigh	1973	No	No	Referendum
Cary	1975	No	No	Ordinance
Charlotte	1977	No	No	Referendum
Greensboro	1983	No	No	Ordinance[c]
Statesville	1985	No	Yes	Consent decree
Fayetteville	1986	No	No	Ordinance
Greenville	1986	Yes	No	Ordinance
Henderson	1986	Yes	No	Ordinance
High Point	1986	Yes	Yes	Consent decree
Lexington	1986	No	Yes	Settled
Enfield	1987	Yes	No	Ordinance, lawsuit threat
Mooresville	1987	No	No	Ordinance
Thomasville	1987	No	Yes	Settled
Albemarle	1988	No	Yes	Settled
Edenton	1989	Yes	No	Ordinance
Benson	1989	No	Yes	Settled
Siler City	1989	No	Yes	Plan adopted after suit filed
Smithfield	1989	No	Yes	Plan adopted after suit filed

SUMMARY (Were changes accompanied by lawsuits?)
Yes 12 (44%)
No 15 (56%)

[a] This column in tables 6.8 and 6.8A is unique to this chapter on North Carolina. It indicates whether the county or city in question is covered by section 5 of the Voting Rights Act. Only 40 of North Carolina's 100 counties—and the towns and cities within—were in 1989 included in the preclearance provisions of section 5.

[b] The laswuit was settled after two injunctions had been granted and after the city's alternative plan had been rejected by the Justice Department.

[c] The city council passed an ordinance to create the plan after it had been defeated in five referendums since 1968. Under the at-large scheme, however, blacks had been elected to the city council and school board in roughly proportionate numbers since the 1950s.

TABLE 6.8A
Cause of Change from At-Large to Mixed or District Plan between 1973 and 1989, North Carolina Counties with 10 Percent or More Combined Black and Indian Population in 1980

County	*Year of Change*	*Covered by Section 5?*[a]	*Did Lawsuit Accompany Change?*	*Reason for Change*
		Changed to Single-Member Districts		
Guilford	1983	Yes	Yes	Settled
Wilson	1985	Yes	Yes	Summary judgment
Vance	1987	Yes	Yes	Settled
Craven	1987	Yes	No	Ordinance
Nash	1988	Yes	Yes	Preliminary injunction, then settled
Pitt	1988	Yes	Yes	Consent decree
Duplin	1989	No	Yes	Consent judgment
Anson	1989	Yes	No	Ordinance
Granville	1989	Yes	Yes	Court-ordered remedy
Harnett	1989	Yes	Yes	Settled
Sampson	1989	No	Yes	Settled
		Changed to Mixed Plan		
Mecklenburg	1984	Yes	No	Referendum[b]
Halifax	1984	Yes	Yes	Preliminary injunction, then settled
Camden	1986	Yes	No	Ordinance[c]
Pasquotank	1986	Yes	Yes	Settled
Chowan	1987	Yes	No	Ordinance
Bladen	1988	Yes	Yes	Consent judgment
Lenoir	1988	Yes	Yes	Consent decree
Pamlico	1988	No	Yes	Consent decree
Wayne	1988	Yes	Yes	Settled
Caswell	1989	Yes	Yes	Settled
Forsyth	1989	No	Yes	Settled

SUMMARY (Were changes accompanied by lawsuits?)
Yes 17 (77%)
No 5 (23%)

[a] This column in tables 6.8 and 6.8A is unique to this chapter on North Carolina. It indicates whether the county or city in question is covered by section 5 of the Voting Rights Act. Only 40 of North Carolina's 100 counties—and the towns and cities within—were in 1989 included in the preclearance provisions of section 5.

[b] Voters rejected the referendum for a switch from a five-commissioner at-large system to one with three commissioners elected at large and four elected at large to represent districts. They approved the shift to a mixed system with three at-large and four district seats.

[c] The county commission enacted the mixed plan in 1977. The Justice Department did not approve it until 1986.

TABLE 6.9
Major Disfranchising Devices in North Carolina

Device	Date Established	Date Abolished
Literacy test	1900[a]	1965, 1970[b]
Grandfather clause	1900[a]	1908[c]
Poll tax	1900[a]	1920[d]

[a]Constitutional amendment.
[b]Voting Rights Act of 1965 and amendments of 1970.
[c]Automatic expiration in constitutional amendment.
[d]Repealed.

TABLE 6.10
Black and White Registered Voters and Officeholders in North Carolina, Selected Years[a]

	Black		White	
	N	%	N	%
Registered voters				
1962[b]	—	10.0	—	89.6
1966	281,134	14.2	1,653,796	85.1
1990	635,045	19.0	2,677,162	80.0
Officeholders				
State house				
1962	0	0.0	120	100.0
1966	0[c]	0.0	120	100.0
1990	13[d]	10.8	120	89.2
State senate				
1962	0	0.0	50	100.0
1966	0[e]	0.0	50	100.0
1990	4[f]	8.0	46	92.0

Sources: North Carolina Advisory Committee 1962; North Carolina State Board of Elections (for 1966 and 1990 registration data); U.S. Census of the Population for North Carolina, 1960, 1970, and 1990.

[a]Mean black population in state 1960–90 = 22.8%.

[b]The most recent pre-Voting Rights Act registration figures are those for 1962. These data—and those for 1966—are for blacks and whites only, and do not sum to 100 percent.

[c]The first black representative was elected in 1968.

[d]A Native American was elected in 1990.

[e]The first black senator was elected in 1974.

[f]An additional black senator was elected in 1990.

CHAPTER SEVEN

South Carolina

ORVILLE VERNON BURTON,

TERENCE R. FINNEGAN,

PEYTON McCRARY, AND

JAMES W. LOEWEN

SOUTH CAROLINA, first in nullification and first in secession, was also the first state to challenge the constitutionality of the Voting Rights Act.[1] It was fitting that the state should have taken a central role in this challenge. After all, it had served as the leading advocate for the rights of slaveholders in the debates over the Declaration of Independence and the Constitution. Under the leadership of John C. Calhoun, South Carolina had attempted to "nullify" a federal tariff law in 1832 in order to establish a constitutional precedent for voiding future antislavery legislation. It was the first state to secede from the Union, and a few months later, South Carolinians fired the first shot of the Civil War at Fort Sumter. During the seven decades following Reconstruction, the state legislature devised election laws that effectively disfranchised African Americans; and when the Supreme Court outlawed the white primary, South Carolina led the way in devising substitutes to keep blacks out of the Democratic primary. In 1948 Governor J. Strom Thurmond became the standard bearer of the "Dixiecrat" revolt against the civil rights plank of the Democratic party. A few years later, the South Carolina attorney general's office vociferously defended the principles of public school segregation before the Supreme Court in *Brown v. Board of Education*, and the state's congressional delegation resolutely opposed every civil rights bill proposed in Congress from 1957 to 1965.

Despite this history, South Carolina attorneys, in challenging the Voting Rights Act, maintained that it subjected the state to unnecessary intrusive supervision without proof of intentional discrimination. In denying their challenge and affirming the constitutionality of the act in *South Carolina v. Katzenbach*, Chief Justice Earl Warren stated, "Congress felt itself confronted by an insidious and pervasive evil." He noted the long history of racial discrimination in the voter registration process in South Carolina, directly quoting some of the more outrageous remarks of Benjamin R. "Pitchfork Ben" Tillman at the 1895 disfranchising convention as evidence of the discriminatory purpose of the literacy test suspended by the act. Warren stated that "the constitutional propriety of the Voting Rights Act of 1965 must be judged with reference to the historical experience which it reflects."[2] History had finally caught up with South Carolina.

Voting Rights and Racial Politics from 1865 to 1965

"The central fact in the history of black Carolina," concludes Newby, "has been the racism of white Carolina."[3] The degree to which African Americans have held public office in South Carolina since the Civil War was largely determined by the state's election laws and the manner in which they were implemented. White officials made their intentions clear from the beginning. The South Carolina constitutional convention of 1865, with the approval of President Andrew Johnson, restricted voting and officeholding to white males. "This is a white man's government," explained Governor Benjamin Perry, "and intended for white men only."[4] In an attempt to buttress white supremacy, southern state legislatures enacted "black codes" that severely restricted the rights of freedpersons. The South Carolina black code required agricultural workers to sign away most of their rights as citizens in annual labor contracts with landowners or risk prosecution for vagrancy.[5] The enactment of black codes throughout the South played a key role in persuading Congress to enfranchise African Americans and temporarily restrict the suffrage of some Confederates.

Enfranchised by the Fourteenth and Fifteenth amendments, South Carolina's black majority elected Republican candidates to the bulk of the seats in a new constitutional convention, which then granted the right to vote to every adult male, "without distinction of race, color, or former condition."[6] Subsequently, blacks controlled a majority of seats in the lower house (and from 1874 to 1876 in both the senate and the house), and they won elections as lieutenant governor, secretary of state, and state treasurer. Equally important, they were elected to a significant number of local offices, such as sheriff, county commissioner, magistrate, school commissioner, and alderman.[7] Reconstruction in South Carolina lasted as long as in any other state, and the black Republicans there achieved as great a degree of political power as did African Americans anywhere.

Disfranchisement

Some whites bitterly opposed black equality and endorsed systematic political violence to overcome Republican control. Whether through secretive activity by the Ku Klux Klan or open mob violence, Democrats often resorted to political assassination and murder, although physical beatings, arson, and threats of death were more common. Seven state legislators were murdered between 1868 and 1876.[8] Violence was so severe in nine upcountry counties that the federal government intervened in 1871 and declared martial law, making hundreds of arrests; a few dozen indictments led to guilty pleas and prison sentences. In the black-controlled town of Hamburg, Democrats under former Confederate general Matthew Calbraith Butler's leadership brought a cannon and several hundred armed horsemen to do battle with the African-American militia, killing six (four by firing squad) and pillaging the homes and shops of the town's black population and their white allies.[9] In the wake of the Hamburg massacre, Butler and another former Confederate general, Martin Witherspoon Gary, orchestrated a violent "redemption" of state government from Republican control. Gary had announced as early as 1874 that political contests in South Carolina were "a question of race and not of politics."[10] While Civil War hero General Wade Hampton ostensibly advocated moderation, Gary favored all-out guerilla warfare and organized Democrats into three hundred "rifle clubs" throughout the state. Armed bands of horsemen attired in symbolically defiant red shirts intimidated and attacked potential black voters.[11]

Although violent clashes between whites and blacks occurred in Charleston and in low-country plantation counties, the scale of battle in 1876 was nowhere as great as in Edgefield County, home of Gary and Butler. Over seven hundred armed and mounted Democrats in red shirts seized control of the county courthouse and, despite the presence of federal troops, prevented African Americans from voting. "Gary's doctrine of voting early and often changed the republican majority of 2,300 in Edgefield to a democratic majority of 3,900," recalled Gary protégé and future governor Benjamin Tillman, a participant in the Edgefield violence, "thus giving Hampton a claim to the office of governor." Hampton's victory resulted from the casting of 2,252 more votes than there were eligible voters.[12]

Although Hampton owed his election to the political violence of the "Edgefield plan," in his campaign speeches he pledged to treat blacks fairly in the new order. For Hampton and the "moderates," blacks who "knew their place" had a place in the system, and he did appoint some to local offices. Later, however, as a U.S. senator, Hampton justified fraud, intimidation, and violence to deny South Carolina blacks the franchise, claiming "the very civilization, the property, the life of the State itself, were involved."[13] Black-majority counties elected some African-American legislators, but the overwhelmingly white legislature determined to combat these successes. It adopted a law intended to eliminate federal scrutiny of state affairs by requiring separate ballot boxes for state and federal elections.[14] In addition, the legislature abolished a large number of precincts in heavily Republican counties, requiring voters to travel long distances in order to vote.[15]

After the end of Reconstruction, the Democrats manipulated election laws to institutionalize their control of state politics (see table 7.9). In 1882 a new law required all citizens to reregister or face permanent disfranchisement; registrars had great discretion in applying the law so that they could avoid striking white voters from the rolls. A companion statute, the Eight Box Law, intended as a de facto literacy test, required voters to place ballots for various offices in separate boxes, which election officials periodically shuffled. These discriminatory tactics effectively cut the African-American electorate in half.[16]

Even so, black voters remained numerous enough to be troublesome to white supremacists. Consequently, the legislature adopted a congressional redistricting plan that packed blacks into a malapportioned district where they made up 82 percent of the population, thereby diluting their voting strength in the rest of the state. The "black district," as it was called, ran from the city of Columbia to the coast, divided six counties, incorporated most black neighborhoods of Charleston, and, according to the *New York Times*, resembled a boa constrictor. Although this district generally elected a black Republican to the U.S. House of Representatives until 1896, the gerrymander assured Democrats safe contests for the remaining seats.[17]

The second stage of disfranchisement, designed to eliminate the African-American vote altogether, took place in the 1890s after former "red shirt" Ben Tillman gained control of the Democratic party. Brown has described Tillman as the "best known and most vitriolic Negrophobe in America" and the undisputed leader of black disfranchisement.[18] Tillman's biographer, Simkins, maintained that between Reconstruction and World War I, "Ben Tillman fostered the modern reaction against the Negro. This stance was one of his most significant influences on American life."[19] Tillman's movement to purge the black vote in South Carolina was as openly racist and its postdisfranchisement regime as rigidly committed to white supremacy as any in Dixie. In the U.S. Senate, Tillman declared defiantly: "We have done our level best. We have scratched our heads to find out how we could eliminate every last one of them. We stuffed ballot boxes. We shot them. We are not ashamed of it."[20] Openly avowing their intention to disfranchise blacks through the rewriting of the state constitution, the Tillman forces secured passage of a new registration law designed to eliminate as many African-American voters as possible before the referendum on calling a constitutional convention (see table 7.9). Governor John Gary Evans, Tillman's successor and General Gary's nephew, ordered election officials not to issue registration forms to blacks.[21] "The whites," Tillman announced, "have absolute control of the government, and we intend at any hazard to retain it."[22]

In 1895, now U.S. Senator Tillman chaired the convention's committee on the rights of suffrage. At his urging the convention established as prerequisites for registration the payment of a poll tax at least six months before the election and proof of payment of all other taxes. In addition, a prospective voter had to satisfy a literacy test or demonstrate an understanding of any constitutional provision read to him by the registrar. The discretion of the registrar was unlimited. The convention also adopted a "petty crimes" provision that disfranchised all those convicted of certain crimes that whites believed blacks frequently committed. Conservative historian David Duncan Wallace referred to this provision as "the black squint of the law."[23]

In 1896 the South Carolina legislature authorized statewide party primaries.[24] Henceforth the State Democratic Executive Committee prohibited all African Americans from voting in the primary, which was, in the one-party system after disfranchisement, the only election that mattered. The state poll tax requirement never applied to these primary elections, presumably because party rules already excluded African Americans.[25]

These changes affected both black and white political participation. As of October 1896, only 5,500 blacks were registered to vote in South Carolina, a mere

10 percent of all registered voters.[26] Kousser estimates that 45 percent of white adult males and 11 percent of black adult males voted in the 1896 presidential election.[27] This low turnout was the norm between 1920 and 1946. On average, only 27 percent of the state's adults voted in the Democratic primaries for governor and U.S. senator.[28]

Controlling election laws and voter registration was crucial to maintaining white supremacy. Congressman James F. Byrnes, who eventually became a U.S. senator, Supreme Court justice, U.S. secretary of state, and governor of South Carolina, cautioned in 1920: "It is certain that if there was a fair registration they [African Americans] would have a slight majority in our state. We cannot idly brush the facts aside. Unfortunate though it may be, our consideration of every question must include the consideration of this race question."[29] A year later, historian Francis Butler Simkins confirmed the intent of his native state's legislation. "Reviewing the South Carolina law in respect to the Negro since 1876, it is apparent that its frank purpose is to perpetuate the division of society into two distinct castes—the white, or dominant ruling class, and the Negro, or subject class."[30]

Democratic party officials unabashedly did their part for the cause of white supremacy. "There are dam [*sic*] few negroes registered in any way," observed a local executive committee spokesman to a journalist in 1940. "If a coon wants to vote in the primary, we make him recite the Constitution backward, as well as forward, make him close his eyes and dot his *t*'s and cross his *i*'s. We have to comply with the law, you see."[31] The effect of disfranchising legislation was profound: only fifteen hundred African Americans in South Carolina were registered to vote in 1940.[32]

When the Supreme Court overturned the white primary in 1944,[33] Governor Olin D. Johnston called a special session of the legislature to repeal all laws relating to primary elections in the hope that this would remove the element of "state action" and make the white primary invulnerable to legal challenge. "After these statutes are repealed," Johnston told the legislature, "we will have done everything in our power to guarantee white supremacy in our primaries."[34] Voters then approved a constitutional amendment erasing all mention of primaries from the state constitution, and the Democratic party adopted rules excluding African Americans from its "private" primary elections.[35]

When the NAACP challenged the private primary in federal court, Judge J. Waties Waring of Charleston ruled that because the Democratic primary was the vehicle through which all public officials were chosen, it remained a state action. Because the governor and legislature acted "solely for the purpose of preventing the Negro from gaining a right to vote," the judge ruled the change violated the Fourteenth and Fifteenth amendments.[36] The Democratic party then adopted new rules, not explicitly barring African Americans but requiring voters to swear to uphold segregation and for the first time extending the literacy test required for general elections to the primary.[37] Judge Waring struck down the required oath and prohibited the party from barring black participation.[38]

In 1950 the general assembly adopted a new election law restoring state regulation of primary elections.[39] The proposal to extend the literacy test to party primaries occasioned great debate. Some up-country legislators feared the measure would disfranchise their poor white constituents. In the end, however, the appeal to racial solidarity was successful, and Governor J. Strom Thurmond signed the bill into law.[40]

Among the electoral devices restored to the primary election laws were statewide full-slate and majority-vote requirements, which would dilute the votes of blacks now eligible to participate in the Democratic primary.[41] Although these features of the statute were reenacted without comment, contemporary accounts attributed the same purpose to the statute as a whole. "Conservative lawmakers admit that the bill is designed to control Negro voting in primaries," reported a Charleston newspaper in 1950.[42]

At the same time, Governor Thurmond was pushing to remove the state poll tax requirement from the state constitution, apparently with the intention of weakening congressional support for a federal anti–poll tax bill. Ogden noted that "many South Carolinians recognized that their tax had little significance since it did not apply to primary elections nor to women, was non-cumulative and amounted to only $1.00 per year."[43]

These machinations in election law, such as the repeal of the poll tax, mark a departure from the hard-line posturing of other states. In 1950 James F. Byrnes ran for governor and continued South Carolina's shift toward a "calculated moderation." Byrnes's experience on the Supreme Court and in national politics provided him a sophisticated and subtle approach in resisting racial integration. In order to forestall desegregation, for example, he used a significant portion of a new sales tax for the education of black children, and white leaders throughout the state began equalizing the facilities of white and black schools in a desperate attempt to salvage segregation. Byrnes urged the creation of a committee to find ways to maintain segregation and staffed it with some of the state's most prominent lawyers. Chaired by state senator L. Marion Gressette, this special school committee coordinated efforts to maintain the racial status quo.[44] This technique of bending a little to prevent larger changes, aptly termed "firm flexibility" by Sproat,[45] gave the state another decade of segregation. Byrnes's approach also ostensibly brought South Carolina back to the constitutional high ground. Just as it had argued for states' rights instead of slavery in both nullification and Civil War, so South Carolina appealed to constitutional precepts in opposing civil rights and voting rights in the modern period.

African-American Activism

During these many years of oppression, blacks regularly sought to reassert their right to vote. When women secured the ballot in 1920, a group of black women tried to exercise this newfound right, but were forcibly ejected from the registration office in Columbia.[46] In 1939 an African-American labor group in Greenville joined with the local NAACP and the Negro Youth Council in a voter registration drive, only to be quashed by police intimidation. To raise money to challenge the white primary and to increase voter registration, blacks founded the South Carolina Negro Citizens Committee in 1942. Led by black journalist John McCray in 1944, they formed a statewide protest organization, the Progressive Democratic party, with chapters in every South Carolina county. This group unsuccessfully challenged the seating of South Carolina's all-white delegation at the 1944 Democratic national convention, and sponsored Osceola McKaine, an African American, as a candidate for the U.S. Senate against Democrat Olin Johnston.[47] Between 1940 and 1946 the Progressive Democrats and the NAACP mounted a registration drive that increased the number of black voters on the rolls from 1,500 to 50,000.[48] Despite Klan marches and cross burnings, 35,000 black voters went to the polls in the 1948 primary. In the primary race that year for the U.S. Senate seat between William Jennings Bryan Dorn and Burnet Maybank, Dorn denounced Judge Waring because of his decision outlawing the white primary. The black vote went solidly to Maybank, sending a clear signal to the state's Democratic politicians that black voters would seek to punish blatant appeals to white supremacy.[49]

During the next decade journalist McCray, NAACP leader Reverend I. DeQuincey Newman, activist Modjeska Simkins, and other African Americans encouraged sustained activism as a means of effecting racial change. Esau Jenkins, a black businessman from Charleston, with help from NAACP activist and native Charlestonian Septima Clark, Highlander Folk School founder Myles Horton (who was white), beautician Bernice Robinson, and Guy and Candie Carawan (whites who moved to Johns Island), began citizenship schools in the late 1940s and early 1950s to help African Americans obtain the right to vote and overcome the "yoke of [white] domination."[50] The Southern Christian Leadership Conference established citizenship schools in low-country Georgia in the early 1960s under Clark's direction, where African Americans from South Carolina and other states of the Deep South learned about their legal rights and about strategies for civil disobedience. These schools became one of "the most effective organizing tools of the [civil rights] movement." Citizenship schools taught democratic rights and encouraged thousands to take part in demonstrations.[51]

African Americans believed that education was a key to freedom; consequently, separate and unequal education was the foremost target of the civil rights movement in South Carolina. In the early 1940s the NAACP brought court cases to equalize teachers' salaries. Black South Carolinians' most dramatic and influential success against institutionalized white racism involved the *Briggs v. Elliot* case against Clarendon County. This case led to the *Brown* decision, which eventually outlawed segregated schools.[52]

Other important developments in South Carolina included James McCain's work with the Congress of Racial Equality (CORE). Under the leadership of McCain, CORE launched a sustained effort to register African Americans during the late 1950s. A former head of the black teachers' association in South Carolina, McCain established throughout the state seven CORE groups, which later proved instrumental in the South Carolina sit-in movement during the 1960s.[53] In 1958, McCain's troops actually gained control of the Democratic organization in a black-majority precinct in Sumter and supported, without success, an African-American candidate for city council. Despite the urging of CORE's national leadership that he enlist as many whites as possible, McCain found that for white Carolinians, joining an interracial civil rights organization or even supporting a black voter registration drive was unthinkable at the height of "massive resistance" to school desegregation. Rivalry with the NAACP was also a problem, but the two organizations eventually worked out a tacit division of the state.[54]

Black voter registration did not increase dramatically for more than a decade; in 1960 it was still only 58,000, 16 percent of the black voting-age population.[55] By 1962 around 91,000 blacks (23 percent of the black voting-age population) were on the rolls.[56] As in the rest of the South, black registration in South Carolina was still low in counties with a high percentage of African Americans in their population.[57] These old plantation counties, mostly in the low country but including some Piedmont counties, provided most of the members of the White Citizens' Councils formed in the state in the 1950s to rally opposition to school desegregation.[58]

White Reaction to the Civil Rights Movement

Many whites in South Carolina agreed with Governor James F. Byrnes's 1954 declaration that if the state could not "find a legal way of preventing the mixing of the races in the schools, it will mark the beginning of the end of civilization in the South as we have known it."[59] South Carolina whites bitterly opposed federal court decisions that ruled segregated schools unconstitutional, and the NAACP, which organized most African-American plaintiffs in desegregation lawsuits, became the focus of white resistance. NAACP members and their relatives were fired as teachers, and in some cases black leaders fled the state to avoid terrorist activity and legal prosecution.[60] In 1956 the general assembly adopted laws making NAACP members ineligible for state employment, requiring investigation of NAACP activity at traditionally black South Carolina State College, and revising the state's barratry laws so that they could be used against NAACP lawyers who "stirred up" civil rights litigation.[61] CORE organizer Frank Robinson was forced out of his real estate and home-building business when local banks cut off his credit because of his voter registration activities. Students engaging in demonstrations went to jail throughout the state in the early 1960s.[62]

In 1964 South Carolina whites revolted openly against the national Democratic ticket; the Democratic party's commitment to civil rights so alienated Senator Strom Thurmond that he permanently switched to the Republican party. Conservative whites voted as a bloc for Republican presidential nominee Barry Goldwater, enabling him to win 59 percent of the state's vote. Despite overwhelming support from those African Americans able to cast ballots, incumbent Lyndon B. Johnson garnered only 41 percent.[63] More important than all other issues, according to

Fowler, was "the race question, and, more specifically, the fact that Goldwater voted against the Civil Rights Act of 1964 while Johnson was chiefly responsible for its passage."[64] An intensive case study of Ridgeway, South Carolina, found that "a large number of nominal Democrats consistently vote Republican. Virtually all of them cite the Civil Rights issue as their reason."[65]

On the eve of passage of the Voting Rights Act, South Carolina remained thoroughly in the grip of white supremacy. Although 37 percent of the 1964 black voting-age population was registered, this represented only 17 percent of the state's voters on the rolls.[66] South Carolina elected no black officials in the twentieth century before the Voting Rights Act.[67] Whites kept black registration down and sometimes did not count all the votes cast by blacks who did register. Charged with telling a black voter during the 1964 presidential election "to place his ballot in the wrong box," precinct manager Wade H. Ratcliffe explained, "I knew this was wrong but we have always done these things."[68] Immediately following the enactment of the Voting Rights Act, African-American leaders formally complained about white officials' deliberate slowdown of the voter registration process for blacks in Allendale, Barnwell, Charleston, Dorchester, Jasper, and Orangeburg counties, and federal observers were sent to Clarendon and Dorchester.[69]

Despite heroic voter registration drives mounted by CORE, the Voter Education Project,[70] the Southern Christian Leadership Conference, and the NAACP—all involved in "combined efforts" in July and August 1965—these organizations faced great difficulty in overcoming the effects of long years of racial discrimination.[71] Education in particular failed the black community of South Carolina. In his 1911 inaugural gubernatorial address, demagogue Cole Blease stated, "I am opposed to white people's taxes being used to educate Negroes."[72] An analysis of educational expenditures from 1896 to 1960 demonstrates how inequitably the state funded black education.[73] In 1940, for example, South Carolina spent only 30 percent as much to educate a black child as a white child, a lower percentage than any southern state except Mississippi. By 1952, per-pupil expenditures for black children were only 60 percent of the amount spent to educate white children, still behind all southern states except Mississippi. In 1960, half a decade after *Brown*, South Carolina still spent on average 50 percent more per white than per black pupil, a greater disparity than had existed in 1896.[74] Students graduating from high school in 1940 were only in their forties in 1964; those who finished in 1952 were just turning thirty; and those who graduated in 1960 were barely old enough to vote. Thus, given the well-known correlation between educational attainment and voter turnout, the effects of educational disparities lingered for decades as a deterrent to African-American political participation.

Despite the insistence of some Carolinians upon white supremacy, during the 1960s the state continued its move toward "calculated moderation," parting company with the forces of hard-core resistance. Black voter registration drives aroused sporadic violence from angry whites and occasional stalling devices from local officials, although not the massive opposition found in Mississippi, Alabama, Louisiana, or Georgia.[75]

At this time, federal intervention could have proven quite useful. Since adoption of the 1957 Civil Rights Act, the Justice Department had been empowered to bring lawsuits challenging racial discrimination in the registration process. However, because it concentrated its meager resources on even more recalcitrant states, the department's Civil Rights Division as late as 1965 had not filed a single lawsuit challenging South Carolina officials with racial discrimination.[76] Thus, during the debate that year over the Voting Rights Act's section 5 provisions, South Carolina attorney general Daniel R. McLeod and U.S. Representative William Jennings Bryan Dorn pointed to Justice Department inaction to buttress the charge that their state was being labeled guilty without trial. The act's extraordinary intrusion into matters reserved to the states, they argued, was unjustified without proof of intentional discrimination by state or local registration officials. McLeod and Dorn attributed the low level of black voter registration in South Carolina to apathy, not official discrimination.[77]

After the act's passage, the state echoed these protestations of innocence in *South Carolina v. Katzenbach*, but, speaking for an eight-to-one majority, Justice Warren made clear, even while conceding that evidence of recent voting discrimination was more "fragmentary" for South Carolina than for states in the Deep South, that Congress had assembled ample proof that white officials in the covered southern states enforced the literacy test and other devices in a purposefully discriminatory manner against black citizens. The formula for determining the jurisdiction of the act was "rational in both practice and theory," declared Warren, because long-standing use of tests and devices was a direct cause of low black voter registration.[78]

The Continuing Struggle over Voting Rights

With passage of the Voting Rights Act in August 1965, black voter registration soared.[79] By 1967 it had climbed to 51 percent of the age-eligible population. By and large, South Carolina's white officials grudgingly conceded that as in the rest of the South, the Voting Rights Act made it impossible to prevent African-American citizens from registering and casting their ballots.[80] Yet barriers to registration and voting have continued until recently, especially in some rural areas. State law specified that voter registration always occur in a public place, often the courthouse, a potentially intimidating place to many black southerners, for whom it symbolizes the locus of white power. As recently as 1987, according to the director of the Voter Education Project, "in rural areas, some precincts are in all-white areas, and blacks just don't cross the railroad tracks." Local voting registration boards had the discretion to appoint deputies and set office hours. Often offices were not open when black laborers might be available to register.[81]

Registration procedures in Fairfield County exemplify the complications that African Americans encountered as late as the 1980s. The local NAACP, the Progressive Citizens Organization, and Fairfield United Action had been successful in increasing black registration from about 20 percent of potential voters prior to the Voting Rights Act to a majority of them in the mid-1980s. But the county's board of registration continued to resist black registration efforts. The governor, who appoints each county's board upon recommendation from the senate (that is, the county senator), in 1986 appointed two white members and one black member (a domestic worker employed by the Fairfield senator).[82] The board refused requests to allow door-to-door registration drives. It also refused to accept one black deputy registrar's voter applications because the deputy registrar used a computer code instead of the full name for precincts; the following week the board rejected the same deputy's applications because the computer code was not supplied. In 1983, only five deputy registrars were appointed for all the African-American communities in the county. The board refused fourteen applications because a check was not on the registration form next to an item that had no box to check. Only an appeal to the South Carolina Elections Commission forced the acceptance of these new applications.[83] South Carolina now has a postcard registration procedure, which has significantly diminished registration restrictions in South Carolina.[84]

In 1965 it seemed to some observers that black registration increases augured significant change in South Carolina in the near future. The act's ban on the literacy test had "the potential for a political upheaval," warned one reporter, who projected the election of at least twenty-two blacks to the general assembly under the existing districting plan.[85] Two developments, among others, helped avert black officeholding. First, even as black registration increased, so did white registration: from 76 to 82 percent in 1967. Thus, in spite of sharp black registration gains, African Americans that year still comprised a mere 21 percent of total registrants in a state that was 30 percent black.[86]

Another strategy for minimizing the effectiveness of the growing black vote was to enact election laws designed to "dilute" minority voting strength, such as at-large elections, full-slate requirements, or runoff provisions. South Carolina already had a full-slate law (prohibiting the casting of a "single-shot" vote) and a majority vote requirement for most elections. These procedures enhanced the racially discriminatory effects of at-large elections and multimember legislative districts, which were the cornerstone of southern efforts to minimize the impact of increased black voting strength after 1965.[87] When the Voting Rights Act was passed, however, nineteen South Carolina counties elected at least some members of their county governing body by single-member districts, according to a survey by the U.S. Bureau of the Census. By 1973, the bureau's survey indicated that eleven counties had switched entirely to at-large elections.[88]

Many of these changes were challenged in federal court during the next two decades, and their purposes often became a matter of public record. This was not true of the switch to at-large elections for the Charleston County Council in 1969. Available evidence suggests, however, the possibility of an underlying racial purpose. J. Mitchell Graham, who had formerly chaired the county council, explained to a reporter not long after passage of the Voting Rights Act that the existing election plan gave Charlestonians "the guarantee of representation from their own districts."[89] In 1967, however, with blacks running for office throughout the state, the county council asked the local legislative delegation to draft a statute requiring countywide election of council members.[90] The person who chaired the council and pushed successfully for the adoption of at-large elections was Micah Jenkins, who ten years earlier had been among the most visible leaders of the Citizens Council movement in South Carolina.[91] Because a constitutional amendment was a prerequisite for other features of Jenkins's proposed reform of county government, the legislature did not adopt the change until 1969.[92]

The Nexus between Legislative Redistricting and Home Rule

All politics, it is said, is local. Thus when the Voting Rights Act was passed, African Americans hoped it would enable them to wield significant influence at the community level through the election of black candidates. These hopes did not materialize. Political power in South Carolina was not directly responsive to local electorates. A system of legislative county government, established by the Tillman forces during the struggle for disfranchisement in the 1890s, had eliminated county and township elections because conservative whites disliked elected local governments with their "identification with black political power, as well as with high taxes."[93] Since that time, the general assembly provided that the governor appoint county officials upon recommendation of a county's state senator and representatives. This law effectively eliminated the opportunity of African Americans to elect local officials of their choice, even where they were an overwhelming majority of the population.[94]

The power of legislative delegations over county government remained largely intact from 1895 until 1965, even in those few counties where some form of elected councils had been established through local legislation.[95] The general assembly was the center of governmental power in South Carolina, and the senate was clearly the dominant house. Each of the forty-six counties had one senator, elected countywide, and one or more representatives, also elected at large. In no other state was legislative dominance over local government so strong. Key put it succinctly: "County legislative delegations constitute the real governing bodies of their respective counties."[96]

The local legislative delegation often appointed the county governing body as well as local school boards, public service districts, and park boards. Sometimes the legislators themselves served as members of the county council. The delegation supervised the selection of employees and appointments to boards and committees. Most importantly, the delegation set tax levels and submitted the county budget, which was adopted by the entire legislature as the county's "supply bill."[97] Each county's senator, because he could veto any local legislation, usually became its "first-ranking politician."[98]

In December 1965 this system suddenly faced the risk that rural counties would lose their resident senator when the federal court in *O'Shields v. McNair*[99] gave the legislature four months to redistrict the state senate according to the one-person, one-vote principle articulated by the U.S. Supreme Court.[100] Senator Edgar A. Brown of Barnwell County, a thirty-six-year veteran known as the dean of the senate and described as "the most powerful man in South Carolina's government,"[101] characterized reapportionment as the "political crisis of my time." The court's decision, he declared, "invites a return to the kind of government that Wade Hampton had to stamp out in 1876."[102] Warning of a resurgence of the evils of "Black Reconstruction" was a time-honored tactic of southern white Democrats concerned about black voting strength.[103]

Brown and other veteran legislators, however, devised a redistricting plan that minimized the chances of the election of African-American legislators.[104] Its essence was to use as many at-large multimember districts as possible. In order to satisfy the one-person, one-vote rule, the all-white general assembly reapportioned the state senate by shifting from a plan in which all senators were elected from single-member districts (i.e., one per county) to a system relying primarily on multimember senatorial districts. Reapportionment did not require use of multimember districts, however, even in rural areas and certainly not in urban counties.[105] In *O'Shields* the court in 1966 approved an interim reapportionment plan that replaced many of the existing single-member districts with multimember districts.[106] A year later the legislature adopted a permanent plan that included only five single-member districts, dividing the state into fifteen multimember senatorial districts, all of which had a white majority.[107] Only one African American was ever elected to the senate under either of these plans.[108] With that exception, the senate maintained its all-white membership and its at-large elections until 1984, when it became the last southern state legislative body to acquire either single-member districts or African-American members.

Multicounty senatorial districts created a major difficulty for many rural counties because under the redistricting plan adopted in response to *O'Shields*, those counties would no longer be represented by a senator residing within county borders. Having an "outsider" exercise the extraordinary control over local government traditionally accorded the local senator was unacceptable to many Carolinians.[109] The movement to secure local autonomy for South Carolina counties and cities, which culminated in the adoption of a statewide Home Rule Act in 1975, grew directly from resentment over the effects of court-ordered redistricting.[110]

As if increased black voter registration and court-ordered redistricting were not enough for South Carolina whites, a new element entered the picture in 1969. In *Allen v. Board of Elections*, a consolidated case involving various Mississippi and Virginia voting changes, the U.S. Supreme Court ruled that under section 5 of the Voting Rights Act, potentially dilutive procedures such as at-large elections, numbered posts, residency districts, majority-vote requirements, and districting plans were not legally enforceable until submitted for preclearance, either by a three-judge panel in the District of Columbia or by the Department of Justice.[111] Section

5 provided a powerful weapon for enforcing minority voting rights if the jurisdiction had altered its electoral procedures since 1 November 1964 in a manner that had the potential for diluting minority voting strength. The Justice Department then created a special section to review such electoral procedures.[112]

When the South Carolina legislature redistricted after the 1970 census, plaintiffs challenged the plan for each house in court, and each plan underwent section 5 review by the Justice Department.[113] On 6 March 1972, in the first of a series of controversial decisions, the Attorney General objected to the use of multimember districts, numbered posts, majority-vote requirements, and some of the specific district lines in the senate plan, which had no black-majority seats.[114] The general assembly then drew a new plan, which a three-judge court in South Carolina ruled constitutional; the Attorney General, deferring to the court, did not object to its implementation.[115]

A three-judge court also rejected the claim of African-American plaintiffs that the house plan was racially discriminatory; on the other hand, however, it struck down the state's full-slate law on the grounds that to require a person to vote for every office on the ballot was an unreasonable restriction on the right of suffrage.[116] The South Carolina legislature immediately replaced the full-slate law with a numbered-place rule, which required each candidate to qualify for a particular seat (that is, place no. 1, place no. 2, and so forth).[117] Every seat would then be decided through a head-to-head contest in which only one vote could be cast, making single-shot voting impossible.[118] The Department of Justice, in turn, objected to this change under section 5.[119] The house plan was implemented in the 1972 house elections, but without the full-slate requirement. In 1973 the U.S. Supreme Court summarily reversed the decision of the three-judge court that had upheld the constitutionality of the house plan.[120] Forced to redistrict once again, the general assembly nevertheless rejected the complaints of African-American legislators against multimember districts, numbered seats, and the majority-vote requirement. The Department of Justice cited these dilutive devices as evidence of racial discrimination when it objected to the plan under section 5.[121] The legislature finally acquiesced and adopted a single-member district plan, under which the number of African-American representatives increased from four to thirteen in the 1974 elections.[122]

The presence of these new members made a significant difference in the debate over the Home Rule Act in 1975. This omnibus legislation transferred much of the authority for local legislative or administrative decision making away from the county delegation in the general assembly to a popularly elected county council. The Home Rule Bill, as originally passed by the house at the urging of the black caucus, would have required all counties to elect their governing bodies by single-member districts. At one point, racial tensions in the debate threatened to get out of hand when a black Democrat and a white Republican from Columbia "exchanged heated remarks on the single-member provision . . . punctuated by mild profanity."[123] White legislators accepted single-member districts in part because of general awareness that the changes resulting from the Home Rule Act had to undergo Department of Justice scrutiny.[124]

The all-white senate, however, adamantly refused to require district elections, even at the risk of passing no bill at all. Ultimately, a compromise provision required all county councils to be elected from single-member districts, with two exceptions: (1) the voters could approve the use of at-large plans in a referendum; or (2) counties that failed to hold a referendum would be assigned one of five specific forms of government by default. Under the second option, a county was assigned the form most closely approximating its current system, which usually included at-large elections.[125] More than half the counties (twenty-five of forty-six) held referendums; citizens of twenty opted in the referendums for single-member district elections.[126] The Home Rule Act accounted for more than 40 percent (fifteen of thirty-five) of the changes from at-large to district election plans that have occurred in South Carolina county councils between 1974 and 1989 (see table 7.8A).

In South Carolina, the civil rights movement, the Voting Rights Act, one-person, one-vote senate reapportionment, and the rise of the Republican party were intertwined. At the same time that the state's traditional white leadership was faced with increased black and white voting, it was also losing control of day-to-day oversight of county offices. With a political culture constructed on constituent service, loss of control at the local level was a critical challenge. Court-ordered redistricting, which suddenly rendered the traditional system of legislative county government unacceptable to political leaders throughout South Carolina, provided the major stimulus for the home rule movement after 1965. The state legislature and many county governmental bodies shifted to at-large election methods.

In the early 1970s African-American plaintiffs filed and lost a challenge to the process that left the South Carolina senate all white. Plaintiffs, however, won their challenge to the electoral system that resulted in a nearly all-white house of representatives. Consequently, African Americans were a significant force in the new general assembly when the Home Rule Act came up for final passage in 1975. On the county level, however, it was not until the mid-1970s that voting rights lawyers filed the first racial vote-dilution challenges to at-large county governments; almost all the suits were wholly unsuccessful.

The Nexus between Section 5 Enforcement and Litigation

In the 1970s South Carolina had few active voting rights lawyers. Black attorney Matthew Perry, retained by the NAACP, handled much of the civil rights litigation in South Carolina until he was named to the U.S. Court of Military Appeals in 1976.[127] In legislative redistricting cases Perry was cocounsel with Armand Derfner of Washington, D.C., with the Lawyers' Committee for Civil Rights Under Law. Derfner, who had litigated voting rights cases in Mississippi in the 1960s with the Lawyers' Constitutional Defense Committee, moved to Charleston in 1974 and opened a private practice. He was involved in many of the key South Carolina cases, often in cooperation with Laughlin McDonald, a white native of Fairfield County who has directed the Southern Regional Office of the American Civil Liberties Union (ACLU) in Atlanta for over two decades. Other attorneys, both white and black, like John Roy Harper II, an African-American native of Greenwood who grew up in Camden, occasionally brought voting rights cases in the 1970s, but the ACLU was virtually the only source of funds available in South Carolina in the 1970s to cover the heavy expenses of vote-dilution lawsuits.[128]

The experience of private attorneys convinced them that the federal bench in South Carolina was generally unsympathetic to African-American plaintiffs in civil rights cases.[129] In Lee County, for example, where a change from district to at-large elections in 1968 had been precleared by the Department of Justice, Derfner and McDonald thought the facts in the case might nevertheless sustain a constitutional challenge. In 1966, following increased black voter registration in this 60 percent black county, an African-American candidate ran for the board of commissioners and lost by only a few votes. Before the next election Lee County switched to a county council elected at large. Although the plaintiffs provided undisputed evidence of racially polarized voting, racial disparities in socioeconomic status and education, and the virtual exclusion of African Americans from the ranks of poll workers and election officials, Judge Robert F. Chapman in 1976 decided in favor of the county.[130]

The same fate awaited a 1977 challenge to the at-large election of city council members in Columbia filed on behalf of members of the local NAACP by McDonald, black attorneys I. S. Leevy Johnson and John Roy Harper II, and white Columbia attorney Herbert Buhl and tried once again before Judge Chapman.[131] Both Chapman and the three-judge appeals court ruled against the plaintiffs, finding that racially polarized voting was significant but did not "approach totality" because an estimated 25 percent of the vote in predominantly white areas went to an African-American candidate in the most recent election.[132] The courts also rejected the NAACP's claim that the city had been unresponsive to the needs of the African-American community, and dismissed the significance of earlier discrimination such as the literacy test, poll tax, and full-slate requirement on the grounds that, having been struck down by the federal courts or outlawed by the Voting Rights Act, these devices were no longer a barrier to African-American participation. The courts also ruled that the city had adopted at-large elections in 1910 with no discriminatory purpose.[133] Following this ruling, however, the city held a referendum in which voters approved a change to a mixed election system, with four council members elected from single-member districts and two at large, in addition to the mayor. Although devised by a biracial committee and supported by the mayor, the change to district elections occurred only because of overwhelming support in African-American precincts.[134]

Faced with the prospects of trying cases before unsympathetic judges, the voting-rights bar in South Carolina came to appreciate the virtues of the preclearance requirements of section 5, which put the burden of proof on the jurisdiction proposing election law changes, not on minority citizens. Justice Department objections under section 5 caused about one-fourth of the changes in county election method from 1974 to 1989 (nine of thirty-two; see table 7.8A); section 2 litigation prompted about 29 percent of changes (ten of thirty-two); and one county voluntarily changed its method of election after pressure from the NAACP.[135]

The Attorney General objected to the adoption of at-large elections for nine county councils and four school boards during the 1970s.[136] Often litigation was necessary to enforce these objections. With the exception of Charleston County, which successfully challenged the timeliness of the objection in court, all thirteen governments ultimately adopted single-member districts.[137]

Some cities as well as counties switched to district elections as a result of Department of Justice scrutiny. Most cities and towns in South Carolina already used at-large elections, and the Home Rule Act did not require a change. Municipal annexations had to be precleared, however. In 1974, for example, the Attorney General objected to seven annexations of predominantly white areas by the city of Charleston.[138] Polarized voting patterns had characterized recent city elections, and the votes of whites in the annexed areas had a substantial impact on the outcome of the close mayoral election in 1971, swinging the victory to the incumbent mayor.[139] In order to secure preclearance of the annexations, Charleston agreed to adopt a ward election system.[140] As of 1990, the city had six African-American council members out of twelve. Section 5 objections to annexations of white subdivisions led to single-member districts in other cities as well.[141]

Attorneys for plaintiffs were sometimes able to use requirements of section 5 to good advantage in forcing political jurisdictions to change from at-large to district elections. Dorchester County, for example, came under section 5 scrutiny following a previous challenge for faulty redistricting on the basis of the one-person, one-vote rule. In 1973 Derfner and McDonald successfully challenged the districts used in Dorchester county council elections on one-person, one-vote grounds.[142] Rather than redress the malapportionment through redistricting, the county adopted at-large elections. The Department of Justice refused preclearance, noting that racial bloc voting had prevented all African-American candidates from being elected to the council in a county that was 35 percent black.[143] Dorchester then devised a seven-district plan, with two black-majority districts, which the department approved.[144]

Private voting rights attorneys and the Department of Justice have cooperated in attacking South Carolina's at-large voting system. Still, because the department had precleared some changes before the Home Rule Act, some voting rights attorneys believe that in the early years of the Voting Rights Act, "while concentrating on cleaning up barriers to black voter participation, the Justice Department failed to enforce preclearance requirements which allowed many South Carolina counties to establish at-large election methods without objection."[145] Wherever the department failed to file an objection, private attorneys had to bring costly and time-consuming lawsuits. Key cases in South Carolina involved Sumter and Edgefield counties.

Litigation in Sumter County

Litigation regarding the use of at-large elections was complex and produced important struggles on both sides. The Sumter County Council case involved legislative redistricting, fear of black influence after the Voting Rights Act, objections by the Department of Justice, and private litigation. In 1967 Sumter County adopted an elective form of government to replace its appointive system.[146] Sumter was among those counties which chose not to hold a referendum under the 1975 Home Rule Act. The act, therefore, assigned to Sumter the council-administrator form of government, with council members to be elected at large. On 3 December 1976, however, the Attorney General objected to the at-large feature of the plan. Both the Department of Justice and local African-American plaintiffs, represented by white attorney Herbert Buhl of Columbia and black attorney Donald Sampson of Greenville, challenged the unprecleared use of at-large elections for county council in 1978; the court agreed that under the terms of section 5, the county's at-large system was legally unenforceable.[147] In November 1978, the county held a referendum to determine the preference of the electorate, and, in a racially polarized vote, a majority supported the at-large option over a district plan.[148] The county asked that the previous objection be withdrawn in light of the referendum results, but the Department of Justice declined.[149] The county then persuaded a three-judge court in South Carolina that its request for reconsideration was actually a new submission and that, because the department had failed to object within the required sixty days, it had, in fact, precleared the change.[150]

The Department of Justice chose not to appeal this ruling. Sampson, joined by attorney Armand Derfner, took the case to the U.S. Supreme Court and won a reversal.[151] Sumter County then filed a lawsuit seeking preclearance by a three-judge panel in the District of Columbia. After a full trial on the merits, the court refused to preclear the switch to at-large elections, ruling that the county had not met its burden of proof that the original change in 1967 was racially discriminatory in neither purpose nor effect. The court found that the decision to eliminate the legislative appointment of county government was motivated in part by a concern "that a black senate district would be created and the person elected from that district might control appointments to the Sumter County governing body."[152]

Expert testimony in the trial clarified the racial motivation behind the shift from appointive to at-large elected officials in 1967. Sumter was a bastion of racial conservatism, and its resident senator, Henry Richardson, had actively supported the county's White Citizens Council in the 1950s.[153] When the senate redistricting committee broached a plan that would have put Sumter County into a black-majority senatorial district with Clarendon and Williamsburg counties, Richardson and his colleagues threatened a filibuster. The incumbent senator from Williamsburg predicted bluntly that the proposed three-county district might actually elect a black senator.[154] The more likely prospect, at least for the near future, was the election of a white who, in order to attract the support of black voters, might agree to appoint African-American members to the county governing body. The influential Richardson pushed through the legislature a statute creating an elected county council, with all members elected at large, and then managed to force black-majority Williamsburg into another district. Under the state's full-slate law, such a council was more likely to remain all white than it would be under the traditional appointive system.[155] In 1984, after eight years of litigation, Sumter County adopted a plan with seven single-member districts. The council held its first election since 1976; African Americans won three seats.

Litigation in Edgefield County

An even more complex lawsuit, *McCain v. Lybrand* arose in Edgefield County, home of U.S. senator J. Strom Thurmond, who had bitterly opposed the original Voting Rights Act in 1965 and who fought not only the extensions of section 5 in 1970, 1975, and 1982, but the 1982 amendment to section 2.[156] Ten years of lawsuits and proceedings, with an ultimate objection by the Department of Justice in 1984, finally ended the use of at-large elections for the Edgefield county council. In 1969 black activist Tom McCain began efforts to open local governing bodies to African Americans. In 1974, on behalf of African-American plaintiffs led by McCain, attorneys Derfner and McDonald filed a lawsuit challenging the county council's at-large elections. After a trial on the merits in 1975, Judge Robert Chapman took five years to rule.[157] In following the Supreme Court guidelines set forth in *White v. Regester*,[158] Chapman decided that the plaintiffs' expert had presented statistical evidence of "bloc voting by the whites on a scale that this Court has never before observed."[159] When, in 1980, the judge ruled in favor of the plaintiffs, Derfner almost cried. "I have never been more surprised in my life as a lawyer," he said.[160]

Chapman vacated his own opinion, however, when the Supreme Court abruptly enunciated a new "intent standard" in *City of Mobile v. Bolden*, which meant that plaintiffs would have to prove that at-large elections were adopted or maintained with a racially discriminatory purpose.[161] Because of Edgefield's long history of racial discrimination, which continued up to the time of trial, Derfner and McDonald pressed their constitutional claim and began amassing "smoking gun" evidence concerning the change from appointed to elected county council in 1966.[162] At the same time, they amended their complaint to challenge the county's failure to submit the 1966 change to at-large elections for section 5 preclearance. In 1981 a weary McDonald wrote to interested parties of "this seemingly interminable lawsuit."[163] The three-judge district court in South Carolina, however, ruled that the Department of Justice had already precleared this change when it failed to object to a 1971 modification of the at-large system.[164] On behalf of the plaintiffs, McDonald, Derfner, and Buhl appealed to the Supreme Court, which finally in 1984 unanimously reversed the South Carolina panel.[165] The department then objected to the change to at-large elections, and Judge William W. Wilkins, Jr., former assistant to Thurmond, ordered implementation of a single-member-district plan, under which African Americans won three of five seats on the Edgefield county council.[166]

Immediately following this case, black parents sued the Edgefield school board to change from at-large to single-member districts. Because of the tremendous costs incurred by the county during *McCain v. Lybrand*, some prominent Edgefield citizens wanted to change to single-member districts. Instead, school board members insisted on retaining at-large districts. In *Jackson v. Edgefield County, South Carolina, School District*, the school board, like the county council, spared no expense in the defense of discrimination.[167]

Plaintiffs presented evidence at trial of the school board's racially discriminatory behavior for years after the adoption in 1968 of at-large elections to reinforce the inference that the change was racially motivated and that at-large elections were maintained with discriminatory intent. When Congressman Butler Derrick, a native Edgefieldian, testified as a witness for the school board, he conceded that Edgefield County voting was racially polarized. Again Edgefield African-American plaintiffs prevailed; again the cost to the county's citizens was extraordinary. This time the school board did not appeal.[168]

The Edgefield and Sumter cases were important precedents for other counties, cities, and school districts. They encouraged other municipalities to settle out of court. In the city of Sumter, for instance, which was 39 percent black but had only had one African American on council in more than one hundred years, the Justice Department objected to the annexation of a white suburb, and the local NAACP approached the city council about changing to district elections.[169] Mayor W. A. "Bubba" McElveen, having observed Sumter County spend eight years and more than half a million dollars in an unsuccessful attempt to preserve at-large elections, introduced single-member districts in the city. As a result, blacks won three of six single-member-district seats.[170] Following *Jackson v. Edgefield County, South Carolina, School District*, Edgefield County African Americans filed lawsuits to change the method of election from at-large to single-member districts in the cities of Edgefield, Johnston, and Trenton. These cities immediately negotiated settlements.

"When Sumter and Edgefield fell, the rest came tumbling down," said longtime NAACP activist Adell Adams. The *Columbia State*, arguably the most influential newspaper in South Carolina, agreed. Coming on the heels of the 1982 revision of section 2, which made it possible for minority plaintiffs to win vote-dilution lawsuits without proof of discriminatory intent, the lengthy and costly court losses by Sumter and Edgefield counties "marked the beginning of the end of at-large governments in South Carolina."[171] *McCain v. Lybrand* clarified section 5 preclearance in the state, and gave the section 5 unit of the Justice Department firmer precedents with which to insist on changes in other jurisdictions.

After the *McCain* Supreme Court decision affecting Edgefield, adjacent Saluda County settled out of court. Several other counties and cities adopted single-member districts under similar litigation or threat thereof. In 1987 Laurens County, facing objections from the NAACP, the ACLU, and the Justice Department to its at-large system, approved a single-member-district plan, and two African Americans were elected to its council. Abbeville County had never elected a black county council member until the NAACP and ACLU sued the county and the city. When the county went to district elections in 1989, two African Americans were elected. In Barnwell County the NAACP and ACLU again sued, and the county, under its first district elections, elected three black council members. In 1988 Columbia attorney John Roy Harper II and NAACP attorney Willie Abrams sued Richland County. The county settled before trial; eleven districts were drawn, and four African Americans won election out of the first six districts phased in that year (see table 7.8A).[172]

Role of the NAACP in Litigation

In voting rights litigation, local NAACP members and officers were generally the plaintiffs in suits brought by Buhl, Derfner, Harper, McDonald, and other attorneys in the 1970s and early 1980s. At its annual meeting in 1980, the South Carolina State Conference of Branches resolved to dismantle all at-large systems of elections that diluted African-American voting strength. In 1981 the national NAACP's general counsel, Thomas Atkins, visited the state and brought Margarett Ford, an assistant general counsel. Ford was assigned to South Carolina and worked primarily on the South Carolina House and Senate redistricting as well as on congressional issues. In 1985, Dennis Hayes, NAACP staff attorney responsible for the voting rights docket, joined Ford in South Carolina to work on reapportionment and redistricting. Hayes encouraged local NAACP branches to broaden their grass-roots activism and local participation. His proddings to file section 2 lawsuits in South Carolina fell on the receptive ears of Adell Adams, chair of the Political Action Committee of the state NAACP; John Roy Harper II, general counsel of the South Carolina NAACP; Dr. William E. Gibson, president of the South Carolina State Conference of Branches; and Nelson Rivers, who was hired as executive secretary of the state conference at about the same time Hayes began work in the state. With a statewide network of local branches, the NAACP, beginning in November 1986, made its primary focus local at-large election systems that diluted the votes of South Carolina's African Americans. Rivers, who characterized the at-large system as a dinosaur and "a thing of the past," told NAACP branch presidents that "where there is an NAACP branch president and at-large voting system in the same city or town, one of the two must go."[173] Thus in the late 1980s the South Carolina NAACP, with the full backing of the national office in Baltimore, initiated a number of successful voting rights lawsuits.

Beyond litigation, the NAACP branches have been successful in political negotiations to convince counties, cities, towns, and school boards to voluntarily dismantle at-large systems. For example, the city of Spartanburg, which is 41 percent black, had one African-American city council member, a successful and popular high school football coach. Black citizens wanted more representation, and the local branch of the NAACP in 1987 convinced Hayes, along with Greenville black attorney Michael Talley, to bring suit against the city council. The Justice Department subsequently intervened (having objected to the annexation of a predominantly white area in Spartanburg as early as 16 July 1985). The case in Spartanburg was settled, and African Americans were elected in three of the six single-member districts.[174] Following the successful settlement of the suit against the city, the local NAACP approached the county council with its maps and plans; the county council, in light of the city's decision to settle its lawsuit, agreed to adopt a district plan. A referendum passed in March 1990, and a district plan was implemented that year.

Although litigation was not involved in the Spartanburg County Council change, threat of litigation was clear to all involved. In response to the question, "Do you know the reason the county changed to a district method of electing county officials?" a city official answered, "The NAACP forced the district method."[175] The ACLU, often working with the NAACP, continued its attack in other jurisdictions as well. Cases were often settled; believing that chances of successfully defending citywide or countywide voting were small, local governments adopted district election plans (see table 7.8A). As a result, black representation increased dramatically (see tables 7.5 and 7.5A).

Racial Bloc Voting

Proof of racial bloc voting was a crucial element to the success of lawsuits. In 1965 a Columbia newspaper concluded that "bloc voting in the Piedmont State exists, among Negroes and whites." As evidence, the paper pointed to the 1964 Democratic primary for the South Carolina House of Representatives. "In several local elections of recent vintage," it continued, "with Negro and white candidates in the field, both races have voted with color-consciousness, as blocs."[176] Even in recent years, courts have found that racially polarized voting characterized South Carolina jurisdictions.[177] Defendants in other lawsuits agreed to go to district plans after courts ruled that plaintiffs had established a prima facie case of racial bloc voting.[178] In a recent statewide redistricting lawsuit, the court relied on extensive expert testimony demonstrating ongoing evidence of racially polarized voting.[179] The Department of Justice has also referred to evidence of bloc voting in thirty-eight separate section 5 objections between 1974 and 1992.[180]

A recently published statewide study reinforces judicial findings for particular jurisdictions in South Carolina. Loewen examined precinct-level data from 130 contests held from 1972 to 1984 between black and white candidates. Over two-thirds were elections for local office in both rural and urban jurisdictions from every section of South Carolina. An average of 90 percent of white voters cast their ballots as a bloc for white candidates; African Americans were almost as cohesive, voting for candidates of their own race 85 percent of the time.[181] With such racially polarized electoral behavior, at-large elections in majority-white jurisdictions inhibit African-American representation to a substantial degree. State officials conceded in 1987 that "there are few methods other than at-large election methods to dissuade blacks from voting or seeking council seats."[182] And the research director of the Atlanta-based Voter Education Project observed that "the at-large election system is the most effective tool to deny blacks equal representation. Until the fundamental question of at-large systems is addressed, we're going to have places like South Carolina and North Carolina where blacks are largely underrepresented."[183]

The Impact of Single-Member Districts

A simple method of measuring the impact of election methods on minority representation is to compare the percentage of black officeholders in at-large systems with the percentage elected under district plans.[184] A better method is to compare the proportionality of black officeholders in the two types of system, using an "equity measure," such as the ratio of blacks on council to blacks in the city population. As in the other state chapters in this volume, we have used such measures of black representation to examine the impact of changes in election structure on black officeholding.

County governing bodies are the primary focus of our analysis of South Carolina for several reasons (although data on cities are presented in several tables). Relatively few cities had changed to single-member districts by 1989, and the paucity of cases made it difficult to draw firm conclusions. Moreover, in recent years county councils (along with the state legislature) have been the central battleground in the conflict over election methods. At the time of our survey, voting rights lawsuits and objections by the Department of Justice had affected South Carolina counties to a greater degree than cities. Black electoral efforts, as well as black electoral success, had come mainly on the county level. Finally, we focus on county government because of its significance in South Carolina, especially in rural counties. As recently as 1980, 49.1 percent of all the state's African Americans still lived in rural areas. County governments maintain roads and operate schools. As Blough puts it, counties "have been the most important kind of local government during much of the history of this rural state . . . [and] in recent years counties have undergone the most radical transformation of all local governments."[185]

The indisputable finding of our survey is that African Americans in white-majority counties are more fully represented under single-member-district plans than under at-large systems (see table 7.1A).[186] Counties with mixed plans also elected a higher percentage of African Americans than those with at-large systems, but no blacks were elected to the at-large seats within mixed plans in 1989 (see table 7.3A). Only in black-majority counties did method of election make little difference. Where African Americans were no longer in the minority, at-large elections did not prevent them from winning. The equity measures presented in table 7.4A reveal the same pattern, but demonstrate that even in counties using district elections, African Americans were not elected in numbers corresponding to their percentage of the population.

A before-and-after comparison, as displayed in table 7.2A, demonstrates that changes from at-large to single-member district systems substantially increased minority representation on South Carolina county councils between 1974 and 1989. Whatever their racial composition, counties using at-large elections in 1974 had only a small share of African-American council members. The equity ratio employed in table 7.5A measures the same trend more effectively. In counties between 10 and 29.9 percent black that changed from at-large to districts, the proportionality of black representation increased from a score of 0.15 to 0.82 between 1974 and 1989. In counties between 30 and 49.9 percent black, it increased from 0.08 to 0.72. Although single-shot voting (i.e., voting for only one person when more than one could be elected—a method that sometimes enables blacks to win at-large seats) was possible in at-large systems in South Carolina, counties that retained at-large elections witnessed only a minimal increase in black representation between 1974 and 1989, except where blacks were a majority.[187]

The discriminatory effects of at-large elections are consistent with the evidence presented earlier that voting behavior in South Carolina remains highly polarized along racial lines. The district-by-district results presented in table 7.6A further strengthen this conclusion. In districts less than 30 percent black, only 2 percent of the council members elected in 1989 were African Americans; in those between 30 and 49.9 percent black, only 10.2 percent were. Districts between 50 and 59.9 percent black were, in effect, swing districts; blacks made up, on average, 54.3 percent of the population but comprised only 36.4 percent of the council members elected. In districts 60 percent and above, by contrast, a minimum of 82.2 percent of the council seats were filled by African Americans.

Only a few cities had adopted single-member districts by the time of our survey.[188] For purposes of comparison with other states, we display election results in tables 7.1 through 7.6 for cities of at least 10,000 with a black population of at least 10 percent. (South Carolina has no cities in this category with an African-American majority.) The small number of cities involved minimizes the statistical significance of the findings. We have, however, included every city in each category.

City election results are similar to our findings concerning county councils. The most obvious finding is that single-member-district plans in cities afforded African Americans the best opportuntity to elect candidates of their choice (see table 7.1). Although minority representation in mixed plans was also significantly higher than minority representation in at-large plans, black candidates won only in the district portions of these plans; none won at-large seats in cities with mixed plans (see table 7.3).

The effectiveness of single-member districts in terms of minority representation in cities can be seen clearly from table 7.4. By 1989 the nine white-majority cities that used single-member-distict plans had gone beyond representational parity. The dramatically divergent record of the seven white-majority cities that still used at-large elections demonstrates the detrimental effects of this dilutive device on minority officeholding.

The pattern of change over time in cities is also analogous to the pattern found in county councils. The change from at-large to single-member disticts in white-majority cities greatly increased minority officeholding between 1974 and 1989. While black representation in the nine cities that changed to single-member districts increased tremendously in 1989 over 1974, in the seven cities that retained at-large systems black representation increased only modestly (see tables 7.2 and 7.5).

Table 7.6, showing city data, reinforces our conclusion in Table 7.6A, showing county data, that voting patterns in South Carolina remain divided by race. White-majority districts elected not a single African American to city office. In black-majority districts, on the other hand, African Americans held three-quarters of the seats in districts between 50 and 59.9 percent black and all seats in districts 60 percent black or greater.[189]

Conclusion

Although the struggle for fair elections continues in South Carolina, the Voting Rights Act brought enormous change to the state's politics. The increase in African-American voter registration and turnout almost immediately eliminated the white supremacist rhetoric that had been a hallmark of the state's political leaders. Increased African American representation has come more slowly. Even today, black representation on county councils, city governing boards, and school boards is in general far from proportional. The number of African Americans in state elected offices remains woefully small (see table 7.10). Still, the equity ratio for all county councils at least 10 percent black more than tripled between 1974 and 1989, from 0.21 to 0.71; for the cities we surveyed it increased from 0.07 to 0.85. Most of this increase resulted from the change from at-large to single-member-district plans.

Lawsuits by private plaintiffs, along with Department of Justice objections and litigation, have played a significant role in the shift of South Carolina counties to single-member districts since 1974. Often litigation, or the threat of litigation, prompted a county to submit a change to the Department of Justice, leading then to an objection. Voluntary changes, especially those adopted pursuant to the Home Rule Act in 1976, indicate a growing willingness on the part of some whites in some counties to accommodate minority representation, as well as a growing preference for district elections among whites for nonracial reasons. Not all were as resistant as Edgefield or Sumter.

Nowhere in the state were the changes wrought by the Voting Rights Act more dramatic than in Edgefield County, home of "Pitchfork Ben" Tillman and Senator J. Strom Thurmond. On 1 January 1985, three African Americans were sworn in as county council members, giving them majority control. The ceremony took place in the same courthouse seized at gunpoint by the "Redeemers" of 1876 to prevent African Americans from voting and to control the ballot count.[190] Even when whites later recaptured the majority on the county council in 1986, African Americans retained political influence. In 1984, when African Americans won majority control of the county council, the lame-duck white incumbents responded by signing an unprecedented two-year contract with the incumbent white administrator, in an attempt to tie the hands of the incoming black majority.[191] In 1985 the newly inaugurated county council replaced the incumbent anyway with Dr. Thomas McCain, the black educator who had led the court battles responsible for the victory.[192] When the 1986 elections swung the margin back to a three-two white majority, however, the new council did not replace Dr. McCain, and he remains as Edgefield County administrator today. In the words of local white businessman and publisher of the *Edgefield Citizen-News*, Bettis C. Rainsford, "I think he's done a helluva job and everybody else does, too."[193] The white-majority council's and white Edgefieldians' acceptance of McCain as county administrator proves that single-member districts can make a difference, even in the home county of "Pitchfork Ben" Tillman.

TABLE 7.1
Black Representation on City Councils in 1989 by Election Plan, South Carolina Cities of 10,000 or More Population with 10 Percent or More Black Population in 1980

Type of Plan by % Black in City Population, 1980	N	*Mean % Black in City Population, 1980*	*Mean % Black on City Council, 1989*
SMD plan			
10–29.9	2	18.65	25.00
30–49.9	7	41.73	45.24
50–100	0	—	—
Mixed plan			
10–29.9	1	29.47	25.00
30–49.9	4	40.43	33.33
50–100	0	—	—
At-large plan			
10–29.9	5	15.56	3.33
30–49.9	2	37.08	15.48
50–100	0	—	—

TABLE 7.1A
Black Representation on County Council in 1989 by Election Plan, South Carolina Counties of 10 Percent or More Black Population in 1980[a]

Type of Plan by % Black in County Population, 1980	N	*Mean % Black in County Population, 1980*	*Mean % Black on County Council, 1989*
SMD plan			
10–29.9	9	23.79	14.93
30–49.9	14	40.35	27.45
50–100	9	58.00	41.82
Mixed plan			
10–29.9	2	23.45	19.05
30–49.9	2	34.11	14.29
50–100	0	—	—
At-large plan			
10–29.9	2	22.24	8.33
30–49.9	2	32.77	7.14
50–100	3	56.79	42.86

[a]Colleton had a multimember district plan, but is included in the single-member-district category. Colleton had two large districts that elected three members from each district. Beaufort had one multimember district, three single-member districts, and three at-large seats and is included in the mixed category.

TABLE 7.2
Changes in Black Representation on City Councils between 1974 and 1989, South Carolina Cities of 10,000 or More Population with 10 Percent or More Black Population in 1980

Type of Change by % Black in City Population, 1980	N	*Mean % Black in City Population, 1980*	*Mean % Black on City Council*	
			Before Change (1974)	*After Change (1989)*
		Changed Systems		
From at-large to SMD plan				
10–29.9	2	18.65	0.00	25.00
30–49.9	7	41.73	2.14	45.23
50–100	0	—	—	—
From at-large to mixed plan				
10–29.9	1	29.47	0.00	25.00
30–49.9	4	40.43	4.17	33.33
50–100	0		—	—
		Unchanged Systems		
At-large plan				
10–29.9	5	15.56	0.00	3.33
30–49.9	2	37.08	8.34	15.48
50–100	0	—	—	—

TABLE 7.2A
Changes in Black Representation on County Councils between 1974 and 1989, South Carolina Counties of 10 Percent or More Black Population in 1980

Type of Change by % Black in County Population, 1980	N[a]	*Mean % Black in County Population, 1980*	*Mean % Black on County Council* Before Change (1974)	*Mean % Black on County Council* After Change (1989)
		Changed Systems		
From at-large to SMD plan				
10–29.9	4	25.06	3.85	20.59
30–49.9	11	40.01	3.39	28.75
50–100	7	56.74	11.43	37.21
From at-large to mixed plan				
10–29.9	1	22.13	0.00	16.67
30–49.9	1	35.31	0.00	0.00
50–100	0	—	—	—
		Unchanged Systems		
At-large plan				
10–29.9	2	22.24	0.00	8.33
30–49.9	2	32.77	7.14	7.14
50–100	3	56.79	15.38	42.86

[a] *N*s differ from those in table 7.1A because some counties did not have at-large plans in 1974.

TABLE 7.3
Black Representation in 1989 in Mixed Plans by District and At-Large Components, South Carolina Cities of 10,000 or More Population with 10 Percent or More Black Population in 1980

% Black in City Population, 1980	N	*Mean % Black Councilpersons in District Components, 1989*	*Mean % Black Councilpersons in At-large Components, 1989*
10–29.9	1	33.00	0.00
30–49.9	4	53.33	0.00
50–100	0	—	—

TABLE 7.3A
Black Representation in 1989 in Mixed Plans by District and At-Large Components, South Carolina Counties with 10 Percent or More Black Population in 1980[a]

% Black in County Population, 1980	N	*Mean % Black Councilpersons in District Components*	*Mean % Black Councilpersons in At-large Components*
10–29.9	2	21.05	0.00
30–49.9	2	28.57	0.00
50–100	0	—	—

[a] Beaufort had three at-large representatives, three single-member districts, and one multimember district from which three representatives were selected. Aiken, Horry, and Saluda county chairpersons were elected at large. These three counties listed their method of election as single-member district. However, because one member was elected at large, the counties were categorized as mixed. Saluda County had no black representatives from the four districts. The black population was dispersed throughout the county so that a district could not be created to give black candidates a majority district.

TABLE 7.4
Two Equity Measures Comparing Percentage Black on City Council in 1989 with Percentage Black in City Population in 1980, South Carolina Cities of 10,000 or More Population with 10 Percent or More Black Population in 1980

Type of Plan by % Black in City Population, 1980	N	*Difference Measure (% on Council − % in Population)*	*Ratio Measure (% on Council ÷ % in Population)*
		Changed Systems	
From at-large to SMD plan			
10–29.9	2	6.35	1.34
30–49.9	7	3.51	1.13
50–100	0	—	—
From at-large to mixed plan			
10–29.9	1	−4.47	0.85
30–49.9	4	−7.1	0.82
50–100	0	—	—
		Unchanged Systems	
At-large plan			
10–29.9	5	−12.23	0.23
30–49.9	2	−21.6	0.42
50–100	0	—	—

TABLE 7.4A
Two Equity Measures Comparing Percentage Black on County Council in 1989 with Percentage Black in County Population in 1980, South Carolina Counties with 10 Percent or More Black Population in 1980[a]

Type of Plan by % Black in County Population, 1980	N	*Difference Measure (% on Council − % in Population)*	*Ratio Measure (% on Council ÷ % in Population)*
		Changed Systems	
From at-large to SMD plan			
10–29.9	4	−4.47	0.82
30–49.9	11	−11.26	0.72
50–100	7	−19.53	0.66
From at-large to mixed plan			
10–29.9	1	−5.46	0.75
30–49.9	1	−35.31	0.00
50–100	0	—	—
		Unchanged Systems	
At-large plan			
10–29.9	2	−13.91	0.37
30–49.9	2	−25.63	0.22
50–100	3	−13.93	0.75

[a]These data are calculated directly from 1989 figures in table 7.2A.

TABLE 7.5
Changes in Black Representation on City Councils between 1974 and 1989, South Carolina Cities of 10,000 or More Population with 10 Percent or More Black Population in 1980 (Ratio Equity Measure)

Type of Change by % Black in City Population, 1980	N	*Black Representational Equity on Council*	
		1974	*1989*
	Changed Systems		
From at-large to SMD plan			
10–29.9	2	0.00	1.34
30–49.9	7	0.05	1.13
50–100	0	—	—
From at-large to mixed plan			
10–29.9	1	0.00	0.85
30–49.9	4	0.09	0.82
50–100	0	—	—
	Unchanged Systems		
At-large plan			
10–29.9	5	0.00	0.23
30–49.9	2	0.21	0.42
50–100	0	—	—

TABLE 7.5A
Changes in Black Representation on County Councils between 1974 and 1989, South Carolina Counties with 10 Percent or More Black Population in 1980[a]
(Ratio Equity Measure)

Type of Change by % Black in County Population, 1980	N	*Minority Representational Equity on Council*	
		1974	*1989*
	Changed Systems		
From at-large to SMD plan			
10–29.9	4	0.15	0.82
30–49.9	11	0.08	0.72
50–100	7	0.20	0.66
From at-large to mixed plan			
10–29.9	1	0.00	0.75
30–49.9	1	0.00	0.00
50–100	0	—	—
	Unchanged Systems		
At-large plan			
10–29.9	2	0.00	0.37
30–49.9	2	0.22	0.22
50–100	3	0.27	0.75

[a]These data are calculated from the data in table 7.2A.

TABLE 7.6
Black Council Representation in City Council Single-Member Districts in 1989, South Carolina Cities of 10,000 or More Population with 10 Percent or More Black Population in 1980[a]

% Black Population of District	N	*Mean % Black Population in Districts, 1980*	*Mean % Black Councilpersons in Districts, 1989*
0–29.9	35	9.38	0.00
30–49.9	4	33.75	0.00
50–59.9	4	57.20	75.00
60–64.9	4	63.58	100.00
65–69.9	9	66.13	100.00
70–100	15	77.30	100.00

[a]Complete information was obtained on districts in twelve of fourteen cities.

TABLE 7.6A
Black Representation in County Council Single-Member Districts in 1989, South Carolina Counties of 10 Percent or More Black Population in 1980[a]

% Black Population of District	N	*Mean % Black Population in Districts, 1980*	*Mean % Black Councilpersons in Districts, 1989*
0–29.9	99	15.16	2.00
30–49.9	49	39.82	10.20
50–59.9	22	54.31	36.40
60–64.9	17	62.38	88.20
65–69.9	17	67.20	82.40
70–100	11	75.89	90.90

[a]Complete information was obtained for districts in 30 of 36 counties.

TABLE 7.7
Black City Council Representation in Single-Member Districts in 1989 by Racial Composition of District, South Carolina Cities of 10,000 or More Population with 10 Percent or More Black Population in 1980

Racial Composition of District	N	*Mean % Black Population in Districts, 1980*	*Mean % Black Councilpersons in Districts, 1989*
Black majority	32	70.35	96.88
White majority	39	11.88	00.00

TABLE 7.7A
Black County Council Representation in Single-Member Districts in 1989 by Racial Composition of District, South Carolina Counties with 10 Percent or More Black Population in 1980

Racial Composition of District	N	*Mean % Black Population in Districts, 1980*	*Mean % Black Councilpersons in Districts, 1989*
Black majority	67	63.17	70.15
White majority	148	23.33	4.73

TABLE 7.8
Cause of Change from At-Large to Mixed or District Plan between 1974 and 1989, South Carolina Cities 10,000 or More Population with 10 Percent or More Black Population in 1980

City	*Did Lawsuit Accompany Change?*	*Lawsuit/Reason for Change*[a]
	Changed to Single-Member Districts	
Charleston	No	Change necessary to secure Justice Department preclearance of annexations; redistricting, 1983
Easley	No	—
Greenwood	No	Change to districts, 1988. Voluntary; consulted with NAACP
Greer	No	Voluntary change at the request of local NAACP in 1987; two black-majority districts out of six; phased in, so that the second black district did not elect until 1989
Laurens	Yes	*Glover v. Laurens*
Orangeburg	Yes	*Owens v. City of Orangeburg*
Rock Hill	No	Annexation objection and negotiations with NAACP.
Spartanburg	Yes	*NAACP and United States v. Spartanburg*
Sumter	No	Change necessary to secure Department of Justice preclearance of annexations, 1986. Negotiations with NAACP

(*continued*)

TABLE 7.8 (*Continued*)

City	*Did Lawsuit Accompany Change?*	*Lawsuit/Reason for Change*[a]
		Changed to Mixed Plan
Aiken	No	—
Anderson	No	Voluntary change, Home Rule Act, 1976; redistricting, 1985
Columbia	No	Voluntary change by referendum to mixed plan in 1982 following successful defense of at-large elections in *Washington v. Finlay*
Florence	Yes	*Jones v. Tedder,* C.A. No. 76-831 (D.S.C.), consent decree, 1977; one councilmember elected at large, three from single-member districts, plus mayor; redistricting 1984
Greenville	No	Voluntary change, Home Rule Act, 1977; redistricting, 1983
SUMMARY	Yes	4 (28.6%)
	No	10 (71.4%)

Source: Legal research and interviews with civil rights attorneys; Municipal Association of South Carolina.

[a]Cities of Easley and Aiken could not provide information on reasons for change.

TABLE 7.8A
Cause of Change from At-Large to Mixed or District Plan between 1974 and 1989, South Carolina Counties with 10 Percent or More Black Population in 1980

County	*Did Lawsuit Accompany Change?*	*Lawsuit/Reason for Change*
	Changed to Single-Member Districts	
Abbeville	Yes	Litigation by NAACP and ACLU: *Robinson v. Savitz,* Consent Decree (D.S.C.), 1989
Allendale	Yes	Litigation by NAACP: *Allendale County NAACP v. Henry Laffitte* (D.S.C.), 1976
Anderson	No	Home Rule Act[b]
Bamberg	No	Department of Justice objection, 20 September 1974
Barnwell	Yes	Litigation by NAACP and ACLU: *Houston v. Barnwell County* (D.S.C.), 1988
Berkeley	No	Home Rule Act
Calhoun	No	Home Rule Act
Cherokee	No	Home Rule Act; referendum
Chester	Yes	Department of Justice objection, 28 October 1977; *King v. Roddey,* consolidated with *United States v. Chester County,* (D.S.C.), 1979
Chesterfield	No	Home Rule Act
Colleton	Yes	Department of Justice objections, 6 February 1978, 19 December 1979; *Colleton County Council v. United States* (D.D.C.), 1982
Darlington	Yes	*United States v. Darlington County* (D.S.C.), 1986
Dorchester	Yes	Department of Justice objection, 22 April 1974; *DeLee v. Branton* (D.S.C.), 1974
Edgefield	Yes	*McCain v. Lybrand* (D.S.C.), 1974–84; Department of Justice objections, 8 February 1979, 11 June 1984
Fairfield	Yes	Litigation by ACLU: *Walker v. Fairfield County Council* (D.S.C.), 1988; Council asked the ACLU to bring suit. Majority-black county

(*continued*)

TABLE 7.8A (*Continued*)

County	*Did Lawsuit Accompany Change?*	*Lawsuit/Reason for Change*
		had already elected three of five black council members when elections were at large
Florence	No	Home Rule Act
Georgetown	Yes	Consent Decree; *Watkins v. Scoville* (D.S.C.), 1982–84
Greenville	No	Home Rule Act
Greenwood	No	Voluntary, but NAACP worked behind scenes
Laurens	Yes	Litigation by ACLU; *Beasley v. Laurens County, United States v. Laurens County* (D.S.C.), 1988 Consent Decree
Lee	No	Home Rule Act
Marion	No	Home Rule Act
Marlboro	No	Home Rule Act
Newberry	No	Home Rule Act
Orangeburg	No	Home Rule Act
Richland	Yes	*NAACP v. Richland County* (D.S.C.), 1988
Sumter	Yes	Department of Justice objection, 3 December 1976, *Blanding v. Dubose,* joined with *United States v. Sumter County* (D.S.C.), 1978; *Sumter County v. United States* (D.D.C.), 1982
Union	Yes	*Lytle v. Commissioners of Election of Union County* (D.S.C.), 1974; Home Rule Act
York	No	Department of Justice objection, 12 November 1974; Home Rule Act; referendum
	Changed to Mixed Plan	
Aiken	No	Department of Justice objection, 25 August 1972; Home Rule Act
Horry	Yes	Department of Justice objection, 12 November 1976; *Horry County v. United States* (D.D.C), 1978

(*continued*)

TABLE 7.8A (*Continued*)

County	Did Lawsuit Accompany Change?	Lawsuit/Reason for Change
Saluda	Yes	Litigation by ACLU: *Lewis v. Saluda County* (D.S.C.), 1983–85, Consent Decree
SUMMARY	Yes	16 (50%)
	No	16 (50%)

[a] Beaufort is not included in this table because it changed before 1974. Spartanburg is not included because it changed after 1989.

[b] In 1975 the Home Rule Act (explained in text) required every county to select a form of government. Twenty-four of the forty-six counties held referendums. If a county did not schedule a referendum, the Home Rule Act assigned, of five government systems, that nearest to the county's 1975 form of government.

TABLE 7.9
Major Disfranchising Devices in South Carolina

Device	Date Established	Date Abolished
White primary	Selected places 1876; statewide, 1896	1947[a] 1947[a]
Separate ballots and boxes for state and federal elections	1878	1895[b]
Reregistration of all voters	1882	One-time measure
Eight Box Law	1882	1895[b]
Appointment of all legislature by local officials	1894	1975[c]
Poll tax	1895	1951[d]
Denial of right to vote for commission of certain crimes	1895	1982[e]
Reregistration of all voters	1896	One-time measure
Literacy test	1895	1965[f]
Understanding clause	1896	1965[f]
Short registration hours and time	1896	1967, 1968, 1986[g]
Lengthy residency requirement	1896	1972[h]
Party loyalty oath	1944	1947, 1948[i]
Local private party clubs	1944	1947, 1948[i]

[a] *Elmore v. Rice*, 72 F. Supp. 516 (E.D.S.C. 1947), *aff'd sub nom. Rice v. Elmore*, 165 F.2d 387 (4th Cir. 1947), *cert. denied*, 333 U.S. 875 (1948).

[b] State constitution (1895). Rendered superfluous by disfranchising features in state constitution.

[c] State legislature (1975).

[d] Amendment to state constitution (1951).

[e] State Legislature (1981); influenced by *Allen v. Ellisor*, 477 F. Supp 321 (D.S. C. 1979), *rev'd and remanded*, 664 F.2d 391 (4th cir. 1981).

[f] Voting Rights Act (1965).

[g] Act 443 State Legislature (1967); creation of South Carolina Election Commission (1968); postcard registration (1986).

[h] Unconstitutional in light of *Dunn v. Blumstein*, 405 U.S. 330 (1972).

[i] *Elmore v. Rice* (1947); *Brown v. Baskin, 78 F. Supp. 933* (E.D.S.C. 1948); *aff'd*, 174 F.2d 391 (4th Cir. 1949).

TABLE 7.10
Black and White Registered Voters and Officeholders in South Carolina, Selected Years[a]

	Black		*White*	
	N	%	N	%
Registered voters				
1964	144,000	17	703,000	83
1966	191,000	21	718,000	79
1990	354,000	26	1,000,000	74
Officeholders				
State house				
1964	0	0	124	100
1966	0	0	124	100
1990	16	13	108	87
State senate				
1964	0	0	46	100
1966	0	0	46	100
1990	5	11	41	89

Sources: South Carolina Election Commission 1990 and 1991; Joint Center for Political and Economic Studies 1990 and 1991; U.S. Commission on Civil Rights 1968, 219, 252–53.

[a]Mean black South Carolina population, 1960–90 = 31.4%.

CHAPTER EIGHT

Texas

ROBERT BRISCHETTO, DAVID R. RICHARDS, CHANDLER DAVIDSON, AND BERNARD GROFMAN

TEXAS is not one of the seven states originally covered by the special provisions of the Voting Rights Act,[1] but it has been a major battleground on which the struggle over minority voting rights has occurred. While the African-American population in Texas is proportionally smaller than that in any of the other seven states, in absolute numbers it is larger. In fact, Texas blacks and Hispanics[2] together—6.3 million strong in 1990—slightly outnumbered the black population of the entire Deep South region composed of Mississippi, Alabama, Louisiana, Georgia, and South Carolina.

The proportion of Texas blacks and Hispanics combined is as great as the black proportion in Mississippi, which has the largest black ratio of any state. In 1990 blacks and Hispanics made up 11.9 and 25.6 percent of the state's population, respectively, for a total of almost 37 percent. Over 96 percent of the remaining inhabitants were Anglos, that is, white non-Hispanics.[3]

A review of the history of minority voting rights in Texas provides a short course in the evolution of the federal government's role in protecting the franchise. At the turn of the century the state established by statute and practice formidable barriers to voting.[4] Today, almost entirely as a result of federal litigation, only vestiges remain to remind us of the lengthy struggle by the state's two largest minority groups for access to the ballot. But voting rights encompass more than the right to cast a ballot and have it fairly counted. They include the right of previously excluded minority groups to have an equal chance to elect their candidates to office. The attack on the infringement of this right is of more recent vintage, and it is far from completion. The present chapter tells the story of minority efforts both to vote without hindrance and to overcome barriers to fair representation.

AFRICAN AMERICANS

The emancipation of slaves in Texas began with the arrival of federal troops in Galveston on 19 June 1865, although some slaveholders refused to free blacks until the fall.[5] An all-white constitutional convention met the following year. The new constitution it produced did not extend the suffrage even to literate blacks; and the first legislature thereafter prohibited "intermarriage, voting, officeholding, and jury service by freedmen."[6] Only with congressional passage of the Reconstruction acts in 1867 were the state's African Americans enfranchised.[7] Thus was established a century-long pattern following emancipation in which Texas officialdom denied the political rights of blacks, whose only recourse was to the federal government.

Congressional Reconstruction, as a precondition for Texas's reentry into the Union, required the enfranchisement of blacks and the convening of a new constitutional convention, which was held in 1868–69. It was dominated by Radical Republicans as a result of widespread refusal by white voters to participate, in protest of federal military rule.[8] Although two-thirds of the votes polled on the convention question were cast by African Americans, who were voting in their first election in Texas, only ten of the ninety-three delegates were black. All but one of the black delegates were from heavily black counties.[9]

Edmund J. Davis, a Republican, became Texas's Reconstruction governor in 1870, and over the next three years black participation in state and local politics was greater than at any time until quite recently.[10] Several black political organizations quickly flourished, and two black senators and twelve representatives were elected to the Twelfth Legislature, the first to be convened under the new constitution. They, too, were mostly elected from heavily black counties.[11] Radical Republicans dominated the legislature for a brief period, and among the most important policies they enacted were ones creating a state police and militia, both of which blacks could join. These organizations helped deal with the violence—much of it racial—that was rampant in the state during that era. Many whites resented them for actions they took against the Ku Klux Klan and for guarding the polls during elections.[12]

The heavy influx of white settlers in the early 1870s enabled the Democrats to recapture both houses of the legislature in the elections of 1872, and the number of black lawmakers was reduced to seven. Governor Davis was defeated by a vote of two to one in 1873. A former Texas governor called the Democrats' victory "the restoration of white supremacy and Democratic rule."[13] Reconstruction in Texas was over.

Another constitutional convention was held in 1875, this one, as in 1866, controlled by white Democrats. The six black delegates, however, were among a bloc that prevented establishment of a poll tax as a voting requirement. But they were unable to derail a bill mandating segregated schools. The gerrymandering of predominantly black counties diminished black and Republican candidates' opportunities for judicial and legislative seats.[14] An Austin newspaper, speaking of the black-belt counties, said "districts were 'Gerrymandered,' the purpose being, in these elections, and properly enough, to disfranchise the blacks by indirection."[15]

From the end of Reconstruction to the turn of the century, the political situation of Texas blacks declined, slowly at first and then, in the 1890s, with increasing momentum. The result, as in the other southern states, was disfranchisement.[16] In the 1870s, associations of whites had sprung up in the black-belt counties, the purpose of which was to prevent the election of blacks to office. When this failed, "local whites, as in other parts of the South, resorted to extra-legal devices such as fraud, intimidation, intrigue, and murder."[17] Pitre gives a chilling and detailed account of this terror in the Texas black belt following Reconstruction—a terror that differed little, according to Smallwood, from that in the Deep South states during the same period.[18]

White conservative opposition to black political participation increased with the growth of third parties, in which blacks played a significant though not a leading role. The most famous of these was the Populist party, which developed rapidly as an expression of agrarian discontent and peaked in 1896. As a result of the intimidation and violence that white Democrats directed at the Populists—basically a biracial coalition of impoverished farmers—the extremely high voting rates in gubernatorial races of the 1880s and 1890s dropped sharply from over 80 percent of adult males, black and white combined, to about 50 percent in 1902.[19]

In 1901 the legislature voted to submit a constitutional amendment to the electorate requiring payment of a poll tax as a voting requirement. Ratified the following year, it went into effect in 1904, by which point the turnout rate of adult males had dropped still further to 37 percent.[20] The legislature in 1903 and 1905 enacted laws that codified the poll tax, encouraged use of the exclusive white primary by the major parties, and established an annual four-month registration period that ended nine months before the general election. The effect of these developments, along with the discouragement of black participation by the "lily white" faction of the Republicans, was to depress black voter participation from 100,000 in the 1890s to about 5,000 by 1906.[21] Exclusion of African Americans from the two major parties was virtually complete, and inasmuch as nomination in the Democratic primary was tantamount to election, black disfranchisement was a fait accompli.

The banning of Texas blacks from the political system a generation after emancipation was a terrible blow to them, for they had not only enjoyed the freedom to vote but had elected several of their number to state and local office. Between 1871 and 1895 at least forty-one served in the legislature—thirty-seven in the house and four in the senate.[22] Many more were elected to city and county office during this period, largely from counties that were majority black or contained a significant black minority.[23]

Mexican Americans

Mexican Americans also were gradually disfranchised in Texas in the late-nineteenth and early twentieth centuries, although never to the extent as were blacks. From one perspective, they did not represent as great a threat to local Anglo domination as did blacks at the time because, except in a few counties between the Mexican border and the Nueces River, they made up only a small percentage of the population. In 1887, when blacks comprised 20 percent of the state's population, Tejanos made up 4 percent.[24] Only in the late 1940s did Tejanos numerically surpass blacks, as the black ratio continued to decline. By 1960 "Spanish-heritage" people—to use the census term—constituted 15 percent of the Texas population, while blacks comprised 12 percent.[25] The 15 percent figure, however—the highest up to that point in the twentieth century—overstates the size of the potential Hispanic electorate; throughout the century, many Tejanos were not citizens and could not vote.[26]

Even so, from the state's earliest days Mexicans in South Texas counties were a matter of political concern to the Anglos, some of whom tried during the 1845 Texas constitutional convention to exclude them as voters. While these efforts failed, Tejanos were nonetheless subsequently denied the vote in certain districts. Even where they had voting rights, "protests and threats from Anglo-Americans were constant reminders of a fragile franchise."[27] Their ability to influence election results was greatest in the urban areas along the border, where they were concentrated. In the rural areas they were powerless. Here, it was only as Anglo *patrones* (bosses), typically large landholders whose relation to the *peones* was almost feudal, began to organize the Mexican vote around the time of the Civil War did their vote become relatively secure. But under these circumstances, it was a manipulated vote.

The possibilities for political access that an urban setting offered were demonstrated in San Antonio, which had a large Mexican population when Texas became part of the United States.[28] In the decade between 1837 and 1847, fifty-seven of the city's eighty-eight aldermen were Spanish-surnamed. As the Mexican proportion of the population dropped, however—which it did throughout the century—so did the number of Mexican officials. In the decade between 1875 and 1884, for example, only two of the sixty-nine aldermen had Spanish surnames.[29]

The rise of boss rule along the Rio Grande in the latter half of the nineteenth century led to sharp and sometimes bitter disputes in the early twentieth century between "reformers" and the machines.[30] The conflict was typical of Progressive Era battles over control of the electoral structure in that the challengers, some of whom organized into Good Government Leagues, used the rhetoric of "good government" and "honest elections" to justify their politics of self-interest. Often the reformers were small Anglo farmers newly arrived in the fertile Rio Grande Valley and resentful of the large landholders—also usually Anglos—and their control of the Mexican-American vote. A particularly bitter conflict of this kind in Dimmit County led the reformers to create a White Man's Primary in 1914. The local newspaper announced that the organization "absolutely eliminates the Mexican vote as a factor in nominating county candidates, though we graciously grant the Mexican the privilege of voting for them afterwards."[31] The conflicts between South Texas reformers and machine bosses, therefore, offered Tejanos a choice between disfranchisement and a manipulated vote.

Some of the machines continued into the post–World War II era. Duval County, whose stuffed ballot boxes were crucial for Lyndon B. Johnson's razor-thin senatorial victory in 1948, remained under the control of the notorious Parr machine until 1975.[32] Key found in the late 1940s that several South Texas counties exhibited the tell-tale signs of machine control in their voting returns: many victories of landslide proportions and voters' "remarkable fickleness in attachment to particular candidates." When LBJ defeated former governor Coke Stevenson in the 1948 senatorial election thanks to the lopsided Duval County vote, the loser complained about the landslides there and in surrounding counties. Boss George Parr pointed out that Stevenson had solicited his support in four previous elections and won by similar margins. "And I never heard a complaint from him then about the bloc vote in Duval County," Parr remarked.[33]

The disfranchisement of Tejanos through exclusive primaries was not unique to Dimmit County. Democrats in Gonzales County had barred both blacks and Tejanos from their primaries in 1902.[34] "White men's primaries" at the local level were frequently mentioned in the literature on Tejano politics. M. C. González, for example, a founder of the League of United Latin American Citizens (LULAC) in 1929, listed among the conditions facing Mexican Americans in Texas during the 1920s "the establishment of 'white man's' primaries to prevent blacks and Mexican Americans from exercising their right of suffrage."[35] Kibbe, writing in the 1940s, mentions the existence of a local white primary, called the White Man's Union, in four South Texas counties.[36] De Leon mentions a White Man's party in Duval County existing in 1892.[37] Shelton quotes the constitution of the White Man's Union Assocation in Wharton County as excluding "any Mexican, who is not a full Spanish blood."[38]

Restrictive registration rules, too, were directed at Mexicans. Laws making it difficult for Mexican citizens to vote in Texas were opposed at the time of passage by Jim Wells, a conservative Democrat who was one of the most powerful South Texas bosses.[39] (A county was later named for him.) In 1918 the legislature passed a bill prohibiting interpreters at the polls. This law was clearly aimed at voters who had difficulty with English—a lack of proficiency that was undoubtedly encouraged by discrimination in the schools, including the widespread segregation of Tejanos.[40] Thus, like blacks, Texas Mexicans were not only victims of an oppressive social and economic system that in many respects resembled a classic caste society; by law and custom they were deprived of the means to change their situation through effective political participation.

The Battle to Abolish the White Primary

Soon after turn-of-the-century disfranchising laws were passed, Texas blacks, supported by the newly formed National Association for the Advancement of Colored People (NAACP), began to challenge the system of political discrimination. They focused their first major efforts on the white primary. In varying numbers, blacks actually had continued to vote in some Texas nonpartisan municipal elections after 1905. Through litigation, blacks in Waco successfully challenged a nonpartisan white primary in 1918. This and some notable manifestations of black voter influence in San Antonio were apparently behind the legislature's 1923 law providing that "in no event shall a negro be eligible to participate in a Democratic primary election held in the State of Texas."[41] While county Democratic parties across the state had already pretty thoroughly prohibited black participation by that time, the new law gave explicit state sanction to the practice.

Dr. Lawrence A. Nixon, a black El Paso physician, was quick to challenge this law, and the Supreme Court in *Nixon v. Herndon* (1927)[42] concluded that it violated the Fourteenth Amendment's equal protection clause, holding that "color cannot be made the basis of a statutory classification affecting the right set up in this case."[43] To circumvent the ruling, the legislature soon enacted a replacement statute designed to shift the burden of disfranchisement from the state to political parties. The new law authorized "every political party in the State through its State Executive Committee . . . to prescribe the qualifications of its own members."[44] The State Democratic Executive Committee (SDEC) took this cue and adopted a resolution limiting participation to "white Democrats . . . and none other."[45] Dr. Nixon, with NAACP counsel, sued again, and the Supreme Court in *Nixon v. Condon* (1932)[46] also invalidated that scheme as simply an extension of the earlier unconstitutional exclusion. The Court reasoned that the SDEC did not have the authority to act for the party; consequently, it was simply acting for the state and, in so doing, violated once again the equal protection clause. But the party's state convention, said the Court, had such authority. Within a month after the opinion, to no one's surprise, the convention adopted a resolution prohibiting African Americans from participation in the Democratic primary.

Richard Randolph Grovey, a black Houstonian, attacked the new rule in yet another suit. At issue was whether the party was a private, voluntary organization or an instrument of the state. Plaintiffs argued that the primary was conducted under state authority and thus was protected by the Fifteenth Amendment. The unanimous Court, in *Grovey v. Townsend* (1935)[47] held otherwise, invoking an earlier Texas supreme court decision which declared that political parties were voluntary associations, not creatures of the state.[48]

The single most important organization concerned with African American voting rights in Texas or elsewhere at this time was the NAACP. Urbanization and the growth of a black middle class in Texas cities provided the basis for a black leadership class that was somewhat freer to participate in civil rights activities than was possible in small towns. Beginning in the late 1930s, a new generation of leaders, typified by Dallas businessman A. Maceo Smith, revived existing local chapters, created new ones, and developed a dynamic statewide conference. Working with such figures in the national office as Walter White and Thurgood Marshall, the new black Texas leadership—including Juanita Craft in Dallas; and Lulu White, Carter Wesley, and Hobart Taylor, Sr., in Houston—coordinated and funded a number of major legal efforts.[49]

Largely as a result of this group's work, in collaboration with Thurgood Marshall, general counsel of the newly formed NAACP Legal Defense Fund, the Supreme Court again addressed the constitutionality of the white primary in 1944. The Court's membership was changing. In an earlier case involving New Orleans voting fraud, *United States v. Classic* (1941),[50] it had held that "where the state law has made the primary election an integral part of the procedure" of choice, "or where in fact the primary effectively controls the choice, the right of the qualified elector to vote and have his ballot counted at the primary, is part of the right" protected by article 1 of the Constitution.[51] This led Dr. Lonnie Smith, a Houston dentist, to challenge the Texas white primary using the same logic as the Court espoused in *Classic*. Capping twenty years of litigation on the issue, the Court, in *Smith v. Allwright* (1944),[52] overrode its prior reasoning in *Grovey* that the Texas Democratic primary was distinct from the state electoral apparatus. On the contrary, the Court now said, because state law regulated the Democratic primary, which selected nominees to be included on the general election ballot, the primary was an agency of the state. The exclusion of blacks from the party's nominating process thus violated the Fifteenth Amendment, which forbids denial of the franchise on the basis of race.

The Smith decision was announced in April, and significant numbers of Texas blacks voted in the July 1944 Democratic primary. In 1946 their turnout in the primary was estimated at 75,000–100,000, in about the numbers at which they had voted during the high point of black participation in the 1890s.[53] Yet the raw figures are deceiving. Whereas a turnout of 100,000 in 1896 represented perhaps as much as 90 percent of the black potential (male) electorate of the day, in 1946 it constituted only about 20 percent of the (male and female) black electorate.

Litigation over racially exclusive primaries concluded with *Terry v. Adams* (1953).[54] The Supreme Court there condemned the "Jaybird primary" that had arisen in Fort Bend County in the nineteenth century to exclude African Americans from meaningful electoral participation. Strictly speaking, this device was not a primary but an exclusively white pre-primary conducted by the local Jaybird party to determine the preferred candidate of white voters, thereby avoiding the risk of dividing their vote in the Democrat primary. Defendants, who described their whites-only group in court as a "good government" measure,[55] argued that the Jaybirds, unlike the Democratic party, were not part of the state's official election machinery and, hence, were constitutional. The Court held otherwise.

Barriers to Registration

Texas, unlike most other southern states, never had a literacy test. However, the poll tax in Texas operated as a limitation upon the right to vote in federal elections until 1964 and in state elections until 1966. Statewide constitutional referendums to abolish the tax had failed, although evidence indicated that it still had an impact on turnout in the 1960s, especially among low-income voters. Simmons reported in the early 1950s that the tax, "although a small sum ($1.75), costs the [South Texas Mexican] laborer most of a day's wage."[56] The same was true of many blacks in rural East Texas, and of poor whites generally.

The Twenty-fourth Amendment, prohibiting the tax as a voting requirement in federal elections, was ratified by the required thirty-eight states in 1964. Texas was one of five at that time which still maintained the tax.[57] The Voting Rights Act of 1965 instructed the U.S. Attorney General "forthwith" to challenge in court the enforcement of any poll tax used as a voting requirement. He quickly brought suit against Texas, and a federal court in *United States v. State of Texas* (1966)[58] found that the state's poll tax was unconstitutional, having originally been imposed for the purpose of disfranchising black voters. The legislature, dominated by the conservative Democratic wing led by Governor John Connally, promptly replaced the tax with an almost equally onerous annual voter registration system. The new law, which, like the recently invalidated one, required the voter to register in a four-month period ending 31 January in order to vote in November elections, was ruled unconstitutional by a federal court in *Beare v. Smith* (1971).[59] The court concluded that "it is beyond doubt that the present Texas voter registration procedures tend to disenfranchise multitudes of Texas citizens otherwise qualified to vote."[60]

Texas did not surrender gracefully. In 1975 the legislature enacted a new voter registration statute that would effectively have purged the state's entire election rolls and required reregistration of the state's voters. As Congress the same year had extended coverage of section 5 of the Voting Rights Act to Texas, the new voter registration system became the first Texas statute challenged under it.

The state, in *Briscoe v. Levi* (1976),[61] failed in its attempt to block extension. At about the same time, a federal court enjoined the implementation of the proposed statutory purge of the voter rolls in *Flowers v. Wiley* (1975).[62] Since then Texas has had a registration statute that permits enrollment up to thirty days before any election. The system seems to have operated without objection for a number of years.

An impediment that disproportionately burdened minority candidates for office was removed by elimination of the excessive candidate filing fees required by Texas law. The Supreme Court in *Bullock v. Carter* (1972)[63] concluded that "the very size of the fees imposed under the Texas system gives it a patently exclusionary character . . . [and] there is the obvious likelihood that this limitation would fall more heavily on the less affluent segment of the community."[64] That segment was disproportionately made up of minority persons.

No story of minority registration efforts in Texas would be complete without mention of the prolonged struggle of students at Prairie View A. & M. to register to vote. Prairie View is a predominantly black university located in rural Waller County near Houston, the only Texas county in 1970 with a majority-black population. Texas by statute attempted to prevent students from registering to vote in the communities where they attended college, a limitation declared unconstitutional in *Whatley v. Clark* (1973).[65] Nonetheless, the local tax assessor steadfastly frustrated attempts of Prairie View students to register in Waller County.[66] The extension of section 5 to Texas finally enabled a successful attack upon this exclusion of African American voters in *Symm v. United States* (1979).[67] Immediately thereafter a successful attack was made on the apportionment of the Waller County commissioners court for its failure to include students in determining county population. The resulting reapportionment produced the county's first black county commissioner.[68]

Minority Groups in the Voting Rights Movement

Most of the voting rights litigation in Texas until the 1970s focused on the unconstitutional barriers to participation faced by blacks rather than Mexican Americans, for various reasons: the degree of black exclusion was more extreme; blacks had historically been a larger group in the state; and, perhaps for the first two reasons, blacks were more inclined toward litigation. It was only in the 1960s that Tejanos began to come into their own as a statewide political force, although they had been emerging as an important part of the Texas liberal coalition at least since the 1950s.[69]

The decade of the 1960s witnessed the rise of the Chicano movement, a surge of militant activity among the younger generation of Mexican Americans that quickly spread throughout the Southwest. In Texas, the decade began with the involvement of old-line Tejano organizations in the 1960 presidential campaign. The Viva Kennedy clubs played an important role in carrying Texas by a narrow margin for the Democratic ticket, and gave impetus to a broad-based coalition formed in 1962, the Political Association of Spanish-Speaking Organizations (PASO). In 1963 the teamsters union, PASO, and a number of independent militants joined in a historic uprising in which the city council of a small South Texas town, Crystal City, was entirely filled by an all-Tejano slate. This victory, while short-lived, received nationwide coverage in the news media and presaged a new day for Mexican Americans in Texas politics. A farmworkers movement, along the lines of the one led by Cesar Chavez in California, was also partly inspired by PASO, and confrontations between strikers and the Texas Rangers, long considered by growers and the local Anglo establishments of South Texas as their personal police force, fanned a wave of militance that surged across Texas college campuses, leading to such Chicano groups as the Mexican American Youth Organization (MAYO) that established La Raza Unida party. High school students in South and West Texas towns in the late 1960s boycotted classes in support of fair treatment and greater prominence for the teaching of Mexican culture.

These developments had their roots in self-help groups that Mexican-American veterans founded soon after World War I, such as Sons of Texas, Sons of America, and Knights of America, all of which were united into LULAC in 1929. This organization would play a significant role in politicizing Tejanos locally and fighting discrimination through legal means. Recent scholarship, moreover, has revised the notion that these early organizations, as well as the G.I. Forum, founded by World War II veterans, were primarily concerned with assimilation into Anglo culture and politically ineffective.[70] Considering the racist Texas milieu of the period, the accomplishments of LULAC, the G.I. Forum, and leaders of those groups, such as Professor George I. Sanchez and Dr. Hector Garcia, were in the long term quite effective.

Grass-roots organizations, for example, played a significant role in the 1948 election of Gustavo Garcia to the San Antonio school board, a watershed event in Texas electoral politics. LULAC was active in the 1957 election in El Paso of Raymond Telles, a moderate reformer and the first Hispanic mayor of a major southwestern city in the twentieth century.[71] Such groups were involved in Henry B. Gonzalez's election to the San Antonio city council in 1953 and to the Texas senate in 1956, where he immediately became an eloquent opponent of discrimination against not only Tejanos, but blacks and poor whites.[72]

Yet not until the Mexican-American statewide political mobilization during the 1960s did voting rights litigation begin to shift its focus of concern toward Mexican Americans.[73] This was due largely to the establishment of two organizations. Modeled on the NAACP Legal Defense Fund, the Mexican American Legal Defense and Educational Fund (MALDEF) was created in 1968 with financial support from the Ford Foundation, and the lawsuits brought by its attorneys focused increasingly on the special electoral problems confronting Tejano voters. The Southwest Voter Registration Education Project (SVREP) was founded by San Antonio activist Willie Velásquez in 1974. One of its primary purposes was to register Tejanos, and it appears to have made great strides on that score. When the project began its work in 1976, 488,000 Mexican Americans were registered in Texas. Ten years later, approximately 1 million were, even though their registration rates remained much lower than those of blacks or Anglos.[74] But in addition to its registration drives, SVREP's legal staff also became involved in voting litigation. Between 1974 and 1984 SVREP and MALDEF filed eighty-eight suits in widely scattered Texas jurisdictions.[75]

One of the first successful voting cases brought by MALDEF was *Garza v. Smith* (1970).[76] This action challenged Texas election laws that enabled voting officials to assist physically handicapped voters but did not permit assistance to voters who were not proficient in English. The argument in *Garza* foreshadowed the broadening of section 5 coverage to Texas five years later. In its 1975 extension of the act, Congress concluded that "where State and local officials conduct elections only in English, language minority citizens are excluded from participating in the electoral process."[77] Congress therefore brought under section 5 coverage some of those states and counties that had historically failed to provide multilingual election materials.[78]

Various private attorneys and legal aid lawyers, including liberal Anglos, were also active in voting rights litigation during this period. Litigation by attorneys with the federal Legal Services Corporation was partly responsible for efforts by conservative Republicans during the Reagan and Bush administrations to abolish the organization, or, failing that, to at least prohibit it from filing voting suits.

Minority Vote Dilution

The elimination of barriers to registration and voting in Texas often did not result in the election of minority candidates, even in jurisdictions with significant numbers of minority voters. Several structural roadblocks remained, the most noteworthy of which were multimember districts (including at-large elections), racial gerrymandering, and malapportionment. Such barriers diluted minority voting strength when bloc voting among Anglos combined with certain election rules to prevent a cohesive bloc of minority voters from electing candidates of their choice. Largely for this reason it was not until 1966 that the first African Americans in this century became nominees of the Democratic party for any elective public office in Texas above the level of voting precinct official, even though black candidates had run for office at least as far back as 1920.[79]

Mexican Americans, too, faced numerous barriers to political office, although by 1967 there were ten Tejano state legislators—nine in the house and one in the senate—compared to only three blacks.[80] While Mexican-American voters as early as the 1940s were described as tending to prefer candidates of their own ethnicity "on the rare occasions when they appear on the ballot," the same electoral mechanisms that prevented blacks from winning office operated against their candidates, too. "Anglo American politicians have always recognized this tendency," wrote Simmons in 1952, "and have tried to cope with it, when no other means were available, by putting up a second Mexican candidate of their own choosing in order to split the Mexican vote."[81]

Simmons also pointed to the well-known phenomenon of a nonpartisan slating group operating through at-large elections. He quoted a county commissioner: "Candidates are usually nominated on a ticket which is made up by a private group that invites the candidate to run." While any candidate was free to oppose the ticket, "independent candidates seldom have a chance."[82] Several lawsuits in the 1970s and 1980s pointed to the existence of the standard electoral mechanisms of minority vote dilution operating against Tejano candidates: at-large elections, gerrymandered districts, the numbered-place system, and others.[83]

The first successful challenge to legislative malapportionment in Texas, at least in modern times, occurred after the 1960 census, when population disparities in legislative districts were huge. The boundaries had not changed significantly since 1921.[84] A state constitutional prohibition on the number of legislative seats per county had contributed to overrepresentation of the shrinking rural population at the expense of the rapidly expanding urban one, which contained great numbers of minority voters. The largest senatorial district, for example, contained 1,243,158 persons, while the smallest one had 147,454. A majority of the senators could be elected by as few as 30 percent of Texas voters.[85] *Kilgarlin v. Martin* (1966)[86] was a broad-based attack on the 1960 Texas legislative redistricting plans. In preliminary rulings, the senate and house apportionment was found to violate the one-person, one-vote principle recently established by the Supreme Court in *Reynolds v. Sims* (1964).[87] Texas constitutional provisions limiting the number of senators and legislators who could be elected from any given county were invalidated, and apportionment of the Texas senate was required on the basis of population equality.

The legislature responded with a new apportionment plan that, among other changes, increased the number of legislators in Harris County (Houston) from twelve to nineteen and in Dallas County from nine to fourteen. In the case of Harris

County, for the first time state representatives were to be elected in three county multimember subdistricts rather than countywide. Senate districts—which had been and remained single-member districts—were also carved into subdistricts of Dallas and Harris counties to meet one-person, one-vote criteria. In spite of clear instances of racial gerrymandering against blacks in the Harris County state representative districts under the new apportionment scheme,[88] the initial result of these changes in 1966 was the election of the first three black Texas legislators to serve since 1895.

Barbara Jordan, who had twice failed to win election to the state house of representatives when she ran at large in Harris County, was elected from one of the new Houston senate districts (one, significantly, that contained a black and Mexican-American majority), becoming the first black Texas senator to hold office since 1883. Curtis Graves won a house seat from a multimember Harris County subdistrict. In addition to these two victories resulting from boundary changes, Joe Lockridge, also black, was elected at large to the state house from Dallas County after being slated by the Dallas Committee for Responsible Government (DCRG), a powerful white-dominated slating group that would soon receive federal court scrutiny.[89]

A major breakthrough in minority legislative representation came after the 1970 census. Blacks and Tejanos—aided by a group of minority and Anglo lawyers and political scientists—jointly attacked the system of multimember countywide legislative districts in Dallas and Bexar counties, arguing that, in conjunction with other discriminatory actions, the arrangement diluted minority votes in violation of the Fourteenth Amendment. In *Graves v. Barnes* (1972)[90] the three-judge federal court agreed, mandating single-member legislative districts for both counties. This decision was unanimously affirmed by the Supreme Court in *White v. Regester* (1973),[91] the first case in which it sustained claims of at-large vote dilution.

The Court had earlier asserted in *Whitcomb v. Chavis* (1971) that multimember district systems "may be subject to challenge where the circumstances of a particular case may 'operate to minimize or cancel out the voting strength of racial or political elements of the voting population.' "[92] However, until *White* the Supreme Court had never been persuaded that such circumstances existed. In fact, in *Whitcomb* the Court had rejected a trial court finding that an at-large legislative districting scheme in Indiana operated unconstitutionally to cancel out minority voting strength. Similarly, the Supreme Court had upheld a Texas trial court conclusion in *Kilgarlin v. Hill* (1967)[93] that the state's at-large legislative districts did not unconstitutionally deprive African Americans of their voting rights. Against this discouraging backdrop, the plaintiffs' victory in *White* took on special significance.

The *Graves* decision had both immediate and long-term consequences. The immediate result was a significant increase in the number of blacks and Mexican Americans from Dallas and San Antonio, respectively, elected to the Texas legislature in November 1972. In the second round of *Graves v. Barnes* (1974),[94] the state's remaining multimember legislative districts were also found to dilute minority voting strength. Single-member legislative districts were created in the Texas counties of Tarrant (Fort Worth), El Paso, Travis (Austin), Nueces (Corpus Christi), Jefferson (Beaumont), McLennan (Waco), Lubbock, and Galveston. In most instances, this resulted in the election of the first minorities to the legislature from those counties.

An upsurge in voting litigation across Texas followed *White*. Applying the principles established in that case, minority plaintiffs made a number of Fourteenth Amendment attacks on at-large elections to city councils and school boards. Using one-person, one-vote arguments under *Avery v. Midland County* (1968)[95] and *White* minority vote-dilution principles, black and Tejano voters also attacked county government apportionment schemes throughout Texas, the 254 counties of which have long been governed by a commissioners court consisting of four commissioners elected from single-member districts and a county judge elected at large. The first city to change its at-large council elections as a result of vote-dilution litigation was Nacogdoches in deep East Texas; after black plaintiffs won at trial, the city in 1975 settled a lawsuit while the case was on appeal, and subsequent elections produced the city's first black council member. The first successful legal attack on at-large elections to a Texas city school board occurred in Waco. The trial court ordered the creation of single-member districts for both the city council and school board, and this arrangement was sustained in *Calderon v. McGee* (1978).[96]

After the extension of section 5 to Texas in 1975 as a result of the state's large Spanish-language population, attacks based on Fourteenth Amendment arguments developed in *White* and section 5 objections by the Justice Department produced some form of single-member-district elections in most major Texas cities, including Houston, San Antonio, and Dallas. These changes led to noteworthy increases in the number of elected minority officials, as will be shown below. Vote-dilution litigation, however, has affected not simply the large urban centers but cities as small as Jefferson, with a 1980 population of fewer than 3,000, where plaintiffs won at trial and a single-member-district plan was imposed.[97]

Similar breakthroughs occurred in county reapportionment litigation. For example, a federal court ruling in *Weaver v. Nacogdoches County* (1974)[98] produced a new reapportionment plan and the election of the first black Texas county commissioner in this century. Another East Texas reapportionment case resulted in the first federal court finding of a racial gerrymander in the drawing of district lines. In *Robinson v. Commissioners Court, Anderson County* (1974)[99] the court held that "the most crucial and precise instrument of the Commissioner's denial of the black minority's equal access to political participation, however, remains the gerrymander of precinct lines so as to fragment what could otherwise be a cohesive voting community. . . . This dismemberment of the black community . . . had the predictable effect of debilitating the organization and decreasing the participation of black voters in county government."[100]

The extension of section 5 to Texas was a major advance in securing minority voting rights. Justice Department intervention in Texas after 1975 either prevented many potentially dilutionary measures or required them to be counterbalanced with additional election changes that restored or enhanced minority voting strength. Thus, when the city of Houston annexed territory, some of which included virtually all-white suburbs, and thus diminished the proportion of blacks and Mexican Americans in the city, the Justice Department entered an objection, based in part on evidence of racially polarized voting in Houston council elections presented by plaintiffs in *Greater Houston Civic Council v. Mann*,[101] an unsuccessful constitutional challenge to the city's electoral structure tried in 1975. The city's options were to contest the objection in federal court in Washington, D.C., deannex the territory, or change the council's at-large election system to include at least some single-member districts. The city took the latter course, following a citywide referendum, and adopted a mixed plan of nine single-member districts and five at-large posts, in addition to the mayor's at-large office.[102] Justice Department intervention under section 5 was also instrumental in San Antonio's change from an at-large to a pure single-member-district plan in 1977.

Between the time Texas was brought under section 5 coverage in 1975 and December 1990, the Justice Department interposed 131 objections to voting procedures in the state. Many of these objections were to multiple infractions of voting law within a single jurisdiction.[103] The infractions embraced the spectrum of illegal procedures: racial gerrymandering, discriminatory purges of registered voters, imposition of numbered posts and the majority runoff requirement, annexations that diluted minority votes, a faulty bilingual oral assistance program, reduction in the number of elected officials, transfer of duties from one official to another, and unfair changes in election dates. One can only speculate about the number of discriminatory changes that would have occurred but for the deterrent effect of section 5.

Reviewing the results in the forty-one instances in Texas where they could identify a change from at-large to mixed or district plans in the 1970s, Davidson and Korbel found the percentage of black and Mexican-American officeholders had increased from 11 to 29 percent of the total in those jurisdictions (6 to 17 percent for blacks, 5 to 12 percent for Mexican Americans). Put differently, before the change, minority officeholders were underrepresented by a factor of three; afterward, they were almost proportionally represented. City councils, school boards, junior college boards, and multimember legislative districts were included in the study; increases in minority representation occurred in every type of unit.[104] This was the only before-and-after study published in the 1970s or 1980s that examined the impact of at-large elections on Mexican Americans, and its findings contrasted sharply with most of the research on this issue that utilized cross-sectional data. The reason, we believe, is that cross-sectional studies seldom control for residential dispersion of Mexican Americans, which is greater than it is for blacks.[105] Our own data, reported below, corroborate Davidson and Korbel's findings.[106]

One of the most far-reaching results of Texas voting litigation is contained in the

1982 congressional amendments of section 2 of the Voting Rights Act, passed to overcome the effects of *City of Mobile v. Bolden* (1980),[107] in which a plurality of the Supreme Court held that at-large elections were not unconstitutional unless the they had been "conceived or operated" intentially to discriminate. In amending section 2 to allow a showing of discriminatory result as sufficient proof of dilution, Congress explicitly incorporated into the statute the vote-dilution principles first established in 1972 by the federal trial court in *Graves v. Barnes* and then adopted in the language of *White v. Regester*.[108]

The impact of amended section 2 was clearly seen in *Campos v. City of Baytown* (1988).[109] The appeals court affirmed a trial court finding that the at-large election system for Baytown's city council violated section 2. Despite the presence of sizable black and Mexican-American communities in the city at the time of trial, no minority member had ever been elected to the Baytown council. Yet the plaintiffs would have been hard put to show that the at-large system, which dated from 1947, was adopted to frustrate minority candidates. Under amended section 2, however, plaintiffs used voting statistics to prove the dilutionary effect of the at-large system.

The pace of section 2 voting rights litigation in Texas remained lively at the end of the 1980s. In 1989 courts first heard attacks on the at-large election of trial and appellate judges in Texas. In both cases the trial courts concluded that at-large electoral systems violated section 2, and required single-member districts as a remedy. In *Rangel v. Mattox* (1989),[110] the trial court found that the at-large electoral system of the Thirteenth Court of Appeals, situated in South Texas, discriminated against the Tejano voters of the Lower Rio Grande Valley. The court sanctioned a plan consisting of six single-member districts. In *LULAC v. Mattox* (1989),[111] the trial court concluded that at-large election of district judges in the state's urban counties similarly violated minority voting rights of blacks and Mexican Americans under section 2.

On appeal of the *LULAC* decision, the Fifth Circuit, sitting *en banc*, held that section 2 did not apply to judicial elections. This decision effectively blocked any immediate change in Texas judicial elections. The Supreme Court reversed in *Houston Lawyers Association v. Attorney General of Texas* (1991),[112] holding that judicial elections were indeed covered by section 2. As a result, the issues presented in *Rangel* and *LULAC* are now back before the Fifth Circuit. These cases would seem to portend significant changes in the method of selecting the Texas judiciary.

The extent and diversity of voting rights actions and Justice Department intervention in Texas is suggested by a list compiled by Korbel in connection with lawsuits challenging the method of electing judges. The list contains Justice Department objections or privately brought actions concerning vote dilution between 1972 and 1989 in a mere twenty-county area of South Texas. (The state contains 254 counties.) Targeted were voting procedures for school boards, city councils, county commissioners courts, the state legislature, and justice of the peace courts.

There were fourteen objection letters from the Justice Department in seven of the counties, and at least fourteen vote dilution cases won by plaintiffs or settled out of court in a manner favorable to plaintiffs.[113]

The Impact of Voting Rights Litigation in Texas Cities

We now systematically examine changes in voting structures in Texas cities. As part of a collaborative effort in several states, we measured the extent of change between 1974—the year before section 5 was extended to the state—and 1989 in all Texas municipalities of 10,000 or more persons that had a combined black and Hispanic population of at least 10 percent according to the 1980 census.[114] The purposes were, first, to learn how rapidly black and Tejano officeholding had progressed; second, to determine the extent to which such progress was linked to the existence of single-member-district and mixed plans (the latter composed of both district and at-large seats); and, third, in the event that there was a linkage, to find out whether the creation of districts was the result of litigation under the Fourteenth Amendment (as in *Graves* and its progeny), litigation or Justice Department objections under the Voting Rights Act, or voluntary action by city governments.

Methods

Our research design followed in broad detail the above-mentioned longitudinal study by Davidson and Korbel.[115] However, as Grofman pointed out soon after the research was reported, the design lacked a control group.[116] The design for the present study therefore includes not only cities that abandoned at-large elections for district or mixed plans but those comparable Texas municipalities which did not change their at-large council structure between 1974 and 1989.[117] During this period the number of African-American and Hispanic elected municipal officials in all Texas cities increased from 59 to 138 and from 251 to 463, respectively.[118]

Minority Representation in Texas Cities

Table 8.1 is a cross-sectional view of minority representation on city councils in 1989 by type of election plan and percentage of minority population within each type.[119] Because most studies examining the relation between election plans and minority representation have used a cross-sectional design, table 8.1 provides a point of comparison with them. It shows that in cities that were majority Anglo, combined minority representation in 1989 was greater in district than in at-large systems, when the effects of minority population size were controlled for. However, at-large cities had better minority representation than districted ones in cities where blacks and Hispanics were a majority, although this seemed to be at least partly the result of the at-large cities having, on average, a larger minority population percentage than either mixed or district plans. (In other words, if the effects of minority population were controlled in the 50–100 percent category, as they are, in effect, in table 8.5, the at-large advantage in these cities would diminish.) But this latter finding should not be allowed to obscure the most important pattern in table 8.1: the advantage to minorities in district-based *majority-Anglo* cities—for it is in these cities where the at-large system is said to be particularly dilutive of minority votes.

As explained in the Editors' Introduction, cross-sectional studies typically do not control for a number of factors besides minority population that can affect minority representation. In addition, cross-sectional data collected from a sample of cities after many of them have changed their method of election may reflect a "selection bias" because the remaining at-large cities may not be typical of at-large cities in general—a possibility that is examined in chapter 10.

Table 8.2, utilizing a before-and-after design with a control group, measures minority percentages on all city councils at two points fifteen years apart: in changed cities before and after the shift from at-large elections occurred; and in unchanged cities at the same two points, 1974 and 1989.[120] Among majority-Anglo cities, those changing from at-large to single-member districts between 1974 and 1989 witnessed sharply increased minority (black plus Hispanic) percentages on council following the change. Large changes also occurred in the cities that adopted mixed plans. These positive changes occurred for both blacks and Tejanos separately, generally speaking. Among unchanged at-large cities, on the other hand, there was an actual decrease in minority representation in one population category, and only a modest rise in the other.

So far we have controlled only roughly for the effects of a city's minority population on minority representation, by categorizing the data according to three sets of minority population ranges. To refine this control, we employ the concept of representational equity, or proportionality, which is simply a comparison of cities' percentage of minority council members with their percentage of minority inhabitants. There are two standard measures of proportionality—differences and ratios—the strengths and limitations of which Grofman has discussed elsewhere.[121]

Table 8.4, presenting 1989 cross-sectional data, shows some of the same patterns in tables 8.1 and 8.2. Whether using the difference measure or the ratio measure of equity, we find in majority-Anglo cities that single-member-district and mixed cities were generally more representative than at-large ones, and usually they were strikingly so—at least where blacks were concerned. Tejanos did not follow this pattern so clearly. They were less well represented than blacks in every type of system, except in some minority-Anglo cities (where the majority of the population was overwhelmingly Hispanic, not black). Nonetheless, it was generally true that in majority-Anglo cities, Tejanos were more equitably represented in cities that had adopted at least some districts than in those that had not.

Table 8.5, comparing equity ratios in 1974 with those in 1989, gives an even clearer picture than does table 8.2 of the effects of the shift from at-large elections in those cities of less than 50 percent minority population. It essentially corroborates the findings in tables 8.1, 8.2, and 8.4. The experimental cities underwent sharp increases in combined minority representational equity during the fifteen years, while the control cities made generally unremarkable gains when they made any gains at all.[122] The impact of the new election systems is best seen by focusing on equity ratios in the majority-Anglo cities that changed to pure single-member districts, and comparing them to ratios in the cities that remained at-large.

	1974		*1989*	
	Blacks	*Hispanics*	*Blacks*	*Hispanics*
		Changed to Districts		
10–29.9%	0.38	0.18	1.32	0.35
30–49.9%	0.13	0.15	1.12	0.95
		Remained at large		
10–29.9%	0.62	0.37	0.80	0.21
30–49.9%	0.58	0.24	0.75	0.50

Within each population category, mean minority equity scores in the control cities were better in the early year—1974—than in cities that later changed to districts, a fact that was true for both ethnic minorities. This was at a time, obviously, when all the cities in the table elected council at large. *By 1989, the situation was completely reversed*: the mean equity scores in all categories of the cities that switched to districts were greater than those, in the comparable population categories, in the cities that had kept their at-large systems. Again, this was true for both blacks and Mexican Americans. This consistent reversal was the result, in most cases, of hefty increases in minority equity scores as cities switched to district elections. Part of the reversal, on the other hand, was due to the fact that in the twenty-six cities of less than 30 percent minority population that kept at-large systems—representing one-fourth of the total number of cities analyzed—there was an actual drop in the mean equity score of Mexican Americans (0.37 to 0.21) and only a modest rise for blacks (0.62 to 0.80) over the fifteen-year period. This is an important finding, we believe, in light of the claim by some critics of the Voting Rights Act that Anglo Texas voters were much more likely to vote for minority candidates in at-large settings by the end of the 1980s than they were even a decade or two earlier.

In 1989 both Tejanos and blacks in the majority-Anglo unchanged cities were still underrepresented, although Tejanos were more so. Had the changed cities not adopted new election structures—so the data for the cities in the control group suggest—their minority voters would still be far less well represented than they were in 1989, and perhaps, in some cases, even less well represented than in 1974. In summary, table 8.5 presents strong evidence for a causal link between election systems and proportionality of minority representation in majority-Anglo cities.[123] This link exists for both Tejanos and African Americans.

The findings in table 8.5 contrast to those of a recent cross-sectional study of American cities of at least 50,000 population with minority populations of less than 50 percent, which found a relatively small difference in 1988 black representational equity scores between at-large and districted cities.[124] This may well be the result, in part, of the studies' different population thresholds, assuming that racially polarized voting is greater in smaller cities.

There may be another reason for the different results as well. Table 8.5 shows clearly that the cities that changed election systems had, on average, significantly lower minority equity scores in 1974 than those which remained at-large. This suggests that any cross-sectional study today of Texas cities which attempts to measure the impact of election structures on minority representation may be subject to a bias resulting from the *selection effect*: Our sample of cities that in 1989 were districted contained a disproportionate number that in 1974 were among the "worst cases" of at-large cities, in terms of minority representation. Assuming that the worst cases were most liable to vote-dilution litigation and thus were most likely to change to districts, a cross-sectional study in 1989 would contain a sample of at-large cities from which the worst ones in 1974 were removed ("selected"), in which case the comparison of at-large and district cities would understate the difference in minority representation between at-large and districted cities, in contrast to what it would have been had the changes to district systems not occurred.

Yet another important fact emerges from table 8.5. Despite the frequently heard assertion that the evolving nature of voting rights law now requires at-large cities to adopt district systems, the Texas case shows otherwise. There are 83 cities in the table with a minority population between 10 and 50 percent, yet 38 (46 percent) still maintained at-large systems in 1989, in spite of two decades of aggressive legal challenges to such structures across the state and seven years of section 2 litigation—some of it in these very cities. Nor is it true that these at-large cities failed to change because minorities were proportionally represented on council. As the table shows, minority populations in the majority-Anglo unchanged cities were only about half as well represented as one would expect if ethnicity were not a factor. In 22 of the 38 unchanged cities, moreover, no blacks sat on council in 1989; in 30 of these cities, no Tejanos did; and in 19 cities—exactly half—neither a black nor a Tejano was a council member. The number of cities among the 38 that had neither blacks nor Tejanos on council actually increased slightly between 1974 and 1989: from 21 to 22.

The dynamics of change in the minority-Anglo cities are difficult to fathom, given only the data in table 8.5. Contrary to the facts in majority-Anglo cities, when predominantly minority cities (which in our sample are all predominantly Hispanic ones) switch to districts, there is either little increase in representational equity or an actual decrease. In fact, minority equity of representation increased more sharply in the unchanged cities where, at 0.97, it was greater by 1989 than in either other type of changed cities (0.80 and 0.72, respectively).

What could account for this? The minority-Anglo unchanged cities had an average minority population of close to 80 percent. If voting were racially polarized, as in the case of many at-large majority-Anglo cities, then the Mexican-American population could easily have determined the makeup of city council. Why they were less equitably represented in changed cities—particularly pure district ones—is unclear. One possible answer is that because changes from at-large plans in minority-Anglo cities are less likely to be the result of litigation or Justice Department objections, the drawing of district boundaries may not be as closely supervised, and this might work to the disadvantage of minority voters. On the other hand, inasmuch as there was significant minority representation on these cities' councils even before the changes occurred, one would expect the boundaries not to be patently disadvantageous to minority voters.

Whatever the explanation of this anomaly in majority-minority cities, the focus of our inquiry must be kept on the Anglo-majority cities, because they are the ones that present the classic conditions for minority vote dilution. Our findings in table 8.5 demonstrate clearly that when such cities shifted to districts, minority representation increased sharply, in contrast with cities that retained at-large elections.

The Effects of Mixed Plans on Minority Representation

A significant proportion of cities shifting from at-large plans chose mixed systems. Past research indicates that they typically fall between single-member-district systems and at-large ones in the equity of black representation. The data on blacks in table 8.5 conform to that pattern. The most plausible reason is that a mixed system is made up of both the least and most representative election methods. It is useful to examine the results of these two methods separately in order to see how mixed systems work.

Table 8.3 compares minority representation in the at-large and district components of mixed cities in 1989. It shows that most of the black representation can be attributed to the district rather than to the at-large component of the majority-Anglo plans. For Hispanics, the pattern was less clear, primarily because they were sharply underrepresented in both components. It is noteworthy, in light of these findings on blacks, that a federal court in *Williams v. City of Dallas* (1990) held that the at-large seats in the Dallas city council's mixed system diluted the voting strength of blacks.[125]

The Link between Minority Population Percentage and Minority Representation in Single-Member Districts

Table 8.6 shows 1989 minority representation in single-member districts in cities with mixed or pure single-member-district plans. There were 57 cities with at least some districts, but we were unable to obtain 1980 population data for districts in

12. The data base consists of the 257 districts in the 45 cities for which we did obtain complete information. The rule of thumb often mentioned is that a district must have a population of about 65 percent of a particular minority group in order to provide that group with a realistic opportunity to elect a minority candidate.[126] Table 8.6 indicates that for blacks in Texas, majority-black districts somewhat below that level were usually sufficient. However, about 5 percent of the nonblack population in majority-black districts was Hispanic, and the presence of Hispanics in such districts, as we shall see, can provide an advantage to black candidates.

In contrast to blacks, Hispanic candidates at no level were assured of victory, although their chances increased sharply when districts became majority-Hispanic. Yet even here, Hispanic districts often had significant numbers of blacks in the population. For minorities in general—where African Americans and Hispanics are treated as one group—the finding is much the same as for Hispanics. At the 70 percent level and above, 91.7 percent of officials were minority members.

Tables 8.6 and 8.7 shed light on another question: How well were blacks and Hispanics represented in majority-Anglo districts? If race did not play a significant role in whites' voting behavior, we would expect the answer to be, very well. The most useful data in table 8.6 for addressing this issue is the third set, which allows us to determine how likely it was that either blacks or Hispanics were elected from districts that were less than 50 percent black and Hispanic combined. The answer is, relatively few. Only 2.5 percent of the council members in the 147 districts less than 30 percent black and Hispanic belonged to the two ethnic minorities. The figure increased to 16.7 percent in the 29 districts 30–49.9 percent black and Hispanic. But it is obvious that the overwhelming majority of black and Hispanic council members were elected from districts in which Anglos were a relatively small minority. Data in table 8.7 corroborate this. In the 176 districts that were majority-Anglo, only 4.5 percent of the council members from those districts were black or Hispanic. Anglos did not fare much better in the 32 majority-black and 31 majority-Hispanic districts: they comprised 6.2 and 12.9 percent of the council members, respectively. These findings are consistent with the assumption that racially polarized voting was strong in most Texas cities during this period.

Minority Representation in Multiethnic Districts

Blacks and Tejanos often reside in contiguous or overlapping neighborhoods. Census data indicate that in 1980 both groups' residences were still highly segregated from those of Anglos in most of the larger Texas cities.[127] Many districts contained large numbers of both ethnic groups, although not a majority of either. In this circumstance, did minority candidates have a reasonable chance of winning office? The answer is provided by table 8.7, which contains data on the 257 districts analyzed in table 8.3 above. By examining minority council representation in districts with different ethnic compositions, we are able to see the benefits accruing to minority candidates in situations where minority coalitions are possible.

As might be predicted on the basis of table 8.3, table 8.7 shows that minority candidates had a very good chance in districts with a sizable African-American or Tejano majority and a very poor chance in districts with a sizable Anglo majority. The average black-majority district was 66.5 percent black, and the average percentage of minority officeholders was 93.8 percent. The average Hispanic-majority district was 66.4 percent Hispanic, and the average percentage of minority officeholders was 87.1 percent. The average Anglo-majority district was 82.3 percent Anglo, and the average percentage of minority officeholders was 4.5 percent. The table also shows that minority-plurality districts elected a significant number of minority candidates, as did Anglo-plurality districts in which blacks and Hispanics combined made up a slight majority. This is consistent with the interpretation that the minority groups help each other's candidates in these circumstances.

The Causes of Structural Changes in Texas Cities

In a fifteen-year period, fifty-two cities in our sample changed to some form of district plan; this represents structural change of a magnitude not witnessed in Texas since the widespread adoption of at-large plans in connection with the commission form of government during the Progressive Era.[128] The foregoing evidence, moreover, points to a causal link between the adoption of district systems and greatly increased minority representation on city councils.

To determine the causes of the structural changes, we sent questionnaires to all city attorneys in municipalities in our sample that had shifted from at-large to district or mixed systems between 1974 and 1989. Follow-up questionnaires were sent to nonrespondents after three weeks, and then telephone calls were made to those cities still not responding. The reasons officials gave for the changes were tabulated, and then compared with a data set obtained from voting rights lawyers throughout the state, consisting of lawsuits challenging at-large elections in Texas municipalities going back to the late 1960s. The information from these two sources was then combined and presented in table 8.8.

The table shows that twenty-nine (56 percent) of the fifty-two cities of 10,000 people or more that adopted single-member-district or mixed plans did so after a lawsuit was filed. (An additional city changed solely as the result of a section 5 objection.) In some cases, the suit alleged unconstitutional vote dilution; in others, it alleged violation of sections 2 or 5 of the Voting Rights Act.

There is not always a direct relation between the filing of a lawsuit (several of which were settled out of court) and a change in election structure. In some instances, city councils had already begun to discuss changing the election structure when the suit was filed. On the other hand, it is clear that in numerous cities, suits were necessary to compel councils to create districts in which minority candidates could have a fair opportunity to win.

Even where no suit was filed, it is obvious from the replies of various city attorneys that some of the changes had resulted from petitions by minority citizens for a change or from threats of a suit that the city could well have lost while incurring considerable costs. As one attorney put it who described his city's 1984 change as voluntary: "There was some perception among council members that districts were the wave of the future and would best be determined locally rather than by a lawsuit." Another attorney who described his city's change as voluntary said, "Because of recent changes in the law, [our city] felt a voluntary move to single member districts to be more efficient from an economic and political standpoint." Referring to changes that occurred shortly after the congressional amendment to section 2, these remarks demonstrate that the Voting Rights Act was very much on the minds of city council members in deciding to make the change. Earlier research on the causes of election law shifts in Texas corroborates this fact.[129]

Other city attorneys who described the process in their municipality as voluntary pointed out that there is no sharp distinction between voluntary and legally forced change. In reality, most cities changed because minority leaders or city officials were at least aware of the evolution in voting rights law, the effects of which they had heard about as other jurisdictions underwent legal challenges to their at-large elections. (One of the best-attended sessions of the annual meeting of the Texas Municipal League in the late 1970s was a workshop for city attorneys on voting rights litigation.) While some cities that changed voluntarily may have done so simply because they believed it was the right thing to do, legal developments in neighboring jurisdictions made the decision much easier.

Conclusion

A historical examination of minority voting rights in Texas from 1865 to the present reveals a continuing struggle by blacks and Mexican Americans to realize their voting rights in full measure. The very touchstone of democratic citizenship, these rights confer not only the ability to cast a vote without hindrance in every type of public election, but to have a reasonable chance to elect a candidate of one's choice. At the very least, this means an equal opportunity for a cohesive group of minority voters to elect their candidates when cohesive Anglo opposition systematically prevents them from doing so.

The struggle has been difficult and expensive, and at times has cost the lives of those who have taken part. White Texas officialdom, until the mid-1970s dominated by the conservative wing of the Democratic party, generally opposed the minority communities' quest for equal access to the ballot. The battles won by minority plaintiffs and their Anglo allies—most of whom belonged to the liberal wing of the Democrats—have taken place almost exclusively in federal courtrooms as a result of constitutional challenges, the extension of section 5 coverage to Texas in 1975, and the amendment of section 2 in 1982, which has eased burdens on plaintiffs in proving vote dilution.

Black Texans were actively involved as plaintiffs, lawyers, and fund-raisers in the series of white primary cases from the early 1920s until *Terry v. Adams* in 1953, which opened party activity once again to many southern blacks. Soon after the Voting Rights Act was signed, lawsuits began to challenge malapportioned districts and multimember election structures. The battle between racial liberals and conservatives over restrictive registration laws was fought until 1971, when, in *Beare v. Smith*, the liberals prevailed, even though rearguard efforts by white registrars in various counties to exclude blacks continued into the 1990s.[130]

Invoking the Fourteenth Amendment, MALDEF began its attack, in *Garza v. Smith* (1970), on the failure of registrars to allow assistance to voters not proficient in English. Also in the early 1970s minority plaintiffs and lawyers belonging to the three major ethnic groups, aided by academic experts, launched a series of constitutional challenges against dilutionary structures in municipalities, school districts, community college districts, the legislature, and Congress. These efforts played an important role in increasing the number of black and Tejano officeholders in these bodies. *White v. Regester* (1973), a Texas legislative redistricting case, was the first minority vote-dilution challenge in the United States to win in the Supreme Court.

In 1975, ten years after passage of the Voting Rights Act, its special provisions, including those in section 5, were extended to Texas. Bilingual ballots in Tejano areas became the norm. The Justice Department began to object to changes in election structures, and Texas jurisdictions were soon the target of the largest number of objections in any covered state. In just five years, between 1975 and 1980, the Attorney General objected to eighty-six proposed changes in Texas, significantly more than the fifty-three changes objected to in Mississippi in the fifteen-year period between 1965 and 1980.[131]

In the 110 Texas cities of 10,000 or more persons with a 1980 combined minority population of at least 10 percent, 52, including the state's 4 most populous, changed from at-large to single-member-district or mixed plans between 1974 and 1989. Of those, more than half—29—changed after a lawsuit was filed. Nineteen of the 29 suits were resolved after 1982, when section 2 was amended. This suggests that a decisive majority of the lawsuits that accompanied change were tried under the Voting Rights Act. In 3 of the 52 cities that changed—2 in which a lawsuit was filed, 1 in which it was not—section 5 objections also entered into the process, resulting in change. Finally, of the 22 changed cities in which neither a lawsuit nor an objection was instrumental in the switch, most of them adopted single-member districts after 1982, and city attorneys in some of them acknowledged frankly that the change came about as a result of amended section 2. Their cities decided to adopt districts before a lawsuit would have forced the issue. For this reason it seems probable that the great majority of the 52 cities adopted some form of districting plan as a direct or indirect result of the act.[132] And as we have demonstrated, the creation of districts has been responsible for much of the increase in minority officeholding.

This survey has shown how the evolution in constitutional and statutory law from the 1940s to the 1990s has developed in response to the growing demand for equal participation of previously unrepresented blacks and Mexican Americans. In the course of this evolution, powerful tools have been fashioned that make manipulation of the election system by racial conservatives more difficult. While this achievement alone is not sufficient to enable racial and language minorities to achieve full integration into American society, it certainly represents necessary and important progress toward that goal.

TABLE 8.1
Minority Representation on Council in 1989 by Election Plan, Texas Cities of 10,000 or More Population with 10 Percent or More Combined Black and Hispanic Population in 1980[a]

Type of Plan by % Minority in City Population, 1980	N	*Mean % Minority in City Population, 1980*			*Mean % Minority on City Council, 1989*		
		Black	*Hispanic*	*Black + Hispanic*	*Black*	*Hispanic*	*Black + Hispani*
SMD plan							
10–29.9	12	14.9	8.9	**23.9**	19.6	3.8	**23.4**
30–49.9	10	22.2	14.5	**36.6**	25.5	10.8	**36.2**
50–100	4	3.4	66.5	**69.9**	2.5	53.3	**55.8**
Mixed plan							
10–29.9	15	10.0	12.4	**22.3**	9.9	9.8	**19.7**
30–49.9	14	17.8	22.1	**39.9**	18.5	10.4	**28.9**
50–100	2	3.3	58.3	**61.6**	0.0	35.4	**35.4**
At-large plan							
10–29.9	26	8.5	9.8	**18.4**	6.8	2.1	**8.8**
30–49.9	12	17.7	20.6	**38.3**	13.3	10.4	**23.6**
50–100	15	0.9	76.4	**77.3**	1.7	71.3	**73.0**

[a] One city is omitted from this table because it elected council from multimember districts.

Note: In tables 8.1–8.7, the "Black + Hispanic" percentages are not the summed row values of blacks a Hispanics. Rather, these percentages are derived from the raw data.

BLE 8.2

anges in Minority Representation on Council between 1974 and 1989, Texas Cities of 10,000 More Population with 10 Percent or More Combined Black and Hispanic Population in 1980

e of Change by Minority in City ulation, 1980	N[a]	*Mean % Minority in City Population, 1980*			*Mean % Minority on City Council*					
					Before Change (1974)			*After Change (1989)*		
		Black	*Hispanic*	*Black + Hispanic*	*Black*	*Hispanic*	*Black + Hispanic*	*Black*	*Hispanic*	*Black + Hispanic*
				Changed Systems						
m at-large to SMD plan										
10–29.9	9	14.6	10.6	**25.1**	5.6	1.9	**7.4**	19.3	3.7	**23.0**
30–49.9	9	23.9	12.5	**36.4**	3.2	1.9	**5.1**	26.7	11.9	**38.6**
50–100	4	3.4	66.5	**69.9**	3.1	47.5	**50.6**	2.5	53.3	**55.8**
m at-large to mixed plan										
10–29.9	14	10.3	12.7	**23.0**	2.6	1.8	**4.4**	9.5	10.5	**20.0**
30–49.9	13	17.5	23.2	**40.6**	7.6	3.8	**11.4**	19.0	11.1	**30.2**
50–100	1	5.1	46.6	**51.8**	16.7	50.0	**66.7**	0.0	37.5	**37.5**
				Unchanged Systems						
-large plan										
10–29.9	26	8.5	9.9	**18.4**	5.3	3.7	**8.9**	6.8	2.1	**8.8**
30–49.9	12	17.7	20.6	**38.3**	10.2	4.9	**15.1**	13.3	10.4	**23.6**
50–100	14	0.9	77.0	**77.9**	0.0	65.4	**65.4**	1.8	73.6	**75.4**

[a] The number of cities in table 8.2 (102) is smaller than that in table 8.1 (110) because in five cases the changes m an at-large plan occurred before 1974 or the change was not from an at-large but from a mixed plan; and in ee cases data on minority council members for the year 1974 were not available.

BLE 8.3

inority Representation in 1989 in Mixed Plans by District and At-Large Components, xas Cities of 10,000 or More Population with 10 Percent or More Combined Black d Hispanic Population in 1980

Minority in City pulation, 1980	N	*Mean % Minority, Councilpersons in District Components, 1989*			*Mean % Minority, Councilpersons in at-Large Components, 1989*		
		Black	*Hispanic*	*Black + Hispanic*	*Black*	*Hispanic*	*Black + Hispanic*
–29.9	16	13.8	9.3	**23.0**	2.1	9.4	**11.5**
–49.9	13	24.8	12.3	**37.1**	9.5	7.9	**17.4**
–100	2	0.0	63.3	**63.3**	0.0	0.0	**0.0**

TABLE 8.4
Two Equity Measures Comparing Percentage Minority on Council in 1989 with Percentage Minority in City Population in 1980, Texas Cities of 10,000 or More Population with 10 Perce or More Combined Black and Hispanic Population in 1980

Type of Plan by % Minority in City Population, 1980	N[a]	*Difference Measure (% on council − % in Population*			*Ratio Measure (% on Coun ÷ % in Population*		
		Black	*Hispanic*	*Black + Hispanic*	*Black*	*Hispanic*	*Black Hispa*
				Changed Systems			
From at-large to SMD plan							
10–29.9	9	4.7	−6.9	**−2.2**	1.32	0.35	**0.92**
30–49.9	9	2.8	−0.5	**2.3**	1.12	0.95	**1.06**
50–100	4	−0.9	−13.2	**−14.1**	0.74	0.80	**0.80**
From at-large to mixed plan							
10–29.9	14	−0.8	−2.2	**−3.0**	0.92	0.83	**0.87**
30–49.9	13	1.6	−12.0	**−10.4**	1.08	0.48	**0.74**
50–100	1	−5.1	−9.1	**−14.3**	0.00	0.80	**0.72**
				Unchanged Systems			
At-large Plan							
10–29.9	26	−1.8	−7.8	**−9.6**	0.80	0.21	**0.48**
30–49.9	12	−4.4	−10.3	**−14.7**	0.75	0.50	**0.62**
50–100	14	0.9	−3.4	**−2.5**	1.96	0.96	**0.97**

[a] The cities in this table are the same ones as in table 8.2.

LE 8.5
nges in Minority Representation on City Council between 1974 and 1989, Texas Cities of)00 or More Population with 10 Percent or More Combined Black and Hispanic Population in 0 (Ratio Equity Measure)

e of Change by % ority in City ulation, 1980	N[a]	Mean Minority Representational Equity on Council					
		1974			1989		
		Black	*Hispanic*	*Black + Hispanic*	*Black*	*Hispanic*	*Black + Hispanic*
		Changed Systems					
m at-large to SMD plan							
10–29.9	9	0.38	0.18	**0.29**	1.32	0.35	**0.92**
30–49.9	9	0.13	0.15	**0.14**	1.12	0.95	**1.06**
50–100	4	0.91	0.71	**0.72**	0.74	0.80	**0.80**
m at-large to mixed plan							
10–29.9	14	0.25	0.14	**0.19**	0.92	0.83	**0.87**
30–49.9	13	0.43	0.16	**0.28**	1.08	0.48	**0.74**
50–100	1	3.27	1.07	**1.29**	0.00	0.80	**0.72**
		Unchanged Systems					
large Plan							
10–29.9	26	0.62	0.37	**0.48**	0.80	0.21	**0.48**
30–49.9	12	0.58	0.24	**0.39**	0.75	0.50	**0.62**
50–100	14	0.00	0.84	**0.84**	1.96	0.96	**0.97**

The cities in this table are the same ones as in table 8.2.

TABLE 8.6
Minority Representation in Council Single-Member Districts in 1989,[a] Texas Cities of 10,000 or More Population with 10 Percent or More Combined Black and Hispanic Population in 1980

		Mean % Minority Population in Districts, 1980			*Mean % Minority Councilpersons in Districts, 1989*		
% Ethnic Population	N	*Black*	*Hispanic*	*Black + Hispanic*	*Black*	*Hispanic*	*Black + Hispanic*
Black							
0–29.9	212	6.4	20.6	**27.0**	3.3	16.0	**19.3**
30–49.9	13	37.1	22.8	**59.8**	53.8	7.7	**61.5**
50–59.9	3	55.5	2.4	**58.0**	100.0	0.0	**100.0**
60–64.9	13	62.4	4.2	**66.6**	84.6	0.0	**84.6**
65–69.9	7	67.2	4.8	**72.0**	100.0	0.0	**100.0**
70–100	9	75.7	5.1	**80.8**	100.0	0.0	**100.0**
Hispanic							
0–29.9	200	17.2	8.6	**25.7**	18.0	2.0	**20.0**
30–49.9	26	13.0	39.5	**52.5**	19.2	26.9	**46.1**
50–59.9	10	9.5	54.3	**63.9**	10.0	80.0	**90.0**
60–64.9	6	9.4	63.2	**72.6**	16.7	66.7	**83.4**
65–69.9	6	5.8	67.3	**73.1**	16.7	66.7	**83.4**
70–100	9	2.6	81.3	**83.9**	0.0	88.9	**88.9**
Black + Hispanic							
0–29.9	147	5.3	8.2	**13.5**	0.6	1.9	**2.5**
30–49.9	29	12.4	26.8	**39.2**	6.7	10.0	**16.7**
50–59.9	13	26.9	28.9	**55.8**	53.3	26.7	**80.0**
60–64.9	16	34.1	29.3	**63.4**	58.8	29.4	**88.2**
65–69.9	16	37.1	30.0	**67.1**	43.8	43.8	**87.6**
70–100	36	37.5	41.6	**79.1**	55.6	36.1	**91.7**

[a] Data were available for 45 of the 57 cities with districts.

TABLE 8.7
Minority Council Representation in Single-Member Districts in 1989 by Ethnic Composition of District, Texas Cities of 10,000 or More Population with 10 Percent or More Combined Black and Hispanic Population in 1980

		Mean % Minority Population in Districts, 1980			*Mean % Minority Councilpersons in Districts, 1989*		
Ethnic Composition of District	N	*Black*	*Hispanic*	*Black + Hispanic*	*Black*	*Hispanic*	*Black + Hispanic*
Black majority	32	66.5	4.4	**71.0**	93.8	0.0	**93.8**
Hispanic majority	31	6.8	66.4	**73.2**	9.7	77.4	**87.1**
Anglo majority	176	6.5	11.3	**17.7**	1.1	3.4	**4.5**
Black + Hispanic majority (no single group a majority) with:							
Black plurality	2	46.0	21.0	**67.0**	100.0	0.0	**100.0**
Hispanic plurality	8	22.1	44.9	**67.0**	50.0	50.0	**100.0**
Anglo plurality	8	28.7	27.5	**56.2**	37.5	12.5	**50.0**

TABLE 8.8
Cause of Change from At-Large to Mixed or District Plan between 1974 and 1989, Texas Cities of 10,000 or More Population with 10 Percent or More Combined Black and Hispanic Population in 1980

City	*Did Lawsuit Accompany Change?*	*Lawsuit/Reason for Change*[a]
	Changed to Single-Member Districts	
Beeville	No	City secretary said 1974 change was the result of pressure brought by Hispanic leaders. School district system had recently been overturned through voting rights litigation.
Cleburne	No	City Attorney said change was the result of black leaders' activities.
Corsicana	No	There were no activities or threats by minority leaders, but city attorney said city was mindful of changes elsewhere.
El Paso	No	Threat of a lawsuit from an Anglo civic club that felt its interests were slighted; also some Hispanic involvement.
Ennis	No	Not due to activities of minority leaders, but charter commission was made up of people "from all ethnic groups."
Fort Worth	No	Voting rights attorney George Korbel said change was made "under threat"; city attorney said it was voluntary, but was seen "as necessary and would have been required in the future."
Henderson	No	City attorney said minorities requested change but made no threat.
Jacksonville	No	City attorney refused interview.
Laredo	No	Voting rights attorney Korbel said threat was necessary; city attorney denied it.
Levelland	Yes	*Esparza and Herrera v. City of Levelland;* settled, 1986.
Longview	No	No threat of suit or minority activity.
Lubbock	Yes	*Jones v. City of Lubbock*; plaintiffs won at trial, 1981.

(*continued*)

TABLE 8.8 (*Continued*)

City	*Did Lawsuit Accompany Change?*	*Lawsuit/Reason for Change*
Lufkin	Yes	*David v. Garrison*; plaintiffs won at trial; 5th Cir. reversed; parties settled, 1978.
Marshall	Yes	*Wilson v. City of Marshall*; settled before trial.
Palestine	Yes	*Robinson v. Rodgers;* settled in 1976.
Plainview	No	City attorney imputed change to "recent changes in the law," referring to amended section 2.
Port Lavaca	Yes	*Rodriguez v. City of Port Lavaca*; settled in 1984.
San Angelo	No	Voting rights attorney Korbel said change occurred "under threat"; city attorney said it was voluntary, resulting from a petition from minorities and others.
San Antonio	Yes	*Martinez v. Becker*; after suit was filed, section 5 objection to annexation triggered establishment of new plan. City attorney nonetheless described the change as "voluntary." New plan adopted in 1977.
Sweetwater	No	City attorney said change was voluntary.
Terrell	Yes	*PCVO v. City of Terrell*; plaintiffs won at trial.
Texarkana	No	City acceded in minority leaders' request.
Tyler	Yes	*Square v. Halbert*; settled in 1976.
Waco	Yes	*Calderon v. Waco I.S.D. and City of Waco*; plaintiffs won. Sustained by 5th Cir. in 1978.
	Changed to Mixed Plan	
Alvin	Yes	*Binkerhoff v. City of Alvin*; settled in 1985.
Baytown	Yes	*Campos v. City of Baytown*; plaintiffs won at trial, and city in 1989 adopted an interim plan while case was on remand from 5th Cir. (In 1992 a permanent single-member district plan was adopted.)

(*continued*)

TABLE 8.8 (*Continued*)

City	*Did Lawsuit Accompany Change?*	*Lawsuit/Reason for Change*
Beaumont	Yes	*Moore v. City of Beaumont*; city adopted plan in 1984 after suit was filed. City attorney said process began before suit was filed.
Big Spring	Yes	*LULAC v. City of Big Spring*; settled in 1983.
Brenham	No	City attorney said change was not connected to racial issues.
Brownfield	Yes	*Davila v. City of Brownfield*; settled in 1986.
Corpus Christi	Yes	*Alonzo v. Jones*; plaintiffs won at trial, new plan adopted in 1983.
Dallas	Yes	*Lipscomb v. Wise*; plaintiffs won at trial in 1975. (Mixed system was later challenged and replaced with a single-member-district plan in 1991.)
Denison	No	City attorney said there were no threats, but plan was adopted because it was "the wave of the future."
Denton	No	City attorney refused interview.
El Campo	No	City attorney said there were no threats, no racial activists.
Grand Prairie	No	Blacks filed petition; leadership was provided by white "populist" mayor.
Hereford	Yes	*Aguero v. City of Hereford*; settled in 1985.
Houston	Yes	*Greater Houston Civic Council v. Mann*; city won at trial, but changed system in 1979 following section 5 objection to subsequent annexations. Objection was based in part on data collected by plaintiffs at trial.
La Porte	No	Section 5 objection to intended charter revision led to change in 1979.
Lamesa	Yes	*Sorola v. City of Lamesa*; settled in 1984.
McKinney	No	Request was made by black leaders.
Midland	Yes	*LULAC v. City of Midland*; settled in 1985.

(*continued*)

TABLE 8.8 (*Continued*)

City	*Did Lawsuit Accompany Change?*	*Lawsuit/Reason for Change*
Nacogdoches	Yes	*Weaver v. Muckleroy*; plaintiffs won at trial. Case settled in 1975 while on appeal.
New Braunfels	Yes	*Torres v. City of New Braunfels*; settled in 1984.
Odessa	No	Black council member requested change, according to city attorney.
Port Arthur	Yes	*City of Port Arthur v. United States*; original plaintiffs lost constitutional case (*Mosley v. Sadler*). City then tried to annex white residential areas. Private plaintiffs and the Department of Justice filed suit under section 5 and ultimately won, in a case that was decided by the Supreme Court in 1982. City attorney refused interview.
Snyder	Yes	*Peña v. City of Snyder*; settled in 1987.
Taylor	Yes	*Thompson v. City of Taylor*; settled in 1985. Earlier plaintiffs, who had filed suit in the 1970s, nonsuited in the wake of *Bolden v. City of Mobile*, for lack of evidence of discriminatory intent.
Temple	No	Voting rights attorney Korbel said change made "under threat"; city attorney said it was voluntary. City changed twice: once in 1977, again in 1989.
Texas City	Yes	*United States v. City Commission of Texas City*; the Department of Justice filed a constitutional and section 2 suit in 1977. Shortly before trial in 1978 the city, by referendum, adopted a charter amendment creating a mixed plan; the case was dismissed without prejudice as moot.
Victoria	Yes	*Mata v. City of Victoria*; settled. But city attorney's office, almost a decade after the suit was filed, said the change was "completely voluntary."

(*continued*)

TABLE 8.8 (*Continued*)

City	*Did Lawsuit Accompany Change?*	*Lawsuit/Reason for Change*
Wichita Falls	Yes	*Vasquez v. City of Wichita Falls*; settled before trial in 1985.
SUMMARY	Yes 29 (56%) No[b] 23 (44%)	

Sources: Plaintiffs' attorneys' records; telephone interviews with city attorney's or secretary's office in cities; interviews with George Korbel, voting rights attorney with Texas Rural Legal Aid, and Gerald Hebert, Department of Justice.

[a]There are minor discrepancies between the classification of a few cities' election plans in this table—derived from a telephone survey of the cities in 1989—and that derived from records of plaintiffs' attorneys who tried the cases between 1974 and 1989. In some instances, the attorneys classified a city as single-member district, and the city classified it as mixed, or vice versa. Two cities in table 8.1 are absent from this table because they changed from mixed to single-member-district plans rather than from at-large plans.

[b]One of these twenty-three cases involved a change resulting from a section 5 objection.

TABLE 8.9
Major Disfranchising Devices in Texas

Device	*Date Established*	*Date Abolished*
White primaries (major parties)		
Locally, on a county-by-county basis (Democrats)	At least as early as 1888[a]	Unknown
Virtually statewide, regulated by state party (Democrats)	1904[b]	1923[c]
Statewide, mandated by state law	1923[c]	1927[d]
Statewide, mandated by State Democratic Executive Committee (Democrats)	1927[e]	1932[f]
Statewide, mandated by Democratic state convention (Democrats)	1932[e]	1944[g]
Local so-called nonpartisan white men's parties and preprimary groups	Beginning in 1874[h]	1953[i]
Poll tax		
State elections	1902[j]	1964[k]
Federal elections	1902[j]	1966[l]
Early and short registration period	1903[m]	1971[n]

[a] Barr 1971, 195–96.
[b] Ibid., 201.
[c] Barr 1982, 134.
[d] *Nixon v. Herndon,* 273 U.S. 536.
[e] Key 1949, 622.
[f] *Nixon v. Condon,* 286 U.S. 73.
[g] *Smith v. Allwright* 321 U.S. 649.
[h] Rice 1971, 113.
[i] *Terry v. Adams,* 345 U.S. 461.
[j] Barr 1971, 205.
[k] Twenty-fourth Amendment to the U.S. Constitution.
[l] *United States v. State of Texas,* 252 F. Supp 234 (1966).
[m] Barr 1971, 206.
[n] *Beare v. Smith,* 321 F. Supp. 100 (S.D. Tex. 1971), *aff'd sub nom. Beare v. Briscoe,* 498 F.2d 244 (5th Cir. 1974).

TABLE 8.10
Ethnic Registered Voters and Officeholders in Texas, Selected Years[a]

	Black		Hispanic		Anglo	
	N	%	N	%	N	%
Registered voters						
1964	375,000	12.4	—	—	—	—
1968	540,000	13.2	—	—	—	—
1988[b]	832,610	11.0	1,169,736	15.5	5,549,520	73.5[c]
Officeholders						
1965	<7	<0.1	—	—	—	—
1971	45	<1.0	—[d]	—	—	—
1989	312	1.2	1,693	6.3	25,036	92.5

Sources. The 1964 and 1968 registration data were supplied by the Voter Education Project (1976) of the Southern Regional Council; 1988 registration data were from U.S. Department of Commerce, Bureau of the Census 1989, 39. The 1965 officeholder data are found in U.S. Commission on Civil Rights 1968, 221; 1971 officeholder data are reported in Joint Center for Political Studies 1971, 113–17; 1988 officeholder data are from Joint Center for Political Studies 1989, 11, and the National Association of Latino Elected and Appointed Officials 1989, vi.

[a] Mean black and Hispanic populations 1960–90: 12.3% and 19.9%, respectively.

[b] Registration figures for 1988 are based on postelection surveys of self-reported registration. Respondents tend to overreport their degree of participation; some evidence points to disproportionate overreporting by minority respondents.

[c] Includes a small number—less than 1 percent of total registrants—of Asians and other nonblack, non-Hispanic minorities.

[d] An early attempt at a systematic count of Tejano elected officeholders was made in 1973 by George Korbel, a voting rights lawyer, and revealed a total of 565.

CHAPTER NINE

Virginia

THOMAS R. MORRIS AND NEIL BRADLEY

VIRGINIA has always clung to an image of moderation in race relations, even though it was one of the original six states deemed by Congress to warrant being covered entirely under the special provisions of the Voting Rights Act. In 1960, five years before passage of the act and just as the state's "massive resistance" to school desegregation had been struck down by the courts, blacks made up 20.6 percent of the state's population. Public schools in Prince Edward County had been closed in 1959 and would not reopen until 1964. Only about 23 percent of voting-age blacks were registered to vote.[1] The political organization that had become synonymous with the name of Senator Harry F. Byrd, Sr., reigned supreme in Virginia, easily defeating antiorganization candidates supported by black voters in the Democratic primary and Republican challengers in the 1961 elections.

Key wryly observed in 1949 that Mississippi was a "hotbed of democracy" in contrast with Virginia. Only once between 1925 and 1945 did the winning candidate in the Democratic primary receive more than 8.6 percent of the vote of the adult population.[2] Virginia had the distinction during this period of turning out the smallest proportion of its potential vote for governor of any of the southern states. Suffrage restrictions effectively minimized voting by blacks and poor whites. These restrictions were crucial to the successful operation of the Byrd organization and its predecessor, the Martin organization, headed by U.S. Senator Thomas Staples Martin from the late nineteenth century until his death in 1919. The increasing black voting strength made possible by the removal of suffrage restrictions in the 1960s paralleled the demise of the Byrd organization.

Nineteenth- and Early Twentieth-Century Suffrage Restrictions

After the fall of the Confederacy, Virginia avoided a period of radical Reconstruction such as most other southern states experienced. The Virginia constitutional convention of 1867–68 originally proposed a document known as the Underwood Constitution, which incorporated universal adult male suffrage for blacks as well as whites. Seventy-two radicals (twenty-five of whom were black) had overwhelmed the thirty-three conservatives, and the convention majority delivered its harshest blows by supporting the "disfranchisement" and "test-oath" clauses.[3] Those clauses would have denied the ballot and public office to the vast majority of white Virginians who had held civil or military office under the Confederacy. Shocked by the provisions of the proposed Underwood Constitution, conservatives from both the Whig and Democratic parties came together to form the Conservative party of Virginia. A united assault by white voters against the Underwood Constitution was avoided when moderates from the Republican and Conservative parties joined together to support "universal suffrage and universal amnesty": the enfranchisement of blacks without the disfranchisement of former Confederates.[4] White Conservatives and moderate Republicans accepted a liberal state constitution, which included black suffrage, in exchange for being allowed separate votes on the two disqualifying clauses when the constitution was put before the voters for approval in 1869.

In the 1869 elections, the disfranchisement and test-oath clauses, aimed at secessionist whites, were soundly defeated at the same time the new constitution was overwhelmingly adopted. The gubernatorial candidate supported by most conservative whites, Gilbert Walker, was also elected by a majority of over eighteen thousand votes.[5] Faced with the prospects of dividing the vote of those opposing the biracial Republican ticket, the Conservative party candidates for statewide office resigned in favor of the nominees of the conservative Republicans who ran on the "True Republican" ticket. Some blacks voted for Walker, the True Republican nominee, but most supported the losing Republican candidate.[6] Meanwhile, the Conservative party (destined to become the Democratic party in 1883) won solid majorities in both houses of the legislature and five of the nine seats in Congress.

In the election of delegates to the 1867–68 convention, 95,145 blacks but only 76,084 whites voted; 88 percent of registered blacks voted, whereas only 63 percent of registered whites did. Two years later, in 1869, whites outvoted blacks 125,114 to 97,205 in the referendum on the Underwood Constitution and the statewide and legislative elections.[7] The increased voting by whites ensured that, despite the dominant role played by radicals and blacks in drafting the new constitution, the Conservative party presided over its application and shaped state policies during the 1870s. Reconstruction ended for Virginia in early 1870, and, from the perspective of Virginia traditionalists, the state had been "redeemed" in 1869 from the prospect of rule by blacks and their radical Republican allies, who had controlled the Underwood Convention.[8]

In 1870 the state legislature enacted a statute requiring separate registration books for blacks and whites. This law made chicanery easier by limiting through technical delays the number of blacks who could vote in the allotted time or allowing local registrars to "lose" the black voter list. Gerrymandering to break up black pockets of voters took place during reapportionment in 1874–76, 1883, and 1891, first by the Conservatives and then by the Democrats.[9] In 1876, the Conservatives amended the state constitution to make payment of the poll tax a prerequisite for voting, and conviction for petty larceny grounds for disfranchisement. According to the Richmond *State* and *Petersburg Index and Appeal*, these amendments constituted "almost . . . a political revolution" in reducing the black vote in 1877.[10] Black voting had already begun to decline and was further diminished in importance by the amendments.

A brief period of control by the Readjuster party, which gained broad support from blacks and sought to ease (or "readjust") the burden of prewar debt, led to the repeal of the poll tax in 1882, but the exclusion of blacks from public office continued unabated. Twenty-seven blacks had been elected in 1869 among the 180 members of the new general assembly, but that number fell to 17 two years later and plummeted to 2 in 1885.[11] By 1891 no blacks sat in the state legislature, and only 3 Republicans remained. Moreover, Virginia's first and only black congressman, John Mercer Langston (1890–91), was defeated in the 1890 congressional elections along with all other Republican candidates. (Langston had been elected in 1888 but did not take his seat until 1890 because of an election contest.)

During the early stages of the Democratic organization under Senator Thomas Martin (1893–1919), black citizens were virtually eliminated from electoral participation in Virginia. The two-step disfranchisement included election "reform" and a new constitution. The Democrats passed a secret-ballot law in 1894 known as the Walton Act. It provided for a publicly printed ballot to be marked secretly in booths. Neither party names nor symbols were permitted on the ballots. Provision was made for special election judges (i.e., Democrats) to assist illiterates, but the practical effect was to end voting by most blacks in Virginia. One scholar has estimated that the percentage of blacks voting for the candidate opposing the Democratic nominee dropped from 46 percent in 1893 to 2 percent in 1897.[12]

In 1902 Virginia ranked seventh among the states in the percentage of blacks in its total population (35.7 percent); moreover, blacks constituted a majority of the population in thirty-five of the state's one hundred counties.[13] The Virginia constitutional convention of 1901–02 took the second step in disfranchisement in its provisions for a framework of poll taxes, an "understanding clause," and literacy tests designed explicitly for the purpose of disfranchising black voters. The overall effect of the new requirements, which affected poor whites as well as blacks, was to decrease dramatically the total vote in the state; the presidential vote declined almost 50 percent from 264,240 votes in 1900 to 135,865 in 1904. The restricted electorate once again aided the Democratic organization in tightening its grip on state politics.

Even though voter turnout for all races and regions in Virginia was shockingly low, black voter participation was even more dismal. Of the estimated 147,000 blacks of voting age at the time the 1902 constitution was adopted, only 21,000 were on the registration lists once Virginia's registrars began applying the understanding clause. After the poll tax became a voting requirement in 1905, it was estimated that fewer than one-half of that 21,000 met both poll tax and registration requirements. In Richmond the number of blacks qualified to vote shrank from 6,427 in 1900 to 228 in 1907.[14]

Black Participation under the Martin and Byrd Organizations

With the work of the disfranchising convention completed, the way was cleared for the Martin organization to acquiesce in the demands of the antiorganization reformers for a direct primary in Virginia. Without the dramatic reduction in the black vote, it is doubtful that the organization would have agreed to the primary system.[15] Discriminatory application of registration procedures by local registrars against black citizens also was used to exclude Republicans and other white voters who refused to support organization candidates, thus serving the additional purpose of reducing the competitiveness of the Republican party to which most blacks gave their support. Nomination in the Democratic primary became tantamount to election in Virginia.

Until 1912 blacks were legally eligible to vote in the Democratic primary, although the black vote in the first primary of 1905 was "minuscule and inconsequential."[16] In 1912 the legislature passed a statewide primary law introduced by Richard Byrd, the father of Harry Byrd and speaker of the house of delegates at the time. Known as the Byrd Law, it gave the party wide discretion to regulate its affairs. The Virginia Democratic party promptly affirmed a policy of limiting participation in its primary to qualified white voters.[17]

Little action was taken from 1912 through 1925 to challenge Virginia's white primary policy. But when the U.S. Supreme Court in 1927 struck down a 1923 Texas law prohibiting black participation in Democratic primary elections, blacks attempted to vote in a 1928 primary in Richmond. After election judges denied them the opportunity to participate, one black plaintiff challenged the constitutionality of the Byrd Law. It had been drafted with foresight to avoid charges of discriminatory state action by permitting parties to make their own regulations, but the law fell as a result of one of its progressive elements—public financing of the primary election. A 1930 federal appeals court decision invalidated Virginia's publicly financed white primary, and the state did not appeal. This legal development gave Virginia the distinction of being the only southern state at the time with no racial restrictions on primary participation.[18]

But while invalidated by the federal courts, the white primary statute remained on the books, even though unenforced. As late as 1947 party leaders counseled against updating the party rules rather than creating, according to Key, "an opportunity for intolerant elements to sound off, unnecessarily and undesirably opening the whole race issue, which is little discussed in Virginia politics."[19] Key in 1949 observed an Upper South attitude among Virginia whites toward blacks, which resulted in a proportionally larger black vote in primaries and general elections.[20] Blacks were permitted to vote in primaries and serve as delegates in conventions. The Byrd organization was not troubled by this black participation because blacks made up such a small percentage of the registered voters and other suffrage restrictions were still in force. In addition to being registered, voters also had to be current in the payment of the poll tax six months before an election. Moreover, citizens who had been lax in payment of the tax had to pay for the two preceding years as well, for a total of $4.50, to be eligible to vote.

Blacks rarely sought office prior to 1945, but black voting increased markedly in Virginia cities following World War II, especially where there were black candidates seeking local offices. Oliver Hill, a black attorney in Richmond respected by both races, came within 191 votes in 1947 of being nominated to the state legislature in the Democratic primary. The legislative seat he ran for encompassed the entire city of Richmond. The following year he garnered an estimated 3,000 white votes and won the ninth of nine at-large seats on Richmond City Council.[21] Two years later, in 1950, Hill was narrowly defeated for reelection when blacks opted to support a seven-person biracial ticket rather than cast single-shot ballots for Hill, as they had done in 1948.

Hill's success encouraged other black candidates in the early fifties. The coming of white massive resistance to the U.S. Supreme Court's 1954 school desegregation decision, however, was a sharp setback to black aspirations. In his book on massive resistance, Robbins Gates summarized black participation at the time in this manner:

> In states of the Upper South [including Virginia], Negroes can be conceded political "participation" without a commensurate concession of political "power." Participation without power makes for hat-in-hand politics. Negroes are to be found in both Virginia parties, and in both factions of the dominant party, but in no party or faction do they have any real political power "as Negroes." No party or faction thereof in the state is in a position to yield to any Negro demands that fail to conform to basic tenets of white supremacy.[22]

Between the 1870s and 1960s, therefore, various suffrage restrictions effectively limited black voting to a level that was not threatening to white supremacists and virtually eliminated black officeholding.

Political Change Comes to Virginia

Prior to 1964 the black vote in Harry Byrd's Virginia had not been significant, much less decisive. The end of the Byrd era was foreshadowed when the state Democratic convention repudiated Byrd's position of "golden silence" on the 1964 presidential election and endorsed the candidacy of Lyndon Johnson. Increasingly sophisticated voter registration drives inspired by the successes of the civil rights movement, abolition of the poll tax, and near unanimous black support for the initiatives of the new Johnson administration resulted in blacks providing the winning margin of 76,704 votes for the Democratic ticket in Virginia. Estimates of the number of blacks voting varied from 100,000 to "at least 160,000."[23] Whatever the figure, it was evident that with blacks casting well over 90 percent of their vote for the Democratic ticket, Johnson could not have won in Virginia without them.

The Voting Rights Act, passed the next year, ended Virginia's literacy test for voting. The adoption of the Twenty-fourth Amendment to the U.S. Constitution in 1964 eliminated the poll tax for federal elections, and the Supreme Court's decision in *Harper v. Virginia State Board of Elections*[24] invalidated the poll tax for state elections as well.

The importance of the tax for the Byrd organization was highlighted by the call of a special session of the state legislature in the fall of 1963 to design an alternative way of limiting the electorate, once it became clear that the tax would soon be invalidated. To replace it, legislation was enacted requiring voters to file a "certificate of residence" six months prior to each federal election to prove continuing residence in the state. In May 1964 a federal district court invalidated the legislation, clearing the way for Virginia citizens to vote, for the first time in sixty years, without paying the poll tax.[25] An estimated 55,000 blacks registered as part of an increase of 224,305 new voters from April to October 1964.[26] The number of votes cast by Virginians in 1964 topped 1 million for the first time in history, an increase of 270,000 over the 1960 presidential election. Voter turnout in the state moved from 33.3 percent in 1960 to 41.2 percent of the adult population in 1964; while representing a significant increase, the 1964 figure was still 20 percentage points below the national average.[27]

The 1965 gubernatorial election proved to be a transition to a new political era in state politics. Lieutenant Governor Mills E. Godwin, Jr., who had supported massive resistance as a member of the state senate, acknowledged the changes taking place by endorsing the Democratic presidential ticket in 1964, the year President Lyndon B. Johnson was challenged by Barry Goldwater. He benefited the following year when he received the gubernatorial nomination without opposition and enjoyed labor and black support in the general election. In part because the poll tax still applied to state elections in 1965, far fewer blacks voted than in 1964. The Democratic majorities in black precincts were less than for the Johnson ticket, but once again the victorious Democratic nominee would not have been elected without black voters.[28]

In 1966 a solid black vote was essential to William Spong's upset victory by 611 votes over the aging incumbent senator, A. Willis Robertson, in the Democratic primary. Spong won an easy victory in the general election on the basis of urban and black votes. In the other Senate race that year, blacks overwhelmingly supported the Republican candidate against Harry Byrd, Jr., who had been appointed to his father's seat. The black vote reduced Byrd's support, but not enough to deny him a majority of the popular votes.[29] The decade of the 1960s ended with the 1969 election of the first Republican governor of the century. A divisive Democratic runoff primary enabled the moderate Republican candidate, Linwood Holton, to win this first gubernatorial election after the removal of the poll tax in state elections. Holton's triumph demonstrated that Republicans could run well in urban Virginia in races for state offices, just as their presidential nominees had done for years. Moreover, Holton's 37.2 percent share of the black vote was a key factor in his victory.

The Voting Rights Act was one of a number of interrelated factors shaping the changes in Virginia's electorate during the sixties. The act's elimination of the literacy test, the removal of the poll tax at the federal and state level, the increasing urbanization of the state, and the more competitive status of Republicans were all important components of the changes taking place. The potency of the black vote in general elections from 1964 to 1966 subsided, however, as the registration of white voters, too, increased dramatically. From 1965 to 1973 the black vote steadily declined as a percentage of the total vote in general elections. Voting in selected black precincts during that period remained relatively constant in general elections even as overall participation within the electorate increased.

The erosion of black influence was dramatically demonstrated in populist Democrat Henry Howell's narrow loss to Mills Godwin in the 1973 race for governor. Given the near unanimous black support for Howell, he would have won the election if the black participation rate had approached that of whites. Sabato quoted black leaders as conceding a loss of "intensity" following the initial surge of black registration in the 1960s and interpreted the low participation level as an indication that "many blacks are disillusioned with the political process or question the fruits of participation in the system."[30]

In the Democratic primary, in contrast to general elections, black influence was increasing even as their participation rates in general elections declined. Blacks, labor, and liberals became disproportionately represented in the Democratic primary as conservative voters dropped out of it, shifting their focus to the general election in November. Blacks overwhelmingly supported nominees of the Democratic party who were shut out of the governorship and both U.S. Senate seats during the 1970s. Only in 1977, when a moderate, Marshall Coleman, was elected as the state's first Republican attorney general, did a Republican candidate for statewide office even approach Linwood Holton's 37.2 percent of the black vote in 1969. Coleman received 32.7 percent of that vote against a conservative Democrat who had supported massive resistance legislation in the late 1950s. In the 1980s, only two Republican candidates for statewide offices received any significant black vote. John Warner garnered 21.2 percent when he was reelected to the U.S. Senate in a landslide in 1984. Maurice Dawkins, the black nominee in the 1988 race for a U.S. Senate seat, received 16.3 percent of the black vote, losing badly to former governor Charles Robb.[31]

The major surge in black registration and voting took place in the mid-1960s. But even though increased participation in state elections thereafter was primarily attributable to new white registrants, black registration went forward. From 1960 to 1984 the proportion of blacks among registered voters in Virginia increased from 10 to 17 percent, figures consistent with those for the rest of the southern electorate.[32] The long-term significance of this newly enfranchised minority in statewide elections was evident in the resurgence of the Virginia Democratic party in the 1980s as it swept all three statewide offices in three consecutive elections

(1981, 1985, and 1989). The vital role of black support was underscored by the fact that none of the successful gubernatorial nominees of the Democratic party received a majority of the white vote in the three general elections.[33] Moreover, in all three, the turnout rate of blacks exceeded that of whites. This record of support by black voters undoubtedly contributed to the nomination by convention of state senator L. Douglas Wilder without opposition for lieutenant governor in 1985 and for governor in 1989. Virginia Democrats, who abandoned the runoff primary following the divisive gubernatorial primary of 1969, turned to state conventions for the purposes of nominating statewide candidates in the 1980s.

As the nation's first elected black governor, Wilder is a poignant reminder of the progress being made in overcoming racial barriers. Race undoubtedly continues to be an issue in Virginia politics, but Wilder's victory, although by the closest margin in a Virginia gubernatorial election in this century, means race is not always the determining factor in the outcome of elections. His winning margin came largely from Northern Virginia and Hampton Roads, the fastest growing regions of the state with the largest nonnative populations. So dramatic was the population shift within Virginia that he was able to win by carrying only twenty-two of forty-one cities and twenty-two of ninety-five counties. Wilder received 41 percent of the white vote and benefited from a turnout rate among black registered voters that was 8 percentage points higher than the figure for white voters; four years earlier the black rate had been only about one point higher.[34]

Rarely has a minority candidate been as well positioned to win statewide office as was Wilder in 1989. A majority-black state senate district had assured him electoral security and legislative seniority. As the state's leading black politician for twenty years, and as a candidate who had never lost an election, he had earned a reputation as a seasoned insider within the majority Democratic party. He had moderated his views over the years to espouse fiscal conservativism and hard-line positions on crime, including support for the death penalty. Like his white predecessors, he had used his four years as lieutenant governor to expand his contacts around the state. Wilder pursued a "deracial" political strategy designed to avoid racial polarization and emphasize the nonthreatening nature of his campaign. He ran "not as a black politician, but as a politician who happened to be black."[35] He was nominated without opposition by a fully unified party, was well financed, and ran as the successor to two popular Democratic administrations. Moreover, his prochoice position on the dominant issue of the campaign—abortion rights—gave him an advantage without which it is difficult to imagine him winning. His victory underscores the capability of a black candidate to win the votes of a large number of whites. "Wilder's campaign," in the cautionary evaluation of one observer, "offers a formula, albeit not an easily followed one, for doing that."[36]

Virginia Resists the Voting Rights Act

On key 1965 congressional votes, only Mississippi opposed President Johnson's positions and a larger federal role through Great Society programs more often than

Virginia did.[37] All of the Virginia congressional delegation voted against the Voting Rights Act except for Representative W. Pat Jennings, a liberal Democrat from the southwestern district containing many straight-ticket, anti-Byrd Democrats.

Support for the act and its extensions was limited to a handful of the state's twelve-member congressional delegation. Only Senator Spong, who was defeated for reelection in 1972, and Republican representative William Whitehurst, whose district included a black population of 22 percent, voted for the 1970 extension. However, even Whitehurst voted against extending the act in 1975, leaving only two Democrats elected from northern Virginia in 1974 to cast affirmative votes. In 1982 the only Virginia votes supporting final passage of that year's extension and amendments were two Republicans: Senator Warner and Congressman Frank Wolf of northern Virginia. Overall, the minimal level of support by the delegation for the act's initial passage and its three extensions can best be explained by the predominance of two groups least likely to provide support: Old South Democrats and Republicans.[38] By 1968 Republicans had won half of the state's ten house seats, and at the time of the 1982 vote for extension controlled nine of ten House seats and one Senate seat.

In 1973 the Virginia General Assembly passed a resolution directing the state attorney general to take action necessary to bail out Virginia from coverage of the special provisions of the act, including section 5. Accordingly, Attorney General Andrew Miller filed suit that same year in the U.S. District Court for the District of Columbia, making Virginia the first southern state to seek exemption from the act. The state maintained that it met the statutory requirement at that time—a ten-year absence of any discriminatory device for voting—since its literacy test had been fairly administered in the years immediately before it was suspended by the act. Miller estimated that as many as 90,000 blacks might have registered between 1962 and 1964. He pointed to the growth of black registration prior to 1965 and the failure of the Civil Rights Commission and the Department of Justice to "find substantial discrimination." In fact, no federal observers or examiners had ever been assigned to Virginia under the provisions of the act.[39]

However, estimates of the number of blacks registering to vote in Virginia during the 1960s varied widely. The Civil Rights Commission estimated that almost 100,000 more blacks were registered in 1967 than in 1965, when the act was passed. The commission also found a gap of over 22 percentage points between white and black registration rates prior to passage of the act.[40] The federal district court hearing Virginia's bail-out arguments acknowledged in a footnote the dispute over registration statistics as well as the state's concession that the black registration rate was "significantly lower" than the white rate. The court commended the state for "its good faith efforts in voter registration in the sixties," but estimated that the black registration rate was about 10 percent below that of whites from 1963 to 1965.[41] Virginia was denied exemption from the act on the ground that the state's record of segregated, inferior education for blacks contributed to low literacy rates, which affected the ability of persons to satisfy literacy requirements prior to 1965.

Vote Dilution in State Legislative Redistricting

The state's 1964 reapportionment of the legislature was challenged in federal court for,[42] among other reasons, diluting the black vote by establishing a two-member senate district in Richmond and by combining Richmond with Henrico County into an eight-person at-large district for the purpose of electing members to the house of delegates. While blacks made up 42 percent of the Richmond population, they constituted only 29 percent of the combined Richmond-Henrico house district. In a decision handed down on 9 April 1965, less than four months before the signing of the Voting Rights Act, a federal district court dismissed the complaint on the grounds the state had traditionally used multimember districts in other areas of Virginia.[43]

William Ferguson Reid of Henrico County narrowly lost his campaign for a seat from that Richmond-Henrico district in 1965, but in 1967 he became the first black to serve in the Virginia legislature since 1891. Reid, a physician, placed fourth overall in 1967, winning handily against three opponents in the Richmond-Henrico district, along with the other seven Democratic candidates. Turnout in Richmond, where Dr. Reid led the ticket, exceeded the 1965 turnout for the gubernatorial election by some eight thousand votes.[44] In 1969 attorney Douglas Wilder was elected state senator from Richmond in a special election in which he won slightly less than 50 percent of the vote against two white candidates. There was no runoff requirement. The citywide election took place in a jurisdiction that had a black population majority but a substantial white registration edge. Even though the bulk of his support came from black voters, Wilder acknowledged on election night that he received some white votes and benefited from the decision of some whites not to vote. He said he "look[ed] forward to the time when all men can run as candidates on their qualifications, and not as a 'Negro' candidate or a 'white' candidate."[45]

The decision of the state senate in 1971, under pressure from the Justice Department, to elect all senators from single-member districts signaled the end of Richmond's multimember senate district. Most of the city's black population was put in Wilder's district, giving him a politically safe constituency that was 71 percent black. Wilder ran without opposition and served until he resigned following his election as lieutenant governor in 1985. Delegate Reid was not so fortunate in the changes affecting his district. The new house districts created in 1971 separated Richmond and Henrico County, leaving Reid, a county resident, to run in a single-member floater district composed of the two jurisdictions and containing a black population of 29 percent. In 1971 he won reelection against an independent, but he was unseated two years later by a white Richmond city council member running as an independent in a three-way race involving a Republican candidate and heightened public attention to the busing issue. In 1977 two blacks were elected to the house of delegates from Richmond as part of the victorious Democratic ticket, when two incumbents relinquished their seats to seek statewide offices.

Following the 1970 census count, the Department of Justice objected under section 5 to Virginia's redistricting plans for both houses of the legislature. The objections for the senate plans found that a multimember district diluted the black vote in Norfolk. In 1971 the senate responded to the objections by creating single-member districts, including a heavily black district there. Meanwhile, Henry Howell, the white liberal state senator from Norfolk, complained that he had been placed in a "Goldwater" district as a result. Invoking the one-person, one-vote principle, he challenged the legislature's decision to include all shipboard naval personnel in his district despite the fact they were residentially scattered throughout the Norfolk area.[46] The federal district court agreed with Howell and restored a multimember senate district for Norfolk, subsequently upheld in *Mahan v. Howell*.[47] This litigation headed off the probable candidacy of Delegate William Robinson, Sr., of Norfolk, a black college professor first elected in 1969, for the abolished single-member senate seat.

On the house side, the Department of Justice objected to the retention of multimember districts in areas with heavy concentrations of black voters—Hampton, Newport News, Norfolk, Portsmouth, and Richmond. The house of delegates received an unexpected reprieve, however, when the U.S. Supreme Court declined to invalidate multimember districts on Fourteenth Amendment grounds in an Indiana case, *Whitcomb v. Chavis*.[48] The Department of Justice withdrew its objections, and multimember districts were retained.

As Virginia turned to redistricting for the 1980s, its record of four blacks in the hundred-member lower house and one senator in the forty-member upper chamber gave it the lowest level of black legislative representation in the South. This was in a state with a black population of 19 percent. Legislative redistricting following the 1980 census was not one of Virginia's finer moments. In 1981–82 there were some fourteen legislative sessions, six redistricting plans, a ruling of unconstitutional population disparities by a three-judge federal panel, a gubernatorial veto, and Justice Department section 5 objections to plans for both houses. Buffeted by the court and the Department of Justice, the legislature ended up sharing its power to redraw district lines with lobbyists for the American Civil Liberties Union (ACLU) and the NAACP, and was required to hold house of delegates elections one year after the normal 1981 elections because the districts had been declared unconstitutional. No wonder that syndicated columnist Carl Rowan wrote a well-publicized piece entitled "Don't Carry Us Back . . ." in August 1981, citing Virginia's record of legislative redistricting as a prime reason for the need to extend the Voting Rights Act in 1982.[49]

As had been the case ten years before, single-member districts for Norfolk were a source of controversy. The senate's plan to divide Norfolk so that neither of its two districts would have more than a 37 percent black population was criticized by Wilder for diluting black votes, and it predictably drew an objection from the Justice Department.[50] On the house side, incumbency protection and preservation of 1971 district lines wherever possible received the highest priority in the original plans. These criteria were not utilized for black areas, however.

Applying 1980 census data to the 1971 district lines would have meant the direct election of seven delegates from predominantly black districts. Instead, the initial 1981 house plan decreased the number of delegates elected in such districts from seven to four.

The house of delegates finally shifted to a plan of one hundred single-member districts, nine of which were majority-black. Black community groups uniformly supported the shift to single-member districts, but black legislators were divided in their views. Delegate William P. Robinson, Jr., of Norfolk disagreed with the two black delegates from Richmond about the appropriateness of single-member districts. Delegate Robert C. Scott of Newport News generally agreed with Robinson that single-member districts could isolate minorities and discourage racial cooperation, but he ultimately voted for the single-district plan while Robinson abstained.[51]

Seven of the nine majority-black districts provided for in the final house plan were at least 59 percent black, and as of 1990, all were held by black Democrats; the two districts with smaller black majorities elected white Democrats. On the senate side, black representation increased from one to three members in the 1980s in a body of forty members. Black delegates moved up in 1985 and 1987 to fill vacant seats in majority-black senate districts in Norfolk and Richmond and joined Delegate Scott of Newport News, who won a seat in a senate district that was 65 percent white. Along with Delegate Reid's victory in 1971, Scott's election in 1982 and reelection in 1983 and 1987 to his senate seat constitute the only times blacks have been elected to majority-white, single-member districts for the state legislature. Scott, as an incumbent state senator, ran for a congressional seat in 1986, challenging a Republican in a majority-white district. He lost, garnering 44 percent of the vote.

Vote Dilution through Muncipal Annexations

By 1966, following passage of the Voting Rights Act, black registration in Richmond had surged to over a third of the total, compared with a little over one-fourth in 1964. The white power structure responded by proposing a system of staggered terms—a device that can have dilutive effects by diminishing the probability of a successful bullet-vote strategy—and the endorsement of two black businessmen in the 1966 at-large councilmanic elections. A bitter campaign marked by a record black turnout culminated in the defeat of the staggered-term proposal and the election of three blacks to the city council, including the two backed by the white, business-oriented group Richmond Forward.[52] Turnout in predominantly black precincts reached a new high in 1968 when the black organization Crusade for Voters made a determined effort to win control of the nine-member council. The Crusade did not endorse two black incumbents, B. A. Cephas, Jr., and Winfred Mundle, who had been backed by both the Crusade and Richmond Forward in 1966. The influence of the Crusade became evident when the two white candidates it endorsed ran much better in black precincts than did the two black incumbents supported by Richmond Forward.[53] Even though three candidates endorsed by the

Crusade won, its effort to win control of city council failed, and only one black, Henry Marsh, won a seat on city council.

In the early 1970s, the issue of fair representation of blacks in local government was raised by the annexations of surrounding counties by the cities of Richmond and Petersburg. Richmond did not submit its annexation for review by the Justice Department in accordance with section 5 until after the decision of the Supreme Court in *Perkins v. Matthews*[54] left no doubt about the city's obligation to do so. The Justice Department objected to the dilution of the black vote in both cities. The annexation reduced the black proportion in Richmond, which had recently grown rapidly, from 52 to 42 percent in Richmond and in Petersburg from 55 to 46 percent. Richmond was enjoined by the federal courts for seven years from holding councilmanic elections in what has been described as a classic confrontation "between the powerful white elite and growing numbers of central city blacks."[55]

The U.S. District Court for the District of Columbia, after hearing Richmond's section 5 suit for preclearance, concluded the annexation discriminated against blacks in purpose and effect. It viewed the action as a move by the white political leadership, frightened by the new electoral strength of black voters, to maintain control of city council. The court pointed to Richmond's focus in the negotiations on the number of new white voters and its insistence in the annexation agreement that citizens in the annexed area be able to vote in the 1970 city council election.[56] In 1975, the Supreme Court in *City of Richmond v. United States*[57] held that the reduction in the black proportion of the population was permissible as long as blacks were afforded an opportunity to elect candidates in proportion to their political strength in the newly enlarged city. In lieu of deannexation, Richmond, as had been the case with Petersburg, was permitted to shift from at-large to single-member-district elections. In both cities only one black was sitting on city council at the time of the annexations. Black majorities were installed on the city councils under the new ward systems, albeit in Petersburg the majority was short-lived and became a four-to-three white majority.

Two other jurisdictions received much less attention when they made changes in their at-large electoral systems in the mid-1970s. Lynchburg's annexation of portions of two surrounding counties in 1975 was met by a Department of Justice objection and a suit by a local citizens' committee opposing the annexation. Lynchburg chose to implement a mixed plan, including three at-large seats and four single-member wards, one of which was majority black. In 1972 Nansemond County consolidated with its two small towns as the city of Nansemond. Two years later, Nansemond City merged with the city of Suffolk. The newly enlarged city of Suffolk was precleared by the Department of Justice when Suffolk opted for a mixed plan with one two-member ward and five single-member wards.

Vote Dilution through At-Large City Elections

To assess the impact of changes in local electoral systems on minority officeholding, we surveyed all twenty-six Virginia cities with black populations of 10 percent or higher in 1980. In addition to the consolidated city of Suffolk and the three cities making changes in the 1970s because of the addition of new population through annexation, six cities shifted from at-large city council elections as a result of the Voting Rights Act—Hopewell, Fredericksburg, Franklin, Emporia, Covington, and Norfolk. The first lawsuit challenging at-large city council elections apart from annexation was filed by black plaintiffs, represented by the Lawyers' Committee for Civil Rights Under Law, against Hopewell on 22 January 1982. Hopewell's council had always been all white under its at-large system, despite the fact that blacks constituted about 20 percent of the city's population. As a result of the litigation, which was resolved by a settlement, Hopewell in January 1983 adopted a system of two at-large seats and five wards, one of which was nearly 75 percent black. Subsequently, the council consisted of one black and six whites.

A suit challenging Norfolk's at-large elections was first filed in August 1983. Six years later the U.S. Court of Appeals for the Fourth Circuit, in a two-to-one decision, directed the district court to oversee the establishment of ward-based voting. From 1968 to 1984 Norfolk's city council had a single black member. After the suit had been filed in August 1983, Norfolk's white mayor supported the election of a second black candidate and publicly stated his election could render "the issue of black representation . . . a moot point."[58] Citing *Thornburg v. Gingles*, the Supreme Court's interpretation of amended section 2, the Fourth Circuit panel found the 1984 election of a second black candidate who was reelected in 1988 to be the result of "special circumstances." In 1991 Norfolk, a city with a black population of 39 percent, drew seven single-member districts, three of which were majority-black.

Litigation filed by blacks represented by the American Civil Liberties Union led to the creation in Emporia of three majority-black districts in a mixed plan of eight seats. Emporia, a city with a 44 percent black population, had never elected more than one black to serve on council at any time since 1970. Another ACLU suit prompted Covington (13 percent black) to shift to a five-ward plan with one majority-black district. In Franklin, which elected its council at large, an objection by the Department of Justice led to a new electoral system when an annexation changed the city's voting population from 51.9 percent black to 51.7 percent white. Three majority-black districts were established as part of a mixed plan, increasing the size of council from five to seven with a mayor elected at large. A local referendum establishing a modified ward system in Fredericksburg was followed by a Department of Justice objection. The three-ward, four at-large plan was changed to a four-ward, three at-large system with a majority-black district.

Vote Dilution in Counties, Towns, School Boards, and Judicial Elections

Whereas Virginia cities have traditionally used at-large elections to select their council members, the state's counties have historically utilized magisterial (i.e., "magistrate") districts for electing boards of supervisors.[59] Of Virginia's ninety-five counties, only four rely exclusively on at-large elections. Eleven counties have mixed plans, with one or two supervisors elected at large; nine other counties employ one or more two-member districts, or in the case of one county, a three-member district. Otherwise, Virginia counties utilize single-member districts to elect members of their governing bodies.

Despite the historic use of single-member magisterial districts in Virginia, a number of southside counties made selective use of multimember districts to dilute the black vote. In May 1983 ACLU lawyers filed a lawsuit on behalf of black plaintiffs against Prince Edward County, challenging a three-member district that diluted the black vote. The county promptly changed to a pure single-member-district plan and, in so doing, created two black-majority districts. Subsequent litigation was responsible for the adoption of pure district systems in five counties—Buckingham, Lunenburg, Mecklenburg, Prince Edward, and Richmond. In Dinwiddie County, following litigation, a two-person district was preserved, but districts with 62 and 64 percent black populations replaced districts with black majorities of about 55 percent. Prior to the litigation, the only black to win a supervisor's seat in the county since Reconstruction did so in 1987 with a plurality of the vote in a contest against two white candidates.

A successful district court challenge to the racial makeup of the five single-member districts for Brunswick County was dismissed on appeal on the technical defense of laches, the appellate court ruling that plaintiffs waited too long to sue.[60] After the 1990 census, the county adopted a new districting plan, which was again challenged unsuccessfully by black residents; the court of appeals ruled that the plan did not dilute minority voting strength.[61]

As a result of lawsuits filed by the ACLU on behalf of black plaintiffs, blacks have been elected to sit on county governing boards for the first time in this century in the counties of King and Queen, Lunenburg, and Richmond. In Mecklenburg County, where two blacks had been elected in the 1970s, no blacks were serving when a consent decree was entered in June 1989 in litigation filed by the ACLU that created districts with black population majorities of 57, 61, and 65 percent. Pittsylvania County drew new district lines in 1988 to make adjustments for the loss of population through annexation. A new plan composed of seven districts failed to produce a black-majority district despite the county's 33 percent black population and the failure of any black to serve on the board of supervisors since Reconstruction. A public hearing on the plan attended by over three hundred members of a concerned citizens group organized by local black leaders, and the threat of a lawsuit, eventually led to the drafting of another plan with a 63 percent black-majority district.

Of the 188 towns in Virginia, all but 7 elect their town councils at large; 6 of the 7 changed from at large as a result of litigation filed under the Voting Rights Act.[62] Five switched to mixed systems combining at-large and single-member districts, and another, South Hill, now contains a two-member black-majority district and two three-member districts. Except in Blackstone, where there was a 43 percent black population, no black had ever been elected to the at-large town councils before the voting rights lawsuits led to changes in the 1980s.

Prior to 1992, when the state legislature permitted localities to authorize elected school boards following a local referendum, Virginia was the only state that did not elect any school board members. A proposal for elected school boards had been defeated in the 1901–2 constitutional convention explicitly because the delegates feared blacks would be elected. The convention left the method of selection to the legislature, which adopted an appointive method, and school boards continue to be appointed. The proportion of blacks serving on these boards—about 18 percent—is roughly equal to their proportion in the population, but they are far more likely to be appointed in districts with few blacks than in those with many. In 1988, for example, blacks were underrepresented, sometimes severely, in twenty of the forty jurisdictions with black populations exceeding 30 percent.

For a ten year period between 1947 and 1956, Arlington County had an elected board under state legislation. When the board adopted a school desegregation proposal in 1956, the legislature immediately repealed the provision that allowed it to be elected. A 1988 lawsuit challenging these discriminatory decisions was unsuccessful. Though the courts found the acts intentionally discriminatory, they rejected plaintiffs' claims under constitutional provisions and under section 2 of the Voting Rights Act, holding that the existence of a 1984 legislative study which "set forth solely legitimate reasons" for appointed school boards was sufficient evidence that the school boards "had met their burden of rebutting the inference of discriminatory intent," and that while there was a "significant disparity" in board appointments in a number of jurisdictions, there was "no proof that the appointive process caused the disparity."[63]

Virginia is one of four states in which judges are elected by the state legislature. The election of judges actually takes place in the house and senate caucuses of the Democratic party. A unit rule binds caucus members to vote for the candidates embraced by the caucus majority.[64] In 1990 there was 1 black justice on the 7-person state supreme court, 1 black judge on the 10-person intermediate court of appeals, 5 blacks among the 127 circuit court judges, and 9 among 184 district court judges. In short, fewer than 5 percent of Virginia's judges were black in a state whose black population was 19 percent in 1990.

Litigation and the Civil Rights Community

Voting Rights Act litigation came late to Virginia. After the annexation litigation in the 1970s involving section 5, no dilution suit was filed until 1982. The late start of litigation may be attributed to the lack of a state civil rights organization interested in black political representation, and consequently, to a lack of lawyers within the state willing to undertake such cases. This lack is striking, and several factors could have contributed to it. Some national organizations had placed their resources elsewhere, possibly because they believed that there was a greater need for litigation in Georgia and Mississippi, for example, than in Virginia. Dilution litigation was not well funded in the late 1970s until after the *Bolden*[65] decision in the Supreme Court, and resources were limited. Additionally, dilution litigation is fact-intensive and difficult to handle long-distance. There were no voting rights litigation offices located in Virginia.

The first two lawsuits against at-large city systems in Hopewell and Norfolk were filed by Frank Parker of the Lawyers' Committee for Civil Rights Under Law, in Washington, D.C. The Hopewell case initiated the challenges in the 1980s to Virginia's local governing boards. Meanwhile, the Atlanta ACLU office, headed by Laughlin McDonald, initiated action against Prince Edward County in May 1983. No group of cases was filed until the ACLU of Virginia began operating a voting rights project, with a staff lawyer working on these cases. The project recruited Gerald Zerkin and Steve Bricker, both Richmond civil rights lawyers, to handle voting rights cases. In addition to the eighteen cases handled by the ACLU since the extension of the Voting Rights Act in 1982, local NAACP units have handled two cases, and the Department of Justice has entered section 5 objections in Southampton and Greensville counties, and in Franklin and Fredericksburg. Of the lawsuits that have been resolved, all have resulted in the creation of majority-black districts except for the suit filed against Charlotte County by the local NAACP. The case was dismissed when the plaintiffs were unable to produce a remedy plan with a black district made up of a "minority" population of 65 percent or a black voting-age population of 60 percent.[66]

The absence of an active statewide black organization left most of the initiative for voting rights changes in Virginia to the ACLU and the Lawyers' Committee. In comparison, during the period following *Brown v. Board of Education*, the Virginia Conference of the NAACP put together an impressive team of thirteen lawyers headed by Oliver Hill, a respected Richmond attorney who had served one term on the Richmond city council. More school desegregation lawsuits were filed in Virginia than in any other southern state.[67] Later, the first voting rights staff lawyer, Richard Taylor, also a black, joined the Virginia ACLU, where he worked on a number of voting rights cases for two years. Taylor eventually joined the firm of Hill, Tucker, and Marsh, and along with Henry L. Marsh, Richmond's first black mayor, filed the section 2 case against Henrico County in 1988. But the litigation task in the 1980s largely passed to a new generation of mostly white civil rights attorneys.

An Analysis of Changes in City Election Structures

Our scheme for assessing the impact of city election structure on minority officeholding involves observing the changes in minority officeholding in those cities with a black population of at least 10 percent that changed from an at-large system between 1977 and 1989. The changes in minority officeholding are then compared with those in a control group of seventeen at-large cities that did not change their election structure during the same period.

The total number of jurisdictions surveyed is relatively small because of the state's unique, statewide practice of city-county separation. Cities and counties are entirely separate from each other as governmental entities. This arrangement means that Virginia's ninety-five counties and forty-one independent cities are the primary political subdivisions in the state and helps explain Virginia's small number of local governments. Virginia ranks forty-second among the states in number of local governments, lower than any of the other southern states.[68] Unlike cities, the 188 towns in Virginia remain a part of the county in which they are located, and their citizens are subject to the exercise of power by county government.

Table 9.1 presents a cross-sectional view of the mean percentage of blacks elected to council in independent cities in 1989, by election plan and proportion of black population in the city. Unfortunately, the small number of cities in most black population categories makes generalizations quite tentative. The data in table 9.1 indicate, nonetheless, that in population categories where comparisons are possible, blacks in majority-white cities are significantly better represented in districted than in at-large jurisdictions—a pattern that has generally been found to be true throughout the South.

Changes in black representation over time are shown in table 9.2, which presents data from 1977, two years after Virginia was denied exemption from the Voting Rights Act, and from 1989.[69] Here again, in conformity with the conventional wisdom on the subject, the table shows that in majority-white cities switching from at-large to either single-member districts or mixed systems, blacks increased their percentage on council at a greater rate than in those cities remaining at large, although there were appreciable gains in some of the latter ones. This pattern is corroborated in table 9.5, where the data present black representation in terms of proportionality, as measured by the black percentage on council divided by the black percentage in the city's population. In the cities 10–29.9 percent black—the only category in which comparison is possible between each of the three types of election structure—the data show blacks sharply overrepresented (1.54) in single-member-district plans, slightly overrepresented (1.05) in mixed plans, and underrepresented by a factor of about two (0.56) in plans that remained at large over the twelve-year period. It is also noteworthy that in 1977, blacks in the majority-white cities that later abandoned at-large elections were less well represented than in those cities that remained at large. In the intervening years, the pattern was completely reversed.

All gains in black representation in the seven cities changing from at-large to single-member-district and mixed plans occurred as a result of the creation of black-majority districts where none had previously existed. Covington and Hopewell each elected one black council member for the first time. In both Franklin and Emporia black representation increased from one to three council members and in Fredericksburg it improved from two of eleven to two of seven members.

Table 9.3 examines cities with mixed plans in 1989. It demonstrates, as other studies have done, that most of the black officeholders in such plans are elected from the district rather than the at-large component. This was true even in the majority-black city. In line with this finding, the data in table 9.6, which examines black electoral success within the districts of districted cities, show that black officeholding is closely linked to the racial makeup of the districts. In districts less than 30 percent black, no blacks were elected; and in districts less than 30 percent white, only blacks were elected. Looked at from a slightly different perspective in table 9.7, the data show that in the 26 majority-white districts, the mean proportion of black council members was 7 percent. In the 22 majority-black districts, by contrast, the figure was 91 percent. The data discussed here are consistent with the view that a significant degree of racially polarized voting exists in the cities under analysis.

Table 9.8 lists the nine independent cities that changed from at-large to single-member-district or mixed plans during the period studied. Eight of the nine converted as a result of litigation under the equal protection clause, Justice Department intervention under the Voting Rights Act, or both, and provide a striking example of the effectiveness of the freezing principle of section 5. Six of the nine cities switched to some form of district elections because they wished to change their city boundaries, five by annexation, and one by merger. These cities were compelled by a combination of litigation and Justice Department objection to adopt districts as a way of compensating black voters for the increase in white voters resulting from city boundary changes.

While blacks were still underrepresented, the four Tidewater city councils of Norfolk, Hampton, Newport News, and Portsmouth had two of seven members who were black in 1989. Black candidates in urban Tidewater, unlike their counterparts in rural southside Virginia, obviously benefited from relatively well organized voter mobilization efforts. In Portsmouth, a city with a 1980 black population of 41.1 percent, James A. Holley was directly elected as the city's first black mayor in 1984, with 52 percent of the vote. Moreover, as a result of the 1984 council elections in Portsmouth, blacks held four of the seven seats until the defeat of a black incumbent in 1986 and the recall of Mayor Holley in December.[70]

The fluid nature of black representation in Tidewater cities was poignantly demonstrated in the 1990 elections. Bolstered by citizen discontent over the Portsmouth city council's failure to appoint a black to the school board and united by broad support for a biracial ticket, blacks regained a four-to-three majority in a city where the black percentage of the population increased from 41.1 to 47 percent in the 1980s.[71] In Newport News (with a 34 percent black population), both of the black incumbents, one of whom had been continuously elected since 1970, were defeated, leaving the council with seven white members. The elections were the first held following an objection by the Department of Justice to the city's proposal to replace one at-large member of council with a mayor directly elected by the voters, which would have reduced the opportunity for effective bullet voting. In a 1987 public referendum, the voters had approved direct election of the mayor and nonpartisan city council elections. The Department of Justice's analysis revealed "an apparent pattern of racially polarized voting in city elections."[72] Black candidates had narrowly won election to the third of three seats and the fourth of four seats in the at-large elections of 1984 and 1986, respectively. Moreover, on several occasions when only three seats were being contested, black candidates finished fourth in the at-large voting.

Two other Tidewater cities lost black representation in the 1990 elections. The lone black incumbent on a council of eleven members was defeated in Virginia Beach. In Suffolk, where a mixed plan was implemented in 1974 following an enlarged jurisdiction resulting from a merger of two cities, blacks lost their four-to-three majority on city council with the defeat of a black incumbent. Since 1986 blacks had been able to hold a majority in an electoral system with only two black-majority wards. A white-majority ward alternately selected a black candidate and a white candidate over a period of three terms and, in another district with a white majority, a black candidate won narrow plurality victories against two white opponents.

Direct election of black mayors in two Virginia cities is noteworthy, considering that cities and towns nationwide with majority-white populations have been highly reluctant to choose black mayors. Roanoke and Fredericksburg, with black populations in 1980 of 22 and 20 percent, respectively, elected black mayors over a prolonged period of time. Noel Taylor of Roanoke was first selected as mayor by the city council in 1975 to fill a vacancy and then got elected in his own right in 1976. That same year, Lawrence Davies, who had first been elected to an at-large seat on city council in 1966, was elected mayor of Fredericksburg. Both men are ministers and are now serving their fourth terms as mayor.

Conclusion

The number of local jurisdictions in Virginia switching to single-member districts or mixed plans due to the Voting Rights Act is small yet significant. With Norfolk's change in 1991, nine of the state's forty-one cities (constituting a little over one-third of those municipalities with 10 percent or greater black populations) abandoned at-large council elections. Nine counties created black-majority districts for the first time due to the act, and six towns changed from at-large to mixed electoral plans. Without these changes based on the Voting Rights Act, blacks would have undoubtedly been denied participation or accorded only token representation on governing bodies in many jurisdictions. Even then, only Texas, of the seven southern states covered entirely by the Voting Rights Act, had a smaller percentage of blacks among its elected officials at the end of the 1980s—and Texas had a black population proportion only about half as large as Virginia's.

After a century of suffrage restrictions following the Civil War were lifted, blacks in Virginia have begun to win office in significant numbers, thanks to Justice Department intervention under section 5, litigation under the Fourteenth Amendment and section 2, and the help of various organizations: the Lawyers'

Committee, the ACLU, and the NAACP, in particular. Among the most notable achievements of black candidates have been those of Douglas Wilder, first elected as state senator, then as lieutenant governor, and finally in 1989 as the first black governor of any state in the union. Nor should the elections of four-term black mayors in Roanoke and Fredericksburg be overlooked.

Yet while Virginia today projects an image of moderation in race relations, and the above-mentioned achievements give some evidence of this, the truth is more complicated. The virtual absence of blacks from the state's town councils indicates a continuing racial polarization at the grass-roots level—a polarization also reflected in the difficulty blacks have in winning in majority-white jurisdictions (see tables 9.3, 9.5, 9.6 and 9.7). The continuing underrepresentation of blacks in many at-large county and city governments drives this fact home, as does the resistance of at-large jurisdictions to adopting an election structure that gives blacks a better chance of representation. As we have shown, virtually all of the changes in these structures have come about through federal intervention.

And even within the bosom of the Democratic party, the party with which blacks in Virginia have largely cast their lot, the facts are not as happy as the state's moderate image suggests. It is true that some of the greatest political triumphs on the race front have come about within the party. Wilder's 1989 election illustrates the success of the biracial coalition within it. But black Democrats have not begun to reap the benefits that one could reasonably expect to issue from their vastly increased political participation, their loyalty to the party, and their support of the party's successful white nominees. Democratic white incumbents have been reelected to the legislature in a number of instances where they found themselves in newly created, majority-black districts. And despite the Democratic party's control of the legislature, which directly elects the state's judges, the paucity of blacks in the Virginia judiciary is striking.

Our story of the Voting Rights Act in Virginia, then, is one of successes mixed with failures. There is no question that the act has dramatically reshaped the state's political landscape. But as elsewhere in the South, the work begun by the Second Reconstruction is far from done.

TABLE 9.1
Minority Representation on Council in 1989 by Election Plan, Virginia Independent Cities with 10 Percent or more Black Population in 1980

Type of Plan by % Black in City Population, 1980	N	*Mean % Black in City Population, 1980*	*Mean % Black on City Council, 1989*
SMD plan			
10–29.9	1	13	20
30–49.9	0	—	—
50–100	2	56	50
Mixed plan			
10–29.9	3	21	19
30–49.9	2	44	45
50–100	1	50	43
At-large plan			
10–29.9	11	18	10
30–49.9	6	35	29
50–100	0	—	—

TABLE 9.2
Changes in Black Representation on Council between 1977 and 1989, Virginia Independent Cities with 10 Percent or More Black Population in 1980

Type of Change by % Black in City Population, 1980	N[a]	*Mean % Black in City Population, 1980*	*Mean % Black on City Council*	
			Before Change (1977)	*After Change (1989)*
		Changed Systems		
From at-large to SMD plan				
10–29.9	1	13	0	20
30–49.9	0	—	—	—
50–100	1	51	11	56
From at-large to mixed plan				
10–29.9	2	20	5	21
30–49.9	1	40	10	38
50–100	1	55	20	50
		Unchanged Systems		
At-large plan				
10–29.9	11	18	8	10
30–49.9	6	35	15	29
50–100	0	—	—	—

[a] The number of cities in this table ($N = 23$) is smaller than that in table 9.1 because three of the cities in that table changed their election system prior to 1977.

TABLE 9.3
Black Representation in 1989 in Mixed Plans by District and At-Large Components, Virginia Independent Cities with 10 Percent or More Black Population in 1980

% Black in City Population, 1980	N	*Mean % Black Councilpersons in District Components, 1989*	*Mean % Black Councilpersons in At-Large Components, 1989*
10–29.9	3	23	13
30–49.9	2	58	0
50–100	1	50	0

TABLE 9.4
Two Equity Measures Comparing Percentage Black on Council in 1989 with Percentage Black in City Population in 1980, Virginia Independent Cities with 10 Percent or More Black Population in 1980

Type of Plan by % Black in City Population, 1980	N[a]	*Difference Measure (% on Council − % in Population)*	*Ratio Measure (% on Council ÷ % in Population)*
		Changed Systems	
From at-large to SMD plan			
10–29.9	1	7	1.54
30–49.9	0	—	—
50–100	1	5	1.10
From at-large to mixed plan			
10–29.9	2	1	1.05
30–49.9	1	−2	0.95
50–100	1	−5	0.91
		Unchanged Systems	
At-large plan			
10–29.9	11	−8	0.56
30–49.9	6	−6	0.83
50–100	0	—	—

[a] The number of cities in this table (*N* = 23) is smaller than that in table 9.1 because three of the cities in that table changed their election system prior to 1977.

TABLE 9.5
Changes in Black Representation on Council between 1977 and 1989, Virginia Independent Cities with 10 Percent or More Black Population in 1980 (Ratio Equity Measure)

Type of Change by % Black in City Population, 1980	N[a]	*Black Representational Equity on Council*	
		1977	*1989*
	Changed Systems		
From at-large to SMD plan			
10–29.9	1	0.00	1.54
30–49.9	0	—	—
50–100	1	0.22	1.10
From at-large to mixed plan			
10–29.9	2	0.25	1.05
30–49.9	1	0.25	0.95
50–100	1	0.36	0.91
	Unchanged Systems		
At-large plan			
10–29.9	11	0.44	0.56
30–49.9	6	0.43	0.83
50–100	0	—	—

[a] The number of cities in this table ($N = 23$) is smaller than that in table 9.1 because three of the cities in that table changed their election system prior to 1977.

TABLE 9.6
Black Representation in Council Single-Member Districts in 1989, Virginia Independent Cities with 10 Percent or More Black Population in 1980

% Black Population of District	N	*Mean % Black Population in Districts, 1980*	*Mean % Black Councilpersons in Districts, 1989*
0–29.9	21	10	0
30–49.9	5	32	40
50–59.9	4	55	75
60–64.9	0	—	—
65–69.9	4	67	75
70–100	14	86	100

TABLE 9.7
Black Council Representation in Single-Member Districts in 1989, by Racial Composition of District, Virginia Independent Cities with 10 Percent or More Black Population in 1980

Racial Composition of District	N	*Mean % Black Population in Districts, 1980*	*Mean % Black Councilpersons in Districts, 1989*
Black majority	22	77	91
White majority	26	14	7

TABLE 9.8
Cause of Change from At-Large to District Plan between 1973 and 1989, Virginia Independent Cities of 10,000 or More Population with 10 Percent or More Black Population in 1980

City	*Year of Change*	*Did Lawsuit Accompany Change?*	*Reason for Change*
		Changed to Single-Member Districts	
Covington	1989	Yes	Suit by blacks challenging at-large elections; settled by consent decree
Petersburg	1973	Yes	Annexation diluted black vote; Department of Justice objection; city sought and lost declaratory judgment
Richmond	1977	Yes	Annexation diluted black vote; Department of Justice objection; black plaintiff brought suit; city sought and received declaratory judgment when it adopted ward system
		Changed to Mixed Plan	
Emporia	1988	Yes	Suit by blacks challenging at-large elections
Franklin	1987	No	Annexation diluted black vote; Department of Justice objection
Fredericksburg	1988	No	Local referendum approved modified ward plan; Department of Justice objection to the plan
Hopewell	1983	Yes	Suit by blacks challenging at-large elections
Lynchburg	1976	Yes	Annexation diluted black vote; Department of Justice objection; suit by predominantly white citizens' committee opposing annexation was joined by predominantly black organization favoring annexation if ward system adopted
Suffolk	1974	No	Merger of cities of Nansemond and Suffolk diluted black vote; mixed plan precleared by Department of Justice
SUMMARY[a]		Yes 6 (67%) No 3 (33%)	

[a]Eight of nine cities changed as a result of section 5 intervention, voting rights litigation, or both.

TABLE 9.9
Major Disfranchising Devices in Virginia

Device	Date Established	Date Abolished
Poll tax	1876 1905	1882[a] 1964, 1966[b]
Publicly printed ballot without party names or symbols	1894	Still in effect[c]
Understanding clause	1902	1904[d]
Requirement to apply to registrar "in his own handwriting" stating name, age, date and place of birth, residence, occupation, etc.; to answer all questions submitted by registrars affecting the individual's qualifications as a voter	1904	1965[e]
White primary	1912	1930[f]

[a]Repealed by legislature in response to Readjuster movement allied with the predominantly black Republicans.

[b]Twenty-fourth Amendment (1964) for federal elections; *Harper v. Virginia State Board of Elections* (1966) for state and local elections.

[c]Party names listed today on presidential ballot only.

[d]Understanding clause was a temporary act intended to be window dressing to get other provisions approved in a constitution referendum. See Kousser 1974, 59–60.

[e]Proscribed by the Voting Rights Act.

[f]Struck down by a federal court three years after the Supreme Court first held the Texas white primary unconstitutional.

TABLE 9.10
Black and White Registered Voters and Officeholders in Virginia, Selected Years[a]

	Black		White	
Year	N	%	N	%
Registered voters				
1964	144,259	12	1,070,168	88
1966	243,000	18	1,140,000	82
1990	478,000	17	2,331,000	83
Officeholders				
State house				
1964	0	0	100	100
1966	0	0	100	100
1990	7	7	93	93
State senate				
1964	0	0	40	100
1966	0	0	40	100
1990	3	7.5	37	92.5

[a]Mean black Virginia population, 1960–90 = 19.2%.

PART TWO

The Southwide Perspective

TEN

The Effect of Municipal Election Structure on Black Representation in Eight Southern States

BERNARD GROFMAN AND CHANDLER DAVIDSON

THE PRECEDING CHAPTERS on the eight southern states covered by section 5 of the Voting Rights Act demonstrate how long and difficult has been the struggle for blacks, and Mexican Americans in Texas, to achieve full voting rights, and how various have been the devices and practices hindering their ability to elect their candidates of choice. In this chapter we provide a synoptic overview of the findings from these states about the effects of election type on black representation.

The chapter consists of four sections. In the first, we discuss the nature of the data from the state chapters and the features of the longitudinal design they share. In the second, we summarize evidence from the states on the relation between changes in local election systems and gains in black representation. In the third, we compare our findings with those of other scholars and explain the advantages of our research design over the cross-sectional design customarily employed to examine the impact of election structures. Finally, we consider the implications of our findings.

Data Base and Research Design

The proposal in 1988 to the National Science Foundation that originated the projects reported in this volume had as one of its central aims the generation of a data set that could be used to resolve a continuing controversy about the causes of the gains in black officeholding in the South over the past two decades. The conventional view holds that at-large and multimember election systems are barriers to the election of blacks and that a central cause of gains in black representation at the state and local level in the South has been the change from at-large or multimember plans to single-member-district ones. As the state chapters have shown, black political leaders and interest groups have challenged at-large elections throughout the South in both the nineteenth and twentieth centuries,[1] acting on the premise that in local jurisdictions with substantial black voting strength where previous black success was minimal or nonexistent, the replacement of at-large elections by single-member districts that fairly reflected black population concentrations would increase black representation. Recently, however, some authors have disputed the claim that changes to single-member districts are necessary to increase black officeholding.[2]

In order to measure appropriately the impact of electoral systems on minority representation at the local level for the eight southern states that have been the chief focus of litigation under the Fourteenth Amendment and the Voting Rights Act and to address issues of causal inference that cannot be resolved with cross-sectional analysis—the approach typically used to investigate the impact of election type on minority representation—the authors of the state chapters contributed to the development of a large data base for southern cities. Data collection was linked to a longitudinal research design that required a detailed inventory of the changes that occurred in municipal election structures in these states over the course of recent decades.[3]

Research Design

Generally speaking, each of the state chapters as well as this one use information gathered for the early 1970s and the late 1980s to measure changes in minority representation on city council in two types of cities: those which changed from at-large to either single-member-district or mixed plans and those at-large cities which did not change.[4] The data base for each state identifies the number of black local officials at each of two times for each city in the state above a certain population size and minority percentage.[5] It also identifies the election system in use at each time: at-large, single-member district, or mixed.[6]

Special features of the research design are noteworthy. First, because the data collected are from two different periods, they allow before-and-after comparisons of minority representation in cities that replaced at-large elections with either district or mixed systems. Because each before-and-after comparison pertains to the same city, this approach "holds constant," roughly speaking, those factors which might vary if the comparison were between sets of cities grouped according to their present-day election system.[7]

Second, the design includes a control group of cities that did not change election type. This allows a direct comparison over time between results in the changed cities and those in the control cities, an improvement on certain earlier before-and-after studies of minority representation.[8] The unchanged cities control for other effects besides election structures that might have impinged on all cities over time, such as general changes in political culture resulting from, say, white voters' increased willingness to vote for black candidates.

Third, the chapter authors have generated several data sets that together provide important information about minority representation, changes in election system, and voting rights litigation. In particular, there is information about temporal changes in minority representation in cities that shifted wholly or in part from at-large elections to districts. Too, there are cross-sectional data from all cities both at the starting point and the end point of our studies, allowing comparisons at two different times. There is also information that allows us to compare the representation of blacks in the at-large and district components of mixed plans. Moreover, one type of data enables us to combine information on individual single-member districts in districted cities (both pure single-member district and mixed cities) to determine the extent of black officeholding at each level of black population in these districts and, in particular, the degree to which black officeholding in districts depends upon their having a black population majority.

Characteristics of the Data Set

Table 10.1 presents basic characteristics of the principal data set used in all the state chapters.[9] The data were collected for two points separated on average by about fifteen years. The earlier time was 1974 in a plurality of states, but for Alabama it was 1970; for North Carolina, 1973; for Virginia, 1977; and for Georgia, 1980. The later time was 1989 for all states except Georgia, for which it was 1990.

Another measurement variation in the state chapters is the minority population proportion. In all but two of the states, only cities with a black population of 10 percent or more were examined.[10] Exceptions are Texas, where a combined black and Hispanic population of 10 percent is the threshold for most of the tables in that chapter,[11] and North Carolina, where a combined black and American Indian population threshold of 10 percent is used.[12]

A third variation in the state chapters is city size. Data were collected in each state, using 1980 census figures for cities over a certain size. The population threshold is 1,000 in Mississippi; 2,500 in Louisiana; 6,000 in Alabama; and 10,000 in Georgia, Texas, and South Carolina. In North Carolina all incorporated cities are examined, including cities with population of fewer than 500.[13] The Virginia chapter reports on all cities that are "independent." As a result, cities with as few as 4,840 inhabitants are included for that state.

By focusing on the southern states with the greatest black population proportion and by developing data on a large set of cities, we have enough cases to ascertain patterns of black officeholding in each state and thus to detect variations and similarities among the states. Because most of the state projects gathered data on cities within a broad population range, this is one of the largest data bases (over 1,000 cities) ever used to examine the impact of election structure on minority representation, despite the fact that it is drawn from only eight states.

The Effect of Election Type on Black Representation in Cities in Eight Southern States

The primary purpose of our analysis is to determine the effects of election structure on black officeholding. However, if we were to use election structure as the sole independent variable, we would risk ignoring important nonelectoral differences and reaching erroneous conclusions. Our research design was developed to allow us to isolate certain other factors that are thought to have an independent influence on black officeholding. Because our analysis focuses solely on the eight southern states now covered entirely or in large part by section 5, possible differences between the South and the rest of the country are effectively controlled. Because we have data for individual states, the differential influence of statewide cultural norms or political practices can also be controlled. And because we categorize cities by their black population percentage, the independent impact of that variable is also controlled.[14]

City size is another variable alleged to have an independent influence on minority officeholding in the South. Our data, indeed, suggest that at-large elections have a more constraining influence on black officeholding in small towns than anywhere else. Because the state chapters differ in the population threshold used to select cities for inclusion in their data base, the inclusion of very small cities in some states but not in others could bias our conclusions. Later in this chapter, therefore, we will report certain key data only for cities that are 10,000 or larger in total population.

Tables 10.2A–C reports data separately for each state on the black percentage among elected city council members at the beginning and end of the period under investigation. The last row reports a mean value for the eight states, which is the simple unweighted average of the individual state values.[15] To control for the effects of black population size, we use the same three black population categories in tables 10.2A–C that are used in the state chapters.[16] The figures shown are only for those cities for which we had complete longitudinal data that elected all council members at large at the starting point of our study. Thus tables 10.2A–C presents results in those at-large cities which changed election system and those which did not. The data reported in tables 10.2A–C allow inferences to be made about what happened when at-large elections in southern cities were replaced by district or mixed systems.

There are six basic components in this set of tables. These components are linked together in pairs ("before" and "after"): the initial percentage of black elected officials in cities that changed from an at-large to a district plan and the subsequent percentage in those cities; the initial percentage of black officials in cities that changed from an at-large to a mixed system and the subsequent percentage in those cities; and the initial percentage of black officials in the unchanged cities and the subsequent percentage in those cities. These six values are reported in the first six data columns of tables 10.2A–C. The columns also show the number of cases in each cell. Examination of each of the before-and-after comparisons tells how much black officeholder percentages changed in each of the three types of cities.

The data from Louisiana provide a convenient illustration of how to read the three parts of the table. In that state's cities that were 10–29.9 percent black, table 10.2A shows that in the period from 1974 to 1989 there were dramatic gains in black representation. Among the cities in that population category that changed election system, the black percentage on council rose from 0 to 27 percent in cities that shifted from an at-large to a district plan and from 3 to 19 percent in the those that shifted from an at-large to a mixed plan.[17] While jumps of 27 percentage points (27 − 0) for the single-member-district cities or 16 percentage points for the mixed cities may not look all that large, they are in fact very large relative to black population proportions, since the mean black population in the cities that were between 10 and 29.9 percent black was only 25.4 percent among the Louisiana cities that shifted to single-member districts and only 23.5 percent among the cities that shifted to a mixed plan. Thus the *growth* in black representation *relative to black population* in the Louisiana cities that shifted to single-member districts was 105 percent (26.7/25.4), and it was 69 percent (16.2/23.5) in the cities that shifted to mixed plans—a dramatic increase.[18]

However, not all of the growth in black representation can be attributed to change in election type. Even in the Louisiana cities that retained at-large systems, black representation increased from 0 to 10 percent. Therefore, because the gain in black representation in cities shifting to districts was 27 percentage points as compared to a gain of only 10 points in cities that retained their at-large plan, the shift to single-member districts can be thought of as having yielded a *net increase* in black representation of 27 − 10 = 17 points. In like manner, table 10.2B shows that the shift to districts yielded a net increase of 17 points in Louisiana cities that were 30–49.9 percent black, and table 10.2C shows a net gain of 24 points as a result of changing to districts even for the state's majority-black cities.

The information in table 10.2 can thus be used to gauge the independent effect of adopting a new type of election system. By looking at the difference between the growth in black representation in the jurisdictions shifting from an at-large to a single-member or mixed system and the growth in the jurisdictions that remained at-large throughout the entire period of roughly fifteen years, one can determine whether or not the gains in minority representation were greater in the cities that changed election systems than in those which remained at large. The value of this "difference resulting from change" variable is reported in the last two columns of tables 10.2A–C for single-member-district and mixed systems. In effect, by subtracting values for the unchanged cities from those for the cities that changed election type,[19] we are using change in black officeholding in the units that did not change election type as a base-line control for *maturation effects*—changes in the dependent variable that are unrelated to the impact of the changes whose consequences we are investigating, such as increased willingness among white voters to support black candidates.[20]

The tables show that in a substantial number of states, the level of black representation in majority-white cities that continuously elected at large did not change much over the previous two decades. In Georgia, North Carolina, South Carolina, Texas, and Virginia, the growth in black representation in cities that were 10–29.9 percent black ranged between 1 and 3 percentage points; while in North Carolina and South Carolina cities that were 30–49.9 percent black, the growth was only 4 and 7 points, respectively. Indeed, in the one Georgia at-large city in this population category, there was actually a decline in black representation during the period under investigation.[21]

Majority-White Cities that Changed from At-Large to Single-Member-District Systems

If the conventional view of at-large elections is true, majority-white cities changing to a pure district system are the ones where we would expect to observe the largest increases in black officeholding. That is exactly what we find in tables 10.2A–C. On average, across the eight states, black gains in majority-white cities were considerably larger in those adopting single-member districts than in those that remained at large.[22] For cities that were 10–29.9 percent black, the average gain in those shifting to districts was 23 points, and for cities that were 30–49.9 percent black, 34 points. In contrast, for cities that were 10–29.9 percent black that remained at large, the gain was only 6 percentage points, and for cities that were 30–49.9 percent black, 14 percentage points. The average net gain for cities that changed to districts relative to those that remained at-large was 16 and 19 points for those that were 10–29.9 and 30–49.9 percent black, respectively.[23] Relative to the black population levels in those cities, the gains attributable *directly* to change in election type were quite large.

The same general pattern is found in virtually all eight individual states, in eleven of the thirteen instances for which data are available to make comparisons.[24] Moreover, one of the two deviant cases is based on a single observation. On the face of it, the Texas case would seem to indicate that a 50 percent black council in 1989 was elected in a majority-white city. But although we present the case in this table for consistency of our treatment of the data, it is misleading, inasmuch as the city's population actually changed from majority white to majority black between 1980 and 1990, a change not reflected in the table because we used 1980 as a measure of both our 1970 and 1990 black population proportions.[25] Furthermore, treating this now majority-black city in table 10.2 as a majority-white city visibly increases the eight-state average we report for the at-large cities in the 30–49.9 percent category, inasmuch as the results in this single city are the results reported for the state of Texas a whole. Had we simply excluded that city, the average gains in at-large cities that were 30–49.9 percent black would have been only 9 percentage points rather than 14, and the net advantage of single-member districts over at-large plans would have increased from 19 to 25 points.

The other case with unexpected results involves three Alabama cities that were 10–29.9 percent black and remained at large, whose gains were equal to those in cities which adopted districts. However, we believe this anomaly can also be accounted for. The discrepancy between observed and predicted results is based on the only majority-white cities in Alabama that retained at-large elections in 1989. There were forty-two cities that elected at large in 1970, compared to only three in

1989. To anticipate our discussion of selection bias, the evidence suggests that the three Alabama cities retaining at-large elections as late as 1989 were atypical of the broader set of forty-two cities in the degree to which black candidates were elected.

Majority-White Cities that Changed from At-Large to Mixed Systems

The general expectation is that majority-white cities changing from an at-large to a mixed plan will also witness an increase in black officeholding, although not as great as in cities changing to a pure district plan, given the continued presence of some at-large seats. This is precisely what the data in tables 10.2A–C show, on average, across the eight states. For cities that were 10–29.9 percent black, the average gain among those shifting to a mixed plan was 13 points, and in cities that were 30–49.9 percent black, 25 points, for a gain over equivalent unchanged cities of 6 and 10 points, respectively. This compares to the corresponding net gains in the cities that shifted to single-member districts of 16 and 19 points, respectively.

The same pattern is found in virtually every state, in eleven of the fourteen instances for which data are available to make such comparisons. Moreover, as in the comparison between at-large systems and those changing to districts, the Texas exception results from mischaracterizing a city as majority white in 1989 because we use 1980 rather than 1990 population data; the Alabama exception is based on the only three majority-white cities in our data set that were still electing at large in 1989.

Majority-Black Cities

In majority-black jurisdictions, if blacks voted as a bloc, common sense might suggest that they should be able to elect their preferred candidates and perhaps even exclude whites from office if they wished, just as majority-white populations often have done to black candidates when elections are conducted at large. On the other hand, majority-black cities are disproportionately in the rural black belt, where black registration has historically been low and where whites have been particularly resistant to black strivings for equality.[26] Thus another version of common sense might predict, alternatively, that black representation would be low in majority-black areas electing at large—initially, at least.

In actuality, the mean growth in black representation in the majority-black cities adopting distícts was 53 percentage points in the five states for which there were such cities, while in the majority-black cities that changed to a mixed plan in the six states containing such cities, the gain was 32 points. These changes compare to a gain of 22 points in cities remaining at-large in the four states where there were such unchanged cities. In short, even for majority-black cities, the change to single-member districts yielded a considerable net advantage in minority representation; further, a change to a mixed plan also produced greater gains in black representation than was true for cities that remained at large.[27]

Summary of Findings in Tables 10.2A–C

On average,[28] the greatest effect of a change from an at-large plan to single-member districts occurred in majority-black cities (53 percentage points); the next greatest effect occurred in cities that were 30–49.9 percent black (34 points); and the lowest but still substantial effect occurred in cities that were 10–29.9 percent black (23 percentage points).[29] In terms of the net difference measure, the equivalent net gains were 33, 19, and 16 percentage points, respectively.

Results of changes to mixed systems, measured in terms of net gain, paralleled those of changes to pure district systems in that the greatest net effect of change to a mixed plan occurred in majority-black cities, followed by that in cities that were 30–49.9 percent black, and then by that in cities that were 10–29.9 percent black; but the net change values were not nearly as great: 15, 10, and 6 points, respectively, compared to 33, 19, and 16 points, respectively, for cities that changed to single-member districts.

In sum, the overall patterns in the three tables reveal the effects of change to single-member districts on black representation levels to be quite substantial, relative to black population percentage, even after we imposed a control for possible maturation effects by subtracting the growth in black representation that takes place in unchanged at-large cities. There were smaller but still significant gains in black representation achieved in the cities that shifted to mixed plans. The fact that the greatest net gains occurred in majority-black cities was unexpected, but the pattern of an increasing net impact of change in election systems as black population proportion increases is consistent with the view that whites' concern about black electoral impact becomes greater as the possibility grows that blacks can actually elect their preferred candidates in significant proportions and is greatest where blacks might actually be able to control the system.[30] It is also important to recognize that majority-black cities in the 1970s were likely to have been ones in which white bloc voting was especially high and black registration low. Moreover, many of the majority-black cities in our data base were unlikely to have been majority black in either registration or turnout in the early 1970s. Also, as noted earlier, some of the majority-black jurisdictions in our data set were only slightly more than 50 percent black and may not even have had black voting-age majorities.[31]

The Effect of Election Type on Representational Equity

An alternate use of the data in tables 10.2A–C is to transform the percentages of black elected officials into a ratio measure of black representational equity. Tables 10.3A–B, analogous to table 5 in each of the state chapters, presents a snapshot of the situation in the cities at the beginning (10.3A) and end (10.3B) of the period.[32]

The values of the black ratio equity measure (referred to from now on as *equity scores*) indicate the percentage of black officials on city council as a proportion of the percentage of blacks in the city.[33] A value of 1.00 indicates that black representation is perfectly proportional to black population, while smaller values indicate less, and larger values greater, than proportional representation.[34] The virtue of the ratio measure is that it controls for black population percentage across cities. Our use of this measure, however, is strictly a mathematical convenience.[35] It is not intended to imply that the legal standard for an ethnic minority group's right to participate equally in the political system is or should be proportional representation by officeholders of that ethnic group.

Table 10.3A demonstrates two very important facts. First, on average, majority-white single-member-district cities provided very close to proportional representation for blacks as the 1980s came to a close: cities that were 10–29.9 percent black had a mean equity score of 1.14, and cities that were 30–49.9 percent black had a score of 0.92. Second, black representation in majority-white at-large cities was very much lower: 0.53 and 0.56, respectively.

If we look at the data on a state-by-state basis, there are no exceptions to the first generalization. As for the second one, if we exclude as misleading the at-large Texas city 30–49.9 percent black that was majority black in 1990 but is classified as majority white, the only real exceptions are the three Alabama at-large cities already referred to, although Virginia at-large cities that were 30–49.9 percent black also had unusually high equity scores (0.83), as did Texas at-large cities that were 10–29.9 percent black (0.75).[36]

In majority-white cities, table 10.3A shows that, on average, black representation in mixed plans was intermediate between that in district and at-large plans but closer to the equity scores in the district ones. Cities 10–29.9 percent black had a mean equity score of 0.85, as did those 30–49.9 percent black. The generalization that equity of black representation in mixed plans was intermediate between that in district and at-large plans holds for most of the states where comparisons are possible.[37]

In majority-black cities in all states that had them, districted systems provided very close to proportional representation for blacks; the mean equity score was 0.92. We have data for only four states showing what happens in majority-black jurisdictions that elected at large. (South Carolina and Texas had no majority-black cities in the data set; in Georgia and Virginia, none of the handful of majority-black cities elected at large.) In Alabama, majority-black cities electing at large had high levels of black representation (a mean equity score of 1.09). In two other states black representation was moderate in majority-black at-large cities: Louisiana had a score of 0.80 and Mississippi, 0.70. However, North Carolina was a dramatic exception to this pattern of high or moderate black representation in majority-black jurisdictions electing at large, with an equity score of only 0.14. Black representation in majority-black jurisdictions was actually lower for mixed cities than for at-large cities in three of the four states for which direct comparisons are possible (with North Carolina the exception), but differences were not large.

Table 10.3B demonstrates that in the early period, usually the early 1970s, at-large cities—either those which subsequently changed election system or the ones that did not—were providing nothing close to proportional representation for blacks. Indeed, the equity scores of majority-white at-large cities at this time were minuscule. Only in five categories of cities out of forty-four were mean equity scores above 0.40, and in twenty-one categories the score was 0.00. Data for the 1970s are not shown for Georgia, which has a starting point of 1980. However, even as late as 1980, black representation in the majority-white at-large cities in that state was far from proportional, although it was greater than that reflected in the 1970s data for most of the other states in table 10.3B.[38]

Black Representation at the District Level

If, as tables 10.2 and 10.3 indicate, at-large elections depressed the share of offices held by blacks, the reason seems clear. In many cities employing this method, whites voted largely as a bloc for white candidates, and, constituting the majority of the electorate, they were able to prevent the election of blacks. Thus our findings indirectly lend weight to the view that many whites in southern cities have not been receptive to black candidacies. As this is contrary to the recent views of a number of media commentators and a few scholars, it is useful to pursue the matter of white voting preferences further. Thanks to other information our state chapter authors collected, we are able to do this.

The additional information is contained in two data sets. Unlike the information on which tables 10.2A–C and 10.3A–B are based, where cities are the units of analysis, these data sets include information at the level of individual districts. One set, for cities with mixed plans, allows us to compare the percentage of black officials in 1989 (or in 1990 where Georgia is concerned) who were elected from both district and at-large seats in the same city. Another data set for cities with mixed and pure district plans allows us to compare the percentage of black officials in districts of varying racial composition. If white voting patterns were changing significantly in the 1980s, the evidence should indicate, first, that in mixed cities blacks would be elected from both districted and at-large components in similar proportions and, second (when black population proportion is controlled), that in single-member-district cities, numerous blacks would be elected from majority-white as well as from majority-black districts. Neither of these expectations is fulfilled.

Table 10.4 shows the mean equity score in the at-large and districted components of mixed plans.[39] In a majority-white city the constituency for the at-large seats will be majority white too, while some individual districts will probably have black majorities. The obverse is true for at-large majority-black cities. Therefore, by comparing the results of district and at-large elections in mixed cities, we can determine whether blacks fare better in majority-white constituencies (the at-large component of majority-white cities) than in constituencies of which some are majority black. Inasmuch as the comparison is between results from two types of election *in the same city*, many of the variables that might affect black representation independently of election type are controlled in a way they would not be in a cross-sectional comparison of results *between cities*.

The findings are clear. In majority-white cities, blacks were very rarely elected at large, but in the district components, they were elected in proportions roughly comparable to their population percentage in the cities. Indeed, in Alabama, Mississippi, and South Carolina, *all* black representation in the *majority-white mixed cities* came from the district components.[40] In point of fact, even in the majority-black cities with a mixed election system, blacks were more nearly represented proportionally in the district than in the at-large component. In Alabama, North Carolina, and Virginia, the at-large components in the *majority-black mixed* cities elected *no* blacks at all.[41]

Further evidence bearing on the inability of blacks in majority-white venues to win city council offices in the eight states is found in table 10.5. Containing data from pure district and mixed plans, this table shows the percentage of black officials elected in districts of varying racial composition.

In districts less than 30 percent black, the likelihood of blacks being elected was virtually nil. Indeed, even in districts 30–39.9 percent black, the percentage of black elected officials was zero in four of the seven states for which we have data, although it was not far from proportional in two of the remaining three states. The pattern in districts 40–49.9 percent black was more varied: in two of the four states for which we have data, no blacks were elected from such districts, but in the remaining two states, black representation was close to proportional.[42]

There was also a varied pattern in districts 50–59.9 percent black, but much less so, and a threshold was apparently reached in five of the seven states for which data are available. In these states black representation was greater than black population proportion, and in a sixth state, Louisiana, districts 50–59.9 percent black provided very close to black proportional representation.[43] On average across the states, 74 percent of the districts elected a black representative. In fact, in states such as North Carolina, Texas, and Virginia, a 50–59.9 percent black district population was sufficient to guarantee election of a black. In districts more than 60 percent black, black representation was either 100 percent or close to it in all southern states except Mississippi, where the likelihood of black representation remained below one-half until districts were over 65 percent black.[44]

Summarizing the Findings in Tables 10.4 and 10.5

The patterns in tables 10.4 and 10.5 are even starker than those in tables 10.2 and 10.3 and point to the persistence of racially polarized voting not only in at-large cities but in the at-large component of mixed cities and at the level of individual districts in cities that were districted.[45] However, the level of black disadvantage varied. In pure at-large elections in majority-white cities, the degree of black success, although far below that in the pure district cities, still was considerably greater than that in the at-large components of mixed systems in majority-white cities, or than that in individual districts that were majority white. Indeed, table 10.5 shows black officeholding in single-member districts 10–29.9 percent black to be at or near zero and to be dramatically low even in the single-member districts 30–49.9 percent black.[46]

Comparisons between Southern Regions

Considering the scholarly attention traditionally given to differences in race relations between the Deep South and the Outer South, we compared these two regions in our eight-state sample, treating Alabama, Georgia, Louisiana, Mississippi, and South Carolina as Deep South states and North Carolina, Texas, and Virginia as belonging to the Outer South. Surprisingly, differences between Deep South and Outer South states in the effects of at-large elections on black representation were not that large, and in many ways North Carolina, despite its reputation for liberalism, had one of the poorest records of black representation of any state, especially in at-large settings.[47] However, especially with respect to table 10.5, it is Mississippi, as might be expected, that appears to have white behavior least likely to be conducive to black electoral success.

Comparing Results of Changed Election Plans on Black Representation in Cities and Counties

The findings on minority representation at the county level in the three states for which county data were collected closely mirror those for cities. On the one hand, relatively high levels of minority representation were observed in the majority-white counties that used single-member districts or mixed plans. On the other hand, at-large majority-white counties scored quite low on black representational equity.

Comparing cities and counties with the same levels of black population, we find a consistent pattern of differences between the two levels of governments in only one of the three states. Equity scores were consistently lower in Georgia counties than in Georgia cities for all types of election systems and levels of black population.[48] In North Carolina and South Carolina, however, for given levels of black population and election type, there was higher representational equity sometimes at the city level and sometimes at the county level.[49]

Comparing Results from Cross-Sectional and Longitudinal Data

The findings so far summarized in this chapter might appear to be old news. As we noted in the Editors' Introduction, numerous studies published in the 1970s and 1980s comparing black candidates' success in different election systems led to a scholarly consensus that single-member districts were in general far more advantageous to blacks than were multimember ones. Yet this consensus has been challenged by recent data suggesting that racial polarization is declining and that at-large elections are no longer as pernicious as they once were, even in the South. For example, Thernstrom, in a 1987 book sharply critical of the use, generally, of the Voting Rights Act to compel the creation of majority-minority districts, has argued that racial polarization was a much less serious problem than many minority leaders and voting rights attorneys and experts believed it to be.[50]

The most important study on the effects of election structure on black representation using data more recent than that from the 1970s or very early 1980s is by Welch, a leading specialist in minority representation.[51] Her well-designed and methodologically sophisticated cross-sectional study analyzed all U.S. cities with a 1984 population of at least 50,000 and containing a black or Hispanic population in 1980 of at least 5 percent but less than 50 percent. There were 218 cities with the requisite black population that she analyzed and 155 with the requisite Hispanic population, although many of the same cities composed her two ethnic subsamples.[52] Because her data were gathered in 1988, at least seven years after the previous major study, she could rightly claim to shed light on minority representation near the end of the 1980s and on changes from earlier patterns.[53] Her 1990 study is also important because her previous work had done much to buttress the conclusion that at-large elections sharply reduced minority representation.

Welch's most striking finding was that by 1988, black representational equity in at-large elections in majority-white cities of at least 50,000 population had increased significantly, while it remained high in majority-white cities with district and mixed plans. After controlling for the effects of black population percentage, she reported a significant closing of the gap in black officeholding between at-large and districted majority-white cities above this population threshold. In particular, Welch found that by 1988, black representation in southern majority-white at-large cities of 50,000 or more with a black population of at least 10 percent[54] had grown to the point where the ratio equity score in such cities was 0.83.[55] In contrast, studies of the 1970s had found scores in comparable cities nationwide to range roughly between 0.50 and 0.60.[56] Welch found that at-large cities had progressed in the South by another measure as well: the proportion of cities of at least 50,000 with a black population of at least 10 percent in which no blacks sat on council had dropped to 9 percent as compared to the 44 percent at the national level reported in an earlier study she had coauthored.[57] Moreover, contrary to findings for earlier decades, black representational equity in at-large plans in majority-white southern cities was actually greater than that in comparable cities in the North.[58]

Relying on evidence such as that reported in Welch's 1990 study, and also placing reliance on the results of certain highly visible political contests, particularly the election of Douglas Wilder as governor of Virginia, some observers profess to see a dramatic change in the past decade or so in white willingness to vote for black candidates in majority-white southern venues. A few observers have suggested that some or even most lawsuits in recent years seeking to effect a change from at-large to district elections were unnecessary and perhaps even injurious to the best interests of blacks.[59] This claim, we believe, is erroneous.[60]

It is important not to overstate the extent of differences between Welch's findings and earlier ones—something she herself is careful not to do. As she points out, while black representational equity had risen to 0.83 in the southern majority-white at-large cities of at least 50,000 population with a 10 percent or greater black population, the equity score for comparable districted cities in the South was still higher: 0.95. Also, when Welch compared at-large and district components of mixed systems in 1988, she, like us, found few black officeholders elected from the at-large components. For the southern majority-white mixed cities above 10 percent black, the black equity score she found was 1.05 in the districted component but only 0.24 in the at-large one.[61] Moreover, she found that representational equity in the at-large component of mixed plans in majority-white cities had actually *declined* at the national level since the 1970s. These findings alone undercut an unqualified claim that at-large elections no longer significantly disadvantage black voters, and they raise serious questions about claims of a sharp decline in racially polarized patterns of voting in the South.[62]

However, there are important differences between Welch's findings and ours that need to be discussed and explained. In particular, in majority-white southern cities for 1989–90, our cross-sectional data in table 10.3A show a far greater gap in black officeholding between at-large and district plans than Welch's study revealed for majority-white southern cities in 1988. We find a mean equity score for at-large cities that were 10–29.9 percent black of only 0.53, and we find an equity score of only 0.56 for cities that were 30–49.9 percent black—both far lower success rates than the 0.83 figure Welch reports for the combined set of southern majority-white cities that were at least 10 percent black.[63] And while it is true that in the eight states studied in this volume—with only one exception[64]—cities retaining at-large systems also showed gains in the proportion of black elected officials, these gains were far smaller than those in the cities which abolished at-large elections.

How can we explain the apparent contradiction between the Welch study and the data presented here? There are two reasons for the differences. One critical reason is that her 1988 data are restricted to cities of 50,000 or larger. When smaller cities and towns are examined, a very different picture emerges of the impact of at-large elections on black officeholding in recent years.[65] A second reason is that we employ a research procedure that, unlike hers, allows for a test of the hypothesis that at-large cities today are not representative of at-large cities of twenty years ago because of selection bias. For selection bias renders highly suspect claims about what the level of black officeholding would have been if the cities adopting mixed or district plans had remained at large—claims based on the assumption that the cities that changed would have had the same minority success rates as the cities that remained at large.

In the following section we first present evidence for our conclusion that very populous at-large cities differ from small cities with respect to the relation between election type and the level of black officeholding. Then, in the succeeding section, we examine evidence for a selection bias in cross-sectional research, taking advantage of the longitudinal aspects of our data base for southern cities.

The Significance of Differences in City Size Thresholds

Most careful studies of the effect of election structures have been limited to cities 25,000 or larger or 50,000 or larger. The latter threshold was used by Welch. There are only twenty-three such southern cities 10 percent or more black in her 1988 data base that still used at-large elections and were majority white.[66] Thirteen of those twenty-three cities are also in our data base.[67] For those thirteen we find an equity ratio of 0.70 for cities that were 10–49.9 percent black, closer to her figure of 0.83 than to the equity scores of 0.53 and 0.56 we report for at-large cities in table 10.3A for cities in the 10–29.9 and 30–49.9 percent black population categories, respectively. There are simply few very large southern cities that still elect at large, and almost all of these have elected appreciable proportions of black officials. However, at-large elections in majority-white cities are far less favorable to minority candidates in cities below 50,000. In the remainder of this section we look at city size effects on black representation in our data set. The eight state projects used different city size thresholds, with the result that states with low thresholds or none—North Carolina is a case in point—add a disproportionate number of cases to the category of smaller cities. Barring the use of a weighting procedure, we are therefore unable to control for the possible effects of state-specific influences. To remedy this problem, we decided to impose a size threshold of 10,000 on our eight-state data base and to analyze all cities in the resulting sample. Tables 10.6A–C and 10.7A–B report the extent of changes in black officeholding for all cities of at least 10,000 in 1980 that were at least 10 percent black in a fashion that parallels tables 10.2A–C and 10.3A–B, respectively.[68]

Since all the cities are at least 10,000 in size, and cases from North Carolina no longer dominate the sample, we can also report in tables 10.6A–C and 10.7A–B an average across states that uses cities as the units, in addition to one that averages across states as was done in tables 10.2A–C and 10.3A–B.[69]

The results largely corroborate our earlier ones with respect to the higher levels of black representation in the cities that changed election type as compared with those that remained at large. However, it is clear that in some states city size had a significant independent impact on black officeholding. More generally, we find a higher average level of black representation in the at-large cities 10,000 and above in population than in the full set of cities in our larger data set. For the cities that were 10,000 and up we get results more like those of Welch in her 1990 study of cities above 50,000, especially for cities that were 30–49.9 percent black. For example, using cities as our units for calculating means, we find in table 10.7A an equity score of 0.57 in the at-large cities that were 10–29.9 percent black and a score of 0.78 in the at-large cities that were 30–49.9 percent black.

In Mississippi and North Carolina, the two states where choice of the size threshold had the greatest impact on the number of cities included in the data set, the equity score at the end of the period was substantially higher for cities above 10,000 than for the entire set of cities in the two states' data base. In at-large cities of 10,000 or more, the scores were 0.58 and 0.51, respectively, in cities that were 10–29.9 percent black (table 10.7A), as compared to scores of 0.41 and 0.14 for the larger data set that includes the smaller cities (table 10.3A). Continuing the same mode of comparison, at-large cities that were 30–49.9 percent black in these two states produced equity scores of "not applicable" and 0.82, respectively, as compared to equity values of only 0.26 and 0.14 for the larger data set for the two states.

In Louisiana and Virginia, however, the pattern of greater equity scores in the larger cities as compared to the smaller cities was not present. For at-large cities of at least 10,000 that were 10–29.9 percent black, the scores in 1989 were 0.00, and 0.64, respectively, as compared to values of 0.60 and 0.56 for the larger data set. For the more populous at-large cities that were 30–49.9 percent black, the scores were 1.13, and 0.76, respectively, as compared to 0.52 and 0.83 for the larger data set. In Alabama the same three at-large majority-white cities compose the entire category in tables 10.3A–B and table 10.7A–B, and thus no evaluation of the effect of city size is possible for that state.[70]

All in all, the most striking aspect of these comparisons is that while the influence of city size varies somewhat within states, black representation was abysmally low in the hundreds of very small majority-white jurisdictions in North Carolina and in Mississippi—the former a state in the Outer South long enjoying a reputation for racial moderation, the latter a Deep South state whose name has been synonymous with racial reaction. Another important finding is that majority-white cities above 10,000 were far more likely to have eliminated the at-large plan than were the smaller commmunities. Only 36 percent of the cities above 10,000 still maintained at-large elections in the late 1980s, far lower than the 79 percent of cities in the full data set (which includes the small cities and towns) that maintained at-large elections.[71] Clearly, in some states, voting rights litigation has hardly begun to penetrate barriers to black officeholding in the rural areas. This fact is ignored in research such as Welch's that is limited to larger cities.

The dearth of black representation in the smaller cities of the South is particularly noteworthy because these communities, especially the very small ones, may be those where conditions of life for blacks have changed the least since 1965. If so, the absence of black participation in governance may be especially critical. This possibility takes on additional importance when one realizes that the number of blacks still living in small communities is considerable. In North Carolina, for example, more than two-thirds of all blacks in 1980 lived in cities of less than 25,000.

Problems that May Result from Selection Bias

We now turn to the problem of selection bias. The question we wish to answer is whether the equity scores in at-large election plans in 1989 were typical of scores we would have observed if all the cities that were at large at an earlier period had remained at large. In a strict sense, no one can answer this question because it concerns a counterfactual situation. We cannot know certainly what the facts would have been had the situation been different and none of the cities changed election system.

Nonetheless, a longitudinal design does enable us to approach this question in a manner that a cross-sectional one does not. The results, we believe, are quite suggestive. Because we have two data points for each city, separated by about fifteen years, we can look back to the time of the early data and compare the characteristics of 1989–90 at-large cities at that earlier time, with the characteristics of those at-large cities that later changed. Differences between these two sets of cities, all originally at large, could provide persuasive grounds for concluding that the remaining at-large cities were indeed atypical.

We define selection bias as a situation where the treatment (in this instance, "change in election system") is not causally independent of the dependent variable, that is, "black officeholding." For example, in the situation under analysis, selection bias could occur because a city's abolition of its at-large election system was linked to black success in gaining office under that system. This link is highly plausible. Given the application of the law under the Voting Rights Act and the Fourteenth Amendment since the mid-1970s, an at-large system generally is more likely to be challenged by a voting rights lawsuit or faced with a threat thereof, and litigation is more likely to be successful (or any threat of litigation is more likely to be credible) if minorities have not been successful in gaining office under it.[72] Therefore, cities that are still at large at the end of a period in this time span can be expected to be a nonrandom sample of the cities that were at large at the beginning of the period. In particular, cities that are still at-large at the end of the period may disproportionately be those cities where minorities had achieved some electoral success early on.

If this is true, then these at-large cities—the ones examined by a cross-sectional design at the end of the period—would be "selected" through a biased process. It is now obvious why the longitudinal approach is especially useful in tackling this issue. It enables us to examine all the cities that were at large at the beginning and to see whether the subset of them that were still at large at the end had higher initial black equity scores, on average, than the subset that later adopted mixed or district plans. If this turns out to be true, there is strong evidence that cities still retaining the at-large system were probably more accessible to black officeholders than is true of the full set of at-large cities at the beginning of the period.

The possibility of selection bias in a sample analyzed by the cross-sectional method was obvious to Welch, who herself posed this question: was the recent better showing of black candidates in predominantly white at-large cities due at least in part "to the possibility that those cities with the most egregious previous underrepresentation of blacks were the ones most likely to be challenged in court and thus most likely to have changed from at-large systems?"[73] Welch regarded this question as open.

Is there reason to believe something like this happened? We initially thought it was a good possibility because the cities that remained at large were, in most states, only a relatively small subset of the cities that began the period at large. According to table 10.1, in five of the eight states of our study a clear majority of the at-large cities changed election type over the period in question. In a sixth state, Louisiana, the proportion of cities that shifted election type was almost exactly one-half. Only in North Carolina and Virginia did the vast bulk of cities with at-large elections at the beginning of the period still elect at large at the end. Of course, had the other state chapters included cities and towns of very small size, as did North Carolina, then we would have most probably found that most cities in the South still elected at large.

To increase comparability across states without unnecessary sacrifice of sample size, we again focus on the cities in our data set that are above 10,000. If we confine ourselves to these cities, however, then the extent of changes in election type since the beginning of the period is even greater than for the full set of cities, although North Carolina and Virginia remain exceptions to the generalization that a clear majority of the cities that used to elect at large no longer do so.[74]

We examine the mean black equity score of the 1989–90 at-large cities of at least 10,000 at the beginning of the period, for cities grouped according to what election system they eventually adopted, and controlling for the percentage black in the cities' population.

The evidence for selection bias is easiest to see by examining the entire set of majority-white cities in tables 10.7A and 10.7B. In those sixty-seven cities which changed to single-member districts, the black equity score initially averaged only 0.09. In contrast, the seventy-two cities that retained the at-large plan began with a score of 0.31. These differences are statistically as well as substantively significant and show clear evidence of potential selection bias. The fifty cities that changed to mixed plans had an intermediate mean score of 0.23. There is also evidence of selection bias in the majority-black cities. The six adopting single-member districts had an initial mean score of 0.03; the six adopting mixed plans, 0.18; and the five remaining unchanged, 0.46. The number of majority-black cities, however, was obviously small.[75]

We now turn to a state-specific analysis to better understand some of the complexities of selection bias. The findings are seen in table 10.7A and 10.7B. In Georgia (for both population categories of majority-white cities), in Texas and Virginia (for cities 10–29.9 percent black), and in South Carolina (for cities 30–49.9 percent black), there appears to be a potential selection bias effect in the majority-white cities; minority electoral success was higher initially in the majority-white cities that remained at large than in those changing election type.[76] Thus, for half the states, the representational equity of the at-large majority-white cities might well have been lower if more of the "worst case" at-large cities had retained at-large elections.[77]

Tables 10.7A–B shows no evidence of probable selection bias in four states: Alabama, Louisiana, Mississippi, and North Carolina. But it is possible that our particular longitudinal design is not sufficient to uncover all the evidence that might exist for such bias even in these states, and may possibly underestimate the magnitude of selection bias in the four other states as well. This is because we chose, for each state, only two data points approximately fifteen years apart rather than, say, several data points throughout the period.[78]

Not only were very few southern cities using an alternative to the at-large election system in the early 1970s,[79] but in many areas of the South few cities had even begun to elect blacks to office in this period. This was fortunate for our before-and-after design, inasmuch as it meant that there would be few cases where the change in election type had preceded our starting date, but it was unfortunate for our analysis of selection bias. The hypothesis of selection bias is premised on the assumption that some at-large cities early on became less vulnerable to voting rights litigation by virtue of having elected a substantial percentage of blacks to office, in comparison with other at-large cities. But if virtually no blacks were being elected in the "before" period, no test of the selection bias hypothesis is possible.[80]

Consider Alabama, a state that, according to the table, gives no evidence of selection bias. The authors of the Alabama chapter chose 1970 as their starting point. The three majority-white Alabama cities still electing at large—cities whose 1989 ratio equity score was 1.10—had no black representation in 1970. But black representation that year in the state's other majority-white at-large cities was also virtually nil, as table 10.7B shows. Analogous patterns of complete or nearly complete black exclusion from office in the "before" period of our study existed in Louisiana and Mississippi (and for South Carolina cities that were 10–29.9 percent black). Thus with only data for the 1970 or 1974 starting points in these states, the possibility of selection bias would appear to be nonexistent. However, bias may still be present in these states, but missed because of the lack of data points intermediate between the early 1970s and the late 1980s. Additional data collected for the Alabama chapter underscore this point.[81]

Summary

Our analyses of the eight-state data set lead us to reaffirm the standard view that at-large elections have deleterious effects on black representation for cities with white majorities and a black population of at least 10 percent. As table 10.2 demonstrates, dramatic gains in black representation followed abolition of at-large elections—gains much greater than in cities that remained at large. (The negative impact of at-large elections is felt in county government too, as demonstrated in the three state chapters that examined the question.) In almost all states, table 10.3A shows, black representational equity was near 1.00 for majority-white cities using single-member districts: 1.14 for cities that were 10–29.9 percent black; 0.92 for cities that were 30–49.9 percent black; and a score only slightly above 0.50 for the majority-white cities that elected at large (0.53 for cities that were 10–29.9 percent black and 0.56 for cities that were 30–49.9 percent black).[82]

Also, as anticipated, when the black population percentage was held constant, levels of black officeholding in cities with a mixed plan were generally intermediate between those in at-large and single-member-district systems. Moreover, the data in tables 10.4 and 10.5 show a pattern of total exclusion of blacks in some states (and near exclusion in others) in the at-large component of mixed plans and in the majority-white districts in single-member district plans. Black officeholding in mixed plans was largely or almost entirely the result of black success in the districted component of the plan. Moreover, when we focus on districts in cities that elected by district, black officeholding was practically nonexistent in council districts less than 40 percent black but—except for Mississippi—it was close to 100 percent of all officeholders in districts greater than 60 percent black.[83]

The data analysis in this chapter also allows us to account for the differences between the findings of Welch's important 1990 study and those reported for the state chapters in this volume. Welch noted sharply increased black officeholding in at-large systems by 1988.[84] Our state chapters found that with a handful of exceptions at most, black equity scores in at-large settings were still very low in 1989. We reject the interpretation some authors (but not Welch herself) have placed on her work, and we have presented evidence that the differences between Welch's results and those of the chapter authors are more apparent than real, partly because of the difference in city sizes in the two studies and partly because of the problem of selection bias that Welch's cross-sectional design could not detect.

One way to see the remarkable effect of the changes in election type described in this chapter is to focus on the number of cities that failed to elect even a single black representative. Let us confine ourselves to the cities above 10,000 in our eight-state data base. There were 206, all at large, at the start of the period, of which 141 (68 percent) had no black officeholder; by the end of the period, there were only 77 at-large cities, of which 22 (29 percent) had no black officeholder. Also at the end of the period, however, there was *no* city with a single-member district or mixed plan that failed to have at least one black officeholder. Thus, even if we assume that without a change in election type, the proportion of the 129 changed cities (206 − 77) that would have no black officeholders at the end of the period would have been 29 percent (an estimate we know from our above discussion of selection bias to be very generous), then at least 37 cities over 10,000 in the eight southern states ([.29 − 0] × 129) avoided black exclusion from politics as a result of a change in election type. Of course, this is a very conservative estimate of the consequences of cities' adopting districts, since using the current results in at-large cities as predictive of what would have happened had these cities not adopted districts understates the consequences of change in election rules. In making this estimate of the positive impact of cities' adopting district or mixed plans, we are focusing narrowly on their ability to break the barrier against the election of a single black officeholder in these cities of at least 10,000.

If we broaden our inquiry, however, to include all gains in black officeholding resulting from cities' abolishing at-large elections and if we make use of our full data set, these gains are greater still. Our question now is, how many black officeholders can we be reasonably sure owe their election to single-member district or mixed plans? These are *council members who would not have been elected had black representation in these cities remained at the same level as in the unchanged at-large cities*. We find the net effect of change in election type in 217 cities to have resulted in the election of approximately two hundred more black city council members in 1989–90, even after we control for gains that under very generous assumptions might have taken place even had these cities remained at large.[85] Moreover, because such a relatively small proportion of cities have adopted districts in the South as a whole, there remain potential net gains of hundreds of new black council members in the many cities and towns that still remain at large, if they adopt district systems.

In summary, the longitudinal comparisons permitted by our data base and the variety of data we looked at have allowed us to gauge more accurately the extent to which shifts to single-member districts caused gains in black officeholding.[86] To recapitulate, when we combined the information in tables 10.4 and 10.5 with that shown in tables 10.2 and 10.3, it was apparent that minority underrepresentation was a persistent phenomenon in the South even as late as 1989. Moreover, when we reanalyzed the data to look for possible selection bias effects, we discovered a strong likelihood of them. Also, when we examined tables 10.6 and 10.7, we saw that even though black officeholding was relatively proportional in the handful of large southern cities that still elected at large, there were strong city size effects, such that representational equity in the at-large setting remained minuscule in small towns in some states. In these jurisdictions, especially in North Carolina and Mississippi, blacks continued to go unrepresented, and there were numerous towns that fell into this category. Had we examined at-large cities under 10,000 in Georgia, South Carolina, and Texas, we might very well have found similar underrepresentation there. These findings lead us to disagree strongly with those who dismiss the continuing importance of the Voting Rights Act as a safeguard for the right of blacks to fair representation.

TABLE 10.1
Data Base Characteristics, Cities with 10 Percent or More Black Population in 1980, Eight Southern States Covered by Section 5 of The Voting Rights Act

State	City Population Threshold	(N)[a]	Number of At-Large Cities: At Beginning of Period	Number of At-Large Cities: At End of Period	Period of Analysis
Alabama	6,000	(48)	48	6	1970–89
Georgia[b]	10,000	(34)	15	6	1980–90
Louisiana	2,500	(90)	57	29	1974–89
Mississippi	1,000	(133)	130	59	1974–89
North Carolina[c]	None	(729)	724	702	1973–89
South Carolina	10,000	(21)	21	7	1974–89
Texas[d]	10,000	(46)	42	17	1974–89
Virginia[e]	None	(26)	23	17	1977–89
TOTAL			1,060	843	

[a] The *N*s shown in parentheses in the third column are the total number of cities in a state for which any data are available. The values in the fourth column indicate the number of cities with at-large plans at the beginning of the period for which data are reported in the longitudinal data bases.

[b] In Georgia in 1990, 7 of 34 cities for which data are reported used multimember districts (see tables 3.1 and 3.2). We have omitted the multimember-district cities from the longitudinal data used in this chapter.

[c] The North Carolina data include ten cities with less than 10 percent black population but with a combined black plus Native American population of greater than 10 percent. All are under 5,000 in population; most are under 500. Six are in Robeson County. Five are majority Native American. The city of Goldsboro is identified by data provided by the city as being majority-minority, and is so characterized in Chapter 6. However, it is only 46.6 percent black, according to the U.S. census, and is not treated as majority-minority in chapter 10.

[d] In Texas, one multimember-district city is omitted from the data set. Also omitted is one for which 1974 data are unavailable and two others that did not have at-large systems in 1974. Only cities at least 10 percent black are analyzed in chapter 10, as distinct from chapter 8, where cities at least 10 percent black and Hispanic combined are analyzed.

[e] All independent cities (see chapter 9 for a definition of these cities).

TABLE 10.2A

Changes in Black Representation on Council during the Period of Investigation, Cities *10–29.9 Percent Black* in Eight Southern States

State (1980 Population Threshold)	*Change in % Black on Council*						*Difference ($t_2 - t_1$) in Black Representation*			*Changed Plans: Net Change in Black Representation*	
	From AL to SMD		*From AL to Mixed*		*AL Unchanged*						
	t_1	t_2	t_1	t_2	t_1	t_2	*SMD Plan*	*Mixed Plan*	*AL Plan*	*(SMD Change − AL Change)*	*(Mixed Change − AL Change)*
Alabama	0	20	11	11	0	20	20	0	20	0	−20
(6,000)	(23)	(23)	(1)	(1)	(3)	(3)	(23)	(1)	(3)		
Georgia	0	25	—	—	9	10	25	—	1	24	—
(10,000)	(1)	(1)	(0)	(0)	(5)	(5)	(1)	(0)	(5)		
Louisiana	0	27	3	19	0	10	27	16	10	17	6
(2,500)	(3)	(3)	(7)	(7)	(16)	(16)	(3)	(7)	(16)		
Mississippi	0	20	0	11	0	9	20	11	9	11	2
(1,000)	(5)	(5)	(16)	(16)	(20)	(20)	(5)	(16)	(20)		
N. Carolina	—	—	8	18	1	3	—	10	2	—	8
(none)	(0)	(0)	(5)	(5)	(346)	(346)	(0)	(5)	(346)		
S. Carolina	0	25	0	25	0	3	25	25	3	22	22
(10,000)	(2)	(2)	(1)	(1)	(5)	(5)	(2)	(1)	(5)		
Texas	6	27	7	19	11	14	21	12	3	18	9
(10,000)	(9)	(9)	(11)	(11)	(16)	(16)	(9)	(11)	(16)		
Virginia	0	20	5	21	8	10	20	16	2	18	14
(none)	(1)	(1)	(2)	(2)	(11)	(11)	(1)	(2)	(11)		
STATE MEAN	1	23	5	18	4	10	23	13	6	16	6
(*N*)	(7)	(7)	(7)	(7)	(8)	(8)	(7)	(7)	(8)	(7)	(7)

TABLE 10.2B

Changes in Black Representation on Council during the Period of Investigation, Cities *30–49.9 Percent Black* in Eight Southern States

State (1980 Population Threshold)	*Change in % Black on Council*						*Difference ($t_2 - t_1$) in Black Representation*			*Changed Plans: Net Change in Black Representation*	
	From AL to SMD		*From AL to Mixed*		*AL Unchanged*						
	t_1	t_2	t_1	t_2	t_1	t_2	*SMD Plan*	*Mixed Plan*	*AL Plan*	*(SMD Change − AL Change)*	*(Mixed Change − AL Change)*
Alabama	0	38	0	30	—	—	38	30	—	—	—
(6,000)	(13)	(13)	(2)	(2)	(0)	(0)	(13)	(2)	(0)		
Georgia	13	30	7	32	20	17	17	25	−3	20	28
(10,000)	(3)	(3)	(3)	(3)	(1)	(1)	(3)	(3)	(1)		
Louisiana	2	39	0	24	0	20	37	24	20	17	4
(2,500)	(9)	(9)	(6)	(6)	(7)	(7)	(9)	(6)	(7)		
Mississippi	0	36	0	30	0	9	36	30	9	27	21
(1,000)	(14)	(14)	(13)	(13)	(15)	(15)	(14)	(13)	(15)		
N. Carolina	5	36	11	32	1	5	31	21	4	27	17
(none)	(6)	(6)	(7)	(7)	(216)	(216)	(6)	(7)	(216)		
S. Carolina	2	45	4	33	8	15	43	29	7	36	22
(10,000)	(7)	(7)	(4)	(4)	(2)	(2)	(7)	(4)	(2)		
Texas	0	37	21	42	0	50	37	21	50	−13	−29
(10,000)	(3)	(3)	(2)	(2)	(1)	(1)	(3)	(2)	(1)		
Virginia	—	—	10	33	15	29	—	23	14	—	9
(none)	(0)	(0)	(1)	(1)	(6)	(6)	(0)	(1)	(6)		
STATE MEAN	3	37	7	32	6	21	34	25	14	19	10
						[16][a]			[9][a]	[25][a]	[15][a]
(*N*)	(7)	(7)	(8)	(8)	(7)	(7)	(7)	(8)	(7)	(6)	(7)

[a] The numbers in brackets show what happens when the one unchanged at-large Texas city in the 30–49.9 percent black is excluded. This is the city, as explained in the text, that had a majority-white population in 1980 but that was majority black by 1990.

TABLE 10.2C

Changes in Black Representation on Council during the Period of Investigation, Cities *50–100 Percent Black* in Eight Southern States

State (1980 Population Threshold)	*Change in % Black on Council*						*Difference ($t_2 - t_1$) in Black Representation*			*Changed Plans: Net Change in Black Representation*	
	From AL to SMD		*From AL to Mixed*		*AL Unchanged*						
	t_1	t_2	t_1	t_2	t_1	t_2	*SMD Plan*	*Mixed Plan*	*AL Plan*	*(SMD Change − AL Change)*	*(Mixed Change − AL Change)*
Alabama	0	80	0	51	46	74	80	51	28	52	23
(6,000)	(1)	(1)	(2)	(2)	(3)	(3)	(1)	(2)	(3)		
Georgia	—	—	23	35	—	—	—	12	—	—	—
(10,000)	(0)	(0)	(2)	(2)	(0)	(0)	(0)	(2)	(0)		
Louisiana	0	50	0	25	27	53	50	25	26	24	−1
(2,500)	(2)	(2)	(1)	(1)	(6)	(6)	(2)	(1)	(6)		
Mississippi	0	43	5	37	23	49	43	32	26	17	6
(1,000)	(11)	(11)	(12)	(12)	(24)	(24)	(11)	(12)	(24)		
N. Carolina	6	48	0	40	2	9	42	40	7	35	33
(none)	(3)	(3)	(1)	(1)	(140)	(140)	(3)	(1)	(140)		
S. Carolina	—	—	—	—	—	—	—	—	—	—	—
(10,000)	(0)	(0)	(0)	(0)	(0)	(0)	(0)	(0)	(0)		
Texas	—	—	—	—	—	—	—	—	—	—	—
(10,000)	(0)	(0)	(0)	(0)	(0)	(0)	(0)	(0)	(0)		
Virginia	11	56	20	50	—	—	45	30	—	—	—
(none)	(1)	(1)	(1)	(1)	(0)	(0)	(1)	(1)	(0)		
STATE MEAN	3	55	8	40	24	46	53	32	22	33	15
(*N*)	(5)	(5)	(6)	(6)	(4)	(4)	(5)	(6)	(4)	(4)	(4)

TABLE 10.3A
Black Representation on Council *at the End of the Period* of Investigation, Cities at Least 10 Percent Black in 1980 that Began the Period with an At-Large Plan, Eight Southern States (Ratio Equity Scores)

% Black in City Population by Type of Plan at End of Period	*Mean Ratio Equity Score for Cities*								
	Ala.	*Ga.*	*La.*	*Miss.*	*N.C.*	*S.C.*	*Tex.*	*Va.*	*State Mean*
10–29.9									
SMD	1.10	0.89	1.04	0.84	—	1.34	1.20	1.54	1.14
(*N*)	(23)	(1)	(3)	(5)	(0)	(2)	(9)	(1)	(7)
Mixed	0.69	—	0.83	0.58	0.82	0.85	1.11	1.05	0.85
(*N*)	(1)	(0)	(7)	(16)	(5)	(1)	(11)	(2)	(7)
At-large	1.10	0.47	0.60	0.41	0.14	0.21	0.75	0.56	0.53
(*N*)	(3)	(5)	(16)	(20)	(346)	(5)	(16)	(11)	(8)
30–49.9									
SMD	1.03	0.68	0.90	0.85	0.89	1.08	1.04	—	0.92
(*N*)	(13)	(3)	(9)	(14)	(6)	(7)	(3)	(0)	(7)
Mixed	0.78	0.83	0.65	0.74	0.96	0.82	1.07	0.95	0.85
(*N*)	(2)	(3)	(6)	(13)	(7)	(4)	(2)	(1)	(8)
At-large	—	0.41	0.52	0.26	0.14	0.42	1.37	0.83	0.56
(*N*)	(0)	(1)	(7)	(15)	(216)	(2)	(1)	(6)	(7)
50–100									
SMD	1.08	—	0.80	0.74	0.87	—	—	1.10	0.92
(*N*)	(1)	(0)	(2)	(11)	(3)	(0)	(0)	(1)	(5)
Mixed	0.98	0.66	0.49	0.59	0.52	—	—	0.91	0.69
(*N*)	(2)	(2)	(1)	(12)	(1)	(0)	(0)	(1)	(6)
At-large	1.09	—	0.80	0.70	0.14	—	—	—	0.68
(*N*)	(3)	(0)	(6)	(24)	(140)	(0)	(0)	(0)	(4)

TABLE 10.3B

Black Representation on Council *at the Beginning of the Period* of Investigation, Cities at Least 10 Percent Black in 1980 that Began the Period with an At-Large Plan, Eight Southern States (Ratio Equity Scores)

% Black in City Population by Type of Plan at End of Period	*Mean Ratio Equity Score for Cities*								
	Ala.	*Ga.*	*La.*	*Miss.*	*N.C.*	*S.C.*	*Tex.*	*Va.*	*State Mean*
10–29.9									
SMD	0.00	0.00	0.00	0.00	—	0.00	0.26	0.00	0.04
(*N*)	(23)	(1)	(3)	(5)	(0)	(2)	(9)	(1)	(7)
Mixed	0.11	—	0.11	0.00	0.38	0.00	0.36	0.25	0.17
(*N*)	(1)	(0)	(7)	(16)	(5)	(1)	(11)	(2)	(7)
At-large	0.00	0.39	0.00	0.00	0.04	0.00	0.57	0.44	0.18
(*N*)	(3)	(5)	(16)	(20)	(346)	(5)	(16)	(11)	(8)
30–49.9									
SMD	0.00	0.30	0.04	0.00	0.12	0.05	0.00	—	0.07
(*N*)	(13)	(3)	(9)	(14)	(6)	(7)	(3)	(0)	(7)
Mixed	0.00	0.17	0.00	0.00	0.33	0.10	0.55	0.25	0.17
(*N*)	(2)	(3)	(6)	(13)	(7)	(4)	(2)	(1)	(8)
At-large	—	0.49	0.00	0.00	0.03	0.22	0.00	0.43	0.17
(*N*)	(0)	(1)	(7)	(15)	(216)	(2)	(1)	(6)	(7)
50–100									
SMD	0.00	—	0.00	0.00	0.10	—	—	0.22	0.06
(*N*)	(1)	(0)	(2)	(11)	(3)	(0)	(0)	(1)	(5)
Mixed	0.00	0.42	0.00	0.07	0.00	—	—	0.36	0.14
(*N*)	(2)	(2)	(1)	(12)	(1)	(0)	(0)	(1)	(6)
At-large	0.46	—	0.33	0.32	0.03	—	—	—	0.28
(*N*)	(3)	(0)	(6)	(24)	(140)	(0)	(0)	(0)	(4)

TABLE 10.4
Black Council Representation in Mixed Plans at the End of the Period of Investigation by District and At-Large Components, Cities at Least 10 Percent Black, Eight Southern States

	Mean % Black Councilpersons in Each Type of Component																	
% Black in City	*Ala.*		*Ga.*		*La.*		*Miss.*		*N.C.*		*S.C.*		*Tex.*		*Va.*		*State Mean*	
Population, 1980	*Dist.*	*AL*	*Dist.*	*AL*	*Dist.*	*AL*	*Dist.*	*AL*	*Dist.*	*AL*	*Dist.*	*AL*	*Dist.*	*AL*	*Dist.*	*AL*	*Dist.*	*AL*
10–29.9	13	0	—	—	31	0	15	0	31	0	33	0	14	2	23	13	23	2
(N)	(1)	(1)	(0)	(0)	(13)	(13)	(18)	(18)	(5)	(5)	(1)	(1)	(11)	(11)	(3)	(3)	(7)	(7)
30–49.9	42	0	42	12	31	7	37	0	36	3	53	0	25	10	58	0	41	4
(N)	(2)	(2)	(9)	(9)	(13)	(13)	(13)	(13)	(8)	(8)	(4)	(4)	(2)	(2)	(2)	(2)	(8)	(8)
50–100	59	0	45	39	51	38	46	25	50	0	—	—	—	—	50	0	50	17
(N)	(2)	(2)	(3)	(3)	(4)	(4)	(12)	(12)	(1)	(1)	(0)	(0)	(0)	(0)	(1)	(1)	(6)	(6)

TABLE 10.5

Black Representation on Council Single-Member Districts at the End of the Period of Investigation, by Black Population in District, Single-Member-District and Mixed Cities at Least 10 Percent Black, Eight Southern States[a]

% Black Population in District	*Mean % Black Councilpersons in District*								
	Ala.	*Ga.*	*La.*	*Miss.*	*N.C.*	*S.C.*	*Tex.*	*Va.*	*State Mean*
0–9.9	0	0	0	0	0	4	0	NA	1
(*N*)	(94)	(9)	(37)	(44)	(8)	(23)	(24)		(7)
10–19.9	3	0	0	0	0	0	0	NA	0
(*N*)	(37)	(11)	(10)	(27)	(11)	(15)	(12)		(7)
20–29.9	0	0	8	0	0	0	0	NA	1
(*N*)	(8)	(3)	(12)	(13)	(10)	(4)	(2)		(7)
30–39.9	0	33	0	0	25	0	17	NA	11
(*N*)	(4)	(3)	(9)	(14)	(8)	(3)	(6)		(7)
40–49.9	50	—	40	0	0	—	—	NA	23
(*N*)	(4)	(0)	(5)	(12)	(2)	(0)	(0)		(4)
50–59.9	—	67	50	27	100	75	100	100	74
(*N*)	(0)	(6)	(4)	(11)	(8)	(4)	(2)	(3)	(7)
60–69.9	100	100	100	48	75	100	83	75	85
(*N*)	(20)	(2)	(7)	(21)	(4)	(15)	(6)	(4)	(8)
70–79.9	100	—	100	82	100	83	83	100	93
(*N*)	(16)	(0)	(8)	(11)	(6)	(12)	(6)	(5)	(7)
80–89.9	100	100	100	93	100	100	100	100	99
(*N*)	(11)	(5)	(8)	(15)	(6)	(1)	(4)	(2)	(8)
90–100	100	100	100	100	100	—	—	100	100
(*N*)	(7)	(3)	(14)	(27)	(5)	(0)	(0)	(6)	(6)

[a] The percentage black categories in this table are more numerous than in some of the state chapters. Also, Texas data in this table, as compared with Texas data in the state chapter, are for cities at least 10 percent black rather than black and Hispanic combined. North Carolina data are reported only for cities with a population of at least 10,000. The *N*s in this table may differ slightly from those in the state chapters because data are included here only for cities for which the data set is complete.

Table 10.6A

Changes in Black Representation on Council during the Period of Investigation, Cities of 10,000 or More Population in 1980, *10–29.9 Percent Black*, in Eight Southern States

	Change in % Black on Council						Difference ($t_2 - t_1$) in Black Representation			Changed Plans: Net Change in Black Representation	
	From AL to SMD		From AL to Mixed		AL Unchanged						
State	t_1	t_2	t_1	t_2	t_1	t_2	SMD Plan	Mixed Plan	AL Plan	(SMD Change − AL Change)	(Mixed Change − AL Change)
Alabama	0	21	11	11	0	20	21	0	20	1	−20
(*N*)	(13)	(13)	(1)	(1)	(3)	(3)	(13)	(1)	(3)		
Georgia	0	25	—	—	9	10	25	—	1	24	—
(*N*)	(1)	(1)	(0)	(0)	(5)	(5)	(1)	(0)	(5)		
Louisiana	0	17	4	18	0	0	17	14	0	17	14
(*N*)	(2)	(2)	(5)	(5)	(3)	(3)	(2)	(5)	(3)		
Mississippi	0	17	0	14	0	10	17	14	10	7	4
(*N*)	(2)	(2)	(3)	(3)	(2)	(2)	(2)	(3)	(2)		
N. Carolina	—	—	8	17	4	9	—	9	5	—	4
(*N*)	(0)	(0)	(3)	(3)	(14)	(14)	(0)	(3)	(14)		
S. Carolina	0	25	0	25	0	3	25	25	3	22	22
(*N*)	(2)	(2)	(1)	(1)	(5)	(5)	(2)	(1)	(5)		
Texas	6	27	7	19	11	14	21	12	3	18	9
(*N*)	(9)	(9)	(11)	(11)	(16)	(16)	(9)	(11)	(16)		
Virginia	—	—	5	21	10	13	—	16	3	—	13
(*N*)	(0)	(0)	(2)	(2)	(7)	(7)	(0)	(2)	(7)		
City Mean	0	23	5	18	6	11	22	14	6	16	8
(*N*)	(29)	(29)	(26)	(26)	(55)	(55)	(29)	(26)	(55)		
State Mean	1	22	5	18	4	10	21	13	6	15	7
(*N*)	(6)	(6)	(7)	(7)	(8)	(8)	(6)	(7)	(8)	(6)	(7)

TABLE 10.6B

Changes in Black Representation on Council during the Period of Investigation, Cities of 10,000 or More Population in 1980, *30–49.9 Percent Black*, in Eight Southern States

State	*Change in % Black on Council*						*Difference ($t_2 - t_1$) in Black Representation*			*Changed Plans: Net Change in Black Representation*	
	From AL to SMD		*From AL to Mixed*		*AL Unchanged*						
	t_1	t_2	t_1	t_2	t_1	t_2	*SMD Plan*	*Mixed Plan*	*AL Plan*	*(SMD Change − AL Change)*	*(Mixed Change − AL Change)*
Alabama	0	41	0	30	—	—	41	30	—	—	—
(*N*)	(7)	(7)	(2)	(2)	(0)	(0)	(7)	(2)	(0)		
Georgia	13	30	7	32	20	17	17	25	−3	20	28
(*N*)	(3)	(3)	(3)	(3)	(1)	(1)	(3)	(3)	(1)		
Louisiana	0	41	0	35	15	43	41	35	28	13	7
(*N*)	(4)	(4)	(4)	(4)	(1)	(1)	(4)	(4)	(1)		
Mississippi	0	39	0	43	—	—	39	43	—	—	—
(*N*)	(8)	(8)	(2)	(2)	(0)	(0)	(8)	(2)	(0)		
N. Carolina	18	47	18	33	11	32	29	15	21	8	−6
(*N*)	(6)	(6)	(7)	(7)	(7)	(7)	(6)	(7)	(7)		
S. Carolina	2	45	4	33	8	15	43	29	7	36	22
(*N*)	(7)	(7)	(4)	(4)	(2)	(2)	(7)	(4)	(2)		
Texas	0	37	21	42	0	50	37	21	50	−13	−29
(*N*)	(3)	(3)	(2)	(2)	(1)	(1)	(3)	(2)	(1)		
Virginia	—	—	—	—	15	27	—	—	12	—	—
(*N*)	(0)	(0)	(0)	(0)	(5)	(5)	(0)	(0)	(5)		
CITY MEAN	4	41	9	35	12	29	35	26	17	18	9
(*N*)	(38)	(38)	(24)	(24)	(17)	(17)	(38)	(24)	(17)	(79)	(79)
STATE MEAN	5	40	7	35	12	31	35	28	19	13	4
(*N*)	(7)	(7)	(7)	(7)	(6)	(6)	(7)	(7)	(6)	(5)	(5)

TABLE 10.6C
Changes in Black Representation on Council during the Period of Investigation, Cities of 10,000 or More Population in 1980, *50–100 Percent Black*, in Eight Southern States

	Change in % Black on Council						*Difference ($t_2 - t_1$) in Black Representation*			*Changed Plans: Net Change in Black Representation*	
	From AL to SMD		*From AL to Mixed*		*AL Unchanged*						
State	t_1	t_2	t_1	t_2	t_1	t_2	*SMD Plan*	*Mixed Plan*	*AL Plan*	*(SMD Change − AL Change)*	*(Mixed Change − AL Change)*
Alabama	0	80	0	51	46	74	80	51	28	52	23
(*N*)	(1)	(1)	(2)	(2)	(3)	(3)	(1)	(2)	(3)		
Georgia	—	—	23	35	—	—	—	12	—	—	—
(*N*)	(0)	(0)	(2)	(2)	(0)	(0)	(0)	(2)	(0)		
Louisiana	0	60	—	—	—	—	60	—	—	—	—
(*N*)	(1)	(1)	(0)	(0)	(0)	(0)	(1)	(0)	(0)		
Mississippi	0	48	7	50	0	17	48	43	17	31	26
(*N*)	(3)	(3)	(2)	(2)	(1)	(1)	(3)	(2)	(1)		
N. Carolina	—	—	—	—	20	60	—	—	40	—	—
(*N*)	(0)	(0)	(0)	(0)	(1)	(1)	(0)	(0)	(1)		
S. Carolina	—	—	—	—	—	—	—	—	—	—	—
(*N*)	(0)	(0)	(0)	(0)	(0)	(0)	(0)	(0)	(0)		
Texas	—	—	—	—	—	—	—	—	—	—	—
(*N*)	(0)	(0)	(0)	(0)	(0)	(0)	(0)	(0)	(0)		
Virginia	11	56	—	—	—	—	45	—	—	—	—
(*N*)	(1)	(1)	(0)	(0)	(0)	(0)	(1)	(0)	(0)		
CITY MEAN	2	57	10	45	32	60	55	35	28	27	7
(*N*)	(6)	(6)	(6)	(6)	(5)	(5)	(6)	(6)	(5)	(17)	(17)
STATE MEAN	3	61	10	45	22	50	58	35	28	42	25
(*N*)	(4)	(4)	(3)	(3)	(3)	(3)	(4)	(3)	(3)	(2)	(2)

TABLE 10.7A

Black Representation on Council *at the End of the Period* of Investigation, Cities of 10,000 or More Population in 1980 at Least 10 Percent Black in 1980 that Began Period with an At-Large Plan, Eight Southern States (Ratio Equity Scores)

% Black in City Population by Type of Plan at End of Period	*Mean Ratio Equity Score for Cities*									
	Ala.	*Ga.*	*La.*	*Miss.*	*N.C.*	*S.C.*	*Tex.*	*Va.*	*City Mean*	*State Mean*
10–29.9										
SMD	1.06	0.89	0.65	0.80	—	1.34	1.20	—	1.07	0.99
(*N*)	(13)	(1)	(2)	(2)	(0)	(2)	(9)	(0)	(29)	(6)
Mixed	0.69	—	0.87	0.78	0.77	0.85	1.11	1.00	0.95	0.87
(*N*)	(1)	(0)	(5)	(3)	(3)	(1)	(11)	(2)	(26)	(7)
At-large	1.10	0.47	0.00	0.58	0.51	0.21	0.75	0.64	0.57	0.53
(*N*)	(3)	(5)	(3)	(2)	(14)	(5)	(16)	(7)	(55)	(8)
30–49.9										
SMD	1.16	0.68	0.94	0.95	1.11	1.08	1.04	—	1.03	0.99
(*N*)	(7)	(3)	(4)	(8)	(6)	(7)	(3)	(0)	(38)	(7)
Mixed	0.78	0.83	0.91	1.08	0.95	0.82	1.07	—	0.92	0.92
(*N*)	(2)	(3)	(4)	(2)	(7)	(4)	(2)	(0)	(24)	(7)
At-large	—	0.41	1.13	—	0.82	0.42	1.37	0.76	0.78	0.82
(*N*)	(0)	(1)	(1)	(0)	(7)	(2)	(1)	(5)	(17)	(6)
50–100										
SMD	1.08	—	0.86	0.86	—	—	—	1.10	0.93	0.97
(*N*)	(1)	(0)	(1)	(3)	(0)	(0)	(0)	(1)	(6)	(4)
Mixed	0.98	0.66	—	0.76	—	—	—	—	0.80	0.80
(*N*)	(2)	(2)	(0)	(2)	(0)	(0)	(0)	(0)	(6)	(3)
At-large	1.09	—	—	0.28	1.14	—	—	—	0.94	0.84
(*N*)	(3)	(0)	(0)	(1)	(1)	(0)	(0)	(0)	(5)	(3)

TABLE 10.7B
Black Representation on Council *at the Beginning of the Period* of Investigation, Cities of 10,000 or More Population in 1980 at Least 10 Percent Black in 1980 that Began Period with an At-Large Plan, Eight Southern States (Ratio Equity Scores)

% Black in City Population by Type of Plan at End of Period	*Mean Ratio Equity Score for Cities*									
	Ala.	*Ga.*	*La.*	*Miss.*	*N.C.*	*S.C.*	*Tex.*	*Va.*	*City Mean*	*State Mean*
10–29.9										
SMD	0.00	0.00	0.00	0.00	—	0.00	0.26	—	0.08	0.04
(*N*)	(13)	(1)	(2)	(2)	(0)	(2)	(9)	(0)	(29)	(6)
Mixed	0.69	—	0.00	0.00	0.30	0.00	0.36	0.22	0.23	0.22
(*N*)	(1)	(0)	(5)	(3)	(3)	(1)	(11)	(2)	(26)	(7)
At-large	0.00	0.39	0.00	0.00	0.25	0.00	0.57	0.42	0.31	0.20
(*N*)	(3)	(5)	(3)	(2)	(14)	(5)	(16)	(7)	(55)	(8)
30–49.9										
SMD	0.00	0.30	0.00	0.00	0.43	0.05	0.00	—	0.10	0.11
(*N*)	(7)	(3)	(4)	(8)	(6)	(7)	(3)	(0)	(38)	(7)
Mixed	0.00	0.17	0.00	0.00	0.51	0.10	0.55	—	0.23	0.19
(*N*)	(2)	(3)	(4)	(2)	(7)	(4)	(2)	(0)	(24)	(7)
At-large	—	0.49	0.00	—	0.29	0.22	0.00	0.43	0.30	0.24
(*N*)	(0)	(1)	(1)	(0)	(7)	(2)	(1)	(5)	(17)	(6)
50–100										
SMD	0.00	—	0.00	0.00	—	—	—	0.22	0.03	0.06
(*N*)	(1)	(0)	(1)	(3)	(0)	(0)	(0)	(1)	(6)	(4)
Mixed	0.00	0.42	—	0.11	—	—	—	—	0.18	0.18
(*N*)	(2)	(2)	(0)	(2)	(0)	(0)	(0)	(0)	(6)	(3)
At-large	0.64	—	—	0.00	0.38	—	—	—	0.46	0.34
(*N*)	(3)	(0)	(0)	(1)	(1)	(0)	(0)	(0)	(5)	(3)

CHAPTER ELEVEN

The Impact of the Voting Rights Act on Minority Representation: Black Officeholding in Southern State Legislatures and Congressional Delegations

LISA HANDLEY AND BERNARD GROFMAN

THE VOTING RIGHTS ACT of 1965 has succeeded in eliminating most of the barriers blacks in the South previously faced in attempting to register and vote. But the act sought to do more than this. It was also designed to bring minority groups and their concerns into the halls of government. Progress in this direction has been much slower; years after the act had produced impressive gains in registration, blacks still held only a small fraction of the elected offices in the South. However, as table 11.1 illustrates, blacks have been winning office in increasing numbers since 1970, a phenomenon that has been particularly dramatic in the South. By 1985, the percentage of blacks serving at every level of government with the exception of Congress was higher in the South than elsewhere. The primary reason for the disproportionate increase in southern black officeholding, this essay will show, is the Voting Rights Act.

Our evidence demonstrates, moreover, that the currently popular argument that the Voting Rights Act has served its purpose and is no longer as necessary as it once was is misguided.[1] Proponents of this argument herald the election of prominent black politicians such as Virginia governor Douglas Wilder as examples of a new southern progressivism. But Wilder's 1989 election is the exception rather than the rule, our data show, and even that gubernatorial contest was not devoid of racial bloc voting.[2] In fact, there is little evidence for a widespread increase in the willingness of white voters to cast their ballots for black candidates.[3]

This investigation examines the possible reasons for the growth in the number of black elected officials from the passage of the act in 1965, when virtually no blacks held political office in the South, until 1985, when the election results of the previous round of redistricting were in. It focuses primarily on state legislatures in the South, but congressional level data are examined briefly at the close of the study in order to determine if the conclusions hold at the congressional level as well. We arrive at three basic conclusions. First, the increase in the number of blacks elected to office in the South is a product of the increase in the number of majority-black districts and not of blacks winning in majority-white districts. Second, even today black populations well above 50 percent appear necessary if blacks are to have a realistic opportunity to elect representatives of their choice in the South. Third, the increase in the number of black districts in the South is primarily the result not of redistricting changes based on population shifts as reflected in the decennial census but, rather, of those required by the Voting Rights Act of 1965 and its 1982 amendments. Quite simply, had there been no federal intervention in the redistricting process in the South, it is unlikely that most southern states would have ceased their practice of diluting the black vote. The Justice Department forced many southern states to replace their multimember state legislative districts with single-member seats, especially in areas with black population concentrations, and also denied preclearance to single-member redistricting plans that appeared to fragment black voters unnecessarily. Federal intervention of this nature, as well as voting rights suits brought by private litigants, was primarily responsible for the significant increase in southern black officeholding, at least at the state legislative and congressional levels.

Are Whites Electing Blacks to Office in the South?

Table 11.1 shows that the number of southern black legislators increased sharply after 1965. In that year only 3 blacks were state legislators in the eleven states of the Old Confederacy; by 1985 that number had increased to 176—almost 10 percent of the legislative seats. Of course, because blacks comprise almost 20 percent of the southern population, they were still quite underrepresented proportionally.

To what can this substantial rise be attributed? A major cause was the increase in black voting made possible by the act. But black participation rates have leveled off since the early 1970s; thus the more recent increases must have been due to other factors. Some writers attribute it to a growing willingness among whites to vote for black candidates. If this were true, then we should see more blacks elected from majority-white jurisdictions. But as table 11.2 demonstrates, this is simply not the case. Majority-white legislative districts were no more likely to elect black legislators in the 1980s than in the previous decade. In the 1970s, approximately 1 percent of all state legislative districts that were less than 50 percent black elected black legislators. That did not change in the 1980s. Thus the need remained for districts with substantial black population percentages if blacks were to have a realistic opportunity to elect their candidates of choice.

What did change, however, was the number and percentage of majority-black districts that elected black legislators. As table 11.2 indicates, only 59 percent of the majority-black state house districts in the 1970s elected a black to office, but in the 1980s this increased to 77 percent. The rise was even greater in state senate districts: from 25 to 62 percent. Yet there was no increase in the percentage of blacks elected in majority-white districts. In fact, the proportion actually dropped in the lower houses. Thus the increase in black legislators observed in table 11.1 was due almost entirely to the increase in the number of blacks elected from majority-black districts and to the increase in the number of such districts. In the

1970s there were 126 majority-black state legislative districts in the seven southern states we analyzed; in those same states in the 1980s there were 182 such districts, an increase of over 44 percent.[4] Almost 84 percent of the southern black legislators in the 1970s represented majority-black districts; this figure rose to 90 percent in the 1980s.

How much of the increase in the number of black southern legislators is the result of black-majority districts voting more African Americans into office, and how much is it the result of the increase in the number of black-majority districts? Grofman and Jackson have independently developed a formula to answer this question. Called the *decompositional effects formula*, it assigns causal weights to a compositional effect (the number of majority-black districts); a behavioral effect (the ability of a majority-black district to elect a black); and an interaction effect (the interaction between composition and behavioral effects).[5] Using this formula, we determined that of the 5.1 percentage point gain in black representation between the 1970s and 1980s in the seven states analyzed, 55 percent was due to composition, 26 percent to behavior,[6] and 19 percent to the interaction of behavior and composition.[7] In other words, most of the black increase resulted from an increase in the number of majority-black districts. Moreover, black candidates actually fared worse in the 1980s in the majority-white districts than they had earlier.

The Color-Blind versus the Racial Polarization Model of Voting

Confronted with these facts, those with an optimistic view of southern race relations may say that the reason most black legislators get elected from black districts is that most blacks live in such districts. There are consequently not many blacks in other districts, which is why so few blacks get elected in them. This is the same reason, they might go on to say, that so few people of Scandinavian descent get elected to southern legislatures. It is not because of anti-Scandinavian voting, but because there simply are not very many Scandinavians there.

We call this *the color-blind hypothesis*, because it attributes the failure of blacks to get elected in white districts to the geography of residential dispersion rather than to whites' tendency to vote against blacks. (This hypothesis, as stated, obviously ignores the question of why blacks and whites tend to live in separate enclaves. But for the sake of argument, let us assume the answer has nothing to do with race.) The hypothesis could be tested, however, only if a significant number of blacks, albeit a minority, lived in majority-white districts. In that case, evidence for this hypothesis would be found in a correlation between the percentage of blacks in those districts and the percentage of black representatives elected from them. In a sample of majority-white districts whose mean black population was 10 percent, for example, one would expect about 10 percent of the elected representatives to be black as well; where the mean black population was 30 percent, one would expect about 30 percent of the representatives to be black, and so forth.

In contrast, *the racial polarization hypothesis* asserts the opposite. According to this view, the size of the black population in majority-white districts will have little effect on the ability of black candidates to win in them, at least until some tipping point near 50 percent is reached. Evidence for this hypothesis would be a very low correlation between the proportion of black voters in the majority-white districts and the percentage of black representatives elected from them. At the extreme, no blacks would be elected from majority-white districts, and vice versa.

In point of fact, there was in the 1980s a sizable proportion of blacks in the South residing outside majority-black districts, allowing for a test of these contrary hypotheses. A significant majority of blacks lived outside of majority-black house and senate districts in every southern state. (The exceptions were Alabama and Mississippi, where only 50 percent resided outside majority-black house districts.)[8] In five states, over 80 percent of blacks lived outside majority-black senate districts; in three states, over 70 percent of blacks lived outside majority-black house districts.

Given these facts, we have examined the voting behavior of both majority-black and majority-white districts and compared the proportion of blacks one would expect these districts to elect in the 1980s, assuming the color-blind hypothesis were true, with the actual proportion of black legislators elected from them. The results of this test are seen in tables 11.3 and 11.4. They strongly support the racial polarization model at the expense of the color-blind one. In the majority of southern states, not a single majority-white district elected a black legislator. The most progressive state was North Carolina, where 4 percent of the 111 majority-white districts elected a black during the decade of the 1980s.

Racial polarization was also high in the majority-black districts, although not quite so high as in the white ones (see table 11.5). In districts 65 percent or more black, however, polarization was almost complete: nearly 100 percent of these districts elected blacks to office. The fact that black-majority districts were not quite as polarized as white ones probably stemmed from the relatively low black turnout in the black districts; when the actual electorate (as distinct from the total population) became majority black, the black voters were able and willing to elect a black candidate.

Table 11.6 indicates the numerical increase in these heavily black districts in the 1980s. Table 11.5 also shows the growth in the ability of such districts—those 60 percent black and over—to elect blacks to office. These two trends alone combined to boost the number of black legislators significantly in the 1980s. Contrary to the color-blind hypothesis, majority-white districts figured in this growth of black legislators hardly at all.

However, in looking at the black proportion needed to elect black legislative candidates, it is important to be sensitive to state and local variations.[9] In particular, Mississippi was anomalous in that the proportion of majority-black districts electing black candidates was much lower than in any other southern state (see table 11.4). This may in part have been due to lower rates of black participation in this state.[10] In contrast, virtually all majority-black districts in Alabama elected blacks to office.

The increase in the number of black districts between the 1970s and 1980s is presented in table 11.6. There was a 57 percent increase in the number of districts that were greater than 60 percent black. By contrast, the increase in the number of districts between 50 and 60 percent black was 26 percent, indicating an awareness by those drawing the districts of the need for heavy black majorities if black candidates were to have a fair chance of being elected.

In summary, although there was clearly an increase in the number of blacks elected to state legislative office, there is no evidence to indicate that this rise was the consequence of increasing white support for black candidates. Blacks were no more likely to be elected from majority-white jurisdictions in the 1980s than they were in the previous decade. Rather, states drew more majority-black districts, which had higher black concentrations than in the 1970s, as well as a higher likelihood of electing blacks.

This fact cannot be too strongly emphasized. There are basically three types of factors that might affect minority success. First, if black registration and turnout increased relative to whites, greater black success would have occurred in majority-black districts.[11] But this possibility can largely be ruled out because the racial differences in turnout rates remained relatively constant during this period.[12] Even more important, as has been shown using the Grofman-Jackson method described above, most of the increase in southern black representation over the past decade was due simply to an increase in the number of majority-black districts.

A second possible explanation for increased minority success is a growth in black population and/or a change in the black population concentration; that is, if the black population has shifted so as to allow for the creation of additional black-majority districts, then an increase in the number of blacks holding office might be anticipated. However, growth can be ruled out because the percentage of blacks in the South actually declined slightly over the past decade. This is true for the entire region and for nine of the eleven states; only in Georgia and North Carolina did the black ratio rise slightly. As for changes in black population concentrations, there is little evidence to suggest much change during the period in question. In fact, the majority-black counties in the Mississippi Delta area of the Deep South have been losing black population.[13]

A third factor that might have produced substantial gains in black representation in an area with racially polarized voting is an increase in the number of black-majority districts. This, finally, is the best answer, as table 11.6 shows. How did this come about?

WHY WERE MORE BLACK DISTRICTS DRAWN?

Action by the Justice Department, as well as by private litigants (particularly in the 1980s, when civil rights and minority groups made use of the newly amended provisions of section 2 of the Voting Rights Act), accounts for most of the growth in black legislative representation in the South. This action usually took one of two forms: the state was required to change its election system from multimember to single-member districts, at least in the areas of the state with large concentrations of blacks; or, if the state already employed single-member districts, the state was required to redraw its lines so as not to fragment black voters.

The Justice Department has expressed a decided preference for the use of single-member districts, refusing to preclear state legislative plans with multimember districts, especially in heavily black areas. For example, in the 1970s, section 5 preclearance denials reduced or eliminated multimember districts in the legislative chambers of Georgia, Louisiana, Mississippi, and South Carolina.[14] Then in 1981 and 1982, a series of Justice Department objections also eliminated multimember legislative districts in the covered area of North Carolina.

Voting rights litigation also played a role in forcing states to adopt single-member districts. For example, in Texas in the early 1970s, multimember districts were eliminated as a result of a lawsuit brought by private litigants under the Fourteenth Amendment.[15] In North Carolina, multimember districts in a number of areas not covered by section 5 were eliminated as a result of a section 2 lawsuit brought by the NAACP Legal Defense and Educational Fund.[16]

Table 11.7 lists the type of election system used in each of the eleven southern states in 1965, 1970, 1975, 1980, and 1985. It shows that almost all of the states employed multimember districts in 1965; by 1985 no state had a pure multimember election system, although Arkansas still employed some multimember house districts. Many of the multimember districts in Arkansas were subsequently eliminated as the result of a section 2 suit, however.[17]

States already using only single-member districts have also been subjected to Justice Department intervention. For example, the Attorney General objected to several legislative plans in Alabama, Georgia, and Mississippi because of the fragmentation of black voting concentrations by district lines.

Recent critics of the act have claimed that, in many instances, department interference with the autonomy of state legislatures in drawing redistricting plans is unwarranted;[18] however, without such federal intervention, there is little evidence to suggest that white-dominated southern legislatures would have drawn majority-black districts. On the contrary, these legislatures have fought, often bitterly, to avoid such changes. For example, in the 1970s Mississippi used a variety of legal maneuvers that enabled them to avoid the creation of majority-black districts until 1979.

The Shift to Single-Member Districts

How has the adoption of single-member districts affected black legislative representation? Table 11.8 compares the percentage of blacks elected under multimember and single-member-district systems in three periods. It parallels and updates analyses done by Jewell and by Grofman and his colleagues.[19] Blacks were obviously advantaged in single-member-district systems, and this advantage grew over time—a pattern that held both in the lower and upper houses.

This finding is further supported by a simple bivariate correlation between the dummy variable "use of single-member districts" and the variable "number of black legislators." We performed this analysis using forty-four data points—observations for each of the eleven southern states at four different times: 1970, 1975, 1980 and 1985 (see table 11.7 for the raw data). For the lower chamber, r = .80 and for the upper chamber, r = .52. There is obviously a strong relationship between the use of single-member districts and the election of blacks to state legislative office.

Of course, it might be argued that this relationship is misleading because there may be other reasons why states with multimember districts have a lower percentage of blacks serving in their legislatures: for instance, states with multimember district systems may have fewer blacks than states with single-member systems. We tested this hypothesis with before-and-after analyses in the states that changed election systems, comparing shifts in black representation in those jurisdictions that adopted new systems with shifts in those that did not.

The change in black representation in both chambers in all eleven states was identified for each of the three periods: 1970–75, 1975–80, and 1980–85, providing a total of thirty-three observation points for each legislative chamber (see table 11.7 for the raw data). A dummy variable indicated whether there had been a shift to single-member districts within the specified time period for each of the data points. Regressing change in black representation on the dummy variable ("shift to single-member districts") revealed the extent to which changes in black representation occurred in the period in which states switched to single-member districts. Data from states that did not change their system were included in the analysis as a control group. If black representation were to have increased as much in the unchanged systems as in the changed systems, then the increase would not be the result of system change.

The analysis for the lower chambers of the eleven states produced a bivariate correlation of .74 between a shift to single-member districts and change in black representation. A shift to single-member districts was associated with a mean gain of 6.3 black representatives in the state. In state senates, the corresponding correlation was .37, and the change to single-member districts was associated with a mean gain of 1.1 black senators in the state (see table 11.9, part [a]).[20]

As each of these analyses indicates, the switch to single-member districts was an important reason for the increase in black representation in southern legislatures.[21] And with very few exceptions, states did not make the switch voluntarily; Justice Department refusals to preclear state legislative plans that employed multimember districts and voting rights litigation challenging multimember districts as dilutive were the primary causes of the elimination of multimember districts. Tennessee and Florida—neither of which is subject to section 5—were the only states that clearly shifted election systems voluntarily; every other southern state was required, either by courts or by the Justice Department, to adopt single-member districts in the election of at least one of their legislative chambers.

Section 5 Coverage

Initially, six southern states were entirely covered by the preclearance provisions of the Voting Rights Act: Alabama, Georgia, Louisiana, Mississippi, South Carolina, and Virginia. North Carolina was only partially covered. Coverage was extended to the entire state of Texas in 1975. To ascertain the importance of section 5 on black officeholding, we regressed a dummy variable for section 5 coverage ("1" for all states covered in whole or in part) on the number of black legislators in the eleven southern states. The bivariate correlation was .43 for the lower chamber and .21 for the upper chamber. We conclude that the automatic trigger clearly made a difference in black representation (see table 11.9, part [b]). This difference, however, was not as important as that resulting from the substitution of single-member for multimember districts, as evidenced by a multivariate analysis that included the dummy variables "use of single-member districts" and "section 5 coverage." The multiple correlation coefficient was .82 for state houses, and both variables were statistically significant, although section 5 coverage was significant only at the .05 level. Use of single-member districts led to an average increase of 9.4 black representatives; section 5 coverage led to an average gain of 2.8 black representatives. The relationship was not as strong for state senates; the multiple correlation coefficient was .53 and only the dummy variable "use of single-member districts" was significant (see table 11.9, part [c]).

A time variable was also included in the analysis because time alone, we surmised, might have accounted for the increase in blacks elected in the South.[22] We thought it more likely, however, that the increase resulted from eventual black victories in new majority-black districts that did not initially elect a black to office.[23] The simple bivariate correlation between a time interval variable and the number of black legislators in state houses was .38 (see table 11.9, part [d]). When all three variables—time, use of single-member districts, and section 5 coverage—were included in a single multiple regression, only the latter two variables were significant, and the multiple correlation rose to .83. The use of single-member districts led to a mean increase of 8.8 black representatives; coverage led to a mean gain of 2.8 black representatives.

The bivariate correlation between the time variable and the number of black senators, however, was much higher than that between time and the number of black representatives: $r = .56$. Including all three variables within a single multiple regression produced a multiple r of .67, and the variables "use of single-member districts" and time were statistically significant, while section 5 coverage was not. The use of single-member districts accounted for an average increase of 1.2 black senators; and time, an average gain of 0.8 (see table 11.9, part [e]).

We now summarize this part of our analysis. First, the number of black legislators increased as states shifted to single-member districts. Second, the number of black legislators was higher in states covered in whole or in part by section 5, even controlling for the use of single-member districts. Third, there was a slight long-term gain in black representation due to time alone—especially in state senates—even controlling for the use of single-member districts and for whether jurisdictions were covered by section 5.

Black Success at the Congressional District Level

Our examination of black success at the congressional level is brief, primarily because there were so few blacks elected from southern districts and so few majority-black districts. The growth in the number and percentage of southern blacks in Congress was more erratic and less dramatic than in legislatures, as table 11.1 illustrates. In 1985, there were only two black representatives serving southern jurisdictions: Harold Ford from Tennessee and Mickey Leland from Texas. As a result of the 1986 and 1988 elections, there were four: Ford; Craig Washington, Leland's successor; John Lewis from Georgia; and Mike Espy from Mississippi. Only 3 percent of all southern U.S. representatives in 1990 were black, despite the fact that this region was almost 20 percent black in population. On the other hand, prior to 1973 there had been no black representatives from the South.

Black Success in Majority-White Congressional Districts

Three of the four black representatives serving in 1990 came from majority-black congressional districts. Only the Texas Eighteenth was not one; it was, however, a "majority-minority" district. Blacks were a plurality, and together with Hispanics made up 72 percent of the population. We therefore conclude that blacks recently have been far more likely to gain seats in majority-black districts than in majority-white ones.[24] This was not the case in the 1970s, however. There were then no majority-black districts in the South (although the Texas Eighteenth was already majority-minority), but three black representatives were elected: Andrew Young, Harold Ford, and Barbara Jordan. Therefore, as table 11.10 indicates, there has been a decrease in the percentage of majority-white jurisdictions electing blacks to office.

A test of the color-blind hypothesis indicates that the congressional data fit the racial polarization model almost perfectly, just as did the state legislative data. Table 11.11 presents the predicted percentage of black representatives elected from majority-white and majority-black districts, given the mean percentage of blacks in the population for each of the two groups, for those four southern states that actually had majority-black congressional districts: Georgia, Louisiana, Mississippi and Tennessee. In each of these states at least one of the majority-white congressional districts would have been represented by a black if voting was purely color-blind. What table 11.11 makes quite evident is that there was not a single majority-white congressional district in any of these states that elected a black; conversely, in three of the four states, every majority-black district elected a black.

The size of the black population required to elect a black candidate appears to be only slightly less than the 60 percent required for a black state legislator. But as table 11.12 demonstrates, even in Mississippi a black population of 58 percent was sufficient to elect a black to Congress.[25] Harold Ford's district, the Tennessee Ninth, was only 57 percent black. However, the Louisiana Second, at 59 percent black, had not elected a black as of 1988.[26]

The Reason Majority-Black Congressional Districts Were Drawn

Three of the four majority-black districts created in the 1980s were the result of voting rights litigation: the Georgia Fifth,[27] the Mississippi Second,[28] and the Louisiana Second.[29] This is a clear indication of the importance of the Voting Rights Act for producing black officeholders in the South.

One might ask, if blacks can only be elected from such districts, why not draw more? The answer rests in part with electoral geography: it is much more difficult to draw majority-black congressional districts than state legislative ones.[30] The black population is simply not sufficiently concentrated for these much larger districts. There are also proportionally fewer state senate districts with majority-black populations than there are state house districts: they are larger than house districts.

In summary, the congressional data confirm our earlier conclusions about black legislative success in the South. The simple fact is that virtually all districts in which whites are a majority elect white candidates. This was just as true in the 1980s as in the 1970s. For blacks to win, it is therefore still necessary in the South to draw districts in which blacks are a majority or a supermajority of the population. Redistricting plans that have provided for an increase in the number of majority-black districts have invariably been the result either of a court order following voting rights litigation or a Justice Department preclearance denial. Therefore, the continuing importance of the Voting Rights Act for minority representation in the South simply cannot be denied.

'ABLE 11.1
ercentage of Black Elected Officials in the South and Non-South, 1970–1985[a]

ear	% Black Population	U.S. Congress	State Legislature Senate	State Legislature House	County Councils	City Councils
			South			
985	19.6	1.7 (2)	7.2 (33)	10.8 (143)	5.9 (425)	5.6 (1,330)
980	19.6	1.8 (2)	3.1 (14)	8.3 (110)	6.8 (310)	4.4 (1,043)
975	20.4	2.8 (3)	2.4 (11)	6.2 (83)	4.2 (192)	2.6 (605)
970	20.4	0.0 (0)	1.3 (6)	1.9 (26)	0.6 (24)	1.2 (263)
			Non-South			
985	8.5	5.3 (17)	3.2 (49)	3.8 (159)	1.0 (109)	1.1 (850)
980	8.5	4.0 (13)	2.9 (44)	3.3 (137)	0.8 (84)	1.0 (756)
975	7.7	4.0 (13)	2.7 (42)	3.3 (140)	0.7 (75)	0.8 (621)
970	7.7	2.7 (9)	1.6 (25)	2.6 (111)	0.3 (40)	0.4 (289)

Note: Numbers in parentheses are *N*s.
[a]The percentages for the South are for the eleven states of the Confederacy. The remaining thirty-nine states mpose the Non-South.

TABLE 11.2
Southern Majority-White and Majority-Black Districts Electing Black Legislators[a]

Racial Composition of Districts	*1970s* %	*1970s* (N)	*1980s* %	*1980s* (N)
	Lower House			
Majority white	2	(637)	1	(1,144)
Majority black	59	(102)	77	(181)
	Upper House			
Majority white	1	(294)	1	(390)
Majority black	25	(24)	62	(52)

[a]Percentages for the 1970s are based on Bullock 1983, table 3. The base for the 1970 calculations include Alabama, Georgia, Louisiana, Mississippi, North Carolina (senate only), South Carolina, and Virginia. The figures for the 1980s are based on data for all eleven southern states provided by the Southern Regional Council, Atlanta.

TABLE 11.3
Majority-White and Majority-Black Districts Electing Black State Representatives in 1988: Actual Percentages and Percentages Predicted by the Color-Blind Model[a]

	Majority-White Districts			*Majority-Black Districts*		
	Actual	*Predicted*	*(N)*	*Actual*	*Predicted*	*(N)*
Alabama	0	16	(86)	100	71	(19)
Arkansas	0	11	(89)	55	59	(11)
Florida	3	11	(113)	100	60	(7)
Georgia	1	18	(149)	74	71	(31)
Louisiana	0	21	(87)	83	70	(18)
Mississippi	0	24	(89)	67	66	(33)
North Carolina	4	19	(111)	100	62	(9)
South Carolina	0	22	(97)	59	60	(27)
Tennessee	1	10	(91)	100	79	(8)
Texas	3	9	(141)	100	64	(9)
Virginia	0	15	(91)	78	63	(9)

[a]The actual percentages of majority-white and majority-black districts electing blacks to the upper houses were calculated from data provided by the Southern Regional Council and reflect the number of black representatives as of 1988.

TABLE 11.4
Majority-White and Majority-Black Districts Electing Black State Senators in 1988: Actual Percentages and Percentages Predicted by the Color-Blind Model[a]

	Majority-White Districts			*Majority-Black Districts*		
	Actual	*Predicted*	*(N)*	*Actual*	*Predicted*	*(N)*
Alabama	0	18	(29)	83	65	(6)
Arkansas	0	14	(33)	50	56	(2)
Florida	3	13	(39)	100	65	(1)
Georgia	0	19	(47)	78	66	(9)
Louisiana	0	25	(34)	100	63	(5)
Mississippi	0	27	(39)	15	62	(13)
North Carolina	3	22	(34)	100	61	(1)
South Carolina	0	23	(36)	50	56	(10)
Tennessee	0	10	(30)	100	73	(3)
Texas	3	11	(30)	100	53	(1)
Virginia	3	18	(39)	100	69	(1)

[a]The actual percentages of majority-white and majority-black districts electing blacks to the upper houses were calculated from data provided by the Southern Regional Council and reflect the number of black senators as of 1988.

TABLE 11.5
Southern Majority-Black Districts Electing a Black Legislator[a]

% Black	*1970s*		*1980s*	
	%	(N)	%	(N)
	Lower House			
50–54	11	(18)	30	(30)
55–59	42	(19)	57	(21)
60–64	36	(14)	76	(42)
65 or greater	88	(51)	98	(88)
	Upper House			
50–54	0	(6)	27	(14)
55–59	0	(7)	55	(11)
60–64	0	(3)	64	(11)
65 or greater	75	(8)	94	(16)

[a] The 1970s percentages are based on data reported in Bullock 1983. Included in calculations are Alabama, Georgia, Louisiana, Mississippi, North Carolina (senate only), South Carolina, and Virginia. The 1980s percentages are based on data provided by the Southern Regional Council and include all eleven states.

TABLE 11.6
Number of Southern Majority-Black Legislative Districts[a]

% Black	*1970s*	*1980s*
	Lower House	
50–54	18	25
55–59	19	15
60–64	14	28
65 or greater	51	69
TOTAL	102	137
	Upper House	
50–54	6	12
55–59	7	11
60–64	3	7
65 or greater	8	15
TOTAL	24	45

[a] Data are based on the seven states for which there are comparable data for the 1970s and 1980s: Alabama, Georgia, Louisiana, Mississippi, North Carolina (senate only), South Carolina, and Virginia. The 1970s numbers are based on Bullock 1983, and the 1980s numbers are based on Southern Regional Council figures.

TABLE 11.7
Type of Election System and Number of Black State Representatives and State Senators in Southern States[a]

	1965		*1970*		*1975*		*1980*		*1985*	
	SYS	*#*	*SYS*	*#*	*SYS*	*#*	*SYS*	*#*	*SYS*	*#*
					State Representatives					
Alabama	MMD	0	MMD	0	*SMD*	2	SMD	2	SMD	5
Arkansas	MMD	0	MMD	0	MMD	1	MMD	1	MMD	1
Florida	MMD	0	MMD	0	MMD	0	MMD	0	*SMD*	2
Georgia	MMD	2	MMD	2	*SMD*	2	SMD	2	SMD	6
Louisiana	MMD	0	MMD	0	*SMD*	1	SMD	2	SMD	4
Mississippi	MMD	0	MMD	0	MMD	0	*SMD*	2	SMD	2
N. Carolina	MMD	0	MMD	0	MMD	2	MMD	1	*SMD*[b]	3
S. Carolina	MMD	0	MMD	0	MMD	0	MMD	0	*SMD*	4
Tennessee	MMD	0	*SMD*	2	SMD	2	SMD	3	SMD	3
Texas	SMD	0	SMD	1	SMD	0	SMD	0	SMD	1
Virginia	MMD	0	MMD	1	*SMD*[c]	1	SMD[c]	1	SMD	2
					State Senators					
Alabama	MMD	0	MMD	0	*SMD*	13	SMD	13	SMD	19
Arkansas	MMD	0	MMD	0	MMD[c]	3	MMD[c]	4	MMD[c]	4
Florida	MMD	0	MMD	1	MMD	3	MMD	4	*SMD*	10
Georgia	MMD	0	MMD	12	*SMD*[b]	19	SMD[b]	21	SMD[b]	21
Louisiana	MMD	0	MMD	1	*SMD*	8	SMD	10	SMD	14
Mississippi	MMD	0	MMD	1	MMD	1	*SMD*[d]	15	SMD[e]	18
N. Carolina	MMD	0	MMD	1	MMD	4	MMD	4	*SMD*[b]	13
S. Carolina	MMD	0	MMD	0	*SMD*	13	SMD	14	SMD	16
Tennessee	MMD	0	MMD	6	*SMD*	9	SMD	9	SMD	10
Texas	MMD	0	MMD	2	*SMD*[b]	9	SMD	13	SMD	13
Virginia	MMD	0	MMD	2	MMD	1	MMD	4	*SMD*	5

[a] Type of election system (SYS) is designated as follows: "MMD" is a multimember system; "SMD" is a single-member system. A state has been designated as having a multimember system if it has a combination of multimember and single-member districts or if the entire state is composed of multimember districts. An italicized election system type means there has been a change in election system since the last time period reported. The symbol # refers to the number of black legislators serving.

[b] Predominantly single-member districts in areas of black population, some multimember districts elsewhere in the state.

[c] Arkansas has one black-majority multimember district and one majority-black single-member district.

[d] Single-member-district system but with black fragmentation.

[e] Reduced black fragmentation in single-member-district system.

TABLE 11.8
Percentage of Blacks in Southern State Legislatures with Both Single-Member and Multimember Districts, 1975, 1980, and 1985

	Elected from Single-Member Districts	*Elected from Multimember Districts*
	Lower House	
1975	9.3	2.1
1980	10.7	3.4
1985	11.3	4.0
	Upper House	
1975	3.4	1.3
1980	4.2	1.2
1985	7.6	2.9

TABLE 11.9
Factors Predicting the Number of Black Representatives in Southern State Legislatures, 1970–1985

	Lower Chamber			*Upper Chamber*		
Variables	R	b	S.E.	R	b	S.E.
(a) Shift to SMDs	.74**	6.3**	1.0	.37**	1.7*	.5
(b) Sec. 5 coverage	.43**	5.4**	2.1	.21	0.7	.6
(c) Use of SMDs	—	9.4**	1.4	—	1.6**	.5
Sec. 5 coverage	—	2.8*	1.4	—	0.2	.5
Multiple *R*	.82**	—	—	.53**	—	—
(d) Time	.38*	2.7*	1.2	.56**	1.0**	.3
(e) Use of SMDs	—	8.8**	1.4	—	1.2*	.5
Sec. 5 coverage	—	2.8*	1.4	—	0.2	.5
Time	—	1.0	0.8	—	0.8**	.3
Multiple *R*	.83**	—	—	.67**	—	—

Note: $N = 33$ for all regression runs.
$^{*}p < .05$
$^{**}p < .01$

TABLE 11.10
Southern Majority-White and Majority-Black Congressional Districts That Elected Black Representatives

	1970s		1980s	
	%	(N)	%	(N)
Majority-white districts	2	(108)	0[a]	(112)
Majority-black districts	—	(0)	75	(4)

[a]There was not a single majority-white district in the South that elected a black representative in the 1980s. The Texas Eighteenth, although not a majority-black district, was not majority white either; it was 41 percent black and 31 percent Hispanic.

TABLE 11.11
Majority-White and Majority-Black Districts Electing Black U.S. Representatives: Actual Percentages and Percentages Predicted by the Color-Blind Model[a]

	Majority-White Districts			Majority-Black Districts		
	Actual	Predicted	(N)	Actual	Predicted	(N)
Georgia	0	23	(9)	100	65	(1)
Louisiana	0	26	(7)	0	52	(1)
Mississippi	0	30	(4)	100	54	(1)
Tennessee	0	11	(8)	100	57	(1)

[a]The four states included in this chart are the only four states in which majority-black congressional districts have been drawn. The actual percentages were calculated from data provided by the Southern Regional Council and reflect the number of black representatives as of 1988.

TABLE 11.12
Majority-Black Congressional Districts in the South and the Election of Black Representatives in the 1980s

Congressional District	Percentage Black	Black Representative Elected		
		1984	1986	1988
Georgia 5th	65	No	Yes	Yes
Louisiana 2d	59	No	No	No
Mississippi 2d	58	No	Yes	Yes
Tennessee 9th	57	Yes	Yes	Yes
Texas 18th	41[a]	Yes	Yes	Yes

[a]Although the Eighteenth District in Texas was not a majority-black district, it was a majority-minority district, with Hispanics comprising 31 percent of the population.

CHAPTER TWELVE

The Impact of the Voting Rights Act on Black and White Voter Registration in the South

JAMES E. ALT

MOST OF THE ESSAYS in this volume look at the impact of changes in electoral systems on black officeholding in the South, and relate recent gains to the effects of sections 2 or 5 of the Voting Rights Act or to the effects of litigation brought under the Fourteenth and Fifteenth amendments. In contrast, this chapter focuses on institutional barriers to black registration and voting and on the effects, both short term and long term, of the federal registrars sent to various areas of the South in the early years of the act.

The initial concern of the act's framers was to destroy legal barriers to black registration and voting. Most observers agree that this purpose was accomplished within a remarkably short period. But there is little agreement on exactly how this was achieved. In particular, the question remains as to the relative impact on the gain in black registration in 1965 and thereafter of the act's elimination of literacy tests, the presence of federal registrars in southern counties, the 1964 abolition of the poll tax in federal elections, and the later abolition of lengthy residence requirements. The aim of this chapter is to answer this question and to provide an accurate picture of the nature of the changes in southern registration by race from 1960 to 1988.[1]

My analysis is both similar to and different from earlier work on the nature and causes of changes in black registration. The most important similarity is that, following Key, I argue that the southern legal framework was in large part designed to secure the election of white candidates and to keep blacks in a subordinate position. Second, like various other scholars, including Key himself, I look at the effects of institutional mechanisms like literacy tests and poll taxes as distinct from the individual characteristics of potential voters that may affect registration rates. Third, again following Key, I stress the importance of context, showing that particular mechanisms for disfranchisement work differently depending on the relative proportions of the black and white voting-age populations.

On the other hand, there are four main differences between the models developed in this chapter and most scholarship on registration and turnout. First, I rely primarily on a comprehensive data base at the county level. This permits controlling for the effects of various factors, including the relative sizes of the black and white voting-age populations.[2] Second, unlike previous researchers, I do not look at black registration in isolation from white registration. Rather, I develop a ratio measure that allows the analysis to focus not merely on what proportion of blacks are registered but on *relative* numbers of black and white registrants. Use of this ratio measure as the dependent variable overcomes a major methodological flaw of virtually all previous research, which has focused on black registration rates alone. Such a narrow focus ignores the fact that what has often been most important about elections in the South, from the perspective of both whites and blacks, is whether more whites than blacks will be registered and able to vote and thus able to control who gets elected. Third, I construct a multivariate model with interaction effects. This allows for the possibility that barriers such as literacy tests varied dramatically in their effects on relative black and white registration levels in counties with different black population proportions; the model allows us to quantify and thus more precisely estimate the barriers' effects. Fourth, I model not only the effects particular institutions had on the black/white registration ratio in the pre-act South but also the incentives that whites had to make use of particular types of disfranchising devices in counties with different levels of black voting-age population. That is, while the basic analysis treats disfranchising devices as independent (explanatory) variables, at another point I treat certain devices as dependent variables whose presence or absence is to be explained in terms of factors such as the black proportion in the jurisdiction.

To understand how blacks were prevented from realizing the full potential of their numbers involves modeling a complex interaction between disfranchising devices, black and white efforts at mobilizing and demobilizing voters, and socioeconomic variables whose aggregate-level effects have so far been unclear. But I also want to understand fully the role played by the Voting Rights Act in helping blacks regain the franchise. To do this—by estimating, for example, the degree to which the act's elimination of literacy tests per se permitted growth in black registration—one must supplement the analysis of the effects of disfranchising devices with an analysis of the impact of federal registrars on black registration. Only in this way can we sort out the effects of changes in the law from the effects of enforcement practices.

This chapter is divided into four parts. The first reviews the basic data on registration laws and black participation in the South before passage of the act. In the second part I provide a brief literature review of earlier research on southern black registration. The third section identifies my own hypotheses about the interactive effects of disfranchisement devices and black population levels and about the effects of various socioeconomic variables, and it provides a test of those hypotheses. The final section discusses black registration after passage in 1965 and considers the immediate and long-run impacts on black registration of federal registrars who were sent into some recalcitrant jurisdictions under the act's provisions.

Before proceding, a brief summary of the major findings may help steer the reader through what may appear to be a difficult mass of details and model specifications. While I confirm many of the basic insights of earlier work, especially those of Key, my various methodological innovations give rise to an analysis that sometimes provides quite different (and, I believe, more plausible) interpretations than those of other scholars, some of whom have used the same data sets as I have.

First, in the nation as a whole, disfranchising devices were used almost exclusively in states where there were significant black (or, outside the South, immigrant) populations.

Second, in the pre-act South, I find that the effects of disfranchising devices and what Matthews and Prothro refer to as white "race organizations"[3]—organizations aimed at keeping blacks in their place, especially as these interacted with black population proportion—far outweighed socioeconomic factors in explaining relative levels of black registration.

Third, the effects of a literacy test interacted with black population concentrations so that its greatest relative disfranchising effect occurred in counties with the highest black population proportions. Only in counties with very few blacks did literacy tests disadvantage whites relative to blacks.

Fourth, while the poll tax also kept many whites off the rolls, its effects interacted with black population concentrations so that its lowest relative disfranchising effects on blacks occurred in the counties with greatest black population; in fact, in terms of proportions ultimately registered, the poll tax disadvantaged whites more than blacks in counties with a black voting-age population proportion above 40 percent.

Fifth, the effects of the presence of white race organizations also interacted with black population concentrations (and the presence of black organizations); like literacy tests, white organizations were more prevalent and had their greatest relative disfranchising effects in the counties with highest black voting-age population proportions.

Sixth, residence requirements disfranchised whites more than blacks.

Seventh, following passage of the act in the late 1960s, a far higher proportion of black-majority counties visited by federal registrars achieved black-majority electorates than was true of the black-majority counties not visited by them. In fact, although in 1967 and 1968 roughly three-quarters of the majority-black counties in Alabama, Georgia, Louisiana, and Mississippi did not have majority-black electorates, every county in these states which did achieve a majority-black electorate in that period either had had a federal registrar or was geographically adjacent to one or more counties visited by a registrar.[4]

Eighth, the overall relative impact of federal registrars appeared to wear off over time, in that registration rates in counties not visited by registrars became comparable to the rates in those that were. Nonetheless, black-majority counties visited by federal registrars achieved black registration majorities roughly a decade earlier than did black-majority counties elsewhere in the South.

Ninth, the residual effects of abolished disfranchisement devices also appeared to wear off over time. Thus the act destroyed the basis for the pre-1965 pattern of disfranchisement and created the foundation for a new political system where black registration rates by the end of the 1980s were nearly equal to those of whites and where the black-white registration differential was no longer greatest in the most heavily black counties.

Tenth, and finally, in the post-1965 period following the abolition of the disfranchisement mechanisms, white "mobilization," measured by a rise in white registration rates, was strongest in counties with high black proportions, suggesting a continuing fear among whites of the possibility of black electoral dominance. Blacks, suddenly able to register, reacted to this white response with a countermobilization, that is, with higher than normal registration as well. Their countermobilization in these heavily black counties, however, did not lead to yet another ratcheting up of white registration in the period from 1972 to 1988. Further, the gradual closing of the racial registration gap over the years has dampened this pattern of reaction and counterreaction.

Registration Laws in the South Before the Voting Rights Act

Fifty years ago, no southern state had a black voter registration rate above 7 percent, and the southwide average was 3 percent. As the data in table 12.1 show, by the late 1940s the black voting-age registration rate had risen to the teens or higher outside Alabama, Louisiana, and Mississippi. The proportion rose at different rates in different states through the 1950s, reaching a southwide average of nearly 30 percent by the end of the decade. Indeed, even before the Voting Rights Act, black registration rates in Florida and Tennessee were approximately 60 percent, about as high as they were ever to be, while in some other states the rates exceeded 40 percent, remaining dramatically lower only in Alabama and Mississippi. Table 12.1 also shows the rapid rise of black voter registration by 1968, and the smaller temporal and state variations since then. By the late 1980s, the average rate for the entire South was above 60 percent, and all eleven states were within 10 percentage points of the average. A central purpose of this chapter is to explain these variations systematically, both before and after passage of the act.

An Overview of Legal Restrictions on Voting

The Magnolia formula adopted in Mississippi in 1890 epitomized the post–Civil War disfranchising laws. Widely copied in the rest of the South, it combined literacy or understanding requirements, residence requirements, and poll taxes to deny the franchise not only to blacks in general but to migrant workers, those with less education, and the poor.[5] Kousser describes how the laws evolved and how biased application of the rules resulted in the disfranchisement of over 90 percent of previously registered blacks by the early 1900s, while in the Deep South states at least two-thirds of adult whites remained on the rolls.[6] Rusk and Stucker show how the laws reduced turnout in the period between 1890 and World War I.[7]

Literacy requirements, residence requirements, and poll taxes, moreover, were not the only impediments to registration and voting in the legal codes of southern states at various times, nor was the use of these impediments restricted to the South. For example, early twentieth-century litigation over voter registration laws centered on grandfather clauses and the white primary. The former involved various formulas by which other requirements might be waived for those who were registered—or whose ancestors had been registered—at some previous date, typically when there were few black registrants. One version of the grandfather clause was voided by the Supreme Court in *Guinn and Beal v. United States* (1915)[8] in Oklahoma, a nonsouthern state. All attempts to use these clauses ended after the Court's *Lane v. Wilson* decision in 1939.[9] The white primary excluded blacks from voting in party primary elections on the grounds that political parties were private, voluntary associations whose officers were not government officials, and thus were not subject to the constitutional prohibition against racial discrimination in voting.[10] The white primary's abolition gave blacks access to elections that were decisive in one-party areas of the South, causing much of the increase in black registration in Texas, Georgia, and South Carolina before 1947. Between 1944 and 1964, therefore, the primary legal restrictions on black registration were the literacy test, residence requirements, and the poll tax, although restricted registration periods were also a factor.

Literacy Requirements

Literacy requirements were not directed solely against blacks in the South, although their primary use seems to have been aimed at one or another "undesirable" political or ethnic group. Some early literacy tests were adopted to reduce the growing power of urban political organizations that appealed to immigrant voters.[11] For example, Yankees in Connecticut in 1855 and Massachusetts in 1857 adopted laws aimed at disfranchising recently arrived Irish immigrants. Most of the eleven nonsouthern states with literacy requirements in 1960—Arizona, California, Connecticut, Delaware, Maine, Massachusetts, New Hampshire, New York, Oregon, Washington, and Wyoming—had significant immigrant or minority populations, reflecting the test's original purpose of diminishing the voting strength of marginal groups.

As table 12.2 shows, seven southern states, beginning with Mississippi in 1890, adopted forms of literacy or understanding requirements. Speakers in the Mississippi debate emphasized that the requirement was meant to safeguard by legal means white control of the electoral process, which had been previously secured by fraud and violence.[12] The relation between the state's black population proportion in the late-nineteenth century and the imposition of the literacy requirement is obvious from table 12.2. A majority of counties in at least two states were majority black, in which racial bloc voting would automatically have meant at least partial black control of the state legislature.[13]

In the seven states adopting a literacy requirement, the average black illiteracy rate in 1890 was nearly 75 percent, while the corresponding average among whites was below 20 percent.[14] Thus the race-related impact of a literacy requirement is clear. Moreover, all seven states subsequently attempted to weaken its impact on illiterate whites at least temporarily through property ownership and grandfather-, morals-, or understanding-clause exemptions. Key describes the discretion these measures afforded local registrars, and their consequent discriminatory application.[15] Nevertheless, courts upheld the principle of literacy requirements (with varying requirements of standardization in application) until the Voting Rights Act's automatic trigger in section 4 abolished all literacy requirements in political units where less than 50 percent of eligible voters were registered on 1 November 1964 or less than 50 percent had voted in the 1964 presidential election.[16]

Poll Taxes

Each of the eleven southern states had a poll tax at some time, although those adopted after 1900 in Florida, Louisiana, Georgia, and North Carolina had disappeared even before Key's fieldwork in the late 1940s. Two other states, South Carolina and Tennessee, which had taxed nonelderly men only, abandoned the poll tax between the time of Key's research and that of Matthews and Prothro a decade later.[17] The annual tax of between one and two dollars in the remaining five states—Alabama, Arkansas, Mississippi, Texas, and Virginia—varied in its administration.[18] The tax was abolished as a qualification for national elections by the Twenty-fourth Amendment, ratified in 1964. The Voting Rights Act the following year directed the Attorney General to challenge the tax as a voting prerequisite in state and local elections. He did so, and consequently the Supreme Court in *Harper v. Virginia State Board of Elections* (1966)[19] proscribed its use in all elections.[20]

Other Restrictions

Registration requirements were always remarkably tight in the South. Poll tax payments had been due as long as nine months before elections, and the registration books closed four to five months before elections in Georgia and Mississippi. In Texas, the registration period lasted only four months, beginning in the fall of the year prior to elections and ending a full nine months before them.[21] Even in 1970, of the eleven southern states only Tennessee and Texas had any provision for absentee registration, although twenty-seven of the thirty-nine nonsouthern states had such provisions. State preregistration residence requirements of up to a year (upheld by the Supreme Court as late as 1965) were ubiquitous; in 1960 South Carolina, Louisiana, and Mississippi required two years' residence before registration. These states required one year's residence *in the county* before registration, and all others except Tennessee and North Carolina required six months. Restricted locations, few eligible officials, short daily registration periods, and limited dates for registration also reduced southern voting both before and after the act.[22]

Social Science Research on Registration Rates in the South

There is no question that prior to the act, legal barriers to registration had an impact on low registration rates in the South as compared to the non-South, as well as on the low registration rates in some southern locales as compared to others. Hence, no one in the early 1960s doubted that abolition of these legal barriers would increase black registration and voting. The question political scientists began to address in the years immediately preceding the act was the *relative* impact of these legal restrictions vis-à-vis other variables—socioeconomic and demographic—known to impinge on political participation generally.

The view that the removal of legal barriers was important in effecting gains in black registration permeates early reports of the Civil Rights Commission, which describe rapid increases in black voter registration after passage of the act.[23] Some scholars appeared sure (but offered little systematic evidence) that legal barriers, especially literacy requirements and poll taxes, depressed black registration in the southern states before 1965.[24] Key, in addition, estimated that poll taxes reduced white voting by 5–10 percent and had no effect on the disfranchisment of blacks.[25] However, Key's ability to estimate effects was constrained by the fact that few blacks were registered in any southern state in the late 1940s, when he was conducting his research.

Perhaps the single most important study of pre-act southern registration is that of Matthews and Prothro, who analyzed the effects of individual adults' race, gender, education, income, and occupation, factors that they incorporated into a twenty-one-variable model. Although believing that legal impediments had significant effects on black registration, Matthews and Prothro concluded that "low voting rates of Negroes in the South are, to perhaps a large extent, a result of . . . social and economic factors *more than [they are] a consequence of direct political discrimination by the white community*."[26] Of these factors the most important, they thought, was a jurisdiction's black percentage: "Generally, the higher the percentage of Negroes in an area, the greater the pressure to keep them from voting," at least in heavily black areas.[27] By contrast, they saw legal and extralegal barriers to registration, as well as other political factors like party systems and racial organization, as less important.[28] However, these authors devoted a good deal of attention to the development of black and white racial organizations in the South.[29] They found that about 30 percent of counties had a black race organization and about 20 percent had white race organizations. Other things equal, they concluded that black registration rates declined by about 10 percentage points where white race organizations existed unopposed and increased by about 10 points where both a white and a black race organization (other than the NAACP) were present.[30]

Recent research has challenged their view that legal factors played only a limited role in accounting for low black registration. Stanley has created an impressively large and complex data set by pooling all the Michigan National Election Study surveys from 1952 to 1984. He finds that residence requirements lowered white turnout by 3 to 4 percentage points southwide and black turnout by 16 points. Stanley also finds that the poll tax and literacy requirements had no effect on white turnout and lowered black turnout by an estimated 4 and 10 percentage points, respectively.[31]

From at least the time of Key's *Southern Politics*, research on the South has emphasized the mediating role of the black population proportion. However, scholars divide over whether to model the influence of the black percentage on registration as a "black mobilization" process—in which a greater black percentage should produce higher black registration rates—or a "white fear" process, whereby the opposite would be true. In the pre-act South, in other words, did blacks in heavily black counties manage to achieve higher registration through the sheer force of their numbers or, as several authors have suggested, did the very possibility of a large pool of black registrants in these counties provoke whites, who controlled the legal process, to "batten down the hatches" with extraordinarily repressive mechanisms that would hardly have been necessary in counties with low black percentages?[32]

In a frequently cited study of determinants of black registration that examines these alternatives, Salamon and van Evera contrast several explanations, settling on a combination of three variables they believe operated at the local level.[33] The first involved paternalistic relations resulting from the dependence of wage earners on the good will of employers, as in the case of household servants or agricultural laborers. This political dependence led to political submission, they surmise. The second was a high black population, which the authors believe produced unusual white hostility. The third was outside organizational help for blacks, producing black political mobilization. The first two factors, then, according to the authors, depressed black registration, while the third elevated it.

While suggestive, this study is flawed because it fails to measure the effects of a major variable, legal barriers to registration. The authors also do not estimate white registration levels in addition to black ones. For reasons to be discussed shortly, I believe it is immensely important to model and explain relative levels of black and white registration simultaneously. Moreover, a crucial link is missing from this study since the authors do not demonstrate that white hostility, as measured by the presence of race organizations, resulted directly from a high black population percentage. And because their data are limited to twenty-nine black-belt Mississippi counties, the findings cannot be generalized to other areas of the state or the South.

Modeling Race and Registration in the South before the Act

In trying to understand the influence of different variables on black registration in the South in the twenty years or so preceding passage of the Voting Rights Act, it is useful to make some basic simplifying assumptions. The first is that race was a crucial dynamic in southern politics, overshadowing all others. Insofar as the erection of political barriers to registration is concerned, racial considerations do appear to have been paramount. Second, particularly in the black belt but to a lesser degree in the rest of the South as well, the two racial groups were locked in a zero-sum game, or at least they often perceived the situation as such. One manifestation of this perception would be the tendency for whites to vote for white candidates and for blacks, if they could vote and a black candidate were to run, to vote for black candidates.

From these two assumptions it is easy to proceed to a third, namely, that the dominant political strategy of whites was to ensure the election of white candidates. *From these assumptions it follows that the system of legal impediments to registration which had developed in the region existed to preserve white numerical superiority on election day*. That is, it was designed to ensure that enough whites were registered, regardless of the size of the local black population, so that when voting took place, black candidates would not win, nor could blacks even expect to be the decisive voters in the election of white candidates.

While this proposition may seem obvious, it is remarkable that no scholar of southern politics has ever clearly asserted it, much less made it the foundation for modeling the effects of various impediments to registration.[34] A full understanding of black registration as a measure of potential black political strength is impossible without comparing it to white registration, in a way that takes account of the relative numbers of each race in the eligible population and the effort by each race's members to register.

Our analysis also assumes that the blacks who were actively involved in challenging the southern legal framework, and whites who were intent on maintaining it, were rational in the most direct of ways, in that they measured and compared the costs and benefits of a course of action before undertaking it.

Conditions for Use of Disfranchisement Mechanisms

Generally speaking, then, the severest legal restrictions on black registration would be most likely to be imposed where potential black voters were most numerous.[35] Also, white leaders who in the pre-act South were almost invariably in a position to implement their most favored strategies for maintaining white voting superiority would have considered the advantages and disadvantages of the various combinations of disfranchising options available to them.[36] For example, the poll tax had the advantage of disfranchising blacks but at the cost of disfranchising whites as well. How should the costs and benefits of imposing the tax be weighed in a particular jurisdiction?

Other things being equal, whites would be less likely to pay the tax and would thus "free ride"—let fellow whites bear the burden of maintaining white advantage by going to the polls to outvote blacks—under two conditions: when the white proportion was greatest and the need for white votes the least; or when lower-cost antiblack devices such as the literacy requirement existed.

These general expectations are confirmed both by the quantitative analysis that follows and by direct observation of other changes. For example, as noted above, it was in the states with the largest black proportion that whites went to the greatest effort to implement devices that deny blacks the vote. Also, as shown in table 12.2, the poll tax was eliminated in a number of southern states before passage of the Voting Rights Act, when the literacy test persisted in all of them with a substantial black percentage. Finally, the rapid abandonment of severe residence requirements resonates with the finding in this essay that, other things being equal, such requirements bore more heavily on white than on black registration.

Factors That May Affect the Formation of Race Organizations

Let us assume that blacks would have mobilized resources to fight for black suffrage and whites would have sought to promote white suffrage and to counter black suffrage attempts in the locales where each had the most to gain. We can further assume that these locales were those where the chance of influencing electoral outcomes was most substantial. Then, if we take the presence of black and white "race organizations" as a proxy for each race's local mobilization efforts, we should expect black organizations to have formed where there was more to gain—that is, where there were more blacks in the population—and we should expect the same to have been true for white race organizations, since it was in areas of high black population proportion that the potential electoral threat of blacks to white dominance was greatest.[37]

However, the incentives for race organizations to form should also have been affected by the nature of the structural barriers to black enfranchisement. For example, because the literacy requirement could be applied as an instrument of local discrimination, black organizations should have been more likely where literacy tests were used. Indeed, a natural focus of local black organization was discriminatory application of the literacy requirement. By contrast, a literacy requirement and white race organization were *substitutes*, other things equal, and thus the imposition of a literacy test should have diminished the need for white race organizations. Opposite effects should be observed in the case of the poll tax and residence requirements, because these might have affected white registration as much as or more than black registration.[38]

My analysis reveals that white race organizations, as predicted, were indeed more likely to form where there were poll tax and severe residence requirements (which reduced white registration), but less likely to form where there were literacy tests. By contrast, black organizations formed where there were more blacks to organize and where there were literacy tests,[39] but their presence was made less likely by the presence of a poll tax requirement. Most important of all, racial organizations of one race were more common when racial organizations of the other race were also present, suggesting a pattern of mobilization and countermobilization in the pre-act South.[40]

Hypotheses about Factors Affecting Comparative Levels of Black and White Registration

Based on the arguments developed above, I propose a model in which literacy tests, the poll tax, and white race organizations affected black registration differentially depending upon how numerous blacks were in the local jurisdiction.[41] In particular, I hypothesize that literacy tests were more effective in depressing relative black registration in local jurisdictions where the black proportion was higher.[42] Black race organizations should have had their greatest effects in increasing relative black registration in the same sort of locale, where there would have been most to gain. In contrast, I hypothesize that poll taxes and residency requirements had the least effect in depressing black registration share in locales where the black proportion was higher; that is, they should have had their greatest effect in reducing the relative level of white registration where there were the most whites.[43]

To be sure, socioeconomic determinants of differences in registration rates also existed, and their effects must be measured so that they can be part of a fully specified model. For both races, mobilization and electoral participation should have been made easier by certain factors. For example, greater socioeconomic resources like education and income should have increased registration.[44] Conversely, in agricultural areas economic dependency, such as tenant farming arrangements, may have inhibited black registration as well as the formation of black racial organizations.[45] Religion may also have been relevant. In the early 1950s the Catholic church declared racial segregation immoral. Consequently, the residual registration disadvantage to blacks might have been less in heavily Catholic areas. By contrast, it should have been higher where black Holiness sects were numerous, assuming they focused their members' attention on heavenly rather than worldly goals. It is easy to imagine that other factors may have impinged on relative registration rates. For example, since black population growth could have been more threatening whatever the black proportion in an area, population change may well have been an important variable.

The specification and estimation of our final model is decribed in the next two sections. Only those variables found to be statistically significant are included in it. Some variables found important by previous research—for example, early closing dates for registration periods, the extent of racial violence in a jurisdiction as measured by Matthews and Prothro, and the factional structure of party competition—produced at most small and statistically insignificant estimates in a model with the extensive controls reported below, and are thus omitted from the discussion.

White Numerical Advantage

I focus on the ratio of registered whites to registered blacks as the dependent variable since, as noted previously, it is the ratio of white to black registration, rather than the registration rates of blacks alone, that determines the ability of whites to maintain political control. At low black concentrations this ratio would have very large values even if all blacks were registered, and the ratio is affected dramatically by even small changes in the denominator; so to smooth the data it is better to use the logarithm of this ratio.[46] I refer to this logged ratio value as the logged *white numerical advantage*. It is zero when the registered electorates of the races are equal in number, negative when blacks are more numerous in the registered electorate, and positive when whites are more numerous.

If the ability of whites to affect white numerical advantage were unrelated to racial population levels, then the white/black ratio would fall as the relative size of the black population grows. I construct an *equal effort* curve to reflect this. It is the value of the ratio that would result at all levels of black population concentration if, at each level, blacks and whites registered at equal rates. For instance, where white concentration is about 88 percent (and black concentration is thus about 12), if both races displayed equal effort (that is, had the same registration rates), white advantage would be proportional to 88/12, or a little over 7.3. Finally, as noted above, we take the natural logarithm of 7.3 (which is about 2), so at 12 percent black the logged "equal effort curve" has a value of 2. This same curve takes the value of 1 where black concentration is just below 30 percent. Again, at 50/50 its value is 0. Figure 12.1 shows this equal effort curve (composed of + symbols) and also contains, for the 1958–60 period, the distribution of observed values for logged white numerical advantage.[47] Each square represents a county. Values above the equal effort curve show white advantage greater than what would result from "equal effort."

The average value for the 858 counties over which the white advantage ratio can be calculated for this period was 2.34.[48] Because we used logarithms to the base e, in the average county registered whites outnumbered registered blacks by a factor of $e^{2.34}$ or about 7:1.[49] White numerical advantage shown in figure 12.1 was almost always above the equal effort curve, though the amount of dispersion varied. Most of the few cases where black registration rates exceeded white ones (that is, those cases below the equal effort curve) were in the eastern part of Texas, a state that had a poll tax and no literacy requirement; but only a handful of these counties produced black electoral majorities. Moreover, in spite of black registration gains in the years immediately preceding the act, if figure 12.1 were reproduced to show the less complete data available for 1964, the proportion of points above the line would actually be even greater because of new white registration in the period.

Factors That Affect White Numerical Advantage

In this section, using data at the county level, I will test the above hypotheses about factors that have an impact on white numerical advantage. A discussion of the characteristics of my data base is in the appendix to this chapter. Table 12.3 contains the estimation results of the regression model that best fits the data for

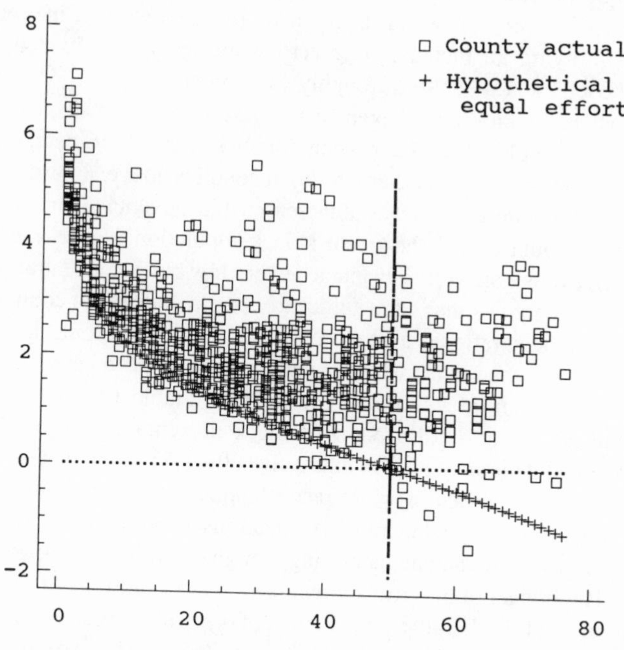

Figure 12.1. Logged White Numerical Advantage and Black Population Concentration, Counties in Eleven Southern States, 1958–1960

1958, explaining logged white numerical advantage with a number of political and socioeconomic variables and including only those interactions between other independent variables and black population concentration that were statistically significant.[50] A negative value for a coefficient means that white advantage is reduced; a positive value means that white advantage is increased. In general, the greater the size of the coefficient, the greater the magnitude of the effect.[51]

Many of the important effects shown in the table involve the interaction between legal barriers or race organizations and the proportion of blacks in the population. To illustrate how to read the table's findings, I review the results for the literacy requirement. This requirement had a composite effect. In counties that were effectively 0 percent black, its effect was to reduce logged white numerical advantage by −0.217 (as shown by the coefficient for the literacy requirement in table 12.3).[52] However, the greater the black population in a county, the more the literacy test tended to advantage whites. For every percentage point increase in black voting-age population, the literacy test increased the logged white advantage ratio by 0.016 (as shown by the coefficient for LR × county VAP % black). Thus, for example, if a county were 20 percent black, the effect of the literacy test was to increase logged white advantage by .103 (that is, $-0.217 + 20 \times 0.016$). Note that to figure out the effect on absolute (unlogged) white advantage, one would exponentiate .103 (as $e^{.103}$), which is equal to 1.11, so we can interpret this coefficient as implying an increase over zero white advantage (which has an exponentiated coefficient of 1.00) of roughly 11 percent.

The point where literacy tests began to increase rather than decrease white advantage can be calculated to occur when counties were 13.56 percent black, since $13.56 \times 0.016 = .217$. In other words, in counties above about 14 percent black, the effect of the literacy test was to increase white advantage, and this effect was greatest in the counties with the greatest black population. Hence, the literacy test had a negative effect on white advantage at very low black concentrations, but a positive effect in counties that were sufficently black. Indeed, in counties with very high black concentrations, a literacy requirement alone could have made white advantage more than twice what it would otherwise have been.[53]

In like manner we can infer from the coefficients in table 12.3 that a poll tax increased white advantage until a county's black percentage rose to about 40 percent, but reduced it thereafter.[54] An interactive effect similar to that for literacy tests is found for the presence of white race organizations. For counties over a quarter black, the presence of white race organizations increased white advantage, with the effect on white advantage increasing at higher levels of black voting-age population.[55] The impact of black race organizations was not found to vary with black population level. Rather, the simple effect of black race organizations was to decrease the logged value of white advantage by -0.265, that is, to decrease white advantage by about 23 percent ($e^{-.265} = .767$).[56] Conversely, residence requirements uniformly reduced white advantage, and a twelve-month county residence requirement cut white advantage nearly in half ($e^{-[.05 \times 12]} = .55$), other things equal. White advantage also was sharply higher in *states* with greater black population shares.[57]

How did socioeconomic variables affect relative registration rates? White advantage was higher where Holiness sects were more numerous in the black population, presumably because these religious organizations were less likely than other organizations to promote secular political involvement, including registration. White advantage was also higher in agricultural areas, where conditions of black dependence were more likely to be found; in areas where the white education level was higher, a situation that probably promoted white mobilization; in areas where population was increasing, perhaps because most inmigrants were white; and in locales where black county population had increased, possibly creating a perceived threat among whites. As expected, white advantage was lower in Catholic and urban areas, and where blacks had higher education on average. Overall, however, the effects of observed variations in socioeconomic context were less pronounced than the effects of the political and legal factors, though they still produced considerable dispersion.

The model in table 12.3 fits all the states.[58] On available data for over 80 percent of the southern counties at the time, no state had an average residual (the discrepancy between observed and predicted white advantage) from the estimates in table 12.3 that was, in terms of statistical significance, different from zero.[59] Thus the model, employing variables that measure legal institutions, levels of organization, and socioeconomic characteristics (including black state and local population concentration), captures in the pre-act period the relevant differences between the Deep and Outer South and among the individual states.

Comparisons with Earlier Research Findings

The principal difference between my work and earlier research is that I show how the effect on white numerical advantage of poll taxes, literacy tests, and white race organizations depended on a locale's black population level, and I provide precise estimates of the nature of those interactions. I confirm the hypotheses that, in the pre-act period, literacy tests had their greatest disadvantaging effects on blacks in areas with high black populations, while poll taxes exerted the opposite effect. But I also show how a variety of other factors—legal, political, and socioeconomic—restricted blacks' ability to register where they stood a chance of challenging white dominance.

Without examining the relative magnitude of the effects of devices such as literacy tests and poll taxes on black/white registration ratios in the pre-act period, we simply could not fully understand what happened in different areas of the South when such devices were removed—as literacy tests were in 1965 and poll taxes were between 1964 and 1966. The findings show that the combined impact of the elimination of literacy tests and poll taxes significantly reduced white advantage generally.

But perhaps even more important, the findings shed light on the differential impact, in various areas of the South, of the abolition of the literacy test and the poll tax. If both were present, their interactions with black population concentration exactly offset each other (.016 − .016 = 0), and so at all levels of black population concentration, white advantage would be given by $e^{(-.217 + .631)}$, which equals 1.51; thus the combined effect of these two devices in counties with both was to increase white advantage by a factor of roughly 1.5, or about 50 percent.[60] The fact that literacy tests rather than poll taxes were found in areas with the largest concentration of blacks means that the elimination of these devices helped blacks even more than the 1.5 figure indicates. On the other hand, the effect of their joint abolition, in those counties where they existed side by side, was more than offset by the contemporaneous elimination of lengthy residence requirements, which allowed white registration to increase in areas where black numbers were greatest.

Registration Patterns in the Post-Act South

I now turn to another feature of the black registration struggle, the dispatch of federal registrars under section 6 of the Voting Rights Act to areas of the South where black participation was lowest, including many counties with black population majorities. I also sketch the basic registration patterns in the post-1965 South. The available data suggest that the southern white registration rate rose from about 65 percent in 1964 to 76 percent by 1967.[61] Reported by the Civil Rights Commission in 1967, the latter rate (in the states covered by the act) represented about a 19-point advantage over the black rate, a difference that still existed over a decade later.[62] Moreover, available data suggest a net increase in the number of southern registered whites from 1964 to 1984 of some 15 million persons, compared to a net increase of 3 million among blacks. The doubling of the black registration rate from 29 to 60 percent in the 1960s only added as many new black registrants (1.7 million) as the much smaller proportionate increases from 61 to 69 percent (1.8 million) added among the much larger eligible white population.[63] A focus on raw numbers, however, would lose sight of dramatic changes in the nature of white advantage.

Figure 12.2 presents average white numerical advantage relative to the equal effort curve in each of the years for which southern data exist at the county level.[64] Each year is represented on this curve as follows. Take 1958, as we did for figure 12.1, and calculate for each county its vertical distance from the equal effort curve, positive if above, negative if below. Then calculate the average of these distances, which turns out to be about 1.4 units: the "average" county is 1.4 units above the line in 1958. Since the vertical axis is in logarithms, exponentiate this number to turn the distance into a numerical multiple. In this case, $e^{1.4} = 3.9$, so in 1958, an average county had a white advantage nearly four times as great as equal effort would have produced, and this value appears in figure 12.2.

The points on the curve in figure 12.2 represent the cumulative effect of everything affecting white numerical advantage, apart from the advantage whites derived solely from their larger population. A value of 1 on the vertical axis of the figure would indicate that blacks were registered in exact proportion to their percentage of the voting-age population. This would happen when, in the underlying data for a given year, the "average" county lay on the equal effort curve.

It is thus obvious from figure 12.2 that while white advantage was declining slightly in the decade before the act, registered whites in the average southern county were still overrepresented by a ratio of almost four to one in 1964. From 1964 through 1967 by far the greatest change in the entire three decades occurred, cutting the white disproportionate advantage by more than half. One can only speculate, given the very modest downward trend between 1958 and 1964, what the disproportionate white advantage would have been in 1968—let alone 1988—had the voting rights bill been defeated. Blacks have continued to advance, though at a much slower pace, since 1972. White advantage was cut again by about a third since the late 1960s, and by 1988 whites and blacks in the South registered in near equal proportions relative to their voting-age populations.[65] If present changes continue, white advantage will disappear: that is, the average county will fall on the equal effort curve sometime in the 1990s.[66]

No one who looks at figure 12.2 can fail to appreciate how striking were the

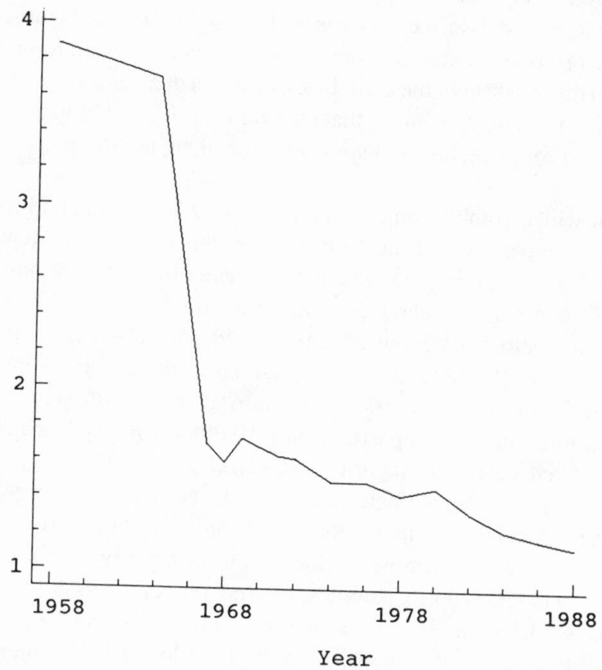

Figure 12.2. White Numerical Advantage as a Multiple of "Equal Effort" in Southern States, 1958–1988

changes in the racial patterns of southern registration in the short period immediately following passage of the act. This fact is hidden by the smoother, flatter trends observed when one considers black voter registration rates (table 12.1) in isolation from their complex interaction with white registration rates, racial organizations, restrictive laws, and demographic conditions. Before the act, an average southern political unit had a white ratio in its electorate that vastly exaggerated the white ratio in its voting-age population. After the act, the disparity diminished dramatically in a few short years.

Federal Examiners and Black Majorities

The elimination of literacy tests by section 4 was an important element in that transformation, but another feature of the act also had an impact on relative black registration. Under section 6, the Attorney General could send federal examiners directly to various counties to facilitate registration of blacks. I use county-level voter registration data after 1965 to trace the effect of the presence of federal examiners.

A fundamental question is whether blacks in black-majority counties actually were able to form majorities of the registered electorate as a consequence of the act. This is an important issue because, as we have seen, the central thrust of white strategy in the pre-act period was to prevent such majorities from forming. Thus, the act created the prospect in majority-black counties of a black numerical advantage at the polls. It seems reasonable that the desire among whites to maintain their advantage would continue, and perhaps even strengthen, as this prospect appeared more likely.

Table 12.4, which combines the data collected by Matthews and Prothro with that available in appendix 7 of the 1968 Civil Rights Commission report and in other sources, shows that in the seven states covered by section 4 in this period, there were 89 such majority-black counties at the time. None had had majority-black electorates before 1965 but 35—nearly 40 percent—had majority-black electorates in 1967 or 1968.[67] Rates of successful majority creation were highest in three Deep South states: 8 of the 10 possible in Alabama, 13 of 26 in Mississippi, and 4 of 9 in Louisiana. In comparison, only 10 of 44 majority-black counties in the other 4 covered states had majority-black electorates.[68]

The presence of federal examiners mattered a great deal for black registration, at least in the transitional period up to 1968. While only 28 percent (16 of 57) black-majority counties without examiners achieved black-majority electorates, 60 percent (19 of 32) of black-majority counties with federal examiners did so during this time. In fact, in Alabama, Georgia, Louisiana, and Mississippi, every county in which a majority-black electorate was registered in 1967 or 1968 either had had a federal examiner or was geographically adjacent to one or more counties that did.

Expanding the scope of the inquiry to include all counties for which interim data on registration are available relative to the base year of 1964, we find that the apparent independent effect of federal examiners having been sent in 1966 was a gain in the black registration rate of 23 percentage points by 1967 or 18 points by 1968. The results for 1967 are shown in table 12.6, while the results for 1968 are omitted because of space considerations. In a larger set of counties in 1968, the average black registration rate was 9 percentage points higher where federal examiners had been sent, relative to its corresponding percentage in 1958–60.[69] These 9 percentage points were added by examiners to what would, in their absence, have been an average predicted black registration rate of 45 percent, so examiners clearly had substantial—double-digit—effects in the short run.

The role of federal examiners in securing *durable* black majority electorates is less clear.[70] On this point there is too little data for firm conclusions. In the three states for which county-level data in 1967 and 1971 are available—Louisiana and the Carolinas—8 of 9 majority-black counties in 1967 no longer had black electoral majorities four years later.[71] In Mississippi, by contrast, 10 of the 11 majority-black electorates in 1967 were still majority black four years later. Examiners had been in 8 of those 10, and they revisited 6 counties in 1969 and/or 1971.[72] Econometric analyses of all southern counties for which we have sufficient data show that as early as 1972 the independent impact of federal registrars had entirely dissipated.[73]

Yet in one important respect the presence of registrars in the early years did have a measurable impact over the long term. As we saw above, in Mississippi and Alabama more than half the majority-black counties had achieved majority-black electorates as a result of the presence of federal examiners as early as 1967 or 1968. No other southern state witnessed this achievement until the late 1970s at the earliest, when South Carolina joined the ranks of the other two states. It was not achieved in other southern states until the mid-1980s. Thus, the use of federal registrars in the transitional years clearly mattered in the majority-black counties to which they were sent. One can only speculate whether a more aggressive policy of deploying registrars might have changed the political landscape of the South. As it was, for all practical purposes the deployment ended by 1970.

Explaining the Contemporary Southern Political System

What has caused the dramatic decrease in registration differences between whites and blacks? Figure 12.2, buttressed by my earlier econometric findings, reveals big differences between 1964 and 1967, which are surely the result of the Voting Rights Act and its related legal and institutional changes. But what about the period since then? The figure also shows a substantial decline in white advantage more recently, from white overrepresentation (relative to "equal effort") of about 60 percent in 1972 to only 10 percent in 1988. Changes of that magnitude demand explanation too, even in view of the much larger changes immediately beforehand.

On the whole, scholars argue that interracial competition of the sort motivating the pre-act politics of registration has become less important.[74] For although some examples of racially motivated mobilization of new registrants exist,[75] nowhere are they part of a systematic pattern. With the legal impediments of the pre-act South swept away—so the usual account of registration in the post-act South goes—blacks and whites both registered in increasing numbers, a phenomenon described by Black, Stekler, and others.[76] Because the number of new white registrants was far greater, blacks remained a small minority of the registered electorate in many areas. Blacks, of course, participated at greater rates than they did before passage of the act, but at rates lower those of whites, other things equal.[77]

This account is correct as far as it goes, but it does not explain the continuing decline in white advantage. That can be explained in part by the fact that while whites have registered in greater numbers, they have registered at lower rates than before in many parts of the South, as we shall see in a moment. However, even this does not address the question of whether the old interracial fight to control the makeup of local electorates that characterized the pre-act South has continued into the present. For that, we again have to consider what is happening to white and black registration rates in the same places and at the same times.

Since 1972 voter registration figures by race have been officially reported on a continuing basis by South Carolina and, with gaps, by North Carolina, Georgia, and Louisiana. These counts of registrants can be transformed into registration rates by dividing them by contemporaneous estimates of white and black voting-age populations.[78] The results, shown in table 12.5, suggest that the decline in white advantage since 1972 could be due to several factors: increases in black registration rates in some states (especially North Carolina and to some extent Georgia), decreases in white registration rates in others (most notably Louisiana), and decreases in registration rates of both races (though a greater decrease among whites) in South Carolina.

Racial Mobilization and Countermobilization

Fortunately, the data are available at the county level in these four states, so we can look even more closely at factors that affected black and white registration in the post-1965 period.[79] One set of factors—what might be called an interaction of opposing forces—has been referred to as the *mobilization-countermobilization hypothesis*. For our purposes, mobilization occurs when one race's registration rates increase in anticipation of an increase in another race's rates, after allowing for the effects of other relevant factors. Countermobilization occurs when the second race's registration rates increase when those of the first race do so, after allowing for the effects of other factors. Simultaneous estimation of white and black registration rates allows for the possibility of measuring mobilization and countermobilization while avoiding bias in estimates attributable to these variables having reciprocal effects. Table 12.6 reports structural models of black and white county-level registration rates in 1967, 1972, 1980, and 1988, based on the four states listed in table 12.5, the only ones for which recent data are available.

The simultaneous structural estimates in the table show that white registration rates in the post-1965 period were directly related to black population concentration, while black registration rates responded to white registration rates, other things equal. That is, white registration rates were now higher where blacks were a larger part of the population (since the act removed the main factors inhibiting black registration in such locales), and blacks reacted, and continue to react, to this white response. These relationships appear in the data for 1972, 1980, and 1988, after controlling for the continuing effects of several demographic factors—including income, urbanism, and population growth—as well as allowing for differences among the states not captured by these other variables.

So the story told by the data is as follows. Where blacks were more concentrated, greater proportions of whites registered, once the legal barriers to black participation fell. Where this happened, other things equal, higher proportions of blacks—now able to register—responded by doing so. But rising black registration rates, as distinct from heavy black population concentrations, did not similarly affect white registration rates, at least before 1988. Therefore, because white registration rates were apparently positively related to black population concentration (other things equal), and black registration rates to white rates, unless we can find other factors to explain why this was so, it is hard to avoid the interpretation that registration politics in these years was characterized by white mobilization and black countermobilization. These results qualify the repeatedly observed finding for the post-1965 South that black registration rates were positively related to black population concentration.[80] In fact, white registration rates were higher where black concentration was higher, but black concentration appears to have had no significant independent effect on black registration rates. That is, black concentration had no apparent effect on black registration rates other than indirectly through its effect on white registration rates, when the rates of both races were estimated simultaneously.

The exact magnitudes of the estimates vary, but the qualitative outlines of the processes just described are robust in spite of considerable experimentation with the specifications and estimating techniques reported in table 12.6. However, the gradual erosion of racial differences in registration levels has somewhat diluted the reactions that its estimation results describe. For instance, the effect of black concentration on white registration rates declined between 1972 and 1988, while the impact of white registration rates on black rates came closer to a one-for-one correspondence. Were such trends to continue, future data would simply reveal areas of higher and lower registration rates of both races, unaffected by racial population concentrations, after allowing for the effects of other socioeconomic variables. This changing structural relationship between black and white registration rates is consistent with the disappearance of the relationship between white numerical advantage and black population proportion.[81]

Other Factors Affecting Relative Registration Rates

Table 12.6 also shows that relative white registration rates were consistently lower in urban areas of the South, possibly reflecting greater relative white population mobility there than in rural areas. Black registration rates were initially higher in areas that were more heavily Catholic, and, more recently, in areas where average incomes were higher. In 1988 black rates were also higher where more of the population was employed in agriculture, reversing a negative correlation that others had reported as surviving into the 1970s, but mirroring the lower white rates in urban areas.[82] Hence, even the effects of agricultural labor dependence, so prominent earlier, had disappeared by 1971. Limited effects of state context also existed. In particular, relative to predicted values, white registration rates were always higher in Louisiana and North Carolina relative to the mean for the four states.[83] Most important, given the absence of the legal impediments of earlier years, table 12.6 shows that these laws had no lasting holdover effects in the aggregate. As suggested previously, the absence of a significant effect after 1967 for the dummy variable reflecting use of federal registrars in a county suggests that the relative impact of federal examiners' presence on black registration rates wore off over time.

Another finding concerns the ebb and flow of registration rates. There was a good deal of volatility in registration rates immediately after the act, as one might expect in the wake of tumultuous changes. Since 1972, however, registration rates for both races were extremely stable within counties over time.[84] Admittedly, there was a regular cycle in registration rates, consisting of a surge in presidential election years and a dropoff in the midterm years—a cycle with greater amplitude for whites than blacks.[85] Once we allow for this cycle, we find the often discussed "Jackson surge" in black registration rates in 1984, the year the Reverend Jesse Jackson mounted the first serious candidacy by a black man for the presidency. My estimate is that the surge was on the order of 5–6 points and had no lasting effects.

The Winds of Change

In this chapter I have analyzed systematic estimates of white and black registration rates before and after the Voting Rights Act became law. I have estimated parameters for a variety of effects on both white and black registration rates in models that fit data for the entire eleven-state South. In the period before 1965, legal restrictions and racial organizations—mediated by black population concentration and some socioeconomic conditions—interacted to produce a system with greatly disproportionate white numerical advantage in southern registered electorates. This system was largely overthrown by 1967, with dramatic changes in relative rates of white and black registration that can principally be attributed to legal and institutional shifts, perhaps most notably the elimination of literacy tests. In addition, federal examiners authorized by the act played a substantial but short-lived role in raising black registration levels and securing local black majorities.

Consequently, it may safely be said that the Voting Rights Act transformed the basis of the southern electoral system, inasmuch as it was the vehicle for destroying the institutional barriers to black registration. Between 1972 and 1988, a pattern of racial mobilization and countermobilization, now possibly in decline, produced a reasonably stable system characterized by a ubiquitous but eroding white numerical registration advantage. The decline in this advantage raised the very real possibility of convergence in white and black registration rates as a percentage of eligible white and black voters, respectively, sometime in the 1990s. If and when that happens, the transformation of the southern registration system that the act began will be complete.

Appendix: Data Sources on Southern Counties

Pre-1960 county registration data for 1,083 of the 1,136 counties in the eleven-state South were taken from the Matthews and Prothro data set, originally provided to me on hollerith cards by James W. Prothro.[86] Registration requirement information about the pre-1965 period was taken from Smith.[87] Interim data on voter registration for 1964 and 1967 were taken from a report by the U.S. Commission on Civil Rights.[88] Subsequent registration data for 1968–71 were provided by the Voter Education Project of the Southern Regional Council and merged with the other data by Philip Wood at the University of Essex, England.[89] Each of the three data sources employed estimates in some cases, and no guarantee of accuracy can be given. Population data for 1970 and 1980 were collected by the U.S. census. Voter registration data for 1972–88 were provided by Election Data Services (EDS) of Washington, D.C. Supplementary data for Georgia in 1980, matching EDS data in other years, were provided by Michael Binford of Georgia State University.

Matthews and Prothro's data set on registration is mainly for 1958, although apparently for Tennessee, at least, 1960 figures were used. No white registration data were available for Mississippi in either year, but 1964 data for some counties (twenty in all) were published by the U.S. Commission on Civil Rights,[90] and were added to the earlier data by Philip Wood. Matthews and Prothro unfortunately did not record numbers of registered whites and blacks. However, as long as there are registration rate and voting-age population data for both races, the ratio of registered whites to blacks can be calculated.

For the 1960s and 1970s, changes occurring between decennial census years are assumed to occur at a constant rate, in order to allow interpolation of voting-age population figures for noncensus years. For the 1980s, population changes occurring between 1970 and 1980 are extrapolated forward year by year. These results will be confirmed or disconfirmed when final 1990 census data become available. The extrapolation probably produces greater measurement error than the interpolation.

TABLE 12.1
Estimated Percentage of Voting-Age Blacks Registered, Eleven Southern States, 1947–1986

State	*1947*	*1956*	*1964*	*1968*	*1976*	*1986*
Alabama	1.2	11.0	23.0	56.7	58.4	68.9
Arkansas	17.3	36.0	49.3	67.5	94.0	57.9
Florida	15.4	32.0	63.8	62.1	61.1	58.2
Georgia	18.8	27.0	44.0	56.1	74.8	52.8
Louisiana	2.6	31.0	32.0	59.3	63.0	60.6
Mississippi	0.9	5.0	6.7	59.4	60.7	70.8
N. Carolina	15.2	24.0	46.8	55.3	54.8	58.4
S. Carolina	13.0	27.0	38.7	50.8	56.5	52.5
Tennessee	25.8	29.0	69.4	72.8	66.4	65.3
Texas	18.5	37.0	57.7	83.1	65.0	68.0
Virginia	13.2	19.0	45.7	58.4	54.7	56.2
TOTAL SOUTH	12.0	24.9	43.1	62.0	63.1	60.8

Source: Data are from Stanley (1987, 97), who lists the original sources, supplemented for 1986 from *Statistical Abstract of the United States* 1990, table 441. These estimated registration rates are based on probably out-of-date values for the growing black voting-age population, and therefore systematically overestimate black registration by several percentage points, the more so the further a sample year is after the last decennial census. Stanley notes this problem for 1968 only. See table 12.5 below for adjusted estimates where alternative data are available.

TABLE 12.2
State-Level Characteristics, Eleven Southern States

		Legal Restrictions in 1960		
State	*Average Black % in State Population, 1880–1900*	*Literacy Requirement? (Date established)*	*Poll Tax?*	*Residence Required in County? (Months)*
South Carolina	60	Yes (1895)	No[a]	Yes (12)
Mississippi	58	Yes (1890)	Yes	Yes (12)
Louisiana	49	Yes (1898)	No[b]	Yes (12)
Georgia	47	Yes (1908)	No[b]	Yes (6)
Alabama	46	Yes (1901)	Yes	Yes (6)
Florida	45	No	No[b]	Yes (6)
Virginia	38	Yes (1902)	Yes	Yes (6)
North Carolina	35	Yes (1900)	No[b]	Yes (1)
Arkansas	27	No	Yes	Yes (6)
Tennessee	25	No	No[a]	Yes (3)
Texas	22	No	Yes	Yes (6)

[a] Some exemptions; abolished after 1948.
[b] Abolished before 1948.

TABLE 12.3
Explanation of Logged White Numerical Advantage,[a] Counties in Eleven Southern States, 1958–1960

Independent Variable	*Estimated Coefficient*	*Standard Error*
Literacy requirement (LR)	−0.217	0.167
LR × county voting-age population (VAP) % black	0.016	0.005
Poll tax (PT)	0.631	0.128
PT × county VAP % black	−0.016	0.003
Black race organization	−0.265	0.062
White race organization (WRO)	−0.530	0.152
WRO × county % VAP black	0.024	0.004
Residence requirement in county (months)	−0.050	0.013
County VAP % black	−0.061	0.005
State population % black	0.052	0.008
% Catholic in county	−0.007	0.002
% Holiness sect members in county	0.018	0.010
% county labor force employed in agriculture	0.012	0.002
White-black difference in median school years completed	0.097	0.027
% change in county population, 1950–60	0.029	0.012
% county population urban	−0.001	0.001
% change in black population proportion, 1900–1950	0.006	0.003
Constant	2.189	0.221
R-squared	0.567	—
Standard error of the regression	—	0.800

Sources: Described in the appendix to this chapter.

[a]Dependent variable is the natural logarithm of the estimated ratio of white and black registered voters in the county. Estimation is by ordinary least squares. Number of observations is 833.

TABLE 12.4
Black Majorities in Voting-Age Population and Electorate, Counties in Seven Southern States, 1967–1968

Did County Have:			
A Majority-Black Voting-Age Population?	*A Federal Examiner in 1966?*	*Number of Such Counties*	*Number Achieving a Majority-Black Electorate*
No	No	469	0
No	Yes	27	0
Yes	No	57	16
Yes	Yes	32	19

Sources: Data are calculated from sources listed in the appendix to this chapter. Data include black majorities in registered electorates in either 1967 or 1968 in the states covered by section 4 of the Voting Rights Act.

TABLE 12.5
Estimated Registration Rates by Race, State, and Year, Four Southern States, 1972–1988

State	*1972*	*1980*	*1984*	*1988*
	Black Voter Registration			
Georgia	—	45.8	52.6	52.2
Louisiana	55.3	54.6	59.9	59.1
North Carolina	46.9	46.7	61.1	59.7
South Carolina	49.4	48.7	53.9	46.4
	White Voter Registration			
Georgia	—	69.1	70.4	70.5
Louisiana	83.9	78.0	77.1	70.5
North Carolina	73.2	72.0	75.5	73.8
South Carolina	63.7	60.8	60.9	53.5

Sources: Data are calculated from sources listed in the appendix to this chapter.

TABLE 12.6
Simultaneous Estimates[a] of Registration Rates after Passage of the Voting Rights Act, Counties in Four Southern States

Independent Variable	*Estimated Coefficient in Year* 1967	1972	1980	1988
(a) Dependent Variable: Black Voter Registration Rate				
Constant	16.430*	−12.700	−5.010	−21.850*
Lagged black registration rate	0.572*	—	—	—
Federal examiner 1966	22.450*	—	—	—
Population % black	−0.050	—	—	—
White registration rate	0.213*	0.617*	0.699*	0.950*
Population % Catholic	—	0.110*	0.093*	0.135*
County median income	—	0.001*	0.000	0.001*
Population % urban	—	—	−0.085*	—
Labor force % in agriculture	—	—	—	0.429*
Louisiana	—	—	—	7.120*
Standard error	15.8	10.2	11.8	12.3
(b) Dependent Variable: White Voter Registration Rate				
Constant	44.490*	58.310*	57.860*	41.080*
Lagged white registration rate	0.572*	—	—	—
Population % black	0.065	0.342*	0.135*	0.128*
Black registration rate	0.053*	0.247	0.251	0.390*
Population % urban	−0.096*	−0.179*	−0.153*	−0.103*
County population % increase, 1960–70	0.040	−0.088	−0.058*	—
Louisiana	5.150*	16.840*	13.490*	8.650*
North Carolina	−6.160*	5.030*	6.170*	9.450*
Georgia	—	—	4.130*	6.370*
Standard error	9.7	10.0	9.1	8.3
Observations	361	202	337	349
System *R*-squared	.541	.567	.434	.407

Sources: Data are from sources listed in the appendix to this chapter.

[a]Estimation is by three-stage least squares. Each year is estimated separately. An asterisk (*) indicates coefficient more than twice its standard error. A dash indicates statistically insignificant effects, as does the omission of any variable included in table 12.3.

CHAPTER THIRTEEN

The Voting Rights Act and the Second Reconstruction

CHANDLER DAVIDSON AND BERNARD GROFMAN

THE VOTING RIGHTS ACT is deeply rooted in American history. It was the last major piece of legislation passed during the southern civil rights movement. That movement, in turn, was but a phase of the battle for black citizenship rights growing out of the Civil War and Reconstruction. And, of course, the war itself was fought over the slavery question and was a milestone in the African-American quest for racial equality. A broad historical perspective is therefore essential to an understanding of the act's significance.

THE FIRST AND SECOND RECONSTRUCTIONS

It is our thesis that the Voting Rights Act must be seen as a mechanism to insure that the Second Reconstruction of the 1960s did not meet the same fate as that of the First Reconstruction of the 1860s and 1870s.[1] In that era, the basic rights of citizenship ostensibly guaranteed African Americans by the Fourteenth and Fifteenth amendments enacted following the war were stripped away with astonishing speed, largely as a result of a ferocious white southern backlash. Table 9 in the state chapters of this volume chronicles in detail the ingenious devices adopted in the southern states from the 1860s forward to prevent blacks from registering and voting. The southern "redeemers" could not have succeeded, however, without the indifference of most northern politicians to the plight of the newly freed slaves, and without the complicity of the federal courts. In the absence of broad support for the Negroes' cause, the forces of reaction effectively gutted the Civil War amendments of their intended powers to secure black people's newly gained rights.

Almost a century later, as the civil rights movement gathered momentum, it was clear to historically informed observers that the white South would not surrender easily as blacks tried once more to obtain rights they had acquired during Reconstruction. Writing in the spring of 1965 before passage of the Voting Rights Act that August, Woodward observed that "the South since 1954 has been more deeply alienated and thoroughly defiant than it has been at any time since 1877."[2] Continued white resistance in the 1960s to school desegregation, the widespread violence against blacks who attempted to desegregate public accommodations, the ominous election of racist demagogues calling for an end to federal pressure for change, and the failure of the Civil Rights acts of 1957, 1960, and 1964 to end systematic exclusion of blacks from the voter rolls in the Deep South convinced civil rights leaders, Congress, and President Lyndon B. Johnson that only extraordinary measures would guarantee black southerners the rights they had long been denied.

Voting rights was a case in point. During and after the First Reconstruction, southern white officials were quick to employ devices that denied newly enfranchised blacks their political rights without blatantly violating the Fifteenth Amendment but that violated it nonetheless. Then, a half century after disfranchisement, when the Supreme Court in 1944 declared white primaries unconstitutional, many southern officials, anticipating a concerted push for black suffrage, once again took steps to prevent it. Simultaneously, as chapters in this book reveal, they began amending electoral laws to prevent black officeholding in the event that substantial numbers of blacks entered the electorate. So strong was white resistance that efforts to minimize the influence of black votes continued and sometimes intensified after passage of the act in 1965.[3]

The failure of the white South to submit voluntarily to the growing demand in the nation at large for abolishing its Jim Crow system was the backdrop for the debate over the Voting Rights Act in the spring and summer of 1965. The framers of the act, which was designed to enforce the Fifteenth Amendment, were well aware of that amendment's failure to effectively protect black voting rights almost from the time it was ratified in 1870. The Justice Department under President Johnson, as well as congressional leaders—pushed hard by civil rights forces—were determined that the Second Reconstruction should not fall victim once more to the same reactionary impulse that had emasculated the First Reconstruction.

The provisions of the act with the most immediate impact were those which temporarily abolished the literacy test in most areas of the southern states still using it and authorized the executive branch to send federal examiners to register black voters in those same jurisdictions—ones that had shown the greatest resistance to granting African Americans their constitutional rights. Also of major importance were the preclearance provisions of section 5, requiring covered jurisdictions to submit proposed changes in voting practices to the Justice Department. Before the department would approve changes in electoral practices, it had to be convinced that the changes had neither the effect nor the purpose, in the language of the act, of "denying or abridging the right to vote on account of race or color."

Two features of section 5 are particularly noteworthy and explain the intense resistance of many white southerners. First, the only appeal of the department's preclearance denial was to the Federal District Court for the District of Columbia, a court then presided over by cosmopolitan and progressive judges.[4] This meant that southern district judges could no longer hamstring private plaintiffs or Justice Department lawyers, as they had done under the Civil Rights Act of 1957 and its successors. Second, because no change in voting practices could legally be implemented without preclearance, southern jurisdictions whose election schemes had been struck down by a federal judge could not immediately implement a different form of voting discrimination and apply it while it was being litigated, as they had been able to do before passage of the act.

In sum, the new Voting Rights Act would shortly bring the force of the federal government to bear directly on what have been called first-generation problems—white southerners' efforts to prevent blacks from registering and voting—and it would provide a powerful tool that could be used to abolish second-generation devices such as vote dilution, a barrier to black officeholding. The act did this primarily by giving the executive branch extraordinary monitoring and enforcement powers in that region of the country where adamant opposition to black voting rights was still widespread.

Once the battle was lost to defeat the act or, barring that, to scuttle key provisions, various southern officials challenged the act's constitutionality, refused to submit changes in election practices for preclearance, tried to retain the poll tax in states where it was still used, and sought to have the act's provisions construed narrowly so as, for example, to permit devices like at-large elections to replace single-member districts without the need for Justice Department approval.

Most of their stratagems failed. South Carolina's challenge to the act's constitutionality was rejected by the Supreme Court in 1966.[5] That same year, in cases growing out of Justice Department challenges to the poll tax in state and local elections—challenges section 10 instructed the Attorney General to file—the Court ruled that the tax was unconstitutional.[6] Then, in a case that was to prove critical for the subsequent evolution of voting rights law, the Court in 1969 rejected Mississippi's claim that the state's massive changes from district to at-large elections did not need to be precleared under the act.[7] Reviewing the act's legislative history, the Court held that such changes fell under the act's definition of voting practice and as such might abridge protected voting rights.

The Impact of Sections 4, 6, and 7

In very general terms, the act's overall enfranchising effect has been known for some time. By abolishing the literacy test in covered jurisdictions, section 4 of the new law accomplished what none of the earlier laws or judicial decisions during the post–World War II period had achieved: a dramatic growth in black registration in the Deep South, and a significant though smaller growth in the Outer South, where blacks had already begun to register in appreciable numbers. As Alt demonstrates in table 12.1, which presents registration trends by race in each southern state, a striking shift occurred shortly after the act was passed.

Alt's chapter should prove to be a definitive study of southern black and white registration in the decades immediately before and after passage of the act. It integrates sociological and demographic factors, data on white and black political organizations, information on institutional practices having a racially exclusionary impact, and events and actions tied to passage of the act—all within the framework of a statistically sophisticated longitudinal research design.

Alt gives precise estimates of the effects formal barriers such as the literacy test had in depressing black registration. Applying econometric techniques to insights

Key had achieved some forty years earlier, he presents a unified model of southern political participation in the decade before 1965, focusing on counties' black population percentage as the major variable, both in isolation from and interaction with other factors. He shows how barriers to voting were most pernicious in locales with the heaviest black concentration—areas in which Key had predicted whites would perceive the greatest threat of black voting because it could result in black electoral control.

Alt's analysis reveals how the act's passage led to a complete breakdown of the old patterns of minority exclusion in which black registration was lowest relative to that of whites in the areas of the South with the greatest black population concentrations. Alt also analyzes the critical role played by federal registrars authorized under sections 6 and 7. Of particular interest is his finding that the registrars' intervention quickly succeeded in achieving increased black registration rates in the majority-black counties where they were sent. A comparable registration level took another ten years to achieve in heavily black counties elsewhere in the South.

The Impact of Section 5

The act's preclearance provisions have had a tremendous impact on southern legislatures during reapportionment because the Department of Justice has not only rejected plans for multimember districts that would submerge substantial black voting strength but plans for single-member districts that would either fragment or pack minority population concentrations. Table 10 in the state chapters demonstrates the extent of growth in black legislators.

Handley and Grofman in chapter 11 show the almost perfect correlation between majority-black districts and black officeholding in state legislative and congressional districts. This correlation also exists in cities and counties with districted plans, as shown in table 7 of the state chapters and in table 10.5. Handley and Grofman further demonstrate that the creation of these majority-black legislative districts is largely the result of Justice Department preclearance denial or southern legislators' expectation of it. In the eight states on which we focus in this volume, the number of black state legislators and U.S. representatives increased from 2 in 1964 to 160 in 1990. Had it not been for section 5, this increase would have been very much smaller, our findings strongly suggest.

Even so, black officeholding in the South by the end of the 1980s was still sharply lower than it would have been were race not a factor in elections. Table 10 in the state chapters demonstrates this clearly. Black elected officials in Texas, for example, made up only 1.2 percent of the state's officeholders in 1989, although the average black population over the past thirty years was 12.3. In Mississippi, with the largest black population proportion of any state in the union—a 37.4 percent thirty-year average—blacks in 1989 made up only 12.2 percent of the officeholders. Georgia was among the states with the highest proportion of blacks in its house of representatives and senate—17 and 14.3 percent, respectively—at the end of the 1980s. And yet the black population in Georgia between 1960 and 1990 averaged 27 percent.

At the local as distinct from the state level the principal impact of section 5 arguably has been more limited. By the time the Voting Rights Act was passed, a clear majority of southern localities already employed at-large elections. Thus section 5—limited to enforcing the retrogression standard in cases where jurisdictions planned to change election type—could not serve as the primary mechanism to attack the discriminatory effects of at-large elections in the South.[8] Instead, challenges initially were mounted in terms of the constitutional standard for equal protection and, after 1982, the revised standard of section 2. During the period before 1982, the act functioned largely at the local level to deter majority-white jurisdictions from imposing changes in election practices, other than the already existing at-large elections, that would dilute minority voting strength.

The Impact of the Constitutional Equal Protection Standard

After holding in *Fortson v. Dorsey* (1965)[9] that multimember district plans might under certain circumstances restrict constitutionally protected rights, the Supreme Court in *White v. Regester* (1973)[10] upheld a lower court's decision striking down multimember legislative districts in Texas that were found to dilute black and Mexican-American voting strength. Building on *White*, minority plaintiffs later in that decade filed constitutional challenges to local at-large elections and often prevailed, although the number of municipal jurisdictions affected was not that large.[11] Even so, *Stewart v. Waller* (1975)[12] caused over thirty Mississippi cities to revert to single-member districts.[13]

In *City of Mobile v. Bolden* (1980)[14] the Supreme Court held that plaintiffs must show a discriminatory purpose in creating or maintaining a challenged election practice in Fourteenth Amendment minority vote-dilution cases, effectively rejecting the results standard that lower courts had fashioned from the language of *White*. Because the evidentiary standard laid down in *Bolden* was seen as virtually impossible to satisfy without "smoking gun" evidence of intentional discrimination, constitutional challenges to at-large elections virtually came to a halt after the *Bolden* decision.[15] When the act was renewed in 1982, section 2 in an amended form became a vehicle to restore a results-based test to the arsenal of voting rights plaintiffs. In *Thornburg v. Gingles* (1986)[16] the Supreme Court upheld congressional authority to impose such a test by statute and provided a simplified standard that has come to be known as the *three-pronged test*.

As chapter 1 makes clear, it would be a mistake to describe the demise of local at-large systems resulting from Fourteenth Amendment litigation such as *White* and its progeny as having no connection with the Voting Rights Act. The essential idea of minority vote dilution implicit in *White* was introduced in the Court's earlier *Allen* decision, which interpreted the act's section 5 preclearance provision as covering changes from district to at-large elections. Had there been no act and consequently no *Allen* decision, it is highly questionable whether the concept of minority vote dilution that underlay the constitutional challenges to at-large systems throughout the South in the 1970s would have been accepted. It therefore makes sense, we believe, to think of these Fourteenth Amendment cases, which had a significant impact on minority officeholding, as progeny of the Voting Rights Act.

The Impact of Section 2

In addition to sketching the history of the struggle to achieve minority voting rights, a central concern of the state chapters is to measure the impact of changes in local election practices on minority representation and to determine the role of voting rights litigation in causing changes. These changes have been profound. Hundreds of southern cities, counties, and other kinds of jurisdictions shifted from at-large elections in the 1980s. In Alabama, where perhaps the most extensive changes have occurred, there has been a virtual elimination of at-large cities of 6,000 or more with black populations above 10 percent. Throughout the eight-state South covered by section 5, most majority-white cities of 10,000 or larger have changed from at-large to district or mixed plans since the early 1970s. In Texas, numerous jurisdictions with significant Mexican-American populations also have switched from at-large systems. What has been the result of the changes, and how has the Voting Rights Act, particularly section 2, figured in this development?

The Effects of Change in Local Election Systems

The individual state chapters as well as chapter 10 show that at the local level, replacement of at-large elections led to remarkable gains in black officeholding that far outstripped gains in the jurisdictions that remained at large. For example, over a period of roughly fifteen years equity scores for black representation in cities that changed from at-large to district systems went from 0.04 to 1.14 in cities that were 10–29.9 percent black, and from 0.07 to 0.92 in cities that were 30–49.9 percent black. By contrast, in the cities that retained the at-large system throughout the period, comparable scores went from 0.18 to 0.53 and from 0.17 to 0.56, respectively.

The focus of our research at the local level was on cities, but the authors of the chapters on Georgia, North Carolina, and South Carolina also examined the impact of the abolition of at-large plans on county officeholding in those counties with a population of 10 percent or more black. The findings for counties in the three states were quite similar to those for cities: sharp increases in black officeholding in single-member-district plans, and relatively small increases in the plans that retained the at-large system. Moreover, as with the cities, many of the changes in county election structures can be attributed directly to the Voting Rights Act or to Fourteenth Amendment litigation. Evidence reported elsewhere indicates that the same pattern of increased black (and, in many locales, Hispanic) officeholding following the adoption of district systems is true for other types of southern governmental units, such as school boards.[17]

In Texas, Hispanic representation also showed noteworthy gains in districted cities. Between 1974 and 1989, in cities that switched to districts the Hispanic equity score increased slightly in cities that were 10–29.9 percent black plus Hispanic from 0.18 to 0.35, while in cities that were 30–49.9 percent black plus Hispanic, the score jumped dramatically from 0.15 to 0.95. The change in comparable at-large cities that did not switch was from 0.37 to 0.21 and from 0.24 to 0.50, respectively. Moreover, evidence indicates that some of the gains in minority officeholding that occurred in unchanged at-large jurisdictions resulted from a conscious effort by local elites to prevent successful voting rights litigation.

Why do minorities fare better in district cities than in at-large ones? The answer, almost certainly, is that racially polarized voting is still widespread, and when whites, or Anglos in the Southwest, are in the majority, minority candidates have difficulty winning. On the other hand, as suggested by Handley and Grofman's findings on southern state legislative districts and by the state chapters' corroborating findings on city council and county commissioner districts, when minorities are in the majority, their candidates are far more likely to win. Without the close federal supervision of boundary drawing in districted cities as a result of the act, it is quite probable that far fewer majority-black districts (and majority-Hispanic districts in Texas) would have been drawn in them.[18]

Moreover, as we argue in chapter 10, drawing in part from data presented in tables 2.5 and 2.5A, it is quite likely that a selection bias causes recent cross-sectional data on black municipal representation to overstate the ability of black candidates to win in typical at-large settings. In a number of states and on average across all eight states, jurisdictions that retained at-large plans at the end of the 1980s originally had higher black representation than those adopting districts. In other words, the "worst case" cities, in terms of black officeholding, were most likely to become districted during the period under investigation, and the "best case" cities were most likely to retain at-large systems.

The Role of Voting Rights Litigation in Provoking Change in Local Election Systems

Contrary to some recent claims, the evidence we have presented provides no reason to believe that the act's prohibition of minority vote dilution was unnecessary or that it has outlived its usefulness.[19] The data presented by Handley and Grofman demonstrate the importance of the section 5 preclearance provision in enabling black candidates to win legislative races. The data in the state chapters enable us to grasp the critical importance of amended section 2 for the success of minority candidates at the local level. The state chapters also underscore the role of the Justice Department, the federal courts, civil rights organizations, and private litigators in guaranteeing enforcement of the act's provisions.[20]

As we have seen, the impact on black representation of replacing at-large with district and mixed systems in the eight southern states was extraordinary. Why did this widespread shift in local election structures take place? By and large the answer is quite simple: the changes stemmed from the Voting Rights Act, especially section 2.

After the amendment of section 2, numerous suits attacking local at-large elections were filed.[21] The number of section 2 cases between 1982 and 1989 dwarfed the number of constitutional challenges brought during the 1970s in the pre-*Bolden* period. Indeed, from 1982 through 1989 (1990 in Georgia) we found over 150 section 2 challenges to municipal elections in the eight states of our study.[22] Nearly 65 percent of all changes from at-large elections in our full eight-state municipal data set can be attributed to litigation or to settlements resulting from litigation,[23] and an additional 6 percent, roughly speaking, to actions related to section 5.[24] Moreover, about 10 percent of the changes in election type not tied to actual litigation are attributed by the city sources consulted by our state authors to threat of litigation.[25] Thus over 80 percent of all changes in election type in our eight-state data set can be attributed to voting rights activity, and this is almost certainly a conservative figure, since some of the unexplained changes and even some of the changes reported to us by city clerks and other city officials as voluntary would not have taken place except for the climate of enhanced concern for voting rights and officials' fear of litigation.

Once the *Gingles* standard was announced, our data show that well over 90 percent of the section 2 challenges to municipal at-large elections in the eight states were successful, either as a result of a trial or of a settlement that implemented a single-member-district or mixed plan.[26] The vast bulk of section 2 actions were brought by minority plaintiffs, often acting through civil rights or civil liberties organizations. Within the eight states covered by our study, section 2 litigation brought solely by the Department of Justice played only a minor role in effecting changes in local election systems.[27] One of the most remarkable results of amended section 2, therefore, is its encouragement of the private bar to take a major role in enforcing public voting rights law. This fact cannot be emphasized too strongly.

In summary, this volume has chronicled the evolution of the Voting Rights Act to the end of the 1980s, focusing primarily on black political participation in the South. The contributors have tried to understand the impact of the act by systematically analyzing, in chapters 2–9, the eight state-specific data sets described in the Editors' Introduction; in chapter 10, the pooled data for the states covered by section 5; and in chapters 11 and 12, data for the eleven-state South as a whole. While many questions remain unanswered, we have nonetheless resolved several issues about the act's accomplishments—in particular, certain controversies about how gains in minority voter registration and officeholding came about.[28]

Our empirical approach throughout this volume stems from the premise that a balanced assessment of the Voting Rights Act over a quarter century requires at the very least an investigation of the basic facts about black-white voter registration rates and black-white officeholding. We asked the authors to limit themselves to research using hard and convincing data that would answer first- and second-generation issues with respect to electoral participation and the effects of election systems on minority electoral success. By the same token, we asked them to resist speculation on third- and fourth-generation questions—how well minority officials have become incorporated into the political decision-making processes of the bodies to which they were elected, and what the social and economic policy consequences of increased minority representation have been. Neither of the latter types of questions could be readily answered with the resources at our disposal.[29] We nonetheless hope that our research has laid the groundwork for systematic investigations of such questions.

Looking Ahead to the Twenty-first Century

The decade of the 1990s will witness new litigation under section 2, particularly in Texas and California, where concentrated populations of Mexican Americans (and, to a lesser extent, Asian Americans) will challenge barriers to full participation. Litigation on behalf of Native Americans will almost certainly increase, as well. We anticipate new suits in the South challenging district boundaries in already districted units, and we expect to see additional litigation in the North as well. But we also expect to see it in the small-town South. This point bears elaborating.

When we began this research, we thought it would demonstrate the success of the Voting Rights Act in changing minority representation in the South. In particular, we anticipated that many southern jurisdictions with a substantial black population and a history of very limited black officeholding would have adopted district or mixed plans as a result of litigation, leading to large gains in minority representation. This is exactly what we found.

However, on closer analysis, we now recognize that in several southern states this success story applies primarily to the larger towns and cities. There are hundreds of smaller towns where the effects of the Voting Rights Act as a means to prevent minority vote dilution have not yet been felt. It will almost certainly be many years before these jurisdictions are as well represented by minority officeholders as are the more populous ones. While these cities may be small in total population, they are the areas of the South least affected by the civil rights revolution of the 1960s and most in need of minority officeholders to protect the interests of black citizens. Thus, while the research reported here shows that the Voting Rights Act has wrought a "quiet revolution" in southern politics and is perhaps the single most successful civil rights bill ever passed, the need for it is far from over. We believe it will be extensively used in coming years to break the barriers to black officeholding in these towns.

With this litigation as well as with that in the Southwest and the North will come new issues and controversies. How can the law accommodate the sometimes conflicting interests of different minority groups—blacks and Hispanics, for example—in the same jurisdiction? How far must political cartographers go in drawing districts for protected minority groups when these clash with other criteria for districting, such as the desire to honor the geographic integrity of various governmental units? How can courts rationally decide among competing districting plans when the computer revolution in political map drawing makes possible hundreds of unique plans, all of which have virtues and shortcomings? Should minority leaders with close ties to the Democrats aim for maximizing minority seats even at the expense of Democratic party strength in a legislature? Are single-member-district plans, as distinct, say, from limited voting or proportional representation schemes, necessarily the best remedy for at-large vote dilution? How much weight, if any, should a court give to claims by defendants in voting suits that minority candidates' party affiliation, as distinct from their ethnicity pure and simple, is the cause of their defeat at the polls? Does the Voting Rights Act require legislatures, where possible, to draw districts in which minority voters can exert maximum influence short of being able to elect candidates of their choice?

These are issues we cannot address here.[30] We mention them only to emphasize that controversies over minority voting rights are a long-standing feature of American politics; they did not begin in 1965, or even in 1865, nor will they soon disappear. They are conflicts woven into the tapestry of our nation of many peoples of diverse origins and interests. Fortunately, the Voting Rights Act is a dynamic statute. To the extent that it resolves these conflicts fairly and rationally—and, in doing so, leads to a more unified, democratic, and participatory society—it will have achieved its purpose.

NOTES

Editors' Introduction

1. For a more detailed review of the provisions of the act and its subsequent amendments and the relevant legal history, see Grofman, Handley, and Niemi 1992.

2. The phrase is taken from the title of McDonald 1989. We refer to the voting changes as a "quiet revolution" because, while the results of the act are widespread and significant, the use of voting rights litigation to counter the resistance of white officials to minority political empowerment has largely escaped public attention—at least until the 1990s round of redistricting—in marked contrast to a white backlash to legal developments connected with the Civil Rights Act of 1964, for example. On the latter, see Grofman 1993a.

3. At various times other states have also been covered. The number of states now covered in whole or in part by the special provisons of the act is sixteen; the maximum number of states or parts thereof that have ever been covered is twenty-two.

4. At-large systems were often used in combination with runoff requirements or numbered place systems, a combination believed to have especially pernicious effects on the prospects for minority representation in circumstances where whites voted as a bloc against black candidates.

5. Wolfinger and Field 1966, 316, 325 (quotation in text). "A one-party system removes temptations to appeal to Negro voters, as does the city manager plan," they write. "With only one party, the partisan ballot is not meaningful. At-large elections minimize Negro voting strength" (325).

6. In the chapters on Georgia, North Carolina, and South Carolina, data on county elections are also examined.

7. We recognize that litigation involving Hispanic voting rights is already of great importance and that the voting rights of Asians are ripe for future litigation. As part of the National Science Foundation project, whose findings are reported in this volume, we also commissioned studies on the voting rights of American Indians (Wolfley and Henderson 1991), Hispanic voting rights issues in California (Avila and Grofman 1990), and voting rights litigation in New York (McDonald 1991). That work has been reported elsewhere. In order to provide a clearly defined research focus for this volume, we have dealt exclusively with voting rights in the South, where slavery and the Jim Crow system have left terrible and enduring scars. Thus with the partial exception of coverage of Hispanics in the Texas chapter and a few comments about Native American issues in North Carolina, our concern in this volume is with southern black voting rights in those states where voting rights litigation and section 5 enforcement have had the greatest impact. Even in the other two states covered entirely by section 5—Alaska and Arizona—and in the two partially covered states with large numbers of blacks and Hispanics, respectively—New York and California—there has so far been relatively little voting rights activity resulting from the act. Nonetheless, as Mundt (1988) points out, the Voting Rights Act has been "moving North," and we anticipate additional research to analyze its effects outside the South following the 1990s round of redistricting.

8. Leslie Winner, an attorney in North Carolina, contributed greatly to the development of the litigation data base used in the North Carolina chapter. The lead author of the Georgia chapter, Laughlin McDonald, a voting rights attorney in Georgia with litigation experience

in South Carolina as well, critically read the South Carolina chapter and made many useful suggestions. Armand Derfner, an attorney in South Carolina, also contributed significantly to the South Carolina chapter. We are grateful to these three attorneys who, though not authors of the North Carolina and South Carolina chapters, respectively, contributed much to them.

9. Those seeking to protect black voting rights included black community leaders, the Department of Justice, and a dedicated group of private civil rights attorneys, many of whom were connected with the National Association for the Advancement of Colored People, the Legal Defense Fund, the American Civil Liberties Union, the Lawyers' Committee for Civil Rights Under Law, and the Legal Services Corporation. Later, when Hispanics and Asians were placed under the act's special protections, organizations such as the Mexican American Legal Defense and Educational Fund, Texas Rural Legal Aid, the Southwest Voter Registration Education Project, the Asian-American Legal Defense Fund, and the Puerto Rican Legal Defense and Educational Fund played important roles. For a discussion of the "voting rights bar," see Caldeira 1992, 230.

10. See for example Karnig and Welch 1979; Engstrom and McDonald 1981; and Grofman 1980–81.

11. Bullock 1989; O'Rourke 1992; Swain 1989, 1992, and 1993.

12. While there has been theoretical work on the issue of the percentage of minority voters in a district necessary for them to elect their preferred candidates (see especially Brace, Grofman, Handley, and Niemi 1988), the empirical data are very limited (Grofman 1982a and b; Brace, Grofman, Handley, and Niemi 1988; Hedges and Carlucci 1987), and there has never been a comprehensive study of this issue for all city councils in a single state.

13. A partial exception to this is a study by Mundt and Heilig (1982), which tries to determine the causes—classified as either litigation or local referendums—of abandoning at-large elections in southern cities.

We have also been struck by the disagreements in the literature on the effectiveness of the Justice Department's role in implementing the act (especially under Republican presidents), but we will not be discussing that topic here. On the department's role, see Ball, Krane, and Lauth 1982; Days 1992; Days and Guinier 1984; Grofman 1992b; Parker 1989 and 1991; and Turner 1992.

14. For examples, see A. Derfner 1984; Edds 1987; Foster 1985; and Lawson 1976 and 1985.

15. See especially Parker 1990; Stern 1985; and the symposium issue of *Publius* containing essays by Colby 1986; Cotrell and Polinard 1986; Thompson 1986; and Wright 1986.

16. The absence of information on the reason for changes in election type characterizes virtually all of the studies on the impact of at-large elections, including Davidson and Korbel 1981; Engstrom and McDonald 1981, 1982, and 1986; Heilig and Mundt 1983; Karnig 1979; Karnig and Welch 1980 and 1982; Welch 1990; and Zax 1990.

17. Symptomatic of these shortcomings is the work of Thernstrom (1987), whose critique of the act makes almost no use of systematically collected empirical data.

18. Ball, Krane, and Lauth (1982), for example, were more concerned with internal decision making at the Justice Department than with the external long-run consequences of decisions reached.

19. While our research goals were relatively simple, no one else had attempted to achieve them. We believe this is partly because they required an expensive and time-consuming effort to gather and cross-check data. Our research teams first met at a planning conference at Rice University in October 1989. After a thorough discussion of methods and

organizational prerequisites, the conferees dispersed and began their research. A conference was held at Rice University in May 1990, where initial findings were announced to the public. Invited scholars and lawyers criticized the findings, and numerous problems were worked out in subsequent drafts submitted to the editors in 1991. All data chapters were submitted for further criticism in the summer of that year to scholars—primarily historians—not connected with the project. Afterward the data from the state chapters were pooled and analyzed by the editors, with results reported in chap. 10.

20. See Davidson and Korbel 1981, 985–92, for a brief summary of the findings on the Progressive Era reform movement so far as election structures' effects on minority participation are concerned.

21. Grofman and Handley 1989a and 1989b.

22. For example see Lane 1959, 270.

23. See chap. 1.

24. Davidson and Korbel 1981.

25. Grofman 1982b.

26. For example, MacManus (1978) found little evidence that district elections helped minority candidates. Her findings were problematic for two reasons. The data base was virtually identical to one developed at almost the same time by Robinson and Dye (1978), who published opposite conclusions in the same issue of the same journal in which MacManus's article appeared. And, as other scholars soon pointed out, MacManus's methodology in analyzing her data base contained serious flaws. See, for example, Davidson 1979; Engstrom and McDonald 1981, 345, 347; Karnig and Welch 1982, 112–13; Welch 1990, 1052.

27. Conway 1991, 185.

28. Vedlitz and Johnson (1982) is a notable exception. When segregation is taken into account, the difference in black representation between at-large and districted systems is much larger than when not taken into account. Other things being equal, a district remedy for vote dilution will not be effective in cities where the minority population is not segregated. Further, because Hispanics in American cities are typically less residentially segregated than blacks are, district remedies for Hispanics are more difficult to fashion (Zax 1990, 342).

29. Davidson and Korbel 1981, 1001.

30. Among the major cross-sectional studies based on data from the 1970s or early 1980s are Engstrom and McDonald 1981; Karnig and Welch 1982; Robinson and Dye 1978; Vedlitz and Johnson 1982; and Zax 1990.

31. See, for example, Taebel 1978.

32. Thernstrom 1987, 240–44.

33. Welch 1990. In contrast to her findings that suggested a change from the patterns reported in earlier research, however, Welch also found that when she compared minority representation in at-large seats and single-member-district seats in mixed cities—the modal election type in her sample—almost no minorities were elected from at-large seats while many were elected from the district ones. We consider this topic in chap. 10, using data from the state chapters.

34. Welch 1990, 1051.

35. Welch (ibid., 1052) also voices this criticism.

36. Grofman 1982b. Grofman's criticism would apply as well to Polinard, Wrinkle, and Longoria 1991, a more recent longitudinal study of this issue.

37. Heilig and Mundt 1983, 394. While the authors refer to a sample of 209 southern

cities, their published data (table 1, p. 396) are based on numbers that sum to 189. See also Heilig and Mundt 1984, 62–63.

38. Heilig and Mundt 1983, 395.

39. Engstrom and McDonald 1986, 214.

40. See chap. 10 for an extended discussion of the issues surrounding alternative experimental designs.

41. It was necessary to choose different points as the "before" years in some chapters for reasons of data availability. Generally the early point was 1974, but it was 1970 for Alabama, 1973 for North Carolina, 1977 for Virginia, and 1980 for Georgia. The "after" year was 1989 for all states except Georgia, for which it was 1990. However, extensive litigation in Alabama in the late 1980s meant that when the Alabama project used a 1989 cutoff, only five cities in the Alabama data set were still electing at large, and two of these were majority-black cities. Thus the Alabama chapter also discusses data for 1986, when the sample of majority-white at-large cities was larger.

42. The city size threshold was 1,000 in Mississippi; 2,500 in Louisiana; 6,000 in Alabama; and 10,000 in Georgia, Texas, and South Carolina. In North Carolina all incorporated cities were examined, and in Virginia, all cities that were "independent." In the Virginia data base cities as small as 4,480 were included. However, in North Carolina, the only cities to shift from at large were above 10,000 in population. The population data—both city totals and minority percentages—are derived from the 1980 U.S. census.

43. In Texas, the threshold was a combined *black and Hispanic* population of at least 10 percent. However, unpublished tables also report data for Texas cities with a *black* population of at least 10 percent and a small Hispanic population, as well as for Texas cities with a *Hispanic* population of at least 10 percent and a small black population, to control for the presence, in both cases, of the other ethnic minority. In North Carolina it was a combined black and American Indian population of at least 10 percent.

44. Few changes from at-large to district or mixed systems took place in the South before the early 1970s. Indeed, a very high proportion of all changes in election systems have taken place since the 1982 amendments to section 2 of the Voting Rights Act.

45. In general, more esoteric variations in election type are dealt with in footnotes; however, the Georgia chapter has a separate category in its tables for systems that are entirely multimember but not at large, since this is a more common variant there than elsewhere. Also, the North Carolina chapter contains a discussion in the text of the minority success rates in at-large elections with a district residence or nomination requirement as compared to rates in at-large systems without such requirements.

46. This applies to the base-level information on cities and minority officeholders. We were able to achieve high coverage in large part thanks to repeated follow-up telephone calls. However, data at the individual district level for those cities with single-member district or mixed plans are far less complete because this information was simply unavailable.

47. Zax 1990, a cross-sectional study of 1981 data, has two of the largest samples we know of that are used to examine this issue. They comprise 602 cities and 420 cities for his analysis of black and Hispanic officeholding, respectively. The two samples overlap substantially, however.

48. The total sample contains a disproportionately large number of cities from North Carolina, the vast bulk of which continue to elect at large.

49. Included in this data base are not only those cases which directly challenged at-large elections but the small number of cases which indirectly led to such a challenge. An

example would be a suit attacking a jurisdiction's failure to seek preclearance for election changes under section 5, resulting, after a favorable ruling, in a suit challenging at-large elections. Given the large number of law cases—many officially unreported—in this eight-state data base, it should come as no surprise that not all of the information on every case was available. What is surprising, in our view, is that the state chapter authors were able to get as complete a record as they did. Nearly two hundred suits challenging municipal election practices filed over almost twenty-five years constitute this data base; we have complete information for the great majority of them.

50. Equity of representation is simply a measure of proportionality of officeholding (comparing the percentage of minority officeholders to the percentage of the minority population in a given jurisdiction), which is used by the authors in this volume to demonstrate the extent of minority candidates' success under different election schemes. We emphasize that the use of this measure is not meant to imply that either constitutional or statutory voting rights law requires proportional representation of minority population or citizens.

51. For discussion of the properties of each measure (and of alternative approaches) see Grofman 1983.

52. We note at this point that the method of calculating the mean equity scores in tables 4 and 5 of state chapters 2–9 differs from the method in the synoptic chapter 10. The state chapter authors averaged, for all cities within a category, the equity ratio calculated for each city. In chapter 10, we took the ratio of the average black representation of all cities within a category to the average black population of those cities. But these two figures—the average of the ratios and the ratio of the averages—are not the same, although they are usually quite similar. Because state chapters use the average of the ratios, it is impossible to obtain the values in tables 4 and 5 of the state chapters by dividing the average values of black representation and black population in table 2. For this, the raw figures from our data base are required.

53. The raw data, so to speak, on which table 8 is based, are drawn from table Z, described above, which is not published but is archived and is also available from the editors.

54. For an elaboration of our views on this point, see Grofman and Davidson 1992.

55. The outstanding example of this approach is Button 1989, an exhaustive study of black participation in six Florida communities from the 1950s into the 1980s that is testimony to the magnitude of the effort required to address third- and fourth-generation issues in even a small sample of small cities.

56. For similar reasons, we discouraged our authors from focusing on recent political events in their states or speculating about the future of race relations. We did not want readers to be distracted from the findings in this volume by questions that cannot presently be resolved with the available data.

57. It is fortunate that the right to elect candidates of choice is not predicated on the assumption that these candidates, once elected, will be more effective than others, inasmuch as forces entirely beyond their control—white racism in the electorate or on city council, for example, or hard economic times—may diminish their ability to deliver.

58. Karst 1989, 94.

59. McDonald 1981, 3–4. For an account of the remarkable Tom McCain's rise to office in Edgefield County, see Edds 1987, 28–50.

60. The circumstances under which black officeholders can achieve goals that benefit the particular interests of the black community is an especially important issue. It is undoubt-

edly true, for example, that black officeholding sometimes produces few measurable benefits because of white resistance to legitimate black goals. See Guinier 1991b. Also, as previously noted, scarce economic resources in a locale may severely limit the possibility of substantial minority gains.

61. However, we commissioned one study (Fraga 1991) as a pilot study with an eye to developing an appropriate research design for exploring third- and fourth-generation issues.

62. This information can serve as a rich resource for scholars interested in a variety of issues, from very general questions about the role of law as an agent of social change to more specific concerns such as measuring the importance for black representation of various election features in addition to the three basic election types we have focused on—features such as council size, residence requirements (about which only the North Carolina chapter in the current volume reports findings), staggered elections, runoffs, and the like. (The most thorough analysis to date of the impact of some of these special election features in combination with at-large elections is Engstrom and McDonald 1993).

Chapter One
The Recent Evolution of Voting Rights Law Affecting Racial and Language Minorities

1. *Smith v. Allwright*, 321 U.S. 649.

2. While not a history of minority voting rights per se, Dixon (1968) continues to command the attention of students of voting rights as they relate to democratic representation. A. Derfner's influential article (1973) provides a basic framework for understanding the evolution of modern voting rights law and the racial problems in the South giving rise to this evolution. McDonald (1989) presents a useful update of the story told by Derfner. Issacharoff (1992) provides a particularly insightful analysis of the evolution of the legal concept of vote dilution from the 1960s to the present. The definitive history of black disfranchisement is told by Kousser (1974), while the leading histories of the twentieth-century movement for black suffrage are by Lawson (1976 and 1985).

3. The Fifteenth Amendment in full reads as follows:

> Section 1. The right of citizens of the United States to vote shall not be denied or abridged by the United States or by any State on account of race, color, or previous condition of servitude.
> Section 2. The Congress shall have power to enforce this article by appropriate legislation.

4. Kousser 1984b, 32–33.

5. This conceptualization of vote dilution has recently been challenged by Guinier 1991a, 1494. While she believes that a definition such as the one I have given underlies federal courts' recent vote dilution decisions, she argues for a more expansive definition—one in which not simply a group's ability to elect its candidates of choice is diminished, but also its ability to secure its interests through legislative policy.

6. McDonald 1982, 46–50; and McDonald 1983, 71–73. See also McDonald 1986, 575.

7. In 1962 a member of the Alabama State Democratic Executive Committee informed his white colleagues as follows: "We have got a situation in Alabama that we are becoming more painfully aware of every passing day, that we have a concerted desire and a campaign to register Negroes en masse. . . . It has occurred to a great many people, including the legislature of Alabama, that to protect the white people of Alabama, that there should be numbered place laws." *Dillard v. Crenshaw County*, 640 F. Supp. 1347, 1357 (1986).

8. See n. 4 above. See also chap. 3 below on the use of some of these devices in Georgia in the 1870s.

9. That these considerations are just as crucial in small southern jurisdictions as in large metropolitan centers is brought home forcefully in Edds's (1987) depiction of the ongoing black struggle for elective office in many southern jurisdictions, large and small.

10. See n. 4 above. On nineteenth-century vote dilution in South Carolina, Texas, and Virginia, see chaps. 7, 8, and 9 below.

11. Rosenberg 1991, 81. Accounts of contemporary dilutionary practices in particular are contained in U.S. Commission on Civil Rights 1968 (chaps. 4–5) and 1975; A. Derfner 1973, 557–58; and Washington Research Project 1972, chaps. 2, 4. See also Parker 1990, 51–55, for an account of what was perhaps the most massive and systematic attempt by a state—Mississippi—to change election laws in the 1960s for dilutionary purposes. Ladd (1966, 103) notes the widespread adoption of at-large elections in the face of a growing black vote. See also Hamilton 1967, 321–25.

12. For other examples of dilutive election practices adopted after World War II see the various state chapters below.

13. Chap. 2 below. See also Norrell 1985, chap. 6, for an account of the efforts of Alabama state senator Samuel Engelhardt, Jr.—the father of the famous Tuskegee gerrymander—in the years following World War II to prod the legislature to pass dilutionary laws.

14. 364 U.S. 339.

15. 364 U.S. 339, 346.

16. 307 U.S. 268, 275.

17. 364 U.S. 339, 342.

18. Chap. 2 below.

19. 257 F. Supp. 901 (M.D. Ala. 1966).

20. Moon 1949, 188; Ladd 1966, 102–3.

21. Chap. 6 below.

22. Chap. 6 below.

23. Chap. 7 below.

24. Chap. 3 below.

25. Chap. 3 below.

26. Chap. 4 below.

27. Young 1965, 21–22.

28. Davidson 1972, 55–67; Davidson 1990, 54–55.

29. Chap. 5 below.

30. Chap. 9 below.

31. Not all or even most of the at-large systems in the South, of course, were created in recent decades. Many such systems are holdovers from the Progressive Era, although they were often created during that era or earlier to dilute the votes of blacks, working-class whites, and political minorities. See n. 67 below.

32. For accounts of post-1960s efforts at dilution at both the local and legislative levels, see the state chapters in this volume.

33. 369 U.S. 186.

34. 377 U.S. 533.

35. For a detailed account of the political and legal aspects of *Reynolds*, see Blacksher and Menefee 1982.

36. 379 U.S. 433.

37. 379 U.S. 433, 439.

38. The first at-large minority vote dilution suit was filed in 1966. See chap. 2 below.

39. 412 U.S. 755 (1973).

40. 412 U.S. 755, 769, 766.

41. Blacksher and Menefee 1982, 22–23.

42. 485 F.2d 1297 (5th Cir. 1973).

43. 485 F.2d 1297, 1305.

44. 485 F.2d 1297, 1305.

45. The federal courts' gradual development, with help from plaintiffs' lawyers and experts, of the concept of minority vote dilution in the 1970s provided guidance to Justice Department lawyers faced with enforcement of the Voting Rights Act, particularly section 5. To this extent, constitutional law was influencing the Justice Department's thinking about what constituted illegal vote dilution. Below, I suggest that the Voting Rights Act, as interpreted by the Supreme Court in a 1969 ruling, had a profound impact on the Court's thinking about vote dilution as a constitutional issue in the 1970s. It is in light of this mutual influence that I have characterized constitutional voting rights law and the Voting Rights Act as having a synergistic relation.

46. 446 U.S. 55 (1980).

47. McDonald 1992, 70; Larry Menefee, plaintiffs' lawyer, interviewed by the author, 4 February 1992.

48. Garrow 1978, 6–7.

49. Congressional Quarterly Service 1968, 115.

50. The Civil Rights Commission, commenting on the failure of the Civil Rights Acts of 1957 and 1960 in this regard, "cited the efforts in 100 counties in eight states where, despite the filing of thirty-six voting rights suits by the Department of Justice, registration increased a measly 3.3 percent between 1956 and 1963, from approximately 5 percent to 8.3 percent" (Rosenberg 1991, 62).

51. See Garrow 1986, chap. 7, for a vivid account of the Selma campaign. See also Matusow 1984, 180–88.

52. Section 203, which mandates language assistance in certain language-minority jurisdictions, was added to the statute in 1975, later extended to 1992, and then again extended to 2007.

The act as originally passed is Public Law 89–110, 89th Congress, S. 1564, August 6, 1965. Subsequent amendments are as follows: Public Law 91–285, 91st Congress, H.R. 4249, June 22, 1970; Public Law 94–73, 94th Congress, H.R. 6219, August 6, 1975; and Public Law 97–205, 97th Congress, H.R. 3112, August 5, 1982.

53. Section 2 as amended and section 5 are discussed below.

54. In addition to the inclusion of certain language minorities under the protection of section 4(f)(4) (and hence section 5), the 1975 amendments—extended in 1992 to 2007—provide protections also to language minorities under a somewhat different trigger formula in section 203(c). This does not bring the jurisdictions covered by it under section 5, but, like section 4(f)(4), it requires the provision of bilingual election materials to the language minorities.

55. Today, states in which all elections are covered by section 5 are Alabama, Alaska, Arizona, Louisiana, Georgia, Mississippi, South Carolina, Texas, and Virginia. States whose elections are covered only in certain counties are California, Florida, Michigan, New Hampshire, New York, North Carolina, and South Dakota.

56. Congress substantially amended the act during periodic extensions of its special provisions. In 1970, for example, it suspended for five years the use of literacy tests as election requirements in all fifty states, and in 1975 it abolished them permanently. The "bailout" provisions, by which jurisdictions could remove themselves from coverage of sections 4 and 5, were changed over the years, most extensively in 1982. In addition to expanding section 5 coverage in 1975 to include other states through the language minority provisions, the act gave private parties the right, which the Justice Department already had, to sue in order to impose on jurisdictions preclearance and federal examiner remedies. It also enabled private attorneys who prevailed in voting suits to receive expenses and reasonable fees for their efforts. (See chap. 2 in this volume. See also M. F. Derfner 1977, 447 n. 36.) Finally, as explained below, one of the most significant amendments was made in 1982, changing section 2, a permanent feature of the act applying nationwide.

57. 383 U.S. 301.

58. 393 U.S. 544 (1969).

59. Parker 1990, 51–55 (quotation on 54).

60. 393 U.S. 544, 565–66.

61. U.S. Department of Justice, 1990.

62. I owe this insight, conveyed in a personal communication, to Samuel Issacharoff.

63. 478 U.S. 30 (1986).

64. 425 U.S. 130 (1976).

65. For an analysis of section 5 and its enforcement, see Days 1992.

66. Blacksher and Menefee 1982, 26.

67. Hays 1964, 162–63; Holli 1974, 137; B. Rice 1977, 29; Weinstein 1962, 173.

68. For two sharply contrasting accounts of the events leading to the amendment, see A. Derfner 1984 and Thernstrom 1987, chaps. 5–6.

69. 42 U.S.C. 1973.

70. 458 U.S. 613 (1982).

71. Blacksher and Menefee 1982, 39, 50–64.

72. 478 U.S. 30, 50, 51.

73. The largeness and compactness tests, as Karlan has explained (1989, 199–213), mean that if a minority group in a jurisdiction is not large or compact enough to constitute a majority of voters in at least one single-member district, it is not entitled to relief. The degree of both compactness and size, however, appears to be a function of the number of council seats under the challenged plan. Thus, for example, a four-member city council might escape a successful dilution challenge while a six-member council with the same demographic makeup and history of white bloc voting might not.

74. Chap. 8 below.

75. The act has been employed to combat other forms of voting discrimination as well, such as the refusal to hire black poll workers, and the practice of abolishing offices or decreasing their number in order to minimize minority officeholding.

Chapter Two
Alabama

In addition to the financial support of the National Science Foundation of this and the other projects in this volume, our research has drawn on earlier grants to McCrary from the Rockefeller Foundation, the Carnegie Corporation of New York, the University of South

Alabama Research Council, the John D. and Catherine T. MacArthur Foundation, and the Joint Center for Political and Economic Studies. Dianne Thompson, Paola Maranon, and Deborah Huntley, and Justin McCrary provided valuable research assistance.

The views expressed herein are those of the authors and do not necessarily reflect the views of any of the institutions with which they are affiliated, including the U.S. Department of Justice.

1. Garrow 1986, 397–400; Fager 1985.

2. Garrow 1978, 81–82; Garrow 1986, 400–409.

3. See *United States v. Alabama*, 192 F. Supp. 677 (M.D. Ala. 1961), *aff'd* 304 F.2d 583 (5th Cir. 1962), *aff'd* 371 U.S. 37 (1962) [Macon County]; *United States v. Alabama*, 7 Race Rel. L. Rep. 1146 (M.D. Ala. 1962) [Bullock County]; *United States v. Penton*, 212 F. Supp. 193 (M.D. Ala. 1962) [Montgomery County]; *United States v. Atkins*, 323 F.2d 733 (5th Cir. 1963) [Dallas County]; and *United States v. Logue*, 344 F.2d 290 (5th Cir. 1965) [Wilcox County].

4. Pub. L. 88–352, 78 Stat. 241 [42 U.S.C 1971(a) (2,3), (f), (h)]. Even so, a constitutional amendment ratified by the voters in 1965 would have required applicants to demonstrate their ability to read and write English: Alabama Department of Archives and History 1967, 687–88, 707–9.

5. *United States v. Hines*, 9 Race Rel. L. Rep. 1332 (N.D. Ala. 1964) [Sumter County]; *United States v. Cartwright*, 230 F. Supp. 873 (M.D. Ala. 1964) [Elmore County]; and *United States v. Parker*, 236 F. Supp. 511 (M.D. 1964) [Montgomery County].

6. Pub. L. 89-110, 79 Stat. 437 [42 U.S.C. 1971, 1973].

7. Scher and Button 1984. In Alabama the U.S. Attorney General appointed federal examiners in twelve of the counties with the worst registration rates: Autauga, Dallas, Elmore, Greene, Hale, Jefferson, Lowndes, Marengo, Montgomery, Perry, Sumter, and Wilcox. U.S. Commission on Civil Rights 1968, 224–27.

8. In *Reynolds v. Katzenbach*, 248 F. Supp. 593 (S.D. Ala. 1965), a three-judge panel headed by Elbert Tuttle, chief judge of the Fifth Circuit Court of Appeals, enjoined registrars in Dallas, Hale, Lowndes, Marengo, Perry, and Wilcox counties from complying with state court orders. State circuit judges in these counties had placed the registrars in an impossible situation by ordering them not to place federally registered voters on the rolls. In *United States v. Bruce*, 353 F.2d 474 (5th Cir. 1965), the court reversed a lower court ruling that had allowed landowners in Wilcox County to keep voter registration activists off their plantations.

9. In *United States v. Alabama*, 252 F. Supp. 95 (M.D. Ala. 1966), the court found that the purpose and effect of the poll tax requirement was to disfranchise black voters.

10. U.S. Commission on Civil Rights 1968, 224–27.

11. Stanley 1987, 50–52, 54–55; Bass and DeVries 1976, 65; Peirce 1974, 255–56.

12. Black and Black 1987, 138–40; Stanley 1987, 5–7, 50–52; U.S. Commission on Civil Rights 1968, 222–23.

13. U.S. Commission on Civil Rights 1968, 214, 222–23. As in the past, Macon County, 84 percent black in 1960, led the way: one black was elected to the five-person Tuskegee city council for the first time in 1964; one of five county commissioners was black, as well as one member of the school board, and two justices of the peace: Norrell 1985, 164–67. In *Sims v. Baggett*, 247 F. Supp. 96 (M.D. Ala. 1965), a three-judge panel ordered a new districting plan into effect that linked Macon, Bullock, and Barbour counties in one house district. The two black candidates failed to win election in 1966, however, due to an

overwhelming white voter turnout. Not until 1970 were the first two representatives elected to the state house, one of whom was Fred Gray, the lawyer who had brought many of the early Alabama voting rights cases. Norrell 1985, 190–91, 200, 234; Joint Center for Political Studies 1971, 1–6.

14. Lane 1959, 270; Banfield and Wilson 1963, 87–96, 307–9; Matthews and Prothro 1966, 4–5, 143–44, 208, 220–21; Ladd 1966, 29–30, 102–3, 307. For early recognition of the legal implications of racial vote dilution, see Jewell 1964 and 1968; and Dixon 1968, 459–62.

15. *Ala. Acts* (1965), no. 10 (2 June 1965), 31.

16. *Clayton Record*, 25 March 1965, 1.

17. Key 1949, 636, 648; Matthews and Prothro 1966, 224–29; Watters and Cleghorn 1967, 79–81. A contemporary example comes from Choctaw County, Alabama, where proponents of at-large elections said that "they advocate the change because of the increasing number of Negro voters that have been qualified in recent weeks," according to the local paper. "They maintain that by electing the commissioners on an at-large basis the threat of an effective Negro bloc vote will be eliminated." *Choctaw Advocate*, 18 November 1965, 1.

18. In 1978, however, the Department of Justice filed a lawsuit challenging the 1965 change: *United States v. Barbour County Commission*, C.A. No. 78–348-N (M.D. Ala.). The county quickly agreed to return to a system of single-member district elections and settled the case.

19. 257 F. Supp. 901 (M.D. Ala. 1966), *aff'd*, 386 F.2d 979 (5th Cir. 1967). In the fall of 1965, it is true, a three-judge court in the state legislative reapportionment case found that in drawing the 1965 house districting plan, "the legislature intentionally aggregated predominantly Negro counties [Bullock and Macon] with predominantly white counties [Elmore and Tallapoosa] for the sole purpose of preventing the election of Negroes to House membership." *Sims v. Baggett*, 247 F. Supp. 96, 109 (M.D. Ala. 1965). At first blush, this might appear to be the first racial vote-dilution case. *Sims*, then on remand from the Supreme Court (*Reynolds v. Sims*, 377 U.S. 533 (1964)), was essentially, however, a one-person, one-vote case.

20. 257 F. Supp. 901 (M.D. Ala. 1966). For a detailed account of the litigation see McCrary 1988, 9–14.

21. 257 F. Supp. 903; McCrary 1988, 9–10.

22. 257 F. Supp. 903. The defendants stipulated to the accuracy of all the facts in the case (McCrary 1988, 10).

23. 257 F. Supp. 904–5.

24. McCrary 1988, 11.

25. Yarbrough 1981, 62–72. According to Clayton, the purpose of the at-large election resolution was to comply with the one-person, one-vote principle set forth by the Supreme Court. The court dismissed this claim as "nothing more than a sham," noting that the defendants retained the malapportioned districts as residency requirements for candidates, rather than choosing "to adjust the population disparities between the beats [districts] themselves" while preserving the traditional single-member districts. 257 F. Supp. 905.

26. 257 F. Supp. 904, quoting the legislative reapportionment decision in which he concurred, *Sims v. Baggett*, 247 F. Supp. 96 (M.D. Ala. 1965).

27. 257 F. Supp. 905. Judge Johnson declined to order new elections, however.

28. *Smith v. Paris*, 386 F.2d 979 (5th Cir. 1967).

29. *Eufaula Tribune*, 20 February 1968; *Clayton Record*, 22 February 1968. At the same

meeting the committee endorsed segregationist George Wallace as a favorite son in the 1968 presidential campaign, although he was running as an independent against the Democratic ticket.

30. *Eufaula Tribune*, 2 May 1968. "Federal intervention" was commonly understood as a reference to federal enforcement of civil rights laws in the South.

31. Quoted in McCrary 1988, 11.

32. Ibid. In an earlier case, however, private plaintiffs raised a section 5 claim in successfully challenging an Alabama statute extending the terms of the Bullock County commission by two years. *Sellers v. Trussell*, 253 F. Supp. 915 (M.D. Ala. 1966). Clearly involving a "practice or procedure with respect to voting," and thus covered by the pre-clearance requirement, *Sellers* was nevertheless not a vote-dilution case. The three-judge court saw the change as involving the right to vote, and found it unconstitutional as racially discriminatory in effect: "Act No. 536 freezes into office for an additional two years persons who were elected when Negroes were being illegally deprived of the right to vote. Under such circumstances, to freeze elective officials into office is, in effect, to freeze Negroes out of the electorate. That is forbidden by the Fifteenth Amendment." 253 F. Supp. 917.

33. *United States v. Democratic Executive Committee of Barbour County, Alabama*, 288 F. Supp. 943, 945, 946 (M.D. Ala. 1968). Judge Johnson ignored the Justice Department's section 5 claim.

34. *Eufaula Tribune*, 28 November 1968.

35. McMillan 1955, 110–13, 124–33, 151–56, 169–74.

36. Wiggins 1977. Scalawags sought to minimize the nomination of black candidates because the Democrats cried "Negro domination" every time a black was elected to office. Many also shared the general white prejudice against having blacks in decision-making roles. More dependent on black votes than were scalawags, carpetbaggers were necessarily more willing than native white Republicans to nominate blacks to state and local office.

37. Blacks won seats from black-majority wards in Montgomery, but most of the Republican council members were native whites. Rabinowitz 1978, 265, 273–74. No blacks ever won election to the city council in Mobile, although the governor or state legislature appointed several in 1868 and 1869. The city's delegation to the 1867 constitutional convention included several black delegates and white radical Republicans, but conservative whites dominated the city's Republican party thereafter. In 1870 the Democrats regained control of the city government. McCrary 1984, 50–52.

38. *Alabama State Journal*, 4 December 1869. The next year the legislature eliminated the ward election system for electing Mobile aldermen. McCrary 1984, 52.

39. Trelease 1971, 81–88, 246–73, 302–10.

40. Wiggins 1980, 60–66; Rable 1984, 114–18.

41. McMillan 1955, 175. White opposition in north Alabama to tax increases under the Republicans also contributed to the Democratic victory. See Thornton 1982.

42. Kousser 1984b, 31–36; McMillan 1955, 217.

43. *Ala. Acts* (1874–75), no. 18 (3 March 1875), sec. 39, p. 85.

44. *Montgomery Advertiser and Mail*, 3 March 1875.

45. *Montgomery Advertiser and Mail*, 5 March 1875. As late as the 1970s this provision was used to prosecute two black civil rights activists in Pickens County, Alabama: see *State of Alabama v. Julia P. Wilder*, No. CC-78–108 (29–31 May 1979), and *State of Alabama v. Maggie S. Bozeman*, No. CC-78–109 (1–2 November 1979), *aff'd* 401 So. 2d 167 (Supreme Court of Alabama 1981). Using the evidence of racial purpose in the law's adoption, however, black attorney Lani Guinier of the NAACP Legal Defense and Educational Fund

was able to have the convictions of the two women overturned and their voting rights restored.

46. Rabinowitz 1978, 273–75; Kousser 1984b, 35.

47. McCrary 1984, 58. The adoption of at-large elections for the county school board in 1876 was found to be racially motivated, and thus unconstitutional, in *Brown and United States v. Board of School Commissioners of Mobile County*, 542 F. Supp. 1078 (S.D. Ala. 1982), *aff'd* 706 F.2d 1103 (11th Cir. 1983), *aff'd* 464 U.S. 1005 (1983).

48. McCrary and Hebert 1989, 119.

49. McMillan 1955, 222.

50. *Selma Southern Argus*, 13 November, 11 December 1874; McMillan 1955, 218.

51. McMillan 1955, 218–25; Kousser 1974, 130–32. See, for example, the following comment from the *Selma Times*, 6 December 1895: "The Times is one of those papers that does not believe it is any harm to rob or appropriate the vote of an illiterate Negro."

52. McMillan 1955, 223–24; Kousser 1974, 132–36. The racially discriminatory purpose and effect of the Sayre Law was first noted in the findings of a vote-dilution lawsuit in *Bolden v. City of Mobile*, 542 F. Supp. 1050, 1062 (S.D. Ala. 1982), where the court relied on the testimony of Professor J. Morgan Kousser. The last remnants of the Sayre Law were eliminated from Alabama's electoral procedures by *Harris v. Siegelman*, 695 F. Supp. 517 (M.D. Ala. 1988).

53. *Birmingham Age-Herald*, 25 December 1892, quoted in Kousser 1974, 134.

54. Kousser 1974, 137–38.

55. Woodward 1974, 69–74; McMillan 1955, 230–31.

56. Anyone who failed the literacy test could still qualify if he possessed at least three hundred dollars worth of property or forty acres of land. For a brief period anyone whose ancestor fought in the Civil War could also register under a "grandfather" clause. McMillan 1955, 280–81, 305–6.

57. Most of the crimes were drawn from a list suggested by John F. Burns, a black-belt planter whose years as a justice of the peace had taught him, he claimed, that blacks were prone to larceny, bigamy, seduction, incest, rape, burglary, vagrancy, wife beating, and forgery. McMillan 1955, 275. Many decades later, this "petty-crimes" provision was struck down by a unanimous Supreme Court decision (written by Justice William Rehnquist), *Hunter v. Underwood*, 471 U.S. 222 (1985).

58. McMillan 1955, 352–53; Kousser 1974, 241–42.

59. Woodward 1974, 84. Pursuant to the state's white primary law, the State Democratic Executive Committee (SDEC) limited the right to vote in the party primary to white males: Minutes, 10 July 1902, bk. 5, p. 67, SDEC Papers, Alabama Department of Archives and History.

60. *Giles v. Harris*, 189 U.S. 475 (1903); Kousser 1984b, 41. In 1909 Frederick Bromberg, who was twice president of the state bar association and publisher of a daily newspaper in Mobile, advocated throughout Alabama an amendment to the state constitution prohibiting blacks from holding office, which he thought would not violate the Fifteenth Amendment. He predicted, however, that the U.S. Supreme Court would soon "overturn the present methods of applying the registration laws." Of the 1901 disfranchising clauses he remarked: "We have always, as you know, falsely pretended that our main purpose was to exclude the ignorant voter, when, in fact, we were trying to exclude, not the ignorant vote, but the negro vote." McCrary 1984, 54–56.

61. McCrary and Hebert 1989, 110, 119.

62. *Ala. Acts*, (1907) no. 797 (15 August 1907).

63. From 1872 through 1906 the city's Democrats had used a ward system for primary elections, from which blacks were largely excluded. The general election, in which black Republicans voted, had always been conducted on an at-large basis. McCrary 1984, 53–54.

64. Ibid., 54–56. In *Bolden v. City of Mobile*, 542 F. Supp. 1050 (S.D. Ala. 1982), Judge Virgil Pitman found, based in part on this historical evidence of racial purpose, that the adoption of at-large elections in 1911 was racially motivated, and thus unconstitutional.

65. 321 U.S. 649 (1944).

66. *Davis v. Schnell*, 81 F. Supp. 872 (S.D. Ala. 1949), *aff'd* 336 U.S. 933 (1949); Lawson 1976, 89–96. Another lawsuit challenging discriminatory practices by registrars in Macon County, *Mitchell v. Wright*, C.A. No. 102 (M.D. Ala. 1945), was terminated after three years of delays, when the registrars announced that their records now revealed the plaintiff had, in fact, registered successfully, Norrell 1985, 60–68, 222–23.

67. Lawson 1976, 96–97, 376; Norrell 1985, 82–83. The amendment placed the state supreme court in the position of abetting voter discrimination by designing a four-page questionnaire requiring applicants to write their names correctly in ten separate places, explain their employment background in three places, and answer two questions about length of residence. See U.S. Commission on Civil Rights 1959, 17–20. A series of lawsuits brought by the Department of Justice in the early 1960s challenged the discriminatory implementation of this and other state laws by local voter registrars. See Garrow 1978, 15–17, 26–27, 243, 249; and see nn. 3 and 5 above.

68. Norrell 1985, 79–80. Engelhardt was scion of an old planter family that owned thousands of acres of rich land, a cotton gin business, and a country store; he saw his class interests as well as racial pride threatened by black political power. "The niggers were just about to take us over," Engelhardt recalled, adding that "because of all our [land]holdings," he was concerned about the tax assessor blacks might elect.

69. Norrell 1985, 91–92, 101.

70. 167 F. Supp. 405 (M.D. Ala. 1958), *aff'd* 270 F.2d 594 (5th Cir. 1959), *rev'd and remanded* 364 U.S. 339 (1960).

71. 167 F. Supp. 405; Yarbrough 1981, 73–74.

72. 364 U.S. 342. "For Frankfurter," notes one legal scholar, the legislation's "obvious racial purpose and effect distinguished the constitutional claims raised in *Gomillion* from those at issue in malapportionment cases." Yarbrough 1981, 75. See also C. Hamilton 1973, 193. In debating the adoption of the Voting Rights Act in 1965, the house relied on the factual circumstances in *Gomillion* as an example of the discriminatory election practices the statute was designed to regulate. Karlan and McCrary 1988, 756.

73. *Ala. Acts* (1951), 1043, no. 606 (4 September 1951), applied to all municipal elections in the state. For an explanation of single-shot voting, see U.S. Commission on Civil Rights 1975, 207.

74. *Mobile Register*, 29 August 1951, 4; *Selma Times-Journal*, 29 August 1951, 2. The quoted legislator was Senator J. Miller Bonner, Engelhardt's father-in-law. Norrell 1985, 82.

75. *Ala. Acts* (1961), 670, no. 221 (29 August 1961). The new statute explicitly repealed Engelhardt's 1951 act.

76. Butler (1982, 864–67) discusses the full-slate and numbered-place requirements. An early court decision striking down these provisions in the North Carolina code is *Dunston v. Scott*, 336 F. Supp. 206 (E.D.N.C. 1972). Young 1965 is a pioneering study of place voting.

77. McCrary and Hebert 1989, 120–21. Based largely on historical evidence concerning

the 1951 anti-single-shot law and the 1961 numbered-place statute, which exemplified a state policy of using at-large elections to dilute black voting strength, Judge Myron Thompson enjoined further use of at-large elections for nine county commissions in Alabama. *Dillard v. Crenshaw County*, 640 F. Supp. 1347 (M.D. Ala. 1986).

78. See, for example, *United States v. Executive Committee of Democratic Party of Dallas County, Alabama*, 254 F. Supp. 537 (S.D. Ala. 1966). The first eleven section 5 objections to changes in election practices in Alabama dealt with such matters as candidate qualification deadlines, requirements for signing poll lists, and absentee registration requirements.

79. *Allen v. State Board of Elections*, 393 U.S. 544 (1969). Alternatively, the jurisdiction can seek preclearance by a three-judge court in the District of Columbia. Under section 5 the burden shifts to the jurisdiction to demonstrate that neither the purpose nor the effect of the change is racially discriminatory.

80. Days and Guinier 1984.

81. Editorial, *Birmingham News*, 29 May 1969.

82. See the objection letters regarding Alabaster, 7 July 1975 and 27 December 1977; Bay Minette, 6 October 1986; and Alexander City, 1 Dec. 1986. All objections by the Attorney General are described in U.S. Department of Justice, Civil Rights Division, "Complete Listing of Objections Pursuant to Section 5 of the Voting Rights Act of 1965," which is routinely updated. Photocopies of objection letters and microfiche copies of the public—though not internal—files for all section 5 submissions can be obtained from the Voting Section of the Civil Rights Division merely by identifying the date of action.

83. The Department of Justice objected to the adoption of staggered terms on 12 December 1975, and precleared the new mixed plan on 9 May 1977. Newspaper coverage makes clear that the racial effects of at-large elections were well understood, and that the Department of Justice was aware of the black community's efforts to secure single-member districts. See *Columbus Ledger*, 11 September 1975, 1B; 19 September 1975, 1B; 21 September 1975, 1A; 24 September 1975, 4A; 12 October 1975, 1B; 14 October 1975, 1A.

84. Joint Center for Political Studies 1979, 7.

85. *Dillard v. Crenshaw County*, C.A. No. 85-T-1332-N (M.D. Ala. 1986), Plaintiffs' Exhibit No. 187.

86. The counties, with the date of the objection letters in parenthesis, are as follows: Autauga (20 March 1972); Pike (12 August 1974); Chambers (8 March 1976); Hale (23 April 1976, 29 December 1976); Barbour (28 July 1978); Clarke (26 February 1979); Conecuh (14 September 1981); Butler (19 July 1982); Tallapoosa (10 May 1983); Monroe (17 February 1984); Houston (15 October 1985). The objections for Autauga and Chambers included the county school boards as well. The Attorney General also objected to the at-large election of school board members in Pickens County (5 March 1976).

87. *Sims v. Amos*, 336 F. Supp. 924, 935–36 (M.D. Ala. 1972), *aff'd* 409 U.S. 942 (1972). The racial vote-dilution claim was first raised by Morris Dees and Joseph Levin, white lawyers who founded the Southern Poverty Law Center, and their black cocounsels Peter Hall and Orzell Billingsley, Jr., in *Nixon v. Brewer*, 49 F.R.D. 122 (M.D. Ala. 1970). *Nixon* was consolidated with *Sims*, a one-person, one-vote case originating in the landmark reapportionment case *Reynolds v. Sims*, 377 U.S. 533 (1964). The court's decision in *Sims v. Amos* emphasized the one-person, one-vote claim (i.e., *quantitative*, rather than *racial*, vote dilution). David Vann, a white lawyer in Birmingham, and Charles Morgan, Jr., then head of the southern regional office of the ACLU, were attorneys of record throughout the litigation.

88. *Alabama Journal*, 4 January 1972, 1, 4; *Birmingham News*, 4 January 1972, 1A, 4A; *Mobile Register*, 5 January 1972, 3B; *Montgomery Advertiser*, 5 January 1972, 1A; *Selma Times-Journal*, 5 January 1972, 1A, 2A.

89. U.S. Commission on Civil Rights 1975, 241.

90. *Selma Times-Journal*, 25 January 1972, 1A, 2A. See also 28 January 1972, 1A, 2A; and 7 February 1972, 1A, 2A. A local black attorney threatened to file a vote-dilution lawsuit if the council retained at-large elections. See Chestnut and Cass 1990, 259–61. One council member who lived in a black-majority district proposed to increase the number of at-large seats to four, so that the white minority in his district could have an opportunity to elect a ward representative of its choice. The municipal election code provided no such option, however; the legislature would have to enact a new statute, and this would have meant postponing city elections. In *Talton v. City of Selma*, C.A. No. 80–0271-H (S.D. Ala. 1980), whites challenged the existing districts as malapportioned; the court ordered a properly apportioned interim plan with ten single-member districts, which resulted in the election of five blacks and five whites (with a council president and the mayor elected at large). In 1988, however, legislation sponsored by black state senator Hank Sanders, with the agreement of the white-majority city council, established a new mixed plan with eight single-member districts and a council president. The Department of Justice precleared the new plan on 27 June 1988.

91. This change is described in a letter from the city's attorney, Knox McMillan, to David Norman, 6 July 1972, Public File, Auburn (Lee County), Alabama, Submission V4620, Department of Justice, Civil Rights Division, Voting Section. The Attorney General precleared the change on 21 July 1972.

92. Heilig and Mundt 1984, 114. In the referendum "heavy votes in favor were recorded in the highest-income white precincts, with more moderate support in black precincts. Low-income white precincts showed the heaviest opposition." Ibid., 41–42.

93. *Montgomery Advertiser*, 6 July 1973, 1A; see additionally 3 July 1973, 11A. In contrast to the mayor and the senate delegation, house members favored electing council members at large, although with a district *residency* requirement. Ibid., 6 May 1973, 12A. See additionally, 26 May 1973, 11A; 5 June 1973, 1A, 2A; 10 June 1973, 8A; 13 June 1973, 1B; 5 July 1973, 13A; 13 July 1973, 2A; 17 July 1973, 1A; 2 August 1973, 17A; 31 August 1973, 1A. Voters supported the change in a referendum, and four of the nine council members elected in 1975 were black. *Alabama Journal*, 17 September 1975. In 1983, a more conservative city council approved a redistricting plan that purposely reduced minority voting strength; the plan was successfully challenged in *Buskey v. Oliver*, 565 F. Supp. 1473 (M.D. Ala. 1983). Black attorney Solomon Seay represented the plaintiff class, and black council member Donald V. Watkins, also an attorney, represented himself.

94. 412 U.S. 755 (1973).

95. 485 F.2d 1297 (5th Cir. 1973) (en banc), *aff'd sub nom. East Carroll Parish School Board v. Marshall*, 424 U.S. 636 (1976).

96. James U. Blacksher and Larry Menefee in Mobile and Edward Still of Birmingham were cooperating attorneys of the NAACP Legal Defense and Educational Fund (LDF). Still also handled cases in conjunction with the Southern Regional Office of the ACLU. Pamela S. Horowitz, Howard Mandell, Stephen J. Ellman, and Ira A. Burnim, northern-born whites employed by the Southern Poverty Law Center, handled a few vote-dilution cases, although their principal focus was on other areas of civil rights law. Barry Goldstein and Pamela Karlan, northern-born white staff attorneys of LDF, also litigated Alabama cases. Black attorneys involved in voting rights litigation after 1973 include Lani Guinier of LDF, J. L. Chestnut, Hank Sanders, and Rose Sanders of Selma; Solomon Seay, Donald V.

Watkins, and Terry Davis of Montgomery; Demetrius Newton of Birmingham; and Joe Lampley of Huntsville. On the importance of funding provided by public-interest organizations such as LDF and the ACLU, see Caldeira 1992.

97. J. Gerald Hebert handled the largest volume of Alabama dilution cases, but Paul Hancock, Sheila Delaney, S. Michael Scadron, John Tanner, Ellen Weber, Robert Berman, Poli Marmolejos, and Christopher Lehman also litigated Alabama cases. Tanner is a native Alabamian; Marmolejos is the only black lawyer in the group.

98. 340 F. Supp. 691, 694 (M.D. Ala. 1972). "If, pursuant to this action, plaintiffs have benefitted their class and effectuated a strong congressional policy, they are entitled to attorneys' fees regardless of defendants' good or bad faith," said the court. Indeed, the award of attorneys' fees "becomes a part of the effective remedy a court should fashion to encourage public-minded suits, and to carry out congressional policy."

99. *Alyeska Pipeline Service Co. v. Wilderness Society*, 421 U.S. 240 (1975).

100. Pub. L. No. 94–73, 89 Stat. 402 [42 U.S.C., 19731(e)]; U.S. Commission on Civil Rights 1981, 11, 45. Congress also enacted a general statute covering all civil rights issues, Pub. L. 94–559, which reinforces the principle that "private attorneys general" benefit the public good and thus should be appropriately compensated for their efforts. M. F. Derfner 1977.

101. Lawson 1985, 106–10, 117, 200–201; Bass and DeVries 1976, 76–78; Peirce 1974, 300–301; Strong 1972, 469–70. The National Democratic Party of Alabama (NDPA), nominally led by Dr. John Cashin of Huntsville, was successful in electing a majority of officeholders in Green County, 83 percent black, and had some strength in a few other black-belt counties. Its separatist outlook made sense in such areas, where cooperation with the local party was an impossibility. After 1972, however, the strength of the NDPA declined dramatically as the ADC demonstrated the advantages of its position as a black caucus within the Democratic party.

102. The ADC files have, in fact, been a principal source of data for this study. In 1986 dissident members of the ADC, many of whom were angry at the organization's endorsement of Walter Mondale rather than Jesse Jackson during the 1984 Democratic presidential primary, formed the New South Coalition. No longer a caucus within the Democratic party, it was technically bipartisan and biracial. See Chestnut and Cass 1990, 401–2. Other than the Huntsville and Madison county cases, however, the New South Coalition was not very active in voting rights litigation.

103. See the objection letters for the Pickens County Democratic Executive Committee (18 February 1976), and for the Pickens County Board of Education (5 March 1976).

104. *Corder v. Kirksey*, 585 F.2d 708 (5th Cir. 1978).

105. *Nevett v. Sides*, 533 F.2d 1361 (5th Cir. 1976).

106. 571 F.2d 209 (5th Cir. 1978).

107. *Yelverton v. Driggers*, 370 F. Supp. 612 (M.D. Ala. 1974). Howard Mandell represented the Dothan plaintiffs. The city continued to use at-large elections as late as 1989.

108. *Hendrix v. Joseph*, 559 F.2d 1265 (5th Cir. 1977). Judge Johnson's unpublished opinion did not delineate the *Zimmer* factors to the satisfaction of the appeals court, which remanded the case for more ample findings of fact. Johnson's subsequent decision, *Hendrix v. McKinney*, 460 F. Supp. 626 (M.D. Ala. 1978), was upheld. Pamela Horowitz was the principal attorney for the Montgomery County plaintiffs.

109. For perceptive discussions of voting rights case law in the 1970s, see Blacksher and Menefee 1982; Butler 1982; O'Rourke 1982; Parker 1983.

110. 423 F. Supp. 384 (S.D. Ala. 1976). In a companion case black plaintiffs persuaded

the court to strike the use of at-large elections for the county school board: *Brown v. Moore*, 428 F. Supp. 1123 (S.D. Ala. 1976). The attorneys in both cases were Blacksher, Menefee, and Still.

111. Senator Bill Roberts, quoted in McCrary 1985, 469.

112. *Mobile Register*, 28 July 1976, 1A, 4A.

113. 423 F. Supp. 387, 389–92, 397, 400.

114. 423 F. Supp. 388. Judge Pittman relied on regression analysis performed by both plaintiffs' and defendants' experts. McCrary 1990, 511, 523.

115. 423 F. Supp. 402–4.

116. *City of Mobile v. Bolden*, 571 F.2d 238, 245 (5th Cir. 1978).

117. *City of Mobile v. Bolden*, 446 U.S. 55 (1980).

118. *Bolden v. City of Mobile*, 542 F. Supp. 1050 (S.D. Ala. 1982). See above, text accompanying nn. 63–64, and McCrary 1984. At this point the United States, represented by J. Gerald Hebert and Ellen Weber, intervened in the case, and in *Brown and United States v. Board of School Commissioners of Mobile County*, 542 F. Supp. 1078 (S.D. Ala. 1982), *aff'd* 706 F.2d 1103 (11th Cir. 1983), *aff'd* 464 U.S. 1005 (1983).

119. A. Derfner 1984, 145–63.

120. *United States v. Board of Commissioners of Sheffield, Alabama*, 430 F. Supp. 786 (N.D. Ala., 1976), *rev'd*, 435 U.S. 110 (1978), established that: (1) when preclearing a referendum concerning a voting change, the department retained the authority to review any subsequent change in election practices, once approved by the voters; and (2) cities were covered jurisdictions, even if they did not register voters. Because the change was from an at-large city commission to an at-large mayor-council system, this legal victory had no direct impact on minority representation in Sheffield.

121. *Hale County, Alabama v. United States*, 496 F. Supp. 1206 (D.D.C. 1980). Earlier the department had to go to court to enforce its section 5 objection, *United States v. County Comm., Hale County, Alabama*, 425 F. Supp. 433 (S.D. Ala. 1976).

122. Sometimes litigation was necessary to compel submission of changes for Justice Department preclearance: *United States v. Barbour County Commission*, C.A. No. 78–348-N (M.D. Ala. 1978); *United States v. Pike County, Ala. Commission*, C.A. No. 79–245-N (M.D. Ala.); *United States v. Clarke County Commission*, C.A. No. 80–547-P (S.D. Ala. 1980). In each instance the county agreed to adopt single-member districts.

123. *Clark and United States v. Marengo County Commission*, 469 F. Supp. 1150 (S.D. Ala. 1979); *United States v. Dallas County Commission*, 548 F. Supp. 875 (S.D. Ala. 1982).

124. *Clark and United States v. Marengo County Commission*, 469 F. Supp. 1150 (S.D. Ala. 1979), *rev'd* 731 F.2d 1546 (11th Cir. 1984), *appeal dismissed and cert. denied*, 469 U.S. 976 (1984), *on remand*, 643 F. Supp. 232 (S.D. Ala. 1986), *aff'd sub nom. Clark and United States v. Marengo County*, 811 F.2d 609 (11th Cir. 1987) (liability) and 811 F.2d 610 (11th Cir. 1987) (remedy); *United States v. Dallas County Commission*, 548 F. Supp. 875 (S.D. Ala. 1982), *rev'd*, 739 F.2d 1529 (11th Cir. 1984), *on remand*, 636 F. Supp. 704 (S.D. Ala. 1986), 661 F. Supp. 955 (S.D. Ala. 1987) (remedy), *rev'd*, 850 F.2d 1433 (11th Cir. 1988). See McCrary 1985, 484–88; McCrary 1990, 512–14, 523–24.

125. See *Burton v. Hobbie*, 543 F. Supp. 235 (M.D. Ala. 1982), *aff'd*, 459 U.S. 962 (1982). Attorneys for the plaintiffs were Blacksher, Menefee, Still, and black Montgomery lawyer Solomon Seay.

126. *Sims v. Amos* 336 F. Supp. 924 (M.D. Ala. 1972), *aff'd*, 409 U.S. 942 (1972). A three-judge panel in Burton ordered the second plan into effect as an interim remedy, but

called for new elections under a fair redistricting scheme in one year, *Burton v. Hobbie*, 543 F. Supp. 235, 239, 248 (M.D. Ala. 1982).

127. *Burton v. Hobbie*, 561 F. Supp. 1029, 1035–36 (M.D. Ala. 1983).

128. In *Harris v. Graddick*, 593 F. Supp. 128 (M.D. Ala. 1984), also called *Harris I*, Judge Myron Thompson issued a preliminary injunction requiring the appointment of more black persons as poll officials. Blacksher, Menefee, and black Montgomery attorney Terry Davis represented the plaintiffs; Still was by this time representing one of the defendants, the State Democratic Executive Committee.

129. See, for example, the following deposition testimony cited in *Harris v. Graddick*, 601 F. Supp. 70, 72–73 (M.D. Ala. 1984), also called *Harris II*: "Where you got 75 percent of the voters are white and you are going to throw them in a black chief inspector," complained the probate judge of Jefferson County, one of the officials responsible for appointing poll workers throughout the county, "that don't make sense. And I can't get re-elected with that kind of program. I will just tell you like it is." The plaintiffs' attorney then asked: "They would vote against you when you ran for office next time?" The forthright probate judge responded, "You damned right," adding by way of explanation that "people that are primarily working at the polls are the most biased, prejudiced, politically affiliated people in the world and they are the ones that go out and make three or four thousand phone calls in every election."

130. *Harris v. Graddick*, 615 F. Supp. 239 (M.D. Ala. 1985), also called *Harris III*. The final opinion in the case contains findings of historical intent as well as current effects. *Harris v. Siegelman*, 695 F. Supp. 517 (M.D. Ala. 1988), also called *Harris IV*.

131. *Underwood v. Hunter*, 730 F.2d 614 (11th Cir. 1984), *aff'd* 471 U.S. 222 (1985). As evidence of disparate impact the plaintiffs showed that in Jefferson and Montgomery counties, where the two plaintiffs resided, blacks were at least 1.7 times as likely as whites to suffer disfranchisement under the petty crimes provision. The testimony of both expert historians, J. Morgan Kousser for the plaintiffs and J. Mills Thornton for the defendants, documented the racial purpose behind the adoption of the petty crimes provision.

132. 640 F. Supp. 1347 (M.D. Ala. 1986). Blacksher, Menefee, and Still represented the plaintiffs initially; in subsequent phases Pamela Karlan of the NAACP Legal Defense and Educational Fund played a significant role.

133. *Dillard v. Crenshaw County* (1986), 640 F. Supp. 1361, 1373. The testimony of the historian is summarized, ibid., 1356–59. ADC Field Director Jerome Gray also testified about the repeated failures of black candidates running at large in the nine counties.

134. Still 1991.

135. Auburn City Attorney Knox McMillan to David Norman, 6 July 1972, plus attachments (see n. 91 above); Strong 1972, 468–69.

136. Thernstrom 1987; Bullock 1989.

137. Academic research documenting the discriminatory impact of at-large elections includes Jones 1976; Karnig 1976; Robinson and Dye 1978; Latimer 1979; Karnig and Welch 1980; Davidson and Korbel 1981; Engstrom and McDonald 1981 and 1987; Mundt and Heilig 1982.

138. Cox and Turner 1981 was the starting point for our analysis of both the methods of electing municipal governing bodies and the degree of black representation in each city. A survey by the Alabama Democratic Conference of selected Alabama municipalities for 1984 provides a valuable supplement to the information on these issues. Many of the changes from at-large to district elections are documented in consent decrees growing out of voting rights litigation; such consent decrees are obtained from the clerks of federal district

courts in Alabama. For other changes, we draw on the public files of section 5 submissions for Alabama cities in the Civil Rights Division of the Department of Justice. For data on black officeholding we rely on the rosters of black public officials published by the Joint Center for Political Studies from 1971 through 1990. Racial composition data come from the 1980 Census of Population, supplemented in some instances by special surveys undertaken by local jurisdictions and reported to the Department of Justice in section 5 submissions.

139. Such an equity ratio is the most common measure of the dependent variable in ascertaining the relationship between methods of election and minority representation; in using this ratio we do not imply that section 2 of the Voting Rights Act entitles minority groups to proportional representation.

140. Alabama "Class 8" cities (those under 6,000 population) are covered by different code provisions, and are excluded from the analysis presented here. Many of them also shifted from at-large to district elections in response to litigation between 1984 and 1989. Our preliminary findings are that these smaller cities followed the same pattern as those with populations above 6,000: blacks were rarely elected at large in white-majority jurisdictions, but almost invariably won in black-majority single-member districts.

141. In this chapter we present our findings for city governing bodies; in an earlier paper we reported similar results for county commissions. See McCrary, Gray, Still, and Perry 1989.

142. Each city had relatively few blacks: Dothan was 26 percent black in 1980, Ozark was 23 percent, and Jacksonville was only 12 percent. For more than a decade each had reelected the same individual; no white person ever ran against the black incumbents. As early as 1980, Dothan, Ozark, and Jacksonville were among the ten majority-white cities in our total sample of forty-eight cities that had elected a black council member. The remaining thirty-five majority-white cities using at-large elections at that time had no black members. The mean equity ratio for all forty-five at-large cities in 1980 was a mere 0.26; for Dothan, Ozark, and Jacksonville the average was 1.16. Thus even in 1980 black representation in these three cities was atypical. In Dothan, moreover, litigation had played an indirect role in securing minority representation. Black plaintiffs challenged the city's at-large system in *Yelverton v. Driggers*, 370 F. Supp. 612 (M.D. Ala. 1974). After the initiation of the lawsuit, the city elected its first black commissioner to represent a residency district that was more than 90 percent black. Because a black had been elected, federal judge Frank Johnson allowed the city to continue using at-large elections, but he retained jurisdiction over the case.

143. The four municipalities with mixed plans also approached proportionality.

144. See the objection letters for annexations in Alabaster, 7 July 1975, 27 December 1977; Bay Minette, 6 October 1986; and Alex City, 1 December 1986. Subsequently all these cities switched to single-member districts, and their annexations were precleared. An objection to staggered terms in Phenix City, 12 December 1975, led to the adoption of a mixed plan including three single-member districts and two at-large seats.

145. As we saw earlier, Montgomery voluntarily adopted a ward plan, and Auburn and Selma mixed plans, in the 1970s. Six white-majority cities (and one black-majority municipality) switched more or less voluntarily to single-member districts, and one white-majority city to a mixed plan in the 1980s. Andalusia, Attalla, Greenville, Jasper, Northport, and Sylacauga were the white-majority cities changing voluntarily to districts (although discussion of possible lawsuits by minority plaintiffs or by the Department of Justice stimulated

voluntarism in most). Black-majority Prichard also voluntarily adopted a ward plan. White-majority Anniston adopted a mixed plan.

146. Even in cases that appear to be purely voluntary, awareness of the Voting Rights Act served at least an educational function. In its ordinance establishing a single-member district plan in 1988, for example, the small north Alabama city of Attalla, only 6,544 in population and 17 percent black, specified that it was "sensitive to the Sec. 5 Preclearance Requirements of the Voting Rights Act," and even cited the specific provisions of the Code of Federal Regulations that sets forth these requirements. Attalla City Council, Ordinance No. 612(88). Both Etowah County, in which Attalla is located, and the neighboring city of Gadsden had previously agreed to go to district elections in order to settle lawsuits by private black plaintiffs.

Chapter Three
Georgia

1. U.S. Commission on Civil Rights 1968, 232–39.
2. Ibid., 216–17, 232–39.
3. Act of March 2, 1867, 14 Stat. 428; Act of March 23, 1867, 15 Stat. 2; Act of July 19, 1867, 15 Stat. 14.
4. Bartley 1983, 59.
5. *Journal of the House*, 9 September 1868, 294–95; *Journal of the Senate*, 12 September 1868, 277–80; Bartley 1983, 62.
6. 92 U.S. 542 (1875).
7. 92 U.S. 214 (1875).
8. Ga. Laws 1871, 74, repealing Ga. Laws 1870, 431–32.
9. Ga. Laws 1872, 64, 279; Foner 1988, 423. Many counties abolished their grand jury appointed boards of education by local referendums, until by 1985 only thirty-four grand jury appointed boards remained. The constitutionality of the 1872 statute was challenged in a class action suit in federal court in 1988. *Vereen v. Ben Hill County*, 743 F. Supp. 864 (M.D. Ga. 1990). After the complaint was filed the general assembly abolished the grand jury selection system in Ben Hill County, the class representative, and provided for the election of a new board of education from single-member districts. Ga. Laws 1990, 4435. The next year the legislature passed a constitutional amendment, Ga. Laws 1991, 2032, requiring all county boards of education to be elected. The amendment was approved by the voters at the 3 November 1992 general election, rendering the legal challenge moot and consigning the grand jury appointment system to history.
10. Ga. Laws 1873, 25; Wardlaw 1932, 25.
11. Drago 1982, 155.
12. Wardlaw 1932, 46.
13. Kousser 1974, 209.
14. Wardlaw 1932, 45.
15. Kousser 1974, 210.
16. Stone 1908, 355.
17. Ga. Laws 1945, 129.
18. "Poll Tax Repeal Voted in House," *Atlanta Constitution*, 1 February 1945.
19. Ga. Laws 1890, 210.
20. Holland 1949, 50, 54; Kousser 1974, 217.

21. Ga. Laws 1894, 115.
22. Wardlaw 1932, 52.
23. Woodward [1938] 1973, 189.
24. Ga. Laws 1908, 27.
25. *Journal of the House*, 24 June 1908, 11.
26. Ga. Laws 1908, 27.
27. 383 U.S. 301, 310–11.
28. Ga. Laws 1913, 115.
29. Wardlaw 1932, 67–68.
30. "The Georgia Disfranchisement," *Nation*, 8 August 1908, 113–14.
31. Wardlaw 1932, 69.
32. 62 F. Supp. 639 (M.D. Ga. 1945), *aff'd*, 154 F.2d 450 (5th Cir. 1946).
33. 321 U.S. 649 (1944).
34. Bernd and Holland 1959, 487–94.
35. McDonald 1983, 14.
36. "Devise Revenue or Scrap Program, Says Executive," *Atlanta Constitution*, 21 March 1947.
37. Southern Regional Council 1984.
38. Frick 1967, 44–45.
39. Southern Regional Council 1984.
40. Ga. Laws 1949, 1204.
41. Ga. Laws 1950, 126.
42. 71 Stat. 634.
43. Ga. Laws 1957, 348.
44. Ga. Laws 1958, 269.
45. Bernd and Holland 1959, 487.
46. Ga. Laws 1964, Ex. Sess., 58.
47. Interview with Robert Flanagan, 30 April 1990.
48. *United States v. Raines*, 189 F. Supp. 121, 125 (M.D. Ga. 1960).
49. *United States v. Raines*, 172 F. Supp. 552 (M.D. Ga. 1959), *rev'd*, 362 U.S. 17 (1960).
50. Lawson 1976, 270–72.
51. McDonald 1982, 77.
52. Ga. Laws 1917, 193.
53. Key 1949, 106.
54. Ibid., 119; Bernd 1960, 16.
55. *Busbee v. Smith*, 549 F. Supp. 494, 499 (D.D.C. 1982).
56. *Gray v. Sanders*, 372 U.S. 368, 381 (1963).
57. *Journal of the House*, 25 January 1963, 301.
58. Ga. Laws 1964, Ex. Sess., 174.
59. "Majority Vote Ordered," *Savannah Evening Press*, 1 April 1964; "State Democratic Committee Increases Fees for Candidates," *Macon News*, 1 April 1964.
60. "Election Methods Face Change," *Valdosta Daily Times*, 21 February 1963.
61. "Majority Vote Requirement in Elections Passes House," *Valdosta Daily Times*, 20 February 1963.
62. "Runoff Bill Revived by Senate Unit," *Atlanta Constitution*, 1 March 1963.
63. *Rogers v. Lodge*, 458 U.S. 613, 627 (1982).
64. Ga. Laws 1968, 977.

65. Voter Education Project 1976; U.S. Department of Justice 1990; McDonald 1983, 71–73, 79–80. Cities switching to majority vote included: Alapaha, Alma, Americus, Ashburn, Athens, Augusta, Bainbridge, Blackshear, Brunswick, Buford, Camilla, Cochran, Conyers, Covington, Crawfordville, Douglasville, Forsyth, Fort Valley, Gainesville, Gordon, Hartwell, Hawkinsville, Hinesville, Hogansville (including the city board of education), Homerville, Jackson, Jesup, Jonesboro, Kingsland, Lakeland, Louisville, Lumber City, Madison, Manchester, McRae, Monroe, Moultrie, Nashville, Newnan, Norcross, Ocilla, Palmetto, Perry, Quitman, Rome, Saint Marys, Sandersville, Sylvester, Thomasville (board of education), Thomson, Wadley, Waynesboro, and Wrens.

66. Civ. No. 1:90-CV-1001 (N.D. Ga.).

67. Civ. No. 1:90-CV-1749 (N.D. Ga.).

68. *Bond v. Fortson*, 334 F. Supp. 1192 (N.D. Ga. 1971), *aff'd*, 404 U.S. 930 (1971).

69. *United States v. Georgia*, No. C76–1531A (N.D. Ga. 1977), *aff'd*, 436 U.S. 941 (1978).

70. *Brooks v. Harris*, Civ. No. 1:90-CV-1001-RCF (N.D. Ga.). Transcript of Proceedings, 13 July 1990, 74–75.

71. Butler 1985, 448–50.

72. *Toombs v. Fortson*, 205 F. Supp. 248, 257 (N.D. Ga. 1962).

73. Ga. Laws 1962, Ex. Sess., 30; "House Acts to Assure County-Wide Elections," *Valdosta Daily Times*, 8 October 1962.

74. Ga. Laws 1962, Ex. Sess., 51; "Redistricting Certain to Win in House, Experts Forecast," *Atlanta Constitution*, 3 October 1962; *Atlanta Constitution*, 5 October 1962; "Countywide Vote Okayed in House," *Atlanta Constitution*, 9 October 1962.

75. *Finch v. Gray*, No. A96441 (Fulton Cty. Sup. Ct. 1962).

76. "Legislature to Adjourn Today After Decision on Urban Senate Races," *Atlanta Constitution*, 8 October 1962; "Fulton Senate Voting Can Be Held by Districts Only, Judge Pye Rules," *Atlanta Constitution*, 16 October 1962.

77. "Who's In That Runoff? Courts Ready to Decide," *Atlanta Constitution*, 18 October 1962; "Count by Districts Changes Results of 3 Fulton Races, One in DeKalb," *Atlanta Constitution*, 19 October 1962.

78. *South Carolina v. Katzenbach*, 383 U.S. 301, 309 (1966).

79. Ga. Laws 1969, 285, repealing Ga. Laws 1964, Ex. Sess., 43.

80. 42 U. S. C. §§1973aa and 1973c.

81. U.S. Commission on Civil Rights 1968, 238.

82. U.S. Commission on Civil Rights 1981, 103.

83. Watters and Cleghorn 1967, 143.

84. O.C.G.A. §§21–2-218 and 21–3-123.

85. Interview with Ed Brown, director of VEP, 25 April 1990.

86. *NAACP DeKalb County Chapter v. Georgia*, 494 F. Supp. 668 (N.D. Ga. 1980).

87. *Fourth Street Baptist Church of Columbus, Georgia v. Board of Registrars*, 253 Ga. 368 (320 SE2d 543) (1984).

88. No. C84–1181A (N.D. Ga. February 19, 1987).

89. Interview with Brown, 25 April 1990.

90. No. C86–1946A (N.D. Ga. September 12, 1986).

91. No. 3–84-CV-79 (N.D. Ga. June 3, 1985).

92. Rosenstone and Wolfinger 1978, 22.

93. 42 U.S.C. §1973.

94. Davidson and Korbel 1981; Engstrom and McDonald 1981.

95. "At-Large Elections Abolished in Baldwin," *Atlanta Constitution*, 8 April 1984.

96. "More Blacks Win Offices in District Voting," *Atlanta Constitution*, 26 August 1984.

97. U.S. Department of Commerce 1990, app. A, A4–A173.

98. See *Carrollton Branch of NAACP v. Stallings*, 829 F.2d 1547 (11th Cir. 1987)[Carroll County]; *Hall v. Holder*, 955 F.2d 1563 (11th Cir. 1992)[Bleckley County]; *Clark v. Telfair County, Georgia, Commission*, Civ. No. 287–25 (S.D. Ga. Oct. 26, 1988)[Telfair County]; *Nealy v. Webster County, Georgia*, Civ. No. 88–203 (M.D. Ga. March 16, 1990)[Webster County]; *Howard v. Commissioner of Wheeler County, Georgia*, Civ. No. 390–057 (S.D. Ga. July 10, 1992) [Wheeler County].

99. The missing data in the 129 Georgia counties precludes an equivalent table for counties.

100. *McCain v. Lybrand*, 465 U.S. 236, 245 (1984).

101. Lawsuits requiring section 5 preclearance were: Calhoun, *Jones v. Cowart*, Civ. No. 79–79 (M.D. Ga. June 11, 1980); Clay, *Davenport v. Isler*, Civ. No. 80–42 (M.D. Ga. June 23, 1980); Dooly, *McKenzie v. Giles*, Civ. No. 79–43 (M .D. Ga. Feb. 22, 1980); Early, *Brown v. Scarborough*, Civ. No. 80–27 (M.D. Ga. 1980); Henry, *Head v. Henry County Board of Commissioners*, Civ. No. 79–2063A (N.D. Ga. June 10, 1980); Miller, *Thompson v. Mock*, Civ. No. 80–13 (M.D. Ga. Feb. 23, 1981); Morgan, *Butler v. Underwood*, Civ. No. 76–53 (M.D. Ga. June 11, 1980); Twiggs, *Bond v. White*, 377 F. Supp. 514 (M.D. Ga. 1974); and Wilkes, *Avery v. Wilkes County Board of Commissioners*, Civ. No. 176–38 (S.D. Ga. 1976), and *Wilkes County, Georgia v. United States*, 450 F. Supp. 1171 (D.D.C. 1978), denying section 5 preclearance. A successful constitutional challenge was filed against McDuffie County, *Bowdry v. Hawes*, Civ. No. 176–128 (S.D. Ga. 1978). An interview with Christopher Coates, 6 April 1990, indicated threats of litigation had been made in Bacon, Crisp, Meriwether, Walton, and Newton counties. House Committee on the Judiciary, Subcommittee on Civil and Constitutional Rights, *Extension of the Voting Rights Act*, 97th Cong., 1st sess., 1981, ser. 24, pt. 1, p. 605. documented a threat in Newton County. See also U.S. Department of Justice 1990.

102. Ga. Laws 1933, 656.

103. *Williams v. Timmons*, Civ. No. 80–26 (M.D. Ga. 28 June 1980).

104. 458 U.S. 613 (1982).

105. 395 F. Supp. 35 (N.D. Ga. 1975).

106. 437 F. Supp. 137 (M.D. Ga. 1977).

107. 412 U.S. 755 (1973).

108. 446 U.S. 55 (1980).

109. McDonald 1989, 1264.

110. *Thornburg v. Gingles*, 478 U.S. 30, 43–60 (1986).

111. 458 U.S. 613, 618, quoting *Washington v. Davis*, 426 U.S. 229, 242 (1976).

112. *Lodge v. Rogers*, Civ. No. 176–55 (S.D. Ga. March 23, 1983).

113. "Threat of Lawsuits Looms," *Atlanta Constitution*, 26 August 1984.

114. 478 U.S. 30 (1986).

115. "More Blacks Win Offices in District Voting," *Atlanta Constitution*, 26 August 1984.

116. *Thornburg v. Gingles*, 478 U.S. 30, 53 (1986).

117. 478 U.S. 30, 73.

118. *Hall v. Holder*, 955 F.2d 1563, 1573 (11th Cir. 1992).

119. *Lodge v. Buxton*, 639 F.2d 1358, 1378 (5th Cir. 1981).

120. *Carrollton Branch of NAACP v. Stallings*, 829 F.2d 1547, 1559 (11th Cir. 1987).
121. *Cross v. Baxter*, 604 F.2d 875, 880 n. 8 (5th Cir. 1979).
122. *Paige v. Gray*, 437 F. Supp. 137, 158 (M.D. Ga. 1977).
123. *Pitts v. Busbee*, 395 F. Supp. 35, 40 (M.D. Ga. 1975).
124. *Bailey v. Vining*, 514 F. Supp. 452, 461 (M.D. Ga. 1981).
125. *Wilkes County, Georgia v. United States*, 450 F. Supp. 1171, 1174 (D.D.C. 1978).
126. *Brooks v. Georgia State Board of Elections*, No. CV 288–146 (S.D. Ga. December 1, 1989), *aff'd mem.* 111 S. Ct. 288 (1990).
127. American Civil Liberties Union Foundation, 1989.
128. *Busbee v. Smith*, Civ. No. 82–0665 (D.D.C. 1982), Young deposition, 9; Plaintiffs' Exhibit 25.
129. Binford 1990.
130. Dubois 1979.
131. Interview with Tyrone Brooks, 5 March 1990.
132. 241 F. Supp. 65, 67 (M.D. Ga. 1965).
133. 277 F. Supp. 821 (M.D. Ga. 1967).
134. *Bond v. Floyd*, 385 U.S. 116, 120 (1966).
135. Bond 1990.
136. Ibid.
137. *Bond v. Floyd*, 385 U.S. 116, 125.
138. *Georgia v. United States*, 411 U.S. 526, 529–30 (1973).
139. *Georgia v. United States*, 411 U.S. 526 (1973).
140. "Blacks Fighting to Gain Six Seats," *Atlanta Constitution*, 3 July 1988.
141. 376 U.S. 1 (1964)
142. Ga. Laws 1964, 468; *Toombs v. Fortson*, 241 F. Supp. 65, 67 (N.D. Ga. 1965).
143. *Pitts v. Busbee*, 395 F. Supp. 35, 40 (N.D. Ga. 1975).
144. *Busbee v. Smith*, 549 F. Supp. 494, 500 (D.D.C. 1982).
145. *Bacote v. Carter*, 343 F. Supp. 330, 331 (N.D. Ga. 1972).
146. Drago 1982, 60.
147. *Busbee v. Smith*, 549 F. Supp. 494, 510 (D.D.C. 1982).
148. 425 U.S. 130, 141 (1976).
149. *Busbee v. Smith*, 459 U. S. 1166 (1983).
150. *Busbee v. Smith*, 549 F. Supp. 494, 507 (D.D.C. 1982).
151. 549 F. Supp. 494, 501.
152. 549 F. Supp. 494, 500.
153. 549 F. Supp. 494, 520.
154. Joint Center for Political and Economic Studies 1990, 10, 129.
155. U.S. Department of Commerce 1989. These figures may understate the black-white gap in voter turnout. See Lichtman and Issacharoff 1991.

Chapter Four
Louisiana

1. Prestage and Williams 1982, 316.
2. The race of registered voters is recorded on voter registration cards in Louisiana. These percentages reflect the official state registration figures at the beginning of 1990 and the voting-age population figures reported in the 1990 Census of Population.
3. Joint Center for Political and Economic Studies 1991, 10, 13, 195–216.

4. 380 U.S. 145 (1965).
5. La. Const. 1921, art. 7, section 1(d), as amended in 1960.
6. Kunkel 1959, 2, 7.
7. *United States v. Louisiana*, 225 F. Supp. 353, 364 (E.D. La. 1963).
8. Kunkel 1959, 11–12.
9. Prestage and Williams 1982, 293–96.
10. Wright 1987, 13.
11. Kousser 1974, 162–63.
12. Quoted in Kunkel 1959, 17.
13. *United States v. Louisiana*, 225 F. Supp. 353, 373 n. 49 (1963).
14. 225 F. Supp. 353, 374.
15. Ibid.
16. 225 F. Supp. 353, 375.
17. 238 U.S. 347 (1915).
18. From 1868 to 1940 Louisiana's constitutions also contained provisions for a poll tax. This tax does not appear to have been employed as a disfranchising device, however (see Kunkel 1959, 21; and Wright 1987, 20).
19. Kunkel 1959, 20.
20. *United States v. Louisiana*, 225 F. Supp. 353, 377 (1963).
21. 225 F. Supp. 353, 377.
22. These figures are taken from U.S. Commission on Civil Rights 1968, 240–43.
23. See Fenton and Vines 1957; and Prestage and Williams 1982, 101–3.
24. See Matthews and Prothro 1966, 115–20; and chap. 12, this volume.
25. Prestage and Williams 1982, 302; see also Fenton and Vines 1957, 709–10.
26. Wright 1987, 23; see also Fenton and Vines 1957, 705–9.
27. See generally chap. 12. Blacks attempting to register in Louisiana were also subject at times to violence or threats of violence from whites and to economic sanctions (see Prestage and Williams 1982, 317; and Wright 1986, 105).
28. See Conaway 1973; Jeansonne 1977.
29. *United States v. Louisiana*, 225 F. Supp. 353, 381 (1963).
30. *Louisiana v. United States*, 380 U.S. 145, 153 (1965).
31. La. Const. 1921, art. 7, secs. 1(c), 1(d).
32. *United States v. Louisiana*, 225 F. Supp. 353, 381 (1963).
33. See Wright 1986, 100; and Lawson 1976, 136, 211.
34. *United States v. Louisiana*, 225 F. Supp. 353, 378 (1963).
35. *United States v. Wilder*, 222 F. Supp. 749, 750 (1963). See also *United States v. McElveen*, 180 F. Supp. 10 (1960); and *United States v. Association of Citizens Councils of Louisiana*, 196 F. Supp. 908 (1961).
36. *United States v. Wilder*, 222 F. Supp. 749, 752 (1963).
37. *Louisiana v. United States*, 380 U.S. 145, 153 (1965).
38. 380 U.S. 145, 150.
39. See chap. 1 in this volume.
40. U.S. Commission on Civil Rights 1968, 243.
41. Wright 1986, 102; see more generally chap. 12, this volume.
42. U.S. Commission on Civil Rights 1968, 243. The number of voting-age blacks in 1967 has been estimated by interpolating between the 1960 and 1970 census figures.
43. Prestage and Williams 1982, 289.
44. The issue resurfaced in 1986, however, when the Republican party attempted to

purge voters in precincts in which Ronald Reagan had received less than 20 percent of the presidential vote in 1984. This criterion of course primarily targeted black precincts in the state. See Sabato 1988a, 83–84.

45. The expression is taken from Mr. Justice Marshall's dissenting opinion in *City of Mobile v. Bolden*, 446 U.S. 55, 104 (1980).

46. See Engstrom 1985a, 14.

47. See the *Roster of Black Elected Officials*, published by the Joint Center for Political Studies, Washington, D.C., for these selected years.

48. Wright 1986, 103.

49. Ibid.

50. Ibid., 106.

51. See generally Engstrom and McDonald 1981 and 1986; Engstrom and Wildgen 1977; Grofman, Migalski, and Noviello 1986; and Lyons and Jewell 1988.

52. See Engstrom 1988.

53. A few objections were subsequently withdrawn after the receipt of additional information.

54. See Grofman, Migalski, and Noviello 1986.

55. See Halpin and Engstrom 1973, 52–57, 64–65.

56. *Bussie v. Governor of Louisiana*, 333 F. Supp. 452 (E.D. La. 1971).

57. 333 F. Supp. 452.

58. See Weber 1981, 138.

59. The redistricting plan for the senate adopted by the district court was revised, over the objections of black plaintiffs, by the Fifth Circuit Court of Appeals. See *Bussie v. McKeithen*, 457 F.2d 796 (5th Cir. 1971).

60. This requirement, applicable to both chambers of the state legislature, was contained in a new state constitution adopted in 1974. La. Const., art. 3, sec. 1(A).

61. Joint Center for Political and Economic Studies 1991, 13.

62. See generally Engstrom and McDonald 1981 and 1986.

63. See Halpin 1978.

64. This was a telephone survey in which the respondents were either municipal clerks or employees in the clerk's office. The voting-age population of Farmerville was not reported by race in the census, so that municipality has been excluded from the analysis. The authors wish to thank John Cosgrove and Kenneth Prados for assisting with the collection of these data.

65. On the use of these measures, see, e.g., MacManus 1978 and Karnig 1976; but see also Engstrom and McDonald 1981 and 1986.

66. The data on black council members in 1974 are taken from the Joint Center for Political Studies 1975.

67. See Brouthers and Larson 1988.

68. Engstrom and McDonald 1986; Welch 1990. This chapter on Louisiana, unlike the other state chapters, focuses its tabular analysis on those tables (4.1A–4.8A) in which cities are classified by percentage of the voting-age population rather than by total population. However, for comparison with the other state chapters, we also include several equivalent tables (4.1–4.5) that categorize cities by total population. There would be no significant differences in these conclusions about the impact of at-large elections in Louisiana if we were to rely on the black percentages of the total populations in these municipalities rather than on the percentages of the voting-age populations.

69. The data on the racial composition of the respective districts are taken from the

available section 5 preclearance requests submitted to the Department of Justice by twenty-three municipalities.

70. 425 U.S. 130.

71. Engstrom 1978, 160; and Engstrom and Wildgen 1977.

72. *Beer v. United States*, 374 F. Supp. 363 (D.D.C. 1974).

73. *Beer v. United States*, 425 U.S. 130, 138–39 (1976).

74. 425 U.S. 130, 141.

75. Ibid.

76. Binion 1979, 171.

77. Engstrom 1978, 162.

78. McDonald 1991, 6–7.

79. 446 U.S. 55 (1980).

80. Ibid.

81. 403 U.S. 124 (1971).

82. 412 U.S. 755 (1973).

83. 412 U.S. 755, 766.

84. 485 F.2d 1297 (5th Cir. 1973).

85. 485 F.2d 1297, 1306–7.

86. Parker 1983, 735–37.

87. See, however, *Rogers v. Lodge*, 458 U.S. 613 (1982).

88. Engstrom 1988, 102–5.

89. Parker 1983, 716.

90. Engstrom 1986.

91. See generally Engstrom 1986, 115–18.

92. 574 F. Supp. 325 (E.D. La. 1983).

93. Engstrom 1986, 118–19.

94. *Major v. Treen*, 574 F. Supp. 325, 351–55 (E.D. La. 1983).

95. 574 F. Supp. 325, 352.

96. Engstrom 1986, 120.

97. 106 U.S. 30.

98. 834 F.2d 496 (5th Cir. 1987).

99. *Citizens for a Better Gretna v. City of Gretna*, 834 F.2d 496, 502 (5th Cir. 1987). The district court's decision is reported at 636 F. Supp. 1113 (E.D. La. 1986).

100. 834 F.2d 496, 503–4.

101. 834 F.2d 496, 503. The all at-large system was replaced by a mixed arrangement with four single-member districts, one of which had a black majority, and one at-large seat. In the subsequent election, a black was elected to the Gretna city council from the majority-black district.

102. See Engstrom 1985b.

103. 106 U.S. 30 (1986).

104. See also *Smith v. Clinton*, 687 F. Supp. 1310 (E.D. Ark. 1988), *summarily aff'd*, *Clinton v. Smith* 488 U.S. 988 (1988).

105. 691 F. Supp. 991 (E.D. La. 1988), *aff'd* 926 F.2d 487 (5th Cir. 1991). See also *Westwego Citizens for Better Government v. City of Westwego* 872 F.2d 1201 (5th Cir. 1989) and 946 F.2d 1109 (5th Cir. 1991).

106. 725 F. Supp. 285 (M.D. La. 1988).

107. Engstrom 1989.

108. *Clark v. Edwards*, 725 F. Supp. 285 (1988).

109. These estimates are based on a weighted double regression analysis in which the votes cast on the proposed amendment in precincts across the state were regressed onto the percentage of voters signing in to vote who were black in every precinct. On this methodology, see generally Grofman, Migalski, and Noviello 1985, 202–9; Loewen and Grofman 1989; Engstrom and McDonald 1988, 181; and Engstrom 1989.

110. *Clark v. Roemer* 777 F. Supp. 471 (M.D. La. 1991).

111. Civ. No. 86-4057A (E.D. La. Sept. 13, 1989).

112. The October 1989 statewide ballot also contained a proposed constitutional amendment that would have provided a New Orleans–based single-member district for the state supreme court. This proposed amendment, like that for the district courts and the courts of appeals, was rejected in a racially divided vote. An estimated 66.4 percent of the blacks voting on this amendment voted in favor of it, compared to only 18.9 percent of the whites (see note 108).

113. *Chisom v. Roemer*, Civ. No. 86-4057A (E.D. La. Sept. 13, 1989), sl. op. 34–35.

114. *Chisom v. Edwards*, Civ. No. 86–4075 Sec. A (E.D. La. 1992) (consent judgment).

115. *League of United Latin American Citizens Council No. 4434 v. Clements*, 914 F.2d 620 (1990).

116. *Chisom v. Roemer*, — U.S. — (1991), sl. op., 17. The Supreme Court also held in 1991, in an appeal from the *Clark v. Roemer* case, that changes in judicial election systems require preclearance under section 5 of the Voting Rights Act — U.S. — (1991).

Chapter Five
Mississippi

The authors are grateful for the research assistance of Martha Roark and Marianne Merritt in the preparation of this chapter.

1. *Greenville Times*, 24 November 1906.

2. *Stewart v. Waller*, 404 F. Supp. 206, 213 (N.D. Miss. 1975) (three-judge court).

3. E.g., Parker 1990.

4. *Redemption* was a term used by white Southerners after Reconstruction to apply to the abolition of black political participation.

5. Morrison 1987, 33.

6. Lynch [1913] 1970, 44.

7. McMillen 1989, 37.

8. Wharton 1965, 138–56; McMillen 1989, 38–41.

9. Colby 1986, 125.

10. U.S. Commission on Civil Rights 1965, 7.

11. Colby 1986, 125–26.

12. Morrison 1987, 45–47.

13. Ibid., 3.

14. 393 U.S. 544, 565, 569 (1969).

15. Colby 1986, 129–30.

16. Colby 1987, 42–44.

17. 301 F. Supp. 1448 (S.D. Miss. 1969) (three-judge court), *rev'd*, 400 U. S. 379 (1971).

18. *Perkins v. Matthews*, 400 U.S. 379 (1971).

19. 404 F. Supp. 206 (N.D. Miss. 1975) (three-judge court).
20. 412 U.S. 755 (1973).
21. 485 F.2d 1297 (5th Cir. 1973) (*en banc*), *aff'd sub nom. East Carroll Parish School Board v. Marshall*, 424 U.S. 636 (1976).
22. 446 U.S. 55 (1980).
23. E.g., Parker 1983, 738–46.
24. 506 F. Supp. 491 (S.D. Miss. 1981), *aff'd*, 663 F.2d 659 (5th Cir. 1981).
25. 534 F. Supp. 1351 (N.D. Miss. 1980), *vac'd and remanded*, 711 F.2d 667 (5th Cir. 1983), *on remand*, 599 F. Supp. 397 (N.D. Miss. 1984).
26. Parker and Phillips 1981, 40–41.
27. Parker 1983, 747–64.
28. 478 U.S. 30 (1986).
29. Civil No. H77–0062(C) (S.D. Miss. March 2, 1984).
30. The figures in this paragraph do not square with those in table 5.8 for two reasons. First, the figures in the text refer to all section 2 cases in all cities, while the table contains data only on cities of 1,000 or more. Second, the table contains data on cities that changed not only as a result of section 2 litigation but Fourteenth Amendment litigation.
31. Davidson and Korbel 1981, 994–95; Engstrom and McDonald 1981 and 1982; Jones 1976; Karnig 1976 and 1979; Karnig and Welch 1980 and 1982; Latimer 1979; Robinson and Dye 1978; Taebel 1978; Vedlitz and Johnson 1982.
32. Davidson and Korbel 1981; Heilig and Mundt 1983.
33. See Editors' Introduction and chap. 10 in this volume.
34. U.S. Commission on Civil Rights 1975. Facets of Mississippi's resistance to voting rights are described in virtually every chapter of this report.
35. Parker 1990, 188; Amaker 1988, 139–56; and Parker 1989.
36. Parker 1990, 34–35.
37. Amaker 1988, 149; Parker 1989, 14.
38. 446 U.S. 156 (1980).

Chapter Six
North Carolina

We gratefully acknowledge helpful comments by Thad L. Beyle, Merle Black, William A. Campbell, William Chafe, James C. Drennan, Donald Horowitz, J. Morgan Kousser, Laurie Mesibov, Paul Luebke, William S. Powell, John L. Sanders, and Leslie J. Winner; the research assistance and comments of Patrick Rivers; and the technical assistance of Julie Daniel and Eloisa Imel.

1. Key 1949, 210.
2. For more on this, see Kousser 1980.
3. Chafe 1980, 13, 53–60, 220–22.
4. U.S. Commission on Civil Rights 1975, 43. While 46.8 percent of the black voting-age population was registered in 1964, this compared to 96.8 percent for whites. Both figures were inflated by the state's failure to purge voting lists of voters who were deceased or had moved. See *Gingles v. Edmisten*, 590 F. Supp. 161 (E.D.N.C. 1984), Exhibit 38 and Stipulation 58, n. 2.
5. Suitts 1981, 78.
6. 590 F. Supp. 161 (E.D.N.C. 1984).
7. North Carolina Advisory Committee 1962, 16.

8. Kousser 1974, 15.
9. Edmonds 1951, 97–117; Anderson 1981.
10. Swain 1993.
11. Edmonds 1951, 124–36.
12. Logan 1964, 26.
13. Edmonds 1951, 124–36.
14. Logan 1964, 57.
15. Mabry 1940, 63.
16. Kousser 1974, 187.
17. Edmonds 1951, 204.
18. North Carolina, Secretary of State 1980, 890.
19. Kousser 1974, 236.
20. *Allison v. Sharp*, 209 N.C. 477 (1936), quoted in North Carolina Advisory Committee 1962, 16.
21. *Lassiter v. Northhampton County Board of Elections*, 360 U.S. 45 (1959).
22. *Bazemore v. Bertie County Board of Elections*, 254 N.C. 398 (1961).
23. North Carolina Advisory Committee 1962, 24.
24. Key 1949, 256; Crowell 1984, 1.
25. North Carolina Advisory Committee 1962, 24.
26. Ibid., 24.
27. *Winston-Salem Journal*, 19 March 1947, 1; 22 September 1948, 1.
28. U.S. Commission on Civil Rights 1981, 47–48; Suitts 1981, 67.
29. *Dunston v. Scott*, 336 F. Supp. 206 (1972). See Suitts 1981, 67–70.
30. U.S. Commission on Civil Rights 1975, 13–14.
31. *Gaston County v. United States*, 395 U.S. 285 (1969).
32. U.S. Commission on Civil Rights 1975, 31–34; 1981, 101–4.
33. See *Gingles* trial transcript, 429; testimony by board of elections chairman Robert Spearman; and defendant's exhibits.
34. Thompson 1986, 143–45. These comparisons should be interpreted with caution because the state began purging registration rolls in 1972. Reports of white registration rates of over 80 percent are almost certainly inflated.
35. Crowell 1984, 6. See also table 6.10.
36. Thompson 1986, 144.
37. Thernstrom 1987, 20.
38. U.S. Commission on Civil Rights 1975, 26.
39. Parker 1990.
40. 393 U.S. 544 (1969).
41. 393 U.S. 544, 565.
42. Suitts 1981, 71–73.
43. Unpublished Justice Department tabulations.
44. Suitts 1981, 72–73.
45. Keech 1981.
46. Swain 1993.
47. See Joint Center for Political and Economic Studies 1990.
48. For an analysis of this contest, see Eamon 1987.
49. If the appointment occurs in the sixty days preceding the election, it runs to the succeeding election.
50. Drennan 1990, 20. See also Drennan 1989.

51. 618 F. Supp. 410 (E.D.N.C. 1985).

52. No. 86–1048-CIV-5 (E.D.N.C., filed 2 October 1986).

53. Chapter 509 of the North Carolina Session Laws of 1987.

54. Drennan (1990, 33) observes that the law "all but guarantees that the judges in at least eight districts will be black."

55. Drennan 1990, 16–21.

56. These were Judges Ernest B. Fullwood in District Five and Quentin T. Sumner in District Seven-A.

57. Nearly two dozen district court judges out of 127 were black (Drennan 1990, 21 n. 28).

58. 590 F. Supp. 345 (E.D.N.C. 1984). On appeal, this case was upheld in part by the Supreme Court in *Thornburg v. Gingles*, 478 U.S. 30 (1986).

59. 590 F. Supp. 345, 367 n. 27.

60. M. Jordan 1989.

61. Christenson 1990.

62. Information on methods of election for county commissions and city councils was obtained from annual issues of *Forms of Government in North Carolina Counties* and *Forms of Government in North Carolina Cities*, publications of the Institute of Government at the University of North Carolina. Tabulations of minority officeholding at all levels were drawn from the annual issues of *Black Elected Officials: A National Roster*, a publication of the Joint Center for Political Studies. Population figures for 1980 were compiled from census material put out by the North Carolina State Board of Elections. Although cities that were less than 10 percent black were excluded, no population size cutoff was used for the city tables. All municipalities with a governing body were analyzed, including 260 with a population of fewer than 500. Data on population and officeholding on the district level were gathered by telephone survey.

63. *Johnson v. Halifax County*, 594 F. Supp. 161 (E.D.N.C. 1984).

64. In these lawsuits challenging the method of electing the Cumberland County Board of Commissioners and the Siler City city council, the defendants had already abolished at-large elections before the districting; the plaintiffs challenged the new districting system.

65. Leslie Winner supervised research on litigation and contributed to our report on this topic.

66. *McGhee v. Granville County, North Carolina*, 860 F.2d 110 (4th Cir. 1988).

67. Crowell 1988, 1989b.

Chapter Seven
South Carolina

Research for this chapter was materially assisted by grants to Vernon Burton, for which he expresses appreciation to the Woodrow Wilson International Center for Scholars, the National Center for Supercomputing Applications, the Graduate Research Board and the Vice-Chancellor for Academic Affairs Office of the University of Illinois at Urbana-Champaign.

In addition, research was assisted by grants to Peyton McCrary while he was professor of history at the University of South Alabama, for which he expresses appreciation to the John T. and Catherine MacArthur Foundation, and the Joint Center for Political Studies. The views expressed herein are those of the authors and do not necessarily reflect the views of the U.S. Department of Justice, where McCrary is now employed.

The authors would like to acknowledge the assistance in research from Adell Adams,

Georganne Burton, Beatrice Burton, Joanna Burton, Morgan Burton, Vera Burton, Alice Burton, Allison Leff, Nicole Jackson, Patricia Ryan, Christopher Villa, Calvin Harper, John Roy Harper II, Jon Smollen, Thomas Ritz, Dennis Hays, Mike Laff, Paula Xinis, Christine Hoepfner, Donald Litteau, Henry Kamerling, Brian Garrett, Thomas Keeling, Ellen Weber, William Hines, John Edmunds, and John Ruoff. We also wish to thank John Sproat, Jack Bass, and Walter Edgar for their useful comments and criticism of earlier drafts of this essay. A particular debt of gratitude is owed to Armand Derfner and Laughlin McDonald for their help with the legal history of modern voting rights in South Carolina.

1. *South Carolina v. Katzenbach*, 383 U.S. 301 (1966). South Carolina filed the original complaint. At the court's invitation, Alabama, Georgia, Louisiana, Mississippi, and Virginia filed briefs as amici curiae supporting South Carolina's claim that certain provisions of the Voting Rights Act were unconstitutional. Numerous other states filed briefs supporting the constitutionality of the act.

2. 383 U.S. 301, 308–9, 310–11 n. 9, 329–30 (1966).

3. Newby 1973, 15.

4. Burton 1991, 166; McDonald 1986, 558.

5. Williamson 1965, 72–79; Foner 1988, 200; Burton 1991, 166–67.

6. McDonald 1986, 560.

7. Foner 1988, 352–54, 357, 538; Holt 1977, esp. 97; Williamson 1965, esp. 363–417; Burton 1989, 27–38.

8. Edgar 1974, 141, 407, 409, 420–22; Reynolds and Faunt 1964, 62.

9. Although President Ulysses S. Grant was reluctant to use federal law enforcement on the scale necessary to counteract a statewide campaign of paramilitary violence, his outrage at this incident prompted Grant to send troops to Aiken, Laurens, Barnwell, and Edgefield counties. Rable 1984, 165–72.

10. Cooper 1968, 89.

11. Foner 1988, 342–43, 427–28, 431; Gergel 1977, 7–8; Kaczorowski 1985, 57–61; Hall 1984, 936–41; Burton 1985, 228, 290.

12. Burton 1978, 42–44; Foner 1988, 570–75; Gergel 1977, 8.

13. Gergel 1977, 11–14, quotation on 13. Hampton referred specifically here to the 1878 election, which repeated the tactics of 1876 and added new chicanery.

14. Current law allowed congressional regulation of elections to national office. Democratic reliance on violence, intimidation, and fraud to carry state and local elections would not bear federal scrutiny.

15. Tindall 1952, 31, 39.

16. Ibid., 69; Kousser 1974, 49–50, 85–87, 89, 91–92.

17. Tindall 1952, 54; Kousser 1974, 32, and 1991, 598–602; McDonald 1986, 568. Kousser shows that the proportion of the five other districts, and probably of the sixth as well, was also majority black. Dilutive and disfranchising methods allowed Democrats to control the outcome of the other districts (1991, 598–602).

18. Brown 1975, 85–86. Simkins 1944, 531–34; Brown 1975, 89; Banks 1970, 26, 29–30, 60–73. One of Tillman's native Edgefield County political lieutenants was J. Strom Thurmond's father.

19. Simkins 1944, 407.

20. Simkins 1937, 167–68.

21. In *Mills v. Green*, 67 F. 818 (D.S.C. 1895), a federal district court ruled that this registration law was racially discriminatory and thus unconstitutional. The appeals court reversed, however; see 69 F. 852 (4th Cir. 1895).

22. Simkins 1944, 289–91; Kousser 1974, 147; Burton 1991, 169–70.

23. Tindall 1952, 82; Kousser 1974, 150–51; McDonald 1986, 571; Burton 1991, 161, 170.

24. In 1878 Gary had proposed that African Americans be excluded from the political process by barring them from the Democratic party primary (*Charleston News and Courier*, 4 June 1878). In 1876 three counties—Anderson, Pickens, and Oconee—adopted a primary system. Eight more counties followed in 1878, nine in 1880, and four in 1882. In 1886 the Democratic party held the first primary for congressional offices.

25. Tindall 1952, 89; Ogden 1958, 42, 123, 188.

26. Tindall 1952, 88.

27. Kousser 1974, 92.

28. Key 1949, 504–5.

29. Burton 1991, 170–71.

30. Simkins 1921b, 177.

31. Burton 1991, 171.

32. Myrdal 1944, 488n. Newby (1973, 291) puts registration at three thousand (0.8 percent of voting-age African Americans in South Carolina).

33. *Smith v. Allwright*, 321 U.S. 649 (1944).

34. Key 1949, 627.

35. Democratic Party of South Carolina 1946, 2. For a discussion of the white primary in South Carolina see Farmer 1965.

36. Yarbrough 1987, 65–66; *Elmore v. Rice*, 72 F. Supp. 516, 527 (E.D.S.C. 1947), *aff'd sub nom. Rice v. Elmore*, 165 F.2d 387 (4th Cir. 1947), *cert. denied*, 333 U.S. 875 (1948).

37. Key 1949, 628–32.

38. *Brown v. Baskin*, 78 F. Supp. 933 (E.D.S.C. 1948), 80 F. Supp. 1017 (E.D.S.C. 1948), *aff'd*, 174 F.2d 391 (4th Cir. 1949).

39. *S.C. Acts* (1950), No. 858. In addition to restoring previously eliminated provisions of the state's election code, the statute includes numerous revisions. Debate over the bill was infused with racial comments. "The white primary is gone," lamented a legislator from Chesterfield County, and "we have a problem of biracial voting in our state." *Charleston News and Courier*, 9 February 1950, 11A. The newspaper also commented that the regulation of primary elections had been removed in 1944 "to avoid having the white primary outlawed in the courts." 14 April 1950, 1A.

40. *Charleston News and Courier*, 24 February, 1B; 15 March, 1A; 14 April, 1A, 1950.

41. Under the full-slate requirement, section 7(13), "if a voter marks more or less names than there are persons to be elected or nominated to an office . . . his ballot shall not be counted for such office." Section 10 provided that "no candidate shall be declared nominated in a first primary election unless he received a majority of the votes cast for the office for which he was a candidate," and section 11 required a runoff primary in the event that candidates failed to secure the requisite majority. Both the full-slate and runoff requirements date from the days of the white primary: see South Carolina Code (1942), Sec. 2365–67. The first adoption of both devices seems to have been in *S.C. Acts* (1915), No. 118, Sec. 1.

42. *Charleston News and Courier*, 12 February 1950, 4B.

43. Ogden 1958, 188–89.

44. Burton 1991, 177; Newby 1973, 274–313; Sproat 1986, 164, 166–69; Synnott 1989, 54–57.

45. Sproat 1986.

46. Tindall 1967, 165.

47. Sullivan 1991, 87, 88; Garson 1974, 117.

48. Myrdal 1944, 488n; Sullivan 1991, 92; *Charleston News and Courier*, 22 July 1948, 1.

49. Lawson 1976, 53–54; Jack Bass to Vernon Burton, 31 October 1992; Bass 1989, 332.

50. A. Morris 1984, 149–55, 238–39.

51. Carawan and Carawan 1989, vii–xvii, 10, 151–55, 168; Morris 1984, 149–55; Woods 1990; Burton 1991, 163–64, 173–75; Sproat 1986, 170, 172; Branch 1988, 263–64, 381–82, 575–78.

52. Burton 1991, 177; Newby 1973, 274–313; Sproat 1986, 164, 166–69. See *Briggs v. Elliot*, 98 F. Supp. 529 (1951), 103 F. Supp. 920 (1952), 347 U.S. 497 (1954), 132 F. Supp. 776 (1955).

53. A. Morris 1984, 128–34; 201.

54. Meier and Rudwick 1973, 80, 83–84, 87–90, 117, 175–76, 217; A. Morris 1984, 128–34, 201.

55. Garrow 1978, 11. This estimate is consistent with the state's official tabulation in 1958 (the last for a decade), showing that less than 15 percent of the total black voting-age population was registered, as compared with 31 percent of the total white voting-age population. Fowler 1966, 44.

56. Garrow 1978, 11, 19.

57. Fowler 1966, 43–47; Matthews and Prothro 1963.

58. Sproat 1986, 173. These areas supported the independent presidential candidacy of Virginia's Senator Harry F. Byrd in 1956. Byrd's leadership in his state's "massive resistance" was the key factor that won him 29 percent of the votes cast in South Carolina, far behind Democratic standard bearer Adlai Stevenson's plurality of 45 percent, but high for an independent candidate. See Bartley 1969, 166–67; McMillen 1971, 77, 313; Fowler 1966, 1, 6–8, 37–41, 48. In 1960, African Americans provided John F. Kennedy with his nine-thousand-vote margin of victory in South Carolina, the first time in the twentieth century that African Americans made a difference in the outcome of a statewide election. (Newby 1973, 291; *Columbia State*, 1 December 1965, 1D; *New York Times*, 16 June 1966.)

59. Synnott 1989, 57.

60. Kluger 1977, 329, 525; Burton 1991, 163–64; Newby 1973, 274–313; Woods 1990; Sproat 1986, 166–70.

61. Bartley 1969, 217–19, 226, 230.

62. Meier and Rudwick 1973, 90, 104, 106, 116–18, 176.

63. *Columbia State*, 14 December 1965, B14. A more comprehensive explanation for Thurmond's switch is found in Bass and DeVries 1976, 24–25, 250, 253–55.

64. Fowler 1966, 12–13.

65. Whitaker and Davis 1967, 19–20.

66. U.S. Commission on Civil Rights 1968, 222–23; *Columbia Record*, 16 March 1965, 1B.

67. U.S. Commission on Civil Rights 1968, 219. Other sources suggest that there were a few African-American elected officials in black-majority districts. Davis 1976, 58–62; Felder 1987, introduction.

68. *Camden Chronicle*, 19 February 1965, 1.

69. *Columbia State*, 3 August 1965, 1B, and 13 August 1965, 12A; U.S. Commission on Civil Rights 1968, 213.

70. At the time of passage of the Voting Rights Act, the South Carolina Voter Education Project was under the direction of Richard Miles, a white youth from Columbia. In 1967 African-American James Felder became director and John Roy Harper II, then a black law student, served as an assistant.

71. *Columbia State*, 13 August 1965, 12A; *Columbia Record*, 6 August 1965.

72. Burton 1989, xxi. Kousser (1980) shows that in North Carolina African Americans' taxes supported the education of whites.

73. Burton 1991, 175–77.

74. Cooper 1968, 90–91; Ashmore 1954, 153; Burton 1991, 175–77; Burton 1987, xxi–xxiv.

75. Meier and Rudwick 1973, 176, 217, 260–61; Sproat 1986, 170–80.

76. The Justice Department did not file a lawsuit against South Carolina until 1972.

77. McLeod 1965, 603–4, 613–14; Dorn 1965, 632–33, 637–40.

78. The state's brief is summarized and quoted extensively in the *Columbia State*, 16 January 1966, 1A, 8A. Its arguments are also systematically addressed in *South Carolina v. Katzenbach*, 383 U.S. 301 (1966).

79. *Columbia State*, 14 December 1965, 14B; 26 December 1965, 3D.

80. U.S. Commission on Civil Rights 1968, 61–64, 72–73, 86–87, 95–96, 117–18, 167–68.

81. *Columbia State*, 26 December 1965, 3D, and 18 October 1987, 9B; *Columbia Record*, 16 March 1965, 1B; Ruoff 1986.

82. *S.C. Code of Laws* (1976), Section 7-5-10 (source for how the boards are appointed).

83. Ruoff 1986.

84. *S.C. Acts* (1986), No. 535 (Sec. 7-5-155, *S.C. Code* [1976]). Voting rights attorney Laughlin McDonald characterizes South Carolina's registration system today as "the best in the entire South," which he attributes to the conscientious public service of elections administrator James Ellisor. Interview, 24 September 1992.

Reregistration of voters has not been a requirement of law since the late 1970s, but it still remains a barrier. Although a voter in South Carolina registers for life, failure to vote in two consecutive elections places a registered voter on an inactive list, commonly known as the "purge list." People on the inactive list found it very difficult to vote before South Carolina computerized registration lists. The list of inactive voters is now placed at the back of the list, and people who have been "purged" can still vote if the poll workers look at the purge list. With encouragement from the NAACP and the League of Women Voters, poll workers are learning to do so. *Columbia State*, 18 October 1987, 9B; Ruoff 1986.

85. *Columbia State*, 13 August 1965, 12A; 22 August 1965, 3D.

86. U.S. Commission on Civil Rights 1968, 252–53. By 1980, however, their registration rate had risen to 56 percent of the black voting-age population, and they comprised 26 percent of total registered voters; they made up over half of registered voters in only five counties (U.S. Commission on Civil Rights 1981, 43; South Carolina Election Commission 1979). The five counties were Allendale (56 percent); Clarendon (51 percent); Jasper (53 percent); Lee (51 percent); and Williamsburg (53 percent).

87. Jewell 1964, 183–85; McCrary and Hebert 1989, 102–3.

88. U.S. Department of Commerce, Bureau of the Census 1965, 1974.

89. *Columbia State and Record*, 5 December 1965, D3.

90. *Charleston News and Courier*, 12 April 1967, 1A, 2A; 13 April 1967, 1A, 2A. In the city, where the African-American percentage of the population was heavier than in the county as a whole, the Democratic leadership was more reconciled than the county council leaders to the new black voters. Charleston mayor J. Palmer Gaillard, in fact, won African-American support for his ticket in the spring primary by nominating black leader St. Julian Devine for a council seat in black-majority Ward 10. *Ibid.*, 2 June 1967, 2A; 12 June 1967, 8A; 13 June 1967, 1A, 2A. Devine, who had no white opponent, won by a landslide over another black candidate. *Ibid.*, 14 June 1967, 1A, 2A.

91. Quint 1958, 44–45, 47–48. Republicans in the county, as throughout South Carolina, were often openly hostile to the Voting Rights Act. For example, one of the Republicans in the legislative delegation, Senator John E. Bourne of North Charleston, was then pushing for passage of a Republican bill that would have required all voters to reregister before the 1968 primary or general elections. According to press accounts, the Republicans were making "a stubborn fight to trim Negro strength in 1968 elections." In opposing a Democratic motion to postpone implementation of reregistration until after the fall elections, Bourne himself said: "If we pass this amendment, it seems to me we will be slapping the federal registrars on the back and saying, 'We were glad to have you. You did a good job.'" *Charleston News and Courier*, 2 June 1967, 1A, 13A.

92. *S.C. Acts* (1969), No. 94. Thus despite the reference in U.S. Department of Commerce, Bureau of the Census 1974, the Charleston Council was elected at large, rather than by districts, in 1973. Similarly, Thernstrom states that "by 1968 the county of Charleston had elected its first black commissioner, at-large" (1987, 167). In 1968 the county council was still elected by districts, and no black candidate even sought a council seat. *Charleston News and Courier*, 10 June 1968; 4B; 12 June 1968, 1A, 6A.

93. Underwood 1989, 68. According to Andrews (1933, 33), among the reasons for the adoptions of legislative county government "was the race problem, which cast all else into deep shadow."

94. McDonald 1986, 570; Underwood 1989, 67–69, 265–66; Andrews 1933, 33; Kousser 1982, 11–12; Burton 1991, 170.

95. *Columbia State and Record*, 5 December 1965, D3, D20; Graham 1984. As the federal court put it in *O'Shields v. McNair*, 254 F. Supp. 708, 719 (D.S.C. 1966): "With the exception of a few counties, the legislative authority in county affairs is still vested in the General Assembly." In practice, the court noted, decision making was exercised by the county's legislative delegation. "When a particular county delegation reaches a conclusion on a county legislative matter, 'local' bills are introduced in the General Assembly which are routinely passed in both houses without scrutiny by other members of the General Assembly."

96. Key 1949, 151; Graham 1984.

97. Andrews 1933; Underwood 1989, 92–96.

98. Key 1949, 152; *Columbia State and Record*, 5 December 1965, D3, D20.

99. Order of 3 December 1965, cited in *O'Shields v. McNair*, 254 F. Supp. 708, 709, 711 (D.S.C.).

100. *Reynolds v. Sims*, 377 U.S. 533 (1964).

101. *Columbia State and Record*, 16 June 1966, 3D.

102. *Columbia State*, 12 December 1965, 5D.

103. Myrdal 1944, 446–48; Woodward 1974, 85–86, 164–65.

104. L. Marion Gressette, who chaired the notorious "Segregation Committee," also chaired the senate's Reapportionment Committee.

105. Defendants in a Barbour County, Alabama, case defended their shift to at-large elections as necessary to comply with the one-person, one-vote principle. Judge Frank Johnson rejected this claim as "nothing more than a sham" because they could easily "adjust the population disparities" by redistricting. *Smith v. Paris*, 257 F. Supp. 901, 905 (M.D. Ala. 1966).

106. 254 F. Supp. 708, 716 (D.S.C. 1966). Under this order, the senate would implement the interim plan for two years; the legislature would have to redistrict the senate again in 1967, and submit the permanent plan for the court's approval. The court ruled against the plaintiffs in a companion case, *Mungo v. McNair*, allowing the existing apportionment of the house of representatives to stand. 254 F. Supp. 708, 720.

107. *S.C. Acts* (1967), No. 540. Each of the multimember districts was divided into a series of numbered seats, and residency requirements assured that at least thirty counties would have their own senator. South Carolina immediately submitted the plan for preclearance under section 5 of the Voting Rights Act, but there is no record that the Department of Justice took any action on the matter. The federal court in *O'Shields* approved the plan on 9 January 1968.

108. U.S. Commission on Civil Rights 1975, 219; South Carolina Election Commission 1984, 19–24. On 25 October 1983 in a special election to fill the unexpired term of a senator and only after litigation to move to district elections, I. DeQuincey Newman, a grand old man of the South Carolina civil rights movement, won election to a numbered seat in a multimember district composed of Richland, Fairfield, and Chester counties.

109. McCrary 1982.

110. Stoudemire and Ascolillo 1969; Paschal 1977; Underwood 1989, 103, 180, 272; Maggiotto 1984.

111. 393 U.S. 544 (1969).

112. By 1971 the establishment of a separate Voting Section within the Civil Rights Division and the development of detailed guidelines for the evaluation of election changes made section 5 a major instrument for protection of minority voting rights. Lawson 1985, 307–28.

113. Blacks and whites challenged the senate, but only blacks challenged the house. One of the three challenges to the apportionment of the senate was *McCollum v. West*, C.A. No. 71-1211 (D.S.C.) brought on behalf of black plaintiffs who argued that the use of at-large elections in multimember districts, together with numbered posts, had a racially discriminatory effect. In *Stevenson v. West*, C.A. No. 72-45 (D.S.C.) African-American plaintiffs challenged the districting plan for the house on the grounds that its use of multimember districts and the state's full-slate requirement diluted black voting strength.

114. Objection letter, 6 March 1972. Officially an objection is interposed by the Attorney General; in practice the actual letter is signed on his behalf by the assistant attorney general for civil rights, who makes the decision based on recommendations from the Voting Section of the Civil Rights Division. These letters are available from the chief of the Voting Section and are cited hereafter as above.

115. The decision to defer to the court and preclear the senate plan was challenged by African-American plaintiffs in two different lawsuits, which were ultimately resolved in the state's favor in *Morris v. Gressette*, 432 U.S. 491 (1977), which summarizes the litigation's complex history. Following the 1980 census the existing senate districts were severely malapportioned, yet not until November 1983 did the general assembly adopt a redistricting plan. In addition to the usual submission to the Department of Justice, South Carolina filed a declaratory judgment action in the District of Columbia: *State of South Carolina v. United*

States and the NAACP, 585 F. Supp. 418 (D.D.C. 1984). On 8 March 1984 the Attorney General objected to the the senate plan, and the trial schedule in the state's lawsuit threatened to postpone new elections until 1985. At that point South Carolina Republicans and the NAACP brought a lawsuit before a three-judge panel in South Carolina and persuaded the court to order implementation of a new senate districting plan so that elections could be held in 1984. *Graham and NAACP v. South Carolina*, C.A. No. 3:84-1430-15 (D.S.C., July 31, 1984). No multimember districts were used in the court's plan, and five African-American senators were elected to the forty-six member body. McDonald 1986, 578–79; Felder 1987, 11, 26, 42, 45; Webb 1990, 47. The Joint Center for Political Studies claimed only four blacks were elected to the senate, Joint Center for Political Studies 1986, 347.

116. *Stevenson v. West*, C.A. No. 72–45, slip op. at 11 (D.S.C. April 7, 1972). A full-slate law prevents voters from using "single-shot voting," that is, marking only one name in a multiseat election. Black voters often used single-shot voting to increase the chances of electing an African-American candidate, while whites distributed their votes among several white candidates. Butler 1982, 864–67. In 1970 three African Americans were elected to the house, marking the first time since 1902 that any black person held state office. Newby 1973, 291.

117. *S.C. Acts* (1972), No. 1204. In addition to a full-slate law and a numbered-place rule, another device that prevents single-shot voting is the requirement that candidates reside in a particular geographic area but run in a countywide election. For this reason the Department of Justice has objected to the adoption of residency requirements on five occasions: Darlington city council, 17 August 1973; Walterboro city council, 24 May 1974; Bamberg county council, 3 September 1974; Sumter County school district, 1 October 1976; Chester County council, 28 October 1977.

118. Butler 1982, 864–67.

119. Objection letter, 30 June 1972. The Attorney General also objected to three local efforts to adopt numbered places. See the objections to numbered-place laws for the Aiken County council, 25 August 1972, and, in Lancaster County, both the school board, 30 July 1974, and the county council, 1 October 1974.

120. *Stevenson v. West*, 413 U.S. 902 (1973).

121. Objection letter, 14 February 1974.

122. U.S. Commission on Civil Rights 1975, 214–17; Davis 1976, 61–62.

123. *Columbia State*, 11 June 1975, 1A, 6A.

124. We base this description on newspaper coverage of the legislative debates from April through June 1975. See esp. *Columbia State*, 5 June 1975, 1A, 6A, and 13 June 1975, 1A, 6A; *Charleston News and Courier*, 12 June 1975, 1B, 2B, and 13 June 1975, 1B, 2B.

125. *S.C. Acts* (1975), No. 283. The various options under the compromise agreement are spelled out in sections 14–3701 (a) and (b), and section 14–3706.

126. Paschal 1977, 2. Of the twenty-five counties that held referendums, the following twenty used district elections as of 1977: Aiken, Allendale, Anderson, Bamberg, Berkeley, Calhoun, Chesterfield, Dillon, Greenville, Lee, Lexington, Marion, Marlboro, Newberry, Oconee, Orangeburg, Pickens, Union, Williamsburg, and York. Counties already using district elections that did not hold referendums were Cherokee, Dorchester, and Florence. Paschal incorrectly identifies Dorchester as electing its council at large and Edgefield as having district elections. Beaufort had a mixed plan, with three elected at large and six from districts.

127. Bass and DeVries 1976, 259. Perry was at one time acting general counsel for the national NAACP.

128. Caldeira (1992) discusses the critical role of public-interest legal organizations such as the ACLU in voting rights cases. Private attorneys in a civil rights practice rarely have the funds to pay the expense of taking depositions, as well as of retaining scholars to do research and testify as expert witnesses, even when willing to wait years before receiving attorneys' fees.

129. In one early case, *McCain v. Lybrand*, C. A. No. 74–281 (D.S.C.), plaintiffs' attorneys filed an unsuccessful motion requesting Judge Donald S. Russell to disqualify himself from serving on a three-judge panel. Among the grounds cited were the fact that Russell, while serving as U.S. senator from South Carolina, had participated in the debates concerning, and voted against adoption of, the Voting Rights Act of 1965.

130. *Lloyd v. Alexander*, C.A. No. 74-291 (D.S.C. 1976). Chapman chaired the state Republican party before his appointment to the bench.

131. *Washington v. Finlay*, C.A. No. 77-1791 (D.S.C. 24 March 1980).

132. *Washington v. Finlay*, 664 F.2d 913, 918 (4th Cir. 1981). The plaintiff's expert witness, Professor Earl Black of the University of South Carolina, testified that Columbia elections typically experienced "widespread racial polarization," adding that "to this point in time, black candidates in the city council races have not been able to find the 30 percent or 33 percent of the white voters that they need to win." McDonald 1982, 89–90.

133. 664 F.2d 913, 917–18, 921–22. The case was tried between December 1979 and March 1980, and was decided before the Supreme Court established the "intent standard" in *City of Mobile v. Bolden*, 446 U.S. 55 (1980). The appeals court refused to remand the case so that the plaintiffs could present evidence that at-large elections were adopted in 1910 for a racially discriminatory purpose. Although African Americans had been disfranchised fifteen years earlier, the plaintiffs found interesting evidence that might have been developed further had the courts permitted a new trial. The sponsor of the shift to at-large elections in Columbia was John J. McMahan, one of the chief exponents of disfranchisement as a "good government" measure at the 1895 convention. The 1910 statute, furthermore, applied the literacy test and poll tax—which state law applied only to the general election—to the city's primary election for the first time. McDonald 1982, 86–87.

134. *Columbia State*, 16 December 1981, 1A, 5A. On behalf of the NAACP, local Columbia attorney John Roy Harper II and NAACP attorney Willie Abrams have challenged the at-large seats in Columbia. No African American has ever been elected to the at-large seats. The case was tried 13 July 1993. *NAACP, Inc. v. City of Columbia, S.C.*, C.A. No. 89–1938.

135. In six counties—Chester, Colleton, Dorchester, Edgefield, Horry, and Sumter—Justice Department objections were accompanied by litigation. The one voluntary change was by Greenwood County which the NAACP reported it assisted. South Carolina Conferences of Branches 1990, 13.

136. Objections were interposed to the use of at-large elections for county councils in the following: Dorchester, 22 April 1974; Bamberg, 20 September 1974; York, 12 November 1974; Horry, 12 November 1976; Sumter, 3 December 1976; Chester, 28 October 1977; Edgefield, 8 February 1979 and 11 June 1984; and Colleton, 6 February 1978 and 19 December 1979. Efforts to enact at-large plans for the following county school boards also triggered objections: Calhoun, 7 August 1974; Sumter County School District No. 2, 1 October 1976; Bamberg, 31 August 1977; Allendale, 25 November 1977.

137. The objection on 14 June 1977 to the adoption of at-large elections for the Charleston County Council was ruled untimely in *Woods v. Hamilton*, 473 F. Supp. 641 (D.S.C. 1979).

138. In the annexed areas under consideration resided 3,456 whites and only 98 African Americans. Objection letter, 20 September 1974.

139. Ibid.

140. As a result, the Attorney General withdrew the objection to these annexations on 13 May 1975.

141. An objection of 21 October 1985 to annexations in the city of Sumter was withdrawn on 17 October 1986, when the city agreed to switch to district elections. The Department of Justice also objected to annexation of a white area in the city of Spartanburg. The initial objection was dated 16 July 1985. After the city agreed to adopt district elections, the objection was withdrawn on 6 October 1987. See discussions of the cities of Sumter and Spartanburg below. The NAACP led a drive for districts in Rock Hill. Maggiotto 1984, 102. The Department of Justice interposed an objection to annexations in Rock Hill on 28 June 1988, which was withdrawn on 18 October 1989, after the city adopted districts.

The Department of Justice also objected to majority vote requirements for the following municipal councils: Darlington, 17 August 1973; Seneca, 13 September 1976; Cameron, 15 November 1976; Bishopville, 26 November 1976; Calhoun Falls, 13 December 1976; Pageland, 22 March 1977; Hollywood, 3 June 1977; Mullins, 30 June 1978; Marion, 5 July 1978; Nichols, 19 September 1978; Lancaster, 19 September 1978; and Rock Hill, 12 December 1978.

142. *DeLee v. Branton*, C.A. No. 73-902 (D.S.C. 1973).

143. Objection letter, 22 April 1974.

144. McDonald 1982, 61.

145. *Columbia State*, 18 October 1987, 9B. The authority cited by the paper was Laughlin McDonald.

146. The county governing body sought a county council with expanded powers, elected at large. McCrary and Hebert 1989, 113. Under the existing system, the governor appointed seven commissioners in Sumter County, on the recommendation of the local legislative delegation; the state senator was by custom the most influential member. This arrangement had been in effect since 1922. See generally Andrews 1933, 34–38.

147. Order of 21 June 1978 cited in *Blanding v. DuBose*, 509 F. Supp. 1334, 1335 (D.S.C. 1981).

148. According to a subsequent ruling in the case, "whites are estimated to have voted for at-large elections by a four to one margin; blacks are estimated to have voted nine to one against at-large elections." *County Council of Sumter County, South Carolina v. United States and Blanding*, 596 F. Supp. 35, 38 (D.D C. 1984).

149. The county's letter, dated 1 June 1979, suggested that its request might also be considered a new submission of the 1976 change to at-large elections. In two subsequent letters, on 1 August and 27 September 1979, the Department of Justice treated the letter as a request for reconsideration and refused to withdraw its previous objection.

150. *Blanding v. DuBose*, 509 F. Supp. 1334 (D.S.C. 1981).

151. *Blanding v. DuBose*, 454 U.S. 393 (1982). The black plaintiffs intervened subsequently in a lawsuit brought by the county seeking alternative preclearance of the at-large system. *County Council of Sumter County, South Carolina v. United States and Blanding*, 596 F. Supp. 35 (D.D.C. 1984).

152. *County Council of Sumter County, South Carolina v. United States and Blanding*, 596 F. Supp. 35 (D.D.C. 1984), see esp. 37. The account in Thernstrom 1987, 155–56, ignores this finding, among others, and misconstrues the burden of proof under section 5; as a consequence, she misinterprets the court's ruling in the case.

153. Sumter County white voters had supported racial conservatism in presidential campaigns, from Harry Byrd's "protest" candidacy in 1956 to the 1964 Goldwater ticket. Fowler 1966, 7, 21. Richardson's racial views were reflected in a 1955 radio address, for example, where he urged support for the Citizens Council and its struggle for "the preservation of our Southern way of life by legal and peaceful means." McCrary and Hebert 1989, 115.

154. According to the *Columbia State*, 30 April 1967, 3D, quoted in McCrary and Hebert 1989, 114n, many legislators opposed the inclusion of Williamsburg County in the district due to "fear of the county's predominantly Negro population at election time."

155. McCrary and Hebert 1989, 113–15. See the findings in *County Council of Sumter County, South Carolina v. United States and Blanding*, 596 F. Supp. 35, 37–38 (D.D.C. 1984). Edgefield County also shifted from an appointed governing body to a council elected at large. Prior to 1966 Edgefield was governed by three commissioners, a supervisor elected at large and two commissioners appointed by the governor at the recommendation of the local legislative delegation. *McCain v. Lybrand*, C.A. No. 74-281 (D.S.C., April 17, 1980), slip op. 8–9. Threatened, like Sumter, with the elimination of its resident senator, the legislative delegation established a county council of three members elected at large but qualifying for one of three residency districts. This council took over the powers of taxation, budget supervision, and local appointment previously exercised by the county's senator and representatives. *S.C. Acts* (1966), No. 1104. Act. No. 521 of 1971 increased the commissioners and their residency districts to five.

156. *McCain v. Lybrand*, 465 U.S. 236 (1984).

157. *McCain v. Lybrand*, C.A. No. 74-281 (D.S.C., slip op., April 17, 1980). The court initially delayed issuing its opinion pending implementation of the Home Rule Act; pursuant to that 1975 statute, however, the county merely readopted its at-large system.

158. 412 U.S. 755 (1973).

159. *McCain v. Lybrand*, slip op. 17–18.

160. Edds 1987, 44; *Columbia State* 18 October 1987, 1B, 5B.

161. 446 U.S. 55 (1980). On 11 August 1980 Judge Chapman vacated his previous order in *McCain*.

162. Edds 1987, 40–44. The record introduced in 1975 included evidence of continuing discriminatory behavior by county officials. The county operated its juries and its chain gang on a racially segregated basis until challenged in federal lawsuits in 1971. The county school board resisted desegregation until 1970 (when white parents established a segregated private academy) and refused to rename the athletic teams at previously white Strom Thurmond High School (whose "Rebels" played "Dixie" at their football games under the banner of the Confederate flag). McCrary and Hebert 1989, 117n.

163. Laughlin McDonald to Vernon Burton, 28 July 1981 (in possession of Burton).

164. *McCain v. Lybrand*, C.A. No. 74-281 (D.S.C., 10 May 1982). The three judges were Chapman, Donald Russell, and Clement Haynsworth.

165. *McCain v. Lybrand*, 465 U.S. 236 (1984).

166. *Columbia State*, 18 October 1987, 1B, 5B; McDonald 1986, 580; Edds 1987, 37, 46–48; Maggiotto 1984, 88–90.

167. The defendants hired Duke Law School professor Donald Horowitz, whom President Reagan had appointed chairman of the North Carolina Advisory Committee to the U.S. Commission on Civil Rights.

168. McCrary and Hebert 1989, 117–18.

169. Objection letter, 21 October 1985, withdrawn 17 October 1986; NAACP 1990, 26.

170. *Columbia Record*, 21 September 1987, 1C.

171. *Columbia State*, 18 October 1987, 9B.

172. This information was drawn from our surveys. Richland County blacks got one more seat in 1990 when the other five districts were phased in. Thus African Americans won five of the eleven single-member districts.

173. *Columbia Record*, 21 September 1987, 1C, 4C; South Carolina Conference of Branches NAACP 1990, 1, 13, 27; Dennis Courtland Hayes to Vernon Burton, 7 July 1992 (in possession of Burton); interview with Adell Adams, July 1993.

174. South Carolina Conference of Branches NAACP 1990, 26. The case was scheduled before native Edgefieldian Judge Joseph F. Anderson, Jr., who informed both defendants and plaintiffs about the long fight, appeals, and expense of the Edgefield court cases.

175. Questionnaire completed by the Spartanburg Registration and Election Board. The respondent also noted that the "NAACP has protested this method to the Justice dept. They want the chairman to be elected by the commission."

176. *Columbia Record*, 3 December 1965, 14A.

177. *Jackson v. Edgefield County, South Carolina, School District*, 650 F. Supp. 1176 (D.S.C. 1986); *Beasley v. Laurens County, South Carolina*, C.A. No. 6-1817-3 (D.S.C.), slip op., November 17, 1987; *Glover v. Laurens, South Carolina*, C.A. No. 6:87-1663-17 (D.S.C.), slip op., March 18, 1988; *Reaves v. City Council of Mullins, South Carolina* C.A. No. 4:85-1533-2 (D.S.C.), slip op., August 5, 1988.

178. *Lewis v. Saluda County, South Carolina*, C.A. No. 83-1514-3 (D.S.C.), slip. op., July 11, 1985; *Thomas v. Mayor and Town Council of Edgefield, South Carolina*, C.A. No. 9:86-2901-16 (D.S.C.), slip op., May 27, 1987; *Owens v. City Council of Orangeburg*, C.A. No. 5:86-1564-6 (D.S.C.), slip op., June 3, 1987; *Jackson v. Johnston, South Carolina*, C.A. No. 9:87-955-3 (D.S.C.), slip op., September 30, 1987; *Broome v. Winnsboro, South Carolina*, C.A. No. 0-88-1160-16 (D.S.C.), slip op., July 20, 1988.

179. The unreported opinion of a three-judge panel in South Carolina, May 1, 1992, is reprinted as appendix 1 of the plaintiffs' Jurisdictional Statement, *Statewide Reapportionment Advisory Committee v. Theodore*, No. 92–155 (U.S. Supreme Court, October Term, 1992). After trial, the panel held that none of the plans proposed by the parties fully satisfied constitutional and statutory requirements, and drew its own legislative and congressional redistricting plans.

180. Indeed, the plaintiffs in *Statewide Reapportionment Advisory Committee v. Theodore*, C.A. No. 3:91-3310-1 (D.S.C.), offered a compilation of these objection letters as Exhibit 120.

181. Loewen 1990. Loewen studied both primary and general elections and found that race was in no sense merely a proxy for party identification.

182. *Columbia State*, 18 October 1987, 9B.

183. Ibid.

184. Karnig 1976; Latimer 1979; Karnig and Welch 1980; Engstrom and McDonald 1981 and 1985; Welch 1990.

185. Blough 1983, 167.

186. We base our conclusions on evidence from several relational data bases constructed between 1988 and 1992. Conducting both written and telephone surveys of every county and city council, we also examined all extant directories of local government associations. We checked Justice Department records for all counties, cities, and school boards, and these records often provided important corroborating evidence. The U.S. Bureau of the Census published a survey of methods of electing county governing bodies in both 1965 and 1973.

Election returns from the published reports of the South Carolina Election Commission enabled us to determine whether an election was conducted at large or by single-member district. The South Carolina Election Commission informed us which precincts were contained in each district. Finally, to confirm the racial compositions of districts, the South Carolina State Budget and Control Board, Division of Research and Statistical Services, provided the population statistics for each voting precinct for 1980 and 1990. In some counties and cities, this agency had drawn district plans and was able to provide racial compositions of the districts. The *National Roster of Black Elected Officials*, published by the Joint Center for Political Studies, provided data on black officeholding.

187. In at-large counties between 10 and 29.9 percent black, the equity ratio increased from 0 to 0.37; in at-large counties between 30 and 49.9 percent African American, there was no increase at all. Some white voters in recent years have tolerated tokenism in elections. They have been willing to accept one African American elected to a county council. Where blacks are not more than 30 percent of the population, tokenism appears most evident. Edds (1987, 191) discusses tokenism and quotes South Carolina NAACP activist Adell Adams: "With at-large districts, we have black councilmen off and on, but that's exactly what it is, off and on. . . . It's a very iffy situation. If there are seven seats, they'll give the blacks one. 'That's yours, but don't ask me for more.'"

188. At the time of the study, the NAACP had begun numerous challenges to multimember districts in South Carolina cities. On one day in 1989, for example, the NAACP filed suit against five city councils (Bennettsville, Gaffney, Kingstree, Saluda, and Union). South Carolina NAACP 1990, 27. Most of these cases had either not been adjudicated or implemented at the time of our survey.

189. We were unable to obtain district population data for Aiken and Anderson, cities that had mixed plans.

190. Burton 1978, 44.

191. For the twelve years that H. O. "Butch" Carter had served Edgefield County, the council "had never seen fit to give him a contract." Edds 1987, 36.

192. Ibid., 44. The ousted white administrator sued the county but soon settled for severance pay and found a job in another county.

193. *Columbia State*, 18 October 1987, 5B.

Chapter Eight
Texas

We would like to acknowledge the generous help of the following people: Sharon Breard Reese, Rita Loucks, Elizabeth Lock, Cathy Monholland, and Kerri Gantz at Rice University; Marivel Dávila and Rodolfo Ruiz at the Southwest Voter Education Project; José Garza of the Mexican American Legal Defense and Education Fund; George Korbel of Texas Rural Legal Aid; Alwyn Barr of Texas Tech University; and Emilio Zamora of the University of Houston.

1. The special provisions of the act, contained primarily in sections 4–9, apply only to certain states and their subdivisions rather than to the entire nation and, unless renewed by Congress, will expire in 2007. The most important of these provisions for Texas is section 5, which since 1975 has required all the state's political jurisdictions to submit proposed voting law changes to the Justice Department or the U.S. District Court for the District of Columbia for preclearance.

2. We shall generally use the terms *black* and *African American* to designate nonwhite

persons of African heritage. In Texas almost all persons listed by the Bureau of the Census as nonwhite are black; there are few Asian Americans or Native Americans. The persons of Spanish heritage in Texas are called by a variety of names, each with a slightly different connotation: *Mexicans*, *Hispanics*, *Spanish-surnamed people*, *Chicanos*, *Tejanos*, *Latinos*, and *Mexican Americans*. In the name of consistency, we shall primarily use the terms *Mexican American* or *Tejano*, although in some contexts this usage might suggest that we are talking solely about United States citizens, which is not necessarily so. Nine out of ten people of Spanish heritage in Texas are of Mexican origin; many of the rest are refugees from Central America who have entered the state in recent years. Writing in 1949, the demographer Lyle Saunders made a point about "the Spanish-speaking group" in Texas that is still true. "The . . . group is not an easy one to delimit or define. The group is not homogeneous, as is popularly supposed, but is made up of persons with a wide range of physical and cultural characteristics." Saunders 1976, 7.

3. As blacks and Mexican Americans tend to be undercounted, these figures are slightly low. The term *Mexican American* in the above sentence refers to the census category "Hispanic origin," which includes some non-Mexican Hispanics. Further, there is a slight overlap between blacks and people of Hispanic origin in Texas: in 1990 45,272 blacks were of Hispanic origin, so that the total black and Hispanic population was slightly less (37.2 percent) than the sum of blacks and Hispanics (37.5). Of the 63 percent of the state's population who were neither black nor Hispanic, 96.4 percent were Anglos. Of the remainder, 2.8 percent were Asians or Pacific Islanders.

4. Kousser 1974, 196–209.

5. Barr 1982, 39–40.

6. Ibid., 42.

7. Ibid., 46.

8. Ibid., 46–47.

9. Brewer 1935, 14–15; Moneyhon 1980, 236–47.

10. Crouch 1978, 352.

11. Barr 1982, 44, 47–48. In the first edition of this work, published in 1973, Barr (1982, 47–48) stated that nine blacks were elected to the house and two to the senate in the Twelfth Legislature. Scholarship has since turned up three more black house members. Barr 1986, 342.

12. Barr 1982, 48–49.

13. Ibid., 52; Brewer 1935, 126.

14. Brewer 1935, 69; Barr 1982, 70–71.

15. Rice 1971, 26.

16. Ibid., chap. 7.

17. Hine 1979, 27–28.

18. Pitre 1985, 130–51; Smallwood 1981, 160.

19. Key 1949, 534.

20. Ibid. For a treatment of the poll tax in Texas, see Ogden 1958 and *United States v. State of Texas*, 252 F. Supp. 234 (1966).

21. Barr 1982, 80.

22. Pitre 1985, 199, 201. The fourteen blacks in the Twelfth Legislature of 1870—Texas's sole legislature in which Republicans had a working majority—are profiled by Barr (1986). Pitre (1985, 199–213) both lists and describes black legislators in the nineteenth century.

23. Rice 1971, 86, 93–111.

24. T. Jordan 1986, 401, 420.

25. Ibid., 392, 420.

26. Simmons 1952, 272n; see also Key 1949, 272–73.

27. Montejano 1987, 38–39.

28. De Leon (1982, 23–49) describes other exceptions during the latter half of the nineteenth century.

29. Montejano 1987, 40.

30. See Anders 1982 for an account of the challenge to these machines in the Progressive Era.

31. Montejano 1987, 144.

32. Anders 1981, 138 n. 35.

33. Key 1949, 273–75.

34. Barr 1971, 201.

35. García 1989, 27.

36. Kibbe 1946, 227. "Though disfranchisement measures have not been directed specifically at Mexican-Americans," wrote Key 1949, 273, "their effective enfranchisement has often been brought about by individuals primarily interested in utilizing their votes." That Mexican Americans were allowed and even encouraged to vote because their vote could be manipulated is beyond dispute. But contrary to Key on this point, they were in some cases disfranchised by measures specifically directed at them.

37. De Leon 1982, 41. The 1903 Terrell Election Law establishing direct primaries and encouraging parties to limit access to them led the Democratic State Executive Committee the next year to suggest that county committees require primary voters to declare: "I am a white person and a Democrat." But, as Barr notes, "with the Rio Grande Valley vote in mind, 'white' was defined to include Mexicans." Barr 1971, 201. Thus the same Democratic party that excluded blacks generally allowed Mexican Americans to vote, on the assumption that the bosses could control them.

38. Shelton [1946] 1974, 11. The Wharton County organization appears to have been formed primarily to exclude blacks. See Barr 1971, 198.

39. Barr 1971, 205–6.

40. Montejano 1987, 143; García 1989, 27.

41. Barr 1982, 133–35; Lewinson [1932] 1965, 113; Key 1949, 621.

42. 273 U.S. 536.

43. 273 U.S. 536, 541.

44. *Nixon v. Condon*, 286 U.S. 73.

45. Key 1949, 622.

46. 286 U.S. 73.

47. 295 U.S. 45.

48. 295 U.S. 45, 52.

49. Gillette 1978, 393–416.

50. 313 U.S. 299.

51. 313 U.S. 299, 300.

52. 321 U.S. 649.

53. Davidson 1972, 84; Weeks 1948, 506; Strong 1948, 512.

54. 345 U.S. 461.

55. *Terry v. Adams*, 345 U.S. 461, 464 (1953).

56. Simmons 1952, 277–78. The classic study of the effects of the poll tax in the South is Ogden 1958; Ogden was a student of V. O. Key. On the effects of abolition of the tax in Texas, see Nimmo and McCleskey 1969.

57. Schroth 1965, 1632.

58. 252 F. Supp. 234 (W.D. Tex.) *affirmed*, 384 U.S. 155.

59. 321 F. Supp. 1100 (S.D. Tex), *aff'd sub nom. Beare v. Briscoe* 498 F.2d 244 (5th Cir. 1974).

60. 321 F. Supp. 1100, 1103.

61. 535 F.2d 1259 (D.C. Cir.).

62. S-75-103-CA (E.D. Tex). See also *Flowers v. Wiley*, 675 F.2d 704 (5th Cir. 1982).

63. 405 U.S. 134.

64. Ibid., 143–44.

65. 482 F.2d 1230 (5th Cir.).

66. *Wilson v. Symm*, 341 F. Supp. 8 (S.D. Tex. 1972), and *Ballas v. Symm*, 494 F.2d 1167 (5th Cir. 1974).

67. 99 Sup. Ct. 1006 (1979) *affirming* 445 F. Supp. 1245 (S.D. Tex. 1978).

68. *Sams v. Waller County*, No. 75-H-965 (S.D. Tex.—Houston Div. 1979).

69. Montejano 1987, 282; Davidson 1990, 43.

70. García 1989, 17; see also Christian 1989, 589–95.

71. On the Telles election, see García 1989, 113–41.

72. After his 1957 filibuster against a spate of segregationist bills before the legislature, Gonzalez was given the NAACP's Man of the Year Award.

73. Castro (1974) captures the spirit of militancy sweeping across Texas as the chicano movement came to a climax.

74. Brischetto 1988a, 75; U.S. Department of Commerce, Bureau of the Census 1989, 39.

75. Montejano 1987, 296.

76. 320 F. Supp. 131 (W.D. Tex.).

77. 42 U.S.C. §1973 b(f)(1).

78. On the provisions of the 1975 extension of the Voting Rights Act affecting language minorities, see Hunter 1976 and Brischetto 1982.

79. Barr 1982, 133. A very small number of blacks had been elected prior to this time, but in nonpartisan elections at the local level.

80. Grebler, Moore, and Guzman 1970, 561.

81. Simmons 1952, 276–77.

82. Ibid., 280–81. Davidson and Fraga (1988) describe the operation of these slating groups generally.

83. The numbered-place system can advantage whites in a situation where there is racially polarized voting and whites are in the majority. It does this by preventing minorities from electing their favored candidate through single-shot voting. The place system requires candidates to declare for a specific "place" on the ballot. Thus, to use a hypothetical example, suppose there are four citywide seats to be filled, and each voter has four votes to cast. Instead of operating like a pure at-large system, in which all the candidates for city council run against each other and the four highest vote-getters win, the place system requires the candidates to split up into four separate contests (one for each "place") and run against a subset of their competitors.

In the absence of place voting, an ethnic minority group can decide before the election to vote for one candidate only—to "single-shoot." Minority voters then mark their ballot for that candidate and withhold their other three votes, depriving competing candidates of votes. The place system, on the other hand, allows the voter one vote in each of the four contests. Thus the voter does not help the minority group's favored candidate by withholding votes, because those votes would not have gone to the favored candidate's competitors in the same contest. The courts have held that the place system is the equivalent of an anti-single-shot provision, and can in some circumstances dilute the votes of minority voters. See Young 1965 for an explanation and historical account of place voting in Texas elections.

84. Montejano 1987, 277.

85. McKay 1965, 432.

86. 252 F. Supp. 404 (S.D. Tex.).

87. 377 U.S. 533.

88. Davidson 1972, 71–72.

89. See *Graves v. Barnes*, 343 F. Supp. 704 (W.D. Tex. 1972). The trial court concluded with respect to Dallas County that the white-dominated slating group, DCRG, "without the assistance of black community leaders, decides how many Negroes, if any, it would slate in the Democratic Primary." The court found that in DCRG's slating procedure, "the black community has been effectively excluded from participation in the Democratic primary selection process" (343 F. Supp. 726).

90. 343 F. Supp. 704 (W.D. Tex.).

91. 412 U.S. 755 *affirming*, *Graves v. Barnes*, 343 F. Supp. 704 (W.D. Tex. 1972). For an account of the reasoning in *White*, see chap. 1 above.

92. 403 U.S. 124, 143.

93. 386 U.S. 120.

94. 378 F. Supp. 640 (W.D. Tex.), *vacated and remanded*, 422 U.S. 935 (1975).

95. 390 U.S. 474.

96. 584 F.2d 66 (5th Cir.).

97. See *Robinson v. City of Jefferson*, No. M-81–107 (E.D. Tex.-Marshall Div. 1983).

98. No. TY-73-CA-209 (E.D. Tex.-Tyler Div.).

99. 505 F.2d 674 (5th Cir.).

100. 505 F.2d 674, 679.

101. 648 F. Supp. 537 (1986).

102. Days 1992, 61–63; Thomas and Murray 1986.

103. U.S. Department of Justice 1990, T1–T11.

104. Davidson and Korbel 1981, 1001.

105. For a cross-sectional study that controls for residential segregation of blacks, see Vedlitz and Johnson 1982. It shows that the difference between at-large and district plans is greatest in cities with high racial segregation. These cities are probably most likely to be sued in vote dilution suits because minority concentration allows a district remedy to at-large dilution.

106. Polinard, Wrinkle, and Longoria (1991), in the second published before-and-after study of Mexican-American representation we are aware of, also report a sharp average increase in that group's city council representation in Texas after jurisdictions abandoned at-large elections sometime between the mid-1970s and the late 1980s.

107. 446 U.S. 55.

108. A. Derfner 1984, 146–47.

109. 840 F.2d 1240 (5th Cir.).

110. No. B-88–053 (S.D. Tex., Brownsville Div.).

111. No. MO-88-CA-154 (W.D. Tex., Midland-Odessa Div.).

112. 111 S.Ct. 2376.

113. Korbel 1989.

114. We decided to examine the cities in which the *combined population* of blacks and Hispanics was at least 10 percent, because it significantly increased the size of our overall

sample. Had we not done so, the subsample size in several of our cells would have been too small to support generalizations with any degree of confidence. The cost of this procedure is that the data on this "bi-ethnic minority" are not precisely comparable to the data in other chapters which, except in North Carolina, are for blacks alone.

115. Davidson and Korbel 1981.

116. Grofman 1982b, 5. Grofman's criticism of the research design of the Davidson-Korbel study was technically correct, as all longitudinal studies of this sort should include a control group along with the experimental group. However, the before-and-after data on minority representation presented by Davidson and Korbel were for the last election before the change from at-large election rules and the first election after the change in each jurisdiction in the sample. The time period between these elections was seldom more than two years, and often less. It is unlikely that "maturation effects" such as measurable changes in white voters' attitudes to minority candidates—effects that would have been observed in a control group of jurisdictions that did not undergo structural changes—could have developed in so short a time. In the study now being reported, however, the changes in minority representation are those between 1974 and 1989, a period of time long enough to make the appearance of maturation effects plausible. Thus the incorporation of a control group in the present research design is even more important than it would have been in the earlier study.

117. All Texas cities of 10,000 or more population in 1980 with 10 percent or more minority (black plus Hispanic) population were contacted through a telephone survey conducted by the Southwest Voter Research Institute during the summer of 1989. City election administrators were asked a series of twenty questions, including a request for a detailed description of election type in 1974 and 1989; for the racial, ethnic, and gender makeup of city council in 1974 and 1989; and for identification of each councilperson according to whether he or she was a district or at-large representative. Respondents were also asked if their city's election plan had been sued for diluting minority votes. In cities with districted systems, respondents were asked to provide 1980 census data on the total, black, and Hispanic populations in each district. (A follow-up survey to legal departments in all fifty-two cities that changed from at-large to districted systems between 1974 and 1989 was carried out by Sharon Breard Reese under the supervision of Chandler Davidson at Rice University in the spring of 1991, to get the city attorney's account of the reasons for the city's changing systems. Fifty cities responded, and data on the other two were obtained from lawyers who tried cases against them.)

Questionnaires were mailed to those who did not respond, and callbacks were made until the researcher obtained as much information as could be obtained from the city clerk or election administrator. A 100 percent completion rate was achieved on some but not all of the questions.

To check for accuracy and fill in some of the missing data, information on the population composition of districts was obtained from section 5 submissions to the Department of Justice. Additional checks for accuracy of election system data and type of litigation filed against cities were made against data from a 1988 survey by the Southwest Voter Research Institute of attorneys involved in voting rights lawsuits.

City population data were obtained from the 1980 census.

118. Brischetto 1988b, 1; Joint Center for Political and Economic Studies 1991, 14; National Association of Latino Elected and Appointed Officials 1990, 72–87.

119. Only one city with the above-mentioned demographic characteristics—10,000 or more total population, and 10 percent or more black and Hispanic combined—is excluded

from this table and all others. The city of Seguin elected two councilpersons each from four multimember districts. Rather than create another category in all our tables for this city, we dropped it from the analysis.

Almost all of our tables reporting minority representation on councils are based on cities meeting a threshold of 10 percent black and Hispanic population combined, and the data presented contain information on black and Hispanic officials combined. However, tables in the other state chapters, as well as those in chap. 10 that use pooled data on black representation from the states, use a threshold of 10 percent black. (The exception is the North Carolina chapter, whose threshold is 10 percent black and Native American, but the state's Native American population is so small as to be negligible.) To present comparable data, therefore, the Texas chapter ideally would have presented two additional tables for each table showing black and Hispanic data combined: one showing black data in cities 10 percent or more black and another showing Hispanic data in cities 10 percent or more Hispanic. This would not only have been cumbersome, but several of the cells in such tables would have been empty or the percentage figure would have been based on an *N* of 1 or 2. Nonetheless, when we pooled Texas data with those of other states for analysis in chap. 10, we used only those cities that were at least 10 percent black, rather than black and Hispanic combined.

120. The assumption of a before-and-after comparison of a city is that the only change in independent variables affecting minority representation is the change in election structures; thus, observed changes in minority representation must be due to changes in those structures. This assumption is most compelling when the time between "before" and "after" is short. In our research design, however, fifteen years elapsed, which is enough time for some factors thought to impinge on minority representation to change. It seems reasonable to suppose, however, that the changes in relevant independent variables *within* the same cities *over fifteen years* are smaller than the changes in such variables *among* the cities *in the same year* (the latter changes being the ones measured in cross-sectional analysis).

121. Grofman 1982a, 19–21.

122. At this point in our analysis, given the importance of table 8.5, we asked whether our decision to study cities many of which contained large proportions of both blacks and Hispanics led to findings significantly different from those we would have found if we had decided to study "single-minority" cities only. In other words, what if we had limited our study of the effects of election structure on black officeholding to cities 10 percent or more black but no more than 10 percent Hispanic, or, alternatively, if we had examined Hispanic officeholding in cities 10 percent or more Hispanic but no more than 10 percent black—thus disaggregating, so to speak, the two minority groups that are combined in the other tables in this chapter? For an answer, we analyzed such "single-minority" cities separately for blacks and Hispanics, and found that the impact of at-large elections was generally the same as table 8.5 shows. In other words, at-large as compared to district elections generally disadvantaged blacks in cities with few Hispanics, and they disadvantaged Hispanics in cities with few blacks. These tables are not published, but are available from the authors.

123. There might, however, be other variables besides election structure changes that account for the relative increases in minority officeholding in changed cities. One possibility is that the increases are the artifact of our measure of the cities' minority population. The measure of this percentage in table 8.2 is taken from the 1980 decennial census. Of reliable population estimates available, this is the single most accurate one for the fifteen-year period. However, the minority populations increased in many of the cities; if a relatively larger minority population increase occurred in the experimental group, this could

account for part or all of the increase in officeholding in that group, thus exaggerating the causal impact of election structures. To test this hypothesis, we substituted 1990 minority population proportions for 1980 ones in table 8.5 to see whether minority population increases were systematically greater in experimental cities. There was only a minuscule mean difference in population changes between the two types of cities.

124. Welch 1990.

125. No. CA3-88-1152-R (N.D. Tex.—Dallas Div.)

126. Brace, Grofman, Handley, and Niemi (1988) and Grofman and Handley (1990) discuss data relevant to this claim drawn from a variety of sources.

127. Hwang and Murdock 1982, 744.

128. See Rice 1977 on the adoption of commission government in Texas.

129. For an account of this phenomenon in Fort Worth, see Cotrell 1980, chap. 12.

130. See, for example, *New York Times*, 27 April 1992, A17.

131. U.S. Department of Justice 1990, M1–M10, T1–T11.

132. The remaining lawsuits were brought and won under the Fourteenth Amendment. As Davidson points out in chap. 1 above, the Supreme Court's conceptualization of minority vote dilution in *White v. Regester* (1973) was influenced by its 1969 decision in *Allen v. State Board of Elections* (393 U.S. 544), interpreting section 5 of the Voting Rights Act to prohibit minority vote dilution. Thus the act indirectly influenced the development of constitutional law that allowed plaintiffs to challenge minority vote dilution in cases where the act could not be directly invoked. Therefore, the act—either directly or indirectly—influenced all the litigation attacking minority vote dilution in the 1970s.

Chapter Nine
Virginia

1. Stanley 1987, 97.
2. Key 1949, 20.
3. Howard 1974, 15.
4. Maddex 1970, 66–73.
5. Ibid., 82.
6. Morton [1918] 1973, 77–78.
7. Ibid., 44, 77; Maddex 1970, 55.
8. Pulley 1968, 8–9.
9. Maddex 1970, 198; Buni 1967, 2.
10. Maddex 1970, 198.
11. Buni 1967, 2, 8–9; Morton [1918] 1973, 77–78, 84–85.
12. Kousser 1974, 173–75.
13. Morton [1918] 1973, 5 and map opposite 147.
14. Buni 1967, 24, 28.
15. Sabato 1977, 14–16.
16. Ibid., 26.
17. Ibid., 48–49; Buni 1967, 61–62.
18. Sabato 1977, 50–52; Buni 1967, 118–20.
19. Key 1949, 624.
20. Ibid., 669.
21. Buni 1967, 157, 166.
22. Gates 1964, 24.

23. Wilkinson 1968, 259; Eisenberg 1965, 31.
24. 383 U.S. 663 (1966).
25. Eisenberg 1972, 58.
26. Wilkinson 1968, 259–61.
27. Eisenberg 1965, 30.
28. Wilkinson 1968, 282–83; Eisenberg 1969, 27.
29. Eisenberg 1972, 67–68.
30. Sabato 1975, 64–72. See also Black and Black 1987, 138–39.
31. Sabato 1988b, 23–24.
32. Black and Black 1987, 139.
33. Sabato 1987, 71.
34. Morris 1992, 189–204; Edds 1990, 239; Sabato 1987, 84.
35. Sabato 1990, 4.
36. Edds 1990, 258.
37. Wilkinson 1968, 362.
38. Black 1978, 446–47.
39. *Commonwealth of Virginia v. United States*, 386 F. Supp. 1319, 1324 (1975); O'Rourke 1983, 776–77, 770 n. 29.
40. U.S. Commission on Civil Rights 1968, 222–23.
41. *Commonwealth of Virginia v. United States*, 386 F. Supp. 1319, 1325.
42. The 1964 reapportionment was a result of the invalidation of the 1962 reapportionment on one-person, one-vote grounds. *Mann v. Davis*, 213 F. Supp. 577 (E.D. Va. 1962), *affirmed* 377 U.S. 678 (1964).
43. *Mann v. Davis*, 245 F. Supp. 241 (1965).
44. *Richmond Times-Dispatch*, 8 November 1967, A-1, A-5.
45. Baker 1989, 80.
46. Austin 1976, 285–94; *Howell v. Mahan*, 330 F. Supp. 1138 (E.D. Va. 1971).
47. *Mahan v. Howell*, 410 U.S. 315 (1973).
48. *Whitcomb v. Chavis*, 403 U.S. 124 (1971).
49. *Washington Post*, 18 August 1981, A-21.
50. Parker 1982, 11–22; Schuiteman and Selph 1983, 47–51.
51. Schuiteman and Selph 1983, 48 n. 5.
52. Moeser and Dennis 1982, 60–70.
53. Rankin 1974, 3–4; Moeser and Dennis 1982, 80–87.
54. *Perkins v. Matthews*, 400 U.S. 379 (1971).
55. Moeser and Dennis 1982, 3–4.
56. Ibid., 166–69.
57. 422 U.S. 358 (1975).
58. *Collins v. City of Norfolk*, 883 F.2d 1232, 1141–42 (4th Cir. 1989).
59. The cities of Poquoson, Virginia Beach, and Waynesboro have districts as residence requirements for candidates only.
60. *White v. Daniel*, 909 F.2d 99 (4th Cir. 1990).
61. *Smith v. Board of Supervisors of Brunswick County, Virginia*, (E.D. Va. 1992) *rev'd.*, 984 F.2d 1393, 1402 (4th Cir. 1993).
62. The lone exception is Hillsville, a small town of 2,100 residents. See below later in this chapter on the distinction between Virginia cities and towns.
63. *Irby v. Virginia State Board of Elections*, 889 F.2d 1352 (4th Cir. 1989), *affirming*, *Irby v. Fitz-Hugh*, 692 F. Supp. 610 and 693 F. Supp. 424 (E.D. Va. 1988).

64. Morris and Sabato 1991, 263.

65. *City of Mobile v. Bolden*, 446 U.S. 55 (1980).

66. *Richmond Times-Dispatch*, 2 March 1988, B-6.

67. Muse 1961, 47–53; Kluger 1977, 471–76.

68. U.S. Department of Commerce, Bureau of the Census 1988, A-215.

69. A chart listing black representation on city councils in 1977 is in O'Rourke 1979. Petersburg, Suffolk, and Lynchburg are not included because the changes in their electoral systems were made prior to 1977 (see table 9.8). Telephone interviews and newspaper accounts were utilized to determine black representation in 1989.

70. The recall was prompted by allegations that Mayor Holley secretly sent hate mail to other black council members.

71. (Norfolk) *Virginian Pilot*, 2 May 1990, D-1, D-4; (Portsmouth) *Currents*, 3 May 1990, 1.

72. Morris 1990, 1–2.

Chapter Ten
The Effect of Municipal Election Structure on Black Representation in Eight Southern States

We are indebted to J. Gerald Hebert of the U.S. Department of Justice and James E. Alt for helpful suggestions on an earlier draft of this chapter. Errors remaining are solely the responsibility of the authors.

1. At the state legislative level, multimember districts have also been challenged. See the state chapters and the overview in chap. 11.

2. See the discussion in Editors' Introduction and below.

3. In three states—Georgia, North Carolina, and South Carolina—data on counties as well as municipalities were collected. We compare below the findings on minority representation at the county level with those for southern cities.

4. For Georgia, data are from 1980 to 1990. See table 10.1 for the beginning and end points for each of the state analyses and a general inventory of the basic characteristics of our data set on a state-by-state basis.

5. As previously noted, our discussion in this chapter will focus exclusively on black representation and will concentrate on data from city council elections. The data bases in Texas included Mexican Americans and in North Carolina, Native Americans. For results concerning these two minority groups, see chaps. 6 and 8.

6. For Georgia, cities with multimember districts are excluded from the analyses presented in this chapter. There were four such cities in the longitudinal data base in chap. 3. Thus $N = 15$ for at-large Georgia cities in table 10.2, four lower than the corresponding N of 19 in table 10.1. For analysis of black representation in Georgia multimember cities, see chap. 3. In South Carolina, the single-member-district category for counties includes one county (Colleton) that had two equal-size multimember districts, one of which had a substantial black population; the mixed category includes Beauford County, which had a multimember district as well as three single-member districts and three at-large seats. See notes to table 7.1A.

7. "Roughly speaking," because the before-and-after comparisons in our design pertain to the same cities about fifteen years apart—a time frame in which some variables besides election structure have surely changed. However, another feature of our research design, a control group, is intended to ameliorate this problem.

8. Davidson and Korbel 1981; and Polinard, Wrinkle, and Longoria 1991. Heilig and Mundt 1983 contained a control group but exhibited other problems. For a discussion of those studies, see Editors' Introduction.

9. The editors gave state chapter authors detailed basic guidelines, but they also allowed flexibility in order to accommodate variations across states in demographic characteristics of cities, litigation patterns, data availability, and data-gathering resources.

The data across states are largely comparable but there are some state-to-state variations in measurement. One concerns the time frame. The choice of a general starting point and an end point was dictated by various considerations. On the one hand, we hoped to track as much change as possible in covered municipal election structures in the period after the act was passed in the fall of 1965. Thus our end point, we decided, should be the year our research actually got underway. But a starting point as early as 1965, we feared, would mean that a considerable amount of our "before" data would be irretrievable because of poor record keeping by local officials and lack of accurate electoral data on race at the municipal level. On the other hand, if the starting point were too recent, many of the changes in election plan whose effects over time on black officeholding we hoped to measure would already have occurred. A reasonable compromise was a starting point in the early 1970s. Yet because of peculiarities of the individual states as well as varying resources available to the research teams, the beginning and end points, respectively, were not identical for each state.

Moreover, as a result of extensive litigation in Alabama in the late 1980s, the use of the 1989 ending point for that state, which the authors had originally decided on, meant that only six cities in the Alabama data set still elected their council at large, and three of these were majority-black cities. Consequently, some data in the Alabama chapter are also reported for the 1980 period, when the number of majority-white cities electing at large was much greater. We discuss below some of the special features of the Alabama data when we consider the problems of causal inference about election system effects.

10. In the Louisiana chapter, a 10 percent black *voting-age* population threshold was used in some tables to supplement the data reported in terms of population. Here we report data for the Louisiana cities that are at least 10 percent black in *total* population. Because of this difference in choice of threshold for city inclusion, there are some (generally quite minor) differences between the data reported in this chapter and that in the tables in the Louisiana chapter that use voting-age population.

11. We report the data in chap. 10 only for those Texas cities which were at least 10 percent black. Thus the data base for this chapter will be smaller than that used for the tables in chap. 8, which include cities that were at least 10 percent black plus Hispanic.

Thanks to another important feature of the data that were collected, the Texas chapter also is able to assess the effect of black population in a district on Hispanic officeholding and, conversely, the effect of Hispanic population in a district on black officeholding. This feature of the Texas data is discussed in chap. 8.

12. The addition of the Native American component in North Carolina only slightly expands the set of cities that meet the threshold conditions. Those cities are included in the data when we summarize the findings of the tables in the North Carolina chapter (tables 10.1–10.5) since that is how the data in that chapter are reported. However, Native American figures have been dropped from the data set when we report only on cities of at least 10,000 (tables 10.6 and 10.7). Those tables include only cities 10 percent or more black. In North Carolina there were three cities above 10,000 in total population (Ashboro, Boone, and Carey) that were less than 10 percent black but more than 10 percent combined black

and Native American. Ashboro was 9.7 percent black; the other two had black populations of roughly 3 percent. Because of these and other minor differences in classifying North Carolina cities according to minority population depending upon whether black population or black plus Native American population is used, some care must be taken in comparing the results for North Carolina in tables 10.1 through 10.5 with those in tables 10.6 and 10.7.

13. Data are reported for 724 of them. There are far more at-large cities from North Carolina than from the remaining seven states combined.

14. We report data on black representation in terms of cities' total population percentage rather than their percentage of voting-age population primarily to increase comparability to earlier research. Because all tables in this book (except for some of the Louisiana ones) use total population rather than voting-age population, a few cities in our data base that are majority-minority in population are not majority-minority in voting-age population. This is most likely to be true for cities that have barely more than a 50 percent minority population. Also, some cities in each state might shift location among our two other black population categories, depending on whether total population or voting-age population was used as a base. In the Lousiana chapter, for example, compare tables 4.1 and 4.1A. The former reports data for cities classified by black population as a percentage of total population; the latter, as a percentage of voting-age population.

Note also that all population data in the tables—the basis for the denominators in our measures of representational equity—are derived from the 1980 census, although data on the number of elected officials—which provide the numerators—are for either the early 1970s or the late 1980s. Our reliance on the single reference point of 1980 for population figures but on two reference points for our officeholding figures was dictated by the fact that our studies were completed before the 1990 census figures were available, and thus city population estimates could not be made by interpolating between 1970, 1980, and 1990. Therefore, equity measures for the late 1980s may need some minor adjustments in light of 1990 population data; however, such adjustments probably would not significantly alter the comparative findings reported in this volume because there is no reason to believe that black population changes between 1980 and 1990 are correlated with adoption of different electoral plans. (A test of this "no correlation" hypothesis using the Texas city population data in the two census years found it to be true.) However, for individual states, in cells with only one or two cases, there may be effects created by differential population changes over the past decades. For example, as discussed below, one of the Texas cities that elected at large throughout the period shifted from majority-white to majority-black between 1980 and 1990. Since it is the only city in its population category and exhibits substantial black officeholding, the Texas data considerably overstate black electoral success in majority-white at-large jurisdictions by our treating this city as if it were majority-white in 1989, when in fact it was not.

15. Because many North Carolina cities retained an at-large election plan, weighting by cities rather than by states would give results that heavily overrepresented the North Carolina data for that category. To avoid this problem, when we provide a similar eight-state comparison only for cities of at least 10,000 (table 10.6) we calculate (a) the mean using cities as the unit of analysis as well as (b) the mean with states as the units used in table 10.2. For the data set consisting of cities of at least 10,000, no single state provides an excessively large share of the data points.

16. While more categories might have been used, the ones we have chosen have the important property of excluding cities with a minuscule black population. In such cities, change in election type ought not to matter in comparisons between district and at-large

plans, since minority population concentrations large enough to form the majority in a single-member district do not exist. Our choice of three categories also allows us to distinguish between cities that were majority black in population and those that were not, since we anticipated that this would be an important threshold.

17. Here we round to two significant digits.

18. In a subsequent analysis (table 10.3) we reanalyze the data in table 10.2 in another way, to generate the ratio of black representation relative to black population in a given time period in cities of various election types. Immediately above we looked at the *growth* in black representation relative to black population.

19. We use values for the at-large unchanged cities as our control because in almost no state were there enough unchanged cities of other types to provide a reliable baseline to estimate changes in minority representation taking place independently of change in election type.

20. Another example of a possible maturation effect is a significant general change over time in the type of black candidate running—for instance, an increase in the number of conservative black candidates with a greater appeal to white voters.

21. The seeming dramatic *gain* in black representation in Texas at-large cities 30–49.9 percent black also is based on a single city in that cell—a city that, in fact, had become majority black by 1990 and thus is almost certainly misclassified as majority white in 1989. We should also point out that a very different picture, one of small gains in minority representation in Texas at-large jurisdictions, is derived from the full Texas data set based on cities at least 10 percent black and Hispanic combined (see chap. 8).

22. As noted earlier, the reported mean is based on averaging across each state's cell values in the table; otherwise the North Carolina data set, which has far and away the largest *N* for the at-large unchanged category (because it includes a large number of very small cities) would swamp all other data points.

23. Trivial differences between the means reported for the last five columns in tables 10.2A–C and the simple differences between means that might be calculated based on the raw data reported in the first six columns of that table are due to differences in the number of states for which means are being calculated (means for the last five columns are reported only for those states for which complete data is available) and rounding effects. A similar caveat applies to calculations of means in all subsequent tables.

24. The two exceptions are the three Alabama cities that were 10–29.9 percent black and the one Texas city that was 30–49.9 percent black.

25. In 1980 this city (Forest Hill, Texas) was only 36 percent black; by 1990 it was 61 percent.

26. See chap. 12 for evidence for this fact.

27. However, there are some state-by-state variations in this pattern, especially with respect to mixed cities. See table 10.2C.

28. Recall that the means calculated are based on states as units.

29. On a state-by-state basis the pattern is somewhat more complicated, although in only one state (if we exclude the Texas city that was not really majority white in 1989) did a shift to single-member districts have a greater effect on black gains in cities 10–29.9 percent black than in cities 30–49.9 percent black.

30. See chap. 12.

31. For example, of the nine Louisiana majority-black cities, only four were majority-black in voting-age population (see tables 4.2 and 4.2A).

32. Again we report data for cities in each of three categories of election type and for each of our three categories of minority population proportion.

33. We again report values for individual states as well as an overall average that simply is the average of the eight state values.

34. Across a set of cities a mean equity score has been calculated by averaging the equity ratio in each of the cities. Alternatively, we might take the ratio of the average black representation in those cities to the average black population in those cities. The average of the ratios is not necessarily the same as the ratio of the averages, but in general the two figures will usually be close. For consistency across tables, we calculated the ratio of the averages. Otherwise one could not obtain the values in table 4 in each of the state chapters by dividing the average values of black representation and black population given in table 2 in each. Rather, access to the raw data would be needed.

35. See Grofman 1983 for a discussion of the ratio measure and a review of its use in other studies.

36. Later we will show that these latter two high at-large equity values also can partly be explained in terms of differences between the kind of cities that shifted election plan and of cities that did not.

37. Recall that tables 10.2A–C are intended to highlight *change* in representation in the cities that changed election type, including a measure of net change that is relative to the unchanged at-large cities, while tables 10.3A and 10.3B show proportionality of representation relative to population at a given point (table 10.3B "before" and Table 10.3A "after"). Of course, we can also look at black equity changes over time by comparing the data in the corresponding cells of tables 10.3A and 10.3B. See the discussion of selection bias below.

38. Virginia, Texas, and Georgia are also among the four states for which there is some evidence for selection bias in majority-white cities. In Virginia and Georgia, for cities that were 10–29.9 percent black and 30–49.9 percent black, the equity score was highest in cities that remained at large; and the same is true for Texas cities that were 10–29.9 percent black. In South Carolina, a very slight potential selection bias effect is found in cities 30–49.9 percent black.

39. Most of the mixed plans for which we have data are majority white. See table 10.4.

40. In all states except Texas and Virginia (see table 10.3A), minority representation in the majority-white cities was clearly diluted by the at-large component of the mixed plans, since these are the only two states where the equity score for mixed cities was near 1.00 in majority-white cities. In these two states, the district seats in mixed plans actually over-represented blacks sufficiently so that even the addition of an at-large component where blacks were dramatically underrepresented did not drive the equity score below 0.95. We also note that in those states there were usually many more districted seats than at-large seats in the mixed cities.

41. Many of the majority-black cities with mixed plans in the various states had only slight black population majorities and were not cities in which blacks constituted a majority of the electorate.

42. It is perhaps not coincidental that some states had no districts that were 40–49.9 percent black, since this is a category that might be seen by the Justice Department as "cracking" black voting strength if there were the potential to create a majority-black district.

43. Recall that our data are in terms of black population proportions, not registration or turnout shares.

44. Data on the 60–64.9 percent and 65–69.9 percent black population categories in Mississippi are not shown in table 10.5 but are reported in table 5.6 in the Mississippi chapter. In Mississippi, districts that were above 70 percent black had a 94 percent probability of electing black city council members.

45. Indeed, in general it appears to us that there is a mirror pattern of racial polarization in majority-white and majority-black units when we take into account the different registration and turnout levels of whites and blacks and imagine what the data would look like if districts were classified by black share of the actual electorate rather than black population share.

46. It might be argued that the imposition of a mixed system allows whites who might otherwise be tempted to vote for blacks to vote their preference for the white candidates who run at large, safe in the knowledge that at least some blacks will be elected at the district level. Thus we might expect even more polarized voting in mixed cities than in pure at-large cities. And the data do indeed suggest greater polarization. By a similar logic, in pure district cities white voters' knowledge that there are majority-black districts may lead some who might otherwise be disposed to vote for blacks to believe that they now have no obligation to vote for black candidates in any district. And once again we find evidence compatible with this view: there appears to be less polarized voting in at-large cities than in majority-white districts in pure district cities. But there are other plausible explanations as well. More blacks may be elected at large in pure at-large cities than in either the at-large components of mixed plans or in individual majority-white districts in single-member district plans simply because, in citywide races, it is more likely that numerous white candidates will contest for office, allowing a black candidate to be a plurality winner, or because white politicians are eager to have some black officeholders in order to preclude a successful voting rights challenge. There may be other reasons as well. An evaluation of the merits of the competing explanations for the observed differences in black success among these three types of majority-white settings must be left to subsequent research.

47. Why should North Carolina's record be so poor in this regard? One answer might be that the state of its race relations has been overrated. Another more likely explanation is that voting rights litigation came late to North Carolina and has not yet penetrated the state's rural areas, whereas Mississippi, whose record in voting rights for blacks has been egregious, became the target much earlier of vigorous and well-funded legal attacks. It is also important to recognize that most of the North Carolina cities in the data set are relatively small and rural—a result of the absence of a size threshold. Later in the chapter we address black representation in cities of different size.

48. For example, in Georgia the equity ratio for at-large majority-white counties was roughly half that of the at-large majority-white cities, averaging around 0.16.

49. Compare tables 3.5A, 6.5A, and 7.5A with tables 3.5, 6.5, and 7.5, respectively.

50. Thernstrom 1987.

51. Welch 1990.

52. Ibid, 1059, table 2, and 1066, table 4.

53. Welch (1990, 1059, table 2, and 1066, table 4) reports data both for cities that met a 5 percent black population threshold and those that met a 10 percent black population threshold; similarly, she reports data both for cities at least 5 percent Hispanic and for cities at least 10 percent Hispanic. To ensure direct comparability with our own results (and because we would not expect significant differences in minority representation by election type in cities with only a minuscule minority population), we focus on the result that Welch reports for majority-white cities that were *at least 10 percent black*, since this is the threshold used in

our state chapters. (Her results do not appear to differ significantly according to which minority population threshold is used, however.) There were 170 majority-white cities at least 10 percent black in her data base, of which 68 were in the South. Of these 68 cities, 23 elected at large, 14 by districts, and 31 by mixed plans.

54. The figure we report is for at-large cities that were 10–49.9 percent black, the same range restriction as used by our chapter authors. We have data on eight of the eleven states in Welch's "South" category.

55. Welch 1990, 1059, table 2.

56. Ibid., 1058. See also Engstrom and McDonald 1981; Karnig and Welch 1982; Robinson and Dye 1978.

57. Welch 1990, 1058–59; Karnig and Welch 1982.

58. Welch 1990, 1059, table 2, and 1061.

59. See, for example, Bullock 1989; O'Rourke 1992.

60. We emphasize that the discussion below addresses only the empirical aspects of the controversy. As discussed in the Editors' Introduction, we have sought to eschew discussion of the complicated normative issues involved in deciding what the conditions are under which race-conscious districting is permissible or required. For our views on some normative aspects of the debate over enforcement of the Voting Rights Act, see Grofman and Davidson 1992.

61. Welch 1990, 1059, table 2.

62. Our findings also contradict Bullock and MacManus (1991a), who claim that election type is not nearly as important a factor in black officeholding as the independent effect of black population proportion. As various students of this issue have noted, blacks are unlikely to be elected in jurisdictions with few blacks, regardless of what type of election system is employed. Moreover, whatever the election type, the proportion of black elected officials will be strongly related to the black proportion in the population, regardless of whether voting is racially polarized. However, the correct policy question to ask—the one we have sought to answer—is whether, for a *given* proportion of minority population, election type makes a difference in rates of minority representation. Our findings show that the predicted effect of at-large election systems held true for all levels of black population in majority-white cities with more than a minuscule black population.

63. Moreover, if we exclude the Texas city in the 30–49.9 percent black category misclassified as majority-white by 1980 population data, the equity score in the 30–49.9 percent black at-large category drops to 0.43.

64. The exception is Georgia, whose at-large cities 30–49.9 percent black had councils that were 20 percent black in 1980 but only 17 percent black in 1990.

65. See our discussion below of the effects of city size.

66. Welch 1990, 1059, table 2.

67. Recall that the data set in Welch 1990 is for 1988, while ours is for 1989 (1990 in Georgia); further, she includes three southern states—Arkansas, Tennessee, and Florida—for which we do not have data.

68. If we restrict the sample to cities above 10,000, the *N*s of our longitudinal data base change for the five states where data are initially reported for cities with population less than 10,000: in Alabama, the *N* is reduced from 48 to 32; in Louisiana, from 57 to 20; in Mississippi, from 130 to 23; in North Carolina, from 724 to 38; and in Virginia, from 23 to 15. For the North Carolina data we report in tables 10.6A–C and 10.7A–B, we also remind the reader that cities with combined black and Native American population greater than 10 percent that had black population smaller than 10 percent have been excluded. In Georgia

four multimember-district cities are excluded from tables 10.6A–C and 10.7A–B as well as from most other previous tables. In Georgia ($N = 15$, after we eliminate the four cities that used multimember districts), in South Carolina ($N = 21$), and in Texas ($N = 42$), the *N*s remain the same as in tables 10.2A–C and 10.3A–B, since these three states are ones where data were already reported only for cities of at least 10,000. Thus for these states, there are no differences in the data reported in tables 10.6A–C and 10.7A–B and that reported in tables 10.2A–C and 10.3A–B. For Texas, however, we would also remind the reader that the *N* in many of the tables in the Texas chapter is larger than that in tables 10.6A–C and 10.7A–B because tables in the Texas chapter include cities whose *combined* black and Hispanic population was above 10 percent.

69. The former averaging procedure is more directly comparable to the data reported in other studies of the effects of election type on minority representation. We have reported both types of averages in tables 10.6A–C and 10.7A–B to permit readier comparison with the data reported in tables 10.2A–C and 10.3A–B.

70. However, in Alabama, voting rights efforts penetrated throughout the state at all levels of government, reaching down even into the smaller towns (Peyton McCrary, personal communication, March 1993; also see chap. 2), and we would thus not expect city size differences to have that great an independent impact on levels of black representation.

71. Roughly 30 percent of the majority-white cities in our data set above 50,000 population retained at-large elections.

72. Compare, for example, Grofman, Handley, and Niemi 1992, chap. 2.

73. Welch 1990, 1073.

74. If we further confine ourselves to cities that were over 50,000 in total population, 31 percent of such cities in the eight states of our study eliminated at-large elections. This is higher than the 21 percent figure for the entire eight-state data set. (For majority-white cities the comparable percentages are 30 and 21 percent.) The larger cities were much more likely to have been challenged in voting rights litigation or to have changed election type in anticipation of such a challenge.

75. If we turn to the larger data set reported in table 10.3, we also see evidence for potential selection bias effects in majority-black cities in Alabama, Louisiana, and Mississippi. In these states, the majority-black cities that remained at-large began the period with higher black electoral success than those which changed election type. As previously noted, a number of these majority-black cities almost certainly lacked a black electoral majority.

76. These are the same four states for which a possible selection bias effect was previously identified in table 10.3.

77. By *worst case* we mean cities at the earlier point that had the worst track record of minority representation relative to population size and hence were more likely to be challenged; conversely, the *best case* cities had the best track record and were least vulnerable to challenge.

78. It will be remembered that our decision to choose, when possible, the early 1970s as the starting point for our data collection was dictated by various considerations. One was that we wanted ideally to include as many cities as possible in the post-act period from 1965 on that had changed election system. But our hunch that data would not be accessible so far back led us to choose 1974 instead. Our worry about this latter date was that a number of cities would have already changed their system by then, preventing our obtaining data for the "before change" point.

79. Indeed, our data show that in most areas of the South, the great majority of changes in election type occurred after the 1982 amendments to section 2.

80. Similarly, when we confine ourelves to majority-white cities above 50,000 in population (of which there are forty-six in our eight-state data set), there is little evidence of selection bias, in terms of cities that remained at large having initially had a higher level of minority representation than the cities changing election type—at least if we use the initial period as the basis for our determination.

81. See chap. 3. Alabama's research team collected data on minority representation and election type in all its cities for 1980 as well as for 1970, and for 1986 as well as for 1989. Using 1980 as an alternative starting point, we can test for selection bias in Alabama to see whether the most striking unexplained anomaly in our data in table 10.3A—the 1.10 equity value for the three majority-white Alabama cities in the 10–29.9 percent black category that still elected at large in 1989—can at least partly be attributed to selection bias efforts.

A comparison of 1980 and 1989 data demonstrates the probability of a very significant selection bias for Alabama cities 10–29.9 percent black, one that is not apparent when data for 1970 and 1989 only are compared. Even as late as 1980 there were still thirty-five at-large majority-white cities in Alabama of 6,000 or above with a black population of at least 10 percent, as compared to forty-two in 1970 and three in 1989. While the three cities retaining at-large plans in 1989 do not appear atypical in their *1970* equity score, that is not true when *1980* becomes the starting baseline. (In 1974, these three cities, like all majority-white cities in Alabama, had no black city council representatives. See the discussion in chap. 2.) In the three cities in question, by 1980 blacks were already *overrepresented*, with a mean equity score of 1.16, far higher than the 0.26 for the thirty-five majority-white at-large cities that year. Thus the three cities remaining at large in 1989 were a small and quite unrepresentative subset of those with at large plans in 1980. This is strong evidence for the existence of a selection bias in Alabama for cities in the 10–29.9 percent black population category.

The Alabama analysis is further illustration of the potential problems of using cross-sectional analysis to draw causal inferences in settings where a strong selection bias is quite possibly at work. The three anomalous cities had a mean equity score of 1.10 in 1989. In other words, blacks at that point were more than proportionally represented in these at-large jurisdictions. A cross-sectional analysis using 1989 Alabama data might well suggest that because the at-large systems provided fair representation, the shifts from at-large to district elections in other Alabama cities had been unnecessary. But that inference would almost certainly be wrong. As early as 1980, these three cities were ones where black success had been much higher than in the at-large cities that subsequently switched. Had an additional intermediate data year been available for comparison in some of the other states, as it was for Alabama, it is possible that evidence of additional selection bias efforts might have been revealed.

82. Recall also that the equity ratio in this category would become 0.43 if the Texas city that was majority white in 1980 but majority black in 1990 were excluded from the data set.

83. Recall that in Mississippi it was close to 100 percent in districts that were at least 70 percent black.

84. Welch 1990.

85. The last two columns in tables 10.2A–C indicate the longitudinal gains in black officeholding in single-member-district and mixed plans relative to those occurring in the unchanged jurisdictions. Taking average council size to be roughly six, we can calculate how many black officeholders were elected in the changed cities relative to what would have been expected had these cities elected black officeholders at the same rate as did the

unchanged cities. Performing such calculations for the 117 cities that shifted from at-large to single-member-district plans (44 of which were 10–29.9 percent black; 55, 30–49.9 percent black; and 18, majority black), we find a net gain of 157 black representatives. For the 100 cities shifting from an at-large to a mixed plan (43 of which were 10–29.9 percent black; 38, 30–49.9 percent black; and 19, majority-black), we find a net gain of 48 black officeholders. The hypothetical net gain resulting from change to pure districts is considerably greater than the gain from change to mixed systems even though the number of cities in each category is not that different. This is because black representation is greater, on average, in pure district plans than in mixed ones. If we examine the longitudinal gains in the changed cities by substracting the number of black representatives at the beginning of the study from that at the end, we find well over 300 new black council members.

86. The Alabama data are particularly instructive. There we might have overlooked the potential for selection bias completely if, employing only a cross-sectional design to investigate black officeholding, we had looked only at the three at-large cities that still elected at large in 1989.

Chapter Eleven
The Impact of the Voting Rights Act on Minority Representation

1. See, for an example of this argument, O'Rourke 1992.

2. According to exit polls, Wilder did not receive a majority of the white votes in his bid for office in 1989. An exit poll conducted by CBS/*New York Times* reported that only 39 percent of the whites voting in the Virginia gubernatorial contest voted for Wilder. If whites alone had voted, the white Republican, Marshall Coleman, would have been elected governor of Virginia (*Time*, 20 November 1989, 54).

3. The one longitudinal study that exists on the subject of racial bloc voting—a case study of South Carolina—shows essentially no change in the degree of racially polarized voting (Loewen 1990).

4. These numbers are based on the seven southern states for which there are comparable data in the 1970s and 1980s: Alabama, Georgia, Louisiana, Mississippi, North Carolina (senate only), South Carolina, and Virginia.

5. Let P_1 be the proportion of all districts that are majority nonblack and P_2 be the proportion of all districts that are majority black. Further, let B_1 be the proportion of nonmajority-black districts that elect a black legislator and B_2 be the proportion of majority-black districts that elect a black legislator. The Grofman-Jackson decomposition-effects formula is: $X_t - X_0 = (\Sigma\Delta P_i \times B_i) + (\Sigma\Delta B_i \times P_i) + (\Sigma\Delta P_i \times \Delta B_i)$

6. The behavioral effect is positive because majority-black districts were much more likely to elect blacks to office in the 1980s than in the 1970s, outweighing the negative effect of majority-white districts being *less* likely to elect blacks in the 1980s than in the 1970s.

7. The interaction effect is positive because the number of white-majority seats decreased but, since those seats were less likely to elect black candidates than previously, we have a positive contribution of the interaction term. Similarly, the number of majority-black seats increased but so, too, did the probability that those seats would elect a black, giving rise to another positive interaction effect.

8. The percentages of the black population in 1980 that did *not* reside in majority-black house or senate districts for each of the states are as follows:

	Senate	*House*
Alabama	57	50
Arkansas	81	60
Florida	88	75
Georgia	61	54
Louisiana	73	59
Mississippi	56	50
North Carolina	95	79
South Carolina	60	57
Tennessee	58	55
Texas	86	68
Virginia	91	70

9. See Brace, Grofman, Handley, and Niemi 1988.

10. On lower black participation rates in Mississippi, see Lichtman and Issacharoff 1991.

11. However, a lower proportion of blacks were of voting age than was true for whites; hence the proportion of black voters within a district was unlikely to equal the proportion of white voters within a district with equal total population proportions, even if blacks were registering and voting at the same rate as whites (see Brace, Grofman, Handley, and Niemi 1988).

12. According to census surveys (U.S. Department of Commerce, Bureau of the Census 1989, table A), the percentages of adult blacks and whites who voted in presidential elections in the South from 1972 through 1988 are as follows:

	1972	*1976*	*1980*	*1984*	*1988*
White	57.0	57.1	57.4	58.1	56.4
Black	47.8	45.7	48.2	53.2	48.0

13. Black and Black 1987, chap. 1.

14. Although the Justice Department objected to plans for both chambers in South Carolina, the state successfully challenged the senate plan objection in court and only the house was required to shift to single-member districts.

15. *White v. Regester*, 412 U.S. 755 (1973).

16. *Thornburg v. Gingles*, 478 U.S. 30 (1986).

17. *Jeffers v. Clinton*, 730 F. Supp. 196 (E.D. Ark. 1989).

18. See, for example, Thernstrom 1987, 190–91.

19. Jewell 1980 and 1982; Grofman, Migalski, and Noviello 1986.

20. Since not all legislatures are of equal size, these regressions were replicated with changes in black representation expressed as a percentage of all legislators in a chamber rather than in terms of the actual number of legislators, but the conclusions are essentially identical and thus the results have been presented in terms of raw numbers for ease of exposition. More important, these analyses were also replicated with a control for the size of the black population in the state, but since this control did not have a significant effect on the findings, these results have been omitted.

21. A look at the raw data in table 11.7 will also confirm that a shift to single-member districts resulted in an increase in the number of black legislators elected. For example, the

elimination of multimember districts between 1970 and 1975 led to a gain of 13 black representatives in the Alabama house, a gain of 7 black representatives in both Georgia and Louisiana, a gain of 13 black legislators in South Carolina, and a gain of 7 black representatives in the Texas house. Similar gains were made in senates following a change from multimember districts to single-member districts, although the gains were smaller. (Because senate districts are larger than state house districts, it is usually more difficult to create majority-black seats in the senate than in the house. That fact, combined with the fact that there are fewer seats in a senate to be filled, means that the effects of electoral system change on black representation are much less pronounced for senates than for houses.)

22. A "census redistricting year" dummy variable was also incorporated in the analysis to test for the simple effect of redistricting (assigning a 1 for the period 1970–75 and 1980–85, and a value of 0 otherwise). Regressing this "redistricting year" dummy variable against change in black representation produced weak correlations of .17 in the house and .31 in the senate that were not statistically significant in either case.

23. It is actually the number of majority-black single-member districts that was the proximate cause of the gain in black representation; the increases in black representation brought about by changes to single-member districts were mediated by the change in the number of majority-black seats that were drawn following the elimination or reduction in the number of multimember districts. Exactly as we would expect, there was a very strong correlation (r = .82) between the number of black-majority seats and the number of black state representatives. This correlation was even further strengthened when we entered an additional variable for the number of black-majority districts with a 60 percent or greater black population (r = .84). In the state senates, the correlations were lower but the relationships were still statistically significant. The correlation between the number of black senators and the number of majority-black districts was .47. The correlation between the number of black senators and the number of districts over 60 percent black was .52.

24. However, not all majority-black congressional districts elected blacks to office; the Louisiana Second (59 percent black) did not elect one until 1990.

25. Yet, it took several attempts before a black candidate managed to win the Mississippi Second. Robert Clark ran in both 1982 and 1984; in 1982 the district was only 54 percent black (and was less than majority black in voting-age population). A federal court ordered the district redrawn in 1984 (*Jordan v. Winter*, 541 F. Supp. 1135 [N.D. 1982], *vac'd and remanded sub nom. Brooks v. Winter*, 461 U.S. 921 [1983], *on remand* 604 F. Supp. 807 [N.D. Miss. 1984]) and a 58 percent black district was created. Mike Espy finally won the seat in 1986.

26. In 1990, a black, William Jefferson, was elected to the Louisiana Second when Boggs retired.

27. *Busbee v. Smith*, 549 F. Supp. 494 (D.D.C. 1982).

28. *Jordan v. Winter*, 541 F. Supp. 1135 (N.D. 1982), *vac'd and remanded sub nom. Brooks v. Winter*, 461 U.S. 921 (1983), *on remand* 604 F. Supp. 807 (N.D. Miss. 1984).

29. *Major v. Treen*, 574 F. Supp. 325 (E.D. La. 1983).

30. Grofman and Handley 1989a.

Chapter Twelve
The Impact of the Voting Rights Act on Black and White Voter Registration in the South

The support of the National Science Foundation under grants #SES 8809392 and #SBR 9223638 is gratefully acknowledged. Thanks for valuable comments on earlier drafts of this paper are owed to Nancy Burns, Robert Erikson, Mo Fiorina, Michael Hagen, Bill Keech, Gary King, Morgan Kousser, Harold Stanley, and Katherine Tate.

1. There are numerous aspects of southern white political behavior that are important for understanding race relations and the maintenance of white dominance which I do not discuss because they are not central to my focus on disfranchisement devices and minority registration. For example, fears of the "black threat" played a pivotal role in state administration, where counties could be abolished or have their powers modified; also, the southern judiciary sometimes condoned violence and discrimination.

2. The exact nature of the data base is discussed in the appendix to this chapter.

3. Matthews and Prothro 1963.

4. The only counties to achieve majority-black electorates were counties with majority-black voting-age populations.

5. The Supreme Court upheld it on the grounds that it did not explicitly discriminate between the races and that bias in its application had not been demonstrated; the Court later upheld it even where the application appeared biased. See Key 1949, 538.

6. Kousser 1974, 49, 241.

7. Rusk and Stucker 1978.

8. 238 U.S. 347.

9. 307 U.S. 268.

10. Lawson 1976, chap. 2, provides an excellent history of the legal and political conflict surrounding this restriction, from the initial enactment of a statewide Texas white primary in 1923 to its demise in 1944.

11. Reitman and Davidson 1972, 16.

12. As quoted by Colby 1986, 124–25.

13. Unit voting schemes like Georgia's, which gave extra weight to the rural areas that tended to have black majorities, increased the incentive for whites to disfranchise blacks. Key (1949, 5) remarks on the important role played by whites in majority-black areas in the politics of disfranchisement.

14. Reitman and Davidson 1972, 18.

15. Key 1949, chap. 26.

16. The Supreme Court had struck down Alabama's Boswell Amendment as too arbitrary but left other literacy tests intact. The 1964 Civil Rights Act had required administration of literacy tests in writing, to restrict arbitrariness in application and possibly to facilitate litigation. Constitutional cases sustaining the Voting Rights Act's abolition of literacy requirements and the use of federal examiners are reviewed in Reitman and Davidson 1972, 145–46.

17. Matthews and Prothro 1963, 1966.

18. The tax was cumulative in Virginia, though other states had dropped this provision. Veterans and the disabled were frequently exempted. See Smith 1960.

19. 383 U.S. 663.

20. Lawson 1976, chap. 3, provides details of the long battles against the poll tax by various civil rights organizations. For an early before-and-after analysis of the impact of the poll tax on voting, see Ogden 1958, chap. 5.

21. As late as the 1950s, neither Texas nor Arkansas had a system of enumerating registered voters other than compilation of poll tax receipts.

22. In the pre-act South my research reveals significant independent effects on registration only for literacy requirements, poll taxes, and residence requirements. Rosenstone and Wolfinger (1978) describe effects of factors other than these three. Some of the factors they discuss, such as early closing dates and the lack of local registration sites, explain differ-

ences between the South and the rest of the country rather than differences within the South. Lengthy residence requirements were eliminated by the Supreme Court in *Dunn v. Blumstein* (1972), 405 U.S. 330.

23. While Black and Black (1987, 126) describe black registration and voting over the last two decades—following passage of the act—as the "limited leverage of a franchised minority," they have little to say in a systematic manner about the causes of variation in racial registration rates from place to place.

24. See Wright 1987, 21; and Thernstrom 1987, 15–16.

25. Key 1949, 576, 605, 617–18.

26. Matthews and Prothro (1963, 24, emphasis added). Unfortunately, Matthews and Prothro do not report their findings in a way that makes it easy to estimate separate effects or to see how the impact of legal barriers was affected by contextual factors like black population proportion.

27. Matthews and Prothro (1963) did not directly report how much of an effect racial composition had independently of its many socioeconomic correlates. Including all their twenty or so extra demographic variables in a model only predicts black registration about one-fifth better than does black concentration alone.

28. Matthews and Prothro (1966, 324) also asserted, "Legal changes in the political system—such as those stemming from the Voting Rights Act of 1965—can increase Negro political activity. But any changes are likely to be small unless or until these changes in the legal climate lead to . . . greater interest, partisanship, information about parties, and general political information." Earlier works stressing different socioeconomic factors include Fenton and Vines 1957; Price 1955.

29. Matthews and Prothro 1966, 164. I use their data on race organizations below.

30. They did not discuss the effects of racial groups on white registration.

31. Stanley 1987, table 7 and p. 93. He also finds that economic dependence (as measured by the concentration of tenant farming) strongly reduced black participation, but his data do not permit him to test the effects of race organizations or to determine whether, for instance, white registration was higher where more blacks were registered, other things equal.

32. Of course, either process could be operative, depending on the proportion of blacks in a jurisdiction or on differing political cultures in various southern locales.

33. Salamon and van Evera 1973.

34. Key clearly comes closest: consider his observation in the 1940s that "almost everywhere the figures suggest that when other conditions are the same the presence of a substantial Negro population brings with it a higher level of white voting" (1949, 516). Blalock, writing after Key, infers that whites, as the dominant group, must mobilize disproportionately as their numerical advantage declines, and thus advocates devising a "measure of discrimination involv[ing] a ratio of white to Negro voter registrations" (1967, 163). Blalock's call for researchers to focus on the combined registration rates of both races was an important step forward, in spite of his lack of empirical data to investigate the dynamics of biracial registration.

35. Naturally, maintaining numerical supremacy after passage of the act would have retained its appeal to whites, but the older institutional strategies were no longer available. In the period before the act, of course, if blacks could have been depended on to support particular white candidates, their registration would not have had to be prevented.

36. The general perspective of my analysis is one in which choices that are efficient in terms of costs and benefits are sought, subject to information and feasibility constraints.

37. As with any other type of organization, it is costly in human and other resources to form and maintain racial political organizations. Matthews and Prothro (1966) do not look at the question of where race organizations of either race should be expected to form.

38. Indeed, as the analysis leading to table 12.3 demonstrates, the effect of a poll tax was to reduce white advantage, particularly at high black population levels. Overall, residence requirements also reduced white advantage.

39. However, ceteris paribus, the existence of severe literacy tests appears to have diminished the likelihood of black race organizations.

40. Also, white race organizations tended to form where white average incomes and education levels were higher and where the population was growing. Black race organizations were more likely to be formed in urban areas, less likely in agricultural areas, and more likely where the black population was more educated. Analyses on which these findings are based are omitted because of space constraints.

41. I also believe that, with the possible exception of residency requirements, states adopted these mechanisms because, on balance, they believed that they restricted the size of the black electorate.

42. Matthews and Prothro (1966, 155) show that in three North Carolina counties where white registrars did not enforce the literacy requirement, the black registration rate appeared to be dramatically high, but they fail to point out that in one of these counties blacks comprised only 1 percent of the county population, and in the other two less than 10 percent.

43. Morgan Kousser (personal communication, 1991) suggests the alternative interpretation that in areas where black concentration was high, whites collected the poll tax from blacks to raise county revenue and keep other tax rates lower. Also see Kousser 1980, 178.

44. Similarly, resources like education and income should have facilitated the development of race-based organizations.

45. Southern congressional Democrats were instrumental in preventing the extension of Social Security legislation to agricultural workers in the 1930s precisely because this would have interfered with the structure of dependence. See Alston 1985. More generally, of course, southern representatives fought to prevent federal legal intervention in local electoral and social practices (Key 1949, 9).

46. Technically, taking logarithms reduces the effect of heteroskedasticity, or larger random error variance, where the black population is very small.

47. Values shown are for the most complete data set for the period. See the appendix to this chapter for a description of the data.

48. Omitted from figure 12.1 are twenty-two counties with some voting-age blacks but a black registration rate of zero. These cases of total exclusion arose at a variety of black population densities and were mostly in Mississippi. The counties had other political and socioeconomic characteristics that, when combined with the parameter estimates for black registration rates in counties in the rest of the South with black populations of more than single figures, imply expected values for black registration of about 3 to 5 percent—which was about average for Mississippi at that time.

49. Exponentiation, or taking the constant *e* to a power, reverses the effects of taking natural logarithms.

50. The inclusion of an interaction between, say, poll tax and black population concentration means that the effect of a poll tax on white numerical advantage depended on the level of black population density or, conversely, that the effect of black density depended on whether or not there was a poll tax.

51. To assess the importance of interaction effects in counties with various levels of black population proportion, one must multiply the coefficients by the appropriate black population percentage. Such a multiplication could increase the coefficient by a factor of up to 100 in the case of all-black counties.

52. I say "effectively" because where there are absolutely no blacks in a county, white advantage is strictly undefined.

53. For example, in a county with a black voting-age population of 60 percent, we would obtain $e^{(-.217 + 60 \times .016)}$, which equals 2.10.

54. Where there was only a poll tax but no literacy requirement, as in Texas and Arkansas, blacks might have been expected to register at higher rates than whites, especially in black-majority counties. In fact, however, very few such counties had only a poll tax, and thus other factors, such as race organizations, need to be taken into account.

55. Other analysis that I do not report shows, as expected, that white race organizations achieved their effect by depressing levels of black registration.

56. If we look at the combined effect of white race organizations and black race organizations, we find white advantage in counties that are over half black.

57. The average difference made by state black population concentration was to increase white advantage by about 4:1, other things equal. Of course, as is almost inevitable because of the definition of the white advantage variable, it declined with *county*-level black VAP share (even "equal effort" would depress the data in figure 12.2 downward from left to right).

58. I have also done extensive econometric analyses that space constraints do not permit me to report, including models with black and white registration rates, respectively, as their dependent variables. These models sometimes give more detail about the interactive effects of restrictive laws on white advantage. For instance, in these models, poll taxes affected both white and black registration rates. They reduced black registration by 14 percentage points on average, but, where there were few blacks, it reduced white registration by up to 27 points. Residence requirements reduced black registration by about 8 points where a strict one-year residence requirement existed, but had a much larger effect on whites, reducing their registration rates by up to 30 percentage points in areas of high black population concentrations. The existence of a literacy requirement reduced white registration rates by a constant amount, nearly 12 points, at all levels of black population. But while a literacy requirement reduced black registration on average by only 5 to 6 points, it affected black registration rates more as black population percentage increased, so that in 50-percent-black counties its estimated effects on black and white registration were equal. Moreover, at high black concentrations the existence of a white race organization had a bigger negative effect on black registration than the positive effect induced by the presence of a black race organization. Finally, for each 10 point increase in a state's black population concentration, there was, on average, a 10 point gain in the percentage of whites who were registered. All these effects appear in a simpler form in the results reported in table 12.3. Of course, models that estimate black and white registration levels separately fail to take into account interactions like the effects of local black registration levels on white registration decisions, which is automatically accounted for by our white advantage variable that measures *relative* levels of black and white registration.

59. Some suggestive findings about geographically clustered areas with high residuals are omitted because of space considerations.

60. All other joint effects can be calculated analogously.

61. In Texas, partial pre-act poll tax records indicate that white registration levels of

about 45 percent rose to nearly 54 percent by 1967. These low rates may include many Mexican Americans counted as whites. Other states where white registration was low, partly as a result of the poll tax, included Arkansas (whose white rate rose from 65 percent before the act to 72 percent afterward) and Virginia (61 percent before, 63 percent after). In contrast, white registration rates of 90 percent and more were reached in Alabama, Louisiana, and Mississippi by 1967, reflecting increases of nearly 20 percentage points on average.

62. For example, the aggregate data in Stanley (1987, 97 and 154) show that in 1980, 58 percent of blacks were registered, and whites comprised 80 percent of the eligible population but 84 percent of the actual electorate. From these numbers we can calculate a white registration rate of 76 percent, virtually identical to the 77 percent obtained in his survey estimates. Stanley's own data make it perfectly clear that black survey responses overestimated black registration rates by something like 10 points (echoing other findings on blacks' tendency to overreport turnout to a greater degree than whites). The exact source of this discrepancy is not known. Of course, the aggregate data used in my essay have problems, too. In particular, the high observed rates for white registration in some states derive from policies that discourage registrars from deleting names of those who have moved or died.

63. However, we also need to be sensitive to the fact that, in the post-1965 period, there were changes in the racial mix in the South caused by net inmigration by whites and outmigration by blacks. Stanley 1987, 6; Black and Black 1987, 12–22.

64. Intermediate values in the figure are based on certain adjustments that were needed to keep changes in voting-age population synchronized with changes in registration.

65. White registration rates were on average higher than those of blacks by perhaps 10–12 percentage points in 1988. This was a smaller difference than was observed a few years earlier. Until 1988, this racial difference existed almost everywhere: there were very few counties where blacks registered at higher rates than whites. The narrowing racial difference was due to a steady decline in white registration from its mid-to-late 1960s peak, while black registration remained stable or rose after 1972.

66. This conclusion is buttressed by econometric analyses predicting black and white registration levels (see below).

67. Majorities are recorded here whether they occurred in 1967 and/or 1968, since some uncertainty exists about the exact dating of estimates for those two years. There are some other data limitations. See the appendix to this chapter.

68. The act's trigger formula enabling the Attorney General to send federal registrars was based on 1964 registration rates, not on the size of the black voting-age population. In fact, the presence of federal examiners never led to a black majority of registrants in a white-majority county.

69. In all cases these estimates of the effects of examiners are independent of the effects of population concentration and the abolition of the legal restrictions discussed earlier. The effect of examiners always looks larger across a shorter time period, partly because over the longer period some of those registered by federal examiners dropped off the rolls, and partly because over longer periods other influences on registration in general came into play, reducing the apparent effect of registrars. The last estimate is consistent with independent figures in Stekler 1983.

70. Note that the number of majority-black counties in the South was declining because of black migration to urban areas, but I have taken this into account (see below).

71. In Georgia, Louisiana, North Carolina, and South Carolina, there were 12 majority-black electorates in 51 majority-black counties in 1968. Not until 1980 were there as many

as 13 (when there were only 45 majority-black counties), although the number rose to 23 of 39 in 1984, to 27 of 39 in 1986, and to 28 of 37 in 1988, assuming the statistical adjustments described in the appendix are correct. Although data are sketchy for certain periods, the biennial data available for South Carolina reveal steady upward movement in majority-black electorates: from 2 of 14 possible in 1971 to 4 of 14 in 1974; then to 6 of 13 in 1976 (the black population was declining), to 7 of 12 in 1980, to 9 of 12 in 1982, and finally to 10 of 12 in 1984. Georgia had 5 majority-black county electorates in 19 majority-black counties in 1980, and 7 of 16 in 1984; and Louisiana had 1 of 7 until 1974, and then none until 1984.

72. The relationship is not simple. There are two counties in Mississippi with durable black majorities of registrants that never had examiners, while examiners went to East Feliciana Parish in Louisiana three times and never secured a black-majority electorate. Unfortunately there are no data to test for the role of black organizations as distinct from the presence of examiners, and there are no interim data at all for Alabama and Georgia, but it is likely that continuing federal enforcement had some effect in securing black-majority electorates.

73. See table 12.6. To some extent, examiners stimulated black registration temporarily to unsustainably high levels. They also pushed rates in their counties up quickly, and blacks elsewhere subsequently caught up. Between 1967 and 1971, black registration rates dropped on average by about a point in the counties visited by examiners in 1966. Outside these counties, the rates rose by about 4 percentage points in the same period.

74. Stanley 1987, 37. Stanley argues that little of the white post-1965 gains in registration could be attributed to white mobilization to counter rising black registration. However, some of what he calls "nonracial" factors affecting pre-1965 registration, like residence requirements, surely were closely connected to racial attitudes. Since residence requirements reduced white registration and advantage (table 12.3), one can conjecture that the relaxation of residence requirements between 1960 and 1970 was motivated at least partly by white officials' desire to increase white registration.

75. Black and Black 1987, 139.

76. E. Black 1976; Stekler 1983.

77. Tate (1988), Stanley (1987, 35–36), and Davison (1986) all show that black turnout in recent times is typically a few percentage points lower than white turnout, except in 1984, when black registration and turnout were stimulated by the Jesse Jackson campaign. Stanley emphasizes the importance of change in registration requirements, increased media usage by blacks, and the effects of newly competing parties in explaining the lessening differences in black and white turnout rates before and after 1968. We draw on this turnout research since factors that raise turnout often also raise registration.

78. The voting-age data by race are available only from the decennial census. Data in intercensus years are estimated by interpolation. Thus, for the period since 1972, the figures for registered voters in these states derive from official counts, but those for voting-age populations derive from estimates, since the voting-age populations of both races change considerably within decades. Indeed, even though the black population in the South is growing more slowly than the white population—accounting for the decline in black concentration and the number of majority-black counties—it is nevertheless growing. Failure to allow for this biases upward any estimates of black registration rates.

79. A justification for using aggregate registration data by race, despite problems with the data, is that minority self-reporting of registration (or turnout) is often exaggerated even more than is true for whites. See for example Tate 1988, and note 62 above.

80. For example, Black and Black 1987, 137; Daniel 1969; Carlson 1980; and Stern 1987.

81. I prepared graphs identical to figure 12.1 in the previous section for subsequent periods. The figures are omitted but are available upon request from the author. The pattern for 1964 is very similar to that for 1958–60, shown in figure 12.1. In contrast, by 1967, after the act's passage, the vertical scatter above the "equal effort" line was much smaller, so the range of observed white advantage had declined sharply. Moreover, by 1971 there were no systematic differences in white advantage at different levels of black concentration, that is, the vertical scatter was about the same at all levels of black concentration. Therefore, by 1971, whatever the sources of white advantage in the post-act South may have been, they had no obvious relation to a county's black population density. One thing had not changed, however: Blacks registered at greater rates than whites hardly anywhere. There were virtually no counties below the equal rates curve. Nonetheless, as described above, there were now cases (in heavily black counties) where blacks formed a majority of the registered county electorate.

82. Also, where population was increasing, white registration rates were initially higher, ceteris paribus, then elsewhere. Subsequently, white population increases were associated with lower white registration rates, while by 1988 they were unrelated to this variable.

83. A few other state-to-state differences appeared. Analysis of them is omitted because of space constraints.

84. The regression standard errors for black rates shown in table 12.6 declined over the years (and would have been considerably larger in 1967 without the inclusion of past registration rates), reinforcing the conclusion that black registration became more predictable as time passed. In fact, when data on Georgia in 1972 are excluded, the registration rates of each race were equally predictable. See table 12.6.

85. This analysis, omitted because of space constraints, is consistent with Davison's study, which shows that turnout variation over time—especially that between presidential and off years—is often greater than interracial differences in turnout. See Davison 1986, especially figs. 1 and 2.

86. See Matthews and Prothro (1963, 25–26) for a description of the data set.

87. Smith 1960, 12–21.

88. U.S. Commission on Civil Rights 1968, app. 7.

89. Some of these data are reprinted in U.S. Commission on Civil Rights 1971.

90. U.S. Commission on Civil Rights 1968, 244.

Chapter Thirteen
The Voting Rights Act and the Second Reconstruction

1. Woodward (1965) coined the term *Second Reconstruction* to point to the parallels but also to some differences, up to the time he wrote, between the movement for civil rights in the 1960s and that following the Civil War. Also see Kousser (1992).

2. Woodward 1965, 128.

3. See chaps. 2–9 in this volume, as well as chap. 1, for detailed descriptions of this response by white officials. See also chap. 12 on southern white reaction to the act after 1965.

4. Strictly speaking, the Attorney General's objections are not subject to judicial review. If a jurisdiction so wishes, however, it may file a case de novo in the U.S. District Court for

the District of Columbia, challenging the Justice Department's finding, and this is colloquially referred to as an "appeal."

5. *South Carolina v. Katzenbach*, 383 U.S. 301.

6. *Harper v. Virginia State Board of Elections*, 383 U.S. 663 (1966).

7. *Allen v. State Board of Elections*, 393 U.S. 544 (1969).

8. Section 5 was relevant, however, for municipalities seeking to annex or consolidate with predominantly white populations. Here the Department of Justice would sometimes object to the annexation unless changes were made in electoral practices within the enlarged jurisdiction. (See, for example, Days 1992, 61–63.) At the municipal level through 1989, or 1990 in Georgia, our authors identify over ten cases involving at-large elections in the eight states where section 5 came into play.

9. 379 U.S. 433.

10. 412 U.S. 755.

11. For example, there were apparently no successful constitutional challenges to municipal at-large elections in North Carolina and only a few in states such as Alabama, Georgia, and South Carolina. Once the 1982 amendments to the Voting Rights Act were in place, challenges to at-large elections were invariably decided under section 2, even in cases where there were also constitutional issues raised. See chap. 1 and discussion below.

12. 404 F. Supp. 206 (N.D. Miss. 1975).

13. However, there was an intent issue in this multijurisdictional case that made the basis of its resolution unique. See the discussion in chap. 5.

14. 446 U.S. 55 (1980).

15. However, the Supreme Court's decision in *Bolden* remanded the case for further evidentiary proceedings about intent to discriminate. Evidence unearthed by Peyton McCrary, a historian and an expert witness for the plaintiffs, showed that the plan was adopted with a discriminatory intent. See chap. 2.

16. 478 U.S. 30.

17. See, for example, Arrington and Watts 1991; Meier and England 1984; Robinson and England 1981; and Stewart, England, and Meier 1989.

18. A comparison of the results of district remedies in Texas imposed during the 1970s showed that when the boundary drawing was monitored by the Justice Department or developed by minority plaintiffs, the increase in minority officeholding was much greater than when the author of the boundaries was unknown or was hostile to minority electoral interests. See Davidson and Korbel 1981, table 3.

The issue of majority-minority districts whose majority is made up of two minority groups as a remedy for minority vote dilution has been before the courts in several cases, including cities as different as Pasadena, California; Boston, Massachussetts; and Baytown, Texas. Combined minority districts raise important strategic questions about the desirability of fostering multiethnic coalition politics as well as empirical questions about the potential for black-Hispanic electoral alliances. Without trying to resolve either issue, we note that even in the absence of an explicit black-Hispanic electoral alliance, the Texas data suggest that even a slightly greater tolerance by one group of minority voters for candidates of another minority group under some conditions may allow districts to be created in which no single minority group has a voting majority but in which there is sufficient combined minority voting strength to elect a candidate from the larger of the two minority groupings. See table 8.7 for an illustration of this point.

19. The act's provisions allow election practices to be overturned only when racial polarization leading to the systematic electoral defeat of minority candidates of choice is

present (Grofman and Davidson 1992, 301–5). Contrary to what is sometimes claimed (see, for example, Thernstrom 1987, 243), there is very little evidence to suggest that white bloc voting has substantially diminished in the South, especially in party primaries. (For an analysis of racially polarized voting in South Carolina involving numerous elections, see Loewen 1990.) Of course, sometimes black candidates will be able to win a Democratic primary contest in an area with a substantial black population because of overwhelming support from black voters and then go on to win the general election with some degree of support from white Democratic voters.

20. As we noted earlier, the overwhelming majority of the succcessful challenges to local at-large systems were brought under section 2 by minority plaintiffs.

21. In *Rogers v. Lodge*, 458 U.S. 613 (1982), decided shortly after passage of the amended act, the Supreme Court softened its test for intentional vote dilution under the Fourteenth Amendment by permitting courts to make use of circumstantial evidence of intent. Nonetheless, virtually all voting rights challenges by private litigants since 1982 have been decided under section 2.

22. There were also section 2 challenges to other types of elections, e.g., county commissioner and school board, as well as a significant number of lawsuits outside the eight states of our study.

23. See table 8 in each of the state chapters.

24. In every state other than Louisiana, half or more of the changes in election type could be attributed clearly to litigation.

25. These figures are approximate because information is missing on why some of the cities changed and because the classifications of changes as voluntary or due to referendums unconnected to litigation may not always be reliable, especially since the sources being interviewed sometimes lacked firsthand knowledge of the period when the change occurred. Also, while in virtually all instances our chapter authors were able to identify the specific litigation and its resolution even when there was no published opinion, for changes not tied to litigation or section 5 related activity, the various chapters differ somewhat in their classification scheme.

26. Some section 2 challenges were also brought alleging racial gerrymandering in single-member districts in the South—local, state, or congressional—but prior to 1990 there were very few. See Grofman and Handley 1992.

27. Even in the handful of section 2 lawsuits the Reagan-Bush era Justice Department brought in the 1980s, the department's role in most of them was that of plaintiff intervenor in a suit first filed by minority litigants. Nonetheless, the participation of the department in lawsuits as a plaintiff intervenor could be critical to the success of the case, especially in situations where the jurisdiction was a large one whose resources were much greater than those available to minority plaintiffs.

28. See the discussion above and the summary of state-by-state findings in chap. 10.

29. For an elaboration on the reasons for this decision, see Editors' Introduction.

30. See, however, Grofman and Handley 1992; Grofman 1993b.

BIBLIOGRAPHY

Alabama Department of Archives and History. 1967. *Alabama Official and Statistical Register*. Montgomery: Alabama Department of Archives and History.

Alston, Lee. 1985. "The Political Economy of the South." Mimeo.

Amaker, Norman C. 1988. *Civil Rights and the Reagan Administration*. Washington, D.C.: Urban Institute Press.

American Civil Liberties Union Foundation. 1989. "Polarized Voting Analysis, *Brooks v. Georgia State Board of Election*, No. CV 288–146 (S.D. Ga. 1989)." Atlanta. Table.

Anders, Evan. 1981. "The Origins of the Parr Machine in Duval County, Texas." *Southwestern Historical Quarterly* 85: 119–38.

———. 1982. *Boss Rule in South Texas: The Progressive Era*. Austin: University of Texas Press.

Anderson, Eric. 1981. *Race and Politics in North Carolina, 1872–1901: The Black Second*. Baton Rouge and London: Louisiana State University Press.

Andrews, Columbus. 1933. *Administrative County Government in South Carolina*. Chapel Hill: University of North Carolina Press.

Arrington, Theodore S., and Thomas Gill Watts. 1991. "The Election of Blacks to School Boards in North Carolina." *Western Political Quarterly* 44: 1099–1105.

Ashmore, Harry S. 1954. *The Negro and the Schools*. Chapel Hill and London: University of North Carolina Press.

Austin, Robert J. 1976. "The Redistricting Process after One Man–One Vote: The Case of Virginia." Ph.D. diss., University of Virginia.

Avila, Joaquin, and Bernard Grofman. 1990. "Hispanic Representation in California." Presented at a conference, "The Impact of the Voting Rights Act," Rice University, Houston, 11–12 May.

Baker, Donald P. 1989. *Wilder: Hold Fast to Dreams*. Cabin John, Md.: Seven Locks Press.

Ball, Howard, Dale Krane, and Thomas P. Lauth. 1982. *Compromised Compliance: Implementation of the 1965 Voting Rights Act*. Westport, Conn., and London: Greenwood Press.

———. 1984. "The View from Georgia and Mississippi: Local Attorneys' Appraisal of the 1965 Voting Rights Act." In *Minority Vote Dilution*, ed. Chandler Davidson. Washington, D.C.: Howard University Press.

Banfield, Edward C., and James Q. Wilson. 1963. *City Politics*. Cambridge: Harvard University Press.

Banks, James G. 1970. "Strom Thurmond and the Revolt against Modernity." Ph.D. diss., Kent State University.

Barr, Alwyn. 1971. *Reconstruction to Reform: Texas Politics, 1876–1906*. Austin and London: University of Texas Press.

———. 1982. *Black Texans: A History of Negroes in Texas, 1528–1971*. Reprint. Austin: Jenkins Publishing Co.

———. 1986. "Black Legislators of Reconstruction Texas." *Civil War History* 32: 340–52.

Bartley, Numan V. 1969. *The Rise of Massive Resistance: Race and Politics in the South During the 1950s*. Baton Rouge: Louisiana State University Press.

———. 1983. *The Creation of Modern Georgia*. Athens: University of Georgia Press.

Bass, Jack. 1989. "Review, *Dorn of the People: A Political Way of Life* by William Jennings Bryan Dorn and Scott Derks (Orangeburg, S.C.: Bruccoli Clark Layman/Sandlapper Publishing, 1988)." *South Carolina Historical Magazine* 90: 329–33.

Bass, Jack, and Walter DeVries. 1976. *The Transformation of Southern Politics: Social Change and Political Consequence since 1945*. New York: Basic Books.

Beard, Charles A. 1912. *American City Government: A Survey of Newer Tendencies*. New York: Century Company.

Bernd, Joseph. 1960. *Grass Roots Politics in Georgia: The County Unit System and the Importance of the Individual Voting Community in Bifactional Elections, 1942–1954*. Atlanta: Emory University Research Committee.

Bernd, Joseph L., and Lynwood M. Holland. 1959. "Recent Restrictions upon Negro Suffrage: The Case of Georgia." *Journal of Politics* 21: 487–513.

Binford, Michael. 1990. "Andrew Young and the 1990 Governor's Contest in Georgia." Presented at the Voter Education Project Workshop, "From Protest to Politics," Clark-Atlanta University.

Binion, Gayle. 1979. "The Implementation of Section 5 of the 1965 Voting Rights Act: A Retrospective on the Role of Courts." *Western Political Quarterly* 32: 154–73.

Black, Earl. 1976. *Southern Governors and Civil Rights: Racial Segregation as a Campaign Issue in the Second Reconstruction*. Cambridge: Harvard University Press.

Black, Earl, and Merle Black. 1987. *Politics and Society in the South*. Cambridge: Harvard University Press.

Black, Merle. 1978. "Racial Composition of Congressional Districts and Support for Federal Voting Rights in the American South." *Social Science Quarterly* 59: 435–50.

Blacksher, James U., and Larry T. Menefee. 1982. "From *Reynolds* v. *Sims* to *City of Mobile* v. *Bolden*: Have the White Suburbs Commandeered the Fifteenth Amendment?" *Hastings Law Journal* 34: 1–64.

Blalock, Hubert M., Jr. 1967. *Toward a Theory of Minority-Group Relations*. New York, London, and Sidney: John Wiley & Sons.

Blough, William J. 1983. "Local Government in South Carolina." In *Government in the Palmetto State*, ed. Luther F. Carter and Davis S. Mann. Columbia: Bureau of Governmental Research and Service, University of South Carolina.

Bond, Julian. 1990. "A Participant's Commentary." Presented to the New England Historical Association, Boston, 21 April.

Brace, Kimball, Bernard N. Grofman, Lisa R. Handley and Richard G. Niemi. 1988. "Minority Voting Equality: The 65 Percent Rule in Theory and Practice." *Law and Policy* 10: 43–62.

Branch, Taylor. 1988. *Parting the Waters: America in the King Years, 1954–1963*. New York: Simon and Schuster.

Brewer, J. Mason. 1935. *Negro Legislators of Texas and Their Descendants: A History of the Negro in Texas Politics from Reconstruction to Disfranchisement*. Dallas: Mathis Publishing Co.

Brischetto, Robert R. 1988a. "Electoral Empowerment: The Case for Tejanos." In *Latino Empowerment: Progress, Problems, and Prospects*, ed. Roberto E. Villarreal, Norma G. Hernandez, and Howard D. Neighbor. New York, Westport, Conn., and London: Greenwood Press.

———. 1988b. *The Political Empowerment of Texas Mexicans, 1974–1988*. San Antonio: Southwest Voter Research Institute.

———., ed. 1982. *Bilingual Elections at Work in the Southwest: A Mexican American*

Legal Defense and Educational Fund Report. Executive Summary. Washington, D.C.: Mexican American Legal Defense and Educational Fund.

Brouthers, Lance E., and James S. Larson. 1988. "On Structure/Representation Linkages for Small Towns in the Deep South." *Journal of Urban Affairs* 10: 387–93.

Brown, Richard Maxwell. 1975. *Strain of Violence: Historical Studies of American Violence and Vigilantism*. New York: Oxford University Press.

Bullock, Charles S. III. 1983. "The Effects of Redistricting on Black Representation in Southern State Legislatures." Presented at the annual meeting of the American Political Science Association, Chicago.

———. 1989. "Symbolics or Substance: A Critique of the At-Large Election Controversy." *State and Local Government Review* 21: 91–99.

Bullock, Charles S. III, and Susan A. MacManus. 1988. "Minorities and Women Do Win at Large!" *National Civic Review* 77: 231–44.

———. 1990. "Structural Features of Municipalities and the Incidence of Hispanic Councilmembers." *Social Science Quarterly* 71: 665–81.

———. 1991a. "Municipal Electoral Structure and the Election of Councilwomen." *Journal of Politics* 53: 75–89.

———. 1991b. "Testing Assumptions of the Totality of Circumstances Test: An Analysis of the Impact of Structures on Black Descriptive Representation." Photocopy.

Buni, Andrew. 1967. *The Negro in Virginia Politics, 1902–1965*. Charlottesville: University Press of Virginia.

Burton, Vernon. 1978. "Race and Reconstruction: Edgefield County, South Carolina." *Journal of Social History* 12: 31–56.

———. 1985. *In My Father's House Are Many Mansions: Family and Community in Edgefield, South Carolina*. Chapel Hill and London: University of North Carolina Press.

———. 1987. Foreword. *Born to Rebel: An Autobiography*. Athens: University of Georgia Press.

———. 1989. "Edgefield Reconstruction Political Black Leaders." In *The Proceedings of the South Carolina Historical Association, 1988–1989*, ed. William S. Brockington. Aiken: University of South Carolina at Aiken.

———. 1991. "'The Black Squint of the Law': Racism in South Carolina." In *The Meaning of South Carolina History: Essays in Honor of George C. Rogers, Jr.*, ed. David R. Chesnutt and Clyde N. Wilson. Columbia: University of South Carolina Press.

Butler, Katharine I. 1982. "Constitutional and Statutory Challenges to Election Structures: Dilution and the Value of the Right to Vote." *Louisiana Law Review* 42: 851–950.

———. 1985. "The Majority Vote Requirement: The Case against Its Wholesale Elimination." *Urban Lawyer* 17: 441–55.

Button, James W. 1989. *Blacks and Social Change: Impact of the Civil Rights Movement in Southern Communities*. Princeton: Princeton University Press.

Caldeira, Gregory A. 1992. "Litigation, Lobbying, and the Voting Rights Bar." In *Controversies in Minority Voting: The Voting Rights Act in Perspective*, ed. Bernard Grofman and Chandler Davidson. Washington, D.C.: Brookings Institution.

Carawan, Guy, and Candie Carawan. 1989. *Ain't you got a right to the tree of life? The People of Johns Island, South Carolina—Their Faces, Their Words, and Their Songs*. Athens and London: University of Georgia Press.

Carlson, James M. 1980. "Political Context and Black Participation in the South." In *Party Politics in the South*, ed. Robert P. Steed, Laurence W. Moreland, and Tod A. Baker. New York: Praeger.

Castro, Tony. 1974. *Chicano Power: The Emergence of Mexican America*. New York: E. P. Dutton.

Chafe, William H. 1980. *Civilities and Civil Rights: Greensboro, North Carolina, and the Black Struggle for Freedom*. New York, London, and Toronto: Oxford University Press.

Chestnut, J. L., Jr., and Julia Cass. 1990. *Black in Selma: The Uncommon Life of J. L. Chestnut, Jr*. New York: Farrar, Straus and Giroux.

Christenson, Rob. 1990. "Blue-Gantt Paradox Reflects Complexity in State Politics." *Raleigh News and Observer*, 8 December 1990, 3B.

Christian, Carole E. 1989. "Joining the American Mainstream: Texas's Mexican Americans during World War I." *Southwestern Historical Quarterly* 92: 559–95.

Colby, David C. 1986. "The Voting Rights Act and Black Registration in Mississippi." In *Assessing the Effects of the U.S. Voting Rights Act*, ed. Charles L. Cotrell. *Publius: The Journal of Federalism* 16 (Fall, Special Symposium Issue): 123–37.

———. 1987. "White Violence and the Civil Rights Movement." In *Blacks in Southern Politics*, ed. Laurence W. Moreland, Robert P. Steed, and Tod A. Baker. New York: Praeger.

Conaway, James. 1973. *Judge: The Life and Times of Leander Perez*. New York: Alfred A. Knopf.

Congressional Quarterly Service. 1968. *Revolution in Civil Rights*. 4th ed. Washington, D.C.: Congressional Quarterly Service.

Conway, M. Margaret. 1991. *Political Participation in the United States*. 2d ed. Washington, D.C.: Congressional Quarterly.

Cooper, William J., Jr. 1968. *The Conservative Regime: South Carolina, 1877–1890*. Baltimore: Johns Hopkins University Press.

Cotrell, Charles L. 1980. *Status of Civil Rights in Texas*. Vol. 1, *A Report on the Participation of Mexican-Americans, Blacks and Females in the Political Institutions and Process of Texas, 1968–1978*. San Antonio: Texas Advisory Committee to the United States Commission on Civil Rights.

Cotrell, Charles L., and Jerry Polinard. 1986. "Effects of the Voting Rights Act in Texas: Perceptions of County Election Administrators." In *Assessing the Effects of the U.S. Voting Rights Act*, ed. Charles L. Cotrell. *Publius: The Journal of Federalism* 16 (Fall, Special Symposium Issue): 67–80.

Cox, Jane Reed, and Abigail Turner. 1981. *The Voting Rights Act in Alabama: A Current Legal Assessment*. Montgomery: Legal Services Corporation of Alabama.

Crouch, Barry A. 1978. "Self-Determination and Local Black Leaders in Texas." *Phylon* 39: 344–55.

Crowell, Michael. 1984. "The Voting Rights Act in North Carolina—1984." *Popular Government* 50: 1–9.

———. 1988. "North Carolina Local Government after *Gingles*." *Popular Government* 54: 15–20.

———. 1989a. "Elections." In *County Government in North Carolina*, ed. A. Fleming Bell, II. 3d ed. Chapel Hill: University of North Carolina Institute of Government.

———. 1989b. "Voting Rights Litigation Update." *Popular Government* 54: 47.

———. 1990. "Redistricting for Local Governments." *Popular Government* 56: 2–7.

Daniel, Johnnie. 1969. "Negro Political Behavior and Community Political and Socioeconomic Structural Factors." *Social Forces* 47: 274–80.

Davidson, Chandler. 1972. *Biracial Politics: Conflict and Coalition in the Metropolitan South*. Baton Rouge: Louisiana State University Press.

———. 1979. "At-Large Elections and Minority Representation." *Social Science Quarterly* 60: 336–38.

———. 1984. "Minority Vote Dilution: An Overview." In *Minority Vote Dilution*, ed. Chandler Davidson. Washington, D.C.: Howard University Press.

———. 1990. *Race and Class in Texas Politics*. Princeton: Princeton University Press.

———. 1992. "The Voting Rights Act: A Brief History." In *Controversies in Minority Voting: The Voting Rights Act in Perspective*, ed. Bernard Grofman and Chandler Davidson. Washington, D.C.: Brookings Institution.

Davidson, Chandler, and George Korbel. 1981. "At-Large Elections and Minority-Group Representation: A Re-examination of Historical and Contemporary Evidence." *Journal of Politics* 43: 982–1005.

Davidson, Chandler, and Luis R. Fraga. 1988. "Slating Groups as Parties in a 'Nonpartisan' Setting." *Western Political Quarterly* 41: 373–90.

Davis, Marianna W. et al., eds. 1976. *South Carolina's Blacks and Native Americans, 1776–1976*. Columbia, S.C.: State Human Affairs Commission.

Davison, Donald. 1986. *An Ecological Regression Method to Estimate the Political Consequences of the Voting Rights Act of 1965*. University of Central Florida. Mimeo.

Days, Drew S. III. 1992. "Section 5 Enforcement and the Department of Justice." In *Controversies in Minority Voting: The Voting Rights Act in Perspective*, ed. Bernard Grofman and Chandler Davidson. Washington, D.C.: Brookings Institution.

Days, Drew S. III, and Lani Guinier. 1984. "Enforcement of Section 5 of the Voting Rights Act." In *Minority Vote Dilution*, ed. Chandler Davidson. Washington, D.C.: Howard University Press.

De León, Arnoldo. 1982. *The Tejano Community, 1836–1900*. Albuquerque: University of New Mexico Press.

Democratic Party of South Carolina. 1946. *Rules Adopted by State Convention, May 15, 1946*. Columbia, S.C.: Democratic Party of South Carolina.

Derfner, Armand. 1973. "Racial Discrimination and the Right to Vote." *Vanderbilt Law Review* 26: 523–84.

———. 1984. "Vote Dilution and the Voting Rights Act Amendments of 1982." In *Minority Vote Dilution*, ed. Chandler Davidson. Washington, D.C.: Howard University Press.

Derfner, Mary Francis. 1977. "One Giant Step: The Civil Rights Attorney's Fees Awards Act of 1976." *St. Louis University Law Journal* 21: 441–51.

Dixon, Robert G., Jr. 1968. *Democratic Representation: Reapportionment in Law and Politics*. New York, London, and Toronto: Oxford University Press.

Dorn, William Jennings Bryan. 1965. "Testimony." *Hearings before Subcommittee No. 5 of the Committee on the Judiciary, House of Representatives, Eighty-Ninth Congress, First Session, on H.R. 6400 and Other Proposals to Enforce the 15th Amendment to the Constitution of the United States*. Ser. 2. Washington, D.C.: 631–40.

Drago, Edmund L. 1982. *Black Politicians and Reconstruction in Georgia: A Splendid Failure*. Baton Rouge and London: Lousiana State University Press.

Drennan, James C. 1989. "The Courts." In *County Government in North Carolina*, ed. A. Fleming Bell. 3d ed. Chapel Hill: University of North Carolina Institute of Government.

———. 1990. "A Recent History of Judicial Selection in North Carolina." Manuscript.

Dubois, Philip L. 1979. "The Significance of Voting Cues in State Supreme Court Elections." *Law and Society Review* 13: 757–79.

Eamon, Thomas F. 1987. "From Pool Hall to Parish House in North Carolina." In *Strate-*

gies for Mobilizing Black Voters: Four Case Studies*, ed. Thomas E. Cavanagh. Washington, D.C.: Joint Center for Political Studies.

Edds, Margaret. 1987. *Free at Last: What Really Happened When Civil Rights Came to Southern Politics*. Bethesda, Md.: Adler and Adler.

———. 1990. *Claiming the Dream: The Victorious Campaign of Douglas Wilder of Virginia*. Chapel Hill, N.C.: Algonquin Books of Chapel Hill.

Edgar, Walter B., ed. 1974. *Biographical Directory of the South Carolina House of Representatives*. Vol. 1, *Session Lists, 1692–1973*. Columbia: University of South Carolina Press.

Edmonds, Helen G. 1951. *The Negro and Fusion Politics in North Carolina, 1894–1901*. Chapel Hill: University of North Carolina Press.

Eisenberg, Ralph. 1965. "The 1964 Presidential Election in Virginia: A Political Omen?" *University of Virginia* [Institute of Government] *News Letter* 41: 29–32.

———. 1969. "Gubernatorial Politics in Virginia: The Experience of 1965." *University of Virginia* [Institute of Government] *News Letter* 45: 25–28.

———. 1972. "Virginia: The Emergence of Two-Party Politics." In *The Changing Politics of the South*, ed. William C. Havard. Baton Rouge: Louisiana State University Press.

Engstrom, Richard L. 1978. "Racial Vote Dilution: Supreme Court Interpretations of Section 5 of the Voting Rights Act." *Southern University Law Review* 4: 139–64.

———. 1985a. "Racial Vote Dilution: The Concept and the Court." In *The Voting Rights Act: Consequences and Implications*, ed. Lorn Foster. New York: Praeger.

———. 1985b. "The Reincarnation of the Intent Standard: Federal Judges and At-Large Election Cases." *Howard Law Journal* 28: 495–513.

———. 1986. "Repairing the Crack in New Orleans' Black Vote: VRA's Results Test Nullifies 'Gerryduck.'" In *Assessing the Effects of the U.S. Voting Rights Act*, ed. Charles L. Cotrell. *Publius: The Journal of Federalism* 16 (Fall, Special Symposium Issue): 109–21.

———. 1988. "Black Politics and the Voting Rights Act, 1965–1982." In *Contemporary Southern Politics*, ed. James F. Lea. Baton Rouge and London: Louisiana State University Press.

———. 1989. "When Blacks Run for Judge: Racial Divisions in the Candidate Preferences of Louisiana Voters." *Judicature* 73: 87–89.

Engstrom, Richard L., and Charles C. Barrilleaux. 1991. "Native Americans and Cumulative Voting: The Sisseton-Wahpeton Sioux." *Social Science Quarterly* 72: 388–93.

Engstrom, Richard L., and Michael D. McDonald. 1981. "The Election of Blacks to City Councils: Clarifying the Impact of Electoral Arrangements on the Seats/Population Relationship." *American Political Science Review* 75: 344–54.

———. 1982. "The Underrepresentation of Blacks on City Councils: Comparing the Structural and Socioeconomic Explanations for South/Non-South Differences." *Journal of Politics* 44: 1088–99.

———. 1985. "Quantitative Evidence in Vote Dilution Litigation: Political Participation and Polarized Voting." *Urban Lawyer* 17: 369–77.

———. 1986. "The Effect of At-Large versus District Elections on Racial Representation in U.S. Municipalities." In *Electoral Laws and Their Political Consequences*, ed. Bernard Grofman and Arend Lijphart. New York: Agathon Press.

———. 1987. "The Election of Blacks to Southern City Councils: The Dominant Impact of Electoral Arrangements." In *Blacks in Southern Politics*, ed. Laurence W. Moreland, Robert P. Steed, and Tod A. Baker. New York: Praeger.

———. 1988. "Definitions, Measurements, and Statistics: Weeding Wildgen's Thicket." *Urban Lawyer* 20: 175–91.

———. 1993. "Enhancing Factors in At-Large Plurality and Majority Systems: A Reconsideration." *Electoral Studies* 12: 383–99.

Engstrom, Richard L., and John K. Wildgen. 1977. "Pruning Thorns from the Thicket: An Empirical Test of the Existence of Racial Gerrymandering." *Legislative Studies Quarterly* 2: 465–79.

Fager, Charles E. 1985. *Selma, 1965: The March That Changed the South*. 2d Ed. Boston: Beacon Press.

Farmer, James O., Jr. 1965. "The End of the White Primary in South Carolina: A Southern State's Fight to Keep Its Politics White." M.A. thesis, University of South Carolina, Columbia.

Felder, James L. 1987. *A Directory of Black Elected and Appointed Officials in South Carolina*. Columbia, S.C.: Lee Marketing Corp.

Fenton, John H., and Kenneth N. Vines. 1957. "Negro Registration in Louisiana." *American Political Science Review* 51: 704–13.

Ferrell, Joseph. 1969–90. *Form of Government of North Carolina Cities*. Chapel Hill and London: University of North Carolina Institute of Government.

Foner, Eric. 1988. *Reconstruction: America's Unfinished Revolution, 1863–1877*. New York: Harper and Row.

Foster, Lorn S., ed. 1985. *The Voting Rights Act: Consequences and Implications*. New York: Praeger.

Fowler, Donald L. 1966. *Presidential Voting in South Carolina, 1948–1964*. Columbia: Bureau of Governmental Research and Service, University of South Carolina.

Fraga, Luis Ricardo. 1991. "Policy Consequences and the Change from At-Large Elections to Single Member Districts." Paper presented at the annual meeting of the Western Political Science Association, Seattle, 21–23 March.

Frick, Mary Louise. 1967. "Influences on Negro Political Participation in Atlanta, Georgia." M.A. thesis, Georgia State College, Atlanta.

García, Mario T. 1989. *Mexican Americans: Leadership, Ideology, Identity, 1930–1960*. New Haven, Conn., and London: Yale University Press.

Garrow, David J. 1978. *Protest at Selma: Martin Luther King, Jr., and the Voting Rights Act of 1965*. New Haven, Conn. and London: Yale University Press.

———. 1986. *Bearing the Cross: Martin Luther King, Jr., and the Southern Christian Leadership Conference*. New York: William Morrow.

Garson, Robert A. 1974. *The Democratic Party and the Politics of Sectionalism, 1941–1948*. Baton Rouge: Louisiana State University Press.

Gates, Robbins L. 1964. *The Making of Massive Resistance: Virginia's Politics of Public School Desegregation, 1954–1956*. Chapel Hill: University of North Carolina Press.

Gergel, Richard Mark. 1977. "Wade Hampton and the Rise of One Party Racial Orthodoxy in South Carolina." In *The Proceedings of the South Carolina Historical Association, 1977*, ed. James O. Farmer, Jr. Lancaster: The South Carolina Historical Association.

Gillette, Michael L. 1978. "The Rise of the NAACP in Texas." *Southwestern Historical Quarterly* 81: 393–416.

Graham, Cole Blease, Jr. 1984. "South Carolina Counties." In *Local Government in South Carolina: The Governmental Landscape*, ed. Cole Blease Graham and Charlie B. Tyer. Columbia: Bureau of Governmental Research and Service, University of South Carolina.

Grebler, Leo, Joan W. Moore, and Ralph C. Guzman. 1970. *The Mexican-American People: The Nation's Second Largest Minority*. New York: Free Press.

Grofman, Bernard. 1980–81. "Alternatives to Single-Member Plurality Districts: Legal and Empirical Issues." *Policy Studies Journal* 9 (Special 3): 875–98.

———. 1981. "Fair and Equal Representation." *Ethics* 91: 477–85.

———. 1982a. "The Effect of Ward vs. At-Large Elections on Minority Representation: Part I, A Theoretical Analysis." Manuscript.

———. 1982b. "The Effect of Ward vs. At-Large Elections on Minority Representation: Part II, A Review and Critique of Twenty-Three Recent Empirical Studies in 1970–1980." Manuscript.

———. 1982c. "Report to the Special Master on Methodology Used to Insure Compliance with Standards of the Voting Rights Act of 1965, *Flateau v. Anderson*." U.S. District Court, Southern District of New York, June 7. Photo-offset.

———. 1983. "Measures of Bias and Proportionality in Seats-Votes Relationships." *Political Methodology* 9: 295–327.

———. 1985. "Criteria for Districting: A Social Science Perspective." *UCLA Law Review* 33: 77–184.

———. 1992a. "Expert Witness Testimony and the Evolution of Voting Rights Case Law." In *Controversies in Minority Voting: The Voting Rights Act in Perspective*, ed. Bernard Grofman and Chandler Davidson. Washington, D.C.: Brookings Institution.

———. 1992b. "The Role of the Justice Department in Enforcing the Voting Rights Act: Compromised Compliance? Republican Plot? Or Great American Success Story?" Presented at the annual meeting of the American Political Science Association. Chicago, 3–5 September.

———. 1993a. "Would Vince Lombardi Have Been Right If He Had Said, 'When It Comes to Redistricting, Race Isn't Everything, It's the *Only* Thing'?" *Cardozo Law Review* 14: 1237–76.

———. 1993b. "Voting Rights in a Multi-Ethnic World." *Chicano-Latino Law Review* 13: 15–37.

Grofman, Bernard, and Chandler Davidson. 1992. "Postscript: What Is the Best Route to a Color-Blind Society?" In *Controversies in Minority Voting: The Voting Rights Act in Perspective*, ed. Bernard Grofman and Chandler Davidson. Washington, D.C.: Brookings Institution.

Grofman, Bernard, and Lisa Handley. 1989a. "Black Representation: Making Sense of Electoral Geography at Different Levels of Government." *Legislative Studies Quarterly* 14: 265–79.

———. 1989b. "Minority Population Proportion and Black and Hispanic Congressional Success in the 1970s and 1980s. *American Politics Quarterly* 17: 436–45. Reprinted in revised and updated form under the title "Preconditions for Black and Hispanic Congressional Success." In *United States Electoral Systems: Their Impact on Women and Minorities*, ed. Wilma Rule and Joseph Zimmerman. New York, Westport, Conn., and London: Greenwood Press, 1992.

———. 1990. "The Impact of the Voting Rights Act on Black Representation in Southern State Legislatures and Congress." Presented at a conference, "The Impact of the Voting Rights Act," Houston, 11–12 May.

———. 1992. "Identifying and Remedying Racial Gerrymandering." *Journal of Law and Politics* 8: 345–404.

Grofman, Bernard, Lisa Handley, and Richard G. Niemi. 1992. *Minority Representation and the Quest for Voting Equality*. Cambridge, New York, and Oakleigh: Cambridge University Press.

Grofman, Bernard, Michael Migalski, and Nicholas Noviello. 1985. "The 'Totality of Circumstances Test' in Section 2 of the 1982 Extension of the Voting Rights Act: A Social Science Perspective." *Law and Policy* 7: 199–223.

———. 1986. "Effects of Multimember Districts on Black Representation in State Legislatures." *Review of Black Political Economy* 14: 65–78.

Guinier, Lani. 1991a. "No Two Seats: The Elusive Quest for Political Equality." *Virginia Law Review* 77: 1413–1514.

———. 1991b. "The Triumph of Tokenism: The Voting Rights Act and the Theory of Black Electoral Success." *Michigan Law Review* 89: 1077–1154.

Hall, Kermit L. 1984. "Political Power and Constitutional Legitimacy: The South Carolina Ku Klux Klan Trials, 1871–1872." *Emory Law Journal* 33: 921–51.

Halpin, Stanislaus A. 1978. "The Anti-Gerrymander: The Impact of Section 5 of the Voting Rights Act of 1965 upon Louisiana Parish Redistricting." Ph.D. diss., George Washington University.

Halpin, Stanley A., Jr., and Richard L. Engstrom. 1973. "Racial Gerrymandering and Southern State Legislative Redistricting: Attorney General Determinations under the Voting Rights Act." *Journal of Public Law* 22: 37–66.

Hamilton, Charles V. 1973. *The Bench and the Ballot: Southern Federal Judges and Black Voters*. New York: Oxford University Press.

Hamilton, Howard D. 1967. "Legislative Constituencies: Single-Member Districts, Multi-Member Districts, and Floterial Districts." *Western Political Quarterly* 20: 321–40.

Handley, Lisa, and Bernard Grofman. 1989. "Electing Black Mayors: The Impact of Black Population and Election Systems." Presented at the annual meeting of the American Political Science Association, Atlanta.

Hays, Samuel P. 1964. "The Politics of Reform in Municipal Government in the Progressive Era." *Pacific Northwest Quarterly* 55: 157–69.

Hedges, Roman, and Carl P. Carlucci. 1987. "Implementation of the Voting Rights Act: The Case of New York." *Western Political Quarterly* 40: 107–20.

Heilig, Peggy, and Robert J. Mundt. 1983. "Changes in Representational Equity: The Effect of Adopting Districts." *Social Sciences Quarterly* 64: 393–97.

———. 1984. *Your Voice at City Hall: The Politics, Procedures, and Policies of District Representation*. Albany: State University of New York Press.

Henderson, Gordon, and Jeanette Wolfley. 1990. "Indian Success in Different Election Systems." Presented at a conference, "The Impact of the Voting Rights Act," Rice University, Houston, 11–12 May.

Hine, Darlene Clark. 1979. *Black Victory: The Rise and Fall of the White Primary in Texas*. Millwood, N.Y.: KTO Press.

Holland, L. M. 1949. *The Direct Primary in Georgia*. Urbana: University of Illinois Press.

Holli, Melvin G. 1974. "Urban Reform in the Progressive Era." In *The Progressive Era*, ed. Lewis L. Gould. Syracuse: Syracuse University Press.

Holt, Thomas. 1977. *Black Over White: Negro Political Leadership in South Carolina during Reconstruction*. Urbana: University of Illinois Press.

Howard, A. E. Dick. 1974. *Commentaries on the Constitution of Virginia*. Vol. 1 of 2. Charlottesville: University Press of Virginia.

Hunter, David H. 1976. "The 1975 Voting Rights Act and Language Minorities." *Catholic University Law Review* 25: 250–70.

Hwang, Sean-Shong, and Steve H. Murdock. 1982. "Residential Segregation in Texas in 1980." *Social Science Quarterly* 63: 737–61.

Issacharoff, Samuel. 1992. "Polarized Voting and the Political Process: The Transformation of Voting Rights Jurisprudence." *Michigan Law Review* 90: 1833–91.

Jeansonne, Glen. 1977. *Leander Perez: Boss of the Delta*. Baton Rouge and London: Louisiana State University Press.

Jewell, Malcolm E. 1964. "State Legislatures in Southern Politics." In *The American South in the 1960s*, ed. Avery Leiserson. New York and London: Frederick A. Praeger.

———. 1968. "Local Systems of Representation: Political Consequences and Judicial Choices." *George Washington Law Review* 36: 790–807.

———. 1980. "The Consequences of Legislative Districting in Four Southern States." Presented at the Citadel Symposium on Southern Politics, Charleston, S.C.

———. 1982. "The Consequences of Single- and Multimember Districting." In *Representation and Redistricting Issues*, ed. Bernard Grofman, Arend Lijphart, Robert B. McKay, and Howard A. Scarrow. Lexington, Mass., and Toronto: Lexington Books.

Joint Center for Political Studies. 1970–1989. *National Roster of Black Elected Officials*. Washington, D.C.: Joint Center for Political Studies.

Joint Center for Political and Economic Studies. 1990–91. *National Roster of Black Elected Officials*. Washington, D.C.: Joint Center for Political and Economic Studies.

Jones, Clinton B. 1976. "The Impact of Local Election Systems on Black Political Representation." *Urban Affairs Quarterly* 11: 345–56.

Jordan, Milton C. 1989. "Black Legislators: From Political Novelty to Political Force." *North Carolina Insight* 12: 40–58.

Jordan, Terry G. 1986. "A Century and a Half of Ethnic Change in Texas, 1836–1986." *Southwestern Historical Quarterly* 89: 385–422.

Kaczorowski, Robert J. 1985. *The Politics of Judicial Interpretation: The Federal Courts, Department of Justice and Civil Rights, 1866–1876*. New York, London, and Rome: Oceana.

Karlan, Pamela S. 1989. "Maps and Misreadings: The Role of Geographic Compactness in Vote Dilution Litigation." *Harvard Civil Rights–Civil Liberties Law Review* 24: 173–248.

Karlan, Pamela S., and Peyton McCrary. 1988. "Book Review: Without Fear and without Research. Abigail Thernstrom on the Voting Rights Act." *Journal of Law and Politics* 4: 751–77.

Karnig, Albert K. 1976. "Black Representation on City Councils: The Impact of District Elections and Socioeconomic Factors." *Urban Affairs Quarterly* 12: 223–42.

———. 1979. "Black Resources and City Council Representation." *Journal of Politics* 41: 134–49.

Karnig, Albert K., and Susan Welch. 1979. "Sex and Ethnic Differences in Municipal Representation." *Social Science Quarterly* 60: 465–81.

———. 1980. *Black Representation and Urban Policy*. Chicago and London: University of Chicago Press.

———. 1982. "Electoral Structure and Black Representation on City Councils." *Social Science Quarterly* 63: 99–114.

Karst, Kenneth L. 1989. *Belonging to America: Equal Citizenship and the Constitution*. New Haven, Conn., and London: Yale University Press.

Keech, William R. [1968] 1981. *The Impact of Negro Voting: The Role of the Vote in the Quest for Equality*. Westport, Conn.: Greenwood Press.

Key, V. O., Jr. 1949. *Southern Politics in State and Nation*. New York: Alfred A. Knopf.

Kibbe, Pauline R. 1946. *Latin Americans in Texas*. Albuquerque: University of New Mexico Press.

Kluger, Richard. 1977. *Simple Justice: The History of* Brown v. Board of Education *and Black America's Struggle for Equality*. New York: Vintage Books.

Korbel, George. 1989. "Findings Involving Dilution in the Twenty County Area Comprising the Thirteenth Appellate District." Manuscript.

Kousser, J. Morgan. 1974. *The Shaping of Southern Politics: Suffrage Restriction and the Establishment of the One-Party South, 1880–1910*. New Haven, Conn., and London: Yale University Press.

———. 1980. "Progressivism—For Middle-Class Whites Only: North Carolina Education, 1880–1910." *Journal of Southern History* 46: 169–94.

———. 1982. "Declaration." *County Council of Sumter County, South Carolina v. United States*. C.A. No. 82-0912 (D.C.C.). Attachment to Motion for Summary Judgment.

———. 1984a. "Are Expert Witnesses Whores? Reflections on Objectivity in Scholarship and Expert Witnessing." *Public Historian* 6: 5–19.

———. 1984b. "The Undermining of the First Reconstruction: Lessons for the Second." In *Minority Vote Dilution*, ed. Chandler Davidson. Washington, D.C.: Howard University Press.

———. 1991. "How to Determine Intent: Lessons from L.A." *Journal of Law and Politics* 7: 591–732.

———. 1992. "The Voting Rights Act and the Two Reconstructions." In *Controversies in Minority Voting: The Voting Rights Act in Perspective*, ed. Bernard Grofman and Chandler Davidson. Washington, D.C.: Brookings Institution.

Krane, Dale. 1985. "Implementation of the Voting Rights Act: Enforcement by the Department of Justice." In *The Voting Rights Act: Consequences and Implications*, ed. Lorn S. Foster. New York: Praeger.

Kunkel, Paul A. 1959. "Modifications in Louisiana Negro Legal Status under Louisiana Constitutions, 1812–1957." *Journal of Negro History* 44: 1–25.

Ladd, Everett Carll, Jr. 1966. *Negro Political Leadership in the South*. Ithaca, N.Y.: Cornell University Press.

Lane, Robert E. 1959. *Political Life: Why People Get Involved in Politics*. Glencoe, Ill.: Free Press of Glencoe.

Latimer, Margaret K. 1979. "Black Political Representation in Southern Cities: Election Systems and Other Causal Variables." *Urban Affairs Quarterly* 15: 65–86.

Lawson, Steven F. 1976. *Black Ballots: Voting Rights in the South, 1944–1969*. New York: Columbia University Press.

———. 1985. *In Pursuit of Power: Southern Blacks and Electoral Politics, 1965–1982*. New York: Columbia University Press.

Lewinson, Paul. [1932] 1965. *Race, Class, and Party: A History of Negro Suffrage and White Politics in the South*. New York: Grosset and Dunlap.

Lichtman, Allan J., and Samuel Issacharoff. 1991. "Black/White Voter Registration Disparities in Mississippi: Legal and Methodological Issues in Challenging Bureau of Census Data." *Journal of Law and Politics* 7: 525–57.

Loewen, James W. 1987. "Racial Bloc Voting in South Carolina." Presented at the annual meeting of the American Political Science Association, Chicago.

———. 1990. "Racial Bloc Voting and Political Mobilization in South Carolina." *Review of Black Political Economy* 19: 23–37.

Loewen, James W., and Bernard Grofman. 1989. "Recent Developments in Methods Used in Vote Dilution Litigation." *Urban Lawyer* 21: 589–604.

Logan, Frenise A. 1964. *The Negro in North Carolina, 1876–1894*. Chapel Hill: University of North Carolina Press.

Luebke, Paul. 1990. *Tar Heel Politics: Myths and Realities*. Chapel Hill and London: University of North Carolina Press.

Lynch, John R. [1913] 1970. *The Facts of Reconstruction*. Indianapolis and New York: Bobbs-Merrill.

Lyons, W. E., and Malcolm E. Jewell. 1988. "Minority Representation and the Drawing of Council Districts." *Urban Affairs Quarterly* 23: 432–47.

Mabry, William A. 1940. "The Negro in North Carolina Politics since Reconstruction." *Historical Papers of Trinity College Historical Society*, Ser. 23. Durham, N.C.: Duke University Press.

MacManus, Susan A. 1978. "City Council Election Procedures and Minority Representation: Are They Related?" *Social Science Quarterly* 59: 153–61.

McCrary, Peyton. 1982. "Declaration." *County Council of Sumter County, South Carolina v. United States*, C.A. No. 82-0912 (D.D.C.). Attachment to Motion for Summary Judgment.

———. 1984. "History in the Courts: The Significance of *Bolden v. the City of Mobile*." In *Minority Vote Dilution*, ed. Chandler Davidson. Washington, D.C.: Howard University Press.

———. 1985. "Discriminatory Intent: The Continuing Relevance of 'Purpose' Evidence in Vote-Dilution Lawsuits." *Howard Law Journal* 28: 463–93.

———. 1988. "Taking History to Court: The Issue of Discriminatory Intent in Southern Voting Rights Cases." Washington, D.C.: Joint Center for Political Studies. Manuscript.

———. 1990. "Racially Polarized Voting in the South: Quantitative Evidence from the Courtroom." *Social Science History* 14: 507–31.

McCrary, Peyton, Jerome Gray, Edward Still, and Huey Perry. 1989. "The Impact of the Voting Rights Act in Alabama." Presented at the annual meeting of the American Political Science Association, Atlanta.

McCrary, Peyton, and J. Gerald Hebert. 1989. "Keeping the Courts Honest: The Role of Historians as Expert Witnesses in Southern Voting Rights Cases." *Southern University Law Review* 16: 101–28.

McDonald, Laughlin. 1981. "The Voting Rights Act Is the Only Hope against a Century of All-White Rule." *Civil Liberties* (June): 3–4.

———. 1982. *Voting Rights in the South: Ten Years of Litigation Challenging Continuing Discrimination against Minorities*. New York: American Civil Liberties Union.

———. 1983. "The 1982 Extension of Section 5 of the Voting Rights Act of 1965: The Continued Need for Preclearance." *Tennessee Law Review* 51: 1–82.

———. 1986. "An Aristocracy of Voters: The Disfranchisement of Blacks in South Carolina." *South Carolina Law Review* 37: 557–82.

———. 1989. "The Quiet Revolution in Minority Voting Rights." *Vanderbilt Law Review* 42: 1249–97.

———. 1990. "From Protest to Politics: Remaining Legal Barriers to African American Political Participation. The Application of the Voting Rights Act to the Election of

Judges." Voter Education Project. Twenty-fifth Anniversary of Voting Rights Act Workshop. Atlanta: ACLU, Southern Regional Office.

———. 1991. "Substantive Standards for the Application of Section 5 of the Voting Rights Act, 42 U.S.C. sec. 1973c: Purpose, Effect, and Results." Presented at CLE Seminar on Voting Rights and Reapportionment, Stetson University College of Law, Clearwater Beach, Fla., 26–27 April.

———. 1992. "The 1982 Amendments of Section 2 and Minority Representation." In *Controversies in Minority Voting: The Voting Rights Act in Perspective*, ed. Bernard Grofman and Chandler Davidson. Washington, D.C.: Brookings Institution.

McDonald, Michael. 1991. "The Effect of the Voting Rights Act in New York." Presented at the Western Political Science Association Meeting, Seattle, 21–23 March.

McKay, Robert B. 1965. *Reapportionment: The Law and Politics of Equal Representation*. New York: Twentieth Century Fund.

McLeod, Daniel R. 1965. "Testimony." *Hearings before Subcommittee No. 5 of the Committee on the Judiciary, House of Representatives, Eighty-Ninth Congress, First Session, on H.R. 6400 and Other Proposals to Enforce 15th Amendment to the Constitution of the United States*. Ser. 2. Washington, D.C.: 598–614.

McMillan, Malcolm C. 1955. *Constitutional Development in Alabama, 1798–1901: A Study in Politics, the Negro, and Sectionalism*. Chapel Hill: University of North Carolina Press.

McMillen, Neil R. 1971. *The Citizens' Council: Organized Resistance to the Second Reconstruction, 1954–1964*. Urbana, Chicago, and London: University of Illinois Press.

———. 1989. *Dark Journey: Black Mississippians in the Age of Jim Crow*. Urbana and Chicago: University of Illinois Press.

Maddex, Jack P., Jr. 1970. *The Virginia Conservatives, 1867–1879: A Study in Reconstruction Politics*. Chapel Hill: University of North Carolina Press.

Maggiotto, Michael A. 1984. "Parties and Elections in Local Government." In *Local Government in South Carolina*, ed. Charlie B. Tyer and Cole Blease Graham. Columbia: University of South Carolina Bureau of Governmental Research and Service.

Manno, Christopher E. 1978. "The Civil Rights Attorney's Fees Awards Act of 1976." *St. John's Law Review* 52: 562–93.

Matthews, Donald R., and James W. Prothro. 1963. "Social and Economic Factors and Negro Voter Registration in the South." *American Political Science Review* 57: 24–44.

———. 1966. *Negroes and the New Southern Politics*. New York: Harcourt, Brace and World.

Matusow, Allen J. 1984. *The Unraveling of America: A History of Liberalism in the 1960s*. New York: Harper and Row.

Meier, August, and Elliot Rudwick. 1973. *CORE: A Study in the Civil Rights Movement, 1942–1968*. New York: Oxford University Press.

Meier, Kenneth J., and Robert E. England. 1984. "Black Representation and Educational Policy: Are They Related?" *American Political Science Review* 78: 392–403.

Moeser, John V., and Rutledge M. Dennis. 1982. *The Politics of Annexation: Oligarchic Power in a Southern City*. Cambridge, Mass.: Schenkman Publishing Co.

Moneyhon, Carl H. 1980. *Republicanism in Reconstruction Texas*. Austin and London: University of Texas Press.

Montejano, David. 1987. *Anglos and Mexicans in the Making of Texas, 1836–1986*. Austin: University of Texas Press.

Moon, Henry Lee. 1949. *Balance of Power: The Negro Vote*. Garden City, N.Y.: Doubleday.

Morris, Aldon D. 1984. *The Origins of the Civil Rights Movement: Black Communities Organizing for Change*. New York: Free Press.

Morris, Thomas R. 1990. "Virginia and the Voting Rights Act." *University of Virginia* [Institute of Government] *News Letter* 66: 1–8.

———. 1992. "Virginia: L. Douglas Wilder, Governing and Campaigning." In *Governors and Hard Times*, ed. Thad L. Beyle. Washington, D.C.: CQ Press.

Morris, Thomas R., and Larry Sabato, eds. 1991. *Virginia Government and Politics: Readings and Comments*. 3d ed. Charlottesville: Chamber of Commerce and Center for Public Service, University of Virginia.

Morrison, Minion K. C. 1987. *Black Political Mobilization: Leadership, Power, and Mass Behavior*. Albany: State University of New York Press.

Morton, Richard L. [1918] 1973. *The Negro in Virginia Politics, 1865–1902*. Spartanburg, S.C.: Reprint Company.

Mundt, Robert J. 1988. "The Voting Rights Act Moves North." Presented at the annual meeting of the Southern Political Science Association, Atlanta, 4 November.

Mundt, Robert J., and Peggy Heilig. 1982. "District Representation: Demands and Effects in The Urban South." *Journal of Politics* 44: 1035–48.

Municipal Association of South Carolina. 1989, 1992. *Directory and Product/Services Guide*. Columbia, S.C.

Muse, Benjamin. 1961. *Virginia's Massive Resistance*. Bloomington: Indiana University Press.

Myrdal, Gunnar. 1944. *An American Dilemma: The Negro Problem and Modern Democracy*. New York: Harper and Brothers.

National Association of Latino Elected and Appointed Officials. 1989, 1990. *National Roster of Hispanic Elected Officials*. Washington, D.C.: NALEO Educational Fund.

Newby, I. A. 1973. *Black Carolinians: A History of Blacks in South Carolina from 1865 to 1968*. Columbia: University of South Carolina Press.

Niemi, Richard G., Jeffrey S. Hill, and Bernard Grofman. 1985. "The Impact of Multimember Districts on Party Representation in U.S. State Legislatures." *Legislative Studies Quarterly* 10: 441–55.

Nimmo, Dan, and Clifton McCleskey. 1969. "Impact of the Poll Tax on Voter Participation: The Houston Metropolitan Area in 1966." *Journal of Politics* 31: 682–99.

Norrell, Robert J. 1985. *Reaping the Whirlwind: The Civil Rights Movement in Tuskegee*. New York: Alfred A. Knopf.

North Carolina Advisory Committee. 1962. "Equal Protection of the Laws in North Carolina" In *Report of the North Carolina Advisory Committee to the United States Commission on Civil Rights, 1959–1962*. Washington, D.C.: U.S. Government Printing Office.

North Carolina, Secretary of State. 1980. *North Carolina Government, 1585–1979*. Raleigh: North Carolina Printing Office.

Ogden, Frederic D. 1958. *The Poll Tax in the South*. University, Ala.: University of Alabama Press.

O'Rourke, Timothy G. 1979. "City and County At-Large Elections and the Problem of Minority Representation." *University of Virginia* [Institute of Government] *News Letter* 55: 17–20.

———. 1982. "Constitutional and Statutory Challenges to Local At-Large Elections." *University of Richmond Law Review* 17: 39–98.

———. 1983. "Voting Rights Act Amendments of 1982: The New Bailout Provision and Virginia." *Virginia Law Review* 69: 765–804.

———. 1992. "The 1982 Amendments and the Voting Rights Paradox." In *Controversies in Minority Voting: The Voting Rights Act in Perspective*, ed. Bernard Grofman and Chandler Davidson. Washington, D.C.: Brookings Institution.

Parker, Frank R. 1982. "The Virginia Legislative Reapportionment Case: Reapportionment Issues of the 1980s." *George Mason University Law Review* 5: 1–50.

———. 1983. "The 'Results' Test of Section 2 of the Voting Rights Act: Abandoning the Intent Standard." *Virginia Law Review* 69: 715–64.

———. 1989. "Voting Rights Enforcement in the Reagan Administration." In *One Nation Indivisible: The Civil Rights Challenge for the 1990s*, ed. Reginald C. Govan and William L. Taylor. Washington, D.C.: Citizens' Commission on Civil Rights.

———. 1990. *Black Votes Count: Political Empowerment in Mississippi after 1965*. Chapel Hill and London: University of North Carolina Press.

———. 1991. "Voting Rights Enforcement in the Bush Administration: The First Two Years." In *Lost Opportunities: The Civil Rights Record of the Bush Administration Mid-term*, ed. Susan M. Liss and William L. Taylor. Washington, D.C.: Citizens' Commission on Civil Rights.

Parker, Frank R., and Barbara Y. Phillips. 1981. *Voting in Mississippi: A Right Still Denied*. Washington, D.C.: Lawyers' Committee for Civil Rights Under Law.

Paschal, Kay F. 1977. "The 1975 Local Government Act of South Carolina." *University of South Carolina Governmental Review* 19: 1–4.

Peirce, Neal R. 1974. *The Deep South States of America: People, Politics, and Power in the Seven Deep South States*. New York: W. W. Norton.

Pitre, Merline. 1985. *Through Many Dangers, Toils and Snares: The Black Leadership of Texas, 1868–1900*. Austin: Eakin Press.

Polinard, Jerry L., Robert D. Wrinkle, and Tomás Longoria, Jr., 1991. "The Impact of District Elections on the Mexican American Community: The Electoral Perspective." *Social Science Quarterly* 72: 608–14.

Prestage, Jewel L., and Carolyn Sue Williams. 1982. "Blacks in Louisiana Politics." In *Louisiana Politics: Festival in a Labyrinth*, ed. James Bolner. Baton Rouge and London: Louisiana State University Press.

Price, Hugh Douglas. 1955. "The Negro and Florida Politics, 1944–1954." *Journal of Politics* 17: 198–220.

Pulley, Raymond H. 1968. *Old Virginia Restored: An Interpretation of the Progressive Impulse, 1870–1930*. Charlottesville: University Press of Virginia.

Quint, Howard H. 1958. *Profile in Black and White: A Frank Portrait of South Carolina*. Washington, D.C.: Public Affairs Press.

Rabinowitz, Howard N. 1978. *Race Relations in the Urban South, 1865–1890*. New York: Oxford University Press.

Rable, George C. 1984. *But There Was No Peace: The Role of Violence in the Politics of Reconstruction*. Athens: University of Georgia Press.

Rankin, Robert A. 1974. "The Richmond Crusade for Voters: The Quest for Black Power." *University of Virginia* [Institute of Government] *News Letter* 51: 1–4.

Reitman, Alan, and Robert B. Davidson. 1972. *The Election Process: Voting Laws and Procedures*. Dobbs Ferry, N.Y.: Oceana.

Reynolds, Emily Bellinger, and Joan Reynolds Faunt. 1964. *Biographical Directory of the Senate of the State of South Carolina, 1776–1964*. Columbia: South Carolina Archives Department.

Rice, Bradley Robert. 1977. *Progressive Cities: The Commission Government Movement in America, 1901–1920*. Austin and London: University of Texas Press.

Rice, Lawrence D. 1971. *The Negro in Texas, 1874–1900*. Baton Rouge: Louisiana State University Press.

Robinson, Theodore P., and Thomas R. Dye. 1978. "Reformism and Black Representation on City Councils." *Social Science Quarterly* 59: 133–41.

Robinson, Theodore P., and Robert E. England. 1981. "Black Representation on Central City School Boards Revisited." *Social Science Quarterly* 62: 495–502.

Rosenberg, Gerald N. 1991. *The Hollow Hope: Can Courts Bring about Social Change?* Chicago and London: University of Chicago Press.

Rosenstone, Steven J., and Raymond E. Wolfinger. 1978. "The Effect of Registration Laws on Voter Turnout." *American Political Science Review* 72: 22–45.

Ruoff, John C. 1986. "Affadavit." *Smalls v. Fairfield, South Carolina County Council*, CA 86-2726-0 (D.S.C.)

Rusk, Jerrold G., and John J. Stucker. 1978. "The Effect of the Southern System of Election Laws on Voter Participation: A Reply to V. O. Key, Jr." In *The History of American Electoral Behavior*, ed. Joel H. Silbey, Allan G. Bogue, and William H. Flanigan. Princeton: Princeton University Press.

Sabato, Larry. 1975. "Aftermath of 'Armageddon': An Analysis of the 1973 Virginia Gubernatorial Election." Charlottesville: Institute of Government, University of Virginia.

———. 1977. *The Democratic Party Primary in Virginia: Tantamount to Election No Longer*. Charlottesville: Institute of Government, University of Virginia.

———. 1987. *Virginia Votes, 1983–1986*. Charlottesville: Institute of Government, University of Virginia.

———. 1988a. *The Party's Just Begun: Shaping Political Parties for America's Future*. Glenview, Ill., Boston, and London: Scott, Foresman.

———. 1988b. "The 1988 Presidential Election in Virginia." *University of Virginia* [Institute of Government] *News Letter* 65: 21–26.

———. 1990. "Virginia Governor's Race, 1989." *University of Virginia* [Institute of Government] *News Letter* 66: 1–8.

Salamon, Lester M., and Stephen van Evera. 1973. "Fear, Apathy, and Discrimination: A Test of Three Explanations of Political Participation." *American Political Science Review* 67: 1288–1306.

Saunders, Lyle. [1949] 1976. "The Spanish-Speaking Population of Texas." Reprinted in *The Mexican Experience in Texas*, ed. Carlos E. Cortés. New York: Arno Press.

Scher, Richard, and James Button. 1984. "Voting Rights Act: Implementation and Impact." In *Implementation of Civil Rights Policy*, ed. Charles S. Bullock III and Charles M. Lamb. Monterey, Calif.: Brooks/Cole.

Schroth, Thomas N., ed. 1965. *Congress and the Nation, 1945–1964: A Review of Government and Politics in the Postwar Years*. Washington, D.C.: Congressional Quarterly Service.

Schuiteman, John G., and John G. Selph. 1983. "The 1981/1982 Reapportionment of the Virginia House of Delegates." *University of Virginia* [Institute of Government] *News Letter* 59: 47–51.

Shelton, Edgar Greer, Jr. [1946] 1974. *Political Conditions among Texas Mexicans along the Rio Grande*. San Francisco: R and E Research Associates.

Simkins, Francis. 1921a. "Race Legislation in South Carolina Since 1865: Part I, 1865–1869." *South Atlantic Quarterly* 20: 61–71.

Simkins, Francis Butler. 1921b. "Race Legislation in South Carolina since 1865: Part II, 1869 and After." *South Atlantic Quarterly* 20: 165–77.

———. 1937. "Ben Tillman's View of the Negro." *Journal of Southern History* 3: 161–74.

———. 1944. *Pitchfork Ben Tillman: South Carolinian*. Baton Rouge: Louisiana State University Press.

Simmons, Ozzie G. 1952. "Anglo Americans and Mexican Americans in South Texas: A Study in Dominant-Subordinate Group Relations." Ph.D. diss., Harvard University.

Smallwood, James M. 1981. *Time of Hope, Time of Despair: Black Texans during Reconstruction*. Port Washington, N.Y., and London: Kennikat Press.

Smith, Constance E. 1960. *Voting and Election Laws: Laws for Voters*. New York, N.Y.: Oceana Publications.

South Carolina Conference of Branches NAACP. 1980, 1990. *Annual Report*. Columbia: South Carolina Conference of Branches NAACP.

South Carolina Election Commission. 1974. *Report of the South Carolina Election Commission for the Period Ending June 30, 1974, and Including Results of November 5, 1974, General Election*. South Carolina State Budget and Control Board.

———. 1976. *Report of the South Carolina Election Commission for the Period Ending June 30, 1977, and Including Results of November 2, 1976, General Election*. South Carolina State Budget and Control Board.

———. 1979. "Voter Registration Statistics."

———. 1984. *Report of the South Carolina Election Commission for the Period Ending June 30, 1984*. South Carolina State Budget and Control Board.

Southern Regional Council (Voter Education Project). 1966. "Voter Registration in the South, 1966." Atlanta: Southern Regional Council. Mimeo.

Southern Regional Council. 1984. "Forty Years since the End of the White Primary." Fortieth Anniversary Paper. Atlanta: Southern Regional Council.

Sproat, John G. 1986. "'Firm Flexibility': Perspectives on Desegregation in South Carolina." In *New Perspectives on Race and Slavery in America: Essays in Honor of Kenneth M. Stampp*, ed. Robert H. Abzug and Stephen E. Maizlish. Lexington: University Press of Kentucky.

Stanley, Harold W. 1987. *Voter Mobilization and the Politics of Race: The South and Universal Suffrage, 1952–1984*. New York, Westport, Conn., and London: Praeger.

Stekler, Paul. 1983. "Black Politics in the New South: An Investigation of Change at Various Levels." Ph.D. diss., Harvard University.

Stern, Mark. 1985. "Legislative Responsiveness and the New Southern Politics." In *The Voting Rights Act: Consequences and Implications*, ed. Lorn S. Foster. New York: Praeger.

———. 1987. "Black Voter Registration in the South: Hypotheses and Occurrences." In *Blacks in Southern Politics*, ed. Laurence W. Moreland, Robert P. Steed, and Tod A. Baker. New York, Westport, Conn., and London: Praeger.

Stewart, Joseph Jr., Robert E. England, and Kenneth J. Meier. 1989. "Black Representation in Urban School Districts: From School Board to Office to Classroom." *Western Political Quarterly* 42: 287–305.

Still, Edward. 1984. "Alternatives to Single-Member Districts." In *Minority Vote Dilution*, ed. Chandler Davidson. Washington, D.C.: Howard University Press.

———. 1991. "Voluntary Constituencies: Modified At-Large Voting as a Remedy for Minority Vote Dilution in Judicial Elections." *Yale Law and Policy Review* 9: 354–69.

———. 1992. "Cumulative Voting and Limited Voting in Alabama." In *United States Electoral Systems: Their Impact on Minorities and Women*, ed. Wilma Rule and Joseph F. Zimmermen. New York, Westport, Conn., and London: Greenwood Press.

Stone, Alfred Holt. 1908. *Studies in the American Race Problem*. New York: Doubleday, Page, and Co.

Stoudemire, Robert H., and Victor Ascolillo. 1969. "Reorganization of County Government in South Carolina." *University of South Carolina Governmental Review* 11: 1–4.

Strong, Donald S. 1948. "The Rise of Negro Voting in Texas." *American Political Science Review* 42: 510–22.

———. 1972. "Alabama: Transition and Alienation." In *The Changing Politics of the South*, ed. William C. Havard. Baton Rouge: Louisiana State University Press.

Suitts, Steve. 1981. "Blacks in the Political Arithmetic after *Mobile*: A Case Study of North Carolina." In *The Right to Vote*. New York: Rockefeller Foundation.

Sullivan, Patricia. 1991. "Southern Reformers, the New Deal, and the Movement's Foundation." In *New Directions in Civil Rights Studies*, ed. Armstead L. Robinson and Patricia Sullivan. Charlottesville and London: University Press of Virginia.

Swain, Carol M. 1989. "The Politics of Black Representation in U.S. Congressional Districts." Ph.D. diss., University of North Carolina, Chapel Hill.

———. 1992. "Some Consequences of the Voting Rights Act." In *Controversies in Minority Voting: The Voting Rights Act in Perspective*, ed. Bernard Grofman and Chandler Davidson. Washington, D.C.: Brookings Institution.

———. 1993. *Black Faces, Black Interests: The Representation of African Americans in Congress*. Cambridge and London: Harvard University Press.

Synnott, Marcia G. 1989. "Desegregation in South Carolina, 1950–1963: Sometime between 'Now' and 'Never.'" In *Looking South: Chapters in the Story of an American Region*, ed. Winfred B. Moore, Jr., and Joseph F. Tripp. New York, Westport, Conn., and London: Greenwood Press.

Taebel, Delbert. 1978. "Minority Representation on City Councils: The Impact of Structure on Blacks and Hispanics." *Social Science Quarterly* 59: 142–52.

Tate, Katherine. 1988. *Protest to Politics: The New Black Voters in American Elections*. Harvard University. Mimeo.

Thernstrom, Abigail. 1987. *Whose Votes Count? Affirmative Action and Minority Voting Rights*. Cambridge and London: Harvard University Press.

Thomas, Robert D., and Richard W. Murray. 1986. "Applying the Voting Rights Act in Houston: Federal Intervention or Local Political Determination?" In *Assessing the Effects of the U.S. Voting Rights Act*, ed. Charles L. Cotrell. *Publius: The Journal of Federalism* 16 (Fall, Special Symposium Issue): 81–96.

Thompson, Joel A. 1986. "The Voting Rights Act in North Carolina: An Evaluation." In *Assessing the Effects of the U.S. Voting Rights Act*, ed. Charles L. Cotrell. *Publius: The Journal of Federalism* 16 (Fall, Special Symposium Issue): 139–53.

Thornton, J. Mills III. 1982. "Fiscal Policy and the Failure of Radical Reconstruction in the Lower South." In *Region, Race, and Reconstruction: Essays in Honor of C. Vann Woodward*, ed. J. Morgan Kousser and James M. McPherson. New York and Oxford: Oxford University Press.

Tindall, George B. 1952. *South Carolina Negroes, 1877–1900*. Columbia: University of South Carolina Press.

———. 1967. *The Emergence of the New South, 1913–1945*. Baton Rouge: Louisiana State University Press and the Littlefield Fund for Southern History of the University of Texas.

Trelease, Allen W. 1971. *White Terror: The Ku Klux Klan Conspiracy and Southern Reconstruction*. New York: Harper and Row.

Turner, James P. 1992. "A Case-Specific Approach to Implementing the Voting Rights Act." In *Controversies in Minority Voting: The Voting Rights Act in Perspective*, ed. Bernard Grofman and Chandler Davidson. Washington, D.C.: Brookings Institution.

Underwood, James L. 1989. *The Constitution of South Carolina*. Vol. 2, *The Journey toward Local Self-Government*. Columbia: University of South Carolina Press.

U.S. Commission on Civil Rights. 1959. *Voting: Hearings before the U.S. Commission on Civil Rights*. Washington, D.C.: U.S. Government Printing Office.

———. 1965. *Hearings before the U.S. Commission on Civil Rights*, Vol. 1, *Voting*. Washington, D.C.: U.S. Government Printing Office.

———. 1968. *Political Participation: A Study of the Participation by Negroes in the Electoral and Political Processes in Ten Southern States since the Passage of the Voting Rights Act of 1965*. Washington, D.C.: U.S. Government Printing Office.

———. 1971. *Voting*. Washington, D.C.: U.S. Government Printing Office.

———. 1975. *The Voting Rights Act: Ten Years After*. Washington, D.C.: U.S. Government Printing Office.

———. 1981. *The Voting Rights Act: Unfulfilled Goals*. Washington, D.C.: U.S. Government Printing Office.

U.S. Commission on Civil Rights, North Carolina Advisory Committee. 1962. *Equal Protection of the Laws in North Carolina: Report of the North Carolina Advisory Committee to the United States Commission on Civil Rights, 1959–1962*. Washington, D.C.: U.S. Government Printing Office.

U.S. Department of Commerce. 1970–89. *Statistical Abstract of the United States*. Washington, D.C.: U.S. Government Printing Office.

U.S. Department of Commerce, Bureau of the Census. 1965. *Governing Boards of County Governments, 1965*. State and Local Government Special Studies no. 49. Washington, D.C.: U.S. Government Printing Office.

———. 1974. *Governing Boards of County Governments, 1973*. State and Local Government Special Studies no. 68. Washington, D.C.: Superintendant of Documents, Government Printing Office.

———. 1981. *1980 Census of Population*. Washington, D.C.: U.S. Government Printing Office.

———. 1986. "Voting and Registration in the Election of November 1984." Washington, D.C.: U.S. Government Printing Office.

———. 1989. *Voting and Registration in the Election of November 1988*. Ser. P-20, no. 440. [Current Population Reports: Population Characteristics] Washington, D.C.: U.S. Government Printing Office.

———. 1990. *1987 Census of Governments: Government Organization*. Vol. 1. Washington, D.C.: U.S. Government Printing Office.

———. 1991. *1990 Census of Population and Housing*. Washington, D.C.: U.S. Government Printing Office.

U.S. Department of Justice. 1988, 1990, 1991. "Complete Listing of Objections Pursuant to Section 5 of the Voting Rights Act of 1965." Washington, D.C.: Department of Justice.

Vedlitz, Arnold, and Charles A. Johnson. 1982. "Community Racial Segregation, Electoral Structure, and Minority Representation." *Social Science Quarterly* 63: 729–36.

Voter Education Project. 1976. "Election Law Changes in Cities and Counties in Georgia." Atlanta: Southern Regional Council.

Wardlaw, Ralph. 1932. "Negro Suffrage in Georgia, 1867–1930." M.A. thesis, University of Georgia.

Washington Research Project. 1972. *The Shameful Blight: The Survival of Racial Discrimination in Voting in the South*. Washington, D.C.: Washington Research Project.

Watters, Pat, and Reese Cleghorn. 1967. *Climbing Jacob's Ladder: The Arrival of Negroes in Southern Politics*. New York: Harcourt, Brace and World.

Webb, Linda M. 1990. "Legislative Reapportionment in South Carolina from 1960 to 1990 and Beyond: Implications for Effective Planning." M.A. thesis, Clemson University.

Weber, Ronald E. 1981. "Louisiana." In *Reapportionment Politics: The History of Redistricting in the 50 States*, ed. Leroy Hardy, Alan Heslop, and Stuart Anderson. Beverley Hills, Calif.: Sage Publications.

Weeks, O. Douglas. 1948. "The White Primary, 1944–1948." *American Political Science Review* 42: 500–510.

Weinstein, James. 1962. "Organized Business and the City Commission and Manager Movements." *Journal of Southern History* 28: 166–82.

Welch, Susan. 1990. "The Impact of At-Large Elections on the Representation of Blacks and Hispanics." *Journal of Politics* 52: 1050–76.

Wharton, Vernon L.. 1965. *The Negro in Mississippi, 1865–1890*. New York: Harper and Row.

Whitaker, Urban G., and Bruce E. Davis. 1967. *The World and Ridgeway, South Carolina*. Columbia: Institute of International Studies, University of South Carolina.

Wiggins, Sarah Woolfolk. 1977. *The Scalawag in Alabama Politics, 1865–1881*. University, Ala.: University of Alabama Press.

———. 1980. "Alabama: Democratic Bulldozing and Republican Folly." In *Reconstruction and Redemption in the South*, ed. Otto H. Olsen. Baton Rouge: Louisiana State University Press.

Wilkinson, J. Harvie III. 1968. *Harry Byrd and the Changing Face of Virginia Politics, 1945–1966*. Charlottesville: University Press of Virginia.

Williamson, Joel. 1965. *After Slavery: The Negro in South Carolina during Reconstruction, 1861–1877*. Chapel Hill: University of North Carolina Press.

Wolfinger, Raymond E., and John Osgood Field. 1966. "Political Ethos and the Structure of City Government." *American Political Science Review* 60: 306–26.

Wolfley, Jeanette, and Gordon G. Henderson. 1991. "Indian Success in Different Election Systems." Presented at the annual meeting of the Western Political Science Association, Seattle.

Woods, Barbara A. 1990. "Modjeska Simkins and the South Carolina Conference of the NAACP, 1939–1957." In *Women in the Civil Rights Movement: Trailblazers and Torchbearers, 1941–1965*, ed. Vicki L. Crawford, Jacqueline Anne Rouse, and Barbara Woods. Brooklyn: Carlson Publishing.

Woodward, C. Vann. [1938] 1973. *Tom Watson: Agrarian Rebel*. Savannah, Ga.: Beehive Press.

———. 1965. "From the First Reconstruction to the Second." *Harper's* (April): 127–33.

———. 1974. *The Strange Career of Jim Crow*. 3d ed. New York: Oxford University Press.

Wright, Frederick D. 1986. "The Voting Rights Act and Louisiana: Twenty Years of Enforcement." In *Assessing the Effects of the U.S. Voting Rights Act*, ed. Charles L. Cotrell. *Publius: The Journal of Federalism* 16 (Fall, Special Symposium Issue): 97–108.

———. 1987. "The History of Black Political Participation to 1965." In *Blacks in Southern Politics*, ed. Laurence W. Moreland, Robert P. Steed, and Tod A. Baker. New York: Praeger Publishers.

Yarbrough, Tinsley E. 1981. *Judge Frank Johnson and Human Rights in Alabama*. University: University of Alabama Press.

———. 1987. *A Passion for Justice: J. Waties Waring and Civil Rights*. New York and Oxford: Oxford University Press.

Young, Roy E. 1965. *The Place System in Texas Elections*. Public Affairs Series no. 62. Austin: Institute of Public Affairs, University of Texas.

Zax, Jeffrey S. 1990. "Election Methods and Black and Hispanic City Council Membership." *Social Science Quarterly* 71: 339–55.

CONTRIBUTORS

JAMES E. ALT. Professor of Government, Harvard University. He is the author of *The Politics of Economic Decline, Political Economics* (with K. Alec Chrystal), and numerous articles on various aspects of political science and political economy.

MICHAEL B. BINFORD. Associate Professor of Political Science, Georgia State University. He has written about political methodology, public opinion, and Georgia politics. He has also provided data analysis and expert testimony in a number of voting rights cases throughout the South.

NEIL BRADLEY. Associate Director of the Southern Regional Office of the American Civil Liberties Foundation, Inc., in Atlanta. He is a 1970 graduate of the University of Wisconsin Law School and has been litigating voter and election law issues in the Deep South since 1971.

ROBERT BRISCHETTO. Executive Director of the Southwest Voter Research Institute and former member of the sociology faculty at Trinity University. He has served as an expert witness for minority plaintiffs in more than fifty voting rights lawsuits and is the author of a number of articles and book chapters on Hispanic voting and public opinion patterns. In 1992 he received the national award for sociological practice from the Society for Applied Sociology.

ORVILLE VERNON BURTON. Professor of History and Sociology, National Center for Supercomputing Applications, and University Scholar, University of Illinois at Urbana-Champaign. He has written or edited three books and numerous articles on race relations and the American South. He has been a consultant or expert witness for African-American or Hispanic plaintiffs in more than thirty voting rights suits since 1982.

VICTORIA M. CARIDAS-BUTTERWORTH. Doctoral candidate in Political Science, Tulane University. From 1990 to 1993 she was a Program Officer with the Southern Regional Council's Voting Rights Programs in Atlanta, Georgia. Her current research focuses on political theory and ethnic relations in Europe.

DAVID C. COLBY. Political Scientist, Washington, D.C. He has published articles on the Voting Rights Act, black power, AIDS politics and policies, and Medicare and Medicaid issues.

CHANDLER DAVIDSON. Sociologist, Rice University. He has written articles and books on civil rights issues and participated as an expert witness or consultant for minority plaintiffs in cases involving job discrimination, jury selection discrimination, and voting rights.

RICHARD L. ENGSTROM. Research Professor of Political Science, University of New Orleans. He has written extensively on the impact of election systems on minority voters. His articles on this topic, a number of which have been cited by the U.S. Supreme Court, have appeared in the *American Political Science Review, Journal of Politics, Electoral Studies, Journal of Law and Politics*, and other journals. He has served as an expert witness for African-American, Native-American, and Hispanic plaintiffs in vote-dilution lawsuits.

TERENCE R. FINNEGAN. Assistant Professor of History, William Paterson College. He recently completed his dissertation on lynching in South Carolina and Mississippi from

1881 to 1940. Finnegan is the author or coauthor of several articles, including an analysis of methodological problems in voting rights litigation and several works on using computers to teach and study history. He is a coinvestigator of the History Census Database Project at the National Center for Supercomputing Applications at the University of Illinois.

JEROME A. GRAY. State Field Director, Alabama Democratic Conference (the black political caucus of Alabama). Since 1977, he has been actively involved in voting rights issues in the state. His grass-roots political expertise has led to his roles as a court witness, negotiator, and demographer in resolving many voting rights cases, leading to the election of scores of black officeholders in Alabama. Gray has served on numerous panels dealing with voting rights and redistricting, and he is coauthor of *The History of the Alabama State Teachers Association.*

BERNARD GROFMAN. Professor of Political Science and Social Psychology, School of Social Sciences, University of California, Irvine. He is a specialist in mathematical models of collective decision making, with many published articles on topics such as jury verdict choice, reapportionment and voter turnout, and coalition formation models. In recent years he has been involved as an expert witness in numerous cases involving redistricting litigation or as a court-appointed reapportionment expert. He is the editor or author of several books on the subject of elections, redistricting, and the Voting Rights Act, including, most recently, *Controversies in Minority Voting* and *Minority Representation and the Quest for Voting Equality.*

STANLEY A. HALPIN, JR. Associate Professor of Law, Southern University Law Center. Halpin is a political scientist as well as a lawyer by training and has written on minority representation and the Voting Rights Act. Since the late 1960s he has represented African-American, Hispanic, and Native-American plaintiffs in over fifty voting rights cases in the U.S. District and Appellate courts and the Supreme Court, including *Zimmer v. McKeithen, East Carroll v. Marshall, Beer v. United States*, and *Major v. Treen.*

LISA HANDLEY. Senior Research Analyst at Election Data Services, Inc., a political consulting firm. She received her Ph.D. in political science from George Washington University and has taught at the University of California, Irvine; the University of Virginia; and George Washington University. She has worked as a consultant or expert witness in numerous voting rights cases for both plaintiffs and defendants, and has coauthored a book and several articles on minority voting rights and representation.

JEAN A. HILL. Attorney at Law, Lafayette, Louisiana. She has participated in voting rights litigation in Louisiana and New Mexico on behalf of minority plaintiffs.

KEN JOHNSON. Deputy Director of the Southern Regional Council. The recipient of a degree in city planning, he has held research and executive positions with the National Rural Center, the Voter Education Project, the Emergency Land Fund, and the Federation of Southern Cooperatives.

WILLIAM R. KEECH. Professor of Political Science, University of North Carolina at Chapel Hill. He is past president of the Southern Political Science Association and the author of, among other books and articles, *The Impact of Negro Voting* and *Economic Politics: The Costs of Democracy* (forthcoming).

JAMES W. LOEWEN. Professor of Sociology, University of Vermont, and Senior Postdoctoral Fellow, Smithsonian Institution. In 1971 he introduced correlation and regression analysis in voting rights litigation in *National Democratic Party v. Riddell* and, in 1979, two-equation ecological regression in *Boykins v. Hattiesburg* (Mississippi). He has been a consultant or expert witness for black or Hispanic plaintiffs, the Department of Justice, defendants, and political organizations in forty voting rights cases or section 5 submissions. He is the author of, among other books, *Social Science in the Courtroom*.

PEYTON MCCRARY. Historian, Civil Rights Division, Department of Justice. He is author of one book and numerous articles on southern race relations and politics, and of several articles concerning standards of proof in vote-dilution lawsuits. Before taking his current position, McCrary was Professor of History at the University of South Alabama, in which capacity he testified as an expert witness for minority plaintiffs or for the United States in fifteen voting rights cases.

LAUGHLIN MCDONALD. Director of the Southern Regional Office of the American Civil Liberties Union. He has represented minority plaintiffs in numerous civil rights cases and has specialized in the area of voting rights. He is the author of *Racial Equality* and *The Rights of Racial Minorities*, as well as of articles and reviews for scholarly and other publications.

THOMAS R. MORRIS. President of Emory and Henry College and professor of political science. He is coauthor of *Virginia Government and Politics: Readings and Comments*, 3d ed., and author of *The Virginia Supreme Court: An Institutional and Political Analysis*.

MINION K. C. MORRISON. Vice Provost and Professor of Political Science, University of Missouri-Columbia. He has written or edited three books and written numerous articles on American and African politics. Much of his work on America has concerned African-American politics, voting, and elections in the South. He has been an activist and consultant on voting and elections both in the United States and Africa.

FRANK R. PARKER. Professor of Law, District of Columbia School of Law. Formerly Director of the Voting Rights Project of the Lawyers' Committee for Civil Rights Under Law, he has litigated more than seventy-five voting rights cases. Parker is the author of the award-winning *Black Votes Count: Political Empowerment in Mississippi after 1965* and numerous book chapters and articles on minority voting rights.

HUEY L. PERRY. Dean, School of Public Policy and Urban Affairs, Southern University in Baton Rouge, Louisiana. His research focuses primarily on the impact of black political participation in the South, about which he has written numerous articles. Perry is a member of the editorial board of the *Journal of Politics* and *Urban Affairs Quarterly*.

DAVID R. RICHARDS. Attorney at Law, Austin, Texas. He has been primarily involved as plaintiffs' counsel representing blacks and Hispanics in voting rights litigation from 1972 to 1993. He has also, on occasion, represented the State of Texas and other political subdivisions in defense of voting rights challenges.

MICHAEL P. SISTROM. Doctoral Student in American History, University of North Carolina at Chapel Hill. He is studying the civil rights movement and, particularly, the Mississippi Freedom Democratic Party.

EDWARD STILL. Lawyer, Birmingham, Alabama. He has represented African-American plaintiffs in more than two hundred suits against Alabama and its local governments under the Voting Rights Act seeking relief against malapportionment or dilution of black voting strength. He has also written several articles dealing with remedies in such suits.

INDEX OF LEGAL CASES

GENERAL INDEX